The SAGE Handbook of
PERFORMANCE STUDIES

In deep gratitude to and in loving memory of Dwight Conquergood

The SAGE Handbook of
PERFORMANCE STUDIES

Edited by

D. Soyini Madison   Judith Hamera

University of North Carolina at Chapel Hill   Texas A&M University

⑤ SAGE Publications
Thousand Oaks ▪ London ▪ New Delhi

For information:

Sage Publications, Inc.
2455 Teller Road
Thousand Oaks, California 91320
E-mail: order@sagepub.com

Sage Publications Ltd.
1 Oliver's Yard
55 City Road
London EC1Y 1SP
United Kingdom

Sage Publications India Pvt. Ltd.
B-42, Panchsheel Enclave
Post Box 4109
New Delhi 110 017 India

Printed in the United States of America

Library of Congress Cataloging-in-Publication Data

The SAGE handbook of performance studies / edited by D. Soyini Madison and Judith Hamera.
    p. cm.
Includes bibliographical references and index.
ISBN 0-7619-2931-2 (cloth)
  1. Performing arts—Social aspects. I. Title: Handbook of performance studies. II. Madison, D. Soyini. III. Hamera, Judith.
PN1590.S6S24 2006
306.4′84—dc22   2005014281

This book is printed on acid-free paper.

05   06   07   08   09   10 9 8 7 6 5 5 4 3 2 1

Acquisitions Editor:	Todd R. Armstrong
Editorial Assistant:	Deya Saoud
Production Editor:	Kristen Gibson
Copy Editor:	Cate Huisman
Typesetter:	C&M Digitals (P) Ltd.
Cover Designer:	Janet Foulger

Cover image created by Torkwase Dyson.

Contents

Acknowledgments

Sincere thanks to the section editors of, and contributors to, the *Handbook of Performance Studies*. Their diligence, vision, and enthusiasm on behalf of performance studies inspired and sustained the editors throughout this process.

Judith Hamera wishes to thank D. Soyini Madison for the invitation to collaborate on this rich and profoundly important project. Working together has been a joy and a pleasure and I am left with an even greater regard for her intellectual and rhetorical precision, her fierce love of performance, and her rich good humor. I am very grateful for this opportunity.

D. Soyini Madison wishes to thank Judith Hamera whose gracious judgment and extraordinary eloquence enriched the process and development of this handbook beyond measure. As a colleague and friend for two decades, her brilliance, still, never ceases to amaze me.

Thanks, too, to Carl Selkin, dean of the College of Arts and Letters at California State University, for his unstinting support of performance and performance studies.

Deep thanks to Alfred Bendixen, beloved partner in all things.

Thank you to Mejai Kai Dyson and Torkwase Madison Dyson for your support and encouragement.

The editors express sincerest thanks to the staff at Sage Publications, and particularly Todd Armstrong, senior acquisitions editor, and Deya Saoud, senior editorial assistant. They have made this project a pleasure from beginning to end. We truly appreciate their efforts and their complete professionalism.

Dwight Conquergood, scholar, mentor, teacher, and dear friend, passed away as this handbook was being completed. His profound wisdom, generosity of spirit, and abiding love of performance inspired editors and countless others inside and outside of the academy over three decades. His contributions to the field, and to us personally, are impossible to overstate. We humbly offer this handbook as one turn in a larger and life-changing conversation about performance studies that began, for us, with his voice, his words, his care.

Performance Studies at the Intersections

D. SOYINI MADISON AND JUDITH HAMERA

The ongoing challenge of performance studies is to refuse and supercede this deeply entrenched division of labor, apartheid of knowledges, that plays out inside the academy as the difference between thinking and doing, interpreting and making, conceptualizing and creating. The division of labor between theory and practice, abstraction and embodiment, is an arbitrary and rigged choice and, like all binarisms, it is booby-trapped.

—Dwight Conquergood, 2002, p. 153

Performance is often referred to as a "contested concept" because as a concept, method, event, and practice it is variously envisioned and employed. Three founding scholars of contemporary performance studies, Mary S. Strine, Beverly W. Long, and Mary Francis Hopkins, formally set forth the idea of performance as a contested concept in their classic essay, "Research in Interpretation and Performance Studies: Trends, Issues, Priorities." They state,

Performance, like art and democracy, is what W.B. Gallie (1964) calls an *essentially contested concept*, meaning that its very existence is bound up in disagreement about what it is, and that the disagreement over its essence is itself part of that essence. As

Gallie explains, "Recognition of a given concept as essentially contested implies recognition of rival uses of it (such as oneself repudiates) as not only logically possible and humanly 'likely,' but as of permanent potential critical value to one's own use of interpretation of the concept in question" (pp. 187–188). Scholars in interpretation and performance in a valorized category, they recognize and expect disagreement not only about the qualities that make a performance "good" or "bad" in certain contexts, but also about what activities and behaviors appropriately constitute performance and not something else. (1990, p. 183)

On multiple levels performance "means" and "does" different things for and with different people. On one level performance is understood as theatrical practice, that is, drama, as acting, or "putting on a show." For some, this limited view regards performance as extracurricular, insubstantial, or what you do in your leisure time. In certain areas of the academy these narrow notions of performance have created an "anti-theatrical" prejudice (Conquergood) that diminishes performance to mimicry, catharsis, or mere entertainment rather than as a generative force and a critical dynamic within human behavior and social processes. However, in recent history, performance has undergone a small revolution. For many of us performance has evolved into ways of comprehending how human beings fundamentally make culture, affect power, and reinvent their ways of being in the world. The insistence on performance as a way of *creation* and *being* as opposed to the long held notion of performance as entertainment has brought forth a movement to seek and articulate the phenomenon of performance in its multiple manifestations and imaginings.

Understanding performance in this broader and more complex way has opened up endless questions, some of which both interrogate and enrich our basic understanding of history, identity, community, nation, and politics. Performance is a contested concept because when we understand performance beyond theatrics and recognize it as fundamental and inherent to life and culture we are confronted with the ambiguities of different spaces and places that are foreign, contentious, and often under siege. We enter the everyday and the ordinary and interpret its symbolic universe to discover the complexity of its extraordinary meanings and practices.

We can no longer define performance as primarily mimetic or theatrical but through the multiple elements that inhere within performance and within the dynamic of shifting domains of theory, method, and event. The triad of *theory*, *method*, and *event* has generally been understood as the following: performance theory provides analytical frameworks; performance method provides concrete application; and performance event provides an aesthetic or noteworthy happening. Although theory, method, and event are components of the grand possibilities of performance, Dwight Conquergood provides a more precise set of triads guiding us more comprehensively to the substance and nuances of performance through a series of alliterations: the *i*'s as in *imagination*, *inquiry*, and *intervention*; the *a*'s as in *artistry*, *analysis*, and *activism*; and the *c*'s as in *creativity*, *critique*, and *citizenship*. Conquergood states,

> Performance studies is uniquely suited for the challenge of braiding together disparate and stratified ways of knowing. We can think through performance along three crisscrossing lines of activity and analysis. We can think of performance (1) as a work of *imagination*, as an object of study; (2) as a pragmatics of *inquiry* (both as model and method), as an optic and operation of research; (3) as a tactics of *intervention*, an alterative space of struggle. Speaking from my home department at Northwestern, we often refer to the three a's of performance studies: artistry, analysis, activism. Or to change the alliteration, a commitment to the three c's of performance studies: creativity, critique, citizenship (civic struggles for social justice). (Conquergood, 2002, p. 152)

Conquergood challenges us to understand the ubiquitous and generative force of performance that is beyond the theatrical. The question we shall now entertain is: How is this challenge most effectively debated and discussed in the academy?

THE MULTIDISCIPLINARY APPEAL OF PERFORMANCE: PERFORMANCE AS "EVERYWHERE" IN THE ACADEMY?

Across various academic boundaries, performance is blurring disciplinary distinctions and invoking radically multidisciplinary approaches. From the established disciplines of history, literature, education, sociology, geography, anthropology, political science, and so forth—the rubric of performance has found its way into discussions and debate as a topic of interest and inquiry. Teachers and students are seeking to better understand this notion of performance as a means to gain a deeper understanding of their own fields of study, as well as a pedagogical method. The buzz over performance is nearly everywhere in the academy and as a result multiple paradigms and levels of analysis are formed. As these various subject areas adapt performance as an analytical framework and as a methodological tool, something greater has happened to the very concept of performance itself: new and complex questions arise relative to its definition, applicability, and effectiveness. These extended queries into performance have a broad membership ranging from those of us who, before now, never thought much about performance as a scholarly or pedagogical enterprise to those of us who have embraced the dynamic of performance for several decades. Both neophyte and veteran to performance are engaged in the infinite possibilities of performance and therefore expanding, complexifying, and enriching its meanings and practices.

In understanding performance as radically interdisciplinary, how then do we begin to grasp what it is? How do we begin to describe and order the varied manifestations of performance? Are there fundamental principles of performance? We will briefly turn now to specific movements and paradigms to lay forth the broad contours of performance studies and to provide a working definition of performance ranging from the illocutionary movement in the nineteenth century to postmodern art and transnational narratives within this era of globalization and transnationalism.

THE ELOCUTIONARY MOVEMENT

Although performance began in antiquity constituting varied cultural phenomena that ranged from mimesis, ritual, and ceremony, to everyday symbolic acts, one modern tradition that can be understood as part of the history and origins of performance studies, primarily in the United States and Europe, is the elocutionary movement. Elocution or the "art of public speaking" was of major importance in the nineteenth century United States and Europe. In an age where telephones, television, movies, CD players, and the Internet were nonexistent, it was the art of public speaking that became the powerful communicative and entertainment medium of public life and thereby influencing central aspects of community and nation (Conquergood, 2000). The elocutionary speaker was a performer who could leave his audience on the edge of their seats with the turn of an imaginative phrase or a compelling anecdote. The speaker could build the story or the argument to a peak that held the audience captive to the spoken word that was filled with the varying registers of a performing presence wrapped in dramatic gesture and utterance. The public speaker was a performer whose work was to make the audience listen and learn through a drama of communication.

Elocution was a social event. The audience gathered to witness the speaker through a collective that brought friends and strangers together to meet and greet. This event was a moment of communal experience, listening and watching together, but also responding together to what they heard—from reserved claps of appreciation to uproarious laugher to the insulting taunts of hecklers—they listened and responded together. The event was also a ritual with its customary beginnings and endings; it was a ritual of information gathering, persuasion, affirmation, and change.

Just as the art of effective public speaking was a creative force, it was also a force of hegemonic control. It both perpetrated and solidified power relations, as well as the valorization of a bourgeois decorum based on vocal qualities, gestures of gentility, social class, gender hierarchies, and the color of one's skin. Conquergood states,

> Elocution expressed in another key the body-discipline imposed on the bourgeoisie, a way for them to mark "distinction" from the masses. . . . Elocution was designed to recuperate the vitality of the spoken word from rural and rough working-class contexts by regulating and refining its "performative excess" through principles, science, systematic study, standards of taste and criticism . . . elocution sought to tap the power of popular speech but curb its unruly embodiments and refine its coarse and uncouth features. It was the verbal counterpart, on the domain of speech, of the enclosure acts that confiscated the open commons, so crucial to the hardscrabble livelihood and recreation of the poor, and privatized them for the privileged classes. (2000, p. 327)

Conquergood goes on to describe how the elocution of the privileged classes could not withstand such hierarchical exclusivity due to the ubiquitous nature of the spoken word. "The spoken word dimension of elocution provided for the 'spillage' from the enclosed written word that the unlettered poor swept up and made their own" (p. 329). "This spillage of elocution, now appropriated and also owned and enacted by the laboring classes and lumpen proletariat" was revisioned and reformed by the less privileged classes for their own "subaltern needs" (p. 329), audiences, and purposes. The elocutionary labor of enslaved Americans is testament to this juncture in the elocutionary movements, e.g., Frederick Douglass and Sojourner Truth are among such individuals, as well as scores of others: labor organizers, women and children's rights activists, abolitionists, and so forth.

Nineteenth-century public life was profoundly influenced and shaped by the public dynamics of elocution as both hegemonic power and liberating power. The force of public speaking was a site of hierarchical knowledge, value, and bodies marked by whiteness, maleness, and homogeneity that consolidated and celebrated these identities and affiliations. But, it was also a site of liberating expression and a contested space—a site where troubled identities could claim their power and strengthen their hope. The elocutionary movement was less about public speaking and more about a public performance where audience and speaker were changing and changed by the urgent issues of the time and the compelling need to speak and witness. Elocution was empowered by a performance of persuasion and in many instances it moved and changed the nation.

THE ART OF INTERPRETATION

The art of public speaking finds a close relation in the "art of Interpretation" (Bacon, 1979). Just as public speech—from the bourgeois classes, enslaved communities, and the lumpen proletariat—could move the hearts and minds of its audience and persuade the nonbelievers, the art of oral interpretation could bring a work of literature to life, putting flesh, bone, and breath to words and bringing them to life from the stagnant silence of the written page.

Wallace Bacon, considered by some to be one of the forefathers of performance studies, articulated the relationship and evolution of elocution's "just and graceful management of the voice, countenance, and gesture" with that of oral interpretation and the performance of literature (as quoted in Conquergood, 2000, p. 326). Bacon celebrated and theorized in his work the performance of literary texts. He augmented and extended the art of reading and reciting a speech in public to the art of interpreting and enacting a literary text before an audience. Bacon states,

> The literary text is a manmade form, or "skin," that separates it from its environment and makes it definable but also serves as its point of contact with the environment. By first observing (reading) that outer form, the reader seeks to get inside the skin of the work to the inner form, and comes to know it in

much the same way as one comes to know another human being—by observing and listening, by relating what is learned to one's total experience, by talking about it with others, by "talking" with it. (1979, p. 157)

Wallace Bacon further enlivened the art of interpretation through his articulation of "Otherness of the Other" (p. 40). For Bacon, this meeting of the art of interpretation with a literary text is an engagement with another way of being; it is to enter beyond the self and reach respectfully into another's world. "The reader giving rapt attention to the literary work is engaged with the *sense of otherness*" (emphasis mine). He goes on to further state, "For the interpreter, belief in the *otherness* of the text, full awareness of its state of being, is a major stage in mastering the art of performance." Wallace Bacon was fond of the following quote in explicating what is meant by the *Other*:

> A person's sense of presence is likely to be most strongly marked and most incontestably evident in his relationship, at certain heightened moments, with another human person. This is as it should be, for an individual sinks into a deadening egoism (however much he may gild it with idealistic verbiage or mitigate it by outward acts) unless he occasionally exercises and stretches his ability to realize another person as an independent presence to whom homage is due, rather than as merely an interruption of continuity in his environment. To know someone as presence instead of as a lump of matter or a set of processes, is to meet him with an open, listening, responsive attitude; it is to become a *thou* in the presence of his *I*-hood. (Wheelwright, 1962, p. 154)

Wallace Bacon's interventions on elocution and the performance of literature led the field of performance to a more layered and extended conceptualization of the Other, and with it came an interest in integrating performance with paradigms from the social sciences as well as ways of conceptualizing social processes as performance. Bacon's Other had now inspired a movement that extended textual Others toward the politics of worldly Others.

PERFORMANCE AS SOCIAL BEHAVIOR

In performance as behavior, social life is described through an organizing metaphor of dramatic action or what the social critic Kenneth Burke describes as "situated modes of action" (1945, pp. 3–93). Burke asks the important question: "What is involved when we say what people are doing and why they are doing it?" Burke introduces the idea "dramas of living" by providing a dramatistic paradigm composed of five key concepts in response to his question. His pentad illuminates performance in the day-to-day motions of social life. His five key terms of dramatism are *Act* (names what took place in thought or deed), *Scene* (the background of the act, the situation in which it occurred), *Agent* (person or kind of person who performed the act), *Agency* (what means or instruments were used), and *Purpose* (the aim or objective). In explicating the implications of this pentad Burke states,

> Men may violently disagree about the purpose behind a given act, or about the character of the person who did it, or how he did it, or in what kind of situation he acted; or they may even insist upon totally different words to name the act itself. But be that as it may, any complete statement about motives will offer *some kind* of answers to these five questions: what was done (act), when and where it was done (scene), who did it (agent), how (agency), and why he did it (purpose). (Burke, 1945, p. xvii)

Just as "situated modes of action" are framed through Burke's performance paradigm, we may also understand performance through modes of language and the action generated from the words spoken. In 1955 J. L. Austin presented his idea of speech act theory in his lecture entitled: "How to Do Things With Words" for the William James Lecture

Series at Harvard University. Briefly defined, "speech-act" is action that is performed when a word is uttered. He stated that language does more than describe, it also *does something* that makes a material, physical, and situational difference: "I forgive you;" "You cannot enter;" "Guilty!" all *do something in the world*. They create a particular reality. Language can bestow forgiveness, a blessing, freedom, citizenship, marriage, a promise, etc. Language *performs* a reality; therefore for Austin language was not merely constantive, but *performative*. Austin's student, John R. Searle, expanded Austin's performative utterance to assert that language is not only performative at certain heightened moments or ceremonial events, thereby separating the performative from the constantive—but that all language is a form of *doing*. Searle believed that whenever there is *intention* in speaking there is also the performative. While Austin designated particular moments when words produced a speech-act, that is, when words performed, Searle (1969) argued that whenever words are spoken with intention (and they almost always are) words are performative.

Jacques Derrida, however, disagreed with Austin and Searle's suggestion that a performative utterance creates a "doing" or a particular reality. According to Derrida, Austin ignores a reality and context that is beyond the present moment of speaking. Language is not the causal factor; the causal factors are repetition and familiarity. For Derrida, the idea that a speech-act makes something happen within a particular present moment is to deny the fact of a particular kind of history. Speech is citational; that is, what is spoken has been spoken many, many times before, and its effects are a result of its repetition and citational force, not a result of a unique or present moment when words are "newly" uttered. Derrida's critique of speech-act theory is captured in the idea of a "metaphysics of presence." Derrida employs metaphysics of presence as a critical term to describe a thought system that depends on an unassailable foundation—an absolute or immutable truth claim. For Derrida, the term refers to the problematic or faulty belief in an essential truth that guarantees meaning. "For Derrida, all that we know and say is based upon what has gone before and what we have inherited from past actions. If something is done with words, it is because it has happened before and we know out of convention and custom to continue to do it" (Madison, 2005, p. 162).

Through a performance studies lens these varying claims relative to language, meaning, and human behavior are not in contradiction, but form a dialectic and creative tension. Words are indeed performative, and they *do* have material effects. Obviously, words *do something in the world*, and they are reiterative (in terms of Derrida) in that speech, meaning, intent, and custom have been repeated through time and are therefore communicative and comprehensible because they are recognizable in their repetition.

From the elocutionary movement, the interpretation of literature, and speech-act theory, we may extend the operation of performance as it functions in language, culture and social life by turning to the anthropology of *experience* and Victor Turner's three-part compilation of performance: cultural performance, social performance, and social drama. We will begin with experience.

PERFORMANCE AS EXPERIENCE OR EXPERIENCE AS PERFORMANCE

Turner wrote that *expressions* are "the crystallized secretions of once living human *experience*" (1982, p. 17). Once an experience presses forward from the field of the day-to-day it becomes the incentive for expression; it is then no longer a personal reality but a shared one. What we experience may blossom into expression whether in the form of story, gossip, or humor on the one end, or poetry, novels, theatre, or film on the other. "The experience now made into expression is presented in the world; it occupies time, space, and public reality. Experience made into expression brings forth reader, observer, listener, village, community, and audience" (Madison, 2005, p. 151). In the evolution from experience to expression, we have simultaneously crossed the threshold of performance. Experience now becomes the very source of performance. Can we now conclude that performance must first find its origins in experience?

The movement from experience to expression is not so neat or complete. Some argue that performance does not always begin with experience; indeed, they argue that it is experience that begins with performance. Conquergood states that it is actually the reverse; it is the "performance that realizes the experience" (1986, pp. 36–37). Bakhtin states, "After all, there is no such thing as experience outside of embodiment in signs. It is not experience that organizes expression, but the other way around—expression organizes experience. Expression is what first gives experience its form and specificity of direction" (quoted in Conquergood, 1986, p. 85).

In the discussions concerning what comes first, experience or performance, we come to recognize through the insights of Victor Turner that this is similar to the chicken or the egg question. In Turner's work we understand that both came first and second. Performance evokes experience, just as experience evokes performance. The reciprocal relationship between experience and performance is represented in Turner's three-part classification of performance: cultural performance, social performance, and social drama.

Cultural performance: Anthropologist Milton Singer first introduced the term "cultural performance" in 1959, stating that these kinds of performances all possess a "limited time span, a beginning and an end, an organized program of activity, a set of performers, an audience, and a place and occasion" (1959, p. xiii). Cultural performances are therefore understood as more conventional forms of performance because they are framed by cultural conventions. Cultural performances include plays, operas, circus acts, carnivals, parades, religious services, poetry readings, weddings, funerals, graduations, concerts, toasts, jokes, and storytelling. In all these examples, self-conscious and symbolic acts are "presented" and communicated within a circumscribed space.

Social performance: In social performance, action, reflection, and intent are not marked as they are in cultural performances. Social performances are the ordinary day-by-day interactions of individuals and the consequences of these interactions as they move through social life (Turner, 1982, pp. 32–33). Social performances are not self-consciously aware that their enactments are culturally scripted. Social performances become examples of a culture and subculture's particular symbolic practices. These performances are most striking when they are contrasted against different cultural norms, e.g., greetings, dining, dressing, dating, walking, looking, and so forth.

Social Drama. In social harmony the working arrangements within a particular social unit are synchronized. When a social drama occurs there is a schism or break in the synchronization. The social unit is disturbed and the parties involved are in disagreement. Turner states,

> Social life, then, even in its apparently quietest moments, is characteristically "pregnant" with social dramas. It is as though each of us has a "peace" face and a "war" face, that we are programmed for cooperation, but prepared for conflict. (1982, p. 11)

Turner defines social drama through a four-phase structure: breach, crises, redressive action, and resolution. In breach, "there is an overt nonconformity and breaking away by an individual or group of individuals from a shared system of social relations" (Turner, 1974, p. 38).

It is in the second stage, of crises, where conflict becomes most apparent. The opposing forces are openly at odds, the masks are stripped away or magnified, and the conflict escalates. In crises the breach has enlarged; it is made public. In the third stage, redressive action, a mechanism is brought forth to squelch the crises from further disruption of the social system. This may be in the form of a mediator, of a judicial system, or of the opposing forces coming together themselves in an effort to resolve the crises.

The final phase is resolution. It is here, according to Turner, where the "disturbed parties are reconciled and re-integrated back into their shared social system" (1974, 1982). The parties may reunite but with changes, or the other result is the recognition of a "legitimate and irreparable schism between the parties" that will separate them from the social system, or they may establish another social system (1982, pp. 8–19). In reintegration there is usually some kind of ritual act to mark the separation or a celebration of the union.

For Turner, performance, whether it is cultural performance, social performance, or social drama, all takes place under the rubric of structure or antistructure. Structure is all that which constitutes order, system, preservation, law, hierarchy, and authority. Antistructure is all that which constitutes human action beyond systems, hierarchies, and constraints.

These three realms outlined by Turner intend to encompass and order the full range of performance and its functions in culture and identity. However, Turner's explication of performance in social and cultural life is further complicated and deepened by the recent discussions and debates pertaining to the concept of "performativity."

PERFORMATIVITY

For feminist critic Judith Butler (1988), performativity is understood as a "stylized repetition of acts" that are—like Derridean citation—"always a reiteration of a norm or set of norms" which means that the "act that one does, the act that one performs is, in a sense, an act that has been going on before one arrived on the scene" (Diamond, 1996, pp. 4–6). Performativity becomes all at once a cultural convention, value, and signifier that is inscribed on the body—performed through the body—to mark identities. In this view of performativity, gestures, posture, clothes, habits, and specific embodied acts are performed differently depending on the gender, as well as race, class, sexuality, and so forth, of the individual. How the body moves about in the world and its various mannerisms, styles, and gestures are inherited from one generation through space and time to another and demarcated within specific identity categories. These performativities become the manifestations and enactments of identity and belonging. This emphasis on performativity as repetition or citationality is useful in understanding how identity categories are not inherent or biologically determined, but how they are socially determined by cultural norms of demarcation. This is an important insight because it opens the possibility for alternative performativities and alternative ways of being. It causes us to reckon with the fact that these categories and therefore the responses and practices based on these categories are not a fact of life, but are based upon repetitions and fabrications of human behavior. The description of performativity as citationality is a critical move, but, for many performance scholars, it is only *one dimension* of articulating performativity. But, then the question becomes: "What gets lost in the reworking of performativity as citationality?" (Conquergood, 1998). We may understand performativity as citationality, but we may also understand performativity as an intervention upon citationality and of resisting citationality. Just as performativity is an internalized repetition of hegemonic "stylized acts" inherited by the status quo, it can also be an internalized repetition of subversive "stylized acts" inherited by contested identities. "Subversive performativity can disrupt the very citations that hegemonic performativity enacts" (Madison, 2005). Performance studies scholar Jill Dolan describes performativity as "the non-essentialized constructions of marginalized identities" (1993, p. 419). For Dolan, performativity in this light is not simply citation, but a symbiosis of identifying experience that is determined by compilations of differences: sex, class, race, ethnicity, sexuality, geography, religion, etc. The postcolonial critic, Homi Bhaba, adds to the idea of subversive performativity by invoking the "performative" as action that disturbs, disrupts, and disavows hegemonic formations (1994, pp. 146–149).

From Homi Bhabha's and Jill Dolan's descriptions of performativity, we may further clarify the meanings and functions of performativity through the contributions of Mary Strine (1998) and Kristen Langellier (1999) where performativity is a dynamic that comprises the interpenetrations of identity, experience, and social relations that constitute subjects and order context. In other words, performativity is the interconnected triad of identity, experience, and social relations— encompassing the admixture of class, race, sex, geography, religion, and so forth that is necessarily "contradictory, multiple, and complexly interconnected" (Langellier, 1999). In sum, performativities are the many markings substantiating that all of us are subjects in a world of power relations.

The question then becomes, when we rework performativity beyond a "stylized repetition of acts" into the more deeply relevant evocation of performativity as "nonessentialized constructions of identity," what does is it then actually look like? Performativities are significantly and powerfully layered in the day-to-day, yet they are heightened and embossed in cultural performances. It is in cultural performances where performativities are doubled with a difference: they are re-presented,

re-located and re-materialized for the possibility of a substantial re-consideration and re-examination. Elin Diamond reminds us: "When performativity materializes as performance in that risky and dangerous negotiation between a 'doing' (a reiteration of norms) and a thing done (discursive conventions that frame our interpretations), between someone's body and the conventions of embodiment, we have access to cultural meanings and critique" (1996, p. 5). These performances that "materialize" performativity and that open meanings and critique, encompass film, music, theatre— the conventions of embodiment—but they also profoundly constitute and are constituted by the stories we tell one another and the narratives we live by. Langellier explains the necessary interpenetration of performance, performativity, and narration:

> Why add performativity to performance? By *performativity*, I highlight the way speech acts have been extended and broadened to understand the constitutiveness of performance. That is, personal narrative performance *constitutes* identities and experience, producing and reproducing that to which it refers. Here, personal narrative is a site where the social is articulated, structured, and struggled over (Butler, Twigg). To study performance as performativity is, according to Elin Diamond, 'to become aware of performance itself as a contested space, where meanings and desires are generated, occluded, and of course multiply interpreted' (4). In performativity, narrator and listener(s) are themselves constituted ('I will tell *you* a story'), as is experience ('a *story* about what happened to me'). Identity and experience are symbiosis of performed story and the social relations in which they are materially embedded: sex, class, race, ethnicity, sexuality, geography, religion, and so on. This is why personal narrative performance is especially crucial to those communities left out of the privileges of dominant culture, those bodies without voice in the political sense. (1999, p. 129)

In these more consciously subversive renderings of performativity we may now extend our discussion of performativity and take up connections between performance and transnational narratives.

PERFORMANCE AND GLOBALITY

The world has grown smaller. Air travel, the Internet, digital technologies, and telecommunication have brought far away places into our homes and lives, just as representations of who we are and what we do are brought into the lives and cultures of those sometimes so foreign to us that we can not locate or name their homelands on the map. The irony is that distance is no longer solely measured by kilometers or miles, but by time and access for those of us who reap the benefits of "first world" technologies and economies: how many hours flying time to Mozambique or how many cable stations on your TV, or the speed of your computer. Zygmunt Bauman reflects the fact that distance is compressed by time by a global elite class:

> Indeed, little in the elite's life experience now implies a difference between 'here' and 'there,' 'inside' and 'outside', 'close by' and 'far away'. With time of communication imploding and shrinking to the no-size of the instant, space and spatial markers cease to matter, at least to those whose actions can move with the speed of the electronic message. (1983, p. 13)

What are the implications for transnational narratives in this era of globalization or of "the no-size of the instant" for those of us who are particularly concerned about the transnational implications of performance? First, performance becomes the enactment and evidence of stories that literally and figuratively bleed across the borders that national boundaries "cut up" (de Certeau, 1974/1984, p. 12). For example, performing the local is enmeshed in what it means to be a U.S. citizen and that is enmeshed in the facts of U.S. foreign policy, world trade, civil society, and war. Second, we

are who we are in our nations because of our placement—for better and worse—among other nations of the world and that literarily spills into the microstructures of our neighborhood, families, and lives. Third, as we travel to lands far and foreign, performance directs us to the symbolic universe of indigenous life. Signs and symbols hold meanings and histories, but more, they are the expressive formations of local knowledge and desire. Performance leads us to the social dramas, cultural performances, and embodied stories that make culture live. Performance travels transnationally between the local and global so we may be witnesses and co-performers of a politics of culture beyond our own borders. The idea of "territory" in this time of globalization has greater implications than ever before. The way the "local" is affected by transnational communication and affiliations has extended our understanding of "community," "nation," and "identity." Conquergood states,

> According to Michel de Certeau, "what the map cuts up, the story cuts across" (1984:12). This pithy phrase evokes a postcolonial world crisscrossed by transnational narratives, Diaspora affiliations, and especially, the movement and multiple migrations of people, sometimes voluntary, but often economically propelled and politically coerced. In order to keep pace with such a world, we think of "place" as a heavily trafficked intersection, a port of call and exchange, instead of circumscribed territory. A boundary is more like a membrane than a wall . . . our understanding of local context expands to encompass the historical, dynamic, often traumatic, movements of people, ideas, images, commodities, and capital. It is not easy to sort out the local from the global: transnational circulations of images get reworked on the ground and redeployed for local tactical struggles. (2002, p. 145)

The crossings between the local and the global form complex terrains of progress, struggle, and contestation. In this collection, we illuminate performance in its various constellations in ways that consider these crossings and evoke deeper questions about them. The possibilities and political implications from such a constellation of discussions represented in this volume is far reaching, because the authors implicate operations of power at multiple locations and within varied subjectivities. What does this mean? It means the writers in this volume have chosen to examine ethnographically, historically, theoretically, pedagogically, and imaginatively a range of spaces both hidden and apparent that are represented by the silences of the subaltern at one end and by the exegesis of the empowered on the other. This polyvocal range of locations raises questions relative to imbalances of power, forms of resistance, and the symbolic universe of expressive forms of discontent, desire, and alternative possibilities. The politics and praxis of performance open up the multivocality of expressions that are formed under necessity and duress, as well as pleasure and inspiration toward envisioning new and other realities in the everyday acts of both foreign and familiar locations. In performance as praxis, the form of knowledge itself is questioned. Performance asks us to identify and affirm knowledges that are contested, obscure, and often demeaned in the embodied acts and oral traditions of such locations.

PERFORMANCE AND/AS REPRESENTATION

Richard Schechner, another founder of performance studies, famously defined performance as "restored behavior" (1985, p. 33). Schechner brought his considerable experience and reputation as an experimental theatre director to performance studies, and his perspective has inspired scholars to examine the intricate conceptual and pragmatic connections between performance, repetition, and representation (see also Schechner, 2002).

In *Unmarked* (1993) and *The Ends of Performance* (1998), Peggy Phelan offers a politicized reconception of relationships between these three terms. She writes,

> The pleasure of resemblance and repetition produces both psychic assurance and political fetishization. Representation reproduces the Other as the Same. Performance, insofar as it can be defined as representation without reproduction, can be seen as a model for another representational economy, one in which the reproduction of the Other as the Same is not assured. (1993, p. 3)

For Phelan, this translates into a particular ethical stance toward performance and/as representation.

> What lies before the field of performance studies is precisely a discipline: a refusal to indulge the killing possessiveness too often bred in admiration and love. The lessons we most need to learn are lessons in mourning without killing, loving without taking. This is the end toward which performance aims. (1998, p. 11)

Philip Auslander is also concerned with presence and absence in discussions of performance in/as representation. His focus is the issue of "liveness," and particularly the notion that the live performance seems to have a self-evident realness and value that the purportedly secondary "mediatized" ones do not: "However one may assess the relative symbolic values of live events, it is important to observe that even within our hyper-mediatized culture, far more symbolic capital is attached to live events than to mediatized ones, at least for the moment" (1999, p. 59). Auslander argues that performance studies scholars must critically examine this hierarchy of values, and he actively interrogates the presumptions undergirding both the notion of "liveness" itself, and the symbolic capital that accrues to it.

Conceptual reworking of, and interventions in, performance and/as representation appear in works by a wide range of artists. Indeed the interdisciplinary nature of performance studies itself is also reflected in this work, and in the backgrounds of the artists who produce it. This interdisciplinarity, along with irony, pastiche, and a suspicion of master narratives, has led some performance scholars to describe aesthetics in these pieces as "postmodern" (Carlson, 1996, pp. 123–143). Many of these same practices can also be found in the work of early twentieth century avant-garde theatre and performance practitioners (see Goldberg, 1979).

Two examples of performances that actively engage and trouble conventional norms of representation are illustrative. The first is "Food for the Spirit," completed in 1971 by artist and philosopher Adrian Piper (Jones, 1998, pp. 162–164). Piper is a light-skinned African American woman. In one photo-document from this "private loft performance," she stands nude before a mirror, a camera held beneath her breasts (p. 162). Piper's performance exists betwixt and between the moment of "live" performance and the moment in which an audience removed from the event itself confronts the photo. In that liminal space, Piper simultaneously "exposes the assumption of whiteness implicit in the 'rhetoric of the pose'" and challenges the stability and self-evidence of racial identity. She writes,

> I am the racist's nightmare, the obscenity of miscegenation. I am a reminder that segregation is impotent; a living embodiment of sexual desire that penetrates racial barriers and reproduces itself. . . . I represent the loathsome possibility that everyone is "tainted" by black ancestry: If someone can look and sound like me and still be black, who is unimpeachably white? (quoted in Jones, 1998, p. 162)

Consider, too, the work of Spiderwoman, a performance company of three Native American sisters. Mindful of the ways Native Americans enter representation—as "vanished," as archeological "specimens," "noble savages," or the loci of nostalgia, Spiderwoman exposes and critiques these constructions through burlesquing and parodying them. As Rebecca Schneider (1997) observes,

> Laughing, Spiderwoman is sending up something extremely serious. Who are the "primitives" that have been created by white nostalgia? Much of Spiderwoman's work is related to the issue of "Indianness," adroitly played in the painful space between the need to claim an "authentic" native identity and their awareness of the appropriation and the historical commodification of the signs of that authenticity. Their material falls in the interstices where their autobiographies meet popular and aesthetic constructions of the "primitive," specifically the primitivized American Indian. (p. 161)

Performance studies scholars also create performances that rework and interrogate relationships between, and conventions of, performance and/as representation. This work is another example of performance at the intersections of method, of research, object of research, and method of representing research (Alexander, 2002; Jackson, 1998; Johnson, 2003; Jones, 1997).

Performance studies scholars tease out and refashion relationships between performance and representation on the page as well as on the stage. In her influential essay "Performing Writing" (1998), Della Pollock discusses "Six Excursions into Performative Writing." Such writing, she explains, is evocative, metonymic, subjective, citational, and consequential. It is particularly well suited to the complexities of setting bodies—and theories—in motion into language. A number of contributors to this handbook use performative writing in their essays, demonstrating that critique in performance studies, like performance itself, is inventive, generative, and "on the move" (Conquergood, 1995).

WHY A HANDBOOK OF PERFORMANCE STUDIES?

Many of the contributors in this volume cross subject areas; that is, they write from several categories at once. For example scholars and teachers of performance may integrate and overlap several areas, such as ethnography, theory, history, literature, and politics in various other combinations. However, for this collection, we have organized each of these domains as separate topical areas. The editors and contributors for each section all use multidisciplinary approaches; yet, they are experts within their specific domains with an accomplished record of research and teaching. They employ theories and paradigms from various other subject areas of performance to enhance and extend the core concepts within their specific domain of interest. As a result of the multidisciplinary nature of performance, and because, as editors, it is our intent to honor the rich tapestry that constitutes performance, in crossing a range of subjects this collection also crosses a range of readers. This book is meant for students, teachers, practitioners and all those interested in how to understand and employ performance, pedagogically, theoretically, and artistically. The thematic organization is as follows:

Performance and Literature

Performance and literature are intimately linked. Performance is a path by which we enter literary worlds. Performance is polyrhythmic as it conjoins the words, experiences, behaviors, imaginings, and bodies of the reader with those of the literary text. Chapters in this section discuss the use of performance as a critical, analytical tool for examining literature; the institutional formation of performance studies through its links with literature in the oral tradition, in oratory, and in the theatre; the relationship between performance, testimony and the personal narrative; and

performance as, itself, a form of textual representation and artistic production.

Performance and Pedagogy

This section explores the productive intersections between critical pedagogy and performance. Each essay demonstrates that the production, consumption, and dissemination of knowledge are critical performances intimately linked to activism as well as to the formation of institutional practices and identities. This section examines performance as constitutive of pedagogical theory and praxis from varying sites that both trouble and honor the meanings and consequences of knowledge in action. Pedagogy is explored as embodied processes and as a politics of hope.

Performance and Politics

Performance implicates power in the *situated* nature of human interaction as well as in the symbols that simultaneously motivate, sustain, and contest its legitimacy. Performance requires locating the complexly layered micro and macro enactments of politics to identify human conditions and yearnings relative to power, authority, strength, and force. The essays included in this section explore the principles of politics as it encompasses freedom and human desire, particularly within the realms of race, sexuality, gender, globality, caste, and class.

Performance and Ethnography

Performance is variously and simultaneously employed as a theory, method, and event in research and travel to ethically enter the domains of Others. Performance and ethnography combine in this section to explore the value and ubiquity of performance within the ethnographic enterprise: in illuminating relations and theories of space, place, and Other; in the embodied, dialogical dynamics of fieldwork methods; and, in the scholarly representation and advocacy praxis of public performance. Therefore, the essays in this section examine the uses of performance in the analysis, engagement, and presentation of ethnography and its processes.

Performance and History

The relationship between performance and history goes far beyond studies of specific performers and specific periods, though these, of course, are vitally important. Included in this section are discussion of the theatrical construction of the nation, of the relationships between performance and forms of civic and social life, and performance as a heuristic guiding both archival methodology and historiography. Chapters in this section will explore varying aspects of the multifaceted relationship between performance and history.

Performance and Theory

Performance and theory conjoin to explicate the meanings and implications that inhere in human experience and social processes. Performance theory is employed across disciplines to decipher the multiple operations of performance (performativity and the performative) within a written text, a life world, and in domains of cognitive and imaginary expressions. The essays included in this section will examine the dynamics of performance theory, e.g., its taxonomies, interrogations, and queries. Moreover, the essays will reflect the *performance turn* in western academic theory as it invokes more embodied, subjunctive, and transgressive claims regarding the ontology of difference.

CONCLUSION

This handbook serves as both a forum and as a response to a call for those who are interested in employing performance whether it is

through the strategies of performance *theory,* the methods of performance *ethnography,* the politics of performance *pedagogy,* the illuminations of *literature* and performance, the revisionings of performance *history,* the claims in the *politics* of performance, or the overarching ways performance is *performed* as a staged event. All these dimensions of performance are deeply invoked while elements of each richly overlap with elements of the others. The politics, theory, pedagogy, literature, and ethnography of performance are distinct sites of inquiry; however the ways they naturally and inherently intersect with each other becomes a rich montage of meanings, questions, and claims. This volume opens a range of paradigms and meditations on performance to the reader in order to illuminate and clarify the various ways performance can be employed across subjects of interest and disciplinary divisions. Moreover, we have placed various arguments about and ideas of performance together in this collection to create a dialectic of comparisons and contrasts between and within performance studies conversations.

REFERENCES

Alexander, B. K. (2002). Skin flint (or, the garbage man's kid): A generative autobiographical performance based on Tami Spry's "Tattoo Stories." *Text and Performance Quarterly, 20*(1), 97–114.

Auslander, P. (1999). *Liveness: Performance in a mediatized culture.* New York: Routledge.

Bacon, A. W. (1979). *The art of interpretation.* New York: Holt, Rinehart & Winston.

Bauman, Z. (1983). *Globalization: The human consequences.* New York: Columbia University Press.

Bhabha, H. (1994). *The location of culture.* New York: Routledge.

Burke, K. (1945). *A grammar of motives.* Englewood Cliffs, NJ: Prentice Hall.

Butler, J. (1988). Performative acts and gender constitution: An essay in phenomenology and feminist theory. *Theory Journal, 40,* 519–531.

Carlson, M. (1996). *Performance: A critical introduction.* New York: Routledge.

Conquergood, D. (1986). Between experience and meaning: Performance as paradigm for meaningful action. In T. Colson (Ed.), *Renewal and revision: The future of interpretation* (pp. 26–59). Denton, TX: Omega.

Conquergood, D. (1995). Of caravans and carnivals: Performance studies in motion. *The Drama Review, 39*(4), 137–141.

Conquergood, D. (2000). Rethinking elocution: The trope of the talking book and other figures of speech. *Text and Performance Quarterly, 20*, 325–341.

Conquergood, D. (2002). Performance studies: Interventions and radical research. *The Drama Review 46*(2), 145–156.

de Certeau, M. (1984). *The practice of everyday life* (S. Rendall, Trans.). Berkeley: University of California Press. (Original work published in 1974)

Diamond, E. (Ed.). (1996). Introduction. *Performance and cultural politics* (pp. 1–2). New York: Routledge.

Goldberg, R. (1979). *Performance: Live art, 1909 to the present.* New York: Abrams.

Hamera, J. (2002). An answerability of memory: "Saving" Khmer classical dance. *The Drama Review, 46*(4), 65–85.

Jackson, S. (1998). White noises: On performing white, on writing performances. *The Drama Review, 42*(1), 49–65.

Johnson, E. P. (2003). Strange fruit: A performance about identity politics. *The Drama Review, 47*(2), 88–116.

Jones, A. (1998). *Body art: Performing the subject.* Minneapolis: University of Minnesota Press.

Jones, J. (1997). Sista docta: Performance as critique of the academy. *The Drama Review, 41*(2), 51–67.

Langellier, K. (1999). Personal narrative, performance, performativity: Two or three things I know for sure. *Text and Performance Quarterly, 19*(2), 123–144.

Madison, S. (2005). *Critical ethnography: Method, ethics, and performance.* Thousand Oaks, CA: Sage.

Phelan, P. (1993). *Unmarked: The politics of performance.* New York: Routledge.

Phelan, P. (1998). Introduction: The ends of performance. In P. Phelan & J. Lane (Eds.), *The ends of performance* (pp. 1–19). New York: NYU Press.

Pollock, D. (1998). Performing writing. In P. Phelan & J. Lane (Eds.), *The ends of performance* (pp. 73–103). New York: NYU Press.

Schechner, R. (1985). *Between theatre and anthropology.* Philadelphia: University of Pennsylvania Press.

Schechner, R. (2002). *Performance studies: An introduction.* New York: Routledge.

Schneider, R. (1997). *The explicit body in performance.* New York: Routledge.

Searle, J. R. (1969). *Speech acts: An essay in the philosophy of language.* Cambridge, England: Cambridge University Press.

Singer, M. (Ed.). (1959). *Traditional India: Structure and change.* Philadelphia: American Folklore Society.

Strine, M. (1998). Articulating performance/performativity: Disciplining tasks and the contingencies of practice. In J. S. Trent (Ed.), *Communication: Views from the helm for the 21st century* (pp. 312–317). Boston: Allyn & Bacon.

Strine, M. S., Long, B. W., & Hopkins, M. F. (1990). Research in interpretation and performance studies: Trends, issues, priorities. In G. M. Phillips & J. T. Wood (Eds.), *Speech communication: Essays to commemorate the 75th anniversary of the Speech Communication Association* (pp. 181–204). Carbondale: Southern Illinois University Press.

Turner, V. (1982). *From ritual to theatre: The human seriousness of play.* New York: Performing Arts.

Wheelwright, P. (1962). *Metaphor and reality.* Bloomington: Indiana University Press.

PART I

Performance Trouble

DELLA POLLOCK

Every essay in this volume is saturated with theory. Each of the studies of performance history is informed by a particular understanding of the nature of facts, narrative, and time. Each ethnographic moment evoked comes to us with the weight of 20, 30 years of thinking about what it means to "write culture" behind it. At the same time, no number of essays concerned with "performance and theory" (much less the select four included in this section) could ever be fully representative or exhaustive of developments in performance theory. So why a section exclusively on performance and theory? What difference does it make to make theory a particular site of engagement in the pages that follow?

First, these essays are particularly concerned with dramatizing possible relationships between theory and performance—between thinking about and doing performance, between *doing theory* and *thinking performance*. An empirical or even narrowly interpretive approach to the world may rest relatively comfortably with theory as a metanarrative, as an explanatory thread wound around the object-world. Performance won't stand still long enough for theory to wrap it up nicely. It moves in time and space through restless bodies. To track its contingencies, to plumb its affective depths, and to discover the

power and pleasures of its rough currents, thinking about performance must move as well. In these essays, we see and feel theory as something like a collaborator with performance, a cosubject however uncomfortably removed from the stability of a subject/object relation. In embodied relation to performance, theory moves. It is less the primary figure in a new construction of performance than it is a reflexive participant in the *poiesis* of knowing, being, and acting that performance initiates. I would thus have to call performance-and-theory a project of interanimation: of discerning how many more vital possibilities (for performance, for theory, for the world) are wrought by the transactivity of performance and various ways of imagining it.

Second, then, each of these essays makes a significant "detour through theory," taking up Stuart Hall's early charge for cultural studies. For Hall, the question of theory is a question of method. Theory is not or should not be an autonomous practice running at best parallel with history. To the contrary, Hall takes from Marx the imperative that thought must "'rise from the abstract to the concrete' not vice versa" (Hall, 2003, p. 131). As J. Macgregor Wise observes, the "concrete" to which theory rises is not "what is empirically given, but a necessary complexity. It is the result of

1

theoretical work, not its origin" (Wise, 2003, p. 107). Theory would thus produce the "concrete" in the form of a "necessary complexity." Wise summarizes the principle method Hall recommends:

> Take a concept and track its multiple material determinations and then you have the concrete. The process is not that of inserting philosophical abstractions into the 'here and now,' because that neglects these many determinations (1986c: 58). It is not about theory, but 'going on theorizing' (1986c: 60). However, the process of theorizing itself is always grounded in its historical conjuncture; thought presupposes society . . . and therefore is shaped by its own multiple determinations. (Wise, 2003, p. 107)

The "detour through theory" emphasizes the "process of theorizing itself" (as the unfinished work of "'going on theorizing'") and the mutual complexity of theory and history. For Hall,

> Both the specificities and the connections—the complex unities of structures—have to be demonstrated by the concrete analysis of concrete relations and conjunctions . . . . This method thus retains the concrete empirical reference as a privileged and undissolved 'moment' within a theoretical analysis without thereby making it 'empiricist': the concrete analysis of concrete situations. (Hall, 2003, p. 128)

Writing in the mid-seventies, Hall's reading of "Marx's Notes on Method" reflects his encounter with Althusser and his emerging, concomitant interest in "the complex unities of structures." At the same time, it makes a larger claim on the materiality of theory as a means of engaging in "the concrete analysis of concrete situations." Hall preserves the "privileged and undissolved" empirical moment in theoretical analysis while carefully distinguishing theoretical analysis from empiricism. Indeed, by comparison to Hall's version of theoretical analysis as "concrete analysis,"

empiricism is abstract: it entails an abstraction of theory from the world of material determinations of which it is a necessary part.

The "detour through theory" throws off the "givenness" of both the mapped course and destination. Each of the essays in this section moves through and with theory as an alternate, even previously unknown or unmarked route that takes us off the beaten path. The landscape is suddenly less familiar. Gripping the wheel, my car compass proves useless: *Where am I now? What is this place?* Who am I now at this particular intersection of theorizing and historicizing? And who might I be at another?

The detour implicates the subjectivity of the driver (author) as much as it does the passengers (readers). It positions each in the precarious spatial and temporal position of *becoming different*. The detour is thrilling and terrifying in its unpredictability: the child's "When will we get there?" becomes "Will we get there?," "What will 'there' be when we arrive?," and "Who will we be in relation to this place made scarcely or newly recognizable by a course of indirection?"

Third then, for me, making an explicit "detour through theory" is always a strangely utopian gesture. It holds out the (not always or generously consoling) promise of change.

As each of the authors in this section rounds back around the detour, each arrives differently at "performance." The designated destination is the same and different. In each of these cases, the instability of theory redounds to the nominal designation of a "performance" as such, destabilizing it in turn—as if the passengers, disoriented from the alternate path, were to ask: this looks like "it" . . . but is this really where we meant to go? What was once familiar as a ready object of study is now strange, inviting such questions as: What does it mean to call something a performance? What values does doing so attribute or hail? What does siting a "performance" do for the way we think not only about performance(s) but the world "performance" names? And so how does or might binding an interaction or event to the name "performance" affect the way we live in that world?

Each of these essays more or less arrives at a place of what I would have to call performance trouble (echoing Butler, 1990). Through each theoretical excursion, "performance" becomes what it is: a name, a frame, a signifier, a construct. To call even what has become most familiar to us (most naturalized) as performance a "show" is as loaded as presuming gender is a stable, natural identity. Not unlike gender, and historically for many of the same reasons, performance as "show" has been disciplined into an object of spectatorship, formal appreciation, and/or enjoyment. When the nature and status of "performance" is itself disturbed, (1) whatever it is we are calling a "performance" is less immediately knowable: it is less easily assimilated to given bodies of knowledge and convention; (2) the "performance" event or practice becomes less stable and more vulnerable to contest over its nature, meanings, and values; and (3) the designated "performance" may be re-named, re-marked, and/or made to re-signify—to *mean differently.*

Accordingly, these essays and others like them, may lead us less toward *knowing about* performance and more toward feeling, imagining, and/or making *with* performance. Concomitantly we might say that in the end we *know less about* and *make more of* the performances theory calls out.

Jon McKenzie is particularly concerned with what it means to call an event or a practice a "performance." He begins with the troubled space of economic globalization in which "performance" more often than not designates the "fulfillment in form" of technological systems often affiliated with the rise of the U.S. military complex after World War II, including high-performance fighter planes and missile guidance systems. Performance has become the watchword in sales of lower-tech commodities including cars and laundry detergent, and of management styles aimed at eliciting "peak performance" from employees. In each case, performance has come to mean something more than the demonstration of competency that Richard Bauman found essential to the authority of the storyteller in his seminal essay on "Verbal Art as Performance" (Bauman, 1977). Indeed, the stakes have not only been transferred to commodities and corporations but have risen considerably, making "performance" practically synonymous with the highest levels of human-qua-technological accomplishment and productivity. More than gold-star achievement however, performance promises *more*: the car that really performs promises more speed, more power, more control of the road; the company that really performs outperforms others in an ongoing race for the competitive edge in a global market. Entangled with the military-industrial promise of strength and dominion, when "performance" is deployed in comparative global analyses showing that U.S. students do not, apparently, "perform" as well in math and science as their Asian counterparts, it becomes a figure of lack, shame, and discipline. Here, performance becomes accountability becomes "high-stakes testing" education on which the performance potential of a nation hangs.

Performance studies, as McKenzie notes, has by and large ignored these performatives: these acts of naming that constrain whole bodies of human behavior to mechanistic standards for best/better/more accomplishment, or what Marcuse, in an early critique of the rise of consumer culture in the U.S., called the "performance principle." We have disregarded and dismissed the consolidation of multinational interests around "performance," McKenzie argues, in favor of discerning resistance in local, cultural performances. Working his way prismatically through Butler, Foucault, Deleuze and Guattari, and Derrida, McKenzie argues that we have not only systematically ignored prevailing formations of "performance" but their usefulness in seeing and reimagining performance as "an onto-historical formation of power and knowledge." In this light, performance strata above and below that of the nation-state, including inter- and transnational organizations such as the United Nations and the Global Reporting Initiative on the one hand, and small businesses and nongovernmental organizations on the other, become critical sites of alternative performance production. McKenzie's detour through performance theory expands the terrain of potential performance resistance to include global networks, ultimately appropriating the threatening, organizational imperative "perform—or else" to the micro and macro levels of production it would otherwise eclipse.

McKenzie draws on the work of Judith Butler in his final reflections on how we might connect the study of global economic performativities with that of local, discrete, cultural performances. Butler haunts much of the work represented here, although perhaps none so pointedly as Rebecca Schneider's "Never, Again." Schneider's essay is a performance in its own right. Naming it as such, I am calling attention not only to its temporalization of social and linguistic grammars, its evocation of the banality of horror, and its episodic structure, but also to its complex articulation of theory and scene in vexed moments of repetition.

Repetition has been repeatedly declared a definitive characteristic of performance. Performance is, for Richard Schechner, "restored behavior," a repetition in heightened form of a "strip" of human behavior (Schechner, 2002, pp. 28–29). For Butler, it is that "stylized repetition of acts" that repeats itself into invisibility, making the performance seem natural, that is, not a performance at all (Butler, 1990, p. 140). In the end, for Butler, the ultimate trick of performance-as-repetition is to make itself disappear into the appearance of history as "given." It is the performance of this trick, under pressure of disciplinary threat (perform—or else) that Butler calls "performativity."

Repetition intrigues and goads Schneider. In "Never, Again," as in related work (Schneider, 2001), Schneider recovers the performance in performativity—not impossibly wresting it from the networks of repetition in which it is embedded but enabling it to reappear as such in the concrete analysis of reiteration.

"*Yesterday*," Schneider begins. Underscored, yesterday is the day that haunts today. Today (unmarked except by reference to what it is and is not: yesterday) is at once the day on which we are reading the essay and the day on which the September 11, 2001, attack on the World Trade Center twin towers occurs and is simultaneously represented. "First one, then the other," Schneider writes. The fall of the first tower is repeated in the second. The collapse of both is then repeated in "replay upon replay" on TV. Whatever was original in the first televised glimpses of the attack becomes a ghost of simulation:

> Sometimes the second tower was played first, then the first tower was played second. Oddly, as replay led to replay, as forward led to back, the image became only more incredible. The more it reappeared, the more it seemed as if we had missed it and needed to see it again, and each 'again' lent itself less to familiarity than to disbelief. The sense of "how to read" the image became increasingly unsettled with each repetition as the "already seen" began to partake of the uncanny union of overly familiar and impossibly strange. Perhaps the towers had never been there? Or, perhaps they had always been coming down and we had just refused to see it before *now*?

Time shifts. The apparent orderliness of an appalling history—"first one, then the other"—becomes more terrifying yet in its repetition. With each replay—again and again, forward to back—time itself seems to collapse into never and always: "Perhaps the towers had never been there? Or, perhaps they had always been coming down . . . ?" and yesterday becomes the "now" in which in which we seem to be seeing (as if) for the first time.

Immersed in the performance of repetition, Schneider parses the torment of time as it conspires with media replay to produce "a kind of violence of ambivalence." Notably, Schneider does not "tour" the violence from a camera-safe distance but writes in and through the material, structural repetitions that compose our spectatorial "experience" of the terrorist attack. She performs in writing a "detour" that courses through the material formations of extra-canny events: watching Peter Jennings's televised news report at a local coffee shop; teaching class in the wake of the first media blast, surrounded by the gossipy buzz of "have you heard?" (about what has already been and will be *seen*); the repetition of the father (Bush I) in the son (Bush II) in their respective declarations against repetition— "Never again"—that, in the repetition, invokes what was to have been "never" *again;* Gertrude Stein's own literary performances of repetition, here performed as a variation on the kind of *catharsis interruptus* Schneider attributes to the media representation; a tactical diversion through the pages of Michel de Certeau's renowned essay, "Walking in the City," now perhaps most infamous for its representation of the twin towers as "the tallest letters in the world," as a rhetorical figuration of the excess of consumer culture seen grandiloquently from "above," raided, tricked, detoured from below.

The essay moves in precisely the way Schneider's reading of de Certeau suggests our writing-performance of the world might: "in reading the detail *as a practice, in play,*" she argues, "we shift our focus to movement, to moving through, and in shifting to movement, change becomes not only possible but the condition of any myth of stasis (the monument's secret)." Moving through, Schneider *goes on theorizing*. She challenges the monumentalism of ocular memory and its twin image in spectators moved to the point of being unmoved.

She performs the performativity of repetition in writing and, in so doing, finds the tenuous, tremulous grounds of change.

José Muñoz also practices what I would call the motility of performance thinking. In his essay for this volume, "Stages: Queers, Punks, and the Utopian Performative," he moves among and between autobiographical moments, theoretical inquiry, and Kevin McCarty's glittering images of empty stages. The performers here are off-stage: the audience members, lingerers, and subcultures made up of the not-yet-queer and "not-so-kids" that formed around punk groups and Los Angeles gay clubs in the eighties and nineties. In their interactions and refashionings of self-and-other, Muñoz finds what he calls "utopian performatives": the performance of a kind of minoritarian hope that does not so much rest over-the-rainbow as it rebounds back from the far horizon of possibility to create "temporal disorganization." Utopia, for Muñoz, is not a static ideal but a "not yet here" that implodes on the here, now, in the form of "potentialities." Potentialities are affectively charged moments of becoming and belonging that occur at and beyond the edges of anything like a bound event—while the crowd empties out of the club into the parking lot, for instance, or when the activity in the mosh pit upstages the stage. The empty stage, moreover, is never empty: it is as likely to be suddenly overtaken by a flagrant display of sexual excess as it is to be filled with the after-image of boys and young men rehearsing queer subjectivities into being and becoming. For Muñoz, the not here–not now of potentiality propels us into futurity.

Troubling the time/space of performance, Muñoz troubles the signification of queerness as "just a stage." By articulating this familiar/familial gesture at containment with images of actual stages on which Muñoz glimpses queer potentiality, Muñoz resignifies "stage" and "queer." *Thinking with performance* in this way—scouting for potentialities, crossing theory and performance with the same desire and reserve with which Muñoz claims he crossed "a metaphorical threshold between punk worlds and gay life"—becomes then a performative act in its own right, producing the kind of hope Muñoz finds so urgently lacking in many queer and minoritarian discourses.

Muñoz thus qualifies Butler's conception of performativity with immanent hope. He also challenges the kind of performativity that follows on what has become something of a tenet in performance thinking today: Peggy Phelan's 1993 claim that "performance's being . . . becomes itself through disappearance" (p. 146).

Performances disappear. They are here one moment and not the next. For Phelan, they *become themselves* as they disappear into time, each moment hailing the one into which it will irretrievably dissolve. The ephemerality of performance made it particularly attractive to artists of the early modernist avant-garde for whom its elusive immediacies were at once a sanctuary from and a means of assault on the commodification of spatially fixed artwork (e.g., see Goldberg, 2001). Performance temporalities could not be boxed and sold (or so the story goes) and so could trick the swelling commodity market. Disappearance is the ultimate trick: the master magician makes the sequined assistant disappear before our very eyes. He spins the power of performance to make bodies disappear into pure theatricality. The magical wonders of now-you-see-it, now-you-don't snub the very fragility of life— the much less flashy, much more banal disappearance of life into death that defines the performance of mortality.

For Phelan, to the extent that the ontology of performance is realized in disappearance, it is intimately tied into loss. It consequently generates yet another kind of "performativity," the kind J. L. Austin identified in his 1955 efforts to delineate descriptive and effective, or "constative" and "performative," speech utterances (Austin, 1962). "Constative" utterances

describe and report. They *refer to* persons and events and so may be true or false. "Performative" utterances do what they say— they make a bet or a promise, clinch a vow. They are consequential. For Phelan, Austin's constative utterances become performative in the absence of the performance to which they refer. Representing performance does not reproduce the lost object or, in this case, performance. It nonetheless stages the effort to remember what is lost. In performances of reflexive remembering, we learn *again* how loss acquires meaning—not only of and for the object, but of and for the one who remembers. The remembering subject disappears into the object of performative remembering, becoming herself the subject who longs always to be remembered (Phelan, 1993, p. 147)—and the generative figure of ongoing rehearsals and repetitions.

For Phelan, performance disappears into the performativity of reckoning with "what is lost." While, for Phelan, "performance implicates the real through the presence of living bodies," "performance marks the body itself as loss" (1993, pp. 148 and 152). Performance at once hails live bodies into representation of the real and dissolves those bodies into metonyms—associative invocations of something we might call real. The body disappears under its metonymic weight. In turn, it seems, the promise of performativity is limited to a melancholic rehearsal of displacements. The longing to be remembered and the longing to remember may meet only in the irresolution of always longing.

This is not the productive nostalgia Muñoz has elsewhere claimed for performance by people of color (e.g., see Muñoz, 2000). Nor is it the vision he holds for the stages he recites here. Indeed, here the never-empty stage is productive of gay belonging. It is an affective space that is not reproductive of lost subjects but generative of new ones. As Muñoz takes up the image of one of the oldest Latino gay clubs in Los Angeles, La Plaza, for instance, he triangulates memory, theory, and image in an exemplification of what might be called *performative seeing*, a kind of seeing that opens up "another vista" whose particular magic lies in conjuring "stories of migratory crossing, legal and illegal" and positioning "these bodies, whose life world is always in flux about to belong, on the cusp of materialization." Or: tricking disappearance with the prospect of appearance, of making the material body of queer subjectivity *always about to appear*. On these stages, then, in this endless "stage," the live body does not so much implicate as it *becomes* the real.

Judith Hamera takes a different kind of detour. She travels through performance in order to arrive at a concrete analysis of aesthetics. For Hamera, "the social work of aesthetics is especially central to performance, where the labors of creation and the dynamics of consumption are explicitly communal and corporeal, and where corporeality and sociality are remade as surely as a formal event may be produced." In (re)turn, "performance exposes aesthetics' social work as embodied, processual, rhetorical and political and, especially, as daily, as routine, a practice of everyday life." Hamera's aim is to discern the "essential complexities" of art's social lives. Towards this end, she pivots on three instances of performance as divergent as the spectral remains of Khmer dance and music traditions, classical ballet technique, and the exchange of Navajo folk art. With each instance, Hamera expands and contracts the broad field of aesthetics.

Hamera's essay is above all a radical act of naming and renaming "performance." In each instance, Hamera locates an apparently closed performance event (playing traditional music) in concrete relation to intersecting events (remembering playing), thinking their relation into a tight and wide network of social interaction that is, in the end, astoundingly beautiful. Hamera pries conventionally delimited performances free of anything like an object-status, siting them in an open context of contingency, corporeality, and coproductivity. As a result, "performance" becomes a loose knot binding aesthetics and social life. And the frayed remnants of performance traditions all but wiped out under genocide are joined, if not exactly recovered, to the "answerability" of present to past, past to present in the echo chambers of living memory. A dance technique identified with the most elite and gendered Western performance traditions becomes capable of crafting "vernacular landscapes." And the folk art object, so often lost under the press of reading, seeing, and theorizing that reiterates the tourist gaze it deplores, becomes the figure of a thriving performance economy. For Hamera,

> The object, like the performed story, is the membrane across which the performer/artists and audiences encounter and imagine one another, whether from opposite sides of the proscenium or opposite sides of a trading post or gallery counter. Neither is simply a text waiting to be animated but a display that binds communicative competence, history, affect, action and thought together within the commodity situation. Thus, the object in the situation speaks; it is, simultaneously, a story and an event. It animates relations of exchange even as it is, itself, animated in the process.

In her discussion of the residual diaspora of classical Cambodian music and dance, Hamera cites two important turns on "performativity": Elin Diamond's sense of the conjunctural relation between performance and performativity, and Vivian Patraka's adaptation of Diamond in her formulation of "performative goneness." For Diamond, "performativity" describes "the thing done": the what-is-to-be-done that has-already-been-done so many times under disciplinary threat that it is deceptively simply "the thing done" (Diamond, 1996, p. 4). ("It is the thing done," we might overhear a father gently exhort a child.) Performance is the doing. The doing-of-the-thing-done, of course, but nonetheless not a "thing" at all but an act unfolding in time and across space. As much as the-thing-done may structure the doing of it, the doing materializes the structural complexities shaping, pressing, pulling at it. In so doing, performance is, for Diamond, a kind of theorizing: it problematizes conditions of historical determination.

For Patraka, the thing-done is the thing-gone. It is "the pressure of palpable loss" that not only structures but compels the "doing" of Holocaust memories (Patraka, 1999, p. 7). Accordingly performance is, as Phelan suggests, defined by loss but, for Patraka, primarily in the sense that it is "a constant iteration against" loss. Performance does its work of repetition, driven on by what it cannot stand—or will stand for, will materialize, only insofar as it stands *against* "the pressure of palpable" atrocity and genocidal disappearance (see also Taylor, 1997).

In this light, Hamera's work is an insistent performance of "going on theorizing." It repeats and restores classical and folk performances in and among living bodies of thought. Like Schneider, Hamera thinks with the intimacies and intricacies of restored behaviors. Like Muñoz, she finds performance where it's not "done": off-stage, unfinished, going on. Like McKenzie, she challenges the broad economies in which "performance" is too often isolated as a specialized form of practice, whether in the name of "art" or "resistance." And together with Schneider, Muñoz, and McKenzie, she shows the necessary complexity of performing theory in a world in which the performativities of subjectivity, economy, and atrocity invite, if not require, thoughtful reiteration.

REFERENCES

Austin, J. L. (1962). *How to do things with words.* Cambridge, MA: Harvard University Press.

Bauman, R. (1977). *Verbal art as performance.* Prospect Heights, IL: Waveland Press.

Butler, J. (1990). *Gender trouble.* New York: Routledge.

Diamond, E. (1996). Introduction. In E. Diamond (Ed.), *Performance and cultural politics* (pp. 1–14). New York: Routledge.

Goldberg, R. (2001). *Performance art: From futurism to the present* (Rev. ed.). New York: Thames and Hudson.

Hall, S. (1986). On postmodernism and articulation: An interview with Stuart Hall (L. Grossberg, Ed.). *Journal of Communication Inquiry, 10*(2), 45–60.

Hall, S. (2003). Marx's notes on method: A "reading" of the "1857" (revision). *Cultural Studies, 17*(2), 113–149. (Originally published in *Cultural Studies, 6*)

Muñoz, J. (2000). Memory performance: Luis Alfaro's "Cuerpo Politizado." In C. Fusco (Ed.), *Corpus delecti: Performance art of the Americas* (pp. 97–114). New York: Routledge.

Patraka, V. (1999). *Spectacular suffering: Theatre, fascism, and the Holocaust.* Bloomington, Indiana University Press.

Phelan, P. (1993). *Unmarked: The politics of performance.* New York: Routledge.

Schneider, R. (2001). Hello Dolly well hello Dolly: The double and its theatre. In P. Campbell & A. Kear (Eds.), *Psychoanalysis and performance* (pp. 94–114). New York: Routledge.

Taylor, D. (1997). *Disappearing acts: Spectacles of gender and nationalism in Argentina's "Dirty War."* Durham, NC: Duke University Press.

Wise, J. M. (2003). Reading Hall reading Marx. *Cultural Studies, 17*(2), 105–112.

1

Stages

Queers, Punks, and the Utopian Performative

JOSÉ ESTEBAN MUÑOZ

You can't tell who was and who wasn't in a band. We did not like poseurs but we liked to pose for pictures. Because we knew there was something about the night that would be remembered even if we couldn't remember it. We were young and naive in a way that seems to be a lost art. We were snotty and compassionate and deliberate and reckless but we knew exactly what we were doing. We were ghosts then and we are ghosts now. We will haunt your malls and catwalks forever. Ha Ha.

—Exene Cervenka
(in Jocoy, Moore, & Cervenka, 2002, p. 270)

UTOPIAN PERFORMATIVES

How does one stage utopia? Which is to say, how do we enact utopia? As I present work at various universities and conferences from a book I am writing, to be titled *Cruising Utopia: the Performance and Politics of Queer Futurity,* some form of that question is almost always articulated. It is one of those good questions that help writers clarify their arguments, to propel their thinking forward. One thing I have learned from this question is that utopia is an ideal, something that should mobilize us, push us forward. Utopia is not prescriptive, it renders potential blueprints of a world not quite here, a horizon of possibility, not a fixed schema. It is productive to think about utopia as flux, a temporal disorganization, as a moment when the here and the now is transcended by a then and a there that could be and indeed should be.

But on some level, utopia is about a politics of emotion; it is central to what Ernst Bloch called

9

a "principle of hope" (Bloch, 1959/1986).[1] It is my belief that minoritarian subjects are cast as hopeless in a world without utopia. This is not to say that hope is the only modality of emotional recognition that structures belonging; sometimes shame, disgust, hate, and other "negative" emotions bind people together—certainly punk rock's rejection of normative feelings stands as the most significant example of the emotional work of negative affect. But in this instance, I dwell on hope because I wish to think about futurity; and hope, I argue, is the emotional modality that permits us to access futurity, par excellence.

Queers, for example, especially those who do not choose to be biologically reproductive, a people without children, are, within dominant culture, people without a future. They are cast as people who are developmentally stalled, forsaken, who do not have the complete life promised by heterosexual temporality (Edelman, 2004). This reminds one of the way in which worried parents deal with wild queer children, how they sometimes protect themselves from the fact of queerness by making it a "stage," a developmental hiccup, a moment of misalignment that will, hopefully, correct itself, or be corrected by savage pseudoscience and coercive religion, sometimes masquerading as psychology. In this essay, I want to consider the idea of queerness as "a stage" that rescues that phrase from delusional parents and others who attempt to manage and contain the potentiality which is queer youth. In this essay I want to enact a utopian performative change in the signification of the phrase "it is only a 'stage'" deployed in the name of the queer child. More specifically, in this case, the queer wild child of punk subculture. I will enact this change through a reading of visual artist Kevin McCarty's representations of illuminated stages at gay bars and independent rock clubs, and through a more general reading of punk rock's ethos as conjured and connoted by McCarty's images and my readings of them. I will argue that the artist's work indexes a

punk/queer utopian scene that I read for its utopian potentiality and also, furthermore, that the work itself is a photographic instance of the utopian performative.[2]

This argument is not aligned with many of the dominant performance theories that held sway during the early nineties, like Peggy Phelan's axiom that the ontology of performance was disappearance and that performance itself represented a unique mode of representation without reproduction. Instead, a materialist current influences this analysis. For example I see this project working in tandem with a book like Miranda Joseph's *Against the Romance of Community*. In that book, Joseph offers an important critique of Phelan's version of the performance's power:

> In order to claim that performance resists exchange value, or equivalence, and thereby approaches the unrepresentable Real itself, Phelan discounts the work of the audience; their productive consumption of the work, their act of witness is for her the memory of something presented by somebody else. (2002, p. 64)

This then suggests that performance's temporality is not one of simple presence but instead of futurity. In Joseph's lucid critique we see that performance is the kernel of a potentiality that is transmitted to audiences and witnesses and that the real force of performance is its ability to generate a modality of knowing and recognition among audiences and groups that facilitates modes of belonging, especially minoritarian belonging. If we consider performance under such a lens, we can see the temporality of what I will describe as a utopian performativity, which is to say a manifestation of a "doing" that is in the horizon, a mode of possibility. Performance, seen as utopian performativity, is imbued with a sense of potentiality. Georgio Agamben has outlined the temporality of the philosophical concept of potentiality by following a line of thought that begins with Aristotle. Agamben underscores a distinction made by Aristotle between potentiality and possibility (1999). Possibilities exist, or more nearly, they exist within a logical real, the possible, which is within the present and is linked to presence. Potentialities are different insofar as while they are present they do not exist in present things. Thus potentialities have a temporality that is not in the present but, more nearly, in the horizon, which we can understand as futurity. Potentiality is and is not presence and its ontology cannot be reduced to presentness. Agamben reads this notion of potentiality alongside Jacques Derrida's notion of the trace. It is something like a trace or potential that exists or lingers after a performance. At performance's end, if it is situated historically and materially, it is never just the duration of the event. Reading for potentiality is scouting for a "not here" or "not now" in the performance that suggests a futurity.

I begin this writing then by readjusting my opening question "How do we stage utopia?" by suggesting that utopia is a stage. Not merely a temporal stage, like a phase, by also a spatial one. Sir Thomas More initially positioned Utopia as a place, an island, and later that formulation was amended to become a temporal coordinate. Utopia became a time that is not here yet, a certain futurity, a could be, a should be. Utopia, according to Bloch, a philosopher associated, to some degree, with the Frankfurt School, is a time and a place that is "not-yet-here." Bloch, along with other Frankfurt School thinkers like Thedor Adorno and Herbert Marcuse, contended that that utopia is primarily a critique of the here and now, it is an insistence that there is, as they put it, "something missing in the here and the now." Capitalism, for instance, would have us think that it is a natural order, an inevitability, the way things would be. The "should be" of utopia, its indeterminacy and its deployment of hope, stand against capitalism's ever expanding and exhausting force field of how things "are and will be." Utopian performativity suggests another modality of doing and

being that is in process, unfinished. It is to be deciphered by noting what Bloch has called the *anticipatory illumination* that radiates from certain works of art (Bloch, 1974/1996).

Also pivotal to my formulation is the work of the previously discussed Italian philosopher Agamben. I have outlined his emphasis on potentiality and his privileging of this concept over that of possibility. Furthermore, the notion of the utopian performative that I am attempting to outline in this essay is a notion that is inspired by Agamben's notion of a "means without an end." For Agamben, politics is disabled by a certain emphasis on "ends," which is to say politics depends on a performative doing, a perpetual becoming. Performances that display and illuminate their "means" are, like punk, a modality of performance that is aesthetically and politically linked to populism and amateurism. The performative work of "means," in the sense I am using it, is to interrupt aesthetics and politics that aspire toward totality. This too is one of the ways in which I want to resist the Hegelian shell game of absence and presence, appearance and disappearance, that dominates previous performance theories. An emphasis on means as opposed to ends is innately utopian insofar as utopia can never be prescriptive of futurity. Utopia is an idealist mode of critique that reminds us that there is something missing, that the present and presence (and its opposite number, absence) is not enough.

Two years ago, I spent a sabbatical in Los Angeles. I grew up listening to X, the Germs, Gun Club, and other bands that made up the LA punk scene of the eighties. I lived in the LA punk scene via my semisubcultural existence in suburban Miami; this was possible through a grungy alternative record store located in a strip mall, called Yesterday and Today Records; a few punk and new wave clubs like Flynn's on the Beach and Club Fire and Ice; and issues of *Creem*, a magazine that covered the edgier rock scene but could still be purchased in a Miami supermarket. Through my deep friendships with other disaffected Cuban queer teens who rejected both Cuban exile culture and local mainstream gringo popular culture, and through what I'll call the utopian critique function of punk rock, I was able to imagine a time and a place that was not yet there, a place where I tried to live. LA and its scene helped my protoqueer self, the queer child in me, imagine a stage, both temporal and physical, where I could be myself or, more nearly imagine a self that was in process, a self that has always been in the process of becoming.

While in Los Angeles, I started hanging out with an artist, Kevin McCarty, with whom I shared an interest in punk and post-punk music, subculture, and utopia. Our friendship has endured various mutations, moments of volatility and great fun, and our mutual neuroses have fueled our queer intimacy. Our friendship is ultimately based on convergent worldviews in relation to politics and aesthetics. On a recent studio visit I saw a series of works that helped me organize and substantiate my thinking about the time, space, and utopian function of punk in relation to queer subcultural becomings. Writing about living artists helps one further debunk the false principle of the critic's objectivity. Queer intimacies underwrite much of the critical work I do. Yet I reject the phrase "advocacy criticism" and instead embrace the idea of the performative collaboration between artist and writer.

With that stated, I must add that from my side this connection between theory and art feels incredibly one-sided, and not only in the case of McCarty, but also in my work on Carmelita Tropicana, Vaginal Davis, Isaac Julien, and others, because their work and the queer friendships and the intimacies I share with them enable my critical project. Attempting to imagine a convergence between artistic production and critical praxis is, in and of itself, a utopian act in relation to the alienation that often separates theory from practice, a sort of cultural division of labor.

I will discuss a series of photographs that McCarty has titled *The Chameleon Club*. The series is named after a space from the artist's biography that I will soon get to. The series lines up portraits of stages from different club spaces in Los Angeles like Spaceland or Catch One. Spaceland is a bar and music venue in the now hipster section of Los Angeles called Silverlake. Spaceland is where the indie music kids and "not-so-kids" (I position myself within this bracket) go to hear the cutting edge music of the day. Catch One is a predominantly black gay space where lesbian and transgendered people also go. It is a space that is not on the West Hollywood–centered gay map of Los Angeles. McCarty's extraordinary pictures exercise a great deal of formalist mastery that render the stage as monumental. While the space is empty of people, the dark and dramatic lighting is set to make the performance sites look as though they were shot while the club was open and running. After I left LA, Kevin gave me a large print of the Catch One picture. The stage is small but appears large and luminous. The stage itself is black and it rises from a black-and-white checkerboard stage. The black curtains that flank the stage are layered with gleaming silver hubcaps. The hubcaps sparkle through the photographer's gaze and its photographic representation. The back of the stage is illuminated by rows of simple white light strings. They are separated by a world of difference but they nonetheless remind me of the light strings utilized by Felix Gonzalez-Torres. Gonzalez-Torres's light strings symbolized the flickering status of queer lives in an epidemic, but they did not hang in the uniform fashion of the lights in McCarty's imaging of Catch One. I nonetheless look at these images, lighting up the photograph from its deepest point of the picture and offering a warm secondary illumination from their reflection on the actual stage's shiny black floor and I think of that city, Los Angeles, a city, a place I grew to love and this one queer predominantly black space that I had access to.

The only negative critique I have heard of this picture that rests on my wall is from people who have seen it in my apartment and think that it is perhaps too beautiful. The suggestion is that it is too pretty in the face of the adversity that queers of color face on a daily basis. I have presented on this series at different professional conferences and on more than one occasion a gay black man in the audience has recognized the space and approached me afterwards. What I have learned from those encounters is that seeing this space of queer belonging framed by McCarty's meticulous attention makes this space of black queer belonging one that helps us see our connectedness outside of the actual temporality of club life. The utopian performative charge of this image allows one to see the past, the moment before an actual performance, the moment of potentiality; and the viewer gains access to the affective particularity of that moment of hope and potential transformation that is also the temporality of performance.

The stage at Catch One juts out at the audience; it looks like a catwalk and its edges are lit up with small shimmering light bulbs. The catwalk feature makes one think about a queer appropriation of high fashion that my opening quotation from Exene Cervenka refers to. Cervenka's commentary, like McCarty's image of the stage from queer Catch One, calls attention to the way queer and punk subcultures have been informing and haunting the world of mainstream fashion for quite a while. The bluish lighting of Catch One reminds one of a moment in Samuel Delaney's memoir *The Motion of Light in Water*, especially the moment where he describes seeing a mass of gay men having sex under a blue light at the now closed St. Mark's Bath in the East Village. It was during this moment of utopian rapture where he first realized he was not a solitary pervert but part of a vast world of gay men, who fucked, connected, and had actual lives (Delaney, 1988).

The theatricality of the images has much to do with the lighting, which seems to be generated from the stage itself, bottom-up instead of top-down light, giving the effect that the space is glowing with possibility. This recalls Bloch's formulation in regard to certain aesthetic modes, like, for example, what he called the *ornamental*. Bloch privileges the ornamental over the functional. The functional does not let us see anything in it except the use that capitalism has mapped out for it in advance. The ornamental, on the other hand, has an indeterminate use value that challenges the protocols of capitalism and in it one can view Bloch's anticipatory illumination of art. The glow that these photos generate is that anticipatory illumination, that moment of possibility right before an amazing band or performance manifests itself on stage and transforms the world for the performance's duration and, for many of those in attendance, beyond. The best performances don't disappear, but instead linger in our memory, haunt our present, and illuminate our future.

When McCarty displays these images he wants them to be one piece, the two images side by side, adjacent, giving a sense that there is a door between them, joining the space of punk and queer subcultures. Popular culture is the stage where we rehearse our identities. McCarty's work stands as a powerful amendment to this formulation by displaying the actual and metaphorical stages where queers and punks rehearse self. The artist explains his rationale for his objects of study in an autobiographical artist statement:

> Located somewhere in the middle of nowhere, surrounded by cow fields, and suburban home developments, situated in between the ruins of downtown Dayton, Ohio, a post industrial wasteland, and Wright Pat Air Force base, sat the Hills and Dales shopping center. In a retail space, in

the rear of a strip mall the Chameleon Club opened. One entered what would be the sales floor and made their way back, though a single doorway to the storeroom, which had been converted, into a punk rock club. The only furnishings were a plywood stage at the far end flanked by a PA. The dry walling was incomplete exposing cinder blocks. To the right of the stage was a doorway that led to 1470's, the largest gay bar in Dayton. When you paid admission to the Chameleon Club you could buy drinks at 1470's. The punks would pass back and forth, but no one from 1470's came to the Chameleon Club. With their costumes and their lyrics the kids on the music scene performed their identities at the temporary venue. For the punks geographic location was not relevant as long as there was a stage, a soundman and an audience. Behind the bare cinder blocks of the Chameleon Club one could hear the beats of dance music. The sweating bodies of intoxicated gay men crowded the dance floor only to be revealed through the artificial fog by streaks of red, blue, and green lights circling above their heads. Here men forgot about the blue-collar oppressive city they called home and imagined a world where they could be free from shame and embarrassment. Neither place was mine. I observed both from the outside. My utopia existed at the doorway on the threshold—neither space at one time and in both simultaneously. (McCarty, 2005, pp. 427–428)

This statement resonates alongside my own autobiography. I was certainly crossing what was for me a metaphorical threshold between the punk world and gay life. Punk made my own suburban quotidian existence radical and experimental. So experimental that I could imagine and eventually act on queer desires. Punk rock style may look apocalyptic, yet its temporality is nonetheless futuristic, letting young punks imagine a time and a place where their desires are not toxic. McCarty talks about a space between these two zones—between the queer of 1470 club and the punk Chameleon Club. In part, he is narrating a stage of in-between–ness, a spatiality that

is aligned with a temporality that is on the threshold between identifications, life worlds, and potentialities. The work and the artist's statement resonate beyond my own biography.[3]

In an early gay and lesbian studies anthology edited by Karla Jay and Allen Young, *Lavender Culture,* there is another report about queer bars in Ohio. In a short piece by John Kelsey titled "The Cleveland Bar Scene in the Forties," the author reports the fundamental importance of these spaces:

> There was, of course, nothing spectacular about Cleveland's gay male bars in the forties, but the point is simply this: they existed. Gay men had places to meet, not only in San Francisco or New York, but in a city easily scoffed at or ignored by sophisticates on either coast. (1994, p. 146)

Kelsey's narration of the forties resonates powerfully next to McCarty's artist statement. McCarty's impressions from the nineties, fifty years after Kelsey's moment, would probably still agree with a point Kelsey makes: "The curious combination of exploitation and liberation helped define the mood in gay bars then as it is now, though perhaps both elements were more extreme in those days" (p. 146). The calculus of exploitation and liberation dogs queer culture. Kelsey talks about seeing a few good female impersonators and also states that "If the professional entertainment was bad, the amateurs were unbelievably awful" (pp. 148–149). He characterizes a typical afternoon at the Hide-Out Club Sunday afternoon of amateur performances as a scene where

> male typists in Grandma's cast-off finery would take the stage, forget lyrics, and flee in tears. And stockroom boys would take absolutely dreadful spills during their ballet-tap routines. One I much enjoyed was a short, middle-aged man who would sing part of it in the voice of Nelson Eddy, and part in the voice of Jeanette MacDonald. (Kelsey, 1994, p. 149)

The celebration of an aesthetics of amateurism are reminiscent of punk rock's aesthetics. The performances of amateurism, in both punk and this example of queer performance, signal a refusal of mastery and an insistence on process and becoming. Again, such performances do not disappear but instead remain and, like performatives in J. L. Austin, do things in the future. In the above example, the short squat singer of "Indian Summer" is loved decades after his performance, and that one audience member's testimonial stands as one of the things that remains after the performance. The performance, in its incompleteness, lingers and persists, drawing together the community of interlocutors. Utopian performativity is often fueled by the past. The past, or at least narratives of the past, enable utopian imaginings of another time and place that is not yet here but nonetheless functions as a doing for futurity, a conjuring of both future and past to critique presentness. McCarty's work is fueled by a past recollection from his biography that he takes to another time and place and uses to capture this ideality that is the potentiality of utopian performativity. His stages are lit as though a performance is about to emerge from the realm of potential to actuality. The lure of the work is its performative dimension, which I would describe as a *doing as dwelling,* which is to say that I am particularly interested in the way in which the images dwell in potentiality, aestheticizing that moment, transmitting the power of its ideality. Thus the aesthetic fuels the political imagination.

I am especially partial to the image of La Plaza. The club itself is one of the oldest Latino gay clubs in LA. The place has a sort of *ranchera* or country-western feel to it. Often many of the patrons dress to go with the decor. It is not a very glamorous country-western feel. Instead it is, more nearly, a sort of grungy Mexican cowhands feel. But that is not true of the stage at this humble little bar. The curtains shine with an extravagance that seems out of place with the rest of the locale. As soon as showtime starts, the heavy theatrical lights burst on and illuminate the seemingly beaded curtains. Once the show begins, old-school glamorous transvestites take the stage. The entire spectacle is in Spanish. The hostess glimmers with the same intensity as the curtains. All the performances are standard exercises in lip-syncing. About two-thirds of the songs are Spanish anthems and the rest are English pop songs. When contestants come on stage, they are introduced in relation to the province or village they are from in Mexico. The codes that organize time and space are disrupted in this performance space. The first time I visited the club I felt as though I was in Guadalajara in the 1950s. This spatial and temporal displacement mimetically resonates with the lush photograph of the stage. Again we see potentiality, another vista is offered, and in Los Angeles the site, La Plaza, conjures stories of migratory crossing, legal and illegal, and one sees these bodies, whose life world is always in flux about to belong, on the cusp of materialization.

A white neon sign that reads "Salvation" hangs over the stage at the Silver Lake Lounge, another predominantly Latino gay club where I have seen rough strippers and messy drag queens perform their crafts. Queer culture, in its music and iconography, often references salvation. One hears the refrain of a famous club anthem, "A DJ Saved My Life Last Night." There is indeed something about the transformative powers of nightlife that queers and people of color have always clung to. The contrast in Silver Lake Lounge composition is a strong one, a contrast between the idea of salvation and the clear seediness of the actual space. The bright shining ideality of salvation hangs over a space that is dark and not very promising except that the concept literally is writ large on top of the picture—in this visual study the embedded nature of a utopian performativity within subaltern spaces. Sometimes the utopian spectator needs to squint to

see the anticipatory illumination promised by utopia, yet at other times, its visuality and (non)presence cannot be denied.

The stage from Spaceland is lit a certain deep pink that makes it feel like a band of screaming angry teens will hop on stage and tear it up with their savage guitars. The photograph returns me to my early punk shows. I remember the potentiality that those scenes of spectatorship promised even before performers showed up on stage. The hum of other men's bodies, bodies that for whatever reason, for that moment, rejected a trajectory that was attuned to the normal. Being at Spaceland makes me feel old. I remember the Cat's Cradle in Chapel Hill, North Carolina, and seeing my favorite bands there during the relentless social tedium of graduate school. That's where I started to feel too old to go to shows yet nevertheless felt the show and stage,

the transformation of time and space offered by the performance, as forgiving and still permitting me access to this network of queer belongings.

I feel the sense of belonging with even greater intensity when I look at the opulent image of the Parlor Club on Santa Monica Avenue. The tiny stage is clearly overdecorated with its elaborate chandelier and its rich red drapes with golden tassels. I am at the club during my regular visits to Los Angeles since my dear friend and frequent object of study Vaginal Davis hosts her Friday night party Bricktop there. Bricktop's tiny stage often looks like it is about to buckle under Davis's massive frame as she inhabits the stage, perhaps performing some surprisingly delicate flapper dance.[3] Of all the spaces McCarty has chosen to depict, this one is mostly clearly and concretely the space where punk and

queerness meet. Indeed, in the pagan church of punk queerness, Davis is both high priestess and black pope. Davis is one of my favorite people in Los Angeles and something of a heroine from my queer coming of age. In her 'zines such as *Fertile LaToya Jackson* and *Shrimp* (a journal dedicated to the sucking of toes), I found an incredible resource for imaging a futurity where my—for lack of a better word—"anti-normativity" could flourish. Through our friendship and queer intimacy we have performed, through a certain sick reappropriation, a reimagined modality of the patronage system. She does her work and I testify to the *New York Times* and the *Los Angeles Times*—with my academic credentials and letterhead well in place—that she is a certified art star in

the tradition of Dada and Surrealism. I then get to see her work that inspires me to no end. Her Friday night emporium of queer punk vintage retro sleaze is like no other venue I know of. McCarty's picture of the Parlor Room and its stage, with its dense Victorian luster, beautifully captures the ethos of the party. I would summarize that ethos as a use of past decadence to critique the banality of our presentness for the purpose of imaging and enacting an enabling of queer futurity.

Installed at a gallery, the images of punk clubs are hung next to images of a gay bar's stage. The placement of these images next to each other speaks to subjectivities that travel through the swinging door between both temporal and spatial coordinates. For those of us

Copyright © Kevin McCarty

whose relationship to popular culture is always marked by aesthetic and sexual antagonism, these stages are our actual utopian rehearsal rooms where we work on a self that does not conform to the mandates of cultural logics like late capitalism, heteronormativity and, in some cases, white supremacy.

The empty stage is used in pieces by the generation of queer artists before McCarty. Felix Gonzalez-Torres brought a blue platform into the gallery that was also outlined with light bulbs. Paid go-go dancers, who would appear at odd moments, often wearing Walkmen™, would dance suggestively on the stage. That stage was always one of potentiality, empty one moment and overflowing with sex and movement the next. While that work shares a utopian impulse with McCarty's, the empty stages of Jack Pierson look melancholic and emptied out of possibility. Pierson's

images are snapshots of the disappointment that is part of utopia—the hangover that follows hope. At this moment it seems that queer visual culture needs to nourish our sense of potentiality and not reinforce our feeling of disappointment. If we are to go on, we need a critical modality of hope and not simply dramatization of loss and despair.

The source material for McCarty's images is the past—not a nostalgic past, but a past that helps us feel a certain structure of feelings, a circuit of queer belonging. When I look at his images, I remember the sexually ambiguous punk clubs of my youth where horny drunk punk boys rehearsed their identities, aggressively dancing with each other and later lurching out, intoxicated, to the parking lot together. For many, the mosh pit wasn't simply a closet; it was a utopian subcultural rehearsal space. In an earlier image of McCarty's, a makeshift

subculture is shown in a collection of concert tickets pinned to a white wall with pins that resemble those used to mark places on maps. This reminds us of one of Oscar Wilde's best lines from *The Soul of Man Under Socialism:* "Any map of the world that does not include utopia is not worth glancing at" (p. 141). This piece helps us understand the temporality of utopia, the way in which the past is used in the service of mapping a future, a place of possibility and transformation. Heteronormative culture makes queers think both the past and the future do not belong to them. All we are allowed to imagine is barely surviving the present. This mapping of hope and affect on a white wall brings me back to the various shows were I rehearsed and planned a future self, one that is not quite here but always in process, always becoming, emerging in difference.

I opened with Exene Cervenka's recent writing from the catalog called *We're Desperate:* *The Punk Rock Photography of Jim Jocoy* (Jocoy, Moore, & Cervenka, 2002). There is a performance shot in that book of Darby Crash, one of punk history's most fucked-up and damaged queer teens. In the recent punk biography *Lexicon Devil: The Fast Times and Short Life of Darby Crash and the Germs,* the late Tomata Du Plenty, lead singer for rival band the Weirdos, describes Darby offstage in relation to his staged self:

> Darby was fascinating in a parking lot. I think that's where he was really a star. Watching his behavior in a parking lot, that's what made Darby Crash, that's what made him a legend, certainly not his onstage performances! Oh, They were so boring! I couldn't sit through a Germs set, please. Torture! But I could certainly sit on the curb with a 40-ounce and listen to him for hours. He was an interesting, interesting boy. (Mullen, Bolles, & Parfrey, 2002, p. 47)

The stage and the parking lot are adjacent in much the same way that there is phantom door between Catch One and Spaceland in McCarty's work. On one asphalt stage in Los Angeles, one queer punk watches another hold forth, and across this country, under a different shape of palm tree, but still in a parking lot, my best friend Tony and I sit in his beige Nissan Sentra and we speculate about this band the Germs and the provocative lyrics to songs like "Sex Boy" and "Richie Dagger's Crimes"—what can they possibly mean, we asked ourselves, almost already knowing. While we sat in that car, my parents worried about where I was and what I was doing with whom, and I know they must have been trying to comfort themselves by letting themselves think that I was merely at a stage. What we were learning in that parking lot as the Germs song "Forming" played was that there was another stage out there for us, both temporal and spatial, one in which potentiality, hope, and the future could be, should be, and would be enacted. Today I write back from that stage that my mother and father hoped I would quickly vacate. Instead, I dwell on and in this stage because I understand it as one brimming with a utopian performativity that is linked to the ideality that is potentiality. This potentiality is always in the horizon and, like performance, never completely disappears but, instead, lingers and serves as a conduit for knowing and feeling each other.

NOTES

1. I am grateful to Kevin McCarty for his friendship and pictures.

2. This project is beautifully continued in the artist's current Web site: imnotlikeyou.la. That site documents a youth culture scene in LA inhabited by Latino punks. In this aspect of the artist's project race and ethnicity are examined with the same attentiveness and care as sexuality in the Chameleon Club series.

3. In his dissertation, "When the Little Dawn Was Grey," Shane Vogel discusses Bricktop's life and performance practice and Davis.

REFERENCES

Agamben, G. (1999). *Potentialities*. Palo Alto, CA: Stanford University Press.

Bloch, E. (1986). *The principle of hope* (N. Plaice & S. Plaice, Trans.). Cambridge: MIT Press. (Original work published 1959)

Bloch, E. (1996). The artistic illusion and the visible anticipatory illumination. In J. Zipes & F. Mecklenburg (Trans.), *The utopian function of art: Selected essays* (pp. 141–155). Cambridge: MIT Press. (Original work published 1974)

Delaney, S. R. (1988). *The motion of light in water: Sex and science fiction writing in the East Village, 1957–1965*. Minneapolis: University of Minnesota Press.

Edelman, L. (2004). *No future*. Durham, NC: Duke University Press.

Jocoy, J., Moore, T., & Cervenka, E. (2002). *We're desperate: The punk rock photography of Jim Jocoy, SF/LA 1978–1980*. New York: PowerHouse Books.

Joseph, M. (2002). *Against the romance of community*. Minneapolis: University of Minnesota Press.

Kelsey, J. (1994). The Cleveland bar scene in the forties. In K. Jay & A. Young (Eds.), *Lavender culture*. New York: NYU Press.

McCarty, K. (2005). Autobiographical artist statement. *GLQ: A Journal of Lesbian and Gay Studies, 11*, 427–428.

Mullen, B., Bolles, D., & Parfrey, A. (2002). *Lexicon devil: The fast times and short life of Darby Crash and the Germs*. Los Angeles: Feral House.

Vogel, S. (2004). *When the little dawn was grey*. Unpublished doctoral dissertation, New York University.

Wilde, O. (2001). *The soul of man under socialism and other critical prose*. London and New York: Penguin. (Original work published 1891)

2

Never, Again

REBECCA SCHNEIDER

I lost two cities, lovely ones. And, vaster,
some realms I owned, two rivers, a continent.
I miss them, but it wasn't a disaster.
—Even losing you (the joking voice, a gesture
I love) I shan't have lied. It's evident
the art of losing's not to hard to master
though it may look like (Write it!) like disaster.

—Elizabeth Bishop

Yesterday the twin towers came down. First one, then the other. We watched TV—replay upon replay.

One tower imploding on itself. Then another. Screen scramble. If we'd found a screen in time, many of us had watched the first tower come down the first time, "live." Missing the first, others might have seen the second tower the first time it came down. Then: replay upon replay frenzy.

Sometimes the second tower was played first, then the first tower was played second.

Oddly, as replay led to replay, as forward led to back, the image became only more incredible. The more it reappeared, the more it seemed as if we had missed it and needed to see it again, and each "again" lent itself less to familiarity than to disbelief. The sense of "how to read" the image became increasingly unsettled with each repetition as the "already seen" began to partake of the uncanny union of overly familiar and impossibly strange. Perhaps the towers had never been there? Or, perhaps they had always been coming down and we had just refused to see it before now?

To write about disaster as it reverberates, with less attention to the event than to its articulation, feels, at first, disrespectful of the dead. But as war is so obviously composed of the rhetoric that whips it into being, and as terror so obviously occurs as much in the telling (the passing of the news, mouth to mouth, screen to screen), the project of telling the telling seems imperative.[1]

THE TELLING, THEN

First the telling occurred in images, reflected in trillions of pixels across millions of eyeballs around the globe, punctuated by the voices of "news" in a towering Babel of airwaves. The fall of each tower was accompanied by the repeating image of a body against the gridded face of the building. The body, falling between the grid lines, never hit bottom. The repeated sound of a woman screaming, the same scream. These replays hardly made the scene more legible, even as it became incredibly familiar. The body fell not only down the tower but across our collective eyes—again and again it fell without resolution. The planes had sliced the retinal screen of the vision machine, hailing the nervous system laced through living rooms and barrooms and waiting rooms across the globe. The twin nature of the attack, a kind of violence of ambivalence, made the terror manifest at the level of "replay"—but replay as real. Thus the event was choreographed brilliantly for trauma—terror's talk. The space of time between one tower and the next was itself the space of a replay in the realm of the "real," making the inevitable televisual replays that followed also (impossibly) "real." The repetition at the level of the image seemed to evidence the primal lie of trauma: something has been missed, we were not there, it must be seen again, it must be replayed as it cannot have happened "once"—in time or in singularity. It cannot

have happened except to have both already happened and to have not yet occurred.[2]

DOUBLE ARTICULATION

How many times did I hear fellow Americans say, "It's too much like Hollywood—it cannot be real"?

On that morning, I left my office in search of a screen. I stood in a crowd in a coffee shop in Ithaca, New York, where a TV hung from the back wall. I had missed the first tower's fall. (Or, in truth, I'd heard it on the radio—and that hearing compelled me to find a television, as the obvious specularity of the attack beckoned me to participation.) I stood, now, with others. The replay of the first tower's fall caught me up, but mostly the cameras were trained on the second tower—the "about to be seen" was a question mark in the air over the dust of the "already seen." Then the second tower fell. I watched. We watched. It was an again, for the first time.

Peter Jennings, ABC anchorman, was the human face of the camera as we zoomed in, replayed, zoomed out, replayed, body fall, replay, body fall, replay. Accident replayed like a long run of *Oedipus,* over and over again almost to the point of realization: *catharsis interruptus,* again and again. The question of whether the "incident" could have been an "accident" had dissolved, absolutely, the minute the messenger brought the news that a second plane was seen approaching the second tower. Accidents, it seems, don't happen twice, are not subject to repetition. Strange, in fact, how a second time renders a first time purposeful, as if it were the second that came first, or as if the second orchestrated the first from a past that has not yet occurred.

After the fall of the second tower—that is, after the tower fell again—the coffee shop was quiet. So was Jennings. It was clear that at moments the messenger wasn't sure he believed what he was seeing, or wasn't sure that he believed that he was seeing it again.

This is what he said: "If it were a novel, no one would believe it." He paused. Then: "Well believe it, exclamation mark! It's true, period." This is exactly what Jennings said. Or, this is exactly as I remember it—telling myself in that horrible moment: "Remember this. Remember that as Jennings spoke, his words appeared in teletype." It was because the words were teletyped that I even noticed the oddness of his remark. To see "exclamation mark" written out and followed by (!). "Period" followed by (.) . . . I was struck by the doubleness of the articulation and by its inadequacy—to double articulate, to render twice what was only once said, was both not enough and a strangely appropriate indication of the problem both of representation and of terror itself. That the punctuation should interrupt the rhetoric, overcome it, display the sentencing as both absurd and inadequate (but in that absurdity and inadequacy, startlingly appropriate) was only one level of the issue. More important, it seemed to me, the punctuation beside the articulation of the punctuation displayed the sentence as sentence, and situated the pronouncement as the very site of contest, the very vehicle for the terror it both could not contain and yet that was contained by it. All of us were scrambling after words, for words, and words were images—lines that never hit the ground except as dots: !! It was as if the Tower of Babel, citadel of modernity, itself were under siege.

I looked around the shop. It seemed impossible. People were still ordering coffee and bagels—maybe. So it seemed. ("It was too much like Hollywood—it could not be real.") I wanted to ask a stranger standing next to me why he thought Jennings had uttered the exclamation mark and period—why he had rendered them spoken? Did the articulated grammatical framework somehow make his spoken words more real? By uttering his spoken words as (if) written, was this famous news bearer, this most modern messenger, attempting to underscore a certain "truth"

only available to writing? Or only conceivable as/by punctuation? Could there be believability in the mark that was somehow greater than the words to which they added emphasis, the words to which they gave pause? Somehow this stood out to me as important, as if a clue to the terror, as if a clue to the nightmare that would be (and had already been) dead bodies in Afghanistan, Israel, the Americas, Palestine, Pakistan, Iraq—bodies that hung, suspended, falling like question marks—ghosts from the future haunting the "already seen."

"Well believe it, exclamation mark! It's true, period."

In the same moment that I read the spoken grammatical marks as making text apparent, it seemed that the spoken grammatical marks also underscored the "liveness" of Jennings's claim. The double articulation of speech and teletype, with the double articulation of "exclamation mark" and (!), and with, as well, Jennings's spoken emphasis, his exclamatory tone—made the entire sentence overburdened with multiple marks of affect. It also made that affect appear as constructed (as opposed to a seamless "natural") even as it was a construction that fortified the sense of "liveness" and worked to impel "belief."

"If this were a novel, no one would believe it." (Pause.) "Well believe it, exclamation mark! It's true, period."

It is strange how these words repeat in my memory almost more clearly than the image of one tower followed by another. I can hear Jennings's voice and see the teletype in my mind even as I struggle to see the towers I saw again and again and again. Even as I speak with friends who survived, of friends who did not. For me, the voice pronounced an impasse and a passage at once. The first sentence declared that the event would be unbelievable in the modern medium of realism and narrative, the novel—as if to say that writing could not contain the event. But the second sentence, as if to double back or pass through the first, rendered writing (on the level of the affective mark) the very medium of event and belief. In Jennings's second utterance, writing appears not as narrative, but as punctuation, the bearer of affect, inflection, temporality, the material index of voice underscoring performativity. The two exclamation marks fell against each other: the messenger's spoken phrase and, a few seconds afterward, the teletype translation. Both struck me as surrogate for a disaster that was at once the "limit of writing" *and* (write it) the very force of catastrophe.

The disaster, unexperienced. Disaster is what escapes the very possibility of comprehensive experience—it is the limit of writing, the limit of telling. And yet we recognize and hail "Disaster!"—writing, gesticulating, speaking, telling—even as disaster undoes articulation. This must be repeated: disaster de-scribes. This does not mean, however, that the disaster, as a force that compels telling, writing, gesticulating, is excluded from writing, or is beyond the pale of writing or entirely extratextual (Blanchot, 1986, p. 7). Text, like gesture, like word of mouth, like muscle tone, carries the aftershock that founds—backwards—the implosive force of something only retroactively rendered initial: Shock!

The moment when I might have asked the stranger next to me what he thought of the teletype had passed—and in any case it had seemed like (and it would have been) a radically inappropriate question. Jennings was already replaying the scene: the plane slice, the implosion of the first tower. Everyone watched, again. No voice this time. No text underneath. We could almost hear Jennings breathing (comma, breath, comma). Almost . . .

(Pause.)

I was struck by the scene beyond the screen, on the street, outside the coffee shop. I saw the following happen several times (again and again): people who didn't know yet were stopped and asked: "Did you hear?" "Have you heard yet?" Through the coffee shop window I saw the scene several times. Those of us who already knew could say to ourselves: I can't hear them but I know what they are discussing. Look, she seems shocked. Look, he is gesticulating strenuously. Look, they are silent. Now moving quickly.

I had already heard. I had been called at my office on the telephone. "Have you heard?" No, I hadn't heard. I turned on the radio. And at first I did not believe it: "A plane has hit one of the twin towers." An accident? It was only an accident in anyone's mind in the space of minutes between the first plane crashing into the tower and the second plane slicing through the twin like cake. Twice renders purpose. Twice, by virtue of repetition, founds the first as first. Double articulation—to prophesy after the event, and also to found backwards.

I write this on *September 12, 2001*, though I will pass over it again several times, make alterations, remark, and no doubt the text will not be the text it is as I write, but a text revised. Seen again. Perhaps at the threshold of war. Perhaps in the midst of it. But *"today,"* survivors are still uncovered from the rubble. It is a difficult day to be writing—and stranger still to write for a collection on *déjà vu*.[3] Of course, *déjà vu* is an idiomatic French phrase meaning, literally, "already seen." The phrase suggests repetition, and often the uncanny sense that it is a "first time" that one is "seeing again"—the sense that the present has already occurred.

According to the *Oxford Dictionary of Current English Usage*, *déjà vu* is used to suggest the feeling of having already experienced the present or the feeling that something is "tediously familiar." *Today*, the media piles on more and more replay and news "coverage" like bandages that are themselves the harbingers of wounds. We tell ourselves what happened like a question: What happened to the double towers, the repeating world trade, the monument beside itself, twice seen, twice disappeared? The horror of this telling, today, is that it is both clear and extremely unclear what will happen next. What retaliation will this retaliation bring (will again follow again again)? The eye of any storm implies less a present clarity of vision than the uncanny clarity of the sense that one has already seen what one will see again—impending déjà vu, or perhaps the dizzy *jamais vu* that is its twin[4]—the space between one tower and the next, after one tower has collapsed—the horror of return, of coming again, of retaliation, of waiting for the already seen.

Today, underneath boldface headlines urgently reiterating "War on America," "Not Since Pearl Harbor," "America Under Attack," we are bombarded by individual details, punctuating the replay, to build upon each other like brick on brick to (re)construct the towering edifices of the event: "Alice Hoglan, the mother of a passenger on one of the crashed planes, received a call from her son Matthew Bingham in the air after his flight had been hijacked. He told her that if he didn't *see her again*, he wanted her to know that he loved her."[5] Seeing again would render knowing unnecessary—as "seeing again" would be, in itself, to know?

NEVER, AGAIN

At noon on September 11, 2001, in one of my classes on theatre and modernity, an Israeli graduate student who had only been in the United States for one month articulated his surprise that Americans were shocked by the fall of the twin towers (some students in class were crying and the president of Cornell had suspended required class attendance). During the next class, *several days later*, the same student asked whether the inundation of video images was an attempt on the part of the United States to catch up with the rest of the world—to acclimate to the terrorism experienced elsewhere as "tediously familiar." A debate ensued. Was the obsessive repetition of the falling towers on our screens an attempt to render the strange familiar—to make of

terrorism an "already seen"—or was it an attempt to sacralize, to render extraordinary in order to fit the bill put forward by President George W. Bush: "Never again"?

"Never again" was the famous post–World War II phrase that George W. Bush's father, George Bush, had used emphatically in his March 6, 1991, principal policy speech about the post–Gulf War order (his "New World Order") in the Middle East. Bush the First had said: "Our uncommon coalition must now work in common purpose to forge a future that should *never again* be held hostage to the darker side of human nature."[6] Bush's "never again," however, was subject to the comma it left out: "Never, again" would have been more appropriate. Or, simply, "Again." The Second Bush, attempting to render purpose to the First, used the language of "never again" again when defending his responses to September 11 (or, supposedly to September 11). The Second Bush echoed the First Bush's "never again" in his November 2001 authorization of military courts to try noncitizen suspects, to interview hundreds of people of Middle Eastern descent, and to have secret detentions and the monitoring of jailhouse conversations between lawyers and clients. In defense against criticisms that his policy threatened civil liberties and violated due process rights, Bush said: "We must not let foreign enemies use those forms of liberty to destroy liberty itself. Foreign terrorists and agents must *never again* be allowed to use our freedoms against us."[7]

Seemingly singular events, such as the double collapse of the World Trade Towers, appear to defy understanding. It is, apparently, the "singular" status that renders shock. Seeing again offers to make a first time comprehensible. Indeed, comprehensibility appears to be a matter of repetition—that is, comprehension appears to come after an event, in its narration, as a kind of second to the event itself. And yet, much current critical theory struggles to unpack the ways in which symbolic conditions of possibility precede occurrence. David Blakesley describes this prearticulation as Kenneth Burke's notion of "prophesying after the event" and reads prearticulation as a kind of fundamental déjà vu:

Déjà vu (the "already seen") may be more common than we might have thought, occurring at the very moment of perception itself and in the gestational moment when attitude, an incipient act or precognition, comes into being as symbolic action. . . . On the perceptual level, we've already seen what we're about to see, having preordained it conceptually or imaginatively. (Blakesley, 2001)

Recognition as a precondition of vision means that we see only what we can recognize by virtue of having seen it or imagined it, or something like it, before. Precondition is arguably at the Kantian base of many contemporary theories of sociality. Judith Butler's influential work, for example, turns repeatedly on the ritual and performative aspects of power, subject formation, and the social. By virtue of habit in "sedimented sets of acts," we deploy (and are deployed by) symbolic codes that performatively institute and reinstitute the very object relations and identity formations such codes appear to simply describe.[8] Thus an event, recognized as event, is never a "singular" event. Whether catastrophic or banal, an event relies on reiteration and is composed in repetition in that it is hailed as "unique" or "event" or "singular" only in *relation* to precondition and repetition. That an event be recognized *as* event, as having taken place, means that the event exists in relationship to its (failed or successful) articulation—its Double, if you will. Of course, it is an ancient Western truism that "disaster," generating a messenger, is then written across the bodies of hearers and tellers, undoing any possibility of singularity, even in the name or in the guise of the singular.[9]

"Never again," then, is oxymoronic. Rather than the forgetful thrust of "never

again" (which has not been realized in any case), we might *look again* (and again and again). In this vein of thinking, theatre artist Vsevelod Meyerhold called for "vigilant spectatorship" on the eve of the Russian Revolution—vigilance directed toward art *and* life (1969, p. 50). In this vein, Bertolt Brecht borrowed from Meyerhold to call for a critical spectator with a habit of looking and thinking twice—of expecting the "never" that is disaster, again. Brecht advocated the second look, with emphasis on *again* rather than *never,* as an alienation technique that might help us gain distance from the knee-jerk habits of precondition (1964). *Looking again* we acknowledge that our socialities are composed in reiteration. We must critically see again and acknowledge the tremendous foundational power of the double. Disaster takes place as recurrence: "Never"—again. What do we do to respond *differently*?

QUESTION MARK?

Gertrude Stein, whose mantra was "begin again," begins A Novel of Thank You: "How many more than two are there"

Question mark? She doesn't provide it. How many replays make "once"?[10] If I don't see you again, I want you to know that

NEVER, AGAIN

One and a half years ago, the Twin Towers came down. First one, then the other. We watched TV—replay upon replay.

One tower imploding on itself. Then another.

Oddly, as replay led to replay, as forward led to back, the image became only more incredible. The more it reappeared, the more it seemed as if we had missed it and needed to see it again, and each "again" lent itself less to familiarity than to disbelief. The sense of "how to read" the image became increasingly unsettled with each repetition as the "already seen" began to partake of the uncanny union of overly familiar and impossibly strange. Perhaps the towers had never been there? Or, perhaps they had always been coming down and we had just refused to see it before now?

In the United States in *spring 2003,* we watch our civil liberties coming down and with them, like some twin tower, the end of even the pretense of reasonable or respectful international relations on the part of the U.S. government. When violence—of any sort—is done in one's name, violence is done by and to oneself. In my opinion, the horror of war casting itself into the future, masquerading as "preventive," is close to unspeakable. The lack of *other means* to conflict resolution is deeply suspect. If historically the U.S. has attempted to keep its violences, global and national, covert, in the case of "Operation Iraqi Freedom," covert has given way to coverage throughout this spring, until the war is falsely declared "over" on May 1, 2003. And yet, the extent of the so-called coverage of the so-called war on terrorism strangely renders agendas as covert as they have ever been—as if Jennings's abundance of punctuation has continued *ad infinitum,* having forgotten the context of its articulation. *This spring,* journalists are "embedded" with soldiers, and government approved (i.e., censored) images of war are so constant and continual that there seems to be as little news in news as there is reality in the current thrall of "reality TV." All day every day, in the months before Bush's specious claim aboard the USS *Abraham Lincoln,* one can see sanitized death in operation— "live"—piped into one's living room, one's bedroom, one's kitchen, wherever one has hooked up the televisual box, the digi-video porthole to corporate America, running AV like an IV—the TV—pulse of outside on the inside, inside become outside, giving away the ruse of any distinction between such binaries as distance inverts instantaneously into breath, rubble, dust—sand.

What does one see? Mostly, one sees buildings blowing up, then soldiers in desert khaki walking through rubble. Just as often one sees soldiers, in line, kicking down a front door. Inside are women, scripted by news narrators as "happy"—happy to "greet the American liberators." Their faces register confusion and hope, but also shame and fear. My face registers the same—at the other portal end of the televisual network. Is it my eyeball that bangs down the door? The box threads its network way across America, displaying Iraqi insides, while every second car and truck in the U.S. displays the American flag. The new fad of sporting televisions inside one's car (to occupy one's kids) means that the "war on terrorism" can be mobile, carted about from soccer game to church supper to academic lecture to golfing match.

THE BANALITY OF DETAIL

In a diner in Manhattan in *mid-March 2003,* I hear my waitress, two booths away, call back to the kitchen: "Hamburger and French fries." In a moment, a manager or a cook shouts quite loudly back: "Freedom fries! We only serve Freedom fries!" Over such a scene—the entire conflict at the level of a sliver of potato— columns of potatoes served in bowls or sometimes in paper cartons, or on plates, dashed in salt, smothered in ketchup—over such a banal object of ingestion: the most current war. Then this manager, or this cook, comes out of the kitchen. This is the cast: the manager, a large, middle-aged, African American man in a suit— yes, a manager, not a cook—and this waitress, a tall, middle-aged, platinum blond, white with a deep Queens accent—I cannot see the patrons two booths away who ordered the offending fries—but then there is me, midlife white academic from Rhode Island, the smallest state in the Union—*up on my feet now*— struggling to take a stand, to articulate the international situation on the level of nationalized food. Am I going to leave the restaurant over this? I wonder at this manager's vehemence. Has he lost someone in the towers?

Is his son, his daughter, in Iraq? He shouted "Freedom fries" so angrily I have jumped out of my seat. The waitress hardly misses a beat: "French fries/Freedom fries—whatever." Then she says to me, out of range of his hearing, "Sit down, honey." She practically coos: "I'll bring you coffee." I sit down. I drink my coffee.

Every day we witness the constant negotiation between the monumental and the banal— the larger-than-life image or event and the stream of life that passes by, that courses through, that navigates the ordinary through the wider edifices of our collective symbols (monuments) and collective actions (war). Writers like Michel de Certeau and Naomi Schor argued in the 1970s and '80s[11] that to focus on the banal (the stray detail), to shift our sites of discourse away from the grand perspective—from the skyscraper to that which passes by or is easily overlooked or discarded— is a shift in attention that can be, in some ways, resistant to master narratives, master plans, and events of mastery (such as war).

I would like to discuss the opening of de Certeau's well-known essay, "Walking in the City," in some detail. De Certeau begins the essay with, strangely, a sentence fragment— or, at least, the sentence is incomplete when translated into English: "Seeing Manhattan from the 110th floor of the World Trade Center" (1974/1984, p. 91). It fascinates me that this opening in translation from French should be a fragment, truncated of itself, interrupted by a void. The sentence itself is thus a column of words reaching only so far, but no farther—interrupted by a period, falling off, cut to a quick end. "Seeing Manhattan from the 110th floor of the World Trade Center, period." But we read on—we look beyond this first pedestal-like sentence to get the view, and we are given a lyric description of expanse—complete, punctuated to aid flow, and beautiful:

> Beneath the haze stirred up by the winds, the urban island, a sea in the middle of the sea, lifts up the skyscrapers over Wall Street,

sinks down at Greenwich, then rises again to the crests of Midtown, quietly passes over Central Park and finally undulates off into the distance beyond Harlem. (de Certeau, 1974/1984, p. 91)

We are rescued by this second sentence into sense and delivered to the promise (the promise of a perspectival gaze) that there is space "beyond Harlem." But the flow of the second sentence, and its lyrical beyond, is haunted by the fragment that set its stage: "Seeing Manhattan from the 110th floor of the World Trade Center, period." By the end of the page that stretches beneath these two sentences (one truncated, the other languid), de Certeau has called the towers "the tallest letters in the world" and told us that they "compose a gigantic rhetoric of excess in both expenditure and production." Turn the page and de Certeau is orchestrating his famous "Icarian fall" (p. 92) in order to bring his readers down among the footsteps of the passersby:

> The ordinary practitioners of the city live "down below," below the thresholds at which visibility begins. They walk—an elementary form of experience of the city; they are walkers, *Wandersmänner*, whose bodies follow the thicks and thins of an urban "text" they write without being able to read it. . . . The paths that correspond in this intertwining, unrecognized poem in which each body is an element signed by many others, elude legibility. . . . The networks of these moving intersecting writings compose a manifold story that has neither author nor spectator, shaped out of fragments of trajectories and alterations of spaces: in relation to representations, it remains daily and indefinitely other. (1974/1984, p. 93)

The hope, as de Certeau's famous essay unfolds, is that in and through the "daily" and the "indefinitely other" of the banal detail (the footstep, say), we can somehow interrupt the agendas of the monumental, or better, understand the frenzied ways in which they work in tandem. What are the ways they work in tandem? The banal detail of the everyday props the whole, bit by bit composing the whole, and yet (in Proustian and Barthesian logic) the detail simultaneously serves as the hole that might serve as puncture point, or *punctum,* through which the edificial could be completely reorganized. As Naomi Schor reminded us in her important feminist study *Reading in Detail,* the whole depends upon the relegation of the detail to insignificance, to the "soon to be forgotten" or to "the feminized," the "overlooked." And yet this very banality—articulated *as banal*—creates what de Certeau calls an "oceanic rumble"—it both composes the ocean, and is, like any "single" drop, in extreme distinction to the monumentality it composes (de Certeau, 1984, p. 5).

De Certeau wanted to read the way in which the ordinary, as a spatial practice, might interrupt the myth of the monumental, or at least let us see the monumental as it works through and around the *passage,* or the *movement,* of details it scripts as disappearing. There is also the suggestion, in both De Certeau and Schor, of resistance—through refocusing our analytic energies onto the banal, the detail, we unsettle the prerogatives of the dominant order that that detail has been given to prop.[12] But there is more to this shift to the ordinary (which is, for de Certeau, a *spatial* shift), and that is that in reading the detail *as a practice, in play*—we shift our focus to movement, to moving *through,* and in shifting to movement, change becomes not only possible, but also the condition of any myth of stasis (the monument's secret). Twenty years after these two books, the project of thinking about the space between the grandly monumental, or the "whole" of a master text, and the deployment of the detail in either its service or in resistance is still resonant.

If the French fry anecdote I told earlier illustrates the banal as a site of negotiation and exchange, the strategy of "coverage" in this recent war also makes apparent the tangle of complicity between the monumental and banal. This tangle asks us to continue to render the relations between monument and banal detail (the period, the comma, the exclamation point) deeply complex. The grandiose terms of this war—"Operation Iraqi Freedom"—already bespeak the master narrative upon which monumentality has historically been erected. But this operation and this monumental narrative were also thick with detail: an oceanic buildup of minutiae of daily life on a constantly running televisual "reality TV-scape" in which "embedded" journalists sent back details of soldier life on the front until government censorship increased and until viewers got bored. We were given to read this latest war through a screen of anecdote—like a sandstorm of stories that found a predictable *dénouement* in the dragging down of the monument of Saddam Hussein, replayed across our screens again and again, in the name of "Never (,) again."

At a recent Brown University conference in memory of Naomi Schor, Christie McDonald argued that the soldier anecdotes perform a kind of flip-side response to the "Portraits of Grief" that ran in the *New York Times* for the year following September 11, 2001 (McDonald, 2003). The *Times* "Portraits" had attempted in every case to find something extremely ordinary about each 9/11 victim. The portraits excavated stories about the way X would put the toothpaste on his wife's toothbrush every morning and leave it for her by the sink, or about the way Y would stroke his niece's hair while he told her fairy tales. That is, these deaths were memorialized though an accumulation of daily anecdotes in which each victim was remembered not by grand acts or professional accomplishments, but by incidental particulars usually overlooked. Similarly, the war that followed was initially waged on U.S. sentiment through a barrage of visual and anecdotal detail, like a sandstorm of punctuation, rendering the scene almost illegible. So massive was the televisual stockpile of images in the spring of 2003 that the larger, more monumental project (world domination for the pancapital interests of multinational corporations and the global elite) may be "overlooked" by U.S. citizens in sentimental thrall to X and to Y as particular suffering soldiers. Here, arguably, the monumentalizing agendas of the war are both propped *and obscured* by the constant feed of affective, sentimentalized details leveled at the televisual screen on the home front under the rubric "LIVE."

The ban on showing the images of the literal dead Americans and Iraqis, of course, begs enormous questions. Images that leaked out, like the victim/soldier portraits from Abu Ghraib taken in *winter of 2003* that "surfaced" *between March and June of 2004*, reminded us that we had not, in sitting before our visual screens, been *seeing*. The prisoners of Abu Ghraib are tortured by our eyes, as the site of their torture is cast into a future that will never have fully occurred. This is because their torture is at least in part *about* theatricality and display in a medium of dissemination; their torture is meant to take place in dissemination and circulation of their images, again and again. The Abu Ghraib images are stagey strike-the-pose snapshots of abuse that underscore the theatricality of torture and terror as well as terror's dependence on reiteration and *telling*. Ironically, such images were telling in that they interrupted the sentimental feed of daily soldier life and made apparent the ways in which sanitized patriotic sentiment is, like terror, similarly theatrical, staged for affect and dissemination across bodies not necessarily willing but necessarily complicit: theirs *and* ours; yours *and* mine.

Watching television now and then between *then* and *now,* I begin to formulate a question. Have American consumers, interpellated primarily as viewers, become as fixed and forgetful as stone monuments—or the twins to monument—rigidly planted, seemingly unmoving, overlooking Never Again, again?

NOTES

1. On talking terror, see Michael Taussig (1992). See also Diana Taylor, "Disappearing Bodies: Writing Torture and Torture as Writing" (1997). Taylor is excellent in examining the ways in which terror claims an ambivalent space in which an event both occurs and does not occur. She labels this "percepticide" and discusses the ambivalence of terror as composed in the often blatant theatricality she finds again and again in her examination of the use of spectacle in the Argentine Dirty War.

2. Here I refer the reader to the considerable production of "trauma theory" in recent years in literary studies, performance studies, historiography, and art history. The discourse provocatively takes up Freud's *Beyond the Pleasure Principle* and his "novel" *Moses and Monotheism* and, deploying a powerful mix of Blanchot, DeMan, Lacan, and others, applies the repetition compulsion (to repeat what one has repressed) to the sociological spheres of collective memory, commemoration, spectatorship and witnessing, and museological exhibition. See the work of Shoshana Felman, Cathy Caruth, Avital Ronell, and Dominick LaCapra. In general, trauma theorists call for a working through (*Durcharbeiten*) of textual or secondary materials that carry the trace of an event as a means of getting to the political, historical, or ideological complexities of the event itself. Some, such as Foster (1996), read the compulsion to repeat as aimed at puncturing the facade put into place by the "mythic reproduction" of the event.

3. This text was first written for the collection *Déjà vu: In literatur und bildender kunst,* edited by Gunther Oesterle (Paderborn, Germany: Wilhelm Fink Verlag, 2003). The invitation to write on déjà vu preceded, by many months, the occasion of this writing, and I had almost completed another text when, on September 12, I decided to *begin again*. The second half of this essay does not appear in the *Déjà vu* collection, as the events I discuss in that section had, apparently, *not yet* occurred.

4. Déjà vu is a sense of events as "already seen" or as if "seen again." This results in a sense of the present returning as "tediously familiar." But *jamais vu,* the "never seen" or "never, again" has a more medical connotation. According to the *Concise Medical Dictionary, jamais vu* is one of the manifestations of temporal lobe epilepsy in

which there is a sudden feeling of unfamiliarity with that which has already occurred, what has already been experienced.

5. Quote taken from Cable News Network's Web site on September 12, 2001. See http://www .greatdreams.com/trade_day2.htm as well.

6. See the speech on the Web site: http:// www.al-bab.com/arab/docs/pal/pal10.htm.

7. See Ron Fournier, "Bush Defends Investigation Tactics," http://multimedia.beloint eractive.com/attack/bush/1130bushspeech.html. In an Associated Press report on November 30, 2001, Ron Fournier reported that one in ten Americans approved of Bush's remand of freedom in freedom's name.

8. See, for example, Judith Butler's *Excitable Speech* (1997). Here, writing is not in opposition to performance or "liveness." Rather, writing is a word used to suggest the ways in which the surrogate, the copy or the second, founds the first backward through *telling*. Thus "writing" can happen in multiple media, from gesturing to whispering to painting to singing (see Roach, 1996; Derrida, 1976). Writing, then, is both memory and memorial—the medium of Heidegger's *Gedächtnis* of Being—even as it is a memory that forecasts, remembers the future, the "already seen." The critique that "writing" is a metaphor obsessed with textuality, or the literary, and the suggestion that writing therefore forgets performance (or "the body") is an important, though limited, critique. Such a critique often forgets that writing is a gesture that takes place always in the live space of exchange with a reader or orator—taking place again and again and again in the living hands, mouths, and eyes of readers, speakers, or hearers who, alive, necessarily rewrite. To divide writing or reading completely from performance, or performance from writing, is arguably to reinstitute a delimiting binary.

9. Foucault's *The Archaeology of Knowledge* (1972) posits meaning as located in the *practice* of language, which is to say in bodies in time. It is important to remember, however, that the meaning-effects that are produced in language (gestic, textual, or aural) escape (or at least slip beyond) both the intentions of speakers and the regulations of a particular episteme, or system of knowledge. An event (and its meaning) exceeds that which appears to fix it, even as that which appears to fix an event (or a body) prescribes the conditions of possibility for that event's articulation *as*

event. See also Shoshana Felman (1983). For Felman, the event that cannot be fixed is linked to the unfixedness of the live body—the "scandal of the body"—always in free fall, perhaps, against a grid.

10. This endnote is actually meant for the sentence that follows it. In this way, the endnote comes before. I intend the last nonsentence of this section (as well as footnotes 5 and 6) to resonate with Diana Taylor on "percepticide" (1997).

11. Michel de Certeau's *L'invention du Quotidian* was first published in 1974 (Vol. 1, Arts de Faire). The book was translated into English as *The Practice of Everyday Life* in 1984 (translated by Steven F. Rendall, Berkeley, CA: University of California Press). Naomi Shor published *Reading in Detail: Aesthetics and the Feminine* in 1987 (New York: Routledge).

12. Reading in detail is a methodological exercise in tandem with poststructuralism generally, although Schor is eager to point out how poststructuralist analyses (pre-1987) so often forgot the historical feminization of the debased detail in order to prop its new, and masculine, grand literary promise (Schor, 1987, p. 6).

REFERENCES

Blakesley, D. (2001, March). *Prophesying after the event*. Paper presented at the Conference on College Composition and Communication, Denver, CO. Retrieved January, 2002, from http://www.sla.purdue.edu/people/engl/dblake sley/burke/prophesying.html.

Blanchot, M. (1986). *The writing of the disaster* (A. Smock, Trans.). Lincoln: University of Nebraska Press, 1986.

Braun, E. (Ed.). (1969). *Meyerhold on theater*. New York: Hill and Wang.

Brecht, B. (1964). *Brecht on theater*. (J. Willet, Trans.). New York: Hill and Wang.

Butler, J. (1996). *Excitable speech*. New York: Routledge.

de Certeau, M. (1984). *The practice of everyday life* (S. F. Rendall, Trans.). Berkeley, CA: University of California Press. (Original work published 1974)

Derrida, J. (1976). *On grammatolog* (G. Spivak, Trans.). Baltimore: Johns Hopkins University Press.

Felman, S. (1983). *The literary speech act: Don Juan with J. L. Austin, or suction in two languages* (C. Porter, Trans.) Ithaca, NY: Cornell University Press.

Foster, H. (1996). *Return of the real: The avant-garde at the end of the century.* Cambridge MA: MIT Press.

Foucault, M. (1972). *The archaeology of knowledge* (A. M. Sheridan Smith, Trans.) London: Tavistock.

McDonald, C. (2003, April). *Grieving in portraits.* Paper presented at The Lure of the Detail: A Conference in Honor of Naomi Schor, Providence, RI.

Roach, J. (1996). *Cities of the dead: Circumatlantic performance.* New York: Columbia University Press.

Shor, N. (1987). *Reading in detail: Aesthetics and the feminine.* New York: Routledge.

Taussig, M. (1992). *The nervous system.* New York: Routledge.

Taylor, D. (1997). Disappearing bodies: Writing torture and torture as writing. In D. Taylor, *Disappearing acts: Spectacles of gender and nationalism in Argentina's "Dirty War"* (pp. 139–182). Durham, NC: Duke University Press.

3

Performance and Globalization

JON MCKENZIE

More than forty years ago, U.S. President Dwight Eisenhower gave his farewell speech to the American people. Near the end of his farewell, the president spoke the following words:

> So—in this my last good night to you as your President—I thank you for the many opportunities you have given me for public service in war and peace. I trust that in that service you find some things worthy; as for the rest of it, I know you will find ways to improve performance in the future. (1962, p. 1040)

"Improve performance in the future." Today, some forty years later, we might ask: what performance did Eisenhower have in mind, and how was it to be improved? Eisenhower served as the U.S. president during the coldest years of the Cold War. He weathered the first phase of the nuclear arms race, the 1957 Sputnik launch, and the shooting down of a U-2 spy plane over the Soviet Union. And this was just his peacetime service, for prior to becoming president, he had also served as supreme commander of the Allied forces during World War II.

So which performance was Eisenhower talking about? Decades later, could it be that his "improved performance" has become "our" performance, the performance of art, the art of performance, or more generally, aesthetic or cultural performance? "Surely not!" we may want to insist. And yet, what is performance? And what is its relation to contemporary processes of globalization?

In 2001, at the Performance Studies international conference held in Mainz, Germany (PSi 7), I was part of a series of panels addressing the topic of performance and globalization. I noted then that the organizers' description had cast globalization in two ways: either as something that threatened the production and study of performance, or conversely, as something that performance must somehow resist at all costs. Either way, the descriptions assumed "performance versus globalization." However, my own research suggests another, very different relation between performance and globalization, and that is: performance *as* globalization.

TOWARD A GENERAL
THEORY OF PERFORMANCE

To give some sense of how I came to this formulation, allow me to present some of the main ideas contained in my book, *Perform or Else,* one goal of which is to rehearse a general theory of performance. Significantly, the official publication launch of the book occurred at the Mainz PSi conference.

In contrast to the early researchers of cultural performance—e.g., Richard Schechner, Dell Hymes, Victor Turner—whose task it was to identify and theorize different cultural practices as "performance," I set out several years ago with a slightly different task: to track down how the term "performance" had been formalized in other paradigms of research over the past half century. Thus I wasn't out to identify new practices and name them "performance." Rather, I sought out the name "performance" in order to study what other types of practices had already been produced and studied under this term.

To get at these other practices, let me cite some of the performances we don't often find discussed at international conferences on cultural performance. For starters, there are usually no papers on the performance of guided missiles, or computer facilities, or public infrastructures. I bring these up because over the past fifty years, engineers and computer scientists have developed sophisticated practices for creating and studying the performances of technological systems, many of which came out of the U.S. military-industrial complex: high-performance fighter planes, guidance systems, and composite materials.

Such research has been explicitly institutionalized. In 1991, the U.S. Congress passed the High Performance Computing Act (1992) to support the development of massively parallel computer systems, and today there are dozens of High Performance Computing Centers. In 1995, the National Research Council published a wide-ranging report titled *Measuring and Improving Infrastructure Performance* (Committee on Measuring and Improving Infrastructure Performance, 1995). Such performance research has trickled down into low-tech commodities, such as cars and stereos and mop handles. These technological performances are not evaluated in terms of their cultural efficacy but rather by their technical effectiveness, their ability to meet such criteria as speed, endurance, and reliability. As with cultural performance, technological performances can only be defined and studied in highly specific and localized ways.

There are usually no presentations on the technological performance of missiles or mop handles at international conferences on cultural performance. Nor do we find papers on improving the performance of factory workers, or evaluating work-team performance, or creating "peak performance" organizations. But here again, over the past half century, there has emerged a whole field of performance research quite distinct from performance studies. Though it has its origins in Frederick Taylor's scientific management, which dominated the first half of the twentieth century, "performance management" emerged around the time of the Second World War. Its proponents in industry and business schools countered Taylorism's stress on the rationality and conformity of factory work by arguing that management in the service and information economy must encourage workers' creativity and diversity.

This organizational performance paradigm has also been formally institutionalized. To give one example: In 1993, the U.S. Congress passed the Government Performance and Results Act (1994), which sought to improve the performance of federal departments and agencies. It led to the establishment of the National Performance Review. And yet for decades, U.S. companies have been conducting annual "performance reviews" of their employees and managers. At the heart of this field of performance research is not cultural efficacy or technical effectiveness, but rather organizational efficiency: maximizing outputs and minimizing inputs.

To sum up, then, there are at least three paradigms of performance research: cultural, technological, and organizational, and each is guided by different evaluative criteria and different norms of defining and analyzing performance: cultural efficacy, technological effectiveness, and organizational efficiency.

What is the relationship among these performative values, these different kinds of performance? From the perspective of performance studies, with its emphasis on resistance, mutation, and transgression, the other two performance paradigms appear highly, if not exclusively, normative in their social functioning. Indeed, taken together, technological and organizational performance research appears almost synonymous with Big Science and Big Business, with what in the 1960s was called in the United States "the Establishment" or "the System."

Here resides the generative paradox of my research: performance contains both normative and deviant valences. While performance studies scholars have spent over four decades producing and theorizing performance as a force of social resistance, others have been studying and producing performances that we readily identify as dominant in the contemporary world. How to make sense of this paradox? Are these simply different meanings of the term "performance," or do the three research paradigms share some common traits that bind them together at a different level of analysis?

Far from existing in disconnected spheres, these paradigms increasingly overlap and intersect: For instance, just as theatre takes place in institutional contexts constrained and enriched by technological and economic imperatives, the theatrical model has come to inform organizational theory and web design. To understand the mutual embedding of cultural, technological, and organizational performance, I began studying performance from a genealogical perspective, using methods drawn from Derrida, Foucault, and Deleuze and Guattari. What I found was this possibility: below the three research paradigms, at a more general level of analysis, performance could be understood as an ontohistorical formation of power and knowledge.

PERFORMANCE STRATUM

To put this possibility as succinctly as possible: performance will have been to the twentieth and twenty-first centuries what discipline was to the eighteenth and nineteenth: a stratum of power and knowledge. This power operates through the conflicts and compromises of different types of performance, for example, cultural, technological, and organizational performance. This performativity demands that we be effective one moment, efficient the next, and efficacious at another—and sometimes to be all three at once. In short, performative power and knowledge challenges us in different ways to perform—or else (McKenzie, 2001).

I am certainly not the first person to recognize the power of performance. To my knowledge, Herbert Marcuse was the first to theorize the powerful normativity of performance. In 1955, Marcuse argued that postindustrial societies were governed by a reality principle that he called the "performance principle." Writing about the repressiveness found in contemporary civilization, he wrote: "We designate it as performance principle in order to emphasize that under its rule society is stratified according to the competitive economic performances of its members" (Marcuse, 1955, pp. 40–41). According to Marcuse, the performance principle consists of a positivist, technological rationality that has spread from factories to offices, homes, and indeed all spheres of social life. Marcuse, writing in the wake of World War II, conceived performative power as centralized, monolithic, and highly conformist, a conception informed by his experience of Nazi Germany, Stalinist Russia, and Cold War America.

Other important and more recent theorists have also analyzed performance as a form of power. In the late 1970s, Jean-François Lyotard explored the "postmodern condition" explicitly in terms of the performative legitimization of power and knowledge. In his now-famous formulation, Lyotard argued that such modern "grand narratives" as progress and revolution had given way to a new type of power: performativity. "In matters of social justice and of scientific truth alike, the legitimization of that power is based on its optimizing the system's performance—efficiency" (Lyotard, 1979/1984, p. xxiv). While Marcuse stressed the uniformity of the performative principle, Lyotard instead emphasized the heterogeneity of diffuse, agonistic language games ruled by this performativity.

More recently still, of course, Judith Butler has called our attention to the "punitive performatives" that govern gender and sexual identification (Butler, 1990). While Butler's early theorization of performativity drew on Turner's fieldwork research of ritual performance, she soon turned to Austin's linguistic studies to theorize the role of performative speech acts in both constituting and maintaining gender identity. Combining Butler's notion of the citationality of discourse with Schechner's restoration of behavior, we can say that discursive performatives and embodied performances, when bound together by normative forces of iteration, together form the basic building blocks of the performance stratum.

To say that the performance stratum will have been to the twentieth and twenty-first centuries what discipline was to the eighteenth and nineteenth is more than an analogy, for in many ways, performative power is precisely a displacement and radical reinscription of the disciplinary power analyzed by Foucault. There are tremendous differences, however, that can only be sketched here.

While Foucault located the rise of discipline in Western Europe, I believe performative power mechanisms crystallized in the United States just after World War II, precisely the time when Marcuse formulated the performance principle and J. L. Austin lectured on performative speech acts. Significantly, it was just after the Second World War that the paradigms of cultural, technological, and organizational performance began to really take shape. According to Foucault, discipline produced unified subjects through a series of institutions such as school, factory, and prison, each with its own discrete archive of statements and practices (Foucault, 1975/1979). By contrast, performative power blurs the borders of social institutions by connecting and sharing their digital archives. Financial information, criminal records, and school transcripts once stored in separate file cabinets are now being uploaded to silicon databases and electronically networked. Bodies that once passed neatly through a linear sequence of power mechanisms are now learning to switch rapidly between conflicting evaluative grids; the resulting subjects tend to be fractured, multiple, or hybrid. In the U.S. workplace, for instance, we have witnessed the rise of multitasking; in schools, children are routinely diagnosed with attention-deficit disorders; and in everyday life, people have begun "culture-surfing," moving through different styles and traditions almost as quickly and easily as changing channels on the television. From a wider historical perspective, while discipline functioned as the power matrix of the Enlightenment, the Industrial Revolution, liberal capitalism, and European colonialism, performance operates as the matrix of the post-Enlightenment, the information revolution, neoliberal capitalism, and postcolonialism. But let me stress again that performative power and knowledge is really a thing of the future; the disciplinary formation wasn't built in a day, nor has the performance stratum fully installed itself.

CLARIFICATIONS

Here I would like to offer some clarifications. Contrary to objections that are sometimes raised to me, I am not saying that performances exist only in the United States, nor that one cannot study performances that took place before the Second World War. The Mainz conference—and more recently, major conferences on cultural performance held in Berlin, London, Tokyo, Lima, and Canterbury, New Zealand—all demonstrate that performance research is global, and there exist many important texts on cultural performances from earlier centuries. Nor am I denying that some performances can resist or critique globalization. Indeed, significant research has begun to address such resistance and critique.

What I am saying, however, is that performance concepts and practices have a history, and that this history is related to the history of other performance research, both applied and theoretical, and to the corresponding institutions that support and produce such research. Concepts of technological high performance, for instance, grew out of the U.S. military-industrial complex, while those of organizational performance emerged from internal, postwar critiques of scientific management. The study of cultural activities as "performance" arguably began in the United States, and it is no coincidence that the first official departments of performance studies were established in the United States, or that the first four meetings of Performance Studies international also took place there.

Indeed, from my own travels and contacts, I sense a growing suspicion of the "Americanness," or, more accurately, the "U.S.-centrism" of performance studies, and perhaps of performance research more generally. This suspicion may, in part, inform recent attempts to articulate alternative genealogies of performance research, genealogies that are often nationally or linguistically based. Such attempts include Erika Fischer-Lichte's keynote address at PSi 7 in Mainz, which surveyed the development of performance research in Germany over the past half century (Fischer-Lichte, 2001), and Diana Taylor's recent exploration of the Spanish term *performatico* as an alternative to the logocentric "performative" (Taylor, 2003). Performance research has been U.S.-centric I would assert, but it is going global, as contemporary cultural performance research makes clear—but so does performance research carried out by the United Nations, the International Monetary Fund, and other organizations associated with processes of globalization.

PARADIGMS 4, 5, 6 . . .

Whether one understands performance research as emanating from the United States or from multiple nodes around the world, performance has gone global, and not only cultural performance but also technological and organizational forms of performance. To make matters even more complex, allow me to cite three additional paradigms of performance research.

Building on the above discussion, a fourth paradigm of performance research is that of *government performance*. Conducted by political scientists, sociologists, and public policy analysts, this research largely concerns the performance of national governments, i.e., how well such governments perform or carry out their public duties in the opinion of their constituents. Frequently, this performance is evaluated through large-scale public surveys or "barometers," such as the Eurobarometer, the Latinobarometer, and the African and Asian Barometers, all of which are carefully designed and translated for consistency in order to facilitate comparison analysis between different nation-states and geographic regions (McKenzie, 2003).

A fifth paradigm is that of *financial or economic performance,* which involves the use of performance concepts to analyze individual financial instruments (e.g., stocks and bonds), the economic activities of small businesses and large firms, and even entire markets, industries, and economies. To give you the big picture: officials of the International Monetary

Fund (IMF) frequently cite the impact of IMF policies on "global economic performance" (International Monetary Fund, 2000). Financial performance differs from organizational performance in that it concerns overall financial or economic activities rather than the internal management of workers.

And last, a sixth paradigm is that of *environmental performance*. Over the past several decades, under increasing pressure from environmentalists and, more recently, governmental regulators, companies around the world have begun systematic programs to evaluate how well they meet environmental standards. Such programs produce regular environmental performance reviews concerning such areas as biosafety, airborne emissions, and water quality. Moreover, the Organization for Economic Co-operation and Development (OECD) now sets environmental performance guidelines for its member states, some thirty of the world's most highly industrialized countries, as well as three associated nonmembers.

As is the case with cultural, organizational, and technological performance, "performance" in these governmental, financial, and environmental paradigms refers to highly specific, yet highly contested sets of practices. Further, as should be obvious, each paradigm entails contested sets of evaluative criteria that, in the end, are socially and politically determined. Further, as can be seen from the examples mentioned in all three of these paradigms, performance research has become crucial to contemporary processes of globalization, from governance to finance to ecological concerns.

GLOBAL PERFORMATIVITY

As politically influential and geographically extensive as all of these performance paradigms may be individually, the performativity of contemporary globalization is best revealed by attempts to integrate different performative criteria.

We can see one attempt at integrating multiparadigmatic performances in the summary of *The Shell Report*, prepared by the Royal Dutch/Shell Group of Companies and verified by the accounting and auditing firms of KPMG and PricewaterhouseCoopers. The title of this report summary is, significantly, *People, planet and profits*. Why is this title significant here? Because "people," "planet," and "profits" correspond directly to the annual report's three main sections, which respectively are "social performance," "environmental performance," and "economic performance." In short, the entire annual activity of this major multinational corporation is presented and assessed for its stakeholders—and for the world at large—in terms of the integration of three different types of performance: social, environmental, and economic, or in Shell's terms, the performances of people, planet, and profits (Royal Dutch Petroleum Company, 2002).

Royal Dutch/Shell's attempt to integrate multiparadigmatic performances exemplifies the nature and functioning of performativity's operation at a global level. First, performativity is not "one thing"; it is not composed of one single and coherent set of performative discourses, practices, and values. Rather, it consists of many conflicting and, at times, contradictory performativities: cultural, organizational, technological, governmental, financial, environmental . . . and this list is not exhaustive, for there are still other paradigms of performance research, including educational, physiological, psychological, sexual, and pharmaceutical paradigms. Second, the performance stratum functions precisely through ongoing attempts to negotiate multiple and competing performativities. While Lyotard stressed performativity as optimization or the maximizing of efficiency, a more accurate understanding of performativity is "satisficing," first theorized by Herbert Simon (1957). Efficiency may often need to be compromised with other values, such as efficacy or effectiveness. Decision-makers thus seek to satisfy competing demands, but because they work with limited knowledge, they must also make sacrifices; hence they *satisfice*, making not the best or optimum decision but one that is "good enough."

Likewise, global performativity operates through what we might call *satisficial rituals*, routinized performance review programs that consist of highly formalized attempts to measure, evaluate, and improve different types of performance. Such evaluative programs are in no way limited to Royal Dutch/Shell. Quite the contrary: the focus on studying, evaluating, and integrating social, environmental, and economic performances is becoming increasingly important to companies and countries who dedicate themselves to sustainable development. Using guidelines established by the Global Reporting Initiative (GRI), some 323 organizations in 31 countries use social, environmental, and economic performance measures to assess the impact their activities have on the natural environment and the social well-being of their workers, customers, and communities. These organizations include small and large companies, governments, and nongovernmental organizations (NGOs). Now an independent organization itself, the GRI was founded in 1997 by the Coalition for Environmentally Responsible Economies and is an official collaborating center of the United Nations Environment Programme.

We can sense the breadth of global performativity by turning to the Global Compact Performance Model developed by the United Nations. In 1999, UN Secretary-General Kofi Annan announced the Global Compact, a global initiative aimed at encouraging private companies to work toward sustainable and inclusive global economic development. The Global Compact focuses on three main areas of concern: human rights, labor standards, and the environment. The program became operational in 2000 and is today composed of a network of five agencies. Coordinated by the Global Compact Office, this network includes the Office of the High Commissioner for Human Rights, the United Nations Environment Programme, the International Labour Organization, the United Nations Development Programme, and the United Nations Industrial Development Organization. Currently, over 1,130 companies from 59 nations participate in the UN's Global Compact. At the heart of the program is the goal of encouraging private companies to incorporate human rights, labor, and environmental standards into their strategic planning and production processes. To this end, in 2002, a Global Compact Policy Dialogue consisting of UN representatives, business practitioners, and labor and civil society organizations developed the Global Compact Performance Model. The dialogue group explains,

> By *model*, we mean a system of rules, practices and means to achieve a set of results. By *performance* we mean a minimum of inputs and efforts to achieve the best results in the shortest period of time. In other words this [performance model] describes a blueprint or road map to help business to embrace the Global Compact principles and move toward a satisfactory performance without detracting from their other business goals. (*Company Performance Model*, 2002)

Without going into the details of the Global Compact Performance Model, we can see that the dialogue group defines performance at the most general level as minimizing inputs and optimizing outputs in a timely manner. Such "minimaxing" of input and output ratios is central to Lyotard's concept of performative optimization. At the same time, we can also say that to achieve the Global Compact's criteria of "satisfactory performance," companies must negotiate between traditional business performance measures (in paradigmatic terms, those of organizational and financial performance) and new, emerging performance measures (those of environmental performance and social performance—which here includes human rights and fair labor practices). Such negotiations, again, can best be understood as satisficing rather than optimization.

The Global Reporting Initiative and the UN's Global Compact provide ample evidence of how performativity is going global and, indeed, in doing so they also reveal a third characteristic of global performativity. Not only does it entail a multiplicity of performativities and formal programs that attempt to integrate and satisfice these performativities. In addition, global performativity operates through a complex network of social institutions, working not only at the level of nation-states, but also above them at the level of international and transnational organizations, such as the UN and the GRI, and below them, through businesses and NGOs. It is precisely this global networking of institutions that helps distinguish the performance stratum from the much more hierarchical and nationally based institutions found on the disciplinary formation described by Foucault.

PERFORMATIVITY'S PERVERSITIES AND AMBIGUITIES

On the face of it, there is clearly a progressive dimension of global performativity, as seen in the issues and values embodied in the Global Compact and the Global Reporting Initiative: improvement of human rights, environmental protection, fair labor standards, and sustainable and inclusive economic development. These causes have long been championed by social activists and progressive political groups, and especially so in light of contemporary processes of globalization. The same holds true with other issues often promoted by institutional agents of global performativity, such as diversity, creativity, education, and AIDS/HIV treatment and prevention programs. Global performativity is normative, yet creating norms that promote progressive values seems well worth supporting.

At the same time, however, programs such as the UN's Global Compact and, more generally, the widespread introduction of performance models into public institutions have come under increasing scrutiny and criticism. Interestingly, many of these criticisms echo the analyses of performative power made decades ago by Marcuse and Lyotard.

In January 2002, an international group of NGOs called the Alliance for a Corporate-Free UN issued a blunt letter to UN Secretary-General Kofi Annan criticizing the effectiveness of the Global Compact. While praising Annan's motivation in creating the Global Compact, the sixteen signatories argued that its design allows corporations to improve their public reputations via association with the UN without, however, committing themselves to real changes in their corporate behaviors regarding human rights, labor standards, and environmental protection. To support this charge, the Alliance enclosed documentation of guideline violations by five corporate members of the Global Compact. Further, the Alliance charged the Compact's own operation with inadequate transparency of its operation and a fundamental lack of regulatory strength.

In order to correct these problems, the letter proposed a redesign of the Global Compact, one that would transform it into the Global Accountability Compact and thereby convert it from being a partnership between the UN and corporations and into a watchdog organization that monitors companies' performance. Member corporations' adherence to its guidelines would no longer be voluntary but mandatory, and continued membership in the Compact would require any companies found in violation to take corrective action. At one point in their letter, the Alliance urged Annan's office to "clarify that the Compact's purpose is not to advance a business agenda regarding trade and investment rules" (Alliance for a Corporate-Free UN, 2002). Using the terms of the Global Reporting Initiative discussed above, we can read the Alliance's letter as arguing that the UN Global Compact must show greater commitment to social and environmental performance issues by distancing itself from economic performance values.

A far more explicit and extensive critique of performativity can be found in Hans de Bruijn's 2001 text, *Managing Performance in the Public Sector*. De Bruijn, a professor of organization and management at Delft University of Technology in the Netherlands, provides a substantive critique of the adoption of performance measurement programs by governments and public authorities around the world. He notes that while such programs potentially offer greater transparency and public accountability, their actual implementation often produces what he calls "perverse effects" (de Bruijn, 2001). Among the perverse effects de Bruijn identifies are (1) *"gaming the numbers,"* whereby carefully selected inputs or outputs allow government agencies to meet performance goals, while other valuable inputs or outputs are simply ignored; (2) *inhibition of innovation and ambition,* caused by public authorities developing efficient processes and then only encouraging workers to maintain these processes, rather than seek innovations; (3) *veiling of actual performance,* whereby aggregation of performance measures at upper organizational levels obscures information about lower-level performance; (4) *deadening of professional responsibility,* caused by internal and external competition to meet performance standards, which in turn leads to the compartmentalization of information, rather than its cooperative, responsible sharing; and, perhaps most perversely, (5) *punishment of performance,* for example, in cases where one group is rewarded for "good performance" that is only "achieved" by its veiling of key data, while another is sanctioned for "poor performance" made visible precisely by its transparency of information.

De Bruijn notes that while it is possible for public organizations to counter such perverse effects of performance measurement, governments and agencies that have established these programs may often vigorously resist corrective measures. Among the reasons for this resistance are the fact that such programs require both time and money to establish and, once established, they inform both budgets and work processes. Furthermore, biases in performance measurement programs tend to reflect biases in the agency's internal political culture, and thus correcting them may very well require a dramatic organizational restructuring. Finally, even when perverse effects are recognized, directors may come to rely on performance programs not only for assessment purposes but also for steering or controlling the organization to meet demands made upon it by outside agencies or superiors. For a variety of reasons, then, organizations often resist attempts to correct the perversities of performativity.

The criticisms raised by the Alliance for a Corporate-Free UN and by Hans de Bruijn echo critiques of performativity made long ago by Marcuse and Lyotard. Both theorists targeted the economic and technological imperatives that define the performativity of advanced capitalism. The overriding values behind these imperatives are efficiency and expediency, values embodied in the high performance demand to achieve maximum results with minimum resources in the shortest period of time. In short: *profits now.*

Marcuse, writing in the 1950s, focused on the technological rationality emanating from factories outward to society, whereas Lyotard later stressed the sophisticated operational optimization that digital computers make possible. For both theorists, performativity demands quantification, in particular, the calculation of input/output ratios. Social and moral concerns, when not totally ignored by decision-makers, must become measurable in order to count, to matter, to have significance, indeed, to be. Thus under performativity, public accountability increasingly entails the forced quantification of the nonquantifiable, the qualitative, and this forced quantification, I would argue, accounts for many of performativity's perversities.

While Marcuse gave little to no credit to the performance principle he diagnosed at work in postindustrial societies, Lyotard was willing to acknowledge the ambiguities of performativity. In particular, he noted that decision-makers immersed in performative legitimization did address the question of their own decision-making and the rules or "metaprescriptives" that guide them. Indeed, we witness this ambiguity at work today in all the ongoing performance review programs, all the incessant satisficial rituals for integrating diverse performative values. For not only is performance evaluated: these evaluations are themselves evaluated. Indeed, there now exists an entire industry of competing performance consultants, each armed with programs, models, and "best practice" case studies designed to create cycles of constant performance improvement. In addition, given the increasing importance of service industries and the rise of public sector performance programs, the stakeholders of both private and public organizations often no longer include only "insiders." At first dismissively, then reluctantly, and now strategically for both operational and public relations reasons, many organizations have begun to listen to consumers, clients, affected populations, social activists, and even political protestors. To give one widely reported example: President Bill Clinton surprised many people at the 1999 meeting of the World Trade Organization—known to activists around the world as the "Battle of Seattle"—by saying that the organization needed to listen to the people protesting outside its doors.

The emerging global performativity is thus highly ambiguous. On the one hand, we should affirm the inclusion of such issues as human rights, respect for diversity, fair and safe working conditions, protection of rights for women and children, and the improvement of air and water quality within the performance models of the UN's Global Compact, the Global Reporting Initiative, and innumerable other organizations around the world. In each case, the inclusion of these issues comes only after years and years of struggle by local, national, and international groups, from community activists to national advocacy groups to large nongovernmental organizations. However, as the Alliance for a Corporate-Free UN and other activist groups suggest, such victories are easily co-optable and may be Pyrrhic in nature: socially efficacious values may all too quickly be sacrificed to other performative values. Marginalized voices may be listened to but not heard, qualitative matters may be crudely quantified, and highly publicized pledges of corporate and government responsibility may function merely as a fig leaf for business-as-usual. Nonetheless, getting activists' issues "on the table" in public discussions and, more crucially, getting them "on the books," that is, written into laws, contracts, and mission statements, are important achievements. Once on the books, it may become possible for activists to turn the table and use the very same performance models to hold organizations to their word and effect changes in both procedures and behavior (Keck and Sikkink, 1999).

"BUT WHAT ABOUT *PERFORMANCE?*"

I'd like to conclude by entertaining one possible, even likely, objection to these reflections on performance and globalization: "But what about *performance?* What does any of this have to do with theatre, performance art, the performance of everyday life, etc.?"

First of all, concepts and practices of cultural performance have a historical relation to *other* concepts and practices of performance, including some *very* powerful ones, as I hope this essay has shown. While global performativity may seem far removed from the production and study of discrete cultural performances, it must be stressed that performativity operates through a complex network that operates at the macro and meso levels of large institutions and smaller organizations, as well as at the micro level of subjectivity theorized by Butler. In short, global performativity operates both top-down and bottom-up, both globally and locally, both impersonally and intimately. It affects not only political and business organizations, but also cultural institutions and the comings and goings of everyday life.

To give an example at the micro level: in the late 1990s, WNYC, the local public radio station in New York City, launched a show called *The Juggling Act* that focused on how working mothers juggle the demands of both family and professional life. It was co-sponsored by the online magazine *Salon*'s "Mothers Who Think" project, which provides working mothers an opportunity to post stories of their own experiences online. The women editors behind the show dedicated it to "honoring the juggling act that we perform every day." As a performance of everyday life, raising children and pursuing a career simultaneously entails negotiating conflicting sets of expectations, responsibilities, and values. "Juggling act" is "satisficing" played out at an intimate level; it entails responding to diverse demands to perform—or else, demands made by partners, children, doctors, teachers, bosses, and employees. In some cases, performing the juggling act may touch on one's deepest sense of identity while also being informed by global flows of labor and migration. One working mother, Cecelie Berry, an African American lawyer, writes in a *Salon* commentary of the lifelong guilt she has felt as a privileged black woman, guilt that became acute when hiring caretakers for her children. "As a young lawyer, I didn't do the hiring, so like many women, I first became an employer when I hired a nanny. The nannies I hired came from Panama, Jamaica, Israel, Sweden, France, England, Ghana, and the United States. Though the cultures changed, the tactics of the power struggle between mother and nanny remained the same. The mother lode of guilt I carried from childhood made

me—'How you say?'—dead meat every time" (Berry, 2000).

Shifting from the juggling act of everyday life to the day-to-day operations of cultural institutions, we can see how performativity is coming to inform the production, presentation, and evaluation of works by theatres and other arts organizations. Giacomo Pignataro, an Italian researcher of cultural institutions, writes that

> the use of performance indicators in the arts is quite widespread nowadays. The basic reason for the development of this practice is that the scope for commercial profit-oriented activity is very limited, and the size of public and private contributions can be large. The different stakeholders cannot refer to any market signal, however imperfect it may be, to evaluate different aspects of arts production. Therefore there is a need to define "virtual" measures of arts organizations' performance so as to provide some empirical support to the judgment on the value of arts productions. (Pignataro, 2003, p. 366)

The growing use of performance measures and management models within arts institutions reflects their attempt to meet conflicting demands, not only aesthetic and cultural ones, but also economic, political, and social ones. While it is tempting to criticize this increasing performativity as simply the corporatization of arts institutions, one must also recognize the ambiguities at work here. Just as the UN's Global Compact Performance Model valorizes such progressive causes as human rights and environmental justice, so too do new methods of assessment and accountability in the arts stress such criteria as cultural diversity and community outreach, criteria that may apply to both institutional operations and the production of individual shows.

A recent prospective study by the Dutch Ministry of Education, Culture and Science is instructive here. Titled *Culture as Confrontation: Principles on Cultural Policy in 2001–2005*, the study recommends four criteria for assessing individual arts institutions, including Amsterdam's Municipal Theatre and Theatre Company Amsterdam. These four criteria, drawn from the Dutch Council for Culture, are aesthetic quality, social outreach, ticket subsidy ratio, and the position of the particular institution within the larger system of Dutch cultural institutions. The study suggests that the

> assessment will normally be based on the institution's policy plan and on an estimate of the feasibility of this plan in the light of current performance. The extent to which the council relies on future predictions or current performance may vary from one criterion to another. (van der Ploeg, 1999)

It should be noted that the study begins by highlighting the need to maintain the Netherlands' place within the cultural spheres of both Europe and the world.

I'll end by suggesting that not only has the production and study of cultural performances come to be influenced by powerful forms of performativity, but also that cultural performance plays an important role in global performativity. Within the field of human geography, theorists often distinguish three eras of globalization: the mercantilism of the sixteenth and seventeenth centuries; the colonialism of the eighteenth and nineteenth centuries; and the contemporary globalization that began in the twentieth century. The Australian sociologist Malcolm Waters argues that at the forefront of mercantilism was economics (the establishment of global trade routes and trading companies). At the cutting edge of colonialism was geopolitics (the creation of nation-states and colonial empires). Finally, contemporary globalization is guided by culture (the exchange and mixing of cultural traditions such as art, religion, and folklore). Obviously, each era has cultural, political, and economic dimensions. Waters's point is that at different historical times, different social institutions and activities come to the fore, and that

today, cultural factors organize and legitimate the political and economic factors.

Surprisingly, another body of research supports this claim, while returning us to our point of departure. I refer to research undertaken by the RAND Corporation, a nonprofit organization with close ties to the U.S. Department of Defense. Since its inception during the early years of the Cold War, RAND has conducted research on weapons technology, military strategy, and other defense-related topics. Recently, however, RAND has developed what it calls "new areas of research . . . not traditionally part of its agenda." In the late 1990s, RAND established a research program devoted exclusively to the arts. Significantly, the first book produced by this program is titled *The Performing Arts in a New Era* (McCarthy, Brooks, Lowell, & Zakaras, 2001). A second book is titled *A New Framework for Building Participation in the Arts* (McCarthy & Jinnett, 2001). The fact that the RAND Corporation has turned its attention to the performing arts should be a wake-up call. In effect, RAND agrees with many performance studies scholars: cultural performances aren't just about entertainment; they also have social efficacy. And here we might wonder: what other cultural performance research is RAND reading? Are our books on their reading list? If so, would this be a bad thing—or a good one? And, finally, what if RAND is, in its own way, merely carrying out Eisenhower's goal of "improving performance in the future?"

REFERENCES

Alliance for a Corporate-Free UN. (2002, January). Letter to Kofi Annan recommending redesign of global compact. Retrieved May 19, 2005, from http://www.globalpolicy.org/reform/2002/012902letter.htm

Berry, C. (2000). Commentary. *The juggling act: WNYC's series on work and family*. Retrieved May 19, 2005, from http://archive.salon.com/mwt/feature/2000/01/04/wnyc/index1.html

Butler, J. (1990). *Gender trouble: Feminism and the subversion of identity.* London: Routledge.

Committee on Measuring and Improving Infrastructure Performance. (1995). *Measuring and improving infrastructure performance.* Washington, DC: National Academy Press.

Company performance model for achieving the global compact principles. (2002). Retrieved May 19, 2005, from http://www.uneptie.org/outreach/compact/docs/GC-Dialogue2002-Model.pdf

de Bruijn, H. (2001). *Managing performance in the public sector.* London: Routledge.

Eisenhower, D. D. (1962). Farewell Radio and Television Address to the American People. In *public papers of the presidents of the United States, 1960–61.* Washington, DC: U.S. Government Printing Office.

Fischer-Lichte, E. (2001, March). *Text and performance: Reversing the hierarchy.* Keynote address delivered at Performance Studies international conference, Mainz, Germany.

Foucault, M. (1979). *Discipline and punish: The birth of the prison* (A. Sheridan, Trans.). New York: Vintage Books. (Original work published 1975)

Government Performance and Results Act, Pub. L. No. 103–162, 107 § 1 (1994).

High Performance Computing Act, Pub. L. No. 102–194, 105 § 2 (1991).

International Monetary Fund. (2000, February). *IMF survey special supplement.* Retrieved May 19, 2005, from http://www.imf.org/external/pubs/ft/survey/sup2000

Keck, M. E., & Sikkink, K. (1999). *Activists beyond borders: Advocacy networks in international politics.* Ithaca, NY: Cornell University Press.

Lyotard, J. F. (1984). *The postmodern condition: A report on knowledge* (G. Bennington & B. Massumi, Trans.). Minneapolis: University of Minnesota Press. (Original work published 1979)

Marcuse, H. (1955). *Eros and civilization: A philosophical inquiry into Freud.* New York: Vintage Books.

McCarthy, K., Brooks, A., Lowell, J., & Zakaras, L. (Eds.). (2001). *The performing arts in a new era.* Santa Monica, CA: RAND Corporation.

McCarthy, K., & Jinnett, K. (2001). *A new framework for building participation in the arts.* Santa Monica, CA: RAND Corporation.

McKenzie, J. (2001). *Perform or else: From discipline to performance.* London: Routledge.

McKenzie, J. (2003). Democracy's performance. *The Drama Review, 47*(2), 117–128.

Pignataro, G. (2003). Performance indicators. In R. Towse (Ed.), *A handbook of cultural economics* (p. 366). Cheltenham, UK/Northampton, MA: Edward Elgar.

Royal Dutch Petroleum Company. (2002, March). *People, planet and profits: The Shell report 2001 summary.* The Hague, the Netherlands: Author.

Simon, H. A. (1957). *Models of man.* New York: John Wiley and Sons.

Taylor, D. (2003). *The archive and the repertoire: Performing cultural memory in the Americas.* Durham, NC: Duke University Press.

van der Ploeg, F. (1999). Section 2.1: A new method of assessment and accountability. *Culture as confrontation: Principles on cultural policy in 2001–2004.* Retrieved May 19, 2005, from http://www.minocw.nl/english_oud/internat/english/index.htm

4

Performance, Performativity, and Cultural Poiesis in Practices of Everyday Life

JUDITH HAMERA

When Victor Turner characterized performance as making, not faking, he did more than challenge the antitheatrical bias. He placed performance at the center of a larger view of culture as constructed, embodied, and processual. The consequences of this move both include and exceed a focus on the theatrical, or even on "actors" loosely defined. They extend to larger issues of cultural poiesis and enactment, including the development and maintenance of communities, the social life and force of memory, and the production and consumption of material culture and its contexts.

Likewise, Judith Butler's use of the performative to explain the construction and stability of identity illuminates more than just gender and sexuality. Performance studies theorists have extended her insights to include performance per se, something Butler herself resisted in her early writings. In so doing, these theorists raise possibilities for a generative nexus of performance and performativity that can, in turn, extend our understanding of the very ground of social life.

This essay offers multiple examples of the theoretical and analytical potentials of performance and the performative. It employs performance theorists who have enlarged upon the works of both Turner and Butler. Further, it explores the multiple theoretical and methodological compatibilities between performance studies and critical scholarship across the humanities. Finally, these examples highlight the discipline's contribution to an expansive view of aesthetics, one committed to recasting this realm of inquiry in explicitly social terms.

In his classic essay "Rethinking Ethnography," Dwight Conquergood discusses the relationship between performance and cultural process. He asks, "What happens to our thinking about performance when we move it outside of Aesthetics and situate it at the center of lived experience?" (1991, p. 190). Yet, as he acknowledges in later work on Chicago street gang graffiti, *aesthetics always already is lived experience;* performance studies reveals this interrelationship in clear and compelling ways. Aesthetics is inherently social. The formal properties and presumptions intrinsic to the production and consumption of works of art are communicative currency circulating between producers and consumers, binding them together in material and highly situated interpretive communities, serving as bases for exchange in the public and private conversations that constitute art's relational, political, and affective lives.

Aesthetics offers vocabularies for exploring how art works and how it generates meaning. But even more importantly, aesthetic principles, values, and vocabularies organize *where* art works and means: in social time and in social space. Aesthetics are integral to finished creative products and also to the myriad ancillary socialities that never take the stage. Scholars have argued forcefully for more nuanced, politicized readings of the relationships between art, society, and culture (see Matthews & McWhirter, 2003). Central to all such readings are aesthetics, the animating principles of art's social lives. These principles emerge in the objects and events that aesthetic practice leaves behind, and in the routine transactions of those for whom art making is, and happens in, a neighborhood, a set of corporeal possibilities, comforts and constraints linking private self- and object-fashioning to community practice. Janice Radway makes precisely this point in her discussion of "mass culture aesthetics" when she writes,

> Commodities like mass-produced literary texts are selected, purchased, constructed and used by real people with previously existing needs, desires, intentions, and interpretive strategies. By reinstating those active individuals and their creative, constructive activities at the heart of our interpretive enterprise, we avoid blinding ourselves to the fact that the essentially human practice of making meaning goes on even in a world increasingly dominated by things and by consumption. In thus recalling the interpretive character of operations like reading, we restore time, process and action to our

account of human endeavor and therefore increase the possibility of doing justice to its essential complexity and ambiguity as practice. (1991, p. 221)

The social work of aesthetics is especially central to performance, where the labors of creation and the dynamics of consumption are explicitly communal and corporeal, and where corporeality and sociality are remade as surely as a formal event may be produced. Performance exposes aesthetics' social work as embodied, processual, rhetorical, and political and, especially, as daily, as routine, a practice of everyday life.

Victor Turner (1982) attested to the potentially world-making power of performance in his notion of *communitas*: the spontaneous moments of ego-dissolution that bind performers to audiences and audience members to one another. But this world-making power can also be found in the daily mechanisms—the rhetoric and the rituals—that produce performance in specific communities. Here we move beyond Erving Goffman's (1959) germinal notion of the presentation of self in everyday life to examine how performance illuminates the deep structures of community in/and aesthetic practice. How, for example, do performance and the performative contribute to our understanding of what Radway calls the "essential complexities" of art's social lives?

THE THING DONE AND THE THING GONE: PERFORMANCE, MEMORY, AND KHMER CLASSICAL DANCE

> The Khmer Rouge surrounded Phnom Penh, and on April 17, 1975, after five years of civil war, they took control, waving their flag in the streets. Until January 1979 they forced all Cambodians to live in labor camps and work fourteen-to-eighteen hour days. They fed us one daily bowl of watery rice; they separated families; they destroyed all Cambodian institutions and culture; they systematically tortured and killed innocent

people. It is estimated that during this time nearly a third of the Cambodian population was killed due to disease, starvation, or execution. (Pran, 1997, p. 10)

James Brandon observed that, while "performing arts do not die, performers do" (in Sam, 1994, p. 47). As Dith Pran's terse summary above states, Pol Pot and his Khmer Rouge forces set out to systematically and ruthlessly destroy classical Cambodian performance and culture. Benedict Anderson may be correct when he notes that classical Angkor, "emblazoned on the flag of Marxist Democratic Kampuchea," was a "rebus of power" (1991, pp. 160–161), but neither power nor piety spared the material bodies of the Apsaras, the dancers who served as incarnations of Angkor's reliefs. Pich Tum Kravel, and former Minister of Culture Chen Phon, estimate that 90 percent of Cambodian dance teachers and performers were murdered or starved to death; the exact number may never be known (P. Chen, lecture, December 5, 1993). Those few who managed to escape either remained in the country posing as peasants or, more commonly, made their way to refugee camps along the Thai-Cambodian border.

Cambodian artists have generated numerous moving accounts of the fate of the arts during and after the era of the killing fields. These are extraordinary testimonials to the social powers of aesthetics to heal both individuals and communities. For many of these artists, performance itself became both the means by which they survived and a legitimation of that survival. Daran Kravanh's story is illustrative:

I cannot tell you how or why I survived; I do not know myself. It is like this: love and music and memory and invisible hands, and something that comes out of the society of the living and the dead, for which there are no words. (Lafreniere, 2000, p. 3)

Kravanh describes a remarkable moment when, exposed by his compulsion to play his

accordion despite warnings that this marked him for death, he used music to bind him in solidarity to his Khmer Rouge would-be executioner:

If I was going to die, I wanted to die playing my accordion. . . . I played that song with all the joy I had ever felt. The soldier did not shoot me. He listened until the end of the song. Then he said in a small, quiet voice, "Will you teach me to play?" "Yes," I said. Yes was all I had left to say. (Lafreniere, 2000, p. 152)

Khmer Rouge survivor Arn Chorn-Pond's attempts to save formerly outlawed Cambodian classical music, a mission documented in Jocelyn Glatzer's film *The Flute Player* (2003), likewise attests to these artists' commitment to both remember and restore both personal and collective memories of Cambodian culture.

In these accounts, performance serves as a technology of subjectivity through which survivors wrestle with and justify their own survival. Further, classical Khmer performing arts serve as templates organizing a new sociality among survivors, and an archive that links subjectivities and socialities to the glories of Khmer history. In this archival incarnation, performance actually becomes personal and collective memory; it is what Paul Connerton calls an "inscribing practice." It "traps and holds information long after the human organism has stopped informing" its individual enactments (Connerton, 1989, p. 73). But this archive, and its residues and traces, its inscribing practices, are not only cognitive and corporeal, as Connerton might lead us to believe. It is not just physical labor that constructs specific archives of performance, not simply cognitive labor that fills them, but also the unrelenting dailiness of emotional and relational labor that impels survivors to work on behalf of Khmer art and culture.

Performance theorists offer bracing and nuanced strategies for engaging this nexus of survival, memory, and cultural continuity. In

Spectacular Suffering: Theatre, Fascism, and the Holocaust, Vivian Patraka employs Elin Diamond's (1996) notion of performativity, itself a reworking of Judith Butler's view, and reimagines it in light of the Holocaust:

> According to this model of the performative, "the thing done" is a kind of yardstick, a system of beliefs and presuppositions that has taken on an authority and become a hegemonic means of understanding. The "thing done," then, represents particular discursive categories, conventions, genres and practices that frame our interpretations, even as we try to perceive the present moment of doing. As we are in the doing, then, there is the pressure of the thing done. The doing is not knowable without the thing done, and the thing done is all the discursive conventions that allow us to think through a doing. (Patraka, 1999, p. 6)

In the case of "the Holocaust performative," Patraka identifies

> the thing done as *the thing gone.* . . . It is the goneness of the Holocaust that produces the simultaneous profusion of discourses and understandings. . . . The absoluteness of the thing done [gone] weighs heavily on any doing in the Holocaust performative. . . . [It] acknowledges that there is nothing to say to goneness and yet we continue to try and mark it, say it, identify it, memorialize the loss over and over. This is the doing to which Diamond refers, the constant iteration against the pressure of palpable loss. . . . (1999, p. 7)

While I do not want to understate in any way the specificity of Patraka's theorizing the Holocaust performative (per her observations in Patraka, 1999, p. 3), it is striking to note how forcefully it resonates with the testimony of Khmer Rouge survivors against the goneness of classical Khmer culture in the aftermath of the Pol Pot regime. Indeed the invocation of goneness is explicit in both general and highly personal "introductions of [Khmer Rouge] atrocity into representation" (p. 7; see also Sophiline Cheam Shapiro's

"Songs My Enemies Taught Me" in Pran, 1997, pp. 1–5).

Patraka writes that doing/performance is always accountable to the thing gone (1999, p. 7). It is also useful to imagine this accountability in Bakhtinian terms. Here, the survival of Khmer performance becomes the vehicle through which artists perform *answers*, both for their individual survival and for that of Khmer culture. At its simplest, Bakhtin's "answerability" is very like accountability, predicated on an interanimation of art and guilt, life and blame. In "Art and Answerability" (1990), his earliest known publication, he writes,

> I have to answer with my own life for what I have experienced and understood in art, so that everything I have experienced and understood would not remain ineffectual in my life. But answerability entails guilt, or liability to blame. It is not only mutual answerability that art and life must assume, but also mutual ability to blame. . . . Art and life are not one, but they must become united in the unity of my answerability. (pp. 1–2)

Answerability is ambivalent. At its most generative, it seems to offer an ethical opportunity to deploy art to speak back, both to life and to goneness, as well as the reverse. At its most impotent, answerability seems to circumscribe agency, limiting it to reactions of singular subjects condemned to answer to, or "rent" meaning (Hitchcock, 1993, p. 10). Central to this ambivalence is Bakhtin's emphasis on the mutuality of art and life congealed into a unity through answerability-in-practice.

Answerability to goneness through performance cuts across many accounts of Khmer survivors. Likewise, after the collective trauma of the Khmer Rouge, coalitions of performers mobilized to use performance technique as an affective and social infrastructure of answerability for healing and renewal (see, for example, Charlé, 2001; Coburn, 1993; Mydans, 1993; Turnbull, 1999).

Just as the Holocaust performative enables us to theorize the exigencies of Khmer survivors' personal and social relationships to classical arts and aesthetics, performance theory enables us to tease out the complexities in these aesthetic practices themselves. In so doing, it forges connections between performance studies and immigrant studies in the critical humanities. For example, according to media scholar Hamid Naficy, the refugee or the exile faces

> two types of immanent and imminent threats simultaneously: the threat of the disappearance of the homeland and the threat of themselves disappearing in the host society. Fetishization [as a strategy for negotiating these threats . . .] entails condensing all the meanings of home . . . into substitute fetishes and frozen stereotypes. (1993, p. 129)

Naficy concludes, the net result of this fetishization of past and future is that "[t]hrough controlling 'there' and 'then,' the exile can control 'here and 'now'" (p. 132).

The fetish of Cambodia as it was and never was has an especially acute pull for refugee survivor artists, for whom answerability to and through Khmer culture is seen as rooted in a sacred, utopian past while mired in a degenerate present. No matter that the exact nature of this past is unclear as Khmer traditions are, to a great degree, contested constructs among Khmer themselves. Juxtaposition between sacred past and degenerate present permeates Khmer discourse, as does the sense that the future may hold only greater remove from utopian antiquity and, ultimately, perhaps abyss, though this has been modified considerably by the death of Pol Pot and the collapse of the remaining Khmer Rouge forces, as well as a concomitant investment of both Cambodian and American resources and commitment.

Literature, lectures, and performances authored by Khmer artists are replete with assertions of this necessity for reproducing the pure Khmer product/fetish, even as they freely admit there are few existing models to which reproductions can be compared, and even as they acknowledge the exigencies which disrupt such reproduction. Consider ethnomusicologist and musician Sam-Ang Sam's discussion of the contingencies surrounding the assembly of a *pin peat* musical ensemble:

> In performances, Khmer musicians (myself included) both consciously and unconsciously borrow instruments from other Khmer ensembles and mix them with those of *pin peat*. Because of the scarcity and distribution of musicians and musical instruments this borrowing is difficult to avoid. In addition, Khmer traditionally hold great respect for elders. In performance situations, we cannot tell our older musicians . . . not to play with us just because they do not know how to play a *pin peat* instrument. Moreover, excluding them from the group would reduce the ensemble even further, thus making it impossible to produce a full accompaniment. Worst of all, discouraging other musicians from playing might be seen as a break in the continuity of Khmer musical life. (1994, p. 45, italics added)

Yet "fidelity" was still the god-term for Khmer artists, even if, in reality, it can only be approached asymptotically.

The acute investment in "there and then" evident in the concerns of Khmer artists points to larger relationships between performance, space or place, and time. Performance rewrites the body's, and the community's, relationships to space, to time, and to the intersections of both. It transforms "context" into a product of aesthetic activity and supplies us with the theoretical and methodological tools we can use to examine this process.

MARKING TIME AND MAKING PLACE IN BALLET

Auden once observed that all ballets are made in Eden. They are not. They are made in sweaty rehearsal halls, in storefront studios, and in community centers. And as surely as ballets are made in these spaces, the spaces themselves are remade in the process, becoming, perhaps through the repetition of this epitome of classical technique, a kind of Eden both inside and outside of everyday space and time.

Marking Time

Dance and time are intimately linked; in ballet, this linkage is especially acute. Indeed, ballet technique makes the embodied experience of time communicable. Steps are counted into the future, beginning "on the ones" and proceeding through "five and six and seven and eight." Classes are organized ritualistically, beginning with barre exercises and ending with *reverence*, a bow or curtsy to the instructor and, if present, the musical accompanist as well. Advancement in technique is tied to age and measured by "levels"; in the Cecchetti method, these are actual "grades" assessed by exams though, in many studios, these levels are enforced less programmatically. The limits of the body are temporal markers: too young for pointe shoes, too old for quick jumps or fast footwork. Time, for those committed to ballet, always seems to be running out: training should not start "too late," generally not after age 10, and careers are over "too soon," in a dancer's thirties or, with injuries, even younger. The repertoire itself is replete with backward glances: to royalty and dancing peasants, and to Romanticism, both historically and more broadly construed.

Yet, whatever its general contours, details of the relationship between ballet and time are always local, always contextual. Time in/and technique is very different for an American Ballet Theatre principal dancer, for whom the demands of career and chronology are intimately and fairly publicly connected, than it is for the thousands of girls and boys, men and women, taking classes in recreation centers and neighborhood studios, and for dancers performing with semi-professional companies.

In each of these locations, in myriad idiosyncratic ways, communities of dancers deploy and circulate rituals and stories through and about performance that help them examine and navigate relations between the body, agency, and time.

Making Place

Performance, and ballet in particular, revisions and recreates space by literally "placing" it in dialogue with the body. Space, writes de Certeau, is a practiced place (1974/1984, p. 117). Space is multivocal, characterized by perpetual possibilities for transformation. Place is univocal, stable, proper. I would argue that the construction and reproduction of place from space can be explored in performative terms.

Judith Butler characterizes the performative as the "power of discourse to reproduce effects through reiteration" (1993a, p. 20); these "effects" constitute "identity," which repetition then stabilizes. While Butler is reluctant to claim rhetorical power for the theatrical 1993b, p. 278), Elin Diamond argues for a more generative relation between performance per se and performativity, one especially conducive to reading places of performance and performance's placement. Diamond writes,

> When performativity materializes as performance in that risky and dangerous negotiation between a doing (a reiteration of norms) and a thing done (discursive conventions that frame our interpretations), between someone's body and the conventions of embodiment, we have access to cultural meanings and critique. (1996, p. 5)

As useful as Diamond's reformulation of the relationship between performance and performativity is, I would put this another way. Individual performances, I suggest, do make performativity material but such negotiations are not always risky; they may be, or seem, perfectly banal. The performative production of place is one example.

Cultural meanings of place in dance, including the most sublime and the most ritualistic, the most familiar and the most sedimented ones, are generated by iterations of bodily doings, organized by technique's protocols, its "discursive conventions" for reading corporeality and geography (the thing done). That such doings may be banal rather than obviously subversive makes them no less meaningful or constitutive. Home places can be performatively stabilized through performances of the banal. Yet, as Diamond (1996) suggests, there are also other possibilities—chances to undo place, to enact erasures of technique's protocols containing "doings," to challenge sedimented meanings in performance and disrupt the readability offered by the thing done, or even feign that readability to insinuate something else. In such operations, space might be performatively generated from place. As geographer Yi-Fu Tuan observes, "Place is security, space is freedom; we are attached to one and long for the other" (1977, p. 3). This performative negotiation of space into place, and the reverse, is implicit in Michel de Certeau's geopoetic essay "Walking in the City." He writes,

> The long poem of walking manipulates spatial organizations, no matter how panoptic they may be: it is neither foreign to them (it can take place only within them) nor in conformity with them (it does not receive its identity from them). It creates shadows and ambiguities within them. It inserts its multitudinous references and citations into them (social mores, cultural norms, personal factors). Within them it is itself the effect of successive encounters and occasions that constantly alter it and make it the other's blazon. . . . (1974/1984, p. 101)

In her introduction to *The Geography of Identity*, Patricia Yaeger asks, "Are there 'rules' if not laws driving the narration of space?" (1996, p. 4). Are there regulations that dictate protocols for the performative transformation of space into place, or the reverse? Here, critical close readings of performance

practice reveal that, in ballet as in walking, the answer is both yes and no.

There are in fact some "laws" by which ballet transforms space into place and these are explicit. The technique performatively constructs place by, first, "placing" mapped bodies into it. These bodies are themselves viewed as spaces to be organized by technical protocols, then performatively stabilized. Even in preballet classes reserved for children ages three to six, students are inserted into the Euclidean imaginary of the technique: shoulders and hips form the four corners of a "square." Squares are always perfectly balanced; ballet dancers are to achieve the same. Bodies stay square by ensuring that the hips and shoulders remain aligned and in the same plane during the execution of a movement. The illusion of two-dimensionality is the ideal, as in "turn out," which rotates the upper thighs and, in turn, knees and toes, away from the body so that, when feet are positioned with heels together, they form a line at a perfect 180 degrees.

The body in ballet is "centered"; movements originate from the torso, which is "pulled up," always poised between yielding to and resisting gravity, occupying a metaphoric middle place of stability and balance. The center is also a reference point, a corporeal prime meridian running down the torso lengthwise; turning "outside" (*en dehors*) is to move away from this imaginary axis, while an "inside" turn (*en dedans*) initiates an action toward it. Arms and feet are mapped onto five positions; all movements begin in, go through, and end in a position, theoretically if not literally. Further, unlike de Certeau's walkers in the city, practitioners whose improvisatory negotiations of the landscape rewrite it in the most protean and anonymous terms, ballet dancers are given seven basic movements that govern interactions with space: one can bend at the knees toward the ground, rise on the balls of the feet or toes away from the ground, jump or stretch into space, turn around in it, or glide or dart through it.

Rules for corporeal placement in ballet are echoed by maps organizing studio space. Walls and corners are numbered; there are eight positions or spatial orientations possible in a room. Dancers in class may, as directed, face corners, generating a diagonal alignment, or face walls, appearing "straight on." The proscenium stage is the architectural paradigm for studio space; "front" is where the audience will be, though this spot is occupied by a mirror in most studios, transforming "front" from a dialogic location between dancer and audience into a "screen wherein dancers enact [and display] their competence" for themselves (Sadono, 1999, p. 164). Thus, the mirrored front of the studio is both a model of the performance stage, the goal, and a metaphoric and pedagogical "'stage' on which the dancer enacts her acquisition of the ballet ideal," and through which she must pass, as she engages "'the socio-cultural construct of an ideal image' reflected back to her" in the process of training (p. 165).

While the paradigm of the proscenium figures prominently in the logic governing ballet's negotiation of space and place, it is important to note that the studio is simultaneously configured, both geographically and chronologically, as onstage *and* backstage. Dance barres typically line three of four studio walls, exempting only the front or audience position. One-half to two-thirds of a ballet class takes place at the barre. Here, drills of basic movements enforce steps and skills to be reassembled later into choreography. Warming up and stretching happen here. The barre is backstage, where isolated mechanics are perfected. Generally, a time break separates barre work/backstage from center work/onstage, which emphasizes the combinations of steps intrinsic to choreography in performance before the gaze of the mirror/audience. The ballet studio is a panoptic place; even the barre as backstage is a place of surveillance by instructors, and

self-surveillance by dancers looking in the mirror at (some would say "for") themselves. There are also "back backstages," escapes from ballet's official panoptic regime. These are waiting and dressing rooms, though they, like the barre, may be tactically appropriated for self-display beyond the rubric of official pedagogy and for audiences other than the mirror or instructor.

And yet, despite the labeling of bodies, walls, and corners, the answer to Yaeger's question of laws narrating space is also "no." Whatever ballet's strategic ambitions for bodies in/and space, individuals inevitably seize opportunities to narrate studio space, and performatively construct place, differently, in turns of physicality and of phrase that insinuate themselves into and redeploy ballet's rituals of proprietary power. In these cases, ballet creates vernacular landscapes, transforming the sparseness of studios into home places and bodies into maps; it organizes relationships to form affective environments, geographies of the heart. The vernacular landscapes constructed through performance are the settings, the literal and psychic grounds, for the daily, routine time and talk that shape art in communities of practitioners. As J. B. Jackson argues, such landscapes are always local, regardless of the ideals incarnated there; they are stabilized by idiosyncratic ways of seeing the world (1984, p. 149) as well as by the community's "distinct way[s] of defining and handling time and space" (p. 150).

Jackson suggests that such landscapes are not "political," in the sense of engaging those superstructures that "official" discourses erect to maintain "the public" (p. 150). Yet, just as "most buildings can be understood in terms of power or authority—as efforts to assume, extend, resist, or accommodate it" (Camille Wells as quoted in Hayden, 1997, p. 30), just as there is, in effect, a politics of use, vernacular landscapes made through dance are deeply and thoroughly political. These landscapes are shot through with contested notions of appropriate gender performances and gendered resistances, class-inflected expectations of the relationship between art and life, and issues of discipline and authority, all negotiated using ballet as a road map for navigating family, as a stage for the self, or as a refuge from routine. Ballet technique constructs intimate, familiar places for a politics of self- and community-building that Leonard Hawes characterizes in spatial terms; this politics "disclos[es] ways of escaping from and relocating to different subject positions at the same time [it] redraw[s] ideological boundaries" (1998, p. 273).

Performative theories of place and time emphasize the relational, embodied nature of context. In so doing, they mesh with other scholars' critical formulations of the literal ground of aesthetic experience. In "Forms of Time and of the Chronotope in the Novel," Mikhail Bakhtin theorizes time as a social location. The chronotope, he argues, names "the intrinsic connectedness of temporal and spatial relationships." Here, "time, as it were, thickens, takes on flesh, becomes artistically visible; likewise, space becomes charged and responsive to the movements of plot, time, and history" (1981, p. 84). Chronotopes are plural; they describe organizing and support functions of representation and meaning, much as technique serves as the infrastructure shaping corporeality and narrating space in dance:

> What is the significance of all of these chronotopes? What is most obvious is their meaning for *narrative*. They are the organizing centers for the fundamental narrative events of the novel. The chronotope is the place where the knots of narrative are tied and untied. It can be said without qualification that to them belongs the meaning that shapes narrative. (1981, p. 250)

Further, chronotopes, like technique, are prospective, delimiting "a field of possibilities" and specifying "the possibility of events" (Morson, 1994, p. 106).

Bakhtin developed the chronotope to examine historical poetics in literature, though he also offered possibilities of more expansive readings. He writes, "Out of the actual chronotopes of our world (which serve as the source of representation) emerge the reflected and *created* chronotopes represented in the work (in the text)" (1981, p. 253). Thus, the chronotope functions as a dialogic intersection of the world and the representational grammars and protocols that organize and reproduce it, like technique. As Katerina Clark observes, "The chronotope is a bridge, not a wall" between materiality and technologies and products of representation (Clark & Holquist, 1984, p. 279). The metaphors Bakhtin uses to characterize the relationship between the "actual world as sources of representation and the world represented" are generative (Bakhtin, 1981, p. 253). He writes,

> However forcefully the real and the represented world resist fusion, however immutable the presence of that categorical boundary line between them, they are nevertheless indissolubly tied up with each other and find themselves in continual mutual interaction; uninterrupted exchange goes on between them, similar to the uninterrupted exchange of matter between living organisms and the environment that surrounds them. . . . Of course this process of exchange is itself chronotopic. . . . We might even speak of a special *creative* chronotope inside which this exchange between work and life occurs. (p. 254)

Bakhtin's organic imagery here recalls his other physiological metaphor used to characterize the chronotope: where "time takes on flesh" (1981, p. 84). As Clark notes, "Time assuming flesh is something more than a trope here, for those who enflesh the categories are people" (Clark & Holquist, 1984, p. 280). More specifically, they are bodies.

I suggest that performance theory reveals chronotopes as corporeal as well as textual. They are enacted by material bodies who invigorate formal, representational grammars and protocols like ballet technique and, in turn, manipulate these grammars and protocols for their own ends. Here the ballet studio, in all its temporal and geographical specificity, becomes the membrane facilitating this chronotopic process of exchange between particular bodies and the technologies of representation, between art and life.

Two additional aspects of the chronotope make it especially useful for characterizing the busy intersections of bodies, space, and time in the ballet studio. In *Dialogism: Bakhtin and His World*, Holquist notes an apparent antinomy in the concept:

> Certain chronotopes are treated by Bakhtin as if they were transhistorical structures that are not unique to particular points in time. There is a tension, if not a downright contradiction, between these examples and the claims Bakhtin makes elsewhere for the chronotope's ability to be in dialogue with specific, extra-literary historical contexts. (1990, p. 112)

Holquist suggests resolving such a contradiction by thinking of the chronotope "bifocally": "invoking [the chronotope] in any particular case, one must be careful to discriminate between its use as a lens for close-up work and its ability to serve as an optic for seeing at a distance" (p. 113). Holquist makes a valid point but corporeal chronotopes in ballet suggest thinking differently about "bifocality"; perhaps less discrimination rather than more is called for. As I mentioned above, ballet technique—including its grammar of bodies and/in space, and its repertoire, places its participants in a "both-and" relationship to here and now, there and then. In ballet, participants literally follow in the transhistorical footsteps of other dancers, though their pointe shoes may be made from high-tech composite materials rather than layers of fabric and glue. Both the convergences and the discrepancies between here and there, now and then matter, and the

corporeal chronotope of ballet holds them in tension, not as antinomies but as partners.

As a formal category, the chronotope links the organizational mechanics of telling (*szuzhet*) to the messiness of the told (*fabula*); it is the place "where the knots of narrative," those intersections of events and plots, "are tied and untied" (Holquist, 1990, p. 113; quotations from Bakhtin, 1981, p. 250). Corporeal chronotopes in the ballet studio inhabit and enact these same dynamics as they performatively constitute space and time. Here, ballet's technical protocols of reading and writing the body generate "formal and rational design" in class and "enslavement to narrative" onstage, particularly in the action ballet warhorses that so often figure in the repertories of semiprofessional companies (Foster, 1998, pp. 258, 262). Yet corporeal chronotopes also organize the just-so stories of self-creation in community, stories that redeploy ballet's technical rhetorics to other, infinitely more idiosyncratic ends (Clark & Holquist, 1984, p. 68). They emerge in those banal and essential moments of reminiscence where events retrospectively become narrative: "Remember when?" These stories both reflect and construct corporeal chronotopes similar to those Bakhtin finds in the novel.

One corporeal chronotope is particularly useful for describing how ballet organizes bodies, time, space, and stories. "Roam" is a performative version of Bakhtin's chronotope of the road; it reflects the process of moving, as well as the location of movement, that characterizes the corporeality of time and space in ballet. "Roam" refers to

> both a point of new departures and a place for events to find their denouement. Time, as it were, fuses together with space and flows into it (forming the road); this is the source of the rich metaphorical expansion on the image of the road as a course: "the course of a life," "to set out on a new course," [or a course of training]. (Bakhtin, 1981, p. 244)

Moreover, the road may be "one that passes through *familiar territory,* and not through some exotic *alien* world" (Bakhtin, 1981, p. 245). In ballet, the chronotope of "roam" often unites both the familiar and the exotic.

To roam is to move away from home, narrowly construed as the domestic sanctuary of/for the family, perhaps toward a new home in technique. Both popular representations of ballet and the chestnuts of the classical repertory bear this out. Pursuing ballet means leaving home, whether such leave-taking involves moving across town or to another part of the country, as in the popular films *Flashdance* and *Billy Elliot.* Typically in these accounts, the terminus of roaming, like Bakhtin's road, is a point where "social distances collapse," if only, as in these examples, through fantasies of pure merit that admit the hardworking seeker to the exotic and hallowed inner sanctum of technique. Likewise, the repertory is filled with images of roaming: Clara and her nutcracker prince journey to the "Kingdom of Sweets," where familiar confections become dancing marvels; Albrecht goes slumming incognito in a peasant village and Giselle travels back from the dead; James follows the Sylphide into the literal and affective woods.

Roaming is, in fact, logistically central to a professional ballet career; frequently this involves moving, or aspiring to move, to New York where not one but two highly esteemed companies beckon like the promised land. It may mean touring with the relative minor leagues and small markets of semi-professional and regional companies across the country. Even with a position in a comparatively secure major company, roaming means touring, not only in the United States, but across the world as well. Most dramatically, chronotopes of roaming in ballet link geopolitics to bodies, as in the famous Cold War defections of Rudolf Nureyev, Natalia Makarova, and Mikhail Baryshnikov, or in less publicized contemporary dancers' flights from Cuba.

In ballet, as in all aesthetic enterprises, spatial practices, like chronological ones, are locally enacted. However they may be legitimated by appeals to transhistorical precedent or ahistorical purity, space and time in performance are uniquely inflected by the bodies and stories that put them in play. Yet performance's potential for theorizing the daily, social dimensions of aesthetics is not limited solely to what bodies do. Artifacts perform. They become animated by, and animate, the commodity exchanges that also constitute the material ground of aesthetic experience.

THE SOCIAL LIVES OF THINGS

> *Commodities, like persons, have social lives.*
>
> —A. Appadurai

> *A study of commodity culture always turns out to be an exploration of a fantastic realm in which things act, speak, rise, fall, fly, evolve. . . .*
>
> —T. Richards

After Arjun Appadurai, consider the commodity as "anything intended for exchange" (Appadurai, 1986, p. 5). This definition avoids any binarism between art and commodity, thus also avoiding what Appadurai calls "an excessively positivist conception of the commodity, as being a certain *kind* of thing, thus restricting . . . debate to the matter of deciding *what kind* of thing it is" (p. 13). This is in contrast to Bill Brown, who distinguishes between the "object" and the "thing." The former is characterized by its use value and symbolic capital, i.e., its commodity potential, and the latter by its misuse value, its potential to be deployed counter to its purpose (2003, p. 399).

For Appadurai, a contextual, social life is intrinsic to the commodity. He writes,

Let us approach commodities as things in a certain situation, a situation that can characterize many different kinds of thing, at different points in their social lives. This . . . means breaking significantly with the production-dominated Marxian view of the commodity and focusing on its *total* trajectory from production through exchange/distribution, to consumption. (1986, p. 13)

The commodity situation in the social life of any thing can be productively enlarged by reading with and against the notion of "commodity fetishism" wherein objects are animated, appearing "as autonomous figures endowed with a life of their own, which enter into relations both with each other and with the human race" (Karl Marx as quoted in Bennett, 2001, p. 117). In classical Marxist terms, things perform and "living, laboring persons are deadened" (Bennett, 2001, p. 117). Yet, as both Appadurai and philosopher Jane Bennett suggest, the commodity situation is not quite so simple. Bennett suggests that "Marx is too dismissive of this animation of the object" (2001, p. 117). "Within his frame," she argues, "it is reduced to the atavistic of commodity fetishism." In contrast, Bennett sees the animation of objects as a source of productive questions:

What does it mean for ethics and politics when objects appear as animate or as capable of making claims upon us? Is this best described as "fetishization"? . . . What are the theatrical techniques by which commodities exert power over human bodies? What is the role of repetition in commodification? What dimensions of the consuming self does such repetition act upon? (2001, p. 116)

Viewed from a performance perspective, there are several striking elements about this list of questions. Implicit here are the assumptions that "theatrical techniques" and repetition are intrinsic to the commodity situation; our task is only to discover which ones and how. Further, in commodity situations, objects are not only animated; they not only

enter into relations with us but, potentially, make claims on those who enter these situations as well. As Richards observes, "Things act, speak, rise, fall, fly, evolve" (1991, p. 11).

Performance theory's emphasis on the embodied, contested notions of culture makes it a particularly useful tool for examining which theatrical techniques animate specific commodity situations, and how particular objects assert their claims, in their individual contexts. Further, it clearly illuminates the macro and micro politics involved in these transactions. Native American art, and Navajo folk art in particular, offer rich opportunities to employ performance-based theories of the commodity.

THE COMMODITY SITUATION OF NAVAJO FOLK ART

"Navajo folk art" is a contested and elastic term. In their book *Navajo Folk Art: The People Speak*, the first and only systematic book-length treatment of the subject, Chuck and Jan Rosenak argue that the category is characterized as

work by untrained, self-taught artists that is nonutilitarian, highly personal, even idiosyncratic. The craft may be derived from communal traditions, but something personal must be added to qualify it as art. In other words, the craft may be learned but the art is self-taught. (1988, p. 5)

However, the distinction between craft/learned and art/self-taught is difficult to uphold in practice. Further, the emphasis on being self-taught presupposes a level of isolation from institutions that is often more imagined than real, particularly for younger Navajo artists. Many folk artists have had formal art training in high school; others have attended community colleges or universities, or conservatories like the Institute of American Indian Arts in Santa Fe. Finally, boundaries between folk art and fine art are likewise complex.

I opt for a more emic definition: pictorial rugs, carvings, pottery, baskets, and paintings can be considered folk art if they fit within, or expand, the existing range of objects already included in the category and/or if the creator of the piece, or the trader or collector who buys it, considers it part of the category. Thus, "Navajo folk art" describes a set of relationships between people, objects, and history, not the biographies of individual artists or the properties of the objects themselves.

Appadurai's definition is particularly relevant to Navajo folk art, which functioned at its very outset as a medium for exchange rather than solely and simply as an aesthetic practice. I suggest that objects animated in and by commodity situations, and Navajo folk art in particular, perform in multiple senses of the word. Here I am working closely from Richard Bauman's definition, developed in the context of his work with the folktale:

> I understand performance as a mode of communication, a way of speaking, the essence of which resides in the assumption of responsibility to an audience for a display of communicative skill, highlighting the way in which communication is carried out, above and beyond its referential content. . . . Performance calls forth special attention to and heightened awareness of both the act of expression and the performer. Viewed in these terms, performance may be understood as the enactment of the poetic function, the essence of spoken artistry. (1986, p. 3)

Bauman's references to "speaking" and "spoken artistry" are not impediments to my view of the commodity as performance. In de Certeau's discussion, "An Art of Speaking," also focused on the folktale, he argues for a view of story that makes a movement rather than simply telling about it (1974/1984, p. 81). For de Certeau, stories bind the art of speaking to the art of operating (p. 79):

> The same practices now appear in a verbal field, now in a field of nonlinguistic actions;

they move from one field to the other, being equally tactical and subtle in both; they keep the ball moving between them—from the workday to evening, from cooking to legends and gossip, from the devices of lived history to those of history retold. (p. 78)

After de Certeau, I see a praxical and procedural homology between stories, performance in the verbal field, and Navajo folk art objects as "nonlinguistic action." All are devices of lived history, all move from the verbal field into those of the visual, tactile, kinesthetic. All assume and demonstrate what de Certeau calls *savoir-dire*, the "know-how-to-say," the communicative competence integral to a story's, or an object's, social and poetic functions. The object, like the performed story, is the membrane across which performer/artists and audiences encounter and imagine one another, whether from opposite sides of the proscenium or opposite sides of a trading post or gallery counter. Neither is simply a text waiting to be animated but a display that binds communicative competence, history, affect, action, and thought together within the commodity situation. Thus, the object in the situation speaks; it is, simultaneously, a story and an event. It animates relations of exchange even as it is, itself, animated in the process.

These relationships between stories in performance and the Navajo folk art object as performance are not simply theoretical. Acquiring these objects in commodity situations is suffused with performance. Indeed, it is possible to view the purchase of these objects as the purchase of stories in performance. An anonymous article in *Brush and Pencil*, 1905, asserts,

> One may view an olla or a basket and admire, in a casual way, its odd designs, and turn away with but a slight thrill of pleasure. Let the maker of that article interpret the significance of those colors, pattern, and shape, and he has found a feast for his soul. These are poems, histories, and creeds

woven into every Indian basket and imprinted upon every decorated piece of pottery. ("Art of the American Indian," 1986, pp. 84–85)

This desire for story in performance and/as the commodity is not purely historical, as Barry Simpson, a member of one of the major Southwest trading families and owner, with his brother Steve, of Twin Rocks Trading Post indicates in the following narrative. The Simpsons are known for their commitment to, and advocacy on behalf of, Navajo basketry. They are widely credited with raising the profile of the form and with the development of the spectacularly complex "art basket." Here, Barry relates how Jonathan Black, whose wife Alicia Nelson is also a gifted weaver, negotiates performance in/as the commodity situation.

> On a recent visit . . . Alicia made her way into the trading post with a very interesting basket, which portrayed an ear of corn on a white background, surrounded by a green and black border. There were a number of people in the store, and everyone was drawn to the basket; they all wanted to know what it meant. Alicia quickly let everyone know that she had not woven the basket; her husband did and he was in the car. . . .
> The people were happy to meet Jonathan, and they shook his hand, congratulated him on his artistic accomplishment and asked him to interpret the basket's hidden meaning. Poor Jonathan gulped, took a deep breath and began. Pointing to the ear of corn he said, "That's us." He then pointed to the white background and said, "That's the dawn." Finally he pointed to the encircling pattern and said, "This is protection." He smiled uneasily and exited the trading post, escaping back to the car and his child care duties. Everyone looked after him, feeling, I am sure, a little short changed. Their interest had been sincere and they wondered what had happened. (B. Simpson, personal communication, October 11, 2002)

Barry Simpson notes, "the manner in which Jonathan teaches us about his art" forces the spectator to engage both the object and the story more directly and specifically (2002), though other artists opt for different strategies. For example, Betsy Emerson uses humor to "animate" her fired mud toy horses; she noted that the hair for their manes and tails came from her own animals. "So," she said, "if you're riding around Navajo country and you see a horse with no tail, he's mine" (B. Emerson, personal communication, February 9, 2002).

The Rosenaks subtitle their book *The People Speak,* but, in the performances of these commodities, who and what speaks is not always obvious. Specifically, I would suggest that commodity performances in the case of Navajo folk art are complex acts of ventriloquism where objects enact stories of disruption and continuity created or imagined by all involved in the commodity situation.

In the examples above, the artist/performer animates the object in the commodity situation through story; the residues of these stories continue to be ventriloquized through the object across the contexts of trading post and collection. Yet there are two other options for commodity ventriloquism. In the first, the objects themselves perform stories seemingly intrinsic to their own design. In the second, the object performs the projections of its owners in a manner that recalls the character Seymour Polatkin's observation in Sherman Alexie's film *The Business of Fancydancing:* "Indians must see visions and white people can have some visions if they are in love with Indians" (Estes, Rosenfelt, & Alexie, 2002). The following example explores both of these performances, as well as issues of continuity and disruption, map and story, as all are concretized in the performance of a particular genre of folk art object.

The Hathale family, Bruce and Dennis, paint images on old bedsheets dyed the rosy brown hue of red rocks. The resulting images are themselves performatively constituted small worlds; they feature clouds, corn, trolls, mountains, water horses and water oxen, and rainbows: geographies organized into narratives and further organized into images. But these sections of dyed bedsheet do more than represent the world in a nonmonumental format. Through a complex interplay of continuity and disruption, these textiles create and perform the world as both map and story.

The Hathale brothers are the primary artists working in a genre called "memory aids," a variation on Navajo sandpainting. The Navajo word "hataalii" can be generically translated as "healer," or more specifically, as a healer specializing in ritual performances that treat both individuals and the community. The late Roger Hathale, Bruce and Dennis's father, used sandpaintings, complex multicolored reproductions of ceremonial motifs, to effect individual and communal cures. Mark Bahti writes,

> Sandpainting images require the careful attention of the hataalii, as a slight error could result in harm rather than a cure. The image itself, which must be started at sunrise and completed by sunset, can cause harm to those present. To prevent this from happening, the image is first "erased" with a wooden stick with praying feathers attached. In some instances the sand on which the image has been created rests on a tarp in order to facilitate complete removal of the sand and image. The material is disposed of some distance from any home, trail or corral. A final prayer is said over the remains, which some say "discharms" the sands. (2000, p. 9)

The sandpainting is a performance. It is an action as well as an object. Exact or inexact, its animation has consequences for the performers and for the world. It is, simultaneously, object, story, performance, and event. The paintings, and not only the performers, "work" in the performance context.

Reproductions of sandpaintings have been widely circulated as both tourist art and fine art for decades. The Hathales' paintings on muslin, however, are especially interesting. According to the Rosenaks, the late Roger Hathale suggested to his boys that they reproduce sandpaintings. However, the strict

taboos on "fixing" these performances, particularly for an audience of outsiders, had to be both managed and disrupted. The Rosenaks quote Roger as saying,

> I ... felt [his sons] could reproduce the sandpaintings I made for ceremonies as long as they were accurate. If others did this type of art they would be harmed, but I have the power to protect my boys. The idea was mine, but I have never made one myself. Certain figures would bring harm, but I will not let these be sold. (1988, p. 77)

Here it is worth noting the influence of the Rosenaks' book; it both contributed to the creation of, and legitimated and codified, the commodity situation for Navajo folk art. Certainly such an authoritative testament to the authenticity of the Hathales' paintings generated heightened interest in, and marketability of, this work, particularly on the part of collectors who knew of the cultural taboos around preserving actual sandpaintings. For collectors, the vision of vicarious participation in the real thing would be inextricably linked to the social life of the memory aid. They could both buy and be in the performance.

Yet the Rosenaks' account does not stand alone. James Ostler, owner of the Cow Canyon Trading Post, recalls Roger Hathale offering a different account, one emphasizing disruption of, rather than continuity with, the "authentic." According to Ostler, Hathale told him that his experience as a medicine man did indeed protect his sons, but it was because of his advice on details to alter in the paintings precisely to disrupt their authenticity. Because of the intricacies of the form, changes of color or breaks in lines effectively neutralize any threat posed by either fixing exact copies of sacred forms or making gravely consequential, though unintended, mistakes. The issue here is not which story is true, but rather how multiple and even contradictory narratives often embrace one another in the commodity performances that are Navajo folk art.

Notions of the performing object, or the object as an act of ventriloquism, are not in themselves new. Indeed they are prefigured in Marx's theory of commodity fetishism and Bennett's critique discussed above. Elaine Scarry adopts and modifies this Marxist framework in support of her argument that "artifacts are (in spite of their inertness) perhaps most accurately perceived as a 'making sentient of the external world'" (1985, p. 281). Scarry posits the object as a "projection of the human body," intimately linked to subjectification. This process of projection "ultimately suggest[s] that by transporting the external object world into the sentient [subject's] interior, that interior gains some small share of the blissful immunity of inert objecthood" (p. 285). Further, the projective animation of the object deprives it of "its privilege of being irresponsible to its sentient inhabitants on the basis that it is itself nonsentient."

An explicitly theatrical example of a performing object illustrates Scarry's point while illuminating specific dynamics of the commodity situation of Navajo folk art. This is the stage prop that, like a folk art object, occupies "an uneasy position between text [as story] and performance" (Sofer, 2003, p. vi). According to Andrew Sofer, props, like the folk art object, are animated by performance and, in the process "trace spatial trajectories and create temporal narratives as they track through a given performance" (p. 2). Just as Scarry argues for the object's capacity to animate the external world, Sofer posits that the function of the prop (and, indeed, of theatre) is "to bring dead images back to life—but with a twist" (p. 3). In a sense, props are part of the larger poiesis of "drama's opportunistic reworking of its own past" (p. 202).

Likewise, Navajo folk art, animated by artists, traders, and collectors, ventriloquizes and accommodates a variety of spatiotemporal narratives with a variety of political valences, from Jonathan Black's truncated glossary of Navajo iconography to fantasies of encountering an Indian other in another place, now preserved both in and out of time. The folk art object becomes both the (imagined) voice of, and a synecdoche for, a tribe or a place or a fantasy of authentic contact or expression. Some authors and critics suggest that "the opportunistic reworking of the past" is central to the commodity situation of Native American art generally because the complex political dimensions of native subjectivity are "beyond the ken of most Americans, for whom Indians largely remain a people of myth and fantasy" (Bordevich, 1996, p. 40). In this view, the "vanishing" native is both brought to life and frozen in forms that could be superficially viewed as naive, politically innocent, and timeless—products of a homogenous "folk" whose artists, nevertheless, speak with amusing idiosyncrasy. Further, the object functions as a perpetual performance of inclusion and appreciation for collectors, a performance that simultaneously offers them absolution for their positions of relative privilege vis à vis the artist; exemption from the often sordid history of non-Indian desires for, and designs on, Indian objects; and recognition for a good eye, aesthetic savvy complete with multicultural sophistication. Scarry's "blissful inertness" is a privilege transferred from the performing object, and the residues of its production, to the passive, innocent, appreciative audience even as the Hathales' memory aids, for example, enact their responsibility for cultural exactitude or cultural disruption, depending on the account.

In Navajo folk art, and in social aesthetic transactions generally, object/performances create and stabilize small worlds of creativity and commerce replete with history and desire, with contested "tournaments of value" and politics of discipline, "diversion and display" (Appadurai, 1986, p. 57). In so doing, these performances remind us of what Bennett has called "the uncanny ability of nonhuman things to act upon us" (2001, p. 127).

CONCLUSION

These examples demonstrate the generative utility of performance and the performative in addressing two clarion calls from contemporary critical cultural theory. The first is Michel de Certeau's (1974/1984) advocacy of a science of the singular in *The Practice of Everyday Life*. He argues that consumers, including consumers of culture, are engaged in complex acts of poiesis always already in motion. The atomizing practices of conventional quantitative social science are

> virtually ignorant of these trajectories, since [they are] satisfied with classifying, calculating, and putting into tables the "lexical" units which compose them but to which they cannot be reduced. . . . Statistical investigation grasps the material of these practices but not their *form*. . . . (p. xviii)

Performance and performativity, however, proceed from the premise that culture, and the myriad acts of daily poiesis that produce it, are always already in motion: memory is continually produced in ongoing dances between there and then, here and now; places are created out of spaces; artifacts become animated through consumption. In the second of these clarion calls, Donna Haraway (1991) advances an intellectual program of situated knowledges, rooted in the recognition that truth claims are embodied, contingent and accountable, as a way to reinvigorate objectivity as a social and epistemological force. Haraway writes, "Feminist objectivity is about limited location and situated knowledge, not about transcendence and splitting of subject and object. In this way we might become answerable for what we learn how to see" (p. 190). Haraway's use of "answerable" recalls Bakhtin's answerability discussed above: the idea that art and life are partners in a profoundly political duet. Performing objects reveal that de/recontextualization in the collection is neither absolute or innocent. Ballet's inscription of its corporeal geography exposes the performative investments all techniques—performance and otherwise—make in mapping their object-bodies.

Even as it embraces, indeed depends, on embodied, situated knowledges of the particular, performance studies heeds Joan Scott's (1991) warnings against the uncritical valorization of experience as the ultimate referent, the final arbiter of truth claims. To the contrary, the view of cultural poiesis (and cultural poets) that performance studies offers to scholars in the human sciences is predicated on the kind of dialogic exchanges between multiple texts, conversations, and perspectives often labeled "triangulation" in qualitative research. It sees the research enterprise itself as a form of cultural poiesis, an ensemble performance, if you will, replete with all the political, aesthetic, and affective fields central to memory, to place, and to the human and nonhuman actors that live there.

REFERENCES

Anderson, B. (1991). *Imagined communities*. London: Verso.

Appadurai, A. (1986). Introduction: Commodities and the politics of value. In A. Appadurai (Ed.), *The social life of things* (pp. 3–63). England: Cambridge University Press.

Art of the American Indian. (1996). In L. Dilworth, *Imagining Indians in the Southwest*. Washington, DC: Smithsonian Press.

Bahti, M. (2000). *A guide to Navajo sandpaintings*. Tucson, AZ: Rio Nuevo.

Bakhtin, M. M. (1981). *The dialogic imagination: Four essays* (M. Holquist, Ed.; C. Emerson & M. Holquist, Trans.). Austin: University of Texas Press.

Bakhtin, M. M. (1990). *Art and answerability: Early philosophical essays* (M. Holquist & V. Liapunov, Eds.; V. Liapunov, Trans.). Austin: University of Texas Press. (Original work published 1919)

Bauman, R. (1986). *Story, performance, event*. England: Cambridge University Press.

Bennett, J. (2001). *The enchantment of modern life.* Princeton, NJ: Princeton University Press.

Bordevich, F. (1996). Revolution in Indian country. *American Heritage 47*(4), 34–46.

Brown, B. (2003). The secret life of things: Virginia Woolf and the matter of modernism. In P. R. Matthews & D. McWhirter (Eds.), *Aesthetic subjects* (pp. 397–430). Minneapolis: University of Minnesota Press.

Butler, J. (1993a). *Bodies that matter: On the discursive limits of sex.* New York: Routledge.

Butler, J. (1993b). Performative acts and gender constitution: An essay in phenomenology and feminist thought. In S. E. Case (Ed.), *Performing feminisms: Feminist critical theory and theatre* (pp. 270–282). Baltimore: Johns Hopkins University Press.

Charlé, S. (2001, August 12). With monkeys and giants, rescuing a lost world. *New York Times,* p. AR6.

Clark, K., & Holquist, M. (1984). *Mikhail Bakhtin.* Cambridge, MA: Belknap/Harvard University Press.

Coburn, J. (1993, September 26). Dancing back. *Los Angeles Times Magazine,* pp. 14ff.

Connerton, P. (1989). *How societies remember.* England: Cambridge University Press.

Conquergood, D. (1991). Rethinking ethnography. *Communication Monographs, 58*(2), 179–194.

de Certeau, M. (1984). *The practice of everyday life* (S. Rendall, Trans.). Berkeley: University of California Press. (Original work published 1974)

Diamond, E. (1996). Introduction. In E. Diamond (Ed.), *Performance and cultural politics.* (pp. 1–12). New York: Routledge.

Estes, L., Rosenfelt, S. (Producers), & Alexie, S. (Writer/Director). (2002). *The business of fancydancing* [Motion picture]. United States: Falls*Apart* Productions. (Available from Falls*Apart* Productions, www.fallsapart.com)

Foster, S. L. (1998). *Choreography and narrative: Ballet's staging of story and desire.* Bloomington: Indiana University Press.

Glatzer, J. (Director/Producer). (2003). *The flute player* [Motion picture]. United States: Over The Moon Productions. (Available from National Asian American Telecommunications Association, distribution@naatanet.org)

Goffman, E. (1959). *The presentation of self in everyday life.* Garden City, NY: Doubleday.

Haraway, D. (1991). *Simians, cyborgs, and women: The reinvention of nature.* New York: Routledge.

Hawes, L. (1998). Becoming-other-wise: Conversational performance and the politics of experience. *Text and Performance Quarterly, 18*(4), 273–299.

Hayden, D. (1997). *The power of place: Urban landscapes as public history.* Cambridge, MA: MIT Press.

Hitchcock, P. (1993). *Dialogics of the oppressed.* Minneapolis: University of Minnesota Press.

Holquist, M. (1990). *Dialogism: Bakhtin and his world.* New York: Routledge.

Jackson, J. B. (1984). *Discovering the vernacular landscape.* New Haven: Yale University Press.

Lafreniere, B. (2000). *Music through the dark.* Honolulu: University of Hawaii Press.

Matthews, P. R., & McWhirter, D. (Eds.). (2003). *Aesthetic subjects.* Minneapolis: University of Minnesota Press.

Miller, D. (1998). Why some things matter. In D. Miller (Ed.), *Why some things matter* (pp. 3–21). Chicago: University of Chicago Press.

Morson, G. S. (1994). *Narrative and freedom: The shadows of time.* New Haven, CT: Yale University Press.

Mydans, S. (1993, December 30). Khmer dancers try to save an art form ravaged by war. *New York Times,* pp. C11ff.

Naficy, H. (1993). *The making of exile cultures: Iranian television in Los Angeles.* Minneapolis: University of Minnesota Press.

Patraka, V. (1999). *Spectacular suffering: Theatre, fascism, and the Holocaust.* Bloomington: Indiana University Press.

Pran, D. (1997). *Children of Cambodia's killing fields: Memoirs by survivors.* (K. DePaul, Ed.). New Haven, CT: Yale University Press.

Radway, J. (1991). *Reading the romance.* Chapel Hill, NC: University of North Carolina Press.

Richards, T. (1991). *The commodity culture of Victorian England.* London: Verso.

Rosenak, C., & Rosenak, J. (1988). *Navajo folk art: The people speak.* Flagstaff, AZ: Northland.

Sadono, R. F. (1999). Performing symptoms. *Text and Performance Quarterly, 19*(2), 159–171.

Sam, S. A. (1994). Khmer traditional music today. In M. E. Ebihara, C. A. Mortland, & J. Ledgerwood (Eds.), *Cambodian culture since 1975: Homeland and exile* (pp. 39–47). Ithaca, NY: Cornell University Press.

Scarry, E. (1985). *The body in pain: The making and unmaking of the world.* New York: Oxford University Press.

Scott, J. W. (1991). The evidence of experience. *Critical Inquiry, 17*(4), 773–797.

Sofer, A. (2003). *The stage life of props.* Ann Arbor: University of Michigan Press.

Tuan, Y. F. (1977). *Space and place: The perspective of experience.* Minneapolis: University of Minnesota Press.

Turnbull, R. (1999, July 25). Reconstructing Khmer classics from zero. *New York Times,* p. AR6.

Turner, V. (1982). *From ritual to theatre.* New York: PAJ Publications.

Yaeger, P. (1996). Introduction. In P. Yaeger (Ed.), *The geography of identity.* Ann Arbor: University of Michigan Press.

PART II

Performing History

A Politics of Location

LISA MERRILL

SHARING THE TOOLS

This section of *The SAGE Handbook of Performance Studies* deals with the field of performance history. The past—shimmering with its ghosts—infiltrates the present moment and the future, as I write these words, anticipating the histories new theories and ways of seeing call into being. History, like performance, is both a *subject* of study and the *object* or fruits of that study. The *doing* of history, inquiring into the past, then, is an act which results in "histories" the narratives or stories or performances which are the objects and products of that study.[1] And history, however it is performed, is an embodied interaction with traces found in the material evidence of artifacts, whose interpretation demands other performances of meaning-making. These traces are rendered significant through the historian's imaginative acts of reconstruction and deconstruction. Performance history, then, like other forms of historicizing, involves the performative act of telling a story—literally calling it into being.

Historians of performance endeavor to place into temporal and social context particular cultural practices or aesthetic acts. We know of any past instance of cultural production by the traces it leaves for the historian to question and to analyze. But traces are fragmentary at best and not all cultural practices are preserved or documented. Significant efforts have been taken to save some cultural events, document their physical production, and celebrate their reception, while other cultural events have been overlooked, erased, or discarded.

Within the field of performance history there has been a productive tension between a focus on "recovering" as objects of study a broad range of historical acts *as performances,* and a focus on "uncovering" and analyzing agendas in texts, artifacts, and embodied practices so as to challenge the conceptual categories that frame much historical work and transform the disciplinary paradigms within which such concerns have been addressed traditionally.[2] *Thus, the practice of performance history inevitably involves various disciplines sharing their tools.*

Performance historians are particularly well-positioned to examine the connections between spectatorship and the power relations intrinsic to the processes of identification and objectification, so as to explore how dominant ideologies were constructed, resisted, and disturbed in spectatorial processes in a given time period. Suren Lalvani (1996) has contended that "concepts of seeing must be viewed as historically specific—not only embedded in particular epistemologies . . . but linked to specific discourses and forms of social power, and consequently a particular matrix for organizing the relations between observer and observed, the visible and the invisible" (p. 2). Thus, performance historians need to question how spectators in earlier time periods saw and understood performing bodies, focusing on the discourses and material practices that shaped the representations and readings available to audiences.

THE ARCHIVE AS BOTH REPOSITORY AND "CLOSET": A POLITICS OF LOCATION

Locating oneself as a performance historian implies a positionality, and an acknowledgment of a politics of location. For example, we must recognize how the institutional space of a given archive directs and enables *some* ways of seeing, while obstructing others. In my own work on the performance of sexual, gender, ethnic, class, and national identities in the nineteenth century, I have engaged with material artifacts housed in the institutional contexts of archives, frequently preserved for reasons having more to do with the performance of history than the history of performance. I have come to these artifacts and the repositories that contain them as a translator, attempting to locate them in their historical moment, as well as to consider them *as performances*.

In so doing, I have noticed that the erotic economy of the archive and its holdings is charged by its potential as both repository and closet—a collection, and a house for a collection—containing, hiding, erasing, and potentially revealing strategies for secrecy and discovery, as well as offering the performance historian the tactile pleasures of interacting with the actual objects touched by historical subjects. Encountering fragmentary objects—such as manuscript letters, diaries, broadsides, illustrative material, props, costumes, and scripts, for example—prompts me to question ways in which representations and performances of race, gender, and sexuality in an earlier period drew upon and constructed legible bodies as potential objects of identification, of desire, or of vilification for audiences. Part of the challenge and pleasure of the "doing" of such historical work lies in recognizing and teasing out multiple and often contradictory meanings inherent in these objects and the stories told about them. Implicated in this act, of course, are the historian's own choices to attend to or disregard any of the relics he or she encounters, as well as to acknowledge the limitations inherent in the form, function, and setting of the closet/archive as well as its fragmentary contents.

Performance historians frequently look for what is missing as well as what is present. We often assume a role Michel de Certeau (1998) likens to that of a "prowler" in the margins of accepted narratives and disciplinary practices; paying particular attention to the absences and rationalizations in the archive as we attempt to "circulat[e] around acquired conventions" of theatre, literary, cultural, and social history, reading the spaces, silences, and rationalizations in the archive and "deciphering hidden relations held in discourses of other times" (p. 79). In my work on nineteenth century American actress Charlotte Cushman (Merrill, 1999) and her artfully managed presentation of self, in addition to analyzing Cushman's public theatrical appearances, I examined her unpublished letters as a series of autobiographical performances in which she played multiple parts. The stories performers like Cushman told in their personal correspondence or authorized to be told in interviews and articles, and even the photographs or paintings for which they sat, can be considered attempts (albeit not always conscious ones) to position themselves both within and against dominant cultural narratives of gender, sexuality, race, and class.

Archives, as I have noted above, are repositories of artifacts considered by some agency as worthy of saving and are thus subject to all of the limitations and interests of the agency or institutions that have preserved them. Nonetheless, they offer a rich—and often underutilized—source of primary material to performance historians. In a recent project on homoeroticism in the cultural critical constructions of American actors Edwin Forrest and Edwin Booth (Merrill 2002), I have drawn upon official texts, such as periodicals, as well as unpublished personal correspondence to argue that public reception of Forrest and Booth—the two foremost nineteenth century male actors in the United States and the matinee idols of their times—was shaped at a nascent point in the career of each by pseudonymous critical reviews and articles which I discovered to have been authored and authorized by men with deep personal attachments to Forrest and Booth respectively.

Prowling has its rewards, as I recognized in the unpublished letters and articles of these little-known cultural critics the role played by an economy of homoerotic desire in the theatrical reviews published in the periodical press. Reading the published criticism alongside private letters to and from critics James Oakes and Adam Badeau, I found that such pseudonymous cultural critics set the tone for ways in which their subjects would be received by others, operating as metonymic representatives for the communities that informed or motivated their judgments. Moreover, I discovered ways in which the development of the popular cultural institutions of the American theatre and the American press were closely related. Each of these discourses and material practices served as a platform for representations of a form of nineteenth century white American masculinity; in so doing, they inevitably helped produce the various publics they addressed. And each built upon the visibility and accessibility of the other.

Exploring nineteenth century representations of cross-dressing, same-sex desire, and "passing" or shifting racial identities provides particular challenges for archival research, given the ephemeral quality of performance, coupled with the need to recover *intentionally* censored material. Just as Martha Vicinus (1994) considers it imperative that historians of sexuality explore the absences and silences in the historical record of subjects who would today be considered gay or lesbian, "argu[ing] for the possibilities of the 'not said' and the 'not seen' as conceptual tools" (pp. 58–59) for the writing of history, it is critical that performance historians read as significant absences as well as presences in the historical record, particularly when engaging with subjects whose traces may be intentionally missing, hidden, or not saved by institutional bodies.

THE ELUSIVENESS OF PERFORM[ANCE]/ING HISTORY

Part of the elusiveness of history lies in the inchoate longing for a story to fill up the spaces—to make both the "now-ness" of the present and the absent past make sense. Intrinsic to current debates about performance history are constructs imposed by the various disciplinary genealogies, practices, and effects of both history *and* performance. At the center of the study of many events performed in the past are tensions between the embodied and ephemeral nature of live performance and the narrative structure and discursive approach to history as story.

Dwight Conquergood (2002) has critiqued as "scriptocentric" the assumptions and practices that underlie much theatrical and literary history—noting how the valuing of literacy over orality privileges elites and leads researchers to draw upon written texts as the exclusive or primary artifacts to be studied, and even to deploy the trope of "reading" cultural practices to describe ethnographic engagements. Following Conquergood's injunctions, Diana Taylor (2003) urges performance studies scholars and students to look beyond the traditional archive of written texts, to include for analysis a repertoire of embodied acts and scenarios as paradigms for understanding social structures and their history, noting that, "writing and embodied performance have often worked together to layer the historical memories that constitute community" (pp. 26 and 35).

In addition to shining a light on the neglected, silenced, or transgressive performances and performers in an earlier period, performance historians, along with other postmodern theorists, must necessarily trace the elusive ways that culture serves power. Thus, the politics of performance history can be one of its most elusive features. In terms similar to those Joyce Appleby (1998) claims beset national histories, we need be mindful that performance histories may do more than *account for* a particular kind of progress narrative, but rather, may serve to *proselytize* for it (pp. 9–10). Artifacts and relics of performances can be rearranged, accidentally or willfully discarded, evacuating a past too painful to remember, or magnifying and distorting relatively obscure traces into a retrospective primacy in service of a particular politicized narrative of an elusive past. In keeping with this largely unarticulated aspect of historical narratives, Peter Fritzsche (2004) has suggested that what he refers to as "the melancholy of history" is based upon the historical knowledge of shared losses, wherein "people consume and produce historical texts as a way to connect their personal ordeals with larger social narratives" (p. 8).

Moreover, inevitably the economy of the archive or the academic milieu within which most performance historians labor reflects the class interests these institutions support. As Michel de Certeau (1998) reminds us,

All historiographical research is articulated over a socioeconomic, political, and cultural place of production. It implies an area of elaboration that peculiar determinations circumscribe: a liberal profession, a position as an observer or a professor, a group of learned people, and so forth. It is therefore ruled by constraints, bound to privileges, and rooted in a particular situation. (p. 58)

This performance history section of The *SAGE Handbook* offers a range of examples and applications of performance history. Certainly the essays included below are subject to the challenges de Certeau notes, however, as examples of *performance* history, they demonstrate complications additional to those constraints, privileges, and positionalities that beset more conventional historiographic projects. In this section, we explore some of the ways performance historians engage and interact with objects or documents or embodied acts, as well as to note the performative nature of their engagement.

Some of the performance texts and practices discussed in this section, such as the scripts for preparedness and response to nuclear war analyzed by Tracy C. Davis, and the oral histories of integration explored by Della Pollock, are located primarily in the social and political dimensions of everyday life and are offered here as examples of performance history in which the tropes of theatrical performance, when deployed by theorists and historians, offer insights into the ways everyday social and political life is staged, heard, remembered, and understood. Others, such as the essays by Gay Gibson Cima and Shannon Jackson, ask us to question the archive of performance history—to note strategic absences of accounts of cultural performances by women in Cima's case, and in Jackson's essay, to note the disciplinary investments in a politics of location that has valorized elite ways of knowing, to the detriment of performance.

Perhaps as a result of the need to grapple with the here-and-now of live performance, performance historians are uniquely prepared to observe ways in which *accounts* of acts performed in the past serve both as cultural artifacts of the moments that produced them, and, as historian Greg Dening (1996) reminds us, "they also become cultural artifacts of all the moments that give them permanence." Thus, the past "is only known through symbols whose meaning is changed in the reading of them and in the preserving of them" (p. 43).

This historical contingency is demonstrated most clearly in Gay Gibson Cima's essay, "Minstrelsy and Mental Metempsychosis: Mid-Nineteenth Century American Women's Performance Criticism." In this essay, Cima examines ways women's identities were formulated through concrete institutions and material practices and through rhetorical identifications with surrogate bodies, particularly bodies of persons of color. As Cima's work on cultural critics' responses to public speaking performances by nineteenth century women demonstrates, historically contingent beliefs about race, gender, and sexuality shaped the discursive frames through which cultural critics viewed performers and public speakers. Cima's nuanced readings of these texts and performances illustrates what Catherine Gallagher and Stephen Greenblatt have called "the tension between certain artifacts . . . and their cultures" and explores ways her subjects may have expressed "resistance as well as replication, friction as well as assimilation, subversion as well as orthodoxy" (2000, p. 16) to norms about gender, sexuality, and race in a given era.

In an attempt to find that which has not been noticed before, historians perform a figure/ground sleight of hand, attempting to see what others have not. In an oscillating consciousness of context and text, performance historians, in Michel de Certeau's terms, "deal with physical objects in order to transform them into history." In fact, "the work of the historian," according to de Certeau, involves transporting the raw material of a primary source "from one region of culture (curiosities, archives, collections, etc.) to another (history)" (p. 71). This transporting is clearly the case in Tracy C. Davis's essay. In "What to Do When Nuclear War Breaks Out," Davis explores 1950s nuclear preparedness scripts in Canada and in the United States as a rehearsal for a performance that, thankfully, did not occur.

Drawing upon tropes of theatricality and performance theory, Davis's chilling account of anticipatory scripted responses to nuclear war demonstrates how performance theory has a necessary place in historical examinations of the public sphere. Like Jennifer Terry (1999), who describes herself as a historian of effects, interested in "exposing the points at which certain ideas came to be accepted as truthful and analyzing what conditions made their ascent to the status of truth possible" (p. 21), Davis's project traces how authority on Cold War safety was staged, as she explores the discursive moves that produced "common knowledge" about nuclear threat in an earlier era. Furthermore, Davis's use of performance theory complicates and broadens conventional notions of temporality, in that Davis reminds readers that the scripts she examines were not merely *relics* of the past, but—as with all play scripts—formed the blueprint for potential, and in this case, chilling, future performances as well.

In an interview published in the *Radical History Review* (1976), historian E. P. Thompson asserted that "the historian has to be listening all the time. . . . The material has got to speak through him" (p. 15). Della Pollock's project of oral history *as performance* literally enacts this injunction, as she explores her student performers' engagements with oral histories of racial desegregation as told to them by others. In "Memory, Remembering, and the Histories of Change: A Performance Praxis,"

Pollock provides an account of a pedagogical technique for doing performance history which she describes as "listening out loud." While the connection between history and storytelling has now become a fundamental axiom of history-making, Pollack's essay reminds readers of the importance of *listening* as a performance praxis, crucial to the historiographical project. Drawing upon performed memories of racial desegregation in the United States, Pollock explores the effects of students' re-performance of the oral histories and memories of others. Pollock's self-reflexive analysis of the challenges and rewards of engaging with these performed histories draws readers into the politic of the construction, performance, and reconstruction of accounts of critical moments in U.S. racial politics.

Finally, Shannon Jackson's essay on performance genealogies traces a particular disciplinary history, tracking some of the ways performance was understood, deployed, and denigrated in academic departments in the U.S. institutions of higher education. Jackson's genealogy traces the relative privileges and constraints experienced by academics in departments of English, Speech and Rhetoric, Theatre, and Performance Studies in elite academic institutions in the United States, particularly focusing on how texts and their analysis came to be valued over theatre and the *performance* of literature and drama. Jackson's essay illustrates ways the subject matter and skill set constitutive of elite knowledges in the academy have served particular classed interests and shifted over time. Thus, Jackson's essay demonstrates that one of the tasks appropriately taken up by performance historians is to question, reconstruct, and analyze dominant narratives, to attend to "the cultural matrix" out of which such representations emerge.

Each of the following examples and interventions into the practice of performance history has value for the student or practitioner of performance studies. As you read them, consider Greg Dening's (1996) suggestion that

[a] history writer should think of him or herself as a composer. That way it is the *reader* who is the *performer* and the thing performed . . . the history I write is the score for all sorts of flights of the imagination." (p. 102, my emphasis)

The essays here offer such models to readers of the breadth of technique and application for performance history.

NOTES

1. As performance theorist Elin Diamond has observed, "performance is always a doing and a thing done. On the one hand, performance describes certain embodied acts, in specific sites, witnessed by others (and/or the watching self). On the other hand, it is the thing done, the completed event framed in time and space and remembered, misremembered, interpreted, and passionately revisited across a pre-existing discursive field" (1996, p. 1).

2. Karen Offen, Ruth Roach Pierson, and Jane Rendall have made this case about the discipline of women's history (1991). I believe a similar tension exists in the development of the field of performance history.

REFERENCES

Appleby, J. (1998). The power of history. *The American Historical Review, 103*(1), 1–14.

Conquergood, D. (2002). Performance studies: Interventions and radical research. *The Drama Review, 46*(2), 145–156.

de Certeau, M. (1998). *The writing of history* (T. Conley, Trans.). New York: Columbia University Press.

Dening, G. (1996). *Performances*. Chicago: University of Chicago Press.

Diamond, E. (Ed.). (1996). *Performance and cultural politics*. New York: Routledge.

Fritzsche, P. (2004). *Stranded in the present: Modern time and the melancholy of history*. Cambridge, MA: Harvard University Press.

Gallagher, C., & Greenblatt, S. (2000). *Practicing new historicism*. Chicago: University of Chicago Press.

Lalvani, S. (1996). *Photography, vision, and the production of modern bodies*. Albany, NY: SUNY Press.

Merrill, L. (1999). *When Romeo was a woman: Charlotte Cushman and her circle of female spectators.* Ann Arbor: University of Michigan Press.

Merrill, L. (2002). Appealing to the passions: Homoerotic desire and nineteenth-century theater criticism. In K. Marra & R. A. Schanke (Eds.), *Staging desire: Queer readings of American theater history* (pp. 221–261). Ann Arbor: University of Michigan Press.

Offen, K., Roach Pierson, R., & Rendall, J. (1991). *Writing women's history: International perspectives.* Bloomington: University of Indiana Press.

Taylor, D. (2003). *The archive and the repertoire: Performing cultural memory in the Americas.* Durham, NC: Duke University Press.

Terry, J. (1999). *An American obsession: Science, medicine, and homosexuality in modern society.* Chicago: University of Chicago Press.

Thompson, E. P. (1976). Interview with Edward Thompson. *Radical History Review, 42,* 15.

Vicinus, M. (1994). Lesbian history: All theory and no facts or all facts and no theory? *Radical History Review, 60,* 57–75.

5

Genealogies of Performance Studies

SHANNON JACKSON

In the last decade, several scholars have innovated in the practice of performance historiography. Significant for this body of scholarship is the notion of a "genealogical" consciousness, one that calls for history writing that recognizes the multireferentiality of particular terms and that takes seriously patterns of discontinuity in apparently linear historical progressions.[1] As performance scholars use the concept of genealogy to write histories of performance, I will argue for a similar consciousness in our histories of performance studies as a discipline itself. Any introduction to performance studies must include an understanding of the many, often contradictory, ways that our field has been incorporated into the academy. By scrutinizing the arena of academic knowledge production in which many of us learn, teach, and are employed, we will better define the predicament of performance as a cultural practice, as a historical body of knowledge, and as a discipline in higher education. Through such an encounter, the study of performance history comes to terms with the history of performance study.

DISCIPLINARY GENEALOGIES

My approach in this essay derives from a larger project, one that itself derives from a larger mission, to reconcile if not exactly to resolve the relationship between the study of performance and the structures of higher education (Jackson, 2004). Many of us who identify as scholars of performance have found it necessary to adopt a heuristic as well as ironic perspective on what exactly it means to affiliate with such a protean, productive, and impossible discipline. As a field recently consolidated under the umbrella of "performance studies" —incorporating literary, media, theatrical, art historical, and anthropological analyses of diverse cultural forms—performance draws from newer discursive currents in cultural studies and in feminist, critical race, postcolonial, and queer theory.[2] As such, the field can be said to be both an activator and a symptom of new trends in humanities scholarship, incorporating interdisciplinary approaches and responding to political critiques of identity that have circulated throughout the cultural field. Such larger trends have of course been the subject of conflicted discussion as scholars such as Gerald Graff (1987, 1992), Sander Gilman (2000), John Guillory (1993), and (posthumously) Bill Readings (1996) consider the future of the humanities and, indeed, the field of the cultural more generally. It will be my contention throughout this essay that performance and performance studies actually play a partial, multireferential, and ambiguous role in such discussions, an instability whose consequences come into higher relief when current discussions are placed next to disciplinary histories.

To exemplify the predicament of performance in larger discussions of higher education, consider Cathy Davidson and David Theo Goldberg's "A Manifesto for the Humanities in a Technological Age" (2004, p. B7), a much-circulated document that called for a firm embrace of new trends in "literary theory," "science studies" and "post-colonial" classics. While celebrating the fact that the "humanities in 2004 are a many-splendored thing" they also lamented the fact that "humanists do not receive credit for the contributions they make" (¶ 11). In the document, Davidson and Goldberg offered bullet-pointed lists of different "characterizations of the humanities," deciding to position it "normatively" as a site for disseminating an "historical" imagination, an understanding of "relationality," a "conscience and critical memory," the "social values" behind social policy, and a respect for cultural and linguistic "diversity" (¶ 16–23). They argued that such moral and critical skills were part and parcel of the cultural education now offered in a modern research university, a realm of "insight" and "value" that surpassed the technical training in "expertise," "vocational training," or "specialized . . . skills" offered "in a trade school" (¶ 11–12). Interestingly, "performance theory" made an appearance on their list of humanist contributions, credited with having "(at long last) broken down the barrier between humanistic writing about the arts and actual artistic

production" (¶ 7). The "arts" also reappeared again as a domain that was "vital" to the humanities, "co-terminous and codependent . . . both are concerned with representation. . . . Both are based on assumptions that there are multiple forms of intelligence." However, their elaboration had a slightly different tone: "The relationship of the humanities to the arts, however, cannot be simply subject and object (the aesthetic production as an object for humanists). Artists have traditions of expression, voice, and performativity from which those of us in the humanities have much to learn" (¶ 19). Rather than simply another normative characterization of the humanities, the domain of the arts was less securely under the humanist umbrella, even if its potential contribution warranted inclusion in a humanist manifesto. By suggesting that humanists still had much to learn from artists, Davidson and Goldberg somewhat unselfconsciously qualified their own previous assertion that performance theory had ("at long last") broken down the barrier between these realms. Interestingly, their text seemed both to celebrate and defer the undoing of the boundary between the humanities and "actual artistic production."

While it is exciting to have luminaries such as Cathy Davidson and David Theo Goldberg inscribe a place for performance and the arts in their program for the humanities, there is an unprocessed quality to their incorporation. Indeed, several performance scholars would be frustrated to hear that the breaking down of the binary between the humanities and actual artistic production was all that performance theory had to offer a modern research university. Meanwhile, others affiliated with theatre, dance, and oral rhetoric would be more chagrined to hear that that breakdown only just happened and, moreover, that performance theory was the responsible party. Those same field specialists—along with artistic counterparts in the fields of music and the visual arts—might feel an odd mixture of hope and cynicism to hear that humanists feel that they have "much to learn" from artists, wondering for how long this sentiment will be couched in terms that leave it perpetually unfulfilled. It is at such times that a consideration of disciplinary genealogies becomes crucial, for the perceived newness of performance studies can perpetuate a somewhat partial, if well intentioned, understanding of what the study of performance might mean to the humanities.

While performance is often appropriately aligned with newer fields and theories in the humanities, it is in fact also a very old form of study in the academy. And as an older form of study in the humanist academy, its varied and conflicted history reflects forward on how the future of the humanities gets charted. What are those old forms of study? Consider, for instance, disciplinary traditions that worked to undo boundaries between performance practice and humanistic inquiry (or proceeded as if the boundaries did not need to be there). Performance pedagogy appeared classically in oratorical form, as training in the *technē* of rhetorical speech and oral poetics.[3] That tradition of education has reappeared and been revised in a variety of educational formations across the conventional periods of western history and now serves as a productive tool in comparative analyses of western and nonwestern cultural practices. In its twentieth century, Euro-American guise, oral rhetoric most often appeared as "public speaking" while, in some universities, the tradition of oral poetics continued as the oral interpretation of literature. There are other newer old versions of performance pedagogy, however. Classics students of the mid-nineteenth century and Shakespeare students of the late-nineteenth century increasingly sought opportunities to actually produce the plays that they read, eventually prompting university professors to move this extracurricular practice into the standardizing domain of the curricular.[4] The phenomenon of the "acting class" became the staple of many university theatre departments, incorporating the

monologues and "scene study" of contemporary drama into its performances of Sophocles and Shakespeare. Meanwhile, another genealogy of performance study appeared in the educational context of visual art practice. In fact, the first American theatre department appeared at Carnegie Mellon's School of Fine and Applied Arts in 1914. Later, when performance served as a provocative means of artistic innovation in the sixties and seventies, visual art pedagogies altered as well. As avantgarde painters and sculptors began to experiment with the durational, environmental, and embodied techniques of performance, art schools around the country found it necessary to incorporate performing arts into an otherwise "fine" curriculum.[5]

Those three genealogies only begin to chart the heterogeneity of performance as an educational object and an educational practice in higher education. In other disciplinary derivations from anthropology, sociology, folklore, and literature, the boundary between art practice and humanistic writing is less of a concern than is the understanding of performance as social form, as a model of identity, or as literary genre of dramatic form. What exactly these genealogies have had to do with each other is an ongoing question. Do the acting student's "objectives and obstacles" have any compatibility with the performance art student's experiments with duration? Can the performance art student reconcile her explorations of image and movement with the highly verbal, lectern-centered performances of oral interpretation? Does the "public speaker"—the student who is often honing preprofessional skills for law and business—understand or care about any of the above? Meanwhile, these already contradictory institutional genealogies bear an even more ambiguous relation to the late-twentieth century scholarly formation called performance studies. As an interdisciplinary formation in the arts and humanities that draws from the social sciences, performance studies attempts to incorporate theoretical models and methodological conventions from fields with fundamentally different reality principles. Additionally, participants are trained in home departments with different ideas of what it means to be a professional academic and with different assumptions of what constitutes the basic skills of undergraduate and graduate students. When the divided unions of performance studies meet the divided histories of performance study, we can find ourselves asking even more complicated questions. Is there a relation between the study of "objectives and obstacles" and the analysis of the "social drama"? Between the how-to's of oral argument and the history of minstrel performance? Between the oral interpretation of literature and the interpretation of oral cultures? Between dance technique and queer performativity? Can the same department prepare graduate students professionally for the Modern Language Association, the National Communication Association, the Association for Theatre in Higher Education, *and* the American Anthropological Association? Can that same department prepare undergraduates professionally for careers in theatre and film and dance and the visual arts? Can that same department prepare undergraduates professionally for careers in law and business?

My questions about professionalization anticipate the central preoccupation of the next section, for I want to suggest that an analysis of the self-contradicting dynamics of professionalist discourse—as well as the self-defeating effects of professionalist ultimatums—provide an alternate way of organizing disciplinary history. Such a reorganization will in fact require more reflection on the opposition between the humanities and the preprofessional skills of the vocational school that often appears as the object of denigration in many a humanist manifesto. The concept of "genealogy" offers the analytic mixture of irony and history necessary to embark on such a project, a mixture that does justice to institutional

discontinuity and that allows speculation on performance as a perpetually unfulfilled possibility. In his famous revisions of Nietzsche, Michel Foucault developed the concept of genealogy as a counter to a model of history that aims "to restore an unbroken continuity." Rather genealogists attempt to "maintain passing events in their proper dispersion"; to think genealogically "is to identify the accidents, the minute deviations—or conversely the complete reversals—the errors, the false appraisals, and the faulty calculations that gave birth to those things that continue to exist and have value for us" (Foucault, 1977/1980, p. 146). Earlier in the *Archaeology of Knowledge* (1972), Foucault had found that "the non-unity of discourse" had to be a principle operating assumption in disciplinary history. By extension, my excavation of performance in its many institutional forms is an examination of its many references and its shaky self-oppositions, requiring an awareness of their "non-identity through time, the break produced in them, the internal discontinuity that suspends their permanence" (Foucault, 1969/1972, pp. 32–33). As it happens, performance turns out not only to be internally discontinuous itself, but also a tool with which to isolate larger discontinuities in the academic arts and humanities. As such, its historical genealogies expose the larger institutional issues behind the "non-identities" and "minute derivations" of the humanist manifesto. My hunch is that actualizing a partnership between the arts and the humanities actually requires a more careful interrogation—rather than totalizing denigration—of the role of "technical" and "specialized skills" in humanistic education more generally.

JUMP FORWARD TO THE PAST

The notion of "professing performance" is ambiguous partly because of its multiple referents in several fields. To many ears, however, and despite many histories, the idea of professing performance sounds not only ambiguous but oxymoronic, largely because of the barriers between art practice and humanistic writing to which Goldberg and Davidson refer. But what might this oxymoronic status, the improbability of the connection between the verb ("professing") and the noun ("performance"), say about the institutions, structures, and disciplinary genealogies already sketched above?

One way to investigate this question is to put some pressure on the term "profess" and, with it, the terms "professional" and "professor" with which it might be associated. I have been inspired in this vein by Gerald Graff's formative explorations into the institutionalization of literary studies.[6] Graff (1987, 1992) joined and would be joined by other scholars such as Richard Ohmann (1976), John Guillory (1993), and Michael Bérubé (1998) who took a critical stance on their field's development within conventions of professionalism and rigor and while addressing (or disavowing) the economic pressures of a changing student body and a modernizing, technocratic university. Later, Bill Readings's posthumously published *The University in Ruins* (1996) considered how those economic effects continue to exert pressure and continue to remain underanalyzed, even in the domains of interdisciplinary humanities scholarship that sought to progressively redefine the space of culture studies (pp. 89–118). Barbara and John Ehrenreich's influential work has served as a springboard for much of this discussion, for many have felt compelled to engage their Marxist critique of an emerging "professional-managerial class" (PMC). The Ehrenreichs (1979) included "college professors" in what they identified as a group "consisting of salaried mental workers who do not own the means of production and whose major function in the social division of labor may be described broadly as the reproduction of capitalist culture and capitalist relations" (p. 12). PMC members measure and confer value by

their ability to participate in field-based domains of expertise, providing an expert knowledge that is both distinctive and rigorous. The Ehrenreichs identify a paradox in that, despite their role in the reproduction of capitalist relations, PMC members often invoked an anticapitalist rhetoric. Whether through an appeal to socialism or through a moral appeal to cultural preservation, academic humanists in particular tried to create a legitimating sphere of cultural capital outside of the domain of business—despite the social location of the university within relations of class mobility and economic advancement and despite professors' own emulation of expert models.

This made for a messy, complex, and occasionally self-contradicting context for humanist self-definition, one that reveals a Foucaultian disunity at the so-called center of humanistic professionalization. Indeed, it has made the idea of joining the term *professional* to the term *professor* somewhat unsavory to professors on both the right and the left who imagine themselves existing outside of such careerist—certainly, *vocational*—domains. Nevertheless, academics have borrowed various professional terms of legitimation, using concepts of rigor, research, and expertise in order to solidify the autonomy of the professional academic. There is, moreover, a particular way that the addition of "performance" further unsettled this already shaky definitional situation. When theatre and performance appeared in the professorial context, it was both a practice and an object that could be too easily characterized as the opposite of a modern academic field. Performance's status as both a practice and a liberal art also meant that it was not purely either one, neither a fully skill-based vocation nor a securely cultural object. As such, it has occupied an institutional chiasmus, perplexing the domain of cultural knowledge with a so-called technical pragmatism, perplexing the domain of technical knowledge with a so-called cultural imagination.

That ill fit has vexed many a professor of performance and resulted in a variety of defensive strategies.

Rather than defending against pejorative labels, however, I find it more intriguing to argue that performance has had a troubled life within the academy precisely because it makes the disavowals of a "professorial-managerial class" discomfortingly explicit. If the life of the mind already has an unsavory alliance with professionalism, even in its humanistic guise, then the study of performance makes those professional contingencies less easy to disavow. That institutional ambiguity provides an analytic opportunity. Tracking performance's ill fit within the academy can defamiliarize academic processes and reframe current thinking about the employment and mission of the arts and humanities. It is in the cultural/technical chiasmus that performance can be particularly productive, even if paradoxically it is because of that chiasmus that such an opportunity remains continually deferred.

In a recent essay entitled "Rude Mechanicals and the *Specters of Marx*" (2002), theatre theory scholar Alice Rayner meditates on the "rude mechanicals" necessary to produce the "actual artistic production of theatre" and intriguingly alights upon the cultural versus technical divide. Joining Jacques Derrida's own Artaudian-inspired disquisition on what they called the "theological stage" to Derrida's later attempt to come to terms with Marx's specters, Rayner finds in the domain of technical theatre a productive, self-different mechanism for institutional critique:

> The theological stage still requires the services of labor and defines its value as pragmatic. But it is also *merely* pragmatic, i.e., at a discount. Labor is excluded from participation in the guarantees of the word and in the idea except as service. . . . The exclusion of technical theatre, no matter how accidental, is inherited from the theological position that consigns the real labor of theatre to servitude. That inheritance has profound

effects, particularly in academic theatre. It plays out institutionally in the traditional hierarchies of academic practices in which the discourses of literary, critical, or historical researchers are of far greater economic value and intellectual capital than the manual labor that theatre requires. The valuation and cultural capital of the written word—known as publication—exposes the theological structure of both theatrical and educational institutions. (Rayner, 2002, p. 544)

Rayner's essay is sensitive to how the habitual devaluation of the technical in academic theatre is an accident that, in Foucaultian terms, continues to "exist and have value for us." Indeed, the cultural field of "literary, critical, and historical researchers" that humanities manifestos attempt to defend appears as the theologically dominant in this picture, sidelining technical labor with classically classist indifference.

I want to take Rayner's line of thought back through some earlier genealogies of performance in higher education. While I am inspired by her use of Jacques Derrida in "Rude Mechnicals," I will situate his work somewhat differently, for the paradox of using Derrida to conduct this analysis is that the institutional effects of Derrida's own philosophical contributions have often contributed to the forgetful devaluation of what stands in for the technical. Derrida's critique of presence, most prominently theorized in *Of Grammatology* (1967/1974), would greatly affect the terms under which performance scholars of various stripes could argue for the materiality of theatre. Indeed, while that materiality had been variously devalued before the 1960s, deconstruction's critique of metaphysics would give it a particular spin, couching appeals to the nontextual elements of performance as a naïve reification of presence. Sometimes performance appeared as orality, as in Derrida's critiques of Rousseau; sometimes it appeared as a theatrical artist's desire for the "closure of representation," as in his roundabout critiques of Artaud. In either, both, and subsequent cases, however, the appeal to performance as spoken and embodied too easily assumed a naïve representational structure, misrecognizing its material condition as pre-representational rather than as the epiphenomenon of representation (writing) that it really was.

I agree with the Derridean critique and also take a great deal of pleasure from it. Its thought structures have also supported many of the newer critical formations to which I referred in my introduction. Because performance scholars are interested in the mediating work of realms other than print, we can make the adaptation that he did not make in those arguments, mapping the pro-representational argument to the representational work of performance. Indeed, Rayner's own essay is one of many illuminating examples of an alternate use of his theories. This productivity and pleasure notwithstanding, there is also reason to be suspicious of the critique's effects, particularly in its vulgarized forms, particularly in their relation to the modernizing pedagogical structures of a print-based university. While Derrida's "writing" did not mean print, per se, its curricular manifestation most often turned up on a printed page, challenging conventions of close reading with the innovations of critique but not challenging close reading and publication as basic occupational practices.[7] To profess performance in a twenty-first century context is, in some way, about re-engaging nonwritten speech and nonprint corporeality and about believing that it is possible to do so without succumbing to metaphysical naiveté. However, the ubiquity of a Derridean thought structure in humanities gatherings often short-circuits the argument, making the attempt to grapple with performance look like a kind of throwback, as the regressive ponderings of irrepressibly literalist imagination. I would argue that this knee-jerk neutralization is not necessarily or purely intellectual, since a careful reading of Derrida does not automatically support this reaction, but is more specifically institutional, based upon a longer history of

professionalization of the humanities. In order to suggest what I mean, let me return to my opening comments on the older histories of performance in the academy in order develop a few concrete examples.

In their introduction to *The Origins of Literary Studies in America* (1989), editors Gerald Graff and Michael Warner described the emergence of literary studies as a discrete professional field by painting a picture of its earlier, less discrete, practitioners. In nineteenth century universities, Graff and Warner humorously describe the rhetoric-and-oratory professor as the type of person most often responsible for "introducing boys to the golden passages in Shakespeare and the poets." "To be a rhetoric-and-oratory professor," they continue, "one had only to know the classics, have a pretty way of talking, and what some at the time referred to as 'a general society-knowledge of literature'" (p. 4). In the history of literary studies, the rhetoric-and-oratory professor serves as a useful counterpoint, retroactively emerging as the denigrated "amateur" to the English professor's "professional." As such, he shadows the rest of their book, serving as a marker for disciplinary transformations such as a shift from a classical to vernacular curriculum as well as the consolidation of the fuzzy generalist who increasingly served as foil to the humanist specialist. Interestingly, to "have a pretty way of talking" is also an index of his generalized amateurism; it divides implicit delineations between a retroactively defined amateurism and the rigor and expertise of the Ehrenreichs' professional-managerial class. Elsewhere, the rhetoric-and-oratory professor appears as a "spellbinder," as a mystifying "belletrist," or as a "rearguard" spiritualist. With less and more self-consciousness, the pretty talker is framed historically and in the present as the opposite of everything that the humanist academic would become—the opposite, that is, of professional, rigorous, scholarly, rational, theoretical, disciplinary, modern. Indeed, in some institutions, the denigration or excision from the curriculum of speech, oral English, and theatre was fundamental to the intellectual redefinition and professional rise of the literary. Neither Graff nor Warner has much interest in unsettling the feminizing and primitivist associations attached to this spellbinder who "only" talked prettily to boys. Instead, the rhetoric-and-oratory professor functions as a source of amusement in the otherwise disputed origin narratives of literary studies.

It might be the Michael Warner of *Letters of the Republic* (1990) (rather than the Michael Warner who edited *Fear of a Queer Planet*, 1993) who decides not to see anything radical in this homosocial talking scene. And while I am not exactly committed to its celebration either, I am interested in the historical occlusions and institutional effects of personifying "belletrism" in the image of the performing professor. For one thing, this mystifying figure further mystifies and homogenizes a great deal of heterogeneity. Stories of Hiram Corson's spiritualist quests notwithstanding, for many teachers of rhetoric, oratory, and other of its compatriot fields in elocution, expression, argumentation, platform reading, and theatre, the how-to's and wherefores of oral performance were complex, varied, and debated; and they subscribed to a range of theoretical principles. Paul Edwards's (1999) and Margaret Robb's (1954) studies of early proponents demonstrate a range of philosophies and practices in the work of expression figures such as Samuel Curry, Charles Wesley Emerson, and Elizabeth Stebbins; meanwhile, early theatre proponents' (George Pierce Baker, Thomas Wood Stevens, Brander Matthews, Frederick Koch) constant arguments for the performance of drama had another kind of rationale for oral pedagogy. All of them attempted to make a claim for the academic professionalism of performance at a moment when performance had become a signal of a maligned antiprofessionalism within literary-humanism. The specter of an amateur, unrigorous, feminized belletrist's

dog and pony show thus deflated the professionalist hopes of professorial performance. From another angle, we can also see that it was institutionally efficient, though not necessarily philosophically consistent, to pin the professional hopes and symbolic claims of literary and humanistic studies onto something other than the inefficient, less reproducible form of oral performance pedagogy. John Guillory makes a similar point in his discussion of the deracinating effects of school culture on the production of literacy and cultural capital, where a modernizing university incorporated print objects of study and their concomitant practices of teaching:

> It is not a mere contingency that oral works must become "written" in order to be brought in the arena of curricular conflict as "noncanonical" works, excluded or devalued by the Western text tradition. In fact, oral work cannot otherwise enter the institutional field, since orality as cultural condition can only be studied at all ethnographically, as the "writing of culture." When the condition of oral production is on the other hand ignored in the context of interpreting or evaluating these works (by treating oral works as though they were other written works), the real difference between school culture and the culture which gives rise to works disappears from view. (Guillory, 1993, p. 43)

While the pedagogical practice of buying books, attending lecture, turning pages, and reading closely all are ways of eliciting the pleasures of the text, they also can be seen as part of an efficient infrastructure, a set of techniques that facilitates the incorporation of certain knowledges into the educational project of the modern university. The problem is that if education in the arts and humanities wants to make good on the idea of valuing multiple forms of intelligence, the effort will often require a more varied pedagogical infrastructure.

The issue of infrastructure brings to mind another type of institutional obstacle that inhibits engagement with performance. In addition to belletristic amateurism, the phenomena of performance have also been located historically in the domain of the technical and of the basic skill. To the extent that performance was aligned with art-making, its pedagogy had associations with the manual and the industrial. As such, it fell to the wrong side of what Guillory calls the "constitutive distinction between intellectual and manual labor" on which the classed history of the professoriate rests, a constitutive distinction that continues, however accidentally, to reinforce barriers between humanistic writing and artistic production. To the extent that performance was associated with oral argumentation and "public speaking," such pedagogy was an antecedent of the composition class, what is known variously as freshman or expository writing. As such, it has associations with what has been characterized as the least interesting type of teaching, as the opposite of a research field, and as something to which emerging graduate students in the humanities learn to turn up their noses. This kind of move, one made by professors of both right and left persuasions, exemplifies the class disavowals in the formation of the professorial-managerial class.

To show its history, consider an excerpt from an exchange between two rhetoric professors at Harvard in the late-nineteenth century, Barrett Wendell and George Pierce Baker. The former is a somewhat notorious figure in the history of literary studies, one who produced an eclectic body of scholarship in literary history but who was most famous for his book, *English Composition* (1918), a success that would have deleterious consequences for his professional life. The latter, whose later history in the formation of academic theatre is well known to theatre scholars, was a younger professor whose courses in oral argumentation were receiving congratulatory boosts of support from both President Charles Eliot and the Harvard Corporation, helpful as such courses were in supporting the preprofessional curricula of undergraduate careers in law and business. While Baker's applied humanities teaching addressed the perceived needs of what John and Barbara Ehrenreich would recognize as an early professional-managerial class, Barrett Wendell was already jadedly suspicious of whether such teaching addressed the career needs of the teacher, that is, of whether they advanced a member of the professorial-managerial class. Wendell advised Baker to learn from his own abjected example:

> As the writer of *English Composition*, I believe myself to be commonly grouped with elocutionists rather than with scholars. Kittredge's reviews, and Monty's *Specimens,* meanwhile—to say nothing of Child's *Ballads*—have forced respectful recognition not only for them but for their subjects from scholars of the widest rarity and range. You see my conclusion. I honestly believe that in maintaining prescribed argumentation you are unwittingly crucifying yourself. Martyrdom is normally admirable; but is the faith in this case worth martyrdom? (Wendell, 1899)

A picture of Barrett Wendell's self-crucifixion as Harvard's composition instructor actually appears in Warner and Graff's collection, inside William Lyon Phelps's memory of Wendell's office where stacks of student compositions lay on every available surface. When Wendell wanted to rest from the Sisyphean task of grading, he reportedly used a pile of student essays for a pillow. "It seemed to me," Phelps remembered, "that this work was not University work at all, and that any primary school ma'am would probably have been more efficient in the correcting job" (Graff & Warner, 1989, p. 160), testifying to what James Berlin (1987) identifies as the tendency of college professors to define technical and skill-based training as something other than our own responsibility. Composition may be a necessary skill to support and serve humanistic critique but, by virtue of being technical, it is not a valued subject of humanist pedagogy. That this siphoning off of responsibility had a gendered dimension is apparent in Phelps's invocation of the "school ma'am." That this gendering could also be wrapped up in the delegitimated domain of oral performance is apparent in Wendell's invocation of the "elocutionist," the increasingly feminized figure who, as Elizabeth Bell (1993) has argued, would become the convenient foil for just about any humanist, literary, or rhetorical attempt to define its own professional credentialization. As performance teachers continued to enmesh themselves in the workaday domain of technique—whether as the teacher of speech and elocution or as the teacher of acting and voice—they immersed themselves in a pedagogy that signaled antiprofessionalism to many a humanities professor.

BACK TO THE FUTURE

I want to pause for reflection now, for I am not arguing for a collective de-skilling to embrace belletrism, technicality, or talking prettily. I am, however, interested in pointing up an institutional legacy that has persistent discursive effects. More recent attempts to take the phenomena of performance seriously, variously, as object of study, as method of understanding, and as mode of analysis inevitably encounter these institutional genealogies. The specter of the fuzzy belletrist, the dunderheaded technicist, and—more recently—the naïve metaphysicist linger in a humanist imaginary and can be quite easily invoked to end experimentation in performance study. It is the persistence of the stereotype of the rude mechanical and his gendered or amateur compatriots that can interfere with the attempt to follow through on the optimistic hopes for a meeting between the arts and the humanities. Indeed, whatever the pleasures of a critique of presence, whatever its formative intellectual contribution, it is also a discursive formation that interacted with and still interacts with an

institutional context that is much less supple. I know that I am not the first to notice that deconstruction's critique of presence has rationalized the largely decontextualized practices of close reading in new form, one that also lent itself well to the efficient syllabification and grand lecturing of a modernizing university. Additionally, deconstructionist knowledge, whatever its innovations in understanding relationality or the social assumptions behind social policy, also participated in an occupational context that needed academic requirements for gauging rigor in humanist expertise. Even when humanists have been loathe to call literary, critical, or historical research "specialized skills," the fruits of critical labor can circulate in a way that satisfies the "only a few can do it" pretensions of a professorial-managerial class. This is what is often missing from humanist manifestos, a way of considering how the critical paradigms of humanist inquiry can also be used to come to terms with the professional politics of humanist inquiry.

If there is a technical, expert-driven, preprofessional dimension to humanist knowledge, there are particular ways that the incorporation of performance threatens to expose this oft-disavowed component of the liberal arts. However, we can also say that the opposite is true, that performance's association with the realm of the cultural—whether conceived morally as cultural capital, politically as cultural studies, or philosophically as critique—is also a force that more explicitly technical and professional fields must face. This is the other side of the institutional chiasmus, the reversed mirror that refracts within and outside the genealogies of performance studies. If performance is the technical supplement to cultural knowledge production, it is also the cultural supplement to technical knowledge production. While critiques of the professorial-managerial class tend to position all capacities and practices as reiterating enactments of a capitalist economy, the space of the cultural is also a domain—however partial, unsystematic, and imbricated—that tries to enable an alternate way of imagining human enactment. A number of curricular objects and objectives ride on the impulse to perpetuate such a space. Schools of the humanities rely upon it; departments such as literature and philosophy rely upon it; research fields such as performance history rely upon it. Whether one defines that imagining in philosophical, political, artistic, or ethical terms, its resilience is testament to the importance of understanding both its promise and its limiting conditions.

The paradigm of performance might be most promising for the way that it can perpetuate a cultural space that does not automatically position the technical as a symbol of philistine encroachment. Performers—and art-makers more generally—have to resist such limiting characterizations of the technical largely because they know that they cannot do without the service of the technical itself. When art-makers accept the necessity of a technical apparatus, they implicitly endorse a fuller and more varied representation of its material function; art-making means understanding that the technical might also, like the humanities, be a many-splendored thing. In departments devoted to performance pedagogy—whether in oral rhetoric, theatre, performance art, or dance—the question (and consistent bureaucratic headache) has always revolved around whether the promise of a sustained imagination can find a self-reflexive way of engaging domains of infrastructural labor to which humanists have been quick to oppose themselves. Consequently, a changed institutional relationship between the humanities and performance—and between the humanities and the arts more generally—will require an interrogation rather than a reproduction of the opposition between the technical and the cultural, between basic skills and the liberal arts. Rather than using definitions of humanist value to prop up a defense against vocational invasion, the "coterminous and codependent"

relationship between the arts and humanities will require experimentation in what it means to use the technical humanistically. It will mean avowing the infrastructural labor that constitutes humanist knowledge in order to refashion that infrastructure more creatively and more critically.

If this is one thing, if not the only thing, that performance theory has to offer to a modern research university, it is also one that might bring us closer to acting on Davidson and Goldberg's sense of what the arts and the humanities have to learn from each other. Indeed, their longer characterization of what it means for creativity to count in the humanities gestures to the differences that are both stumbling blocks and opportunities:

> The very highest standard of collaboration, for example, is what dance troupes, actors, and musicians do as a matter of course: combine an array of individual talents into a whole. . . . By insisting on the interconnections among our endeavors, and by acknowledging that those trained in expressive cultural forms may be better communicators of certain messages than humanists, we can shape intellectual projects that widen the scope, audience, and importance of our intertwined endeavors. (Davidson & Goldberg, 2004, p. B7)

Incarnating this vision requires a taste for cultivating a humbling, sometimes utopian, always workaday space for testing, re-skilling, and incorporating many talents and techniques. Of course, the highest form of collaboration that performing artists do as a matter of course has not historically honored their multiple forms of intelligence. Moreover, the theological practice of evaluating the individuated publication of humanities professionals has not often positioned collaboration very high on its professional barometer. If, as Davidson and Goldberg also suggest, humanists are trying "to stop talking around the issue of the single-author monograph as the benchmark for excellence" (2004, ¶ 25), then they might be interested in talking to those whose work has historically fallen outside those standards of evaluation for quite some time. Meanwhile, artists might want to seek out humanists whose interests in collaboration could propel a larger institutional reflection. This is another place where a pragmatic insight into the academic humanities can be brought round to help us understand what it means institutionally to link the humanities and the arts.

For me, the appeal to actual artistic production is in fact less interestingly understood as an appeal to a metaphysics of presence. However, it is interestingly, if disconcertingly, understood as a valuing of different representational practices, even forms of intelligence that may initially seem technical to humanist eyes. Widening the scope of our intertwined endeavors means understanding that some critical practices do not always take shape within the professionally imaginative conventions of critique. A general acceptance of this possibility does not always go far enough to question the technical and cultural division that underlies our professional habits. That division hangs in the air in many domains of the academy. It underwrites exchanges in faculty meetings, in curricular planning, in cross-campus committees, in campus art agencies, and in the meetings of scholarly bodies. It is broached and deflected at the communication conferences, every time a black-turtlenecked cultural studies scholar and black-suited public speaking professor sit near each other at the conference's hotel bar. In the registration line of academic theatre conferences, blazered scholars stand behind acting teachers who are "ready-to-move" in their loose-fitting clothes. Occasionally one of those scholars carries a plastic bag with a change of clothes for a late afternoon workshop; occasionally a sweatshirted studio teacher can be seen in the scholars' auditorium, listening near the EXIT sign with back against the wall, surreptitiously stretching his calves. At the current moment, the ambiguities of these concurrent genealogies elicit a great deal of confusion and

prompt debates where tables are continually turned. Upon reflection, it turns out that no domain can be said to be purely preprofessional or purely cultural, purely technical or purely liberal in its approach to the arts. Preprofessionalism has many faces, making it necessary to see a similarity if not an equivalence among the acting instructor, the public speaking teacher, and the humanities professor, each of whom renews respective professional memberships. The space of the cultural is also similarly hybrid, something made more explicit by tracking the contradictory life that performance study has had inside its gendered and classed discourses of legitimation.

In university contexts that are working to imagine new knowledges and new pedagogies, whether in programs that locate themselves in theatre, performance studies, dance, or other wings of the liberal arts, I think that it is important to analyze this discontinuity. Current efforts may find themselves reinventing older wheels and, in the process, fending off familiar pejorative attributions—literal, mechanical, hysterical, preprofessional, technical, spiritual, amateur, feminine, ornamental, drill-like, artificial, theatrical, belletrist, vocational. Rather than seeing any of these terms as referential, it might be worth asking how this noncoincident series of adjectives functions and what anxieties are addressed by such a contradictory discourse of delegitimation. I think that it is particularly important lest our own defensive counter-response to a variety of antitheatrical, antiprofessional, antitechnical, antihumanities prejudices replicate rather than critique their contradictions. Doing so, however, might mean admitting to some of the contradictions in our own professional lives. Without denying the fact that an appeal to the pragmatic and the technical has a legitimating force in the academy, performance's suspect status in the domain of the humanities can have an effect on our own claims and aspirations as performance scholars. In particular, it can cause us to replicate the blind spots and class disavowals of a professorial-managerial class rather than to use the equivocal status of performance as a tool to expose the fundamentally equivocal ground on which professorial self-definition rests. The result, I have found, is not necessarily one that will righteously justify each one of my or your occupational choices; nor will it confirm our predetermined sense of who the good guys are and who the bad guys are in our departments, universities, or larger scholarly bodies. Indeed, I had to give up hoping for such personal and professional ratification from this project long ago. It might, however, give a more complicated picture to fellow scholars and graduate students of what we are defending and of why we are being defensive. The recognition of such a heterogeneous disciplinary history might also allow us to imagine a future in which the collection of divided positions within theatre and performance study can be seen as a symptom of larger paradoxes in higher education and, therefore, as a tool in a larger project of professorial redefinition.

NOTES

1. Joseph Roach's *Cities of the Dead* (1996) was one of the most provocative instances of this reorientation.

2. For commentary on these and other disciplinary trajectories, see Jill Dolan (2001), *Geographies of Learning: Theory and Practice, Activism and Performance*; Peggy Phelan (1998), "Introduction: The Ends of Performance," in J. Lane & P. Phelan (Eds.), *The Ends of Performance* (pp. 1–19); and Richard Schechner (2002), "What Is Performance Studies?" in R. Schechner (Ed.), *Performance Studies: An Introduction* (pp. 1–21).

3. See Christopher Stray (1998), *Classics Transformed: Schools, Universities, and Society in England, 1830–1960*; for an example of contemporary histories of speech education, see Karl Richards Wallace (1954), *The History of Speech Education in America*.

4. For accounts of early theatre departments, see Shannon Jackson (2004), "Institutions and Performance: Professing Performance in the Early Twentieth Century," in *Professing Performance: Theatre in the Academy from Philology to*

Performativity (pp. 40–78); Wisner Payne Kinne (1954), *George Pierce Baker and the American Theatre*; and Walter Spearman (1970), *The Carolina Playmakers: The First Fifty Years*.

5. For a study of the twentieth century history of visual art practice in higher education, see Howard Singerman (1999), *Art Subjects: Making Artists in the American University*.

6. This section reworks and revises examples that appeared in Chapters 2 and 4 of Shannon Jackson (2004), *Professing Performance*: "Institutions and performance: Professing performance in the early twentieth century," and "Practice and Performance: Modernist Paradoxes and Literalist Legacies" (pp. 40–78, 109–145).

7. Sue-Ellen Case is particularly interested in pursuing this issue in *The Domain-Matrix: Performing Lesbian at the End of Print Culture* (1996).

REFERENCES

Bell, E. (1993). Performance studies as women's work. *Text and Performance Quarterly, 13,* 362.

Berlin, J. (1987). *Rhetoric and reality: Writing instruction in American colleges, 1900–1985.* Carbondale: Southern Illinois University Press.

Bérubé, M. (1998). *The employment of English: Theory, jobs, and the future of literary studies.* New York: New York University Press.

Case, S.-E. (1996). *The domain-matrix: Performing lesbian at the end of print culture.* Bloomington: Indiana University Press.

Davidson, C. N., & Goldberg, D. T. (2004). A manifesto for the humanities in a technological age. *Chronicle of Higher Education, 50*(23), B7. Retrieved June 24, 2004, from http://chronicle.com/free/v50/i23/23b00701.htm

Derrida, J. (1974). Nature, culture, writing. In *Of grammatology* (G. C. Spivak, Trans.) (pp. 96–164). Baltimore: Johns Hopkins University Press. (Original work published 1967)

Dolan, J. (2001). *Geographies of learning: Theory and practice, activism and performance.* Middletown, CT: Wesleyan University Press.

Edwards, P. (1999). Unstoried: Teaching literature in the age of performance studies. *Theatre Annual, 52,* 1–147.

Ehrenreich, B., & Ehrenreich, J. (1979). The professional-managerial class. In P. Walker (Ed.), *Between labor and capital* (pp. 5–49). Boston: South End Press.

Foucault, M. (1972). *The archaeology of knowledge; and, the discourse on language* (A. M.

Sheridan, Trans.). New York: Pantheon Books. (Original work published 1969)

Foucault, M. (1980). *Language, counter-memory, practice: Selected essays and interviews* (D. F. Bouchard & S. Simon, Trans.; D. F. Bouchard, Ed.). Ithaca, NY: Cornell University Press. (Original work published 1977)

Gilman, S. (2000). *The fortunes of the humanities: Thoughts for after the year 2000.* Palo Alto, CA: Stanford University Press.

Graff, G. (1987). *Professing literature: An institutional history.* Chicago: University of Chicago Press.

Graff, G. (1992). *Beyond the culture wars: How teaching the conflicts can revitalize American education.* New York: W. W. Norton.

Graff, G., & Warner, M. (Eds.). (1989). *The origins of literary studies in America: A documentary anthology.* London: Routledge.

Guillory, J. (1993). *Cultural capital: The problem of literary canon formation.* Chicago: University of Chicago Press.

Jackson, S. (2004). *Professing performance: Theatre in the academy from philology to performativity.* England: Cambridge University Press.

Kinne, W. P. (1954). *George Pierce Baker and the American theatre.* Cambridge, MA: Harvard University Press.

Ohmann, R. (1976). *English in America: A radical view of the profession.* England: Oxford University Press.

Phelan, P. (1998). Introduction: The ends of performance. In J. Lane & P. Phelan (Eds.), *The ends of performance* (pp. 1–19). New York: New York University Press.

Rayner, A. (2002, December). Rude mechanicals and the "Specters of Marx." *Theatre Journal, 54*(4), 535–554.

Readings, B. (1996). *The university in ruins.* Cambridge, MA: Harvard University Press.

Roach, J. (1996). *Cities of the dead: Circum-Atlantic performance.* New York: Columbia University Press.

Robb, M. (1954). The elocutionary movement and its chief figures. In K. R. Wallace (Ed.), *History of speech education in America* (pp. 178–201). New York: Appleton-Century-Crofts.

Schechner, R. (2002). What is performance studies? In R. Schechner (Ed.), *Performance studies: An introduction* (pp. 1–21). London: Routledge.

Singerman, H. (1999). *Art subjects: Making artists in the American university.* Berkeley, CA: University of California Press.

Spearman, W. (1970). *The Carolina Playmakers: The first fifty years.* Chapel Hill: University of North Carolina Press.

Stray, C. (1998). *Classics transformed: Schools, universities, and society in England, 1830–1960.* England: Oxford University Press.

Wallace, K. R. (1954). *The history of speech education in America.* New York: Appleton-Century-Crofts.

Warner, M. (1990). *The letters of the Republic: Publication and the public sphere in eighteenth-century America.* Cambridge, MA: Harvard University Press.

Warner, M. (Ed.). (1993). *Fear of a queer planet: Queer politics and social theory.* Minneapolis: University of Minnesota Press.

Wendell, B. (1899, February 11). Letter to George Pierce Baker. In the papers of George Pierce Baker, Harvard Theatre Collection, Pusey Library, Harvard University, Cambridge, MA.

Wendell, B. (1918). *English composition.* New York: Scribner.

6

Memory, Remembering, and Histories of Change

A Performance Praxis

DELLA POLLOCK

The feminist philosopher, Julia Kristeva, recently declared that, "faced with the invasion of the spectacle, we can still contemplate the rebellious potentialities that the imaginary might resuscitate in our innermost depths. It is not a time of great works, or perhaps, for us, contemporaries, they remain invisible. Nevertheless," she argues, "by keeping our intimacy in revolt we can preserve the possibility of their appearance" (1997/2002, p. 13). Referring primarily to the intimacies of psychoanalysis, Kristeva articulates a praxis of mundane transference and disclosure that goes well beyond claims for compassion and unproblematized "empathy."[1] What she calls the "invasion of the spectacle" describes in many ways the introversion of the extroversion Guy Debord found in the rise of capital. The essential movement of the spectacle, for Debord, "consists of taking up all that existed in human activity *in a fluid state* so as to possess it in a congealed state as things which become the exclusive value by their *formulation in negative* of lived value" (1977/1983, entry 35). The society of the spectacle Debord describes is one in which appearance subsumes lived relation:

> The world at once present and absent which the spectacle makes visible is the world of the commodity dominating all that is lived. The world of the commodity is thus shown for what it is, because its movement is identical to the estrangement of men among themselves and in relation to their global product. (entry 37)

Capital, once the operative secret of the ideological machine, now becomes mirrored in the extent of goods produced: "Capital is no longer the invisible center which directs the mode of production; its accumulation spreads it all the way to the periphery in the form of tangible objects. The entire expanse of society is its portrait" (entry 50).

For Kristeva, this expansionism is also an "invasion." The consolidation of production and its products as "spectacle" turns inward on the subject, surrogating the self-*seen* for the *scene* of subjective interaction. Accordingly, sustained and deliberate intimacy may be a nascent form of revolt. At this juncture of psychoanalysis and social theory is the counteractive movement of *lived relation* and the vitality of a collective imaginary that may turn spectacle inside out into visionary possibilities and the "rebellious potentialities" of "great works."

In this essay, I will address a critical performance practice that links the work of preservation and imagination in order to "preserve the possibility" of great acts through what Kristeva considers the revolutionary work of intimacy. This evolving praxis entails paring down the exchange of memory to the unsteady contingencies and risks of mutual remembering. It in turn suggests the power to intervene on Debord's "society of the spectacle" through the resurgent, lived value of public re-remembering.

I will focus on two aspects:[2] first, one version of historical intimacy I have come to call "listening out loud," and, second, its manifestation in a recent public event, "Desegregation and the 'Inner Life' of High Schools," which in many ways took spectacular claims for integration as its nemesis. The event did not so much question or critique pervasive, sedimented conclusions about the achievement of integration or even the lack thereof but mobilized a rough concord about work yet to be done. Through its modest but hard-won intimacies, it preserved the possibility of a critical and hopeful racial politics covered over by triumphalist (or declensional) accounts of *Brown v. Board of Education*.[3]

Integration is a good story. It embeds a vision of radical breach and redress into a narrative hardened by repetition into fact and the "past." A story of change may thus become a history hardened against change. In general, and in the particular instance of the desegregation performance project, "listening out loud" interrupted the spectacular condensation of story and history, drawing on oral history exchange to dissolve even liberal pride into a pool of (re)new(ed) rememberings.

Oral histories draw (historical) fact and (storied) symbol into the precarious, cocreative process of memory-making. Doing oral history involves staging a conversation in the relatively artificial context of the interview.[4] It engages its participants in a heightened, reflexive encounter with each other and with the past, even as each participant and the past seem to be called into being and becoming by an as-yet unknown future. The interviewer is herself a symbolic presence, invoking not only other, unseen audiences but promising—as if by bodily contract alone—that what is heard will be incorporated into public memory and acted on in some way, that it will make a difference. Oral histories thus write the past into the present on the promise of an as yet unimagined, even unimaginable future. They *dream* the past—performing *what happened* as an image of *what might happen*. Entwining *what is* with the normative claims of *what might be*, oral histories tell the past in order to tell the future—not to predict, to reveal, or to foreclose on it but to catch it in ethical threads drawn in the act of telling.

It was with this performative vision of oral history in mind that, in the spring of 2001, I embarked on a collaborative project with my colleague in the Department of History at the University of North Carolina at Chapel Hill and the director of the Southern Oral History Program there, Jacquelyn Dowd Hall, a project that we came to call "Desegregation and the 'Inner Life' of High Schools." The project involved coordinating our respective courses on oral history, and oral history and performance, around issues of desegregation in Chapel Hill and the southeastern region more generally. It culminated in an afternoon of performances and presentations that retold the substance of student interviews to a gathered audience of approximately one hundred friends, interview participants, invited guests, interested local residents, scholars, and family members.

The event drew into tight focus the open, uneasy correlation between two social and aesthetic *goods*—integration and identification. While desegregation may be described as the restructuring of major institutions for formal equity, integration suggests a more personal, often unquestioned commitment to *knowing the other as one's self* on the logic that: if I become you, I know you as me, and social differentiation—and the hierarchies tenuously balanced upon it—collapse into "color-blind" sameness. Integration as or by identification recommends the assimilation of the raced "you"/other to the unraced "I"/one—or, at best, I to you, ignoring altogether the limits of "becoming" an-other in the name of eliminating strangeness and estrangement. What we discovered, among so many other things, was that intimate strangeness might be a lived value that could answer to estrangement even insofar as it dramatized the limits of representation. In the end, we achieved what one student called a "fantastic failure": while the temptation was to believe that we could create integration-as-identification-by-imitation (or mimetic representation), it quickly became clear that this was no more possible than it was desirable. In the end, all and everything we could offer was the ashen glow of broken and breaking memories fanned into the fire of creative possibility by the rough intimacies of student interviews and reperformance.

I stumbled onto the process I am calling "listening out loud" over a dozen years ago as part of developing a regional performance tour based on interviews with workers in the textile industry.[5] On the face of it: a simple exercise, listening out loud takes up Trinh Minh-ha's eloquent charge: "To listen carefully is to preserve. But to preserve is to burn, for understanding means creating" (1989, p. 121). Begun in the spirit of preservation that drives much oral history practice—the desire to save stories from both political obscurity and the ravages of mortality, listening out loud sets fire to the thing saved: through the course of conversational interviews, improvised retellings, scenic description, poetic transcription, and public rehearsal, the story as a historical artifact goes up in the flames of committed understanding, becoming the molten energy of re-creation. The stories the students tell in the end are not verbatim. They resemble the first-told versions only or, perhaps, at their best, in their evocation of the "innermost depths" of the storyteller. They reflect as much on the transformative process of listening, telling, and retelling as on what is told. And in the case of the desegregation project: they burned—through distrust and sentimentality—into something like the heart of possibility.

The practice begins with an informal interview, a conversation that focuses primarily on one person and then the other. This conversation may occur over the course of several meetings and days, or in two short periods during a long class session. When I initiate this process, students typically start scrambling for paper and pens and wondering where they can obtain a tape recorder. Assumptions about what composes an interview kick in. Clearly the first assumption is that it involves a recording device of some kind. I tell them they can use only the technology of the ear. That they must listen body to body, heart to heart, not so much recording as absorbing the other person's story. I then generally talk with them some about what it means to *listen hard* and to learn something *by heart*.

The room is suddenly stuffy. The students are nervous. We all shift and fidget. I have taken something away from people I hardly know. Something that is clearly important to them. I stay my course. We talk about their confusion and anxieties. I suggest that the interview conventions they had expected to use might have kept things somewhat cooler; I encourage them to explore—and to use—the rising heat.

Simultaneously invoking and refusing assumptions cultivated by the spectacularity of TV talk shows and conventional social survey techniques generates a performative framework for what is often, then, a supercharged interaction. Challenging some of the residually positivist critique of oral history method, this exercise initiates a subjectivist approach that requires something as yet unnameably *more* of the participants as human beings in intimate, temporal-historical relation, one to the other. I indicate that this is an exercise, an experiment, a first trial, a *try out*, an audition, an auditory experience; you will be *audience* to each other, I tell them, easing a quick slide from the experimental controls and gridlike patterning of some social science to the confusion and chaos of embodiment.

I then ask them to tell each other's story (the story each heard) *in one to two minutes, in the first person*—using "I" but not using names, substituting "This is what I heard:" for the usual "Hi. My name is. . . ." (The room soon echoes with rounds of "*This is what I heard:*" "*This is what I heard:*").

Keen to impersonation as a form of comedy and caricature, the students are immediately leery of exaggerating superficial qualities or details. Their astuteness on this point seems to be enhanced by a sudden, reflexive awareness that they don't want anyone to impersonate *them*. They start looking around the room to see who will *see* them, or is it: who *won't* see them: who will be party to someone else's mis/representation of them? If they weren't already, they are now beginning to feel really out of (representational) control.

I have to say that I don't try to ease as much as to condition this anxiety by, first of all, encouraging them to think of the "return" performances as an extension of the primary act

of *listening hard* and as a variation on the kind of secondhand storytelling that we do everyday, incorporating others' memories into the body of our own and then again into others' through public reperformance.[6]

I also exhort them to work from below appearances. I point them away from both the external features of the performer and their correlate in the surface text—or what could be called the word-score of the performance each received—toward resounding images; patterns of emphasis, hesitation, and silence; qualities of voice and interaction. This is usually enough to shift them out of a kind of deer-caught-in-the-headlights defensiveness into active curiosity. It suggests *a more literary than journalistic interest*, affirms *the listener's role in making meaning*, unburdens the entire project of the kind of text-centrism that favors the text-*artifact* to the relational *art* of telling, and introduces the pleasures of *mutually attentive improvisation*.[7]

Finally, I suggest that their concerns already signify readiness to *get it right*. I can't tell you how often students express their resistance to this process as fear about not "getting it right" and desire to "get it right," their perfectly justified concerns about what might happen to their stories in performance leading them immediately to *get* the ethical issues at the heart of oral history practice—including the impossibility of ever representing another person exactly and the problem of obscuring or patronizing someone else's story by presuming to speak *for* him or her—and so, at least in part: *already* getting it right.

What's "right" in this case is not the kind of empathic identification that is often taken to be a self-evident good in performance and communication studies. Empathy is a good thing. But it is not always the right good thing.

I was consulting with a colleague recently about the possibility of developing a prison writing workshop into a performance. She shared with me some of the remarkably accomplished poems and stories from the workshop. I asked her how she felt about the participants possibly performing each other's work. "No!," she balked. Each should do her own, in her own voice. To some extent, I expected this response. It is a ready claim on voice and narrative as private property that has gained momentum from feminist claims on owning one's voice and that gains a political valence in the context of all other rights denied. I was sympathetic and yet suspicious of the reiterations of (capital) ownership and its implications for, at best, rugged individualism. Despite my colleague's good intentions and the vast body of feminist theory that supported them, I couldn't help but feel that the politics of her quick "No!" reflected more than it resisted the invasion of the spectacle, recreating the story as commodity, and paradoxically, even perversely risking further estrangement.

I offered the listening out loud practice as a rough model for another way of looking at things. When I briefly described performances the students gave in return for each other's accounts, "Oh!" she said, "total empathy!"

I agreed at the time, pleased to think that my short take on narrative exchange had jostled the commonsense stability of the private property model. My colleague quickly identified the difference between a performance that was about separate people telling their separate lives and one that was about what could happen *between* people in that process. The image of "total empathy" carried a utopian vision of alliance and understanding across difference. It suggested qualities of warmth, trust, and solidarity from which the incarcerated women with whom she was working were personally and institutionally guarded. And yet I had to back off from both "total" and "empathy."

There is nothing complete about the kinds of identification that occur in the return performances. Nothing "total." In fact, it seems that it is the incompleteness and sometimes raw partiality of these performances that

makes them both particularly unnerving and exhilarating. Empathy is clearly a principal dynamic here, but it would be a mistake to overemphasize its value, especially at the expense of countervailing dynamics—dynamics that emphasize social difference without reverting to individualism. While I recognize the political power of identification, through the next few examples I want to consider the performative force of *disidentification* along two main axes: *differentiation*, or the delineation of identity boundaries, and *misrecognition*, or the dialectics of identity play and replay. These dynamics work, I would argue, precisely because they *work against* the grain of empathy.[8] In so doing, they distinguish performance from spectacularity in Debord's sense. They keep historical intimacies from being taken up "in a congealed state as things which become the exclusive value by their *formulation in negative* of lived value" by keeping them unstable, ongoing, difficult, highly reflexive (down to the most minute detail), and often very messy.

Differentiation may be most evident in the Brechtian sense of the *Verfremdungseffekt* (roughly, "alienation effect") of the familiar becoming strange, here, however, tuned to the strangeness of sudden familiarity.

A female student recounts—play by careful play—the details of her male interview partner's crowning, high school football game: "I received . . . and then I ran . . . he tried to intercept but I . . ." Everyone laughs with her, gently, recognizing what she clearly knows: that she is not the "I" of whom she speaks. And yet laughter turns to something like awe at the fact that she doesn't miss a beat. With almost no time to prepare, she moves through the long, measured sequence with perfect regard for its integrity and for the meaningfulness of each, apparently slight detail left in her reverberant care. She is like someone trying to speak with due courtesy in her foreign host's tongue.

Another student starts only to find herself suddenly weeping through her friend's account of moving from India to the United States. She didn't know, she says later, she didn't know. The friend trails tears too, her back straight, gazing in silent repose into the eyes of people listening to her although she isn't speaking and, indeed, doesn't have to. Her eyes well with a sense of vindication and recognition; her friend and teller's with sorrow, indignation, surprise, and some dismay. She feels *for*, *with*, *on behalf of*, and *in response to* her friend. This isn't a mimesis of feeling in the sense of a direct copy. The performer isn't feeling—and doesn't pretend to feel—what her friend felt. But the friend's—or first performer's—feelings are doubled, and doubled again—one body to another, and past to present. Both the primary teller and the listener/teller are moved in corresponding but markedly different ways. Both weep now with the power—and grandeur—of bringing the depths of their private encounter into the light of public regard. Both also weep with the genuine pain of becoming isolated in their relationship, of being separated in strangeness: of entering *unknowing*, suddenly *not knowing* what they thought they knew or presumed too well to know: each other.

Misrecognition may mean seeing one's self in a kind of funhouse mirror—with painful clarity and/or pleasurable curiosity:

One student, after hearing his proxy teller faithfully report that "my father left me" at an early age, noted that, in all the years he'd told this story, he'd never used the phrase "left me." We all winced. A violation. A repositioning of the teller as a pathetic victim. The performer apologized, stricken with guilt. No, no, the initial teller responded, to our visible discomfort. This will forever change how I think about my story. We thought he was joking. No, no, he insisted more adamantly, indicating that he neither now saw himself as the distorted image of the abandoned kid, as if the performer's version were the correct one, as if the performer knew better than he who he really was; nor was he bitterly distancing himself

from someone who had been "left." Rather, for the first time, he gave himself permission to think about why he never used this phrase, about how much cultural baggage this conventional locution carried, and how he had alternatively constructed his sense of himself in story. He ended up happily *in between* the story he told and the story he heard, in a place of heightened *reflexivity* and *re-creativity*: pivoting on a phrase, having heard himself remade in another's image, he began to *wonder* about himself and his story, and felt encouraged to rethink/remake both.

Another student responded to hearing herself mirrored in an account of a broken family, alcoholism, and abuse with some consternation: "That was so depressing! I'm a cheerful person!" Coming back hard on her listener-teller's litany of facts, she nonetheless felt confounded by the bleakness of the facts as such, and the extent to which they neglected or obscured her sense of herself as "cheerful." She resisted the apparent elision of the facts of her life and her attitude toward them, finding a difference there that she wanted to hang on to—and yet that continued to hang in the air, despite her protestations: a figure of shifting and contested perspectives. She wanted her story back. We wanted to give it to her—but there was no going back exactly. Her history as story had become irretrievably part of collective rehearsal.

In both of these instances, misrecognition involved an element of *recognition*: I never use that phrase; that was so depressing!—and *refusal*: in response, each student basically said: that's not me. But neither made simply regressive claims on their "original" stories. Neither said *he or she got it wrong; here's what I said.* . . . Both, rather, found themselves in the peculiar place of being critically distanced from the "me" they initially represented and from the "not me" they saw represented by their partners. Each was left to work through the performative dialectics of what Richard Schechner, combining insights from the psychoanalytic work of D. W. Winnicott and ritual studies by Arnold Van Gennep, Gregory Bateson, and Victor Turner, has called the "not not me"—the self who is no more originally defined than he or she is lost in mimetic replay.[9] Beyond the opposition of "me" and "not me" is the possibility of a self turning in a tender spiral outward into remaking. Rather than a foundational reality, "me" becomes the playful figure of a double negative: "not not." We'd normally say that the second negative cancels out the first, returning us to the positive "me." Within the performative grammar of this exercise, however, the "I" is displaced into a reflexive object—"me" twice-removed: That's not me! . . . but it's also *not* not-me!

This student, moreover, might as well have been saying: That's not right or that's *not not-right*, morphing as she did everyone's initial fears about getting it right or wrong into points of collective inquiry—what happened in the transfer from the initial teller to the listener-teller to us? What discursive constraints or imperatives led her listener to convey a more "depressed" or self-pitying tone than she either thought she conveyed or performed in the first place? Is one version more "right" than another? On what basis would we make that call? Accordingly, what's "right" begins to shift tectonically from a figure of either validity (a measure of accuracy: he got the facts "right" after all) or ownership (as in: who has rights to this story?) to a figure of value. The question becomes: what *good* is lost or gained in the triangulation of this story between teller, listener/teller, and secondary listeners, of whom the first teller is now one? Matters of textual fidelity and property rights melted into ethical intimacy; and the smaller, the more intimate the practice of ethical engagement the students pursued, the more passionate the public inquiry that ensued.

There is an element of unrequited love in this practice—a desire for total empathy or perfect mirroring that can never be and maybe should never be fully realized, and yet that propels the exchange forward. The distances provoked by disidentification help to shift the I/you, self/other relationship with which the participants typically begin into a tentative I/thou ethic of respect and appreciation. In turn, the performative relay sets up a play of ideal selves, linking personal investments in being seen and being seen well to desires to see and represent each other as well as possible, resulting in what I can only call consistently and remarkably dignified performances. The strange imbalances and asymmetries of this exchange seem to increase its affective weight, suggesting why one student described the experience in this way: "*I feel what she's feeling so much more . . . and so remember it more.*" It may also be why these stories seem to lodge themselves so fully in collective memory, becoming points of ongoing reference and return, creating *more* yet—more stories, more reflection, more—and more intense—disidentification, more sensuous, embodied responsiveness.[10]

The practice seems to yield at least this hard lesson: a story is not a story until it is told; it is not told until it is heard; once it is heard, it changes—and becomes open to the beauties and frailties of *more* change; or: *a story is not a story until it changes*. Indeed, until *it* changes or until it changes *someone else*,[11] until it becomes part of the vital histories of change it recounts. Finally, then, for now: the practice defies the color-blind fantasy of integration as identification or knowing the other as one's self. In this practice, the "I" who becomes "you" who is "not-not-me" trembles at the shimmering horizon of all that "I" don't know about "you"; the "I" I become in telling your story is one *who doesn't and can't possibly— in any kind of full or total sense—know you*, who learns the limits of representation—and begins to enjoy and to remember the selves that emerge within those limits nonetheless or maybe "*so much more.*"

The desegregation project would elaborate the minimalist "listening out loud" practice into minimalist reperformance by listening, telling, relistening, and retelling again, preserving the stories told in the heat of cocreative understanding. Begun with great enthusiasm, the project came to a sudden halt when Jacquelyn first sought support from the leaders of the alumni association of the local, formerly black high school. The president of the Lincoln High School alumni association, Ed Caldwell, initially refused, arguing that the university had studied the hell out of the black community without making the promised difference, without giving anything back. He invoked the long and painful history of the relationship between the University of North Carolina and the black community when he insisted that our project would be for us alone, to sit on the shelves of the library, never heard from again. He eventually agreed to avail us of critical contacts but cautioned us to tread lightly on ground that had, apparently, already been trammeled.

We proceeded, chastened—even mortified—and tense. The provisional result was an afternoon of presentations and performances for an invited audience of interview participants and invested community members that culminated in these comments from Ed, who returned performance for performance by rising from his seat in the front row, turning toward the audience, and recounting, first of all, his first memories of learning history—learning "who you are," who he is—through stories his grandmother told to him on her front porch while he watched his pals run down the street to play. He then became insistent:

Let me say this:

> I think it's very hard,
> for both
> black,
> white,
> Asian,
> or whatever,

to try to mix,
if they don't feel comfortable.
But you know,
it's the growth,
of the individual:
when you
can step
beyond
what the
tribe—
I'm going to call it the tribe—
expects you to do,
you can start to,
to buck the tribe,
and say,
"That's not for me."
And that means,
within yourself,
you're beginning to grow
and that you're an individual.
Tribe's going to try to knock you
    down
and make you conform. . . .
But you know,
it took me a long time to,
to study religions and whatever,
and I have evolved.
And I am not about to let
no professed Christians tell me how to
    think.

(Audience laughs.)

And I'm going to move about,
based on my growth.
I'm not going to let the tribe tell me,
that this is the way we've always done
    it and this is the way that we do it.
And I think that,

when you begin to grow—
In high school you wouldn't expect
the young people to have the
   emotional
fortitude,
and whatever,
to stand outside
of the peer groups—
just as many black peer groups may,
get on those black kids,
as white kids get on them.
And it's not easy,
to buck them,
and say,
"I'm an individual."
But when you do,
you, you have begun to arrive.
And that's what's going on.
That's why we can't get rid of
the,
the professed segregation,
and whatever
because we as individuals,
will not stand up to our friends,
our peer groups,
our churches,
our buddies . . .
And, what's been so heartfelt,
being here today,
is that you all were beginning to
think.
I cried as much as you did Bob.

(Ed gestures toward a white man sitting in the front row, his friend of many years, Bob Gilgor, who was, at the time, producing a photographic documentary of Lincoln High for the local museum; the audience laughs with them.)

Ah, I mean it's just been,
exhilarating to me.
And,
Jacquelyn Hall,

(Ed points a mock scolding finger at Jacquelyn who is standing on the sidelines of the audience.)

Girl,
I came up there,
to your class,
and I was very strong—

(Jacquelyn smiles broadly and answers, "Yes!")

about what I expected to come out of
   this.
And it has passed
my expectations.
You've got— *(extends his hand out
   over the entire audience)*
you're all just great.
I've got you as missionaries
going out to do . . . whatever.
Okay,
sometimes
you're going to have to be challenged
   by
people that are not as far evolved as
   you are. But you know you've got
   to stand up.

(Gestures toward Bob in the front row.)

This is my best friend.
Okay.
We have lunch every Wednesday.
And we talk about different things.
I give him—

(Bob stands and interrupts Ed with a hug. They remain standing together with their arms

around each other's shoulders. Audience members laugh, clap and make warm, surprised comments. Bob speaks over the tumult: "He's my brother. He is. He is. He's a man of character." Ed continues:)

> And his children,
>
> they come to me as if
>
> I'm Uncle Ed.
>
> They talk to me.
>
> And that's,
>
> that's what,
>
> what *has to happen.*
>
> So, this has been great.

(Ed looks at and addresses one of the performers, Shannon Best, in her seat in the audience.)

> Young lady,
>
> I cried the whole time you talked.

(Audience laughs and nods and comments in agreement.)

> You're a strong person.
>
> You decide to do whatever—
>
> And then you found out that your uncle
>
> had evolved.
>
> So.
>
> That's it.

(He raises both hands up in surrender, tears welling.)

> I'm going to sit down.

(Audience claps as Ed and Bob sit.)

I've let Ed go on here much as he did after the performance for any number of reasons, not the least of which is that it is important to hear and to see how deeply rooted his praise was in personal memory, collective memory,

public reflection, affective investment, political critique, and hope. He sits down on the edge of hope. This was no formal praise. No pat on the back for a job well done. Even what at the time felt like the worrisome length of Ed's comments (would he stall out conversation with monologue?) proved to be a vigorous refusal of another kind: a refusal to let his praise stand uncontextualized, to let the performance go without nurturing its deepest roots and furthest reach, to fail to articulate the depth of his own turnaround from suspicion of the university's part in spectacularizing black history to this final confidence in the promise of the work to which he now paid witness.

I could stop here and make this a story of personal and political heroism: University Project Wins Over Black Leaders; Professors Beat the Political Odds—but I can't, of course, without succumbing to the same logic of liberal apologia and redemption that has secured fantasies of color-blind integration in the U.S. cultural imaginary. Doing so, moreover, would foreclose on the possibility of entering the intimacies of reperformance into the collective memory and imagination of how we might continue to make and remake histories of change. In the next few pages, I'd like to offer any number of examples of how, to the contrary, performances conditioned by listening out loud preserved the possibility of histories of change.[12] I'd like to describe Melanie's explosive improvisation on the memories of a white elementary school teacher nearing retirement whose passion could not be hidden under either her own or Melanie's shy demeanor. I'd like to tell about Kit's interviews with his distant aunt and her best friend, both schoolteachers, who drew Kit into a taut triangulation of gender, generation, and color. I wish I could describe the steady force with which Constance carefully folded and piled clean laundry, performing a kind of homage to her mother's domestic labor while telling us what her mother had never before told her: how class at least as much race kept her

isolated in the first years of integrated schooling, and then kept her out of school, caring for
her home and family under threat of an alco-
holic father. Each of these performances, like
each of the others, was crossed through with
what the student previously didn't know, what
he or she might not have known, and awe-
ful/grateful recognition of how much yet then
remains to be known. At the very moment of
retelling, acquaintance, aunt, mother became
more intimate and more strange, the strangeness of each intimacy revolting against, above
all, the *knowingness*—angry, pious, naïve—
that sustains closed narratives of integration
and preempts ongoing inquiry into the nature
of raced relations.

Each performance opened up issues of racial
politics that far exceeded the relatively narrow
thematics of desegregation. This was perhaps
nowhere more clear than in Shannon Best's
performance—the one to which Ed Caldwell
referred at the end of his comments when he
said "Young lady/I cried the whole time you
talked" and on which I will now focus, if only
as a direct complement to Ed's strongly affective, although in no way simply "empathic,"
backward and forward spiral of remembering
and reflection.

As part of an early assignment that asked
students to reflect on the first time they
encountered color (the first time they recalled
becoming race-conscious), Shannon revealed
her surprise as an eight-year-old watching TV
and seeing her grandfather on the screen
dressed in the garb of a grand wizard of the Ku
Klux Klan. A tough white girl, braced for anything it seemed, Shannon went on to describe
some of what you'll read below: the course of
her engagement to Eddie, the black guy she'd
been dating for some time, her family's bitter
response, and her return dismissal of them.
Shannon was at a loss as to whom to interview for the course project. I encouraged her
to consider talking with members of her
family. She was dumbfounded, sure of what
she would find there: flat bigotry, toxic

hatred, or what she repeatedly called "ugliness."
Why bother?

She proceeded nonetheless, discovering first
of all that the study of desegregation required
as much a study of whiteness as of blackness.
Shannon's assumption that we should all be
talking with African Americans suggests that
the history of desegregation was something
that happened to African Americans alone—
that "they" were integrated into "our" world.
While well-intended, this assumption continues to black out the role of whites in both
enabling and inhibiting integration, sustains
the white myth of integration as a done deal,
and further distances whites from a history
to which they may be otherwise dedicated
by assigning "rights" and implicitly responsibilities elsewhere. Pivoting, however uncon-
sciously, on the assumption that one person or
group can own a historical narrative, Shannon
initially, respectfully disowned this one, in
effect saying: this is not my story.

To the extent that Shannon identified with a
history of oppression, she also separated herself from it by caricature and the performance
of disgust.[13] She not only knew but knew all
too well what fools her family members were
and she wanted none of it. And yet returning to
her family of origin, Shannon, like other white
students, found complexities that challenged
her segregated sense of herself—a sense that,
more often than not, depended on the same
us-them/high-low thinking for which these
students blamed their father's or mother's or
uncle's or grandparents' race hatred.

Shannon was an accomplished performer.
The course of this project can only be described
as a gradual stripping away of her training,
leaving her personally and professionally vulnerable, appearing somewhat less than spectacular, even amateurish and unprepared. She
began working with the interview material
early in the semester, in one presentation staging the whole scene of an emerging race riot at
a high school in Greenville, North Carolina, at
about a ten-foot remove from the audience,

"acting out" the story, mimetically substituting a closed umbrella for the lug wrench pulled from the trunk of a car, and so on. When I suggested that she return to the listening exercise and restart by just telling the story of the interview, she replied, suddenly streaming tears: "I can't. Please don't make me. I can stage it. I can block anything!" Shannon desperately wanted to avoid the kind of vulnerability she knew a less imitative approach would require.

The performance she gave as part of the final afternoon event was a complete surprise to me and to everyone else in class, including, it seemed, Shannon. I'd seen it coming—but not this far. As spectacle, the performance failed brilliantly. The appearance/text were out of rational(ized) control. Shannon began talking too soon. She never managed to get her costume straight; the jacket that was meant to resemble her uncle's remained awkwardly wrapped around one shoulder. Her one attempt at using props mimetically—smoking a cigarette the way her uncle did—never got past the rhythmic tamping down of the tobacco, a gesture that incidentally may have been more telling than any more realistic long drag that might have followed. All smooth surfaces seemed to break against a courageous, extemporaneous confrontation with her past and our present.

Shannon began speaking before she'd fully risen from her seat in the audience. In a quick, defiant voice edged with anxiety, she called out as she strode toward the single chair waiting for her at the front of the room:

My fiancé is black.

>Does that shock anybody?

>>[This is as much a confession as a dare. It is also a setup, positioning the audience in the place her parents occupied in her story of their response to a similar confession.]

>Shocked my parents
>when I

first introduced him

to them, three and half years ago. . . .

(*Shannon sits down as she speaks and looks directly at the audience. She pushes her hair back behind her shoulders and leans into the back of the chair, placing her hands with taut assurance on the armrests.*)

>Their response was:

>"Well there goes your tuition."

>They said they wouldn't pay my tuition any more if I continued to see him.

Well,

my response to that was,

"I'm gonna continue to see him."

>They basically told me that no one in my family was to know

about what I was doing or who I was seeing.

And that was the point where,

I decided to find out a little about my family's history.

>>[*A contest of knowing begins. To the extent that what Shannon told is supposed to remain a family secret, it becomes the basis for unearthing others.*]

And

I found out that my grandfather was a former ah grand wizard of the KKK.

And that,

my uncle was

a junior Klansman,

and was involved in a lot of racial fights the

first year of integration—which was his sophomore year of high school.

And

I was angry,

and I was upset,

and,

I,

I wanted, I wanted

(She sits up tall and leans toward the audience. Her hands seem to search the air for what she "wanted" then and now.)

to interview my uncle

because I wanted to prove to myself how ignorant and closed minded

and just

uneducated my family was.

I wanted to prove that to myself.

> [*Shannon makes an initial reflexive shift beyond her insistent desire to justify her hurt and anger into desire to know what could possibly justify causing such hurt and anger. At the very point of "proof," her family is becoming less known, less familiar, more strange. She expands her inquiry to broader contexts of segregation.*]

But I also wanted to find out how someone's color could bring out that amount of

hatred

in a person

based primarily on

his

race.

And I knew that my uncle had only known,

or had only associated with,

two black people before

schools were integrated his sophomore year of high school—

and these two black men were, ah—

worked for, my, my grandfather

which was his father—

and he told me that,

these two black men they would, ah,

they would come over to his house outside work,

and his father would go outside and they would talk and laugh, and

smoke and drink and just

have a good time.

And he said that he went over with his father to their house one time,

and they sat out under the carport and they,

they smoked and they,

laughed and they

conversated,

but they never went in each other's houses.

Because that's the way things were.

You didn't go into someone of another race's house.

So—

When I went to

interview my uncle,

I went straight into the racial fights.

I wanted to know all about the racial fights.

(Shannon looks down, briefly trying to adjust her jacket, one sleeve of which is turned inside out. She abandons the jacket, looks up again, and begins to speak now as her uncle, telling his story from his/her perspective. Her voice takes on a low, wry tone.)

> [*This is now an explicitly hybrid performance. When Shannon begins speaking as her uncle, it is clear that she is both not herself and not exactly him; she is not-not-him.*]

Oh, (she/he laughs)

you talking about the day of the riot?

Yeah.

I remember.

It was all,

it was all because this ah black kid,

walked in the school

and, ah,

there was this dead raccoon,

hanging by a noose

on his locker.

And I remember: I was walking out of
    school that day,

with this girl—

and there were these twenty black guys

who rushed in from another area.

I didn't know what was going on.

I found out later they had just beat up
    this white kid

across campus.

And ahmmm,

*(Shannon leans back and throws her right foot
across her left knee.)*

they were almost inside the door,
    and stopped.

And one of them looked at me and
    said,

said something like,

"What kind of shit you got to say?"

And when he said that,

they all pretty much stopped.

And I knew at this point,

I was getting my ass kicked.

So,

I just basically looked at him,

and I hit him.

And they commenced to do what I
    pretty much thought they were
    going to do.

(Audience laughs.)

And ahmmm,

*(Shannon has taken out a pack of cigarettes.
She begins to tamp down the pack against the
palm of her other hand, making a loud, rhythmic clapping noise as she speaks.)*

I was on the ground,

and all these people were just walking
    by,

and I'm sitting there kicking and
    screaming.

None of the white kids really wanted
    to get involved in what was going on.

But I had this one friend

that walked by.

He was looking,

and he was like, you know:

"What's going on?" and "who's under
    there?"

And ahmmm,

*(Shannon abandons trying to open the
pack of cigarettes and yet continues banging it against her palm. She continues to
speak in her uncle Ken's, plain, reportorial
style.)*

he saw me kicking and screaming,

at the bottom of the pile,

and he looked at them and he said,

"You black sons of bitches."

Well that got them off *me.*

They jumped on him!

(Audience laughs.)

And we're all scrambling around, on
    the, on the ground,

and these teachers walk out and
    they're all like,

"Y'all need to leave."

And they are screaming.

And I see the National Guard pulling
   up

and all these police, so

we walk out to the parking lot.

To my car.

And I open the trunk.

And

I get out a lug wrench.

And,

by this time, we pretty much know
   it's a full-fledged riot.

At least seven hundred people by then.

*(Shannon pauses briefly, uncrosses her legs
and sits up straight. She begins to talk directly
to the audience as herself now.)*

Well,

when I walked into

my uncle's

place of business that day,

he told me that story,

and then he said he had a little bit of
   work to do on the computer so—

"go back to the back" and introduce
   myself to his partner,

Barry.

*[Her voice still shaded by her uncle's
dry/wry tone, Shannon now draws
the immediacy of talking with us into
tight proximity with the immediacies
of the interview scene itself. She conjoins the vulnerabilities of telling and
having been/being told.]*

So I walk back to the back,

of the office,

and all I see is this black guy standing
   there,

and I walk by him, and he stops me
   and is like,

"Can I help you?"

And I said "Oh, I'm, I'm Ken's niece
   and I'm just looking for his partner."

And he says, "You're looking at him."

And

my face,

turned really red,

right then,

and I held out my hand and

and I shook his hand—to cover up my
   embarrassment—

and I'm thinking to myself, how,

how can I assume that this is not his
   partner,

because he's black?

I mean what does that say about me?
   I'm sitting here,

putting all this criticism on my
   family—

and I'm sitting here assuming the
   same thing.

*[Shannon dis-disidentifies. Here is
the double negative at work, undoing
Shannon's primary sense of herself.
She is the one who is "shocked"
now—although shocked less at the
fact of Barry's skin color than at her
own resilient expectations about it.]*

I was pretty confused at this point, so I
   go back into the room where my uncle is,

and I look at him, and he just starts
   smiling at me,

and he's like, "I know what you're
   going to ask."

And ahmmm,

*(Shannon leans back in the chair. She breathes
in, looks up and begins speaking as her uncle
again.)*

*[Shannon relays her own silence, her
own not-knowing and even her*

uncle's sly kindness in not making her "ask" what he suspects she will ask in deference to Ken's gentle voice. We see and hear now two more expansive selves: Ken's filled out by Barry's and Shannon's filled out by Ken's.]

Barry,

Ah, Barry yeah,

he's my friend.

He'll change someone's whole world,

about, about the way they think about race,

about the way they think about the black race anyway.

I remember in 1985

I put an ad in the newspaper

basically asking for money

to start this business.

I needed some help starting this business.

And he was the only one that responded.

So

I took him up on his offer,

and we started this business.

And up until that point,

slang was used pretty regular around my house.

It was ah,

basically,

'n' this or 'n' that

or jokes about it, and it was just a regular thing.

But it's been at least nine or ten years since that word has come out of my mouth.

He,

he was,

my hero.

(quietly) Barry was my hero.

I am not around it any more.

I do not allow anyone to use it in my house.

And, if I do,

come across the situation where slang is being used, I separate myself from that situation.

And that makes it hard when I get around old friends.

Because for them it's just

an everyday thing.

But ahmmm,

now, the way things are set up at my office,

something happened to me,

that I'm entrusting my children,

and my wife,

and my family,

to Barry.

He is the godfather of my children.

Everything I have will go to him when I die.

And ahmmm,

I don't know,

Barry's just,

just an amazing guy.

(Shannon sits forward and shifts into speaking in her voice, now softened considerably by having passed through her Uncle Ken's.)

Well,

after my interview with my uncle, I am sitting there

realizing how stupid I am,

and how many years I've wasted not getting to know this man that I am related to,

and what a wonderful person he is,

and at that moment,

my fiancé walks in the door looking
  for me,

and my heart pretty much drops to
  the ground,

because nobody's met,

him,

in my family.

And I look at him and I look at my
  uncle and I'm just speechless.

*[Shannon's previous silence—con-
veyed only by echoing witness to her
uncle's words—is now doubled. In
the heightened context of reperform-
ing the interview scene, she becomes
the humble(d) third party to a performance of family/raced relations that
leaves us all on a threshold of hard-
won but tremulous possibility.]*

I don't know what to say.

And my uncle sticks out his hand and
  says,

"It's nice to meet you."

And my fiancé said, "My name's
  Eddie, and I'm, I'm Shannon's fiancé."

And [my uncle] looks at him,

and he said,

"Welcome to the family."

Shannon registered change in the ongoing changes in her own body, mind, heart, voice, and story, change that was homely in appearance and magnificent in its homeliness. Her story is frank, aching, confused. It is a story of being caught out by and now caught in an unfolding history. Soliciting her uncle's memories, she was as much remembered to them as she remembers them now like a second language, a first maybe. A forgotten language of familial love and possibility, in whose grammars she is relieved of both spite and its peculiar clarity. Listening out loud, Shannon testifies to her uncle's transformation, witnessing in

turn her own displacement and reflecting on its meanings. This performance was something like a handshake with history: a start, a touch, a call, an act of remembering and awakening, a performative recollection of what Shannon didn't know and may yet *not know*, all the more tender and resplendent yet for *not know-ing* what happens from here. Uncle Ken has the last and what is in effect the first word—spoken to Eddie and reported by Shannon, all reaching tentatively across great racial divides: "Welcome to the family."

A story is not a story until it changes. Shannon's performance, like others, slid from textual verity and containment to radical con-tingency. It drew her into the vortex of disiden-tifying with a history she knew all too well. Recreating that history meant recreating—refashioning—her most basic sense of herself, allying with her uncle and with our guests and her peers in a compact of cowitness.[14] In so doing, she challenged the performative force of her prior expectations, even insofar as they col-luded with her family's racism in the delimita-tion of precisely this kind of transformation and change. Racism, Patricia Williams argues, is a spectacular discipline:

> [It] is a gaze that insists upon the power to make others conform, to perform endlessly in the prison of prior expectation, circling repetitively back upon the expired utility of the entirely known. Our rescue, our deliver-ance perhaps, lies in the possibility of listen-ing across that great divide, of being surprised by the Unknown, by the unknow-able." (1997, p. 74)

In the end, the desegregation project and the listening out loud practices that fed it were about the great intimacies that may be achieved in small acts of listening across "that great divide," about keeping those intimacies "in revolt" against, especially, performativity as the compulsive reiteration of raced expectations,[15] and so about preserving—in fleeting moments and clumsy gestures—the possibility of great acts. They were and are about embodying listening as an antidote to *knowingness*. They were about feeling *"so much more"* and so remembering *more*, and so, finally, about preserving histories of change as *more*: more feeling, more memory, more—and better—change.

NOTES

1. See Berlant (2004), *Compassion*, for critique of the common sense politics of compassion and empathy.

2. For a supplementary introduction and complementary versions of oral history performance, see Pollock (2005).

3. See Jacquelyn Hall's definitive critique and elaboration of the Brown history, "The Long Civil Rights Movement," in which she observes its foreshortening by accounts of both conclusive triumph and decline (2005).

4. See Sam Schrager's fundamental insight: "What the oral historian does is to provide a new context for the telling of mainly preexistent narrative" (1983, pp. 78–79).

5. This early project is recounted in Pollock (1990).

6. Per Walter Benjamin's now-infamous declaration: "The storyteller takes what he tells from experience—his own or that reported by others. And he in turn makes it the experience of those who are listening to his tale" (1969, p. 87).

7. See Conquergood's critique of text-centrism in Dailey (1998).

8. Judith Butler argues, for instance, that "although the political discourses that mobilize identity categories tend to cultivate identifications in the service of a political goal, it may be that the persistence of disidentification is equally crucial to the rearticulation of democratic contestations" (1993, p. 4). See also Muñoz (1999).

9. See Schechner (1985, pp. 111–115).

10. At its best, oral history performance enacts what Kelly Oliver calls "the response-ability in subjectivity" (2001, p. 139): the self as a responsive agent who speaks what she sees. This self is inextricable from "others." It does not subsume or speak for others any more than it bespeaks an inalienable distinction between self and other. For Oliver, in the praxis of witnessing, "the other is no longer *the* other. There is no other, but a multitude of differences and other people on whom my sense of myself as a subject and an agent depends" (p. 223).

11. Thanks to Laurie Lathem for helping me to extend this formulation. See her essay, "Bringing Old and Young People Together: An Interview Project," in Pollock (2005).

12. All performances quoted and discussed with the students' permission.

13. See Sara Ahmed, "The Performativity of Disgust," (2004, pp. 82–100).

14. See Conquergood's effort to answer Johannes Fabian's call for a turn "'from informative to performative ethnography'" with "an ethnography of the ears and heart that reimagines participant-observation as co-performative witnessing" (2002, p. 149).

15. Per Butler's now-classic formulation of "performativity" (1990).

REFERENCES

Ahmed, S. (2004). *The cultural politics of emotion.* New York: Routledge.

Benjamin, W. (1969). The storyteller. *Illuminations.* (H. Zohn, Trans.) New York: Schocken. (Original work published 1955)

Berlant, L. (Ed.). (2004). *Compassion: The culture and politics of an emotion.* New York: Routledge.

Butler, J. (1990). *Gender trouble: Feminism and the subversion of identity.* New York: Routledge.

Butler, J. (1993). *Bodies that matter: On the discursive limits of "sex."* New York: Routledge.

Conquergood, D. (1998). Beyond the text: Toward a performative cultural politics. In S. J. Dailey (Ed.), *The future of performance studies: Visions and revisions* (pp. 25–36). Annandale, VA: National Communication Association.

Conquergood, D. (2002). Performance studies: Interventions and radical research. *The Drama Review, 46*(2), 145–156.

Dailey, S. J. (Ed.). (1998). *The future of performance studies: Visions and revisions* Annandale, VA: National Communication Association.

Debord, G. (1983). *Society of the spectacle.* Detroit: Black and Red. (Original work published 1977)

Hall, J. D. (2005). The long civil rights movement and the political uses of the past. *Journal of American History, 91,* 1233–1263.

Kristeva, J. (2002). *Intimate revolt: The powers and limits of psychoanalysis* (J. Herman, Trans.). New York: Columbia University Press. (Original work published 1997)

Muñoz, J. E. (1999). *Disidentifications: Queers of color and the performance of politics.* Minneapolis: University of Minnesota Press.

Oliver, K. (2001). *Witnessing: Beyond recognition.* Minneapolis: University of Minnesota Press.

Pollock, D. (1990). Telling the told: Performing like a family. *The Oral History Review, 18*(2), 1–35.

Pollock, D. (Ed.). (2005). *Remembering: Oral history performance* (New York: Palgrave/ St. Martin's.

Schechner, R. (1985). *Between theater and anthropology.* Philadelphia: University of Pennsylvania Press.

Schrager, S. (1983). What is social in oral history? *International Journal of Oral History, 4*(2), 76–98.

Trinh, T. M. (1989). *Woman, native, other: Writing postcoloniality and feminism.* Bloomington: Indiana University Press.

Williams, P. J. (1997). *Seeing a color-blind future: The paradox of race.* New York: Farrar, Strauss and Giroux.

7

Minstrelsy and Mental Metempsychosis

Mid-Nineteenth Century American
Women's Performance Criticism

GAY GIBSON CIMA

Oh! would they but endeavour to realize the bitterness of such a lot [as slavery],
surely, surely, they would rush to the rescue of the thousands who are agonizing
beneath its endurance.

—Elizabeth Margaret Chandler (1836)

DEFINING PERFORMANCE HISTORY

"Performance history" may sound like an oxymoron, a rhetorical linkage of two mismatched or even contradictory terms. What could history—whether it is conceived of as a negotiation with memory (Jacques Le Goff and Pierre Nora), as thick description (Clifford Geertz), as a genealogy of cultural practices (Michel Foucault), or, more recently, as a vexed and partial narrative—have to do with the ephemeral stuff of living performance? And yet, performance scholars always reside at the intersection of these two terms, history and performance, whether they admit it or not.

Writing about performance is, of necessity, writing about events, behaviors, and gestures that have escaped into the past, whether that past has happened just moments prior or centuries ago. Historians, against all odds, try to grasp what was "realized" through past performances, in order to shape the present and future. For example, through an investigation of the ways in which mid-nineteenth century black, white, and multiracial[1] women staged their antislavery and theatrical criticism, I hope to illuminate their overlapping performance strategies and prompt further reflection upon the relationship between women's activism and performance criticism.

106

Performance historians search for traces of past events that remain in the present, sometimes as carefully preserved artifacts housed in well-organized archives. These readily available bits of evidence remain crucial to historians, but they must be approached from new directions. If they are not dislocated from their overdetermined status and remapped in new coordinates, they will not yield new insights. Furthermore, they do not suffice as a record of the past, because they often represent only what the dominant culture has viewed as worth saving and only what has, willy-nilly, survived the exigencies of time. Scholars, therefore, are always broadening the kinds of archives that they investigate, searching for repositories outside of libraries and museums. Evidence may hide in private homes, churches, banks, community centers, hospitals, military headquarters, and other nontraditional performance archives.

With performance studies as a heuristic guide, historians may also use the archives in new ways, angling for an understanding of what is only partially recorded, or what is pointedly not there. Performance scholars learn to be receptive to the fragments, distortions, and silences in the evidentiary record. The gaps and messy contradictions in the extant evidence can lead to a fuller grasp of a particular performance event or custom, precisely because they name the forbidden zones or the contested areas of cultural performance. For example, since it was often imprudent and even illegal for slaves to reveal their print literacy, their antislavery performance criticism is full of gaps and contradictory evidence. There is a telling moment in an 1861 interview with slave critic Louisa Picquet (b. 1828?), who agreed to talk with a smarmy abolitionist named Reverend H. Mattison in order to raise money to purchase her mother's freedom. Mattison represents her as an alluring and victimized "octoroon," a slave with "African" blood, despite the fact that she looks like "an accomplished white lady" (1861/1988, p. 5).

He explains that it is Picquet's performance of herself, not her appearance, that affirms her status as a slave:

> A certain menial-like diffidence, her plantation expression and pronunciation, her inability to read or write, together with her familiarity with and readiness in describing plantation scenes and sorrows, all attest the truthfulness of her declaration that she has been most of her life a slave. (1861/1988, p. 5)

Picquet was certainly aware of the precariousness of her situation. She knew that to Mattison, her literacy would signal that she was not an authentic slave, and while whites routinely wrote fake slave narratives for cash, her ability to gain her mother's freedom was dependent upon her "authenticity." "Authentic" slaves, Mattison's readers believed, were illiterate and compliant, so Picquet pretended illiteracy and performed deference. She gave her interrogator enough of what he desired—a "readiness in describing plantation scenes"—to gain access to what she wanted: an audience to raise funds to free her mother.

However, for a brief moment in her performance of illiteracy, she slipped. She began her interview safely enough, telling how a good friend—conversant with the area of Texas where her mother lived—taught her how to send her mother a letter. She refused to allow Mattison to publish this secret means of communication, for fear of having her letters intercepted, but the effort she expended in protecting her path of communication made her stumble. As Picquet continued the interview, Mattison interjected his comments [in the square brackets]:

> Then he told us how to send a letter, and where to mail it. [There is a kink about mailing a letter, so as to have it reach a slave, that we never before dreamed of; but Mrs. P. does not wish it published, for fear it will hinder her from getting her letters.] Then I wrote a letter [got one written], and

in three weeks I had a letter from my mother. (1861/1988, pp. 29–30)

Straining to protect the only means through which she was able to keep in touch with her mother, Picquet for a moment accidentally dropped her guard and said, simply, "Then I wrote a letter." This statement reveals that indeed, she could write. Unable to recognize this as a slip, however, Mattison simply "corrects" the information for his white readers, translating it into "got one written." What is at stake here is our understanding of how Louisa Picquet performed her sense of herself—the messy, contradictory tangle of an individual life—and also our grasp of how a slave critic in the mid-nineteenth century might manipulate dominant interpretive lenses to her own benefit. In the face of sparse information on slave literacy, at stake also is our notion of who owned language and power in this type of interchange.

Curiously, misprisioned speech and silence may signal performance codes once so pervasive that they did not have to be stated. As historians investigate past performances, they search for these agreed-upon codes that hide within an event, memories meant to be honored but held secret by members of a particular social group. For example, many northern antislavery readers read Picquet's interview as a sad, romantic, and risqué tale stimulating them toward further abolitionist activity, but Southern readers—black, white, and multiracial—may have assumed that as a cultivated "house slave" Picquet was literate. As a result, they may have read her performance in the interview with Mattison as a minstrel act for an abolitionist dupe. They may have realized that she was performing a forbidden role, the role of the manipulator. Some may have championed Picquet's efforts to free her mother, but others would have been outraged by her deceit. Performance historians, aware of their own positionality and activist goals, evaluate evidence based upon specific performance contexts; they reflect on fissures and inconsistencies in the documentary record to tease out an understanding of shifting performance codes and forbidden memories.

Performance historians also notice how events have been framed within historical narratives, and think carefully about how they might be reevaluated as a part of a new narrative. In the present example, the new narrative grants Louisa Picquet a certain kind of power and undercuts the interrogator's and readers' authority. Whether historians are investigating how identity categories such as nationhood, race, gender, and sexuality have been constructed within an historical event, or whether they are examining the highly individualized, jumbled, and random nature of a given event, they are trying to frame something from the past in the present to reshape the future. This is challenging when the evidentiary record is partial, as it is for those investigating feminist and African American performers and performance critics operating within the racialized discourse of mid-nineteenth century America. But it is also crucial to our ability to grasp fully the impact of our own theatre and performance historiographies, to evaluate the stories we have been telling ourselves about the past.

By examining the performance practices of abolitionists in the late 1820s and the 1830s, I seek to reveal not only how they entered the public sphere as cultural critics but also how they interacted with each other and with their audiences to shape notions of race, gender, sexuality, and nationhood at the outset of the reform era. Their appearances in print and onstage, based on a practice they called "mental metempsychosis," paved the way for women theatre critics to try to link a relatively receptive attitude toward slave culture with a receptivity to minstrelsy in the 1840s and 1850s.

WOMEN AS ANTISLAVERY CRITICS

In the 1820s, the number of women performance critics multiplied, primarily because of their participation in the emerging antislavery movement. Black, white, and multiracial women wedged their way into public debates, not only as abolitionist writers but also, for the first time, as antislavery lecturers. This was a radical departure from the norm. During the Revolutionary War era, women had presumed that they could hold individual opinions on matters of national concern. They had shared their opinions with others, sometimes fundraising, boycotting, or petitioning the federal government. As republican mothers dedicated to educating sons—and, in a different way, daughters—for the republic (Kerber, 1980), they had published poems, pamphlets, plays, propaganda, ballads, letters, catechisms, novels, schoolbooks, dialogues, newsletters—a plethora of pieces of performance criticism. Few, however, had performed their criticism onstage in an attempt to rally others to their cause. Women "exhorters" had preached in the streets and actress-playwrights had appeared on the boards, despite social proscriptions against such activity, but they risked losing their respectability each time they spoke. The female antislavery lecturers who stepped into parlors, pulpits, and podiums in the 1830s risked physical violence as well as opprobrium. They were accused of performing "amalgamation" or racial mixing, which many thought a threat to the very fabric of American life.

Consequently, they banded together to form societies in which they could safely perform their activism. From 1820 to 1865, many northern critics focused on abolition: female lecturers crisscrossed the East and Midwest to lobby for an end to auction block rituals. Typically white antislavery critics were middle- to upper-class; black and multiracial critics were free elite and middle-class women, freed women, and slave refugees (Hansen, 1993). The female antislavery associations that flourished in the 1830s and 1840s, and that fostered the woman critic as lecturer, grew out of church groups, benevolent societies, and female literary associations as well as the fiery rhetoric of individual critics like Scottish transplant Frances Wright (1795–1852) and African American Maria W. Miller Stewart (1803–1879).

Antislavery churchwomen were puzzled by the clergy's criticism of their activism, because they themselves viewed their abolitionism as an extension of their work in charitable associations. When the Boston Female Anti-Slavery Society suffered a mob attack in 1835, for example, Maria Weston Chapman (1806–1885) asked the editor of the *Boston Courier*, "when before, in this city, have gentlemen of standing and influence, been incensed against a benevolent association of ladies, for holding their annual meeting, inviting a lecturer to address them, and requesting their friends to attend, after the custom of benevolent societies?" (Yellin and Van Horne, 1994, p. 1). Female antislavery societies were, however, breaking new ground, sharpening women's skills in molding political movements through performance, petitioning, lobbying, and building coalitions in a newly public fashion.

Women's societies differed slightly from men's in terms of their stated ideologies. The women in the New York Chatham Street Chapel society, for example, did not announce that they sought, as their male counterparts did, to "improve the minds, the character, or the morals of the free black population." In fact, they directly stated their desire not to "join hypocrisy to persecution by *dictating* to them how they are to improve their character and their prospects"[2] (Swerdlow, 1994, p. 33). Of course, there are many ways to encourage particular behaviors without "*dictating*" them, but the fact that women made a point of articulating their goals differently from the men is significant. Female societies also differed from one another on ideological and practical grounds, adopting different performance strategies and producing different kinds of critics, depending upon their locale. Some societies were segregated, but many were not.

In Philadelphia and even more strikingly in Boston, they drew heavily on the rhetoric of American republicanism, while in New York—where most members were white—they were more likely to emphasize religious logic. The members of the Philadelphia and Boston societies often complained of the provincialism and racism of the New York associations.

Black women regularly led antislavery efforts. They founded the first female antislavery society on February 22, 1832, in Salem, Massachusetts. The president of that organization, Clarissa C. Lawrence, later became an officer of Salem's integrated Female Anti-Slavery Society as well as a delegate to the 1839 Anti-Slavery Convention of American Women (Sterling, 1984, p. 109). By October 1833, black and white women critics joined to establish the Boston Female Anti-Slavery Society, and two months later Philadelphians followed suit. Women in New York state were slower to take up the antislavery banner, and less likely to do so in integrated associations. For instance, black women in Rochester initiated a female society in 1834, while white women there waited until 1837 to follow suit. Most New Yorkers joined abolitionist ranks through evangelical revivalism and emphasized, like the women of the Chatham Street Chapel society, the sinfulness of slavery and "the principles laid down by our blessed Savior Himself" (Swerdlow, 1994, p. 36).Their black and white Boston counterparts, more motivated by politics, opened their "Address of the Boston Female Anti-Slavery Society to the Women of New England" with references to their responsibilities as "the true descendants of the pilgrims" and their commitment not to Christ but to "Christian freedom." They reminded readers of their interconnectedness, explaining that "while, under any pretense, one human being is held in slavery in a nation of which they form a part, their own freedom is in peril" (1994, p. 36).

Antislavery advocates often staged their inchoate desire for a homosocial—and, for some, a homoerotic—space. Starting in the 1830s, antislavery meetings provided women with a homosocial network of friendships and alliances, which, for some, validated same-sex relationships. In 1893 Jane Campbell, the editor of a new women's journal, published her inaugural article on Mary Grew as one of the nineteenth century's "Representative Women," noting that her name was a "household word" in Philadelphia. Grew served as the corresponding secretary of the antislavery society from 1836 to 1870 and as the president of the Pennsylvania Woman Suffrage Association for 23 years. She spoke from Unitarian pulpits and published frequently on abolition and women's rights in news organs of the day. However, as Campbell closed her article, she admitted, "nothing has been said here of the private life of Mary Grew, beautiful in every respect as it has been, for retiring by nature and inclination she has ever seemed to sink herself in her work" (Campbell, 1893, p. 8). Mary Grew's private life was kept private because of her long term relationship with Margaret Burleigh. When Burleigh died, Grew answered a close friend's sympathy note by confiding,

> You comprehend and appreciate, as few persons do, the nature of the relation which existed, which exists, between her and myself. Her only surviving niece, Miss Ella Jones, also does. To me it seems to have been a closer union than that of most marriages. We know there have been other such between two men and also between two women. And why should there not be. (Grew, 1892)

Grew justified her partnership with Burleigh through language that reverberates in corners of 1960s lesbian cultural feminist discourse: "love is spiritual," she wrote, "only passion is sexual." She privately acknowledged her union with Burleigh, a union which found its history as well as its emotional justification within the antislavery movement.

ANTISLAVERY BODIES
AND CENSUS LABELS

Women's antislavery activism emerged at a time when the 1820 U. S. census had divided bodies into the following categories: free white, other free, persons not naturalized, colored, and slave. These categories had developed over time: the 1790 census, for instance, had counted only free whites, other free persons, and slaves, and had also yielded anecdotal information about the numbers of "English and Welsh," the Scots, Irish, Dutch, French, Germans, "Hebrews," and "all other nationalities." (University of Virginia, 2004). By 1820, these national affiliations were no longer noted, and the racial category "colored" had emerged as a way of separating free black bodies from "other free" bodies. Race was displacing nationality as a means of marking bodies, though nationality still mattered as a means of designating the degrees of American-ness: the category "persons not naturalized" separated new immigrants from old; and "free white" in many regions became a shorthand for perceived Anglo-American-ness, while "other free" was applied variously, at the discretion of individual census-takers, as a label for well-established immigrants of various European nationalities and for any individuals who did not appear "white" or "colored."

Most of the prominent female antislavery lecturers in the 1830s were perceived as free whites or "coloreds," though their families' various national origins doubtless lingered in the minds of audience members, as memories do, creating an implicit class hierarchy within the overall racial category of "whiteness." Between 1820 and 1850, the free status of "colored" Americans was still ostensibly recognized, but its power was offset by the new racial boundaries that implicitly associated free "colored" Americans with slaves instead of free European immigrants. The racial boundaries made explicit in the 1820 census were bolstered by state legislation restricting the movement of free blacks, and by laws leading to the 1850 federal Fugitive Slave Act, which dictated that northerners return slaves to their southern masters. By the 1850s, free northern blacks, including middle-class antislavery critics, had to fear being kidnapped, misidentified as the property of a purported master, and sent south as slaves. Black and multiracial antislavery speakers risked their lives in very precise ways by speaking out against slavery in the mid-nineteenth century. That fact must be given due consideration in evaluating why they sometimes chose to disseminate their cultural criticism through a process that might be called "surrogate activism": they embedded their critiques within whites' lectures and books.

By 1850, however, the census listed new racial categories: "white, native and foreign," "free coloured," and "slave." The last two categories were broken down into "black" or "mulatto."[3] The process implicitly linking freedom with whiteness was completed, so the qualifier "free" was deleted from the category "white," but the effort to distinguish newcomers from established Americans continued in the "native and foreign" designation attached to "white." By 1850, white meant free, and persons of all nations except Africa were, in terms of the census at least, regarded as white. The opposition between "white" and "black" bodies was recoded: not only were free "coloreds" no longer linked to European immigrants, but they were also posed as the clear opposite of whites. The delineation of a "mulatto" population, while acknowledging a middle ground between the seeming opposites "black" and "white" and opening up new opportunities for some women critics to experiment with notions of visibility, invisibility, and identity, also dangerously gestured toward the obvious and yet the unspoken: the forced and unforced interracial sexual contact already embedded in the culture. These shifting census designations help reveal the context in which antislavery activists and theatre critics staged their work from the 1830s through the 1850s, when both female antislavery societies and minstrelsy flourished and fostered complex acts of surrogacy among women critics.

IMAGINING BODIES AND BODIES OF CRITICISM

To deflect the charge that they were performing womanhood inappropriately, nineteenth century women critics adopted various bodily shields for their performances onstage and in print. They created rhetorical "bodies" through which they could safely speak by borrowing phrases or gestures from the mainstream and combining them in new ways and by imagining bodies to serve their ends. These alternative "bodies" acted as shields of respectability as well as sites of desire, fantasy, feeling, learning, and solidarity. Women critics created a variety of bodies to inhabit as the female antislavery meetings of the 1830s transformed into the ladies' physiological and literary societies of the 1840s and the women's rights conventions of the 1850s. As abolitionists, they imagined entering slave bodies to "excite" themselves and each other into antislavery activism; sometimes they pointed to actual slave narrators standing onstage beside them. As medical lecturers, black and white women replaced these imaginary slave bodies onstage with manikins and illustrations. Then, as woman's rights advocates, they fleshed out those skeletons by speaking onstage, side by side, on their own behalf, covering over the memory of the slave bodies and the skeletons that ghosted their performances. Throughout, they imagined various kinds of Christian bodies as a shield. All of these bodies haunt the columns of nineteenth century black and white women theatre and performance critics.

White Antislavery Critics: Empathy, Appropriation, and Desire

The first woman known to lecture onstage in the United States, Frances Wright, tried creating a strictly "rational body" through which to stage her antireligious, antislavery criticism. She presented herself as inhabiting a logical, pragmatic body, the obvious and preferable alternative, in her view, to the hysterical evangelical bodies of women involved in the religious revival of the Second Great Awakening. Her tactic of occupying a rational body, however, not only failed to inspire abolitionist activity but also resulted in the further "blackening" of her reputation.

Other female antislavery critics, consequently, embraced what they felt was a more efficacious performative strategy—but it was also more problematic. They began to adopt the "surrogate bodies" of slaves onstage. Through a process that white critic Elizabeth Margaret Chandler (1807–1834) called "mental metempsychosis," white, free black, and multiracial women critics imagined themselves entering into slave bodies wracked with pain, performing thereby their own womanly sense of violation as well as a tangled and contradictory web of desire and concern. They hoped to generate in their audiences emotions so strong that they would trigger an immediate commitment to antislavery activism. Instead of arguing against the Christian rhetoric of the Awakening, as Frances Wright did, these antislavery critics recycled the suffering Christian body for activist purposes. Even as they staged their idea of enslaved blackness, they reinforced whiteness (as race and as class) through a minstrel surrogacy.

Chandler, the first editor of the "Ladies' Repository" column in the antislavery newspaper *The Genius of Universal Emancipation,* pleaded with her readers as early as 1831 to empathize with slaves through mental metempsychosis (Chandler, 1836, p. 171). Metempsychosis is the process through which a soul is understood to migrate, at death, into another body. This is antithetical, of course, to the individualistic Christian notion that a soul is born within a particular body and lives on intact when that body dies. Plato, borrowing from Hinduism and Buddhism, described metempsychosis as a process through which immortal souls worked toward purity, moving from body to body over time to reach perfection.[4] These souls, detached from their individualistic character, travel bodiless through the realm of ideas. Upon occasion, they can be recollected as ideals. The souls are free to move across bodily boundaries—they are completely fluid—and yet, they also bind bodies together ineluctably across time and space. The performative practice that Chandler called "mental" metempsychosis, then, invited antislavery critics to leave the bodies they occupied, imagine themselves dead, and envision themselves as part of an ancient, fluid soul searching for a body that would propel it toward ideal connectedness. At a time when the U.S. Constitution recognized only the figural (three-fifths) bodies of slaves, Chandler wanted her free white and "coloured" readers to "imagine themselves for a few moments in [the slave's] very circumstances, to enter his feelings, comprehend all his wretchedness, transform themselves mentally into his very self," believing that then "they would not surely long withhold their compassion" (1836, pp. 117–118). Chandler and her fellow antislavery advocates first had to convey the fact that slaves were not, rightly speaking, property but rather *humans*. By adopting slave bodies as surrogate bodies, antislavery workers hoped to fuel empathy, prove that slaves were fully human, and spur activism on their behalf. Slave refugees and narrators themselves, I hasten to add, did not self-identify as victims; their own narratives recount their resistance, moral superiority, and determined self-authorization.

Abby Kelley Foster (1810–1887), among the earliest white female abolitionists to speak at a public lectern, practiced mental metempsychosis in front of audiences of blacks and whites, women and men. She imagined entering slave bodies in a tragic inversion of minstrelsy disguised as cultural criticism, and invited her audiences, packed into private parlors, church sanctuaries, and town halls, to join her. Her performance was charged through with sexuality, violence, and voyeurism, but she saw it as an enactment of specifically Christian love. In an act of surrogate activism, she borrowed the slave body and Christian body to claim attention for antislavery as she spoke:

> When I come to sit down in the cool of the day, alone with none but God to hold communion with, and in the exercise of love to him, become myself the slave—when at such a moment I feel the fetters wearing away the flesh and grating on my bare ankle bone, when I feel the naked cords of my neck shrinking away from the rough edge of the iron collar, when my flesh quivers beneath the lash, till, in anguish, I feel portions of it cut from my back; or when I see my aged and feeble mother driven away and scourged, and then the brutish and drunken overseer lay his ferocious grasp upon the person of my sister and drag her to his den of pollutions . . . when I see you and others standing by to witness it, what do I hear from your lips? (Sterling, 1991, pp. 32–33)

By publicly borrowing slave bodies, critics like Foster staged their own metaphorical deaths, their legal and civic nonexistence as well as the social deaths that abolitionist activity brought them. They leapt into a space Plato associated with the ideal, and Lynda Hart linked to "trauma"—that space between the stage and the stalls, the self and the void—as they entered into the zone of what they regarded as a forbidden body. There they fantasized female same-sex as well as heterosexual desire, interracial lust, sadomasochistic scenes of domination and submission. There they expressed their public outrage at male domination and enacted their misguided sense of a totally shared violation at the hands of men, eliding the material differences between their own middle-class lives and the lives of women and men in chattel slavery.

Through mental metempsychosis, Foster and her fellow abolitionists appropriated slave bodies, but they also made them matter by making them visible, soulful, and inhabitable.

They strove to make the overdetermined slave's body, archived as property, verbally available and fleshly present. As Elaine Scarry explains, "given any two phenomena, the one that is more visible will receive more attention," but the abuses inherent in slavery were covered over with decades and decades of obfuscating rhetoric (Scarry, 1985, p 12). The torture of slaves was at the unspeakable, unrepresentable heart of America, not only because pain is, finally, unshareable and resistant to language, (p. 4) but also because the slave body was not yet widely accepted as a fully human body. Abolitionists performed the slave's pain while humanizing the body subject to that pain so that it could, in fact, be understood and felt by audiences to be pain. Only then, they believed, could sympathy function to prompt political action. Foster attacked the silent witnesses in her audience, whose failure to speak aligned them with the unthinkable, unlivable body of the slaveholder, also silent in the face of the slave's pain. "What do I hear from your lips?" she asked those who witnessed her act of mental metempsychosis. In order to become themselves fully human, antislavery audiences had to accept the humanity of slaves, sympathize with them, and speak out about those feelings.[5] The danger, as always when pain is at issue, was that the body in pain would be appropriated by those describing the pain.

For white women abolitionists, interracial desire as well as moral and religious fervor linked a sentimentalized investment in blacks and black culture with an urge to cast slave bodies as degraded tragic victims. White speakers sought to identify themselves with the romantic tales of slaves and the horror stories of free black women facing northern prejudice, simultaneously casting those black others as victims—and themselves, all too often, not only as fellow "slaves" to men, but also as redeemers to the other women. The most astute whites, like Sarah Moore Grimké (1792–1873), stated at the outset the limits of the "woman as slave" metaphor, honoring

differences in the material conditions of women's lives, but even those white critics who, after emancipation, placed race (in the form of black male suffrage) before gender (in the form of women's suffrage), drew on this metaphor.[6] Lydia Maria Child (1802–1880), in fact, foregrounded it on the title page of her history of women.

Black Antislavery Critics: Self-Love, Solidarity, and Fear

Free black critics—viewed as "free other" in the 1820s and as "free coloured" (either "black" or "mulatto") by the 1850s—also imagined black bodies in danger to spur themselves into action as antislavery advocates. They also practiced mental metempsychosis. But the bodies they imagined at risk were more palpably their own. As more and more laws were passed to restrict their interstate, social, and economic movement, and as the colonization or "Back to Africa" movement gained momentum, many pictured their possible fates and articulated their sudden awareness that their own bodies were linked in the cultural imagination with slaves' bodies. They performed this sense of connection in their stagings of mental metempsychosis. Free black antislavery advocates such as Sarah Douglass (1806–1882) and Sarah Forten (1814–1883) in Philadelphia and Susan Paul (1809–1841) in Boston, serving as officers within integrated antislavery societies or all-black literary societies, imagined entering slave bodies to launch their political engagement. But they did so differently from white critics. They paid much closer attention to the material circumstances of the various bodies involved. Sarah Douglass's speech at a July 1832 meeting of the all-black Female Literary Society of Philadelphia may serve here as an illustration.[7]

The Literary Society was composed of about twenty black women who met in each others' homes on Tuesday evenings "for the purpose of moral and religious meditation, conversation, reading and speaking, sympathizing over the fate of the unhappy slaves, improving their own minds, &c. &c." Feeling for the slaves was matter-of-factly linked to both moral and religious meditation and to self-improvement. The members of the Literary Society performed their bodily connectedness with the slaves: for example, they consumed refreshments designed to make them "feel for those who have nothing to refresh body and mind." Sarah Douglass opened the July 1832 meeting with her "wish that the reading and conversation should be altogether directed to the subject of slavery." Then she proceeded to give a speech. She explained how the changing political climate for free blacks in Philadelphia had sharpened her awareness of slavery and her determination to throw off "the lethargy which had covered [her] as a mantle for years." "One short year ago," she confided, "how different were my feelings on the subject of slavery!" As a member of the black elite, she "had formed a little world of [her] own, and cared not to move beyond its precincts," but the colonization movement had begun to gather steam, and the Pennsylvania legislature had begun to limit the rights of free blacks and to strengthen fugitive slave laws (Rigley, 1991, p. 116). By January 1838 Pennsylvania's free blacks, in fact, were disenfranchised (Lerner, 1967, p. 250). Responding to the emerging threats against her freedom in 1832, Douglass confided, "how was the scene changed when I beheld the oppressor lurking on the border of my own peaceful home!" She performed an act of mental metempsychosis. She reported, "I saw [the oppressor's] iron hand stretched forth to seize me as his prey, and the cause of the slave became my own." As Douglass realized her own status as an embodied target, she linked her body to the slave's. She asked her listeners to reflect on the slaves,

to hold a feast, to feed our never-dying minds, to excite each other to deeds of mercy, words of peace; to stir up in the bosom of each, gratitude to God for his increasing goodness, and feeling of deep sympathy for our brethren and sisters, who are in this land of [C]hristian light and liberty held in bondage the most cruel and degrading—to make their cause our own! (Douglass, 1832, p. 114)

She quoted an "English writer" who believed that "'we must feel deeply before we can act rightly; from that absorbing, heart-rending compassion for ourselves springs a deeper sympathy for others, and from a sense of our own weakness and our own upbraidings arises a disposition to be indulgent, to forbear, to forgive.'" This disposition led her to a pragmatic forgiveness toward slaveholders that is often absent from white critics' work.

This passage also reveals the differences between the ways black and white antislavery critics engaged in the performance of mental metempsychosis. While white critic Elizabeth Chandler concentrated on imaginatively inhabiting the slave body to empathize with the slaves, black critic Sarah Douglass advised sympathy for oneself first, and through that self-awareness, an acknowledgment of the body that she shared with the slave, with her "wronged and neglected race." Douglass was more clearheaded about both her separateness from and her connectedness with the slave body.

The Bible reading for the meeting, Isaiah 54, reveals Douglass's conception of the black womanly body, figured not as a sexualized object of voyeurism but as a pure Christian woman whose "Maker is [her] husband" (Is 54:5). The biblical passage exhorts widows and women without children to celebrate their good fortune and to "enlarge the place of [their] tent" or the sphere of their activities, as God speaks to them: for "behold, I have created the smith that bloweth the coals in the fire, and that bringeth forth an instrument for his work," and "no weapon that is formed against thee shall prosper" (Is 54:1–2, 16–17).

Black antislavery critics like Douglass represented themselves as benevolent, strong, invincible brides of Christ, gathering peoples from the Diaspora to forge a new transnational, transmigrating community of souls. They believed that "no weapon" could stop them.

Like Sarah Douglass of Philadelphia, Boston's Susan Paul—the daughter of a prominent black minister—linked antiracism with antislavery, imagining that emancipation would mean, in effect, an end to racist attacks on free blacks. In an 1834 letter published in *The Liberator,* she related an incident of the racism and "cruel prejudice which deprives us of every privilege whereby we might elevate ourselves—and then absurdly condemns us because we are not more refined and intelligent." "But this is no time for despair," she concluded, for "the rapid progress of the cause which you so successfully advocate will, ere long, annihilate the present corrupt state of things, and substitute liberty and its concomitant blessings."[8] Paul certainly had reason for hope, based not only on the widespread and organized efforts of the abolitionist movement, but also on the individual efforts of such pioneers as Prudence Crandall (1803–1890), a white schoolmistress who desegregated her school and whose Boston visit was noted in the same column in which Paul's letter appeared. But like her republican predecessors who naively believed freedom was just around the corner, she could not anticipate that Crandall's school would be burnt to the ground and that emancipation would not bring an end to racism, but in some ways an intensification of it.

Black female antislavery speakers, newly attuned to the ways in which their own status was linked to the status of slaves, revealed an intraracial, cross-class desire in their performances, even as they staged their class difference from the slaves. When they appeared in front of each other in all-black literary societies, they attempted to evoke slave bodies to establish and perform a sisterly bond

among all black women: those designated in the 1820s as "other free" and "slave," and by the 1850s as "free coloured" and "slave." And when they appeared before integrated antislavery societies, they sometimes used white elite bodies as surrogate bodies for their antiracism, establishing a tentative political alliance with selected white women.

Black and white women abolitionists, and those multiracial abolitionists whose racial identity was equivocal—like the "slightly colored" Ball sisters of the Boston Female Anti-Slavery Society who eventually, it is rumored, passed as white—negotiated their bodies into the public sphere through a complex web of surrogations (Fall River Female Anti-Slavery Society, 1838, p. 6). Just as minstrelsy helped to create "a self-consciously white working class" (Lott, 1993, p. 8), female abolitionist meetings, in their tragic inversion of minstrel performances, helped create a self-consciously white middle- and elite-class feminism, as well as a more radical cross-class black feminism. It is crucial to note also the small seed of a feminism based on the intersection of race and gender: Abolitionist Angelina Emily Grimké Weld (1805–1879), Sarah Grimké's sister, believed that the two were so intertwined that she was "far from keeping different moral reformations entirely distinct"; she believed "no such attempt can ever be successful. They are bound together in a circle like the sciences; they blend with each other like the colors of the rainbow" (Barnes & Dumond, 1934, vol. I, p. 431).

In antislavery meetings, the figure of the slave indeed ambiguously held center stage. While, as Lott explains, white minstrels appropriated certain kinds of masculinity through blackface, white, multiracial, and black female abolitionists appropriated certain kinds of femininity through their staging of slave stories and antiracism narratives (Lott, 1993, p. 52). They staged their sense of violation at the hands of men, their anger at sexual oppression in all its forms—from rape, within or outside of marriage, to the curtailment of their movement in public spaces.

Both white and black antislavery advocates performed their class difference from the slaves. While Chandler used mental metempsychosis to teach white women to feel the pain of slavery, Douglass felt the fear engendered by racism, and likened herself to the slave. But Douglass, unlike Chandler, actually was in jeopardy. Both women focused on feelings as they envisioned a benevolent Christian body of women critics, but Chandler concentrated on empathy and imaginatively inhabiting the slave body, while Douglass advised sympathy for oneself first, and through that self-awareness, an acknowledgment of the "body" that she shared with the slave.

Black Antislavery Critics and Surrogate Activism

Free black antislavery lecturers protected their bodies in a variety of ways. Aware of the racist limitations of whites in their audiences—of their tendency to conflate enslaved bodies with free and refugee bodies through a misguided visual shorthand—they sometimes sidestepped the negative effects of this racism by prompting white surrogates to articulate their viewpoints in public settings. They used "white" bodies to do necessary work. Some multiracial critics, like Paul and Ellen Craft (1826–1891), were just as fair-skinned as the Anglo-American speakers, and either (inadvertently or on purpose) passed as white, or, like Paul, were read as "white" by the black community and "black" by the white community.[9] Some, like Craft, used their "whiteness" to launch unbidden attacks on racism.

Sarah Douglass's critique of racism within Quaker meeting houses may serve here as an example of another type of "surrogate activism": not the donning of slave bodies through mental metempsychosis to spur activism, but the dissemination of a black woman's critique through a white woman's text to activate audiences.

Sarah Douglass participated in a complex chain of surrogacy, a chain which eventually prompted a white English woman to publish Douglass's indictment of Quaker racism. William Bassett, an antislavery advocate eager to stimulate antiracism as well as antislavery activity within the Quaker movement, requested in 1837 that Sarah Douglass provide him with an account of race prejudice within the Arch Street meeting house where she worshipped as a youth, and where her mother still attended Quaker services. She wrote a very useful critique of the racist custom of establishing a "Negro pew." When English Quaker Elizabeth Pease later asked Sarah Grimké about American Quaker practices, Grimké, like Bassett, turned to Douglass for information. She asked Douglass to think about whether or not she wanted to attach her name to the critique (Barnes & Dumond, 1934, vol. II, p. 744). Douglass confided that the Arch Street Quakers "despise us for our color," and provided Grimké with a copy of her Bassett letter, which Grimké forwarded to Pease (Barnes & Dumond, 1934, vol. II, pp. 829–832). As the sister of the first Quaker member of the British Parliament, Pease was more insulated from the American cultural anxieties attendant upon the publication of such a critique. With Douglass's blessing, Pease incorporated Douglass's anonymous critique into her 1840 volume, *Society of Friends in the United States: Their Views of the Anti-Slavery Question, and Treatment of the People of Colour.* Sarah Douglass sent her cultural criticism, then, through three different hands before finding publication in England. She protected herself from becoming visible in the public sphere by publishing her critique anonymously within a white woman's text. All of the individuals in this chain of surrogate activism were mindful of their surrogacy and focused on joint activist goals.

Another free black critic, Sarah Forten, similarly disseminated her critique of racism and slavery through a letter solicited by Angelina Grimké, anticipating that Grimké would speak her critique from abolitionist stages across the Northeast. In muted language, Forten explained that prejudice "originates from dislike to the color of the skin, as much as from the degradation of Slavery" (Barnes & Dumond, 1934, vol. I, p. 379). Colonization, she argued, revealed whites' feeling that "this is not your Country," a prejudiced separatism that could be seen in segregated churches, lectures, and schools (Barnes & Dumond, 1934, vol. II, p. 380). Instead of herself becoming an antislavery lecturer, speaking visibly onstage against racism and colonization, Sarah Forten explained her viewpoint to Grimké, who incorporated it into her speeches in a complex act of surrogate activism. Antislavery women critics, in various ways, moved through one another's bodies, and often through slave bodies, to achieve their goals.

Female Slave Refugees as Speakers: Performativity and Resistance

By the 1840s female slave refugees began to tell their own stories onstage. Twenty-two-year-old Ellen Craft escaped from Georgia by posing as a sickly white boy, with her husband William posing as her slave. She was among the first female refugee speakers. She and her husband joined well-known slave refugee and abolitionist William Wells Brown (1815–1884) on a tour of Massachusetts in 1848. Typically, Brown and William Craft both spoke at meetings, and then "'the fugitive couple'" of the Crafts was ushered "to the front of the platform . . . 'so that all present might have the pleasure of seeing them'" (Sterling, 1988, p. 24). At first Ellen did not speak. According to Brown "so near white that she [could] pass without suspicion for a white woman," she simply sat onstage until she was presented at the end of the program (Brown, 1849, p. 7).

Black women critics, slave and free, were keenly conscious of the performativity of race

during the 1850s. Sometimes they inadvertently or intentionally passed as white, or, like educator Susan Paul, were read variously. But Craft's Massachusetts audiences were unaccustomed to considering the possibility that an escaped Southern slave could look and sound like Ellen Craft, who so closely resembled them: "An expression of astonishment arose" when Ellen stood to be acknowledged at the end of her antislavery programs (Sterling, 1988, p. 25). By her very visible ladylike performance, Craft forced audiences to rethink their understanding of race and gender. If race was not manifest in the skin, then what was race?

Eventually Craft began to speak, offering a "very particular account of [her] escape" (Sterling, 1988, p. 25). Her safety, however, was precarious, and when the Fugitive Slave Law passed in 1850, she fled with her husband and William Brown to London. There, they continued their appearances and Ellen developed a strategy of using her everyday performance of herself as cultural criticism. With the help of British abolitionists, she also planned a high-culture activist performance in what Marvin Carlson calls a "place of performance" (1989) and Joseph Roach calls a "vortice of behavior" (1996).

She strode into the Crystal Palace of the 1851 London Great Exhibition, with its crowds of white visitors. As part of an interracial, international abolitionist delegation, she was escorted by a white member of the English National Reform Association. With fellow abolitionists, she walked right up to the most popular sculpture at the fair, indeed "the most popular American sculpture of the nineteenth century": Hiram Powers's "The Greek Slave" (1841–1843) (Bank, 1997, p. 178; Yellin, 1989, pp. 100, 122). A gleaming white marble statue of a nude female slave in chains, this sculpture evoked and eroticized white woman's metaphorical enslavement as well as blacks' literal enslavement. Powers carved a slave figure permanently resigned to her fate, at a time when refugees like Craft refused to succumb. Ellen Craft, a shifting "mulatto"/"white"/ "black" soul figure who had very publicly and visibly refused to enact the enslaved role represented by this sculpture, performed her resistance. She moved around the curtained statue and contested its statement. She tried to provoke fellow museum-goers, particularly Americans, into a discussion about the sculpture and its relation to American antislavery resistance. American passers-by refused her invitation to an exchange of ideas, registering their contempt for the spectacle of Craft's delegation. This, however, gave the protesters an opportunity to record the museum-goers' prejudice in *The Liberator*. Museums and theatres were active sites of negotiation, where women critics tested out their own theories of race and gender.

White and Black Theatre Critics: Minstrelsy or God's Handiwork?

Eric Lott opens his book on minstrelsy with an anonymous 1855 *New York Tribune* review that hails Jim Crow minstrelsy as "a species of insanity, though of a gentle and pleasing kind" (1993, p. 3). He links this comment, and the blackface minstrel shows that prompted it, to a performance genealogy in which "white male writers have been obsessed with white male-dark male dyads."[10] Lott explains that white male playwrights and critics expressed their homosocial desire and enacted cultural theft through "black" minstrel bodies in a complex nineteenth century interchange. But the *Tribune* review, and the tradition of which it is a part, cannot simply be viewed as the province of white male writers. In fact, a white female critic by the name of Jane Cunningham Croly (1829–1901) wrote Lott's representative review, and Margaret Fuller (1810–1850), another well-known *Tribune* critic, published his secondary example.[11] Cornelia Wells Walter (1813–1898), the editor of the *Boston Evening*

Transcript from 1842 to 1847, routinely wrote reviews of minstrel shows. White women theatre and performance critics are inextricably and problematically linked to what Lott calls "the desire to put moderate racial attitudes and minstrel shows together" in the nineteenth century (Lott, 1993, p 16). They began writing reviews professionally in the 1840s. Jane Croly wrote the minstrel review during her stint as a theatre critic and fashion commentator for Charles Dana's *Tribune* in 1855.[12]

In the mid-1840s, white theatre critic Cornelia Wells Walter edited the *Boston Evening Transcript,* and—like her New York colleagues Fuller and Croly—she celebrated minstrelsy while trying to validate black culture. She praised white minstrel T. D. Rice as "the *inimitable* delineator of Negro character" and "the *original* Jim Crow" (Walter, 1842, p. 2, and 1845, p. 2). However, she also published articles that depicted the origins of minstrelsy in a much more complicated way. In an 1844 essay, for example, she depicted Northerners humming "a fashionable [minstrel] air" during their travels in the South, prompting a complex chain of events:

> In an instant all the negroes within hearing will start and seem delighted. Parts of the tune, no matter how trifling will be remembered, and in the evening when their daily toils are over, you will hear the old Banjo player hard at work fixing the strings of his instrument until he makes a something of what the white man sang, which he christens with a name of his own selection. Thus originated "old Dan Tucker" and many more of the melodies now sung with such rapturous applause at Amory Hall. (Walter, 1844, p. 2)

The process described here is tortured by circularity and contradiction. Southern blacks hear and "remember" minstrel songs with melodies presumed to be lifted from slave culture, but they do not then sing the "original" songs that inspired the minstrel tunes. Instead, they "make a something" out of the northern minstrel song (based on the slave song) and call it by a new name. It is through this new and *original* riff that "Dan Tucker" and other minstrel songs find their way onto the stage.

White women theatre critics' sympathetic attitude toward black performance as well as blackface performance emerged in part from the complex web of interracial desires articulated within female antislavery meetings designed to appropriate blacks' bodies. The reports of these meetings were circulated widely in the early 1840s when Margaret Fuller and Cornelia Wells Walter, in particular, began writing about minstrelsy. The minstrel show mirrored in a comic fashion the mental metempsychosis practiced by the female antislavery critics, and white women theatre critics responded by trying to locate in minstrelsy the traces of the "original" slave culture that prompted blackface's "web of envy as well as repulsion, sympathetic identification as well as fear" (Lott, 1993, p. 8). The tension between claiming black culture as the creation of white actors and validating black authorship and embodied culture is palpable in Cornelia Wells Walter's coverage of minstrelsy. She wanted, like her contemporaries, the white antislavery critics, to acknowledge blacks' humanity while keeping the currency of "soul" moving as she claimed the healthy "white" body of the true woman.

Black performance critics, in contrast, moved beyond the antislavery strategy of mental metempsychosis to stake their claim on American-ness through a universal Christian body. This strategy emerged in the early eighteenth century and reverberates as late as the 1890s, when Lillian Parker Thomas emerged as the first black woman to act as a professional theatre critic. Thomas, a prominent African American elocutionist, reviewer, and editor of the *New York Freeman,* combined her "Stage" and "Church" columns to create a vision of a black Christian arts community whose originality and talent authorized black culture and its claim on America. She tracked black actors,

minstrels, and elocutionists as well as vocalists and instrumentalists across the country, giving her readers a sense of the breadth and depth of black theatrical activity. She documented black women's playwriting for the nineteenth century stage: she noted in a typical column, for instance, that "a three-act comedy drama entitled 'An Autograph Letter,' by Esther B. Tiffany, was presented to the citizens of Hannibal, Mo." (Thomas, 1892, p. 4). Thomas reported on black women elocutionists and lecturers as well as playwrights and actors, and her columns prove that by the turn of the century, black women were engaged in virtually every aspect of theatre, criss-crossing the Northeast and Midwest, in particular. Her columns also reveal that at a time when white-dominated audiences increasingly looked toward New York as the vanguard, new developments in nineteenth century black theatre were not perceived, or perhaps for safety's sake simply not advertised, as limited to one site: black artists, Christians all, were present everywhere. Thomas emphasized women's commonalities, envisioning united Christian women walking side by side as a means of lobbying for African Americans' rights. In "this, a day of great possibilities," she wrote, "the feminine heart yearns for broader paths wherein to walk, an intellectual highway whereon all nations or sex may walk abreast" (Majors, 1893/1971, p. 207).

CONCLUSION

Black, white, and multiracial women performance critics in the middle of the nineteenth century were struggling to find a body—or a set of bodies—through which they could enter the public sphere, either in print or onstage. At first they practiced mental metempsychosis, using the slave body to create sentient bodies for themselves, each other, and the slaves, connecting themselves in a tangled, thorny array of contradictory impulses and activist hopes. Then they imagined, in disparate ways, healthy bodies: black medical lecturers staged universal

Christian bodies through carefully sketched illustrations, while whites introduced ivory bones and charged them with racial "purity." As the woman's rights movement emerged, these performance traditions, of claiming the abstract Christian body and of borrowing bodies and bones, continued to prove useful, not only to those actively engaged in the suffrage movement, but also to women professionals such as theatre critics. Female theatre critics, like their contemporaries in the antislavery movement, tackled the question of how to enter the racialized public sphere by borrowing various bodies or by claiming a universal, abstract Christian body. Both of these strategies proved problematic: the first, with its reliance on invisibility and the fluidity of identity, denied the material differences of those bodies involved in the borrowings, and the second worked only for fellow Christians, within what bell hooks now calls a community of faith. Unless we can acknowledge the bodies of these critics who have preceded us, and for whom we act, in part, as surrogates, we cannot fully perceive the positionality of our own bodies and the challenges inherent within our "bodies of discourse."

NOTES

1. In the early twenty-first century, the term *multiracial* indicates an individual who either self-identifies with, or is perceived as being identified with, more than one racial designation. Within the context of this essay, it stands in for a variety of nineteenth century terms, including the term *mulatto*, to indicate a nineteenth century individual who is perceived as being identified with both black and white "races." Most multiracial antislavery critics self-identified as "black" or "Afric-American," though there were important exceptions. I am defining the term *critic* broadly in this essay, to include women who reshaped the cultural performances of their day by circulating either performance-based criticism (such as interviews or lectures) or print-based criticism (such as journalistic articles or reviews).

2. Quotations in this paragraph and the next are from Swerdlow, 1994, pp. 36 and 33. Italics

in original Constitution. Swerdlow provides an excellent analysis of the local context of the female antislavery societies.

3. In 1870, census-takers also counted "Chinese" and "Indian" residents. It was not until 1900 that the category "mulatto" was struck from the census form and "Japanese" was added to the list of "foreigners" who were not included in the "white" category.

4. Cf. Plato's *Phaedrus*.

5. Jean Fagan Yellin discusses this phenomenon with regard to Chandler's first poem, "Kneeling Slave," which asks if the "lady" will ignore her "sister," or "has thy heart grown selfish in its bliss / That thou shouldst view unmoved a fate like this?" "What is problematic here," Yellin points out, "is [Chandler's] reader's humanity," not the slave's (1989, p. 14).

6. Among white critics, Lydia Maria Child tended not to collapse the "woman" into the "slave": she wrote that she "did not perceive . . . that the doctrine of Women's Rights, as it is called, has a more immediate connection with anti-slavery, than several other subjects" (quoted in Yellin, 1989, p. 60). She is known for creating, through such publications as her 1847 collection of short stories, *Fact and Fiction*, and her 1867 novel *A Romance of the Republic*, the figure of the tragic mulatta, aligning that figure with the true womanhood that she herself rejected (1989, pp. 73–76). However, when Child, who wrote on women's issues but who did not actively join in the meetings, learned of the 1869 split within the movement over whether to focus directly on women's suffrage (as Susan B. Anthony and Elizabeth Cady Stanton and their wing did), or to concentrate on black male suffrage as a first step toward universal suffrage (as Lucy Stone and her wing did), Child sided with Stone and most African American women. She published an article titled "Concerning Women" in the *National Anti-Slavery Standard*, explaining that "few things connected with public affairs have given me so much pain and mortification as to observe occasional indications that some women were willing to set aside the freedmen's right to vote, thinking thereby to hasten the acknowledgment of their own. . . . That there is one woman who would gain freedom for herself by violating principles of freedom with regard to other human beings indicates a latent disease against which it behooves us to take warning in time" (1869, October 30, *National Anti-Slavery Standard*, (53) cols. 1–2, p. 1.

7. C. Peter Rigley, editor of *The Black Abolitionist Papers*, dates this meeting in "late June or early July 1832." "Mental Feasts," the article reporting on the meeting, appears in *The Liberator*, II(29), on July 21, 1832, pp. 114–115. Unless otherwise noted, the passages that immediately follow are all from that article, which was sent to the newspaper by "a lady who was invited to attend the meeting." The article evidently provides the full text of the speech which Sarah Douglass delivered to open the meeting.

8. Letter signed "S. Paul," and dated "Boston, April 1, 1834," in *The Liberator*, IV(14), April 5, 1834, p. 55. From time to time, Susan Paul published examples of how her schoolchildren, or others' interaction with them, exemplified the basic tenets of antiracism and antislavery: see, for example, *The Liberator*, V(31), 1835, August 1, p. 122, for her critique of racism within the Baptist Sabbath School Society; *The Liberator*, VI(33), 1836, August 13, p. 130, for her applause for the antiracism of the Amesbury and Salisbury Sabbath school children; and "Temptation Resisted," in the *American Anti-Slavery Almanac for 1837*, 1(2) p. 42, for her story of a black child's honesty, which she weaves into a critique of slavery.

9. To serve as their delegates to the first national female antislavery convention in 1837, the Boston Female Anti-Slavery Society selected four delegates: Mary Parker, Martha Ball, Susan Paul, and Julia Williams. Parker was white. Ball was described as "slightly coloured" and is rumored to have passed as white. Anne Weston explained that Paul was chosen "'because she was a favorable specimen of the coloured race, Julia Williams because the coloured people regard her as one of themselves, a light in which they do not regard Susan Paul'" (Hansen, 1993, p. 19). Weston's comment about Susan Paul's equivocal position in the community is telling: whites regarded her as black, while many blacks regarded her as white. She clearly self-identified as black. Dorothy Sterling reported that Paul was "the most respected black woman in Boston. She ran her own school, directed the Garrison Junior Choir, which gave benefit concerts for the abolitionist movement, and was active in the Female Anti-Slavery Society. 'She was educated and intelligent and abolitionists associated with her and invited her to their homes as a friend,' a white woman wrote" (Sterling, 1984, p. 184). And yet, she lived a tenuous existence. A series of misfortunes quickly impoverished Paul: her father died, a storm hit her home, her corenters defaulted on the payment for an alternative home, her sister died and the sister's four children became her dependents. As a result of a cold she caught after being chased out of the ladies' cabin and onto the deck of a steamboat, she died of tuberculosis at age 32.

10. From Lott (1993, p. 5), discussing "Leslie Fiedler's Thesis in Love and Death in the American Novel (1960)."

11. See Downs, R. B., & Downs, J. B. (1991), *Journalists of the United States: Biographical Sketches of Print and Broadcast News Shapers from the Late 17th Century to the Present*, p. 99; Paneth, D. (1983), *The Encyclopedia of American Journalism*, p. 105; Schlesinger, E. B. (1971) "Croly, Jane Cunningham," in E. T. James (Ed.), *Notable American Women, 1607–1950: A Biographical Dictionary* (Vol. I), pp. 409–411; "Jennie June" (1904), in *Memories of Jane Cunningham Croly*, p. 6; and "Mrs. Jennie June Croly" (1900, March 11), *The New York Times*, p. 17.

12. Internal stylistic evidence also supports Croly's authorship of this particular column. The *Tribune* theatre reviews from time to time are displaced by Croly's dress reform columns. Cf., for example, "Women's Gear" (1855, May 25), p. 5; and "A Word on the Theatre and Its Audiences" (1855, September 24), p. 5. By the time of her death in 1901, Croly was hailed as the "best-known woman journalist in America" (*New York Times*, 1901, December 24, pp. 3–4).

REFERENCES

Bank, R. K. (1997). *Theatre culture in America, 1825–1860*. England: Cambridge University Press.

Barnes, G. H., & Dumond, D. L. (Eds.). (1934). *Letters of Theodore Dwight Weld, Angelina Grimké Weld and Sarah Grimké, 1822–1844* (Vols. I–II). New York: D. Appleton–Century.

Brown, W. W. (1849). Singular escape. Letter dated 4 January 1849. *The Liberator*, XIX(2), 7.

Campbell, J. (1893). Representative women. *Woman's Progress in Literature, Science, Arts, Education and Politics, 1*, 8.

Carlson, M. (1989). *Places of performance: The semiotics of theatre architecture*. Ithaca, NY: Cornell University Press.

Chandler, E. M. (1836). *Essays philanthropic and moral by Elizabeth Margaret Chandler, principally relating to the abolition of slavery in America*. Philadelphia: L. Howell. Douglass, F. (1832, July 21). Mental feasts. *The Liberator, 11*, 114.

Douglass, F. (1832, July 21). Mental feasts. *The Liberator, 11*, 114.

Fall River Female Anti-Slavery Society. (1838). *Report of a delegate to the anti-slavery convention of American women, held in Philadelphia, May, 1838, including an account of other meetings held in Pennsylvania hall, and of the riot. Addressed to the Fall River female anti-slavery society, and published by its request.* Boston: Isaiah Knapp.

Foucault, M. (1972). *The archaeology of knowledge.* (A. M. Sheridan Smith, Trans.). New York: Harper & Row. (Original work published 1969)

Geertz, C. (1973). *The interpretation of cultures: Selected essays.* New York: Basic Books.

Grew, M. (1892, April 27). Letter to Miss Isabel Howland. In Sophia Smith Collection, Smith College, Northampton, MA.

Hansen, D. G. (1993). *Strained sisterhood: Gender and class in the Boston Female Anti-Slavery Society.* Amherst: University of Massachusetts Press.

Hart, L. (1998). *Between the body and the flesh: Performing sadomasochism.* New York: Columbia University Press.

hooks, b., & West, C. (1991). *Breaking bread: Insurgent black intellectual life.* Boston: South End Press.

Kerber, L. (1980). *Women of the republic: Intellect and ideology in revolutionary America.* Chapel Hill: University of North Carolina Press.

Le Goff, J. (1992). *History and memory.* (S. Rendall & E. Claman, Trans.). New York: Columbia University Press. (Original work published 1977)

Lerner, G. (1967). *The Grimké sisters from South Carolina: Rebels against slavery.* Boston: Houghton Mifflin.

Lott, E. (1993). *Love and theft: Blackface minstrelsy and the American working class.* New York: Oxford University Press.

Majors, M. A. (1971). *Noted negro women: Their triumphs and activities.* Chicago: Freeport, NY: Books for Libraries Press. (Original work published 1893)

Mattison, H. (1988). Louisa Picquet, the octoroon: A tale of southern slave life. In G. Barthelemy (Ed.), *Collected black women's narratives* (pp. 5–30). New York: Oxford University Press. (Original work published 1861)

Nora, P. (1996). *Realms of memory: Rethinking the French past* (L. D. Kritzman, Ed.; A. Goldhammer, Trans., under the direction of P. Nora). New York: Columbia University Press. (Original work published 1981–1992)

Rigley, C. P. (Ed.) (1991). *The black abolitionist papers* (Vol. III: The United States, 1830–1846). Chapel Hill: The University of North Carolina Press.

Roach, J. (1996). *Cities of the dead: Circum-Atlantic performance.* New York: Columbia University Press.

Scarry, E. (1985). *The body in pain: The making and unmaking of the world.* New York: Oxford University Press.

Sterling, D. (Ed.). (1984). *We are your sisters: Black women in the nineteenth century.* New York: W. W. Norton.

Sterling, D. (1988). *Black foremothers: Three lives* (2nd ed.). New York: City University of New York.

Sterling, D. (1991). *Ahead of her time: Abby Kelley and the politics of antislavery.* New York: W. W. Norton.

Swerdlow, A. (1994). Abolition's conservative sisters: The ladies' New York City anti-slavery societies, 1834–1840. In J. Fagan Yellin & J. C. Van Horne (Eds.), *The abolitionist sisterhood: Women's political culture in antebellum America* (pp. 31–44). Ithaca, NY: Cornell University Press.

Thomas, L. P. (1892, December). Stage. *The [Indianapolis] Freeman* (Holiday ed.), p. 4.

University of Virginia, Geospatial and Statistical Data Center. (2004). *Historical census browser.* Retrieved July 1, 2004, from http://fisher.lib.virginia.edu/collections/stats/histcensus/index.html/

Walter, C. W. (1842, September 20). Rice. *Boston Evening Transcript*, p. 2.

Walter, C. W. (1844, February 29). Origin of Dan Tucker. *Boston Evening Transcript*, p. 2.

Walter, C. W. (1845, November 3). National theatre. *Boston Evening Transcript*, p. 2.

Yellin, J. F. (1989). *Women & sisters: The antislavery feminists in American culture.* New Haven, CT: Yale University Press.

Yellin, J. F., & Van Horne, J. C. (1994). *The abolitionist sisterhood: Women's political culture in antebellum America.* Ithaca, NY: Cornell University Press.

8

What to Do When Nuclear War Breaks Out

TRACY C. DAVIS

In Ibsen's play *Hedda Gabler*, first published in 1890, an historian scandalizes and amazes the other characters when he reveals the topic of his second book, still in manuscript.

Lövborg: (smiles, puts down his hat and pulls a packet wrapped in paper from his coat pocket.) [. . .]

Tesman: What's this one about?

Lövborg: It's the continuation. [. . .] Of the book.

Tesman: The new one?

Lövborg: Of course.

Tesman: Yes but, my dear Ejlert . . . it carries on right to the present day!

Lövborg: That is so. And this one deals with the future.

Tesman: With the future! But ye gods, we don't know anything about that!

Lövborg: No. But there are one or two things to be said about it, all the same.[1]

Apparently continuing the narrative of his forthcoming book, Ejlert Lövborg's next work will be a history of the future course of civilization. *Hedda Gabler* highlights how futures are discursively signaled within texts: in the one case Lövborg's book, and in the other Ibsen's own text. Performance historians might be less impressed by Lövborg's feat of intellectual audacity than late-nineteenth century Norwegian social historians such as Jörgen Tesman, for we habitually engage with the multitemporality and intertemporality inherent in scripts and the implications of a text documenting the past and outlining potential future events. This is the basis of our

Waiting for the parade at Trekfest 2004, Riverside, Iowa.

Photo courtesy of Max K. Shapey

faith that a published drama in any way bears on a performance that occurred in the past, as well as the basis of a script's power to call a new event into being in an as-yet-to-occur performance.

The duality of this temporal relationship is not limited to the textual remnants of drama. Performance itself teeters between temporalities, fluidly representing past or future, and sometimes both, whether in a theatre setting or social transactions. For example, a modern site of pilgrimage was created when the councilors of Riverside, Iowa, secured Gene Roddenberry's blessing to dub their town the place "where the Trek begins." In an episode of *Star Trek*, Captain Kirk mentions that he was born in a small town in Iowa, and Riverside (pop. 928) will become—or actually, with Roddenberry's consent—has become that town. In Riverside, a 15-foot model of a spaceship—resembling but

not replicating the version patented by Paramount Pictures—"recalls" that in the year 2233, James Tiberius Kirk, future captain of the starship *Enterprise*, will be born here. No Kirks live in Riverside yet, though the seniors' center invites everyone to "Come in and dine with the ancestors of our own Captn. James Kirk," presumably from the distaff side of the family. On the last weekend in June, every year since 1984, *Star Trek* fans gather in Riverside to commemorate the founding of a television dynasty and to postulate a future of space exploration. They perform their allegiances to *Star Trek* and its spin-off series in costume, parading through the main street and interacting as if Roddenberry's scripts—already accomplished in performance—document a future.

The conceit of Riverside being "where the Trek begins" is that it commemorates a birth that *will* happen there, based on a throwaway line in a science fiction series. Logic tells us that a birth cannot be predicted centuries in advance, nor can the course that such a life will take be known; furthermore, this is the birth of a character who is merely fictive, however much he may be admired and have an active fan base. Science fiction (or speculative fiction), by definition, postulates a future. Commemoration, by definition, recalls a past. One performance event from the past (the line uttered in *Star Trek's* dialogue) and another from the future (Kirk's birth) reciprocally take up elements of each other's temporality without putting the chronology in question. Thus, not only drama exists as events-in-potential, but performance also operates in this manner, though rarely with a claim to a future as concrete as Riverside's.

Even without the narratologically creative fan culture surrounding *Star Trek*, scripts are events-in-potential,[2] cleaving as well as uniting temporalities, making the past and future coterminous in a present moment. As artifacts of writers' imaginations, scripts are tangible products of labor while, at the same time, also events-in-potential. Riverside's claim—and monument—to Captain Kirk's birth demonstrates the public's willingness to suspend disbelief not only in science fiction, but also in sequential logic and in the idea that a script is contained either by its performative or its temporal frames. In fact, theatre historians intent on demonstrating the social relevance of performance rely explicitly on this form of lunacy, which stated in other words would be something like this: *performance scripts are not entirely contained by their performance. They are simultaneously archives and events-in-waiting. Dramatic scripts, unique amongst literary forms, exist in tension with their to-be-performed–ness, and complicate the idea that a performative utterance calls something into being, for they muddle conventional ideas about what is an historical event, when a document is a document of a finite occurrence, and how the conditionality of performance prefigures responses.*

The major case study for this chapter concerns scripts that were written to be broadcast at the outbreak of global nuclear war. Like the United Federation of Planets and Lövborg's book, postulations of global nuclear war have inspired artists and stimulated the imaginations of the public in many contexts. For most of the Cold War, the prospect of massive nuclear attack was a significant influence on the social imaginary, the constellation of preparatory and remedial actions to be undertaken by the public coming under the rubric of "civil defense" in a fashion similar to how the George W. Bush administration, since September 11, 2001, attempts to mobilize government, the civil sector, and the public under the rubric of "homeland security." Civil defense authorities in three close NATO allies—the United States, Canada, and the United Kingdom—constructed dialogic and monologic scripts for the occasion of nuclear war, and held them in readiness, pending authorization from their governments for broadcast. Significantly, these Cold War texts of instruction whose performance was to coincide with imminent war and the immediate aftermath of nuclear Armageddon have the conditional status of scripts in-potential as well as the historical status of rehearsed scripts, for they were tried and practiced in case their performance "for real" was ever necessitated. As scripts instructing citizens in the essential steps for self-preservation in the event of global nuclear war, they challenge the relationship between knowing and theorizing the past and the future as linked phenomena by proposing objects for performance history's analysis that represent events that have never happened, before audiences that have never been constituted, and yet versions closely resembling them are known and were rehearsed, sometimes before enormous audiences. This case study highlights how historians exercise agency to not only document a past through discursive reconstruction but also signal the creation of a future act embedded in the evidentiary potentials and conditionality of scripts, whether delivered in rehearsal or as "the real thing": nuclear war.[3]

REHEARSAL

A RAND Corporation report of 1949, commissioned to help civil defense authorities understand how people were likely to behave in the event of an attack with atomic bombs, predicts that there will be a huge population who "will be extremely disturbed by the appalling sights about them, by the fear that they have been exposed to lethal amounts of radiation, and by the intense suspense of not knowing the fate of their families and their friends." They will likely show disorganized and maladaptive behaviors. They may not help others. They may not take obviously needed precautions. This can be somewhat avoided by training the population prior to the event, though there is a distinct danger that their training may be forgotten in the throes of emotionality resulting from actual war. "Perhaps the most effective device would be a calm, familiar, authoritative voice giving both reassurance and directions as to what should be done," for example through public address systems, an underground communication system that could withstand the bomb damage, or mobile radio broadcasting units.[4] Various versions of these communications were tried in the next decade, for example a "Warning Voice From the Sky" over Cape Elizabeth, Maine, consisting of a civil defense official in a light aircraft who used a megaphone to spread the word about impending attack to those who were out of range of air raid sirens.[5] British authorities used public address systems mounted in terrestrial vehicles, and roved around neighborhoods instructing people when it was safe to emerge from their fallout shelters.[6]

A paper from the *Canadian Medical Association Journal* urged in 1957 that "Previous to disaster . . . it is not enough to communicate a warning. Once this has been given, communication must continue. . . . The guidance, reassurance and social cohesion provided by good communication can prevent the disorientation and confusion that leads to impulsive, irrational behaviour on the part of individuals and groups."[7] Communication was crucial to maintaining civil order. Media theorists observe that "media influence the political agenda and public opinion not necessarily in terms of *what to think* but rather what to think *about*. That is, the media have the capacity to 'prime' audiences."[8] Assuming that the public would be on the move to assembly points and shelter, often in cars, radio was the preferred medium of communication during an impending nuclear attack and in the period immediately following it. Battery-powered radios, and particularly the popularity of transistor radios after 1954, made it feasible to tune in almost anywhere en route to shelter and then once again inside domestic or public facilities.[9]

In the United States, civil defense authorities broadcast on CONELRAD stations (640 and 1240 AM), banning all other simultaneous commercial transmission in order to avoid giving enemy aircraft the opportunity to discern their location from local call signs.[10] But by the mid-1960s, Americans had replaced CONELRAD with the Emergency Broadcast System, yet still had no national plan on a par with the U.K.'s or Canada's.[11] In Britain and Canada, the BBC and CBC national radio networks were used for broadcasting instructions to the public. With Canada's thinly dispersed population, the radio was a more effective means than sirens to disseminate warnings, as well as specific information.[12] Until March 1968, Canada maintained 24-hour-a-day broadcasting capacity at 32 radio stations across the country; stations remained under contract for operation and maintenance of emergency broadcasting equipment for this purpose until May 16, 1991.[13] Every station had a collection of recordings to play in case they received

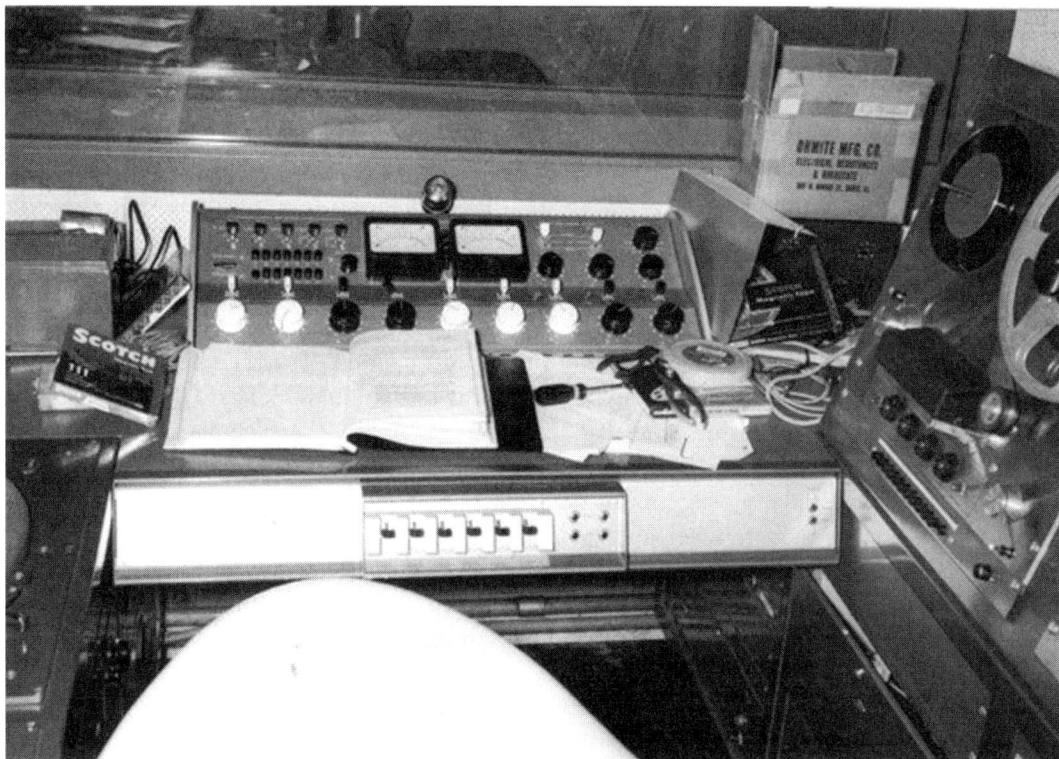

CBC broadcasting studio at Canada's federal emergency government headquarters.

Photo courtesy of the Diefenbunker, Canada's Cold War Museum

word from the Emergency Measures Organization and Department of National Defense that missiles were incoming. In an emergency, commercial AM, FM, and television stations would be alerted (except Frobisher Bay, subsequently known as Iqaluit, in the eastern Arctic), they would cease normal programming, and CBC radio would begin emergency broadcasting within three to five minutes. About fifteen minutes would remain before ICBMs arrived in southern Canada.[14] The continuity of the nation would be ensured by government relocation and broadcast of information through the auspices of the federal government from its blast-proof location in the "Diefenbunker" (Carp, Ontario) where the CBC maintained a special studio for this purpose and where, in an emergency, ten civilians would relocate to staff the Emergency

Public Information Service and nine for the Emergency Broadcasting System.[15] The public's need for information would also be served by CBC broadcast booths in the six federal bunkers located across the country.

Similarly, the British planned to station BBC personnel in each regional seat of government. Despite this, for two days postattack they anticipated that most areas would be without broadcast capacity.[16] This was extensively gamed in CIVLOG 64, a NATO exercise designed to test civil defense preparation amongst civil servants.[17] Another British exercise, Phoenix Five from 1967, asserts,

> The ability to broadcast, personally, would constitute one of the most powerful instruments in the hands of the Regional Commissioner. . . . In the very early stages

after attack the morale of the public would inevitably be at a very low ebb; they would need reassurance from the highest level. Through the medium of broadcasting the Regional Commissioner would be able, personally, to introduce himself and to let it be known that a pre-planned system of emergency administration was in existence. Through this medium, too, news of national importance would be promulgated, together with details of any special measures of importance that it might be necessary to introduce in the interests of the community. It would provide, too, by far the best means of advising the public as a whole on matters concerning fall-out.[18]

But, as civil defense officials frequently noted, plans were not worth anything unless they stood up to testing.

Relying on commercial stations, and thus having to be much more public about its plans, the United States tested its system regularly from 1954 through 1961 in a series of exercises called Operation Alert. In 1955, a five-minute program was broadcast coincident with the simulated attack warning, and another five-minute program was broadcast coincident with the simulated stages when an attack was imminent, including running news accounts of the simulated evacuation.[19] Media executives recommended that President Eisenhower make a broadcast early in the exercise to demonstrate that he was alive and working, that democracy was preserved and government went on.[20] Up to a quarter of the U.S. population tuned in. In 1956, it was assumed that following the simulated attack, only 35 percent of the country—mostly in the southeast—could be covered by radio; within four hours, 90 percent of coverage would be restored, and 100 percent within 24 hours provided that stations could get electrical power. These would be addressed from Highpoint (the presidential bunker in the Blue Ridge Mountains) and signals relayed station-to-station.[21] During the drills to practice communications, all AM, FM, and television stations were mandated to participate by

Radio broadcast for Civil Defense Day, December 7, 1960, the anniversary of the Japanese attack on Pearl Harbor.

Photo courtesy of National Archives and Records Administration RG 397-MA Box 14 folder 8-R.

leaving the air and remaining silent unless they were part of the National Defense Emergency program, in which case they switched to broadcasting on 640 or 1240 kilocycles at 3:10 PM (EST). All citizens were requested to monitor their radios for the next 15 minutes.

Testing communications and broadcasting to the public was a regular part of nuclear civil defense exercises from the late 1950s through mid-1960s. A 90-minute coast-to-coast-to-coast broadcast hosted by CBC personality Byng Whitteker during Exercise TOCSIN B in 1961 specified what the public would hear at each stage of an emergency, and included a 3-minute broadcast by Prime Minister Diefenbaker and taped messages (broadcast regionally) from provincial premiers and territorial commissioners.[22]

TAPE: BEEP WARNING

Whitteker: We rejoin the national network now at the Emergency Headquarters of the Federal Government for Exercise Tocsin, and for the next three minutes I am going to describe to you some of the activities in this centre. (AD LIB DESCRIPTION FOR THREE MINUTES, BASED ON PREVIOUS BRIEFING) Now, I have with me (NAMES TWO CABINET MINISTERS AND THEIR POSITIONS) Mr._____, could you tell the Canadian people of the reasons for sounding National Take Cover just 12 minutes after the Alert Warning? I have understood that we would have two hours' warning of attack by aircraft and that the Take Cover would be sounded in each regional [sic] separately when aircraft approach a major city.

Minister: That's what would happen in an attack involving only manned aircraft. However, in this exercise the assumed enemy is also using missiles, and these have been identified by the BMEWS system.

Whitteker: BMEWS—That's the Ballistic Missile Early Warning System.

Minister: Yes, the one that has been set up in the North for the detection of missiles. For purposes of this exercise, apparently enough missiles have already been launched against North America to justify warning people in all of our likely target areas to take cover.

This was followed by reports from each regional emergency control center until Whitteker was interrupted by a report from the army.

Whitteker: I have just been informed that exercise missiles have exploded in Canada in the general area of Courtney, B.C., Edmonton, Alberta, North Bay, Ontario, Chatham, New Brunswick, and South West Newfoundland. We now take you to Regional Headquarters at Camp Shilo, Manitoba, for the First report.

TAPE: BEEP WARNING

7:36 Shilo: I have just been handed an Army report of an exercise nuclear detonation in Alberta. It reads as follows: "A nuclear weapon exploded in the Edmonton, Alberta area at 5:35 P.M. Edmonton time."

TAPE: BEEP WARNING

Whitteker: "Everyone within 20 miles of Edmonton take shelter against the fallout which will start to come down in that area within 30 minutes."

TAPE: BEEP WARNING

Whitteker: "A much larger area will eventually be affected as the upper winds will cause the fallout to drift southeast from Edmonton toward Saskatoon at about 22 miles per hour."

TAPE: BEEP WARNING

Whitteker: "The estimated times at which fallout will reach localities Southeast of Edmonton will be broadcast in a few minutes. The situation will be easier to follow if you have a road map at hand."

Federal Exercise Headquarters then reported additional detonations, followed by instructions about how to equip emergency shelters and cope during fallout. On-the-spot interviews are held with a prescient man in Esquimalt, British Columbia, who has built a shelter in his home, and a farmer in Alexandria, Ontario, who has made accommodation for his livestock as well as his family. As the 90-minute broadcast script concludes, the lesson is drawn:

Whitteker: If this were a real attack we would, of course, be staying on the air till the immediate danger was over and the All-Clear Message was issued; and there is no doubt that many thousands of Canadians, roused by reality, would be rushing to make preparations for the next attack.

Whitteker then outlines the advice in the government's standard booklet "11 Steps to Survival."[23] Regional correspondents also sign off.

The centralization of broadcast information and regular exercises including public broadcasting had several purposes: by habituating the public to tune to these stations, they could be better controlled through information. Otherwise, as was gamed in Chicago in 1956, eight days after the attack "incipient panic" arose "due to erroneous and alarming information being broadcast over radio" as news reporters relayed information from numerous arms of the federal government—Army, Red Cross, and Department of Agriculture—instead of the official versions passed through the civil defense public information office. Saboteurs, it was thought, could take advantage of this confused situation.[24] In Operation Alert 1959, all commercial broadcasting and telecasting ceased while a quarter of the U.S. population listened to 1,200

stations broadcasting on CONELRAD, but this left a lot susceptible to being misled by other sources,[25] such as the mobile radio stations that simulated broadcasting clandestinely from Manitoba, Canada, and Coahuila, Mexico, beaming psychological warfare propaganda into the United States "urging revolt against authority and surrender."[26] In at least one British scenario, the tracking down and closing of such illegal broadcasting stations is detailed.[27] Cross-border cooperation would be crucial, not only to avoid subversive broadcasting, but in order to coordinate public action.

A joint exercise in 1965 illustrates the problem: nuclear strikes are reported 25 miles southwest of Regina with fallout headed toward South Dakota, and 25 miles east of Minot with fallout headed toward Minnesota and Manitoba. People are moving toward shelter, but they still have some time before danger strikes. What should they do? Should people in North Dakota and Minnesota know of Saskatchewan's strike? Will Minot's strike be made known to residents of Saskatchewan and Manitoba, and if so by what means? The CBC's signal could be picked up across the border, but for whom, exactly, is the CBC broadcasting? Do stations broadcast predictions of fallout trajectories and instructions as to what all people in fallout paths must do? Who is responsible for instructing them? What if instructions for border regions conflict? Do the two governments agree on what people should do at this point?[28]

In 1959, 38 pages of sample scripts were produced for broadcast during the annual Operation Alert drill.[29] All four radio networks in the United States (ABC, CBS, NBC, and the Mutual Broadcasting System) linked up to carry civil defense director Leo Hoegh's address from Highpoint for broadcast by 1,200 stations.[30] Like all the Operation Alert broadcasts, this was punctuated with reminders that this is just a drill and there is no attack.

ANNOUNCER: This is a CONELRAD drill. . . . We cannot close our eyes to the possibility of attack. That is why the radio and television industry has given up valuable time to help make this exercise successful. . . . With CONELRAD broadcasts you would know that the information you were hearing was not only the *latest* information, but *official* information.

Listeners heard descriptions of the typical kinds of information that would be broadcast in the event of nuclear war: shelter supplies, evacuation procedures, warning times, the military's detection system for early warning, how the United States is striking back at enemy forces, and the function of NORAD. Fallout and shielding principles were explained, along with procedures for taking shelter and essential materials for stocking. The *attack alert* and *take cover* signals were described, and actions that should be taken upon hearing them reiterated.

ANNOUNCER: As you leave the city, your government officials will be moving to relocation centers outside the target area in order to maintain government operation and leadership. Under national emergency conditions, local governments will have an immense responsibility. It is here that the attack will first strike—it is here that plans for survival of the people will have to be executed. . . . The threat of nuclear weapons does not end with the explosion of the bombs.

The pretext was simultaneously that all was functioning well at the point of the broadcast's origin, and that the situation was dire enough that Newspoint—a journalists' enclave located in rural Virginia, remote from Highpoint but directly in touch with it—was staffed and reporting official information. Another announcer drew a verbal picture of what

Lowpoint (in Battle Creek, Michigan, the civil defense agency's headquarters and crossroads of information between the military, regional authorities, and federal government) looked like.

ANNOUNCER: #2 This is _____ reporting from one of the secret relocation centers of your government. . . . away from Washington. During an actual attack your government would operate from places like this. We are in the operations room. . . . Young ladies on step-ladders are working at the enormous map of the United States. . . . They are plotting attack information on the map with colored plastic markers attached to tiny magnets . . . the markers indicate which places are being evacuated. Later they will show which have been hit . . . which spared. Across the room is a smaller map covered with clear plastic. A weatherman charts the predicted movement of fallout across the nation . . . historic decisions for the United States . . . and the world . . . will depend on the information reaching this room . . . for the men sitting around me here today . . . in a training exercise . . . are the men who would make the decision . . . in case of attack. The information with which they work comes over a gigantic emergency communications system . . . from the military and from civil defense installations which relay reports from cities . . . states . . . and territories . . . and from other secret government headquarters similar to this one. . . . Man cannot handle this tremendous flow of information fast enough . . . so there are great banks of electronic equipment . . . the brains of the computer . . . ready for use by the men who must make the decisions for survival. . . . This room is the core of Operation Survival. . . . In many other rooms at this hidden headquarters . . . hundreds of experts keep track of . . . how many Americans would have died if this attack were real . . . how many injured . . . how much is left in stockpiled food . . . fuel . . . clothing . . . medical supplies . . . blood.

Transportation experts get reports on which railroads can operate and how many locomotives and cars they have . . . the number of buses . . . trucks . . . aircraft and other vehicles available for the recovery effort . . . medical men get reports on the number of doctors and nurses who survived . . . they also are told how many hospital beds are available and where they are . . . how much medicine is left and where it is . . . the condition of the nearly two thousand emergency hospitals civil defense has spotted strategically around the nation . . . all of this information . . . and much more . . . is fed into the Operations Room. . . .[31]

Exhortations on cooperation and the need for public involvement in civil defense followed.

The National Damage Assessment Center, part of Highpoint, received data on simulated defense conditions, warning times, aircraft tracks, submarine locations, and missile reports which in turn were translated into public warnings. After a simulated attack, the National Damage Assessment Center was fed data on areas of heavy destruction, radiation intensities, and protective action which in turn was translated into information for dissemination to the public. CONELRAD could then give instructions on nuclear, bacteriological, and chemical attacks, personal care, the evacuation situation, and radiation.[32] In a real war, they anticipated relaying this information to Lowpoint which would in turn give press releases on meteorological and radiological information to Newspoint.

Canada and Britain had similar, though more centralized, systems. In Exercise Dustbath, November 7–8, 1964, fallout programs were simulated for the BBC. Broadcasts were short, and telegraphically informational, not unlike the daily shipping forecasts in style. At H+4 (four hours after commencement of simulated nuclear war), an announcer read,

ANNOUNCER: This is the B.B.C. Regional Service for the Counties of AYSHIRE, BEESHIRE, CEESHIRE and the West Riding of DEESHIRE. Alvan Fiddell reporting. Between one o'clock and three o'clock this morning a number of attacks were made on this country by nuclear weapons. The main attack has been directed against London and the Home Counties but this Region has been subjected to attacks on West Middlepoole, Nottington and Darlingham. Serious fires are raging in these places and there are very many casualties. Civil Defence and other rescue services are doing everything they can to rescue survivors. Immediate retaliatory measures were taken by our own forces and there have been no further attacks since 3 o'clock. Radioactive fall-out already affects part of our region and will affect other areas later. If you have not already been warned to go to your refuge room, listen for the public warnings. As soon as you hear maroons [loud explosive devices, used in areas unequipped with sirens] or are instructed by your Civil Defence warden or police go at once to your refuge room and remain there until you are told you can come out. This station is now closing down. A further transmission will be made at 7 o'clock.

Twenty-four hours into the simulated nuclear attack, Alvan Fiddell broadcast again:

ANNOUNCER: Rescue work is proceeding in the towns of West Middlepoole, Nottington and Darlingham and many casualties have been removed to hospital. Many fires have been brought under control and reinforcements of rescue services are on their way to these areas. Apart from the very north of AYSHIRE radioactive fallout covers almost the whole region. It is particularly heavy in the areas around LIVERTON, SOUTHSHORE, STOCKPORT AND NORTHCAPE, and along the REED VALLEY. Do not leave your refuge room. The civil defence authorities are aware of the situation and are keeping a constant check on it. Your warden will tell you when you can come out but it may not be for some considerable time. There will a further news bulletin in one hour. Switch off your radio to conserve the battery and tune in again at 3 o'clock.[33]

This is meant to resemble a news broadcast, not a play: it is informational and nondialogic. The fake yet plausible place names unequivocally designate this as an exercise text. Yet this does not alter its status as a dramatic script. It is precisely because it is part of a speculative exercise that it is more, not less, like drama, for it superimposes one pretext (blatantly untrue) over another (manifestly true) reality. The real time and the real radiological situation that the broadcaster exists in is in tension with but does not negate the unreal time and reported radiological situation of the postnuclear war scenario.

In the late 1950s, the Canadian Department of Health and Welfare produced six dialogic radio scripts on civil defense topics. These posit "what-ifs," not within an emergency situation like Exercise Dustbath but within everyday life which can be spent preparing for the exigencies of catastrophe. They fall into the category of public service broadcasts and many cover basic skills of preparedness adaptable to various kinds of emergency. Operation Get-Together, for example, calls attention to the difficulty of knowing where one's family members are in case of emergency. Bob asks his brother-in-law, Jack, where his wife would be while he is at work and whether he should assume he could contact her in an emergency:

JACK: (*smugly*) Why she'd be at home of course.

ELLA: Honestly, to hear you talk you'd think I never went out of the house from one week to the next. I could be anywhere, Bob. Supermarket, visiting the doctor, having coffee across the street. Anywhere.

Given the logistical problems and the urgency of an evacuation, it is less important to gather families together than to independently get out of harm's way by whatever means possible. Later, families may find themselves scattered in every direction, not knowing where the others are. Bob, an emergency planner, has designed the forms that would be needed to reunite families via local registries and the postage-paid postcards that could be sent to relatives in distant areas to inform them that families are all right. Stockpiles of the cards are ready and waiting at post offices.

JACK: Say, you have got the angles figured Jack. This is pretty urgent business. It's the family unit which holds the community together. Break those up and [the] whole community's in trouble, the whole nation.[34]

This is not great drama—it is corny, contrived, and didactic—yet not dissimilar to much programming from the period. Other programs in the series cover the provision of clothing, food, and shelter for disaster victims and the value of maintaining an emergency seven-day food pack.

The exercise scripts call into being hypothetical futures within the performative temporality of the present moment. In order for the scripts to be efficacious, people would either practice behaviors—embodying what they should do in a real emergency, such as proceeding toward shelter—or learn to connect their everyday behaviors to be adaptively alert to potential problems. Operation Get-Together portrays the latter, and calls into

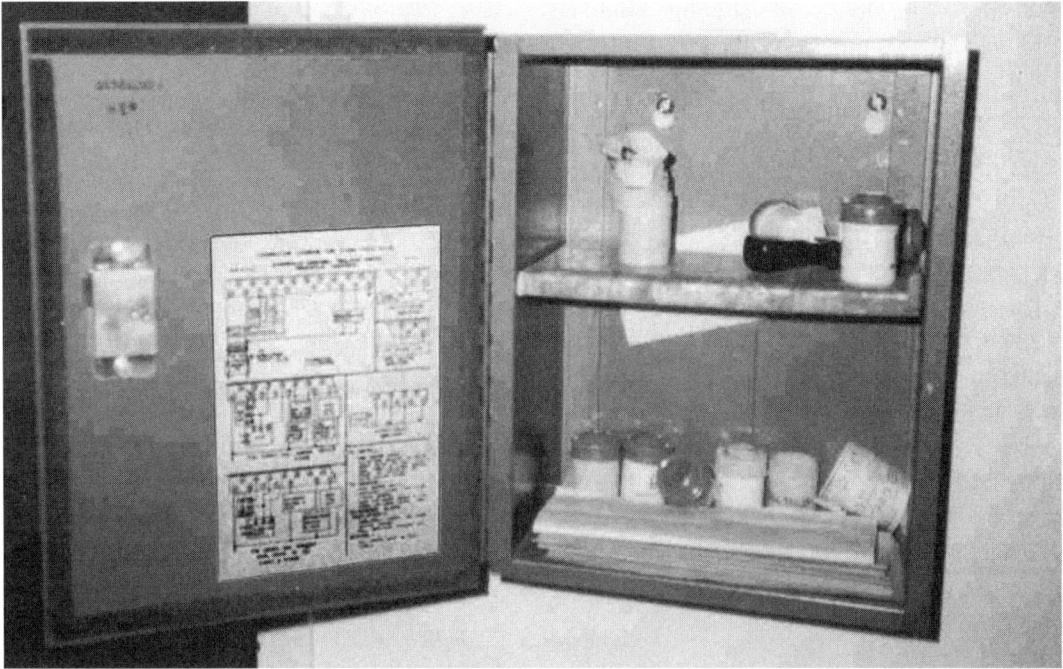

Storage locker for CBC emergency messages at the regional emergency government headquarters, Valcartier, Quebec.

Photo courtesy of the Diefenbunker, Canada's Cold War Museum

being an Everyman sensibility about current actions implicating future consequences.

THE REAL THING

Equally intriguing are the related texts—sometimes prerecorded, sometimes held on deposit in typescript form—that were cached in case nuclear war broke out. These have not been broadcast—yet—but like all scripts have the status of events-in-potential, postulated futures capable of making the transformation to something transacting in time. In this case, it would be an apocalyptic time. Their temporal referentiality, therefore, is entirely dependent upon the act of performance.

In Canada, most postwar objectives would be enhanced through communications: the highest priority, "public education on self-help in first aid, firefighting, and personal survival"—in other words the preservation of life and property—would be supported through second-tier objectives such as continuity of government and broadcasting of fallout information, and third-tier objectives including the conservation of resources, stabilization of the economy, and resumption of governmental peacetime programs.[35] The media would prime listeners to be prepared for certain actions, and in the United States CONELRAD preattack broadcasts would typically focus on informing the public about supplies for shelter, evacuation procedures, warning times, the military's detection system for early warning, NORAD, and the capacity to strike back.[36]

To distinguish these exercises—rehearsals for nuclear war—from the real thing, authenticating scripts were devised. An emergency message from the president, whether broadcast from the White House or Highpoint, would be preceded by two minutes "talk up":

ANNOUNCER: A Presidential message will be heard in _____ minutes and _____ seconds from *NOW*.

This would be repeated until the President came on the air. The closing cue for Presidential messages would be:

ANNOUNCER: THIS CONCLUDES THE PRESIDENTIAL MESSAGE.[37]

When neither a presidential message nor a national program pertinent to the emergency was being broadcast, a constant tone would be transmitted to verify the continuity of the circuits.

In the event of an attack warning, regional CBC stations would repeatedly broadcast the following text, interrupted only by a speech by the prime minister or acting prime minister.

SOUND EFFECT (Undulating sound of sirens for a few seconds.)

ANNOUNCER: This is_____ (well known announcer) speaking. The Canadian Government has declared a national emergency. An enemy attack on North America has been detected. This is a real emergency. Sirens are now sounding or have sounded the "ATTACK WARNING". . . . Take cover immediately in the best available protection against blast and heat, do NOT worry about fallout now. Here are some instructions:

- If you are at home go to the strongest part of your house or building which offers the best protection against flying objects such as glass, wood or bricks.

- Take your battery radio with you, or turn up the house radio so that you can hear it while under cover.
- Stay away from windows.
- Lie down and protect yourself from falling debris.
- Shut your eyes and shield them from the flash of an explosion.
- If you are away from home, at school or work, take cover where you are.
- If you are in a car, truck or bus, stop and take cover in a building, culvert or ditch.
- If you are only a few minutes from a known safer destination proceed and take cover as quickly as possible.[38]

A set of ten draft typescripts from 1962 indicates the content of the taped messages that were issued regionally. The scripts relate to the stages of attack warning, warnings to take cover, instructions for those whose areas come under attack, fallout reports, evacuation planning, and emergence from shelter.[39] These were developed by a working group with input from the CBC, Army, Emergency Health Services, Emergency Supply Planning Branch, and Emergency Measures Organization officials (a branch of the prime minister's office), revising scripts used for the exercise TOCSIN B in November 1961. Attack warning messages were printed on pink paper and kept on file until at least the mid-1980s.[40] To avoid playing messages pertaining to the survival period in the wrong order, they were combined on a single tape.[41] Purely educational and instructional material about sheltering and mitigating the effects of fallout, which would be broadcast prior to an attack if time allows, were produced on video and also stockpiled at stations,[42] though the CBC also retained typescripts for live broadcast with details on personal decontamination, water, food handling, disposal of garbage and human waste, disease prevention, and first aid.[43]

The British government also produced video and audio recordings intended to be broadcast in the precrisis period: the *Protect and Survive* series.[44] Twenty-four-hour-a-day broadcasting would be devoted to the 20 videotapes lasting a total of 47 minutes and audiotapes lasting 37 minutes.[45] Once war broke out, there would be a single BBC sound program, and no television. The public would be urged to tune in continuously for the first 24 hours, then—to conserve battery life—tune in only at specified times or when they heard sirens or maroons. Proposed texts read,

---

ANNOUNCER: The following areas are under Fall-out Warning Black. This means that radioactive fall-out is imminent, or has already arrived, in the area(s). You must therefore take cover immediately and remain under cover until you receive further instructions. This broadcast may not include all areas where there is danger of fall-out and you should therefore act immediately on any warning which has been or will be given by maroon or whistle which you may hear, whether or not your area is included in this broadcast.

Alternately, for regional broadcasts, proposed texts read,

ANNOUNCER This is a broadcast to (South-Eastern) Region. Radioactive fall-out is now affecting the whole of the counties of A, B and C and the following areas in county D as well as parts of adjoining Regions. Stay under cover, and if you have a refuge room, stay in it as much as possible. Do not come out until you receive further instructions. Keep your radio tuned to this station. This broadcast may not include all areas where there is danger of fall-out and you should therefore act immediately on any warning which has been or will be given by maroon or whistle which you may hear, whether or not your area is included in this broadcast.[46]

Resemblance to the Exercise Dustbath scripts is notable. Regional seats of government would also broadcast international, national, or regional situation summaries; the end of the nuclear exchange; forecasts of when broad areas were likely to emerge from cover; specific instructions for emergence applicable to smaller areas; instructions to the public that they would be transported to other regions; instructions that those with transport should travel, along with specific instructions on destination and routes; instructions about rations, food stocks within fallout zones, and local food, including contamination dangers; instructions on how to use their time in the open, especially for specific categories such as nurses, public utility maintenance men, slaughtermen, farmers, etc.; medical advice on caring for radiation victims; and advice on decontamination.[47]

As archival objects, these scripts demonstrate the ideologies and tactics of civil defense programs during the height of the Cold War. Does their nature change if we think of them in the light of their real utility, to instruct people at the outbreak of nuclear war, a performance coincident with the cessation of life for hundreds of millions of people? If indeed the exercise scripts are dramatic because they superimpose the real-time referent (the exercise) over imagined-time referents (the fiction of war), would the same script being broadcast to millions in the midst of crisis *cease* to be dramatic?[48] What does this reveal about threshold events and the standard form of evidence for history, ritual, and theatre history? Can performance supersede and even eliminate drama when the event-in-potential of a script no longer references a future but describes a present reality?

Anne Ubersfeld argues that every performance references three domains: the dramatic text, the performance itself (reflexively), and the natural world.[49] In the case of the civil defense scripts stored in-potential for broadcast during nuclear hostilities, the relationship of these domains to each other becomes particularly interesting. Both the rehearsal texts and the "real thing" texts stimulate behaviors in social life, however in the former case the performance's self-reflexivity inscribes the fictiveness or the simulation, whereas in the latter case self-reflexivity would overcome the realism of a dramatic text in favor of the reality of disaster. Scripts are dramatic because they superimpose real-time referents (the exercise) over imagined-time referents (the fiction of war), but the same script being broadcast to millions in the midst of crisis *ceases* to be dramatic.[50] If, for example, a radio station broadcast the following text, it signaled a rehearsal of a possible future:

ANNOUNCER: We interrupt our normal program to cooperate in security and civil defense measures as requested by the United States Government. This is a CONELRAD Radio Alert. Normal broadcasting will now be discontinued for an indefinite period. . . . In the interest of national security, radio silence *may be prolonged.* If this happens, don't use your telephone. Be patient. Official information will be broadcast as soon as possible.[51]

If, however, this was not an exercise alert but a wartime alert, the performance would become an apocalyptic script describing the present. What does this reveal about threshold events and the standard form of evidence for history, ritual, and performance? These texts raise questions about the circumstances under which the domains of reflexive performance and the natural world abut in order to eliminate the domain of a dramatic text.

What, precisely, is the difference in terms of performance theory? As dramatic scripts, civil defense instructions compress narrative, stimulate unconscious drives, and call a mise-en-scène into being. In other words, they deploy realism. Their reflexivity may take on degrees

of transitivity, but the purpose in peace is to habituate auditors' responses, rehearsing a reaction until it can become realistic in war.[52] As long as the world's first thermonuclear war was merely anticipated, broadcasts of the scripts could only be realistic, not reality. Only if they were broadcast without the exercise caveat did they forfeit realism. After the bombs hit, well-habituated citizens listening to their radios in places of relative safety would, it was thought, seek reliable news in order to stem off the negative effects that would incur from unreliable information. They would seek to correlate their experiences to local and world events, integrating themselves into a broader narrative. Under these circumstances, according to the British Psychological Society, "monitoring the news serves as an attempt to reconstruct a comprehensible set of explanations, and to reduce the uncertainty brought about by uncontrollability," which was not only socially adaptive but psychologically healthy.[53] The Eisenhower administration believed the two most important instruments of social planning for a postdisaster period were maintaining the supply of food and other essential items, and communications (preferably two-way) between the government and the people. This would emphasize national solidarity and facilitate long-term recovery and rebuilding.[54]

During the initial radio broadcast of Orson Welles' *War of the Worlds,* panic ensued despite repeated insistence that there was no invasion from Mars. In the event of nuclear war, the disclaimers of truth would be replaced with disclaimers of falsity, so that "This is not a test; radar stations have detected incoming Soviet missiles; take cover immediately" would be as true in the script as in the world. Whereas the peacetime exercise relies on auditors to accept the alienation of an illusion broken, wartime auditors would need to *not* be estranged, and instead to be absorbed.[55] Lack of a *Verfremdungseffekt* (roughly, "alienation-effect") points to a distinction between realism and reality in these scripts, or rather in the reflexivity of their performance. A change in the world beyond the script (namely, the failure of diplomacy to preserve peace) changes the status of their performance. The difference would be signaled not by a substitution of the whole text but merely a change of disclaimer—from "this is false" to "this is true"—yet it is the status of the "this is true" while it is still false that makes the conceit so recognizable to performance historians.

In its commemoration of James Kirk's birth, the town of Riverside uses dramatic time playfully, commemorating scripts' propensity to create futures, erecting a monument to this, and hosting an annual pilgrimage to it. Likewise, in nuclear drills the public was urged to take shelter: the same shelter they would take if the attack were real. They were urged to listen to their radios: the same stations they would listen to if the attack were real. The context was serious, though the enactment was fundamentally playful: an "as if" of nuclear war, with the radio repeating this essential fact. But closing the shelter door, though the same gesture, might not always have the same reflexive relationship to the natural world.

Does the evolution of these Cold War artifacts from exercise scripts to scripts-in-potential for Armageddon to evidence of civil defense in a bygone era foreclose their status as events-in-potential? Do we assume, as performance historians, that a script (a blueprint for a performance event) ever becomes obsolete, defunct, or undramatic? Is this relative? Is it as applicable to performatives as scripts? What is it about historical context and contemporaneousness that is (and is not) important to the status of a document? What transforms a dramatic document's relationship to time from one of hermeneutics (interpretation) to ontology (being)? Are there precedents to help us understand this unusual case study?

Abbreviations

NAC: National Archives of Canada (Ottawa)

NARA: National Archives and Records Administration (College Park, MD)

PRO: Public Records Office (London)

RG: Record Group

HO: Home Office

NOTES AND REFERENCES

1. Ibsen, H. (1966). *Hedda Gabler* (J. Arup, Trans.). In J. W. McFarlane (Ed.), *Ibsen* (Vol. VII). London: Oxford University Press. p. 216.

2. Jenkins, H. (1992). *Textual poachers: Television fans and participatory culture*. London: Routledge.

3. Because, in retrospect, many civil defense measures seem inadequate, and perhaps even ludicrous, and because of the attempt to disseminate information about them through popular media, populist tactics, and populism, the historiography of this movement is characterized by kitsch history, emphasizing the union between pop culture iconography and dismissive reductionism of what was, at the time, often experienced as the terrifying immanence of death. Kitsch history, epitomized in the United States by the "duck and cover" campaign of Bert the Turtle, displaces attention from the causes of civil defense, namely an arms race of unprecedented destructive power, huge investment in the military-industrial complex, and technologies of paranoia propagated by the ideological opponents. In my work, I attempt to relate the causes to the effects of civil defense and, as a pacifist, to respect the artifacts of history and note our "refusal of coevality" with them, while remembering why these programs arose in the first place. Through estrangement, there is too powerful a temptation to forget the cause while dismissing the effect. See Phillips, M. S. (2003). "Relocating Inwardness: Historical Distance and the Transition from Enlightenment to Romantic Historiography," *PMLA, 118*(3), 436–449.

4. Janis, I. L. (1949). *Psychological aspects of vulnerability of atomic bomb attacks*. Santa Monica, CA: RAND Corporation. p. 38.

5. This was not an isolated incident. During Operation Alert 58, two State Emergency Information staff broadcast loud speaker warnings of impending fallout from a private plane over Readfield, Maine. See NARA RG 396 Entry

1029 650 42/0 5/05 Box 4, "State and Local Participation in OPAL 58. Presentation to the N.A.S.T.D. Conference, Colorado Springs, November 10, 1958," DRAFT, 3 November 1958, p. 4.

6. PRO HO 322/185, Exercises "Review" and "Zeta": Public Control, Establishing Zonal Boundaries, Clearance of Z-Zones, 1954-1957.

7. Tyhurst, J. S. (1957). Psychological and social aspects of civilian disaster. *Canadian Medical Association Journal, 76*, 390.

8. Krajnc, A. (2000). The art of green learning from protest songs to media mind bombs. *International Politics, 37*(1), 25. Italics added.

9. Transistor radios were first marketed in the United States in 1954 (the Regency TR1); by 1959, half of the 10 million U.S. radios made annually were transistor radios. Transistors were far from a panacea for civil defense: "Transistor sets function adequately within buildings, except where they are screened from broadcast signals by metal screening and no external aerial is connected; this could cause difficulties in, e.g., basements in buildings with frames of steel or reinforced concrete. The audience is clearly large enough to make the broadcasting of fall-out information worth while." PRO HO 322/336, Working Party on Broadcasting Fall-Out Information: Meetings and Interim Report, 1964–1965.

10. CONELRAD stands for CONtrol of ELectromagnetic RADiation. Such techniques were used by each side in World War II. A missile's homing instruments could be adjusted to guide it down the path of a broadcast toward a radio transmitter. The only effective countermeasure is to cease broadcasting altogether or not differentiate broadcast frequencies. NARA RG 396 Entry 1013 650 41/32/07 Box 1, "FCDA-OCDM Special Liaison Files of L. C. Frankling [Canada-U.S. Joint Committee], Meeting 7–8 January 1953.

11. NARA RG 397 Entry 39 650 42/26/06-07 Box 1, JRCC D/34-65, "Report on Working Group on Emergency Public Information," [1965]. The United States instituted an emergency broadcast system with approximately 300 participating stations in 1964. By 1971, it could reach only nine percent of the population. U.S. Department of Defense, Office of Civil Defense, *New Dimensions. Ninth Annual Report of the Office of Civil Defense Fiscal Year Ended June 30, 1970*, 1971, p. 18.

12. "Present plans provide for the rapid dissemination of attack and fall-out warnings to all centres of population down to the smallest villages, and that isolated communities outside audible range of warning device will be able to receive *attack* warning messages broadcast by the B.B.C. Consideration is being given to the possibility of broadcasting *fall-out* warnings by the B.B.C. which would cover isolated communities, but many practical difficulties have yet to be overcome." PRO HO 322/192, Staff College Exercises and Studies: Central Exercise Staff (CES): Coordination and Administration of Central Government and Regional Exercises. 1958–1967, "Central Exercise Staff Bulletin January 1963."

13. Emergency Preparedness Canada. (1991). *Wartime public protection in the 1980s. Final report of the task force on war planning and concepts of operations*, 1985. Ottawa: Author. See also Emergency Preparedness Canada (1991). *Public Protection Measures*. Ottawa: Author.

14. Diefenbunker Archive, F. P. Johnson, Director of Special Projects Canadian Broadcasting Corporation, Letter to J. F. Wallace, Director National Civil Emergency Measure Program, 1 July 1969.

15. Diefenbunker Archive, "The Evolution of the Civil Situation Monitoring and Briefing Capability at the Central Emergency Government Headquarters, Canadian Forces Stations Carp (the Diefenbunker) from 1961 to 1992," 1992. Broadcast studios were also maintained at regional headquarters. See also Diefenbunker Archive, "Readiness Status Summary [RGHQ Nanaimo]," 1988.

16. PRO HO 322/336, Working Party on Broadcasting Fall-Out Information, "Interim Report for Period To D+5," February 1965.

17. PRO HO 322/336, "Working Party on Broadcasting of Fall-out Information. Exercise CIVLOG Attack Pattern: Immediate Effects Upon Regional Broadcasting. Paper by A.1 Division," July 1964.

18. PRO HO 322/351, Phoenix Five Hydrogen Bomb Exercise, 1967.

19. NARA RG 396 Entry 1029 650 42/05/05 Box 2, Brig. Gen. Don E. Carleton, "A Report of Participation by the City of Milwaukee in the National Civil Defense Test Exercise of June 15–16, Operation Alert 1955," 1955. p. 6.

20. Oakes, G. (1994). *The imaginary war: Civil defense and American Cold War culture*. New York: Oxford University Press. pp. 88–89.

21. NARA RG 396 Entry 1029 650 42/05/05 Box 2, FCDA Emergency Control Division, Emergency Operations Office, "Intra-Agency

Report on Operation Alert 1956," 12 September 1956. pp. 29–30.

22. NAC RG24, Department of National Defence, Series C-1, Acc. 1983-84/215, Box 252, Files S-2001-91/T19 pt. 1, Canadian Broadcasting Corporation "Radio Script Exercise TOCSIN B 1961 7:00–8:30pm EST November 13th, 1961. All Canadian Stations," Executive Producer Thom Benson, Producer Norman McBain.

23. Canada Emergency Measures Organization and Department of National Defence. (1980). *11 steps to survival. Blueprint for survival no. 4.* Ottawa: Author. (Originally published 1961).

24. NARA RG 396 Entry 1029 650 42/05/05 Box 2.

25. NARA RG 396 Entry 1029 650 42/05/05 Box 6.

26. NARA RG 396 Entry 1029 650 42/05/05 Box 2. See also Office of Civil Defense Mobilization, Executive Office of the President, *Annual Report of the Office of Civil and Defense Mobilization for Fiscal Year 1959,* 1960. p. 12.

27. Campbell, D. (1982). *War plan UK: The truth about civil defence in Britain* London: Burnett. pp. 76–77.

28. NARA RG 397 Entry 39 650 42/26/06-07 Box 1, "U.S./Canada Cross-Border Seminar Exercise January 27–28, Minneapolis," [1965].

29. NARA RG 396 Entry 1029 650 42/05/05 Box 6.

30. NARA RG 396 Entry 1063 650 42/13/01 Box 1, "[Operation Alert 1959] Test Exercise Study Files," 1959.

31. NARA RG 396 Entry 1029 650 42/05/05 Box 6.

32. Diefenbunker Archive, Office of Civil and Defense Mobilization, "Draft Plan for Operations at the Classified Location," 1960.

33. PRO HO 322/336, Working Party on Broadcasting Fall-Out Information, "Broadcasting of Fallout Information. Report by South-West Region," [Dec. 1964].

34. Brown, S. S. (Producer), & Tolowin, D. (Writer). (circa 1958). *Your health, your welfare: Operation get-together* [Radio script]. Ottawa: Canadian Department of National Health and Welfare. pp. 7, 12.

35. Diefenbunker Archive, Public Works Collection, Emergency Measures Organization, *Canada Survival Plan,*1966. pp. 3–4.

36. NARA RG 396 Entry 1029 650 42/05/05 Box 6.

37. Eisenhower Library, White House Office Papers, Office of the Staff Secretary Records of Paul T. Carroll, Andrew J. Goodpaster, L. Arthur Minnich, and Christopher H. Russell, 1952–1961, Emergency Action Series," Federal Communication Commission, "Plan for the Control of Electromagnetic Radiation (CONELRAD) Pursuant to Executive Order No. 10312 Technical Arrangements to Insure Nationwide Continuity of the Emergency Broadcast System During CONELRAD and the Period Following Issuance of the CONELRAD Radio All Clear," 29 July 1960.

38. Diefenbunker Archive, "Emergency Broadcast—Attack Warning," 1967. This closely resembles a contemporaneous publication: Diefenbunker Archive, Public Works Collection, Deputy Chief Reserves, *Civil Emergency Operations—War. Militia Training Material and Guidelines,* 1968: Annex C, Part 2, Sec 1. pp. 36–37. This further corresponds with NAC R06059, Canadian Broadcasting Corporation and Emergency Measures Organization, *Nuclear Attack Clips. Public Service Radio Announcements,* circa 1964.

39. Diefenbunker Archive, "Emergency Broadcasts No. 1-10 (Draft)," 1962.

40. Steed, J. (1985, July 20). Getting ready for doomsday. *The Globe and Mail* (Toronto).

41. Diefenbunker Archive, Emergency Measures Organization, "EMO Working Group on Emergency Broadcasts for the Public Second Progress Report," 1962.

42. Emergency Planning Canada. (1979). *A guide to civil emergency planning for municipalities.* Ottawa: Author. p. 4.

43. Diefenbunker Archive, "Health Maintenance Survival Instructions for the Public" [typescript]. 1962.

44. Central Office of Information. (2000). *Protect and Survive.* Reissued by DD Video, North Harrow, England. (Original work produced 1971).

45. Crossley, G. (1982). *Civil defence in Britain: Peace studies papers* (No. 7). London: Housmans and University of Bradford School of Peace Studies. pp. 85–86.

46. PRO HO 322/336, Working Party on Broadcasting Fall-Out Information, "Interim Report for Period to D+5," February 1965.

47. PRO HO 322/336, Working Party on Broadcasting Fall-Out Information, "Interim Report for Period to D+5," February 1965.

48. Pfister, M. (1991). *The theory and analysis of drama* (J. Halliday, Trans.) England: Cambridge University Press. pp. 246–247.

49. Ubersfeld, A. (1999). *Reading theatre.* Foreword by Collins, F., Perron, P., & Debèche, P. Ontario: University of Toronto Press, p. xvi.

50. Pfister, M. (1991). *The theory and analysis of drama* (J. Halliday, Trans.) England: Cambridge University Press. pp. 246–247.

51. Office of Civil and Defense Mobilization. (1961). *Conelrad* (L-6 ed.). Washington, DC: Department of Defense.

52. The central point about transitivity and intransitivity is drawn from discussion of mimetic fiction and poetry in Lane, C. (2003). The poverty of context: Historicism and nonmimetic fiction. *PMLA, 118*(3), 450–69.

53. Thompson, J. (1985). *Psychological aspects of nuclear war*. Chichester, England: British Psychological Society and John Wiley & Sons. p. 14.

54. Eisenhower Library, White House Office Papers, Cabinet Secretary, Box 22, CI-55, "Human Behavior in Disaster," Cabinet Paper, 22 April 1958. p. 4.

55. Messinger, S. L., Sampson, H., & Towne, R. D. (1975). Life as theatre: Some notes on the dramaturgic approach to social reality. In D. Brissett & C. Edgley (Eds.), *Life as theater: a dramaturgical sourcebook* (pp. 32–42). New York: Aldine de Gruyter. p. 38. (Original work published in 1962, *Sociometry 35*, 98–110).

PART III

Performance of and Beyond Literature

PAUL EDWARDS

Interpretation is an excellent way of studying literature because it demands that the student perceive. . . . The silent reader, skimming and skipping and scavenging often only for particular ideas or images, frequently does not really assimilate whole pieces of literature. . . . But the interpreter cannot so read. He must bring the whole poem close to himself. . . . The act of oral reading before an audience (though that audience may be a single listener—or, indeed, only the reader himself) is . . . a kind of final act of criticism. . . .

—Wallace Bacon, *The Art of Interpretation* (1966, pp. 6, 8–9)

When I choose texts, they're random in a way. I feel I could use any text. That was something that started very early with Spalding [Gray]. I could pick anything in this room. . . . I could take three props here: the printing on the back of that picture, this book, and whatever's in this pile of papers, and make something that would mean as much, no more nor less, than what I've constructed in the performance space downstairs. . . . Finally, it's not about that text. . . . I take [some] chance occurrence and say, that is the sine qua non, that is the beginning, that is the text. I cannot stray from that text. As someone else would use the lines of a playwright, I use that action as the baseline.

—Elizabeth LeCompte (quoted in Savran, 1988, pp. 50–51)

Why "literature"? In the monograph *Unstoried: Teaching Literature in the Age of Performance Studies* (1999) I briefly trace the rise and fall of "interpretation": the study that began in eighteenth century England as "elocution," and flourished in late-nineteenth century America (during the heyday of oratorical culture) under names as quaint

143

sounding as "expression" and "speech arts."[1] Employing a range of examples from parallel histories, I wrote *Unstoried* to suggest to an expanding field of "performance studies" scholars, arriving from many disciplines, how a number of literature professors once got involved.

Having begun my academic career in the now-vanished category of "interpretation teacher," I suppose that I suffered "the misfortune of teaching literature," as Jonathan Brody Kramnick (1998) terms it, "in a moment when its founding rationale has been called into radical doubt" (p. 244). English elocution came into existence alongside "the appearance of the category of 'literature' in the later eighteenth century" (Guillory, 1993, p. 213). The age that gave us the English-language "classic" gave us as well a use-value for literature, a form of "cultural capital" (Guillory, 1993): the rise of "literature" helped to shape the public sphere and its protocols of communication. So did the *performance* of literature, which for two centuries (under various names) capitalized on the trained performing body as a communication medium. From its beginnings, elocution's market-driven goals were divided and sometimes self-contradictory. Did elocution belong in universities or in trade schools? One of its audiences sought enrichment from *belles lettres* through embodied performance, while another (sometimes overlapping) audience sought training in the persuasive delivery of *any* text, as a tool for activism or professional advancement. The manuals on elocutionary delivery that became popular in Georgian England contained training drills on shaping meaningful sounds and exhibiting through gesture the signs of deep feeling. "Passion for Dummies": I find it hard to read these books and not compare them to present-day computer manuals, designed to help us with everything from simply turning on the "machine" to making us appear expressive for the widest possible audience. The oratorically extended body of the eighteenth and nineteenth centuries—whether raving on hustings, imitating the "action" of eighteenth century stage star David Garrick from a pulpit or school podium, or standing at a table in a coffeehouse to read a newspaper out loud—was the laptop-extended or televisualized body of its day.

Elocutionary training attained its greatest respectability in American colleges and universities with the founding in 1914 of the National Association of Academic Teachers of Public Speaking—known since 1997 as the National Communication Association (NCA). Most of the association's members, at the time of its first convention in 1915, were school teachers whose platform oratory embraced both public speaking and literary recitation. Yet as "academically oriented" performers (Rarig & Greaves, 1954, p. 499) they were eager to distance themselves from the "rubbish" of popular platform entertainment with which the label "elocution" had come to be associated during the late-nineteenth century (see Cohen, 1994; Edwards, 1999, pp. 3–4, 16–43, 63–78, 121; Weaver, 1989). As the association grew and diversified, its Interpretation Division became the national gathering place for teachers and scholars of performance-based literary study who worked outside the institutional boundaries of "English" and "theatre." The interests of these educators were diverse enough to permit continual transformations of collective identity. In 1991, the group received approval to rename itself a Performance Studies Division, thereby cultivating what appears to be the first national association of "performance studies" scholars out of its deep roots in literary study, speech arts, and elocutionary training. By contrast, the organization Performance Studies international (PSi), which held its first conference in 1995, arose from the very different institutional identity of the graduate program in Performance Studies at New York University (NYU) and sought to promote interdisciplinary performance scholarship unburdened by association with a history of literary study.[2]

With the rise of performance studies associations from contrasting traditions, scholars like Richard Schechner (2002) have begun to speak of a two-brand model of performance studies pedagogy in American universities: *with* literature, as exemplified by the academic department at Northwestern University, and *without,* as exemplified by the NYU department (pp. 16–19; see also Carlson, 1996, pp. 19–25; Jackson, 2004, pp. 8–11; Jacobson, 1994, p. 20; Phelan, 1998, pp. 3–7). Such myths of institutional origin are unlikely to have any long-term influence on whether performance studies curricula, during the first decades of the twenty-first century, will succeed in inscribing their borders on the departmental terrain of colleges and universities. While commentators on the late-twentieth century scene of performance studies have had fun with the two-brand or two-school model (see, for example, McKenzie, 2001, pp. 46–47), Shannon Jackson (2004) helpfully reminds us that the "two institutional narratives" do not arise fancifully: each suggests a complicated genealogy. The spread of interpretation and later performance studies through the member institutions of the NCA (including Northwestern University) produces a very different "origin" story than the one associated with the founding of the Performance Studies Department at NYU, yet each story "obscures central figures and deliberative societies in other parts of the United States" than New York and Illinois (p. 10). My own sense of institutional histories filled with unstoried figures has grounded my research into the exclusionary, as well as selectively inclusionary, practices that drive the formation and self-definition of academic disciplines and scholarly associations.

"Institutional history," Jackson (2001) observes, "suggests that there are several maps operating simultaneously" (p. 92). My own mapping of what I have called an "NCA tradition" (1999, p. 3) does not seek to demonstrate that performance studies derives from the pedagogy of academically oriented performers of literature. It seeks, rather, to identify the academic study of interpretation as one of the many streams that flowed unpredictably into the current of performance studies, as it began to take shape in the last quarter of the twentieth century. Jackson (2001, 2004) has argued that a deconstruction of institutional blind spots requires a genealogical rather than narrowly ideological approach: a patient willingness to trace the often playful, all-too-human reaccentuations of ideas that eventually harden into the discourses of academic disciplines (2001, p. 85). This was my argument in *Unstoried:* a genealogical approach incalculably enriches the reading of archival materials when we try to make sense of unlikely parallel lives (elocutionists Thomas Sheridan and James Burgh in eighteenth century London), emulous candidacies for leadership (Genevieve Stebbins and S. S. Curry in American "expression" training), or negotiations of disciplinary direction in twentieth century "speech" education.

A question that remains is this. As interpretation vanished from American academic life, why did so many of its practitioners adopt performance studies (rather than a better-established discipline like theatre or English) as the appropriate setting to reinvent the pedagogical practices that first had drawn them to literary study? Within the present-day Performance Studies Division of the NCA (a unit of about 350 members within an association of over 7,000) are rich examples of "the historical entanglements of the already-was and thus still-kind-of-is" (Jackson, 2001, p. 92; see Jackson, 2004, p. 78).

What happened, then, to transform the study of interpretation into an "already-was" and "still-kind-of-is" phenomenon? Across the twentieth century, the market value of Victorian-era elocution's two hottest properties—the performing body as communication technology, and the conceptualization of literacy based on and sustained by literature—would steadily drop. Long before Internet culture, the technologies of film, radio, and television would change our concepts of not only *what* we read but *how* we read. Within the twentieth century university, the "rhetoric-and-oratory professor" and the literary "generalist" became figures of suspicion and even derision among a growing field of specialists; by mid-century, teachers of interpretation began to abandon oratory's claims of relevance and use-value to the "professional-managerial class" (see Guillory, 1993, pp. x-xii; Jackson, 2004, pp. 53–54). When influential teachers began to talk about embodied performance as a mode of literary appreciation that could be practiced *in private*—as seen, for example, in the epigraph drawn from a well-known interpretation textbook by Wallace Bacon, first published in 1966—they were refusing to read aloud the writing that was on the wall of major research universities and trade schools alike.

Such a withdrawal from the public sphere consigns literary study to a deferred value: as James Anderson Winn (1998) expresses this, to the cultivation of "lifelong readers, intelligent appreciators of the arts, people capable of being thrilled by an idea" (p. 128). In *The Pale of Words*, Winn reflects hopefully upon the survival of his subject, English literature, in a university reshaped by a commitment to both interdisciplinarity and performance—and, more specifically, by the use of performance-based pedagogy in humanities classrooms traditionally not associated with performance. But Winn writes without a sense of how such pedagogy has been practiced in American higher education for over a century (even at the University of Michigan, where he directed the Institute for the Humanities at the time he published *The Pale of Words*). More skeptical cultural critics, maintaining that "the category of literature has come to seem institutionally dysfunctional" at the dawn of the twenty-first century (Guillory, 1993, p. x), might accuse Winn of defending the teaching of books and bookishness (with or without performance methods) "in the most banal sense of appreciation" (Kramnick, 1998, p. 244). And such

critics most likely would not be persuaded by the claims of many interpretation teachers, who argued the performing body's radical potential to make the literature classroom a scene of advocacy and even activism. Jill Taft-Kaufman (1985) has summarized these claims, in her astute review of interpretation pedagogy at the very moment when it was fading from the scene of colleges and universities. As advanced by performance theorist Mary S. Strine (1992) such claims provoked a dubious response from Robert Scholes (1992). He found himself "less optimistic" than Strine that performed poetry could "forge 'an effective social force' to deal with immediate problems," even though he remained generally optimistic about the value of poetry

> to help keep human decency alive through periods of barbaric self-interest. . . . Auden, after a decade of lost political causes, wrote that "poetry makes nothing happen." He was wrong. It just makes things happen more slowly than we short-lived and impatient beings could wish. (p. 77)

Far too many of my generation of teachers hungered to see their classroom work change the world at a greater speed. Part of the "pluralist euphoria" that Judith Hamera (1998) describes in the nascent performance studies movement—what she calls a "prison break" toward "anything but literature" (p. 273)—is a break toward the political, the desire of Scholes's "impatient beings" for a more efficacious social praxis than the study of literature has ever seemed to produce.

In *Unstoried*, I had the unfortunate tendency to speak of performance "after" literature—by which I intended to signify the ebbing of literature as a shaping force in what John Guillory (1993) calls the "pedagogic imaginary." But literature (even viewed tartly as a "dysfunctional" institutional category) is not going anywhere anytime soon. At Northwestern, across departments, the Shakespeare courses are more popular than ever. The Borders and Barnes and

Noble stores keeping late hours in so many urban and suburban neighborhoods are remarkable developments of postmodern simulation. On display nightly, from the WiFi hotspot in the Starbucks franchise (coffeehouse of the new public sphere) to the display racks of *Lord of the Rings* DVDs, is an excavation of the layered technologies of words, words, words as we have come to know them since Thomas Sheridan wrote his pronouncing dictionary in the age of Dr. Johnson. In many of these stores, we find the equivalent of what elocutionists once meant by "the platform": spaces designated for public readings, which agents and publicists regularly supply with authors eager to both vocalize and inscribe their products. It has fallen to performance theory, perhaps, to read such institutions of "literacy beyond literature" as phenomena of interest outside merely the history of commerce.

The ludic, punning work of Jon McKenzie effectively charts how far we have traveled (even arriving at a modest frontier trading post like the neighborhood Borders) from the quasi-monastic image of a library where people sat quietly at carrels and read books from beginning to end. The student of interpretation performed the *unity* of a fictional world that could be contained within the covers of a book. But "what's historically specific about the age of global performance is its flagrant anachronisms, its glaring mix of forms and traditions from past and present" (McKenzie, 2001, p. 249). The birth of performance spelled not the death of the book, but what we might call its disclosure or uncovering, its decentering and dispersal.

McKenzie's *Perform or Else* (2001) bears a subtitle, *From Discipline to Performance,* that connects the dots between my two epigraphs. To Wallace Bacon, the preeminent American teacher of interpretation in the postwar decades, an embodied interpretation *"demands"* perception of "the whole poem." Regular practice can cure "skimming and skipping and scavenging," just as the

disciplinary systems advertised in the old elocution periodicals claimed to cure stammering. Although Bacon retired from Northwestern's Interpretation Department in 1979, after serving as its chair for over three decades, he remained active in professional associations (notably the NCA) until close to the time of his death in 2001. He lived long enough, in other words, to see the kind of reading he once regarded as undergraduate hastiness, or curable disorder, elevated to respectability as a theoretical and philosophical stance, a mode of resistance and transgression.

Celebrated avant-garde director Elizabeth LeCompte, in the second epigraph, strikes me as emblematic of a later view when she positions herself against interpretation. In another interview with David Savran, she clarifies that her work with a Flaubert text (staged not long after Arthur Miller's notorious attempt to prevent the Wooster Group's use of his play *The Crucible*) is "not illustrative."[3] It is closer to "paraphrasing" (a tactic also deployed in response to Miller's attorneys) than to interpreting or even "stealing": "that hooks up with my feelings about texts, about the objectness of the written word and its inherent lifelessness without the intervention of an interpretive or outside consciousness" (quoted in Savran, 1986, p. 40). Even in context, LeCompte sounds more than a little like Thomas Sheridan (1762/1798) in his famous elocutionary *Lectures,* seeking to restore life to the "dead letter" of the book (p. xvi). But LeCompte is no elocutionist. (Neither am I, for all my fascination with them.) LeCompte's position is so much a measure of where performance has been for at least the past quarter-century, that it is "now a part of the grain" it once went against. So, at least, suggests Schechner about the state of the "avant-garde" in late-Clintonian America (quoted in Harding, 2000, p. 214).

Performance training transformed me, as a university student over three decades ago, from one of Bacon's "skippers" and "scavengers" into a dedicated close reader. I became one of Winn's "lifelong" reader-appreciators, thrilled by ideas and the words that expressed them. And I continue to bring literary texts into performance classrooms: not as examples of the "dysfunctional category" that Guillory critiques, but as "selected works" whose value I advocate to new readers. My heart's ease for the past several decades has been the excitement of my students as they adapt literature for stage performance. But the excitement of these students is not reverential. It arises in large part from the freedom to reinvent the classics they study, by questioning through the medium of their own bodies the very limits of textual authority. As I have come to realize, my students arrive in class ready to take performance *beyond* literature. My divided loyalties between the book and the performing body exemplify for me the "historical entanglements" of which Jackson speaks, as I continue to teach literature in the age of performance studies.

Other contributors to this section are similarly "entangled." They launched their careers as interpretation students in American schools, but later shifted the direction of their research and teaching. None has abandoned or rejected literature, even in moving away from it. Some have moved further than others. But each of us has reaccentuated the influence of literary study in performance classrooms. In the different ways described below, we are beyond literature in that sense. We all locate our work among the various topics and categories represented throughout the present volume: history, pedagogy, theory, politics, and ethnography, not merely literature.

Kristin M. Langellier and Eric E. Peterson argue that, in the paradigm shift to "performance studies" at the beginning of the twenty-first century, personal narrative displaces literary study as a privileged site of performance. Viewed as a transgressive and *radically contextualized* practice, within an expanded and more inclusive pedagogical context,

personal narrative performance constructs and deconstructs both culture and the life of the subject in culture. The essay articulates a sophisticated theoretical framework for analyzing personal narrative performance in both everyday and formal artistic settings. Langellier and Peterson, who teach in the Department of Communication and Journalism at the University of Maine, Orono, are the authors of *Storytelling in Daily Life: Performing Narrative* (2004).

Lynn Miller and Jacqueline Taylor, editors (with M. Heather Carver) of *Voices Made Flesh: Performing Women's Autobiography* (2003), employ the examples of contemporary public performers to illustrate two modes or categories of autobiographical performance. Both push beyond traditional literary conceptions of the nonfiction genre: "auto/biographical" performances (in which performers stake their own bodies and life-stories in the self-reflexive act of staging historical figures) and "staged personal narratives" (which draw upon and construct the performer/creator's own life experience). Through a series of case studies, Miller and Taylor document the work of public performers whose very "platform" requires the dynamic of audience response; each performance they examine constructs its audience, and is constructed by its audience, in different ways. Miller teaches in the Department of Theatre at the University of Texas, and Taylor in the Department of Communication at DePaul University.

Bruce Henderson employs techniques of personal narrative in his rereading of an instructional tradition. He revisits a painful incident in his university training, when a teacher insensitively critiqued his choices in a literary performance as "autistic" (a term which, clearly, the teacher barely understood). In midcareer, Henderson has returned to graduate school, to pursue a second doctorate in Disability Studies. His recent study of autism encourages him to employ the term as metaphor: in reflecting upon the history of performance pedagogy, he examines the uncommunicativeness of communication teachers concerning aspects of the work they do. Henderson, who teaches in Ithaca College's Department of Speech Communication, is coauthor (with Carol Simpson Stern) of *Performance: Texts and Contexts* (1993).

Ruth Laurion Bowman and Michael S. Bowman set off from the invitation they find in contemporary theory to "think irreverently," not only about performance but about the ways in which we write about performance. They employ techniques of "performative" or "performance" writing to address the challenge of documenting a rehearsed live event: Ruth Bowman's adaptation of Nathaniel Hawthorne's *The Blithedale Romance,* as staged by her at Louisiana State University in November 2003. Exploring alternatives to the conventional production record, the authors attempt their own version of what Jean-Luc Godard (1972) has called "research in the form of a spectacle" (p. 181). With the abruptness of cuts in an experimental film, or the switching of television channels, the essay juxtaposes strips of text: passages from Ruth Bowman's script, quotations from historical research for the script (on topics ranging from mesmerism to labor conditions), narratives and syntheses of this research, and reflections (or better, one frequently interrupted reflection) on the history of the academic discipline in which the research took place. The scholarly "narrative" that emerges has been shaped as much by "electracy"—Gregory Ulmer's term for "cinematic/electronic thinking"—as by "literacy" (see Ulmer, 2003). But it also evokes the old-fashioned stitching of the Seamstress in Ruth Bowman's *Blithedale* script. (In saying even so much, I betray the authors' intention, inspired by the writings of Benjamin, "to communicate without initial conceptualizations.") Michael Bowman currently edits *Text and Performance Quarterly.* Ruth Bowman is the 2003 recipient of the NCA's Leslie Irene Coger Award for lifetime achievement in performance. Both teach in the Speech Communication Department at Louisiana State University.

The view that performers cocreate or recreate the texts they bring before the public suggests a "paradoxical" approach to traditional performance training. My contribution to the section examines this paradox in the art of several practitioners of "adaptation," all of whom began or shifted their careers in a specific local context: the intersection of Northwestern University's performance training and the Chicago theatre community. The essay considers the work of such adapter/ directors as David Schwimmer, Njoki McElroy, Mary Zimmerman, and Frank Galati.

NOTES

1. Earlier versions of several passages in the present essay appear in *Unstoried* (Edwards, 1999). I am grateful to *The Theatre Annual: A Journal of Performance Studies,* published by the College of William and Mary in Virginia, for permission to include a selection of unmarked quotations; and to Nathan Stucky, then the journal's editor, for generous, thoughtful encouragement to develop the monograph.

2. McKenzie (2001, p. 47) traces the origins of PSi to an NYU graduate-student association that began to meet in 1990; see also Phelan (1998, p. 3).

3. The Wooster Group's production of *L.S.D. (. . . Just the High Points . . .)* took shape over several years. A 1983 work in progress combined a 45-minute reduction of Arthur Miller's *The Crucible* with the playing of a record album by Timothy Leary. In October 1984, Miller's attorneys issued a "cease and desist" order to the Wooster Group when it attempted to perform a more fully developed version of *L.S.D.* Miller feared that *L.S.D.* presented "a blatant parody" of his famous work: "I don't want my play produced," he declared, "except in total agreement with the way I wrote it" (quoted in Savran, 1988, p. 193). The ensuing confrontation between Miller and the Wooster Group and the subsequent revision of the production have been occasions for much commentary by theatre and performance scholars. A detailed account appears in Savran (1988, pp. 169–220).

REFERENCES

Bacon, W. A. (1966). *The art of interpretation.* New York: Holt, Rinehart, and Winston.

Carlson, M. (1996). *Performance: A critical introduction.* London: Routledge.

Cohen, H. (1994). *The history of speech communication: The emergence of a discipline, 1914–1945.* Annandale, VA: Speech Communication Association.

Edwards, P. (1999). Unstoried: Teaching literature in the age of performance studies. *Theatre Annual, 52,* 1–147.

Godard, J. L. (1972). *Godard on Godard* (T. Milne, Trans.). New York: Viking Press.

Guillory, J. (1993). *Cultural capital: The problem of literary canon formation.* Chicago: University of Chicago Press.

Hamera, J. (1998). Debts: In memory of Lilla Heston. In S. J. Dailey (Ed.), *The future of performance studies: Visions and revisions* (pp. 272–275). Annandale, VA: National Communication Association.

Harding, J. M. (2000). An interview with Richard Schechner. In J. M. Harding (Ed.), *Contours of the theatrical avant-garde: Performance and textuality* (pp. 202–214). Ann Arbor: University of Michigan Press.

Jackson, S. (2001). Professing performance: Disciplinary genealogies. *The Drama Review, 45,* 84–95.

Jackson, S. (2004). *Professing performance: Theatre in the academy from philology to performativity.* Cambridge, England: Cambridge University Press.

Jacobson, L. (1994, January). What is performance studies? NYU and Northwestern define an elusive field. *American Theatre,* pp. 20–22.

Kramnick, J. B. (1998). *Making the English canon: Print-capitalism and the cultural past, 1700–1770.* Cambridge, England: Cambridge University Press.

Langellier, K. M., & Peterson, E. E. (2004). *Storytelling in daily life: Performing narrative.* Philadelphia: Temple University Press.

McKenzie, J. (2001). *Perform or else: From discipline to performance.* New York: Routledge.

Miller, L. C., Taylor, J., & Carver, M. H. (Eds.). (2003). *Voices made flesh: Performing women's autobiography.* Madison: University of Wisconsin Press.

Phelan, P. (1998). Introduction: The ends of performance. In P. Phelan & J. Lane (Eds.), *The ends of performance* (pp. 1–19). New York: New York University Press.

Rarig, F. M., & Greaves, H. S. (1954). National speech organizations and speech education. In K. R. Wallace (Ed.), *History of speech education in America: Background studies* (pp. 490–517). New York: Appleton-Century-Crofts.

Savran, D. (1986). Adaptation as clairvoyance: The Wooster Group's *Saint Anthony. Theater, 18*(1), 36–41.

Savran, D. (1988). *Breaking the rules: The Wooster Group.* New York: Theatre Communications Group.

Schechner, R. (2002). *Performance studies: An introduction.* New York: Routledge.

Scholes, R. (1992). Response to "Reading Robert Scholes: A symposium." *Text and Performance Quarterly, 12,* 75–78.

Sheridan, T. (1798). *A course of lectures on elocution. . . . A new edition.* London: James Dodsley. (Original work published 1762)

Stern, C. S., & Henderson, B. (1993). *Performance: Texts and contexts.* New York: Longman.

Strine, M. S. (1992). Protocols of power: Performance, pleasure, and the textual economy. *Text and Performance Quarterly, 12,* 61–67.

Taft-Kaufman, J. (1985). Oral interpretation: Twentieth-century theory and practice. In T. W. Benson (Ed.), *Speech communication in the 20th century* (pp. 157–183). Carbondale: Southern Illinois University Press.

Ulmer, G. L. (2003). *Internet invention: From literacy to electracy.* New York: Longman-Pearson Education.

Weaver, A. T. (1989). Seventeen who made history: The founders of the association. In W. Work & R. C. Jeffrey (Eds.), *The past is prologue: A 75th anniversary publication of the Speech Communication Association* (pp. 13–17). Annandale, VA: Speech Communication Association.

Winn, J. A. (1998). *The pale of words: Reflections on the humanities and performance.* New Haven, CT: Yale University Press.

9

Shifting Contexts in Personal Narrative Performance

KRISTIN M. LANGELLIER AND ERIC E. PETERSON[1]

I first learned about performing literature in grade school and high school speech contests, and then later in a graduate classroom, after three years of teaching high school English. As performer and audience, my sure, pure favorite was oral interpretation of prose in its incarnations as solo performance and as chamber theatre, the ensemble staging of short stories and novels. The kaleidoscopic variations of narrators, stories, and audience created an event that never failed to captivate me, although my tendencies to be swept away by the rhetoric of fiction were tempered as I learned about such nuances as unreliable narrators and how to flesh out analytically and onstage the strategic intricacies of telling stories. About the same time, I came to recognize storytellers all around me, creating stories about ordinary and extraordinary experience as their lives unfold. As I look back and tell part of my life story, I credit my father, now deceased, with piquing my curiosity about performing narrative in daily life as he recounted episodes, characters, and images from his childhood and ours; and as we listened and joined him in storytelling during the bustle of suppertime, over card games of euchre and 500, or after a humid summer evening's softball game as we passed pop and popcorn among hands slick with butter. Personal narrative is performed everywhere: in conversation, in print, on radio, television, and stage, and over the Internet. As an elemental, ubiquitous, and consequential part of daily life, its pleasures and power reach far and deeply into our lives.

This brief personal narrative about performing narrative recapitulates a larger disciplinary contingency: the shift from oral interpretation of literature to the more inclusive tradition now called performance studies. Performance studies names a shift from studying literature in performance to performing texts of culture, identity, and experience. Texts are sites where work gets done, where the exchange of pleasure and power becomes visible, where the structures that enable and constrain who we are, how we can act, and what we can think become palpable (Scholes, 1985). Michael Bowman (1998) puts the contextual shift to performance studies in narrative terms: "Oral interpretation's story was how performance will make you a better reader of literature, of texts. . . . Performance studies' [story] is about what happens to us, individually and collectively, when culture is constructed or deconstructed, affirmed or challenged, reinforced or altered by means of performance" (p. 191). As part of that cultural activity, personal narrative has arguably become a privileged site of performance at the beginning of the twenty-first century, witnessed by its presence and placement in this volume. Performing personal narrative reclaims and proclaims both body and voice: the personal gives a body to narrative, and narrative gives voice to experience (Langellier, 1998, p. 207). The embodiment of personal narrative makes textual and performative power—to select or suppress certain aspects of human experiences, to prefer or downplay certain meanings, to give voice and body to certain identities—not only visible, audible, and palpable but also discussable.

The rise of personal narrative in performance studies reflects historical changes that are more broadly cultural as well as disciplinary (see Strine, 1998). In the efficacious words of Sidonie Smith and Julia Watson (1996), we "get a life" by making, performing, and listening to personal narrative: "In postmodern American we are culturally obsessed with getting a life—and not just getting it, but sharing it with and advertising it to others. We are, as well, obsessed with consuming the lives of others" (p. 3). Performing personal narrative is fueled by several broader cultural contingencies burgeoning after World War II in the United States, among them the memoir/ autobiography boom in writing; the new identity movements organized around civil rights, gender, sexuality, age, and ability; the therapeutic cultures of illness, trauma, and self-help; and the many self-performance practices of performance art, popular culture, and electronic media. The turn to technologies of performing the self contributes to what has been called an "interview society" which solicits, consumes, and studies stories of personal experience (Atkinson & Silverman, 1997), a "recited society" which continually performs (cites and recites) stories (de Certeau, 1974/1984), and a "remission society" of storytelling about illness, trauma, and survival (Frank, 1995). A defining condition of postmodernity, personal narrative has also been suggested as a key site in the future of performance studies (Dailey, 1998).

If personal narrative is a means to get a life, and if performance studies is enjoying some new disciplinary life in part through this storytelling, scholars can ask, "What kind of a life are we getting?" This chapter discusses some responses to that question by drawing on insights from theories of performance and performativity. Our emphasis is on how the shift to comprehend personal narrative within the inclusiveness of performance studies raises questions, issues, and challenges different from those raised by the paradigm of studying oral interpretation of literature, which generated theory to comprehend narrative as a text performed in a classroom or on a stage. Briefly put, performing personal narrative is *radically contextualized*. By "radical" we intend its etymological sense of "to the roots." By "contextualized" we refer to the ways text and context are inextricably coarticulated in performance. Performing personal narrative is radically contextualized: embodied in participants who tell personal stories of experience, situated in the interactional and material constraints of the performance event, and embedded within discursive forces that shape experience, narrative, and selves. The chapter develops this argument first by tracing a series of shifts or breakthroughs in defining personal narrative as/in performance. The next sections develop the senses of personal narrative performance as radically contextualized in bodies, situations, and discourse. The argument is illustrated by corresponding examples of family storytelling, staged performance, and illness narrative.

A final section discusses the politics of performing personal narrative: how its pleasures can both legitimate and critique relations of power. Understood as radically contextualized, personal narrative is a normative and transgressive practice in art and daily life, a performative struggle for agency that is always ambiguous and contingent.

BREAKTHROUGHS INTO PERSONAL NARRATIVE PERFORMANCE

It was easier to study and perform literature when, before the contextual shifts broadly called postmodernity, we were more certain about what literature is and is not. The contesting of the literary canon is mirrored by challenges to what is or is not performed or performable. A fundamental tenet of performance studies asserts that no fixed canon defines or delimits performance. Performance studies is a moving focus within a horizon of practices, events, and behaviors arrayed in a broad spectrum variously called an umbrella, tent, caravan, or carnival. Aesthetics and daily life inhabit a shared realm of practices and politics. The term *performance studies* mediates between the inclination in literary and theatre studies for high-culture forms, and the preference in cultural studies for popular culture and media (Roach, 2002). The antidisciplinary impulse of performance studies is complemented by its proclivity for interdisciplinary borrowings (Schechner, 2002). The formulation of performance as an essentially contested concept (Carlson, 1996; Hopkins, Long, & Strine, 1990) gestures to the antiessentialism of poststructuralist theories. In similar fashion, personal narrative eludes definition, blurs genres, and bleeds across boundaries.

The attempt to fix disciplinary boundaries produces two consequences: a preoccupation with what is in and what is out, and a neglect of what falls in the cracks. Personal narrative has suffered both. In earlier work, I referred to personal narrative as a boundary phenomenon

(Langellier, 1989) and as liminal (Langellier, 1999), suspended as it is between art and life, fact and fiction, self and other, natural and stylized performance, the public and the private. Here we suggest how personal narrative morphs across disciplines, each of which has a stake in its study and performance—as autobiography in literary studies, as evidence in oral history, as verbal art in folklore, as life story in psychology, as accounts in sociology, as conversational storytelling in communication and linguistics, or as public moral argument in rhetoric—each of which uses liminality to guarantee personal narrative's authenticity or to invite its dismissal as anecdote. Add to these all varieties of autoperformance— performance art, autoethnography, performative writing, mystory, "and whatever we will have called it tomorrow or the next day" (Gingrich-Philbrook, 2000, p. 376; see Bowman, 2000). One way to read this new context for personal narrative is as a series of breakthroughs into performance.

Sociolinguists William Labov and Joshua Waletzky are credited with the breakthrough into personal narrative in 1967. Their remarkably heuristic essay on "oral versions of personal experience" launched decades of research and performance. Its reprinting in the 1997 special issue of the *Journal of Narrative and Life History* (now *Narrative Inquiry*) is not simply a retrospective of the original essay but a demonstration that personal narrative continues to generate intense interest across numerous disciplines in the humanities and social sciences. Oral versions of personal experience tell "what happened to me." Labov and Waletzky define personal narrative in formal linguistic terms. Fixed referential clauses recapitulate "what happened" in temporal order and yield narrative as the enhancement of experience. Free evaluative clauses answer "so what?" to convey the personal, that is, the significance of the event "to me." Evaluation modifies narrative as personal, and it distinguishes narrative or story from non-narrative, or a report. Labov (1972) also offered a structural model of the fully formed narrative: an abstract (what, in a nutshell, is this story about?), an orientation (who, what, when, where?), complicating action (and then what happened?), evaluation (so what's the point?), resolution (what finally happened?), and coda, which returns from the past to the present and turns speaking over to others (Garrison Keillor's "That's the news from Lake Wobegon where all the women are strong, all the men are good-looking, and all the children above average").

In performance terms, the Labovian model textualizes experience in referential clauses that presume a real event prior to narration. Evaluative clauses feature narrative attitude, that is, a storyteller with a personal point of view. The Labovian model broke through to performance in everyday life along with all sorts of other self-presentational behaviors. Situated within the "narrative turn," personal narrative appealed to both social science and humanities scholars. Elliot Mishler's (1995) proposed typology of narrative analysis usefully maps three models of inquiry into personal narrative. A first model, prevalent among social scientists, takes *reference* as its central problem: "the told" and "the telling" as a correspondence between a sequence of actual events and their ordering in the text. Collected in interviews and ethnographies, personal narrative gives access to the range of lived experiences as a problem of representing experience (Riessman, 1993). Performance holds some place in issues about reference, but Labov from the outset and Anna Deavere Smith (2000) more recently recognized that interviews do not necessarily yield "good," that is, vividly enacted and performable stories. To Labov's "Have you ever come close to death?" question, Smith adds "Do you know the circumstances of your birth?" and "Have you ever been accused of something you did not do?" in order to evoke more dramatic performance in interviews.

A second model focuses less on reference and more on *textualization*, the narrative strategies through which texts achieve coherence and structure to make meaning. This model is more invested in the evaluative function of personal narrative, more interested in "the telling," and more hermeneutic—the project of literary scholars, linguists, and some historians. With only the text available for interpretation, temporal ordering of "the told" is but one among other strategies for ordering narrative. In performance studies, the interest in textualization is perhaps best represented by autobiographical performance and performative writing (e.g., Bowman & Bowman, 2002; Carver, Miller, & Taylor, 2003; Pollock, 1998b). Analytic attention to the strategies of telling and to the aestheticizing of experience evokes performance possibilities of textual poetics, the conventions of voice, form, style, subjectivity, and authority as variable aspects of making personal experience meaningful, coherent, and aesthetic. Poetic and aesthetic strategies appeal to performance interests about what is particularly memorable and performable.

A third model takes the *functions* of narrative—the "work" they do in the social world—as its central problem. This model crosses disciplines and is frequently drawn upon in performance studies where it may include therapeutic functions of narrative (e.g., Park-Fuller, 2000), ritual uses by cultural groups to enact self-definitions (e.g., Madison, 1993), storytelling in interactional and institutional contexts (e.g., Schely-Newman, 2002) and the performative power of personal narrative to tell unheard stories, resist domination, and rewrite history (e.g., Corey, 2003; Pollock, 1999). When the functions of personal narrative are emphasized, reference and textualization are subordinated to the dynamics and pragmatics of putting narrative into action. Storytelling performance as *doing* something and as *something done* in particular bodies, situations, and contexts assumes priority.

Hence, the breakthrough in personal narrative breaks through into performance (Hymes, 1996). Performance highlights the way in which communication is carried out "above and beyond its referential content" (Bauman, 1986, p. 3). The storyteller assumes responsibility for a display of communicative skill, and the audience assumes responsibility for evaluating its effectivity. From a focus on the referential aspects of a narrative text, special attention is directed to the expressive act of the storyteller within the performance event. What we can learn in no other way than through performance is that the "special nature of narrative is to be doubly anchored in human events" (Bauman, 1986, p. 2). In the oft-quoted words of Walter Benjamin, "The storyteller takes what he [sic] tells from experience—his own or that reported by others. And he in turn makes it the experience of those who are listening to his tale" (1936/1969, p. 87). In Richard Bauman's terms, the storyteller takes from experience—the narrated event—and makes it the experience of others—the narrative event. This double-anchor is not a linear sequence of moving an experience through space in the acts of "taking" and "making" but their radical interdependence in time within the situated event of performance in participation with others. The breakthrough into performing personal narrative is variable, ranging from prominent, public cultural events by accomplished performers to the fleeting, mobile, private storytelling of ordinary people.

Performance is distinguished by three qualities that specify text-context relations: it is framed, reflexive, and emergent. First, a breakthrough to performance is framed, that is, marked off from surrounding discourse and keyed by performance conventions of particular speech communities. The performance frame strikes a contract of mutual risk-taking and responsibility between performer and audience to "take this communication in a special way": as a storytelling event. Second, performance is reflexive because the performer

is audience to her or his own experience and turns back to signify this lived world with and for an audience. The storyteller narrates turning points in re-turning to experience; performance is a doing and a re-doing that allows scrutiny of experience, self, and world. As Dwight Conquergood (1998) has noted, the verbal artistry of folkloric texts tends to be conservative, a re-presentation of forms and conventions that stabilize norms. However, and third, performance has the potential of emergence, that is, in re-doing something one may do it differently. Emergence may refer to new text structures, event structures, and social structures, that is, to new stories, new storytelling events, and new identities.

Conquergood conceptualizes emergence not as transcendence to a higher plane but as transgression: "that force which crashes and breaks through sedimented meanings and normative traditions and plunges us back into the vortices of political struggle" (p. 32). The special attention on antistructural emergence as transgressive cultural activity defines performance as a political act. Performance as a political act emphasizes performer creativity to ground possibilities for action, agency, and resistance in the liminality of performance as it suspends, questions, plays with, and transforms social and cultural norms. Personal narrative offers an especially promising candidate for emergence, embedded as it is in the uniqueness of the performer's body narrating a personal experience to construct a self-text for audience evaluation in a particular performance event. The emergence of a self-text different in each body and each performance foments social change. Performance incorporates the feminist slogan that "the personal [narrative] is political" as a way to break through sedimented meanings, normative traditions, and master narratives.

Finally, personal narrative breaks through into performativity: the citing of self and experience as repetition, a re-doing. Granted there is no performativity without performance—until someone's body materializes the norms of embodiment, until someone's experience embodies the conventions of narrative. Performativity, however, underscores the theoretical and methodological move to the *constitutive* nature of performance because a performative speech act does what it says, and it produces that to which it refers. Performativity conceptualizes nonessentialized identities. Hence, storytelling as a performative speech act constitutes self and experience: "I (performer) will tell you (audience) a story about what happened to me" (experience). Personal narrative produces experience and the "I" and the "you" in a symbiosis of performed story and the social relations in which identities are materially embedded: sex, class, race, ethnicity, religion, age, geography, and so on. Identities and experience are recited according to discourse practices "whose regulatory force is made clear as a kind of productive power, the power to produce—demarcate, circulate, differentiate—the bodies it controls" (Butler, 1993, p. 1). The breakthrough to performativity is a way to explicitly theorize relations of power and the normative ordering of events, context, experience, and identity beyond the stage and classroom. In this way, the breakthrough to performativity becomes the daily practice of doing what's done (Pollock, 1998a), of reciting identity and experience in performing personal narrative.

The everydayness of performing personal narrative, the seeming naturalness of "doing what's done," may mask it as a stylized act of repetition, as a re-doing and citation of norms and forms. At the same time, the embodied presence and immediacy of performing personal narrative where storyteller, narrator, character, and audience coincide—my experience, my story, my telling of it in this event—may conceal the thing done, that is, how experience and identity are constituted in discourse. For this reason, Jon McKenzie (1998) calls for retaining but troubling the theoretical distinction between performance and

performativity. He asks, has the valorization of transgressivity itself become normative in performance studies? The theoretical claim that embodied activity transgresses, challenges, and changes text, event, and social structures creates a liminal norm. Consider, for example, the claims that personal narrative performance politicizes the personal, gives voice to marginalized identities, and thwarts master narratives. McKenzie argues that in revisions of her earlier work, Judith Butler usefully theorizes both performative transgression and the normativity of performance. Butler's revisions invite us to bear in mind the citationality of performance and to correct the misreading of performativity as theatrical performance. She resignifies both performativity and performance: "performativity now refers to a *discursive* compulsion to repeat norms of gender, sexuality, and race, while performance refers to an *embodied* theatricality that conceals its citational aspect under a dissimulating presence" (McKenzie, 1998, p. 227).

The breakthroughs into performance and performativity theorize both the transgressive and normalizing potential of performing personal narrative. If both performance and performativity are a re-doing, repeated acts and stylized actions, then the question of how we know what's done in performance cannot rest on identifying—outside the layerings of context—any particular genre, for example, personal narrative, or any performer, for example, a black lesbian, or any event, for example, performance art, to guarantee a liberatory politics. Subversive genres such as personal narrative can be normative, and normative practices, such as the classroom performance of prose, can be subversive. Furthermore, performing personal narrative may entail a compulsory routine, a disciplinary ritual, or punitive consequences "if you don't perform your story right." And, finally, discerning the difference between normative and transgressive citational performances will always be deceptive, elusive, tricky. How does one distinguish between personal narrative performance that reproduces social and aesthetic norms, and performance that produces new possibilities for identity, experience, and performance? As Della Pollock (1998a) writes, "performance is the trick" using a trick-text that turns inside out and against itself, multiplying duplicities and contradictions. Put another way, performing is always implicated in that which it opposes, and power turns against itself, turning itself inside out, over and over in time and space. The "conning" tricks of performance call for its con-textualizing, the "dynamic reconceptualization of [personal narrative] texts as inseparable from processes by which they are made, understood, and deployed" (p. 38). We consider some of these contextualizations of personal narrative performance next.

EMBODYING PERSONAL NARRATIVE

Somebody performs personal narrative. Some *body* performs a story; somebody voices experience through the body. Embodiment makes all performance possible, but even more explicitly so for personal narrative when voice and body coincide in performance. Embodying personal narrative involves two different but related conceptions. One is captured by the term *identity's body* because the text emanates from a performer marked by experience and the discursive forces of sex, race, class, age, illness, and so on. A second sense highlights the *bodily participation* of hearing and voicing, gesturing, seeing and being seen, feeling and being touched, upon which any storytelling depends. Participation in a field of bodily and discursive activities begins in audiencing one's own and others' experience. To revisit Benjamin's storyteller, one "takes," or perceives, from experience and "makes," or expresses, it as a way of turning back on the world to resignify it, to move voices and bodies in space and time. Embodying personal narrative involves listening to others' stories of

experience and telling stories to others. Storytelling is an activity embodied by a performer(s), with others, and within other activities of daily life and ways of speaking.

In performance terms, personal narrative forms a system of relationships among storytellers, audiences, narrators, and characters. The speech act, "I will tell you a story about something that happened to me" situates the performer ("*I* will") in a relationship with a listener in a particular setting ("tell *you*") with a larger audience of potential listeners beyond the immediate context (the "us" implied by performer and listener and a more general or public "you"). Simultaneously, the speech act positions the narrator in relationship with him- or herself as a character ("something that happened to me") and with other characters in the story. Performing personal narrative is a site of interpersonal contact because it brings listeners together in such a way that stories emerge; and performing personal narrative is a site of intrapersonal contact because the storyteller narrates herself as a character. As Maurice Merleau-Ponty (1960/1964) writes, "this subject which experiences itself as constituted at the moment it functions as constituting is my body" (p. 94). The body that touches itself touching makes possible the representation of past experience by occasioning it for a particular audience in a present situation. Performing personal narrative depends upon bodily participation in the system of relations that shift fluidly among storyteller, audience, narrator, and character.

Family storytelling illustrates the embodied context of performing narrative. Elinor Ochs and Lisa Capps (2001) state that "active narrative involvement defines what it means to participate in mainstream American family" (p. 8). Bodily participation in family orders experience, past and present, to make family stories. Family storytelling arises among other bodily activities for doing family and may be told in more extended narrative events such as birthday parties, anniversaries, funerals, reunions, or in fragmentary, fleeting acts around daily interactions and chores—whenever talk turns to family experience. What will become a family story emerges from the embodied participation in particular performance events. For example, a story about "sewing sandwiches" emerged in the kitchen of Gerald and his wife Madeline, with Gerald's cousin Alain, all in their 70s, while I was present conducting research. Gerald was telling about the Monday night sewing circles of the family, but both Alain and Madeline chime in with details as relations among storytellers and listeners rapidly shift. All three have experience, their own and others', of sewing circles, and so each performs as narrator and character, depending upon their angle of experience:

Alain: and of course all the kids we couldn't wait until everybody left

              cause we got the leftovers

                  and sewing sandwiches

              and in *my* family my immediate family my *kids*

              I started making those at home

                  and my kids started calling them *daddy* sandwiches

Madeline: ooh ooh

Alain: but there were the *sew*ing circle's sandwiches

Madeline: his [Gerald's] mother used to make lilies

Gerald: lilies

Madeline: for dessert

This brief narrative segment shows that sewing sandwiches moved through three generations, from sewing circles as site of women's activity in an extended family gathering to the "daddy sandwiches" of a father and his nuclear family two generations later.

In the generation between, Madeline prepared lunches as a member of the sewing circle. If Gerald and Madeline did not know about Alain's daddy sandwiches, Gerald and Alain may not know about making "lilies." The memory signaled by Madeline's "ooh ooh" is developed as she leaves her work at the kitchen sink to join us and describe in sensual detail and with vivid, iconic gestures how her mother-in-law made this special sewing circle dessert. Her information suggests that the experience "taken" to narrate is not just generational but also gendered. She recalls the time and effort of making sewing circle lunches whereas Gerald and Alain recall the fun and food to eat.

Gerald, Alain, and Madeline are not reciting but *making* stories: remembering, innovating, sedimenting, changing "what happened." The shared experience of sewing sandwiches is fleshed out and differentiated in the participation occasioned by my presence and each other's contributions. Family stories are taken from experience and made possible by the bodily participation that embraces gesture and voice, and by the bodily capability to shift among performer, audience, narrator, and character. Family storytelling is a retrospective and an ongoing performance rather than a repository of stories. More a practice than a text or canon of stories, family storytelling both narrates the past and "narratizes" ongoing daily life (Allison, 1994; Park-Fuller, 1995).

The sense of embodiment as identity's body can also be suggested through this brief example. Family is neither simply remembered from experience nor entirely invented from whole cloth but rather pieced together by participants from remnants, resources, genres, and genealogies. As Gerald, Alain, and Madeline perform from personal experience, they take and make not only stories but also their meanings and sensibilities for family. Storytelling about family gatherings, French language, and food orders their group identity as Franco American. Such meanings are neither only personal nor only ethnic but also shaped by generation, gender, and other discursive resources and constraints. As performance, storytelling embodies family relations; and, as performativity, it produces family bodies. Identity's body is always re-cited and re-newed, both transmitted and transformed in performance.

Performing personal narrative is "doing what's done" in daily life with and through bodies as participants take and make stories. That some *body* performs narrative contains a significant ambiguity and multiplicity. The performing body may be one person who shifts among the relations of storyteller, audience-to-self, narrator, and character, for example, when one writes a personal story. Or it may be a few persons who shift among these relationships, for example, a family or group of friends telling stories about work around coffee or over drinks. Or it may be many people gathered in a public setting to hear and discuss someone's story, for example, a staged performance of an illness narrative. Or groups of people might collect to celebrate their culture, such as the *Retrouvailles* (reunion) in 1994 that brought Acadians from the world diaspora to Atlantic Canada. Situating personal narrative in its material conditions further explicates how it is radically contextualized in performance events.

SITUATING PERSONAL NARRATIVE

The embodied context confers the possibility to perform personal narrative, but only *some* of these possibilities are realized in any performance when someone's body materializes the norms of experience and narrative. Personal narrative is always situated, rooted in its setting and circumstances, always subject to ground rules of narrative and performance—in a word, constrained. The term *constraint* in its sense of a boundary defines the conditions of performance. To be constrained means both to be restricted and to be facilitated. An audience, for example, limits performance possibilities

because the storyteller depends on the quality of audience members' participation; and an audience facilitates storytelling because the storyteller can draw on and mobilize shared language, history, culture, and narrative resources in order to tell a story. Performing personal narrative depends upon but is not determined by its material conditions. The ground rules for performing personal narrative include constraints on who tells stories and who listens; typical kinds of stories to tell; conventional story openings, closings, and telling strategies; performance norms; habitual forms of interaction; and so on.

Forms of interaction differ across settings and situations such as the classroom, the coffee shop, the stage. Consider for example, staged performance of personal narrative as a form of habitual interaction practiced within performance studies. A ground rule of such staged performance is the compact between performer and audience by which the storyteller assumes responsibility for an expressive act which the audience evaluates. The compact involves mutual risk-taking and responsibility. It "promises the production of mutually anticipated effects, but the stipulations of the compact are often subject to negotiation, adjustment, and even transformation" (Roach, 1996, p. 219). Performer and audience roles may shift rapidly and fluidly as they do in family storytelling, but in staged performance they are conventionally distributed more unevenly as the performer takes a long speaking turn while the audience listens. The compact confers the storyteller's power and pleasure to "have the floor." The power and pleasure are contradictory and vulnerable, however, because of the audience's scrutiny and evaluation of the "so what?" of performing personal narrative. In terms of personal narrative, one could argue that the coincidence of performer and author, that is, the self-as-text, heightens the vulnerability of the performer and the responsibility of audience; and conversely, that the self-as-text heightens the vulnerability of the audience and responsibility of the performer. Because performing personal narrative is situationally and materially enacted, we must examine its particularities to discuss these dynamics of power and pleasure. Two examples of monologues performed by white males in public settings can suggest variations in the performer-audience compact within the common context of staged performance they share.

The first example draws on Spalding Gray's performance art monologues and Michael Peterson's (1997) study of them. Gray was a widely known performer, and his long career developed the performance art form of autobiographical performance. Gray framed his life as art, filed on mental narrative note cards and performed in a lengthy series of works. He textualized himself and rendered this self as "other" in a speech act which says something like: "Look at me. I am one who sees himself seeing himself." This reflexive performance of his life/art entails specific audience relations because its liminality troubles boundaries between performer and audience as they participate in the self-text. Peterson suggests that the irony and presence of Gray created Gray-as-event, the "sensation of witnessing a present event rather than a simple oral representation of the past" (p. 95). The presence of Gray-as-event was charismatic, quirky, and confessional, indeed a "virtuoso imitation of the personal" (p. 56). Within Peterson's reading of Gray's performances, the personal is neither the disclosing risk of psychic formation nor an analysis of the material forces shaping a life but rather a stylized act of personal presence. The stylizing of "the personal" was situated in the dramatic frame of monologue by a performer whose status had grown to a celebrity, particularly after *Swimming to Cambodia*. The "look at me" became something like a command and a command performance by a celebrity with considerable cultural capital.

What, more specifically, is the audience's part and participation in this performance compact? Peterson argues that a dynamics of identification operated. The audience received a "collective pat on the back" through a liberal humanist recognition of what "we" share with Gray. Gray's self-texts claimed a universality of experience, and his performances offered a seeming naturalness of gesture. The assumptions of universality and naturalness obscured differences between self and other into a "we" of identification and shared experience. Peterson argues that Gray accrued experience, his own and others, as he textualized the world. The eye/I of the liberal humanist subject, albeit an ironic and reflexive one, elides differences among experiences and bodies. In *Swimming to Cambodia*, for example, Gray *narrated* rather than embodied women characters, for example, his lover Renee and Thai prostitutes whom he placed in the imaginary space in front of him. In such strategies, Peterson suggests that Gray consumed the world and the other rather than warning of consumption's dangers. And, in turn, audience members were invited to consume him, accruing cultural capital through their recognition and viewing pleasure.

Audiences can and do, of course, produce other, oppositional, and subversive readings. Students in a graduate course who viewed *Swimming to Cambodia* with their fellow female graduate student from Thailand, for example, exposed rather than confirmed the politics of liberal humanist recognition. In this discussion we are less interested in evaluating the performance success of the storytellers or in an ethnography of audience responses than in thinking through the situatedness of performance and the performer-audience compact. A second autobiographic performance, this one by Craig Gingrich-Philbrook entitled "The First Time" (see Langellier & Peterson, 2004, and Peterson, 2000, for transcription, description, and extended analysis), can suggest a variation in the compact. Gingrich-Philbrook has characterized his work as "stand up theory" and autoperformance. In this piece, Gingrich-Philbrook performs a personal narrative that "takes" from his experience of watching a public service announcement about AIDS and "makes" it a story for the audience who attended a benefit in Carbondale, Illinois. Reflexivity in this performance centers on how Gingrich-Philbrook watches a TV commercial about dancers as the audience watches him. Gingrich-Philbrook interrogates his own experience, that is, his first, easy identification with the heterosexualizing practices of representation found in the commercial. He does this by displaying the moves of the dancers in a character-based perspective that locates action on his body rather than in a narrative-based perspective in the imagined space in front of him. Like the waltz in the commercial, he embodies a woman wearing a dress and then a man spinning a woman. The distance between identity's body and critical commentary results in audience laughter and increased identification between performer and audience, a politics of recognition in a "we."

But as Gingrich-Philbrook challenges his own first, easy identification with the commercial, the performance challenges the audience's first, easy identification with him by refusing their "in the knowness." Gingrich-Philbrook does this by maintaining rather than resolving the ambiguity of "we" and recognition. His performance asks in so many words, "Are you part of the homogenous, heterosexual 'we' used by the commercial announcer, or are you part of 'my people [gay men and lesbians],' used by the narrator?" Performer-audience relations resist the universalizing and naturalizing of experience—his and the audience's—by marking differences and by making explicit the parallels between his viewing of the commercial and the audience's viewing the performance. He performs not only to express his outrage at the commercial but also to disrupt the often imperialist relations by which performers and audiences appropriate their own experiences and others' experiences in

acts of recognition. As the performer-audience compact is called into view and renegotiated in performance, "The First Time" exposes and challenges the conventions of representation, in this instance encapsulated in the heteronarrative (Roof, 1996); and it subverts the ease by which identification with a self-text mutes critique.

Both Gray's and Gingrich-Philbrook's performances draw on the paradoxical position of the audience in monologue performance. That is, the direct address to an audience by the solo performer seems to include and empower that audience at the same time it reasserts its powerlessness. It seems to address the audience directly, and yet to respond would break the dramatic frame established by the performance compact. Audiences to both Gray and Gingrich-Philbrook enjoy the privileged and constrained status as confidante to the self-text performances. However, their performances differ not only in the performer-audience relations discussed above but also in additional aspects of the situation and materiality of performance: in a straight versus a gay body, by a celebrity with accumulated cultural capital versus a performer in educational settings, within performance venues marked by entertainment values versus benefit performances for fundraising and consciousness-raising, and others. Furthermore, although we have viewed both performances only on videotape, it is not immaterial that we know Gingrich-Philbrook personally and have seen several other of his performances live. The audience as well as the performer, in other words, draws on habitual forms of interaction, forms that vary across settings and situations, and forms that may be stabilized or altered within any particular performance event.

The variation of the performer-audience compact merits more attention within educational settings, too. These situations lie somewhere between the relatively fluid and shifting relations characteristic of family storytelling and the more stable frame of monologue in staged performance of personal narrative. In the classroom or in similar dialogic settings, the compact is renegotiated to shift from the dramatic frame of monologue to the (inter)active frame of family storytelling. However, the transition is not always smooth, the renegotiation not always explicit, the shift to different ground rules not always successful. The challenges of how to conduct a critique of a personal narrative performance—the self-text in the narrated event and the performer-audience relations in the narrative event—engage several issues of situation and materiality (Park-Fuller, 2003; Warren, 2003).

ORDERING PERSONAL NARRATIVE

Some bodies tell their stories within their situated and material contexts. What are they doing in telling a particular story in a particular way? Performing personal narrative is known through the discursive regularities in which it participates. A storyteller is not free to narrate just anything in just any way at any place or time to any audience. Some stories can be performed and some stories or parts cannot be performed; some narrative forms can be easily circulated and others cannot be easily understood or credited; some people can speak and others must listen; some identities are acceptable to local norms, some are not. Why this personal narrative event, this story, this speaker and listener(s) and why not another performance event, storytelling performance, and performer? Regulatory principles order discourse and the conditions for performance. Discourse as context entails the formative contexts of personal narrative performance, and how performing personal narrative is formative of contexts because regulatory rules can be broken, breached, transgressed, disobeyed, disregarded, defied.

For purposes here, we follow Foucault (1971/ 1976) in the ordering of discourse according to four principles: external rules, internal rules, speaking positions, and conditions of possibility. First, external rules delimit discourse, forming "just what discourse is." Cultural history authorizes stories and narrative practices. Performing personal narrative is prohibited, for example, in income tax returns, surveys, medical histories, and most types of scholarly writing. External rules also establish divisions between what is meaningful and meaningless: for example, the dismissal of personal narrative as anecdote, mere entertainment, and self-indulgence, or its valorization as epistemological, artistic, and transgressive. Internal rules form discourse through classifications and gradations of sameness to locate series of narratives (e.g., genres, master plots, canonical stories), series of utterances belonging to speakers (e.g., autobiographical/ self-oriented or ethnographic/other-oriented narrators) and characters of all types who lend coherence to action. Another kind of series is neither a textual repetition nor the action of an individual speaker but rather a more anonymous system of rules for generating discourse dispersed across locations and speakers called a "discipline," such as "the arm of the law," "the voice of medicine," or "family values." Discourse is also regularized by governing the conditions of speaking: who is qualified to speak on a specific subject and how are roles for speaking and listening distributed, appropriated, and interchangeable? Does one speak from the authority of experience, as an expert on others, or for others? Who can or has to listen? To what extent can audiences contribute to, interrupt, challenge what is told? Finally, discourse rules frame what can be said, understood, and done in storytelling not in an effort to find and fix meanings but to look at possible conditions of existence for what gives rise to and delimits personal narrative performance. How could this event, this story, this performance have been done differently?

We illustrate the ordering of personal narrative by external rules, internal rules, and conditions for speaking and performance through a particular example of illness narrative: breast cancer storytelling (see Langellier & Peterson, 2004, for extended transcriptions and analysis).

External rules of cultural history authorize the narrative performances of illness. In the latter half of the twentieth century, illness narrative emerged, proliferated, and evolved to a genre of storytelling in daily life, support groups, and memoirs; on stage and the Internet; and as an object of research. The wounded storyteller narrates a story of the body through the body, reclaiming the capacity to tell, to hold onto, her or his own story against the medical chart as the legitimate story of disease (Frank, 1995). The illness narrative orders, interprets, and creates meanings to bind body and spirit together within the biographical disruption of disease (Kleinman, 1988). As modern adventure stories constructed around recovery, illness narratives are "all variations on a long-standing heroic paradigm of the struggle of brave individuals confronting what appear to be insurmountable forces" (Hawkins, 1993, p. 2). Within a culture of illness stories, breast cancer storytelling is sufficiently widespread and widely distributed to compose a subgenre. Barbara Ehrenreich (2001) argues that there is, in fact, a culture of breast cancer constructed through websites, newsletters, support groups, national organizations, and races for the cure. Among rites and rituals of breast cancer culture is the "heavy traffic" in personal narrative.

Breast cancer stories are told by survivors, those who lived to tell their tale. Like other illness stories, they are retrospective narratives, told or written from a relatively secure vantage point of recovery or remission, where threat of recurrence is closed off, even if contingently. Their internal rules, cast in Labovian terms, include the referential function of storytelling to order the events of "what happened" as the medical plot of breast cancer regularly distributed in the same sequence in the narrative: discovery of a suspicious lump, diagnosis of cancer, assessment of treatment options, surgical treatment, adjuvant treatment, and recovery and resolution. G. Thomas Couser (1997) argues the self-reconstruction of the breast cancer narrative follows the comic plot of a happy ending: "Although some of these women suffered recurrences, and some have died of their cancer, their narratives tend to end with recovery of some tentative assurance of health and vitality" (p. 39). Resolution through recovery, if not cure, constructs the narrator as a survivor who is better off not just physically but also in the moral dimensions of achieving normalcy and often self-realization and self-actualization. As to Labov's evaluative function, the point of view of the survivor is positive, even cheerful. Ehrenreich (2001) writes that "the effect of this relentless brightsiding is to transform breast cancer into a rite of passage—not an injustice or tragedy to rail against, but a normal marker in the lifestyle, like menopause or graying hair" (p. 49). The commanding investment in recovery and "brightsiding" drives narrative closure. The comic closure of resolution and cheerfulness serves multiple and compelling interests not just for the performer but for others with and without (at least not yet) breast cancer. Breast cancer narratives end, even if provisionally, and they end "happily" to the mutual desire of performers and audiences.

External and internal rules for ordering breast cancer narratives—survival, comic closure, and cheerfulness—constrain their telling. Jane, for example, a 54-year-old woman with an aggressive and advanced breast cancer, both participates within and struggles against the normative ordering of the breast cancer narrative. Drawing on the authority of her illness experience and building authority for herself as a speaking subject by incorporating her reading, research, knowledge of others with breast cancer, and background in science education, Jane plots her story as a series of decisions she made and assaults she survived, interspersed with interludes of humor and strength. She does, in fact, competently perform the disciplinary "voice of medicine," following internal rules of the medical plot to order her personal, somatic experience. About a woman from the Cancer Society who calls to tell Jane that "I had cancer eighteen years ago and I'm doing so well and you've gotta be positive," Jane says, "I mean it's a nice story but the point is, I mean I know enough to know that every cancer's different."

That "nice story," with its emphasis on the comic plot and cheerfulness, suggests the operation of external rules that prohibit talk about an uncertain prognosis, a treatment's effectiveness, and especially death. Jane reserves her strongest critiques for the enforced cheerfulness—what she calls "that friggin' positive stuff"—enacted by acquaintances, colleagues, and the woman from the Cancer Society:

Jane: I mean this *positive* thing

        I think is the *worst* thing that you can say to somebody

          cause here you *are*

          got this *terrible* news

          you might *die*

        and ah nobody I don't think

        nobody knows what that means

Enforced cheerfulness makes it possible to avoid talking about what it means that "you might die," as Jane voices it. These prohibitions in breast cancer storytelling reposition death and dying as not true to experience. Jane opposes the false cheerfulness of greeting cards and those who say "be positive and pray hard and I know the Lord will be this" with her preference for the truth spoken by "the people that said 'this is shit,' you know, call it what it is." She rejects the acceptable model of illness identity, and she struggles to rework the comic closure of the illness narrative.

Finally, Jane questions the possible conditions of the breast cancer narrative by attempting to launch a counternarrative as "what I forgot to do": to put in "the hormone story." The hormone story works to refashion the implied causality of the linear medical plot where breast cancer "just happens" and a lump is discovered. The focus on the individual in the master plot may incorporate genetics or lifestyle as possible causes for cancer and makes it difficult to speak about environmental factors. "The hormone story" reworks the beginning of Jane's narrative and raises a possible link between Jane's hormone replacement therapy and breast cancer.

In the genre of the illness story, illustrated by breast cancer storytelling, we can observe how the discursive context orders experience, stories, and models of identity. External and internal rules both prohibit and make possible particular narrative performances. Without such rules and speaking positions, performing narrative is not possible; but within them it is always risky and tricky, both for what it can do and what it cannot do. The ordering of experience and identity suggests that performing personal narrative is an ongoing struggle for agency and meaning. It remains to suggest the contours of contextualization in terms of the politics of performance.

POLITICIZING PERSONAL NARRATIVE PERFORMANCE

An analysis of discourse gives the rules and regularities that frame the storytelling event. These conditions of possibility emerge within the specific material situation and embodied context of a personal narrative performance. Performing personal narrative is also political because it does something; and in doing something in and with discourse that is neither uniform nor stable, performing may reinscribe or resist the bodily practices and material conditions in which they are embedded. Performing personal narrative can work to both legitimate and critique relations of power. For this reason we cannot decontextualize performing personal narrative and divide it between bodies with power and bodies which resist, or narratives of power and counternarratives. In the text-trick of doing what's done, of performance and performativity, power can turn on itself, oppose itself, turn inside out.

In order to illuminate the entwined operations of power, we emphasize performing narrative as strategic (Patterson, 2002) in a multileveled system (see Langellier & Peterson, 2004). Strategies concern the goals around which a system is organized, whereas tactics concern how a system goes about accomplishing its goals (Wilden, 1987). Under ordinary circumstances, a strategy envelops or constrains the tactics that carry it out; tactics depend upon strategy. However, tactical innovations may rupture or restructure strategies, but once restructured the hierarchy of strategy enveloping tactics returns. Pollock (1998a) comments, for example, on how performance agency pales next to discursive forces. To discuss some politics of performing personal narrative, we revisit the three performance practices above and ask how tactics carry out or subvert overall strategies: what are the consequences of performing this story in this way?

Family storytelling is an effective tactic for family formation and cultural survival. Participants make family stories as they work and rework information about what happened and what is meaningful to them. The story of the sewing sandwiches is a "good" story to tell because it both transmits information about family culture and reorders information: cultural transformation as the sandwiches move from the grandparents' generation to a father and his nuclear family two generations later. The strategy of cultural survival is facilitated by the generality of the information diffused among multiple participants in the embodied practice of group memory. Generational changes and gendered details suggest the different and often conflicting involvements of multiple tellers. Storytelling tactics support the strategy of family cultural survival, making not only "good" stories but also producing "good" bodies: good fathers, mothers, children, and families.

Family storytelling tactics are constrained by strategies of normalization, for example, "ground rules" of family storytelling that put collective over individual interests; show family in a favorable light; preserve family boundaries; foster institutions of heterosexual love, marriage, and procreation while marginalizing alternative arrangements and choices; reproduce gender roles; naturalize family events and family history as a coherent and linear sequence; and so on. "Good" families align with the environmental interests of social and cultural forces, such as patriarchy, heterosexuality, middle-class identity, and the mythic family. However, the narrative of sewing sandwiches also resists normative regularities, perhaps most strongly an assimilated "American" identity that subordinates race and the embodied differences of the North American French ethnic family.

When we turn to the staged performance, we can view autoperformance as a strategy of identity formation, a way to get a life that matters in a postmodern world. Both Gray and Gingrich-Philbrook perform the personal as an aesthetic and political intervention in social life, of empowering identity's body in staged performance. Tactically, they differ in how they draw on the performer-audience compact in their situated and material performances. Gray carries out the strategy of identity formation through a stylization of the personal as an ironic presence, an I/eye that turns back on itself. His self-texts narrate but rarely embody others in a strategy that amasses experience—his own, that of other characters, and that of the audience—to a "we" of a liberal humanist subject position. In a variation of the performance compact, Gingrich-Philbrook challenges the audience to consider who "we" are and how "we" come to participate in framing the personal *as* personal. His performance marks rather than masks differences between himself and others and among others.

Tactically, Gray takes advantage of forms of interaction and identification that are conventional to staged performance. This decision to mobilize habitual forms of interaction allows him to innovate new texts, that is, self-texts for performance art, and new practices, that is, stylizing the personal as the liberal humanist

I/we. While offering innovation, such tactics may simultaneously firm up more than disturb normative strategies of identity performance and the politics of audience recognition. By contrast, Gingrich-Philbrook's performance keeps open the gap between the "I" and "you" of the commercial, the supposed uniform "we" of heterosexual privilege, by renegotiating performer, text, and audience relations. The "we" of gay men and lesbians, as performers and audiences viewing the commercial or attending the benefit for AIDS, ruptures the heteronormative "we." Such performer-audience relations may be more unsettling to the conventions of performance and more disturbing to the formation of subject positions. Both Gray and Gingrich-Philbrook, however, are constrained by the strategies of normalizing identity, performance texts, styles, and habitual forms of interaction with audience.

The embodied and lived narrative of illness transgresses the medical chart as the story of disease, but Jane's story is contextualized not only within medical discourse but also with the culture of breast cancer storytelling. Instead of the enforced cheerfulness and "that friggin positive stuff" Jane attempts to "call it what it is" and to authorize herself as a speaking subject. Instead of the conventional comic closure of survival and the heroic scenario of victory over cancer, Jane voices the uncertainties of living with breast cancer and the fear of its coming back. Her storytelling works as a tactic to counter the forms of closure on telling a breast cancer story. That Jane almost forgot but did not forget the hormone story points to the coercive power of a medical master plot but also her resistance to it. Her efforts to target pharmaceutical and environmental causes displace the conventional beginning of the breast cancer narrative.

However, power keeps turning back on itself. What is effective tactically may not be effective strategically. Smith and Watson (1996) remark on the ability of dominant discourses to recuperate transgressive efforts. In self-help groups, for example, "a person's

efforts to make a gesture of tactical resistance to a stereotypic communal notion of the unspeakable can be co-opted and re-ordered into the community's normative patterns of speakability" (p. 16). Jane's effort at a counterstory does, however, reveal the "narrative frame-up" by which medical discourse and the comic master plot hide their coercive force through naturalizing and normalizing the content of a breast cancer narrative. Jane's hormone story counters the presumption that breast cancer is inevitable or natural for certain women because of heredity or lifestyle choices. If hormone replacement therapy can affect the growth of cancer or the environment in which cancer grows, then it is reasonable to look to other environmental features as causal factors. Her storytelling likewise contests the normalizing of breast cancer as a rite of passage to survival in her rejection of the "nice story" of achieving a positive attitude and recovery. No amount of narrative repair or counterstorytelling can alter the uncertain trajectory that will eventually end in her death, however. Her storytelling remains complex, contradictory, and contingent.

The politics of personal narrative performance cannot be determined on a single level of tactic or strategy because power opposes itself, texts turn in on themselves, and performing bodies are fundamentally ambiguous. No one element—a canonical story or a counternarrative, a performer's intention or identity's body, a liberatory or ritualized setting— can anchor normativity or guarantee transgression outside the multiple and meshed workings of context. Performing personal narrative as a radically contextualized practice tells a different story from the performance of prose texts many of us first learned as students. This different story may be best told and heard within the evolving context of performance studies. The doing of personal narrative in its shifting contexts of bodies, situations, and discursive forces means that it cannot be "taken out of context" if we want to understand what it is, how it works, and what it does in the world.

So, what kind of a life are we getting by performing personal narrative? The answer is consequential—it matters—because in answering it we take from disciplinary experience and make it a story that will narrate the past and anticipate a future of who "we" are.

NOTE

1. In this essay, the "I" refers to Kristin Langellier, and the "we" refers to Langellier's and Eric Peterson's collaborative research and analysis.

REFERENCES

Allison, J. M. (1994). Narrative and time: A phenomenological reconsideration. *Text and Performance Quarterly, 14,* 108–125.

Atkinson, P., & Silverman, D. (1997). Kundera's *Immortality:* The interview society and the invention of the self. *Qualitative Inquiry, 3,* 304–325.

Bauman, R. (1986). *Story, performance, and event: Contextual studies of oral narratives.* England: Cambridge University Press.

Benjamin, W. (1969). The storyteller. In H. Arendt (Ed.), *Illuminations* (H. Zohn, Trans.) (pp. 83–109). New York: Schoken. (Original work published 1936)

Bowman, M. S. (1998). Toward a curriculum in performance studies. In S. J. Dailey (Ed.), *The future of performance studies: Visions and revisions* (pp. 189–194). Annandale, VA: National Communication Association.

Bowman, M. S. (2000). Killing Dillinger: A mystory. *Text and Performance Quarterly, 20,* 342–372.

Bowman, M. S., & Bowman, R. L. (2002). Performing the mystory: A textshop in autoperformance. In N. Stucky & C. Wimmer (Eds.), *Teaching performance studies* (pp. 161–174). Carbondale: Southern Illinois University Press.

Butler, J. (1993). *Bodies that matter: On the discursive limits of "sex."* New York: Routledge.

Carlson, M. (1996). *Performance: A critical introduction.* London and New York: Routledge.

Conquergood, D. (1998). Beyond the text: Toward a performative cultural politics. In S. J. Dailey (Ed.), *The future of performance studies: Visions and revisions* (pp. 25–36). Annandale, VA: National Communication Association.

Corey, F. C. (2003). Tim Miller's body (of work). *Text and Performance Quarterly, 23,* 253–270.

Couser, G. T. (1997). *Recovering bodies: Illness, disability, and life writing.* Madison: University of Wisconsin.

Dailey, S. J. (Ed.). (1998). *The future of performance studies: Visions and revisions.* Annandale, VA: National Communication Association.

de Certeau, M. (1984). *The practice of everyday life* (S. Rendall, Trans.). Berkeley: University of California Press. (Original work published 1974)

Ehrenreich, B. (2001, November). Welcome to cancerland: A mammogram leads to a cult of pink kitsch. *Harper's Magazine,* pp. 43–53.

Foucault, M. (1976). *The archaeology of knowledge and the discourse on language* (A. M. Sheridan Smith, Trans.). New York: Harper Colophon.

Frank, A. W. (1995). *The wounded storyteller: Body, illness, and ethics.* Chicago: University of Chicago Press. (Original work published 1971)

Gingrich-Philbrook, C. (2000). Revenge of the dead subject: The contexts of Michael Bowman's *Killing Dillinger. Text and Performance Quarterly, 20,* 375–387.

Hawkins, S. H. (1993). *Reconstructing illness: Studies in pathography.* West Lafayette, IN: Purdue University Press.

Hymes, D. (1996). *Ethnography, linguistics, narrative inequality: Toward an understanding of voice.* London: Taylor & Francis.

Kleinman, A. (1988). *The illness narratives: Suffering, healing and the human condition.* New York: Basic Books.

Labov, W. (1972). *Language in the inner city.* Philadelphia: University of Pennsylvania Press.

Labov, W., & Waletzky, J. (1967). Narrative analysis: Oral versions of personal experience. In J. Helm (Ed.), *Essays on the verbal and visual arts* (pp. 12–44). Seattle, WA: University of Washington Press. Reprinted (1997) in *Journal of Narrative and Life History, 7,* 3–38.

Langellier, K. M. (1989). Personal narratives: Perspectives on theory and research. *Text and Performance Quarterly, 9,* 243–276.

Langellier, K. M. (1998). Voiceless bodies, bodiless voices: The future of personal narrative performance. In S. Dailey (Ed.), *The future of performance studies: Visions and revisions* (pp. 207–213). Annandale, VA: National Communication Association.

Langellier, K. M. (1999). Personal narrative, performance, performativity: Two or three things I know for sure. *Text and Performance Quarterly, 19,* 125–144.

Langellier, K. M., & Peterson, E. E. (2004). *Storytelling in daily life: Performing narrative.* Philadelphia: Temple University Press.

McKenzie, J. (1998). Genre trouble: (The) Butler did it. In P. Phelan & J. Lane (Eds.), *The ends of performance* (pp. 217–235). New York: New York University Press.

Madison, D. S. (1993). "That was my occupation": Oral narrative, performance and black feminist thought. *Text and Performance Quarterly, 13,* 213–232.

Merleau-Ponty, M. (1964). *Signs* (R. C. McLeary, Trans.). Evanston, IL: Northwestern University Press. (Original work published 1960)

Miller, L. C., Taylor, J., & Carver, M. H. (2003). *Voices made flesh: Performing women's autobiography.* Madison: University of Wisconsin Press.

Mishler, E. G. (1995). Models of narrative analysis: A typology. *Journal of Narrative and Life History, 5,* 87–123.

Ochs, E., & Capps, L. (2001). *Living narrative: Creating lives in everyday storytelling.* Cambridge, MA: Harvard University Press.

Park-Fuller, L. (1995). Narration and narratization of a cancer story. *Text and Performance Quarterly, 15,* 60–67.

Park-Fuller, L. (2000). Performing absence: The staged personal narrative as testimony. *Text and Performance Quarterly, 20,* 20–42.

Park-Fuller, L. (2003). Audiencing the audience: Playback theatre, performative writing, and social activism. *Text and Performance Quarterly, 23,* 288–310.

Patterson, W. (Ed.). (2002). *Strategic narrative: New perspectives on the power of personal and cultural stories.* Lanham, MD: Lexington Books.

Peterson, E. E. (2000). Narrative identity in a solo performance: Craig Gingrich-Philbrook's "The First Time." *Narrative Inquiry, 10,* 229–251.

Peterson, M. (1997). *Straight white male: Performance art monologues.* Jackson: University Press of Mississippi.

Pollock, D. (1998a). A response to Dwight Conquergood's essay "Beyond the text: Toward a performative cultural politics." In S. J. Dailey (Ed.), *The future of performance studies: Visions and revisions* (pp. 37–46). Annandale, VA: National Communication Association.

Pollock, D. (1998b). Performing writing. In P. Phelan & J. Lane (Eds.), *The ends of performance* (pp. 73–115). New York: New York University Press.

Pollock, D. (1999). *Telling bodies, performing birth: Everyday narratives of childbirth.* New York: Columbia University Press.

Riessman, C. K. (1993). *Narrative analysis.* Newbury Park, CA: Sage.

Roach, J. (1996). Kinship, intelligence, and memory as improvisation: Culture and performance in New Orleans. In E. Diamond (Ed.), *Performance and cultural politics* (pp. 217–236). London and New York: Routledge.

Roach, J. (2002). Theatre studies/cultural studies/performance studies: The three unities. In N. Stuckey & C. Wimmer (Eds.), *Teaching performance studies* (pp. 33–40). Carbondale: Southern Illinois University Press.

Roof, J. (1996). *Come as you are: Sexuality and narrative.* New York: Columbia University Press.

Schechner, R. (2002). Foreword: Fundamentals of performance studies. In N. Stuckey & C. Wimmer (Eds.), *Teaching performance studies* (pp. ix–xii). Carbondale: Southern Illinois University Press.

Schely-Newman, E. (2002). *Our lives are but stories: Narratives of Tunisian-Israeli women.* Detroit, MI: Wayne State University Press.

Scholes, R. (1985). *Textual power: Literary theory and the teaching of English.* New Haven, CT: Yale University Press.

Smith, A. D. (2000). *Talk to me: Listening between the lines.* New York: Random House.

Smith, S., & Watson, J. (Eds.). (1996). *Getting a life: Everyday uses of autobiography.* Minneapolis: University of Minnesota Press.

Strine, M. S. (1998). Articulating performance/performativity: Disciplinary tasks and the contingencies of practice. In J. S. Trent (ed.), *Communication: Views from the helm for the 21st century* (pp. 312–317). Boston: Allyn and Bacon.

Strine, M. S., Long, B. W., & Hopkins, M. F. (1990). Research in interpretation and performance studies: Trends, issues, priorities. In G. Phillips and J. Woods (Eds.), *Speech communication: Essays to commemorate the seventy-fifth anniversary of the Speech Communication Association* (pp. 181–193). Carbondale: Southern Illinois University Press.

Warren, J. T. (2003). *Performing purity: Whiteness, pedagogy, and the reconstitution of power.* New York: Peter Lang.

Wilden, A. (1987). *The rules are no game: The strategy of communication.* London and New York: Routledge.

10

The Constructed Self

Strategic and Aesthetic Choices in Autobiographical Performance

LYNN C. MILLER AND JACQUELINE TAYLOR

The impulse toward narrative is a fundamentally human one. Telling stories about oneself, listening to and learning from the stories of others, helps us to make sense of our world. Stories mentor us and allow us to structure our awareness of the trajectory of our lives. "Though it may seem a strange way to put it," as Jerome Bruner (1993) explains, "we may properly suspect that the shape of a life as experienced is as much dependent upon the narrative skills of the autobiographer as is the story he or she tells about it" (p. 41). While autobiography, in the form of letters, diaries, journals, and other first-person accounts, might be the oldest genre of literature, it has not always been the most respected. Its very subjectivity and particularity, which are what draw us to the form, have caused historians and literary critics to regard it with suspicion as inaccurate or limited by self-obsession and self-interest. In the 1970s feminist critics rescued many women's lives—and literary outputs—from the shallow grave of literary failure. The proliferation of talk shows, memoirs, story circles, life writing, and performance art in the past three decades attests to the continuing appeal of the individual story, and the direct relationship of a reader or spectator to the lyric voice. One legacy of deconstruction remains that while the master narrative—the universal hero's journey, the edifice of the famous, successful life—may be viewed skeptically as too white, too male, too privileged, the particular individual struggle, especially of those on the margins, retains its fascination. The direct communication of the *personal* between the writer or performer and the reader/spectator characterizes the genre. The very lack of the pretense of objectivity conveys a sense of authenticity in a world where institutional authority is seen as questionable.

One-person performances originate in the oral culture of antiquity; in the more recent history of interpretation or performance studies, they date to the lyceum circuits, platform performances, and tent Chautauquas of the late-nineteenth and early twentieth centuries (see Gentile, 1989, for a history of the one-person show). The rise of solo performance at that time is evidenced by, for example, the mesmerizing tours of Charles Dickens and Oscar Wilde. Platform performance may be viewed as an early precursor of performance art. Not all performance art pieces are autobiographical (performance installations in art galleries, or fictional characters and situations enacted by Lily Tomlin or Eric Bogosian are not, for example), yet the raw personal experiences described in works like Holly Hughes's "World Without End" or Tim Miller's "My Queer Body" came, in the 1990s, to embody the edgy simplicity of the genre.

Autobiographical performance encompasses a variety of forms, from testimonials given in self-help groups or monologues in conversation (everyday life performance), to the documentation of an individual life as research (autoethnography), the first-person narrative onstage (personal narrative), and the intermingling of the writer/performer's life with that of an historical figure (auto/biography). In this essay, we consider the parameters and construction of two autobiographical performance structures, personal narrative and auto/biography.

In personal narrative, speakers stage crafted narratives of themselves, whereas in auto/biography, performers present the intersection of a contemporary life with an historical one. While both forms address an audience directly, and are shaped in narrative form, they differ in some marked ways. In the personal narrative, the writer is also the performer—the subject and object are the same as the performer attempts to express an aspect of the subjective self onstage. The personal narrative gains a measure of authenticity from its very subjectivity: writer/performers draw upon the particularity

of their own lives. While speakers may have political aims (to increase awareness or understanding, for example, of issues of sexuality or class or race), they do not pretend to universality; they appeal, rather, to the idiosyncrasy of personal experience. As we explore below, the personal narrative's testimonial character encourages audience members to respond by thinking about their own lives or those close to them. Leslie Marmon Silko (2000) points out this aspect of storytelling: "You have this sense that there's this ongoing story and your story has become part of it" (p. 32). The personal narrative encourages sharing and risk-taking in performer and audience alike. In "Performing Absence," Linda Park-Fuller (2000) speaks to this unique property: "The performer of autobiographical narrative risks exposure and vulnerability in the effort to breach rigid prohibitions that perpetuate silence" (p. 24).

By contrast, auto/biography displays a more embedded subjectivity: as the central focus falls on the historical figure, the writer/performer subsumes him- or herself within the performance. Clearly, when choosing a subject to feature in this kind of first-person recreation, the writer/performer is drawn to a particular figure's life for specific (often personal) reasons; the historical character can become a mentor figure, changing the trajectory of the writer/performer's own life (see for example Miller, 2001). As we will see in the following discussion of a script by Elyse Lamm Pineau, what the artist Pineau has chosen to perform intersects with her life in powerful and intimate ways.

Especially if audiences are familiar with the figure performed, the performer's ultimate test consists of a scholarly and intuitive grasp of why the person was important, an understanding of her historical time, and knowledge of her multiple facets. While the performer of historical figures may evade the charges of narcissism occasionally leveled at the performer of personal narrative, because she is not the central subject, she is held accountable by audience members to present their private versions of what that figure represented—a nearly impossible task with a varied audience. These questions of the quality of research and presentation do not come into play with the personal narrative: we assume the speaker knows much more about herself than the audience does. If the personal narrative is published, however, and performed by others (as when Spalding Gray's monologues are used in speech competitions or acting auditions), these very issues become considerations. Past and present, fact and memory are in flux in the genre itself. As Heather Carver (2003) states: "Autobiographical Performance is inherently fraught with the complexities of the relationship between history and representation—between what happened and what is remembered and performed" (p. 15). In both forms of performed autobiography, audience members implicitly ask the question: Why is this relevant, here and now, to me? The narrative must evoke something of consequence to the spectator; the portrayal must spur some combination of reflection, challenge, and transformation.

The following details the characteristics of these two forms, delineating specific themes, strategies, and individual performances.

AUTO/BIOGRAPHY: HISTORICAL AUTOBIOGRAPHICAL PERFORMANCE

In our introduction to the volume *Voices Made Flesh* (2003), we address the particular components of auto/biography, where the writer/performer encounters an historical subject and produces a performance which documents the encounter of these two identities. Such a performance highlights the writing/performing self in the present as it encounters or struggles with a particular and complex subject of the past; the process of this auto/biographical intertwining shapes and foregrounds the performance. One major challenge of representing the historical figure in the autobiographical mode involves a careful

selection process as the writer/performer chooses which layers of a complex, multifaceted persona to weave into the narrative. We label this process auto/biography as this kind of historical presentation represents a negotiation between the autobiographical self of the writer/performer and the biographical record of the historical personage. (p. 7)

At times, the encounter with the historical persona represents a collision with the self of the writer/performer (as in Catherine Rogers's "Georgia O'Keeffe x Catherine Rogers"; see Rogers, 2003), while at others the selves merge, or take on characteristics of one another, resulting in a third person (as in Elyse Pineau's "My Life with Anais"; see Pineau, 2003). In some performances, writer/performers hide themselves behind the historical other in the interest of giving the audience the illusion of authenticity; a famous example is Hal Holbrook's widely toured performance of Mark Twain. In others, such as Carolyn Gage's "The Last Reading of Charlotte Cushman" (see Gage, 2003), the writer/performer updates the subject, placing her within the mores and values of contemporary culture. Choices inevitably must be made that limit the scope of the original life and focus the perspective of the audience from a particular point of view. Carol H. MacKay (2003) addresses this shaping of the performance: "Although these historical figures presumably take center stage, they in fact compete with their authorial personae, who frequently turn them into reflections of themselves in order to expand their territory beyond traditional boundaries of gender and sexuality" (p. 152).

In any case, the construction of an auto/biography stretches the writer/performer to appreciate new levels of self-awareness: the historical subject becomes a kind of mentor (or possibly a cautionary tale). As with the "mystory," a pedagogical form using autobiographical materials employed by Ruth and Michael Bowman (2002), the resulting performance "becomes an occasion for inventing new knowledge of the self, rather than merely reproducing what is already known" (p. 162).

IDENTITY CONSTRUCTION IN AUTO/BIOGRAPHICAL PERFORMANCE

Frequently seen in the post-1970s neo-Chautauqua revival which features scholars presenting historical personages to general audiences (see Miller, 2003), the auto/biographical performance is a complex one in terms of identity construction. A writer/performer chooses a particular figure to research, script, and perform largely because of an intellectual interest in the figure's life or work, a desire to recreate the historical time period surrounding that contribution, an emotional resonance with the particular person's life, simple curiosity, or any number of factors. Frequently, historians who have taught the time period or literary critics who have excavated a writer's oeuvre are compelled toward this form of historical recreation.

As the scholar/performer speaks in the first person, she is, among other things, obligated to (1) uncover the distinct voice of the persona, through letters, diaries, and other writings as well as through analyzing recorded instances of speech or behavior; (2) provide an audience with insight into the multiplicity of roles the person occupied even while focusing more fully on certain key characteristics or events; (3) show the intersection of the figure with his or her time period; and (4) create a performance context which grounds the figure in a place, time, and exigency. This last contingency, the performance context, will be explored at length below. The context frames the performance in an important way, giving it consequence and point. In personal narrative performance, the subject of the performance and the performer are the same and the performer has the authority and volition to tell her life story publicly. However, if audience members are presented with a recreation of Thomas Jefferson, they in turn occupy a role

as listener. They might wonder a number of things. Why has Jefferson decided to address them? Who are they in the address? When is this interaction occurring? Who are they in relation to the former president?

In *Cast of One*, John Gentile (1989) addresses the role of context in talking about the related genre of the one-person biographical performance: "Very few one-person shows—whether biographical or not—close off the audience behind the fourth wall of stage realism; those that do work on the basis of some conceit" (p. 136). Typically, the audience is "cast" as a character to be addressed. For example, Emily Dickinson in *The Belle of Amherst* by William Luce (1976) confides to audience members as if they were guests invited for tea. Emlyn Williams as Charles Dickens presents Dickens onstage, and the audience performs the theatre-going public who flocked to his performances in Victorian times. In Ruth Draper's celebrated performances (now brilliantly re-created by Patricia Norcia in public performance), the audience is invited to imagine silent characters in a specific scene. Performer and director Frank Galati comments:

> The hardest thing to establish is the conventional agreement between the audience and the performer about the nature of the experience they are about to share. The question that all solo performers must consider is "Why is this person speaking in this situation in front of this group or ignoring this group? Why should the audience listen to one person talk for an hour? What does this person have to say?" (quoted in Gentile, 1989, pp. 138–39)

Here Galati neatly summarizes the problem of motivation when the speaker addresses the audience.

We believe the component of context crucial in auto/biographical performance for reasons of character motivation as well as the imperatives of crafting a theatrical epic situation that locates both speaker and spectator.

In addition to aesthetic considerations, pragmatic considerations of audience familiarity and expectations arise. A portion of the audience often knows something about the history and contribution of the figure performed; often people attend a performance in order to see a favorite writer or politician portrayed. And, in neo-Chautauqua performance (Miller & Taylor, 2003, p. 8), where question-and-answer sessions, both in and out of character, are part of the performance event, audience members also relish the opportunity of addressing in the (fictive) flesh the person who has previously existed only in their imaginations. Yet an audience member who knows that Emily Dickinson lived a famously reclusive life might wonder why Julie Harris, in *The Belle of Amherst,* speaks so freely of her private feelings. If the context strains the credulity of the audience, the suspension of disbelief is shattered. Not only is the performer-audience connection less persuasive in such a situation, but, more importantly, an opportunity is lost for locating the historical figure in a milieu that informs the audience, allowing the spectators to contribute to the portrayal and to their own educations.

In her performance of "Gertrude Stein as Gertrude Stein," for example, Lynn C. Miller (2003) recreates the situation of Stein's actual lecture tour of America in 1934–35. The contemporary audience is constructed, during the first portion of the performance, as interested participants at one of Stein's mid-thirties lectures. Later, Miller steps out of the role of Stein and allows the audience to join her in the present as she entertains questions from the contemporary audience about Stein and Miller's re-creation of Stein. By contrast, Michael McCarthy's portrayal of F. Scott Fitzgerald (performed for the High Plains and Tulsa Chautauquas) illustrates a very private context where the audience is an onlooker, not a participant. Set in the evening before Scott's death, the author, speaking only to himself, reviews his career. Similarly, "The Excitable

Gift," Pam Christian's portrait of Anne Sexton (performed in various theatrical venues in Texas and Illinois), shows the poet contemplating her suicide. Alone, she composes a letter to her daughter Linda; her ruminations compose both an apologia and a deep excavation of the emotions that fuel her poetry. In these two performances, the audience is cast in the role of witness, as we have seen is often the case in the subgenre of personal narrative. The closed approach to the audience in the Fitzgerald and Sexton performances is appropriate: Fitzgerald in 1940 and Sexton in 1974 would not have discussed publicly their mental instabilities, as alcoholism and drug abuse were not subjects of public discourse. Casting the audience in the role of witness also adds depth to each of these performances, as the occasional discomfort of audience members in overhearing such private revelations encourages both introspection and sympathy. The intimacy of the situation creates familiarity, as well as a complex of feelings and reflections through which each spectator apprehends the life and work of these writers, both of whom relied heavily on autobiographical details in composing their literary works. In the case of Sexton, whom Kay Capo (1988) has called a pioneering performance artist, the performance by Christian showcases the poet's merging of personal and public selves. Elizabeth Lee-Brown (2004) writes: "Incorporating portions of Sexton's poems, excerpts from her correspondences with fans and family members and excerpts from interviews, Christian's performance examines the ways in which Sexton constructed herself as a public spectacle" (p. 123).

Even when the writer/performer has chosen to make the performance about the seams between herself and her subject, as we explore below in the discussion of Elyse Lamm Pineau's Anais Nin enactment, clear contextual decisions clarify and heighten the auto/biographical performance, locating the event in a unique space and time. Within a defined context, the performer can more fully embody a persona who exists in the trappings of a specific world, freeing the performer to make similarly concrete decisions about embodiment and interaction with the audience.

MERGING OF SELVES IN AUTO/BIOGRAPHY

We now turn to a more detailed discussion of an auto/biographical performance which highlights the encounter of selves that this kind of performance involves, "Intimate Partners: A Critical Autobiography of Performing Anais" by Elyse Lamm Pineau (2003). In our analysis, we focus on (1) the interweaving of self and other in the construction of the auto/biography, (2) the context created in the performance, and (3) the textual and performative strategies employed by the writer/performer.

Self and Other

Pineau comments on the script by talking about her longtime relationship with the American writer Anais Nin. The two never met, but Pineau's study of the author's work created more than a typical reader-writer bond:

> I first met Anais in the *House of Incest*, seven years after her death. Through her legacy of diaries and novels, essays and public lectures, she drew me into intimate conversation, then heated disagreement, and eventually, the rich and layered complexity of longtime companionship. This essay, and the performance script which it contextualizes, use my relationship with Nin to explore the fecundity of autobiographical subjectivities as they are enacted on and off the stage. I want to track some of the shifting configurations that can mark and mar the intimacy between performer and autobiographical other, foregrounding the incorporeality between the lived body and the embodiment of a literary alter ego. (2003, p. 33)

Pineau delineates three histories she shares with Nin: the biographical, as their lives intersected around Nin's art; the aesthetic, when Pineau spent days immersed in the Nin archives (feeling the presence of the departed writer); and the genealogical, the new life generated from the encounters with as Pineau (2003) terms it, a "storied self."

Pineau began her dance with Nin by adapting her work into a one-person show when she was a master's student at Northwestern. Dazzled by admiration for her subject, she found herself confronted with self-revelation at every step. The correspondence she felt with the writer during her preparation for the performance moves her to write: "'If I could speak,'" I would say to myself at the end of a rehearsal, "'that is what I would say.'" Years went by, during which her relationship with Nin deepened, until she began to imagine herself as a kind of special reader, one left a personal legacy by the writer: "My staged performances seeped into my everyday performativity such that, on or off the stage, my body could slip in and out of hers with such ease that I had difficulty marking the distinctions between myself and the Nin-in-me who had become a kind of alter ego" (2003, p. 35). Here Pineau alternates between narrating the present time and performing the past from the leather-bound journal on stage with her. Inevitably, time and close scrutiny wore away at this elegiac relationship until, at the end of Pineau's doctoral work, "the honeymoon" vanished altogether. She began to regard Nin with a critical eye as hypervigilant as, earlier, her regard was hyperindulgent. Rather than finding Nin an extension of herself, Pineau reveals: "'If I could speak,' I declared in each seminar where I invoked her, 'this is never what I would say.'" While Pineau's body still remained attuned to Nin's, her performance had a deconstructive edge, one where she signaled to her audience her critical detachment; eventually, she ceased to maintain the relationship. Then, ten years after she had first developed her solo performance at Northwestern, Pineau found herself entering a new phase, one where she "entered the rehearsal hall prepared, perhaps for the first time, to listen to what she had to say about me, and particularly, about the ways in which I had been using and abusing her story over the years. And so it was that our partnership took the stage" (2003, p. 37).

At this point in the essay, the script/performance of Pineau/Nin (entitled "My Life with Anais") unfolds as Pineau chronicles her desire to take possession of the now-deceased Nin's tape recordings, never examined by scholars and held by Nin's longtime companion, Rupert Pole. Pineau, overcome by desire to feel and hold the words of the woman she had studied for so long, proclaims,

> I deserved them. After all these years of reading and writing and performing Nin, who else could understand what they were worth? Who else would know that, for Nin, these performances were "the real thing"! I had an obligation to the scholarly community to copy and preserve them. It was my privilege—it was my right to possess them! (2003, pp. 38–39)

She finds it simple to obtain access to Pole's intimate memories. All she has to do is to perform Nin for him, and prove that she truly deserves access to the intimate circle of Pole and Nin's shared life. Despite the fluidity with which she performs Nin's turn of phrase and gestures, her voice, and even her peculiar pre-Raphaelite quality, Pineau by the end of her performance rejects Pole's offer of Nin's final, most private, diary. She realizes her imposture is in danger of morally and ethically overreaching. By dropping her impersonation of Nin, she allows Nin herself to once again occupy her rightful place between Pineau and Pole as "the real thing."

In the final section of "Intimate Partners," Pineau extends Bryant Alexander's notion of "generative autobiography" (see below) into her own construction of *generational* autobiography": "I want to stretch the generative to accommodate the intergenerational family of persons and tales that spin themselves out from encounters with the storied selves of their kin" (Pineau, 2003, p. 42). Specifically, her construction is an embodied one, as over the years her corporeal identity stretched to accommodate the body of Nin (both her works and her physical self in a metaphorical way): "This development of a Nin-in-me, which is the sine qua non of performing autobiographical texts, was formed by the contiguity of Nin's body as present to me in her texts, and my body as present to hers through rehearsal" (2003, p. 43).

Pineau's essay and performance script take the reader/audience member through the intricate steps of her performance with Nin, honed over years of interrelationship, "in terms of how my body constructed itself first *as,* then *against,* and finally *as witness to* Nin's own" (2003, pp. 43–44). In transcribing this progression, Pineau articulates a line of succession from Nin to herself and back again, creating in the process a new persona, "the Nin-in-me." For the spectator, Pineau's performance presents a complex of significations, all of which influence each other; to name just a few, the performance becomes acts of research, of possession, of mentorship, and of sharing (as she invites the audience to enter into her intricate partnership). As in any adaptation, Pineau's efforts reveal one reader's process of apprehension and criticism of a work (in this case the author's persona as well as her texts). Yet, more profoundly, the enactment lays bare how—through dialogue, through space, over time—one self invariably impacts and transforms another.

Context in the Performance

Developed specifically for an audience at the National Communication Association (NCA) in 1994, "My Life with Anais" enlists the audience as fellow explorers in her continuing search for and journey with Anais Nin.

Making the assumption that her audience shares her interest in autobiographical performance, particularly in the pursuit of performance knowledge through adaptation and experimentation, Pineau addresses us as coconspirators. In other words, she acknowledges us as scholars and as audience when she states from down center, "I want to tell you a true story that never happened. A story of ten years in three days. A story of entering the looking-glass house and finding the real thing" (Pineau, 2003, p. 37). Her poetic phrasing both echoes Nin's lyric writing and is a signature style of Pineau's own writing, honed through many years of performative and scholarly works. In this case, her use of language is both a performative strategy and a contextual device, each powerfully underscoring the intimate partnership that is her overriding intention.

Heightening the contextual dimension, Pineau stages her piece in a fluid manner characteristic of auto/biographical performances where the actor must traverse multiple periods of time, as well as engage in both direct address with the offstage audience and dramatic address with absent characters. The performance takes place in three dimensions: (1) the present story time where Pineau engages the audience directly; (2) the past, symbolized by the diary and the single chair, where she conducted her research and felt for the first time the seduction of Nin's works in her hands; and (3) the encounter with Rupert Pole in the house he shared with Nin. Her movement among these three spaces is minimal, yet clear. Pineau, whether Nin or not-Nin, uses her body and voice as narrative glue and stage metaphor. The piece is, after all, about her life change, not Nin's. But such is Pineau's alchemy with her subject that we are able to witness the fusion and frisson of the two women in the performance. As in her title for the essay, Pineau allows her audience to look in on an intimate partnership. Because of the clarity of her context, we spectators are invited to be witnesses, researchers, and cocelebrants

in Pineau's self-enlightenment. As will be discussed further, in the section on personal narrative performance, the opportunity for audience transformation is a characteristic of auto/biographical performance.

Given her literary preoccupation and subject in this performance, Pineau's context allows her audience to function triply as readers, critics, and appreciators. Like her, we worship at Nin's shrine; like her, we critically apprehend Nin's self-dramatizing persona; and like her, we are drawn into the seductive dance of the author's life and work.

Strategies in the Performance

"My Life with Anais," like many auto/biographical performances, displays simple staging and focuses on the direct relationship between performer and audience. A chair, a silk scarf, a leather-bound diary, and an audiotape are the only the physical props. Addressing the audience, Pineau sets up basic stage areas to delineate her confiding in the present about her actions in the past, and particularly, her encounter with Rupert Pole.

Pineau's pacing in front of the audience denotes her mental and emotional churning as she describes the sensuous charge of actually touching the "real" diaries during her research. She comes upon Nin's memory of childhood: "I feel my empathic body taken up, taken in. I taste words on her tongue. Together we wrap our arms around this child, *this child*, whose only wish was to create a world in which everybody loves her and no one ever leaves." What the script of the performance cannot capture is the slow becoming the audience witnesses as Pineau moves into and out of her constructed Nin persona. In her performance, there are three people: herself; Rupert Pole, the executor and former intimate; and the absent/always-present Nin herself. MacKay notes this triangulation which "confounds the reader" (2003, p. 160). The configuration also creates a psychodramatic enactment where

Pineau proves to Pole that she is worthy of his trust, his admiration, and his desire (for Pineau as a surrogate of Nin): in a sense, Nin and Pineau alternate as the object of desire in Pole's gaze. It is from this position, which she ultimately finds almost a violation, that Pineau withdraws when she refuses to accept the secret diary Pole offers.

Language in all its evocative and literary glory, ripe with multiple meanings, remains at the heart of this performance; this seems appropriate, since what initially drew Pineau to her subject were the author's words. Language is a signature throughout the piece that unites contextual and performative strategies. The words resonate inside and outside the body in this performance, but it is in the embodiment of Nin's poetry and Nin's persona that the auto/biographical transformation takes place.

THE STAGED PERSONAL NARRATIVE

We now want to consider the growing body of staged personal narratives that have been created by performance studies teachers and scholars over the past fifteen years. A number of the pieces analyzed here first came to our attention at communication and theatre conferences. During this time, autobiographical performances have come to occupy more and more program space and more and more critical attention. Several of these performances have toured the country, featured not only at colleges and universities but also at festivals, community centers, and professional theatres. The lively influence of performance art can be detected in some pieces; a good example is *Out All Night and Lost My Shoes* by Terry Galloway (1993) which, since its appearance at the 1992 Edinburgh Fringe Festival, continues to be performed on professional and campus stages (see Faires, 2000). But it is important to note that the works generated by scholars coming out of a performance-of-literature background are

marked by a strong narrative thread and a significant emphasis on language—including the foregrounding of numerous literary devices and theatrical techniques that derive, at least in part, from the creators' knowledge of chamber theatre techniques for the staging of narrative literature.

Equally noteworthy is the predominance, in this body of performances, of works that speak from the margins, seeking to position a life as connected to and as a distinctive instance of a particular identity. These pieces draw on a tradition of testimonial literature—bearing witness to experiences and perspectives rarely voiced in the culture's predominant narratives. Many of the creators directly address the absence of stories such as theirs; they desire to move from the position of misrepresented and passive subject to a more powerful position of creative agency, through the shaping of lived experience into performance. Such work regularly contests master narratives: those narratives that presume to represent universal human experience but, in fact, regularly ignore race, class, gender, sexual orientation, and much more. Instead, these performances position themselves as counternarratives—always keenly conscious of the master narrative as background for the rhetorical space they seek to foreground. These staged personal narratives draw on a variety of strategies to make space for the stories that their author-performers believe need telling.

Testimonial performances characteristically invite audience members to draw connections to their own personal experiences. Testimony calls forth testimony. The performer knows she has tapped into this aspect of personal narrative when audience members approach her after the performance and begin telling their own stories. Often, the performance functions as a frame within which audience members view their own experiences.

As personal narrative performances have gained ground in performance studies, a number of concerns have been raised about these works. While these counternarratives are designed as sites of resistance to dominant narratives, it is important to look at the inevitable privilege that adheres to a staged autobiographical performance. By virtue of claiming one's life in public, the performer claims that his or her life is worthy of attention. This makes autobiographical performance both an ideal genre for redistributing power and a locus for continued struggles with the inequitable distribution of power. In other words, the performer makes space for a voice formerly excluded, but immediately has to deal with the assumption that she is now speaking not only for her particular experience, but for all those who share aspects of that experience. The performers cited here try valiantly to resist this universalizing impulse, but in truth there is no simple solution to the problem of speaking for others.

Nor is there an easy solution to the assumption of moral superiority that personal narrative performances may invoke. The very act of taking the stage to narrate one's life asserts, as we have said, the value of that life. The claim that it is *this* life to which we should attend, rather than some other, asserts that this life is in some way (at least in the telling) worthy of others' attention, and thus inherently more important than a "typical" life. Again, performers work to resist these troublesome power dynamics, but not always with unmitigated success.

In her autobiographical performance, "On Being an Exemplary Lesbian: My Life as a Role Model," Jacqueline Taylor (2003) sought to undermine this location of moral superiority by directing attention to and poking fun at the notion of the exemplar as the one from the margins who is allowed to take the stage. Yet the strategy was only partially successful. For whatever one might choose to say about the complications of speaking inside the spotlight, about the impossibility of speaking for others, the fact remains that the performer functions as an exemplar within the context of her performance, however much she might contest it.

Finally, autobiographical performances, by their very nature, are not objective. In some cases the life and the aesthetic object, the performance, seem to have leaky boundaries. Some critics have argued that it is difficult to critique such a performance without seeming to critique the life. Others have noted that such performances are sometimes unclear about their goals; for instance, does the performance seek to evoke an aesthetic, therapeutic, or political response, or something else altogether? If the desired response is therapeutic, whose therapy is sought—the performer's or the audience member's? And is the performance equipped in some way to deal with the responses it might evoke? Or should it be? We attempt to address these questions by examining four personal narrative performances.

"sista docta"

In "sista docta," Joni L. Jones (2003) provides a harrowing account of the demands placed on a young black female professor working toward tenure at a large research university. The solo performance, combining poetry, improvisation, everyday life performance, and audience participation, features drum accompaniment as Jones dances and performs her way through a multiplicity of roles and competing expectations. While Alli Aweusi drums, Jones opens the performance by handing cards to audience members that contain the lines she will have them speak in the "faculty party" section of her performance. Jones, dancing all the while, as she does throughout the performance, asks how many sista doctas are in the house, recognizes these women, and then begins with an adaptation of Mari Evans's poem, "Status Symbol" (Jones 2003, pp. 238–239) that includes details about Jones' experience and sets the theme of dealing with the inherent conflicts an African-American woman encounters as a high-status professional in a white and male-dominated setting. The poem is followed immediately by a scene in which Jones performs her sisters and her daughter commenting on and questioning the work Joni does. The scene, based on a transcript of an actual conversation, evocatively explicates the tensions she faces between family and professional obligations and expectations. The daughter comments,

> I like that Moma and I get to go to plays, and sometimes I go to her classes and I get to help her direct. What I don't like is that Moma travels a lot and I have to stay with babysitters and one time she was at a conference and she couldn't make my costume for Halloween. (quoted in Jones, 2003, p. 240)

One sister notes that "white folks are toxic and oppressive. They can't help it. It's in their genetic coding." Told by another sister that "Joni works with white folks," she replies, "I wouldn't be going to none of their parties and putting on pantyhose. I wouldn't be doing none of it." The dialogue identifies the ability to "hang with white folks" as one of the troublesome demands of the job (quoted in Jones, 2003, p. 240).

In "the faculty party," various audience members stand and deliver the lines Jones earlier distributed. The comments, ranging from encouraging and well intentioned but naïve to blatantly racist, accumulate as Jones transforms from a polite wine-sipping partygoer to a woman staggering, in a series of weighted dance movements, under the weight of her commentators' ignorance and racism. In another section, Jones performs a series of "stupid statements" while enacting self-defense postures. At the end of each statement, the audience is coached to respond in unison, "Be careful, your misunderstandings are dangerous." These strategies allow audience members to consider their complicity in the kinds of remarks quoted here, while recruiting them into the performance in ways that allow them to be part of a response to such racism and obliviousness. This practice of enlisting other voices into the performance

is a familiar strategy in staged personal narratives.

Other segments follow, including: a step routine performed by Jones for the sista doctas; her own poem, "never tell a woman to wear lipstick"; and "girltalk," a series of quotes from black women academics about the institutional racism of the academy. In one memorable scene, messages from her answering machine provide an accumulating series of professional demands on her life. As she dances and jogs her way through the recorded messages, the physical rigors of such a bombardment of expectations are made literal through her sweat and visible exhaustion.

The academic world Jones stages is indeed a chilly one for women and an outright arctic one for African American women. Elizabeth Bell (2003) notes that Jones's script, "almost line for line, parallels the research on African American mentoring: women of color are few and far between in senior positions in academia; feelings of isolation and tokenism abound; and the mentoring load, service responsibilities, and committee work for these women is monumental—often to the detriment of research and publication that would lead to their own advancement in rank and power" (p. 309). The audience literally enters into the world Jones creates by reading the lines she assigns them or joining her onstage for improvisational scenes that draw on the audience members' own related experiences. Through such participatory strategies, Jones performs her own story: solidly situated among the stories of others, hers resonates with them.

Jones's piece both is dedicated to and often directly addresses other sista doctas. For such women the performance offers a powerful jolt of recognition, a sense that often isolating experiences in the academy are in fact shared by a community of other black academic women. But just as powerfully, the performance addresses another audience, one without the direct personal experience of racism and sexism in the academy, but one willing to learn from Jones's account and enter into a dialogue about the effects of race and gender in the university. Interestingly, Jones has placed some of the potential objections, concerns, or misunderstandings of white audience members into the text of her piece (for instance, as lines for the partygoers or in the series of "stupid statements"). In this way, she frames such perspectives quite clearly for her audience and increases the likelihood that even some of those who have not thought much about these issues will begin to share more of her framework and understanding. She performs for such audience members, or even lets them perform, lines that reveal what those attitudes sound like to her.

Clearly, Jones's performance exists as counternarrative to dominant narratives about the academic life. As we have demonstrated, that counternarrative addresses both an audience of insiders (other sista doctas) and an audience of outsiders (those who still don't get it, but with a little more help, just might). Especially interesting about the staging is the use of drumming and dance. The rhythm of the drums and the choreography of the dance become strong conduits for content about the pace and demands of the academic world with which sista doctas contend.

"Refreshment"

"Refreshment" by Craig Gingrich-Philbrook (1997) is a deceptively simple piece. It begins with Gingrich-Philbrook seated in a chair, the performance's only set piece, and uses neither props, music, nor the juxtaposition of stylistically distinct scenes in its account of the author's experiences and thoughts as a spectator at the Gay Pride Parade in New York "a few years ago." Not in any sense a plot-driven narrative, Gingrich-Philbrook's story is worthy of the telling primarily because he tells it so well, with an eloquence and richness that reveal an elegant mind in action and a love of language play.

The piece, originally performed at an AIDS benefit in 1995, posits an audience familiar with Pride parades and gay culture. Yet, even as the piece assumes the intimacy of a conversation between familiars of this world, it inserts enough detail that newcomers can easily come along. For instance, when he describes the moment of silence at the Pride Parade in New York, he says: "I'm standing there and the minute of silence begins to flow up the parade route. You know how that sounds: You ever been there? At a specific time. . . ." (1997, p. 355). Such language invites both insiders and outsiders to share in his reminiscences and reflections.

In the opening moments of the performance, Gingrich-Philbrook recalls sitting in a café prior to the parade as friends describe their favorite Pride Parade moments. While one part of his mind is occupied with getting his own answer ready, he is most attuned to the "reverential tones" with which his friends speak about Pride. He conveys this through a series of similes that build in power through repetition:

> [M]y new acquaintances spoke about Pride the way people sometimes do talking about birthdays—looking back on how far they've come over the past year, taking stock of their life. They spoke about Pride the way people sometimes talk about the future, making resolutions on New Year's Eve about how far they want to go in the coming year. They spoke about Pride the way we speak, on the Fourth of July, about freedom. And they spoke about Pride the way that people speak, on Memorial Day, remembering the price some have paid for that freedom, with a kind of nostalgia. (1997, p. 354)

Moments later, in what first appears to be an aside, but soon takes its place as a central element in this performance, Gingrich-Philbrook explains his inability to join his friends in marching and his consequent location as a spectator. He tells a story about high school bullies assaulting him while he was in junior high, stomping on and breaking multiple bones in both his feet as they demanded that he admit that he was queer.

He remembers, as he reflects on his friends' reverence for Pride, the way his mother and stepfather would scoff at the notion of gay pride, saying, "What is there to be proud of for goodness sake? . . . We're not proud of being heterosexual." This memory is the springboard for a fanciful scene in which he imagines telling them, "You are too proud: You wear your heterosexuality on your chest just like it was a big blue ribbon from the state fair for best big hairdo or best menacing gesture made with a plate of vegetables toward a child." (Note how these images depict a heterosexuality that prides itself at the point of unappealing excesses.) He then imagines flying them over the Pride parade and forcing them to look down on what they see with an understanding that these people are "trying to make a community, just trying to refresh their identities." The scene juxtaposes the angry, argumentative style of a young child ("You are too proud") with his adult eloquence and poetic repetition: "And see how the city, stretching out on either side of them, pushes in behind them, closes in behind them, closes in behind them after they've gone, closes in behind them like they were never there" (1997, p. 355).

Eventually, searching for the "refreshment" of a raspberry sorbet, Gingrich-Philbrook passes a vendor hawking "Neuter Newt" buttons. This sight occasions a lengthy reverie on what besides alliteration could make this a good political slogan. In order to make real the slogan's implied violence, Gingrich-Philbrook describes in unbearable detail what "we" would have to do if we were to neuter Newt, and the scene that he depicts hauntingly echoes the violence of the school-yard bullies he told earlier.

Finally, he happens upon what he first takes to be melted raspberry sorbet spilled in the street but soon identifies as a pool of blood. Now, in yet another series of repetitions, he refuses us the comfort of even identifying the victim, as he reminds us once again of our shared vulnerability:

> And I thought,
>   Oh God. Here, here some gay man has been stabbed, here on this, the safest, the most holy day of the year.
>   And then I caught myself, and thought,
>   Here, here maybe some lesbian has been stabbed, here on this, the safest, the most holy day of the year.
>   Or, here, here maybe a bisexual person has been stabbed, here on this, the safest, the most holy day of the year.
>   Or, here, here maybe a transgendered person has been stabbed, here on this, the safest, the most holy day of the year.
>   Or, here, here maybe one of those "straight but not narrow" folks has been stabbed, here on this, the safest, the most holy day of the year
>   . . . where we are all still vulnerable. All of us. (1997, p. 359)

Gingrich-Philbrook simultaneously performs resistance to the master narrative (as in the scene where he imaginatively flies his mother and stepfather over the Pride Parade and forces them to see the scene through his eyes) and his commitment to reinscribing his own story as another master narrative. For what is he doing in the section quoted above with the "Or, here, here maybe" refrains, if not reminding us of the range of stories that might be told instead?

It is through these detailed and poetic musings that Gingrich-Philbrook asks us to attend more carefully to the world around us and the language with which we describe and sometimes attempt to simplify it. Moving deftly between humor and utter seriousness, he invites us into a world of what he has described as "performed theory," where the questions about language, location, and power that theory seeks to explicate are constantly investigated in the thoughts he shares with us. His is a meditation that seeks to complicate and unsettle our perception of the world, to share not only his own location as a gay man but his own carefully inscribed resistance to universalizing that location or imposing it on others as a final site of authority.

"Skin Flint (or, The Garbage Man's Kid)"

"Generative autobiography" is the term Bryant Keith Alexander employs to describe the performance that develops in response to and in dialogue with another performed autobiography. In a carefully reasoned essay, Alexander (2000) offers his own performance, "Skin Flint (or, The Garbage Man's Kid)," as a case study to illustrate his thinking about generative autobiographical performances. Witnessing "Tattoo Stories," the second of Tami Spry's paired performances exploring her relationship with her now deceased mother (see Spry, 2003), Alexander finds himself considering his own autobiography and in particular his relationship with his father, but not, perhaps, for any of the reasons Spry, in the creation of her work, might have been inclined to expect. Spry describes, first in "Skins" and then in "Tattoo Stories," a mother-daughter relationship that is at once extremely close and marked by contradiction and ambivalence. In the second of these pieces, she recreates a scene where she shares with her friends the joke her mother used to enjoy with her, a "joke" in which she insisted that Spry's real father was actually the garbage man, who would return one day to retrieve her (like an almost-forgotten piece of trash, the jest implies but does not quite say). The mother would insist on the truth of this tale of paternity until the child Spry was in tears, then laughingly reveal the joke. It is not until the adult Spry shares this joke with her friends and they respond with unexpected sympathy that she begins to fathom the enormity of the injustice done to her childhood self.

For Alexander, however, this tale, something of an aside in the narrative Spry is weaving, becomes the trigger for his own "reflection

and self-exploration." The joke, Alexander reminds us, is grounded in assumptions about race and class, about the incongruity of the divide between Spry's location as a white privileged child and the location of "the garbage man's own children" (p. 105). But Alexander is, in truth, the son of a garbage man, and so this performative moment not only foregrounds issues of race and class as they operate in both Spry's performance and in Alexander's life, but also becomes the catalyst for his own autobiographical exploration and performance, written, as he says "between the lines of her performance."

Alexander's performance describes witnessing Spry's piece and uses the metaphor of the closet to portray the silence and denial which have surrounded his response to his father's work:

> Today I take the public opportunity to *out* myself:
> [*As myself—in a confessional mode*] "I am the son of a garbage man."
> I say that for first time after 34 years of subterfuge and euphemistic descriptions such as:
> [*As myself—embarrassed, hesitantly grappling*] "My dad is a . . . My dad is a . . . My dad is a . . . a truck driver."
> "My dad works for . . . the . . . the city."
> [*With an increasing rate and frustration*] "My dad is a san . . . ni . . . tational engineer." (2000, p. 106)

Alexander returns twice more to segments where he struggles to find language for his father's work. These repetitive sections function as a literary device that accumulates in power with each return and variation. He includes as well sections where he describes his experiences in scenes that enact his childhood exchanges with each of his hardworking and proud parents, struggling to instill their family values into their son in the face of a society that often diminished them. References to Spry's narrative abound, not only through direct discussion of her performance, but also stylistically. For instance, he tells his own bitter family joke:

> "Did I ever tell you the Alexander family joke? No? Well it goes something like this: The Alexander kids never really went to the dentist. Most of us have relatively straight teeth. You know why? Because whereas some kids had their teeth controlled and directed by wires and braces—ours were controlled by slaps to the mouth. Isn't that funny?" (2000, p. 107)

Later, and more directly, he confronts head-on the impact of the Spry family joke on him and his family:

> (*As myself—eager, once again recreating the tone of Spry's self-disclosive moment in* Tattoo Stories) "Did I ever tell you the story of the garbage man? I never told you that story? . . . Well! When I was growing up my dad was a garbage man—and even though other people found that funny—well, it was not one of *our* family jokes." (2000, p. 109)

Alexander explains his inability to laugh at the Spry family garbage man joke (which in truth is not funny in Spry's performance either, as it reveals a cruelly manipulative maneuver by mother against child):

> I did not laugh at the garbage man joke . . . because the incomprehensible projection of self as other, which is the crux of the joke as she tells it, reflected my own otherness—reflected my own denial of being a garbage man's kid. (2000, p. 109)

Alexander's performance, in dialogue with Spry's, moves through a journey of coming to terms with the shame society visited on Alexander and his family and a reworking of his understanding the past to finally proudly claim and honor the father who worked hard and honorably to care for his family. He closes with a powerful and empowering proclamation and tribute:

> Her performance was a flint struck against the steel of my resistance, sparking my reflection, my own self-critique. Today I out myself as a garbage man's kid. In doing so I re-claim my identity. I proclaim an identity. I declaim my respect and unending gratitude to my dad. . . . Today I proudly profess that I will always be the garbage man's kid . . . and that's alright. The joke is not on me. (2000, pp. 109–110)

Alexander's performance is a powerful and moving piece that works in its own right, even if one approaches it without previous knowledge of Spry's performance. Indeed, Alexander is careful to describe Spry's performance sufficiently for anyone who has not seen it to understand its significance as the catalyst for his own reflections. It is also, in a manner reminiscent of Gingrich-Philbrook's notion of performed theory, a performance that enacts theories of generative autobiography and of analysis of classism and racism as embedded in the autobiographical narratives we spin about our lives. Yet one does not need a background in literary theory to understand the clear points Alexander is making about class and race. Look through my eyes, it tells us, and see what you might not have noticed in the performance that went before. Look through my eyes and see how my particularity connects to a web of social and cultural meanings that inscribe on my life and on all our lives notions of whose stories matter, notions that this performance takes the stage to contest.

Finally, it is a moving enactment of the testimonial impulse of personal narrative performance, as it both responds to the frame of Spry's performance and simultaneously reframes that piece with another narrative. In doing so, it powerfully portrays the act of silencing that can inhere in a performance designed to break silence and counter a master narrative.

"A Clean Breast of It"

A number of personal narratives have explored illness and recovery through staged performances. "A Clean Breast of It" by Linda Park-Fuller (2003) is one in a strongly testimonial style that recounts her breast cancer diagnosis, treatment, and recovery, and uses narrative to educate the audience about this disease. This is one woman's story, but it is quite consciously and carefully not just one woman's story. Instead, she employs a number of strategies to connect her story to the larger context of breast cancer experiences. She describes herself as inspired to create "A Clean Breast of It" in part by the AIDS narratives she witnessed at the 1993 Arizona State University conference, "HIV Education: Performing Personal Narratives" (see Corey, 1993). She has frequently performed her piece in educational and therapeutic settings, encouraging other cancer survivors and their loved ones to enter into postperformance dialogues.

Park-Fuller's performance is more of a straightforward personal narrative than any of the other pieces discussed here. She employs a largely chronological organizational structure as she narrates her experience from the moment she discovers a lump in her breast through diagnosis and treatment and the first few months of reorienting her life after cancer. She wants to make sure the audience understands the emotional and practical impacts of breast cancer. The communication teacher in her is apparent as she carefully explains, in clear and simple language, what she has learned about how cancer attacks the body with its own cells:

> What fascinates me most is that cancer is all about communication—intercellular communication, about how the cells communicate (or fail to communicate) with one another. When you think about it, cancer is just one big misunderstanding! (2003, p. 228)

As she learns more about her disease, she also learns more about the need to take an active role in her own healing, questioning the medical establishment's inability to address the human side of this disease, or even to assist in recognizing the lifestyle changes that might promote healing.

> So I was making all these resolutions to eat right, yes? And at the same time, I was eating hospital food! Which, as you may know, doesn't taste that great, but I don't think it's particularly good for you either. . . . The funniest thing occurred at lunch one day, when they served me a six-ounce can of diet Shasta soda pop. As I was pouring it into the glass, I noticed some printing on the side of the can. It said: "Warning: This product contains saccharine, which has been known to cause cancer in laboratory animals." Hah! Doesn't anyone talk to anyone else in this hospital? I mean, what am I in here for?
> . . . So that's when I realized that if I thought behavioral changes were going to make a difference in preventing recurrence, . . . then I would have to initiate them myself. (2003, pp. 229–230)

This is a narrative account from a woman who is actively involved in reflecting on and learning about her disease and in shaping her own recovery. Thus, the audience stands to learn a great deal by following her journey.

In the early moments of her performance, Park-Fuller picks up an acoustic guitar and, with an untrained voice and the accompaniment of simple chord changes, she sings, "It'll Come to Me," a song that emphasizes the improvisational nature of much of life, which requires us to "make it up as [we] go along." This moment positions her as a kind of folk raconteur. There is nothing particularly polished or professional about this musical number, but it is pleasant and provides a thematic notion to which the performance will return. Three more times she punctuates the performance with her singing as she continues with additional verses of the opening song. The guitar playing, we learn in the performance, is something she had always wanted to learn to do, but only gave herself permission to pursue as she sought to balance her life after diagnosis and surgery. She explains that she needed to learn to do something amateurishly, simply because it brought her pleasure, and so the simplicity of the music becomes an integral manifestation of what she has learned about living from her cancer experience.

Park-Fuller's language is simple, too, intentionally vernacular, as she sprinkles the script with "you know," "oh," "oh boy," "oh man," and "you see."

Yet the hand of the seasoned director, literary scholar, and teacher is everywhere apparent in this simple narrative. Park-Fuller wants to resist any suggestion that she can stand and speak for all cancer survivors. In a piece like this, she inevitably does so, and yet, to do so is problematic, for no two breast cancer experiences are the same. To counter any suggestion that hers is a universal breast cancer story, Park-Fuller employs several devices. First, she opens the performance with a dedication:

> This performance is for all those who have struggled with breast cancer—those who have survived and those who have not. They all have their own unique stories, and I do not claim to speak for them. But I dedicate this performance to them. (2003, p. 222)

At the outset she has called into the room all those who have experienced breast cancer and has stated clearly her inability to speak for them. Yet she makes it clear all the same that there is a sense in which she speaks on behalf of them.

A second strategy Park-Fuller employs is a timer, set to go off at thirteen-minute intervals, "symbolizing the death rate of breast cancer in the United States" (2003, p. 218). She sets the timer near the beginning of the performance, as she gives the audience statistics about the incidence and mortality rates of the disease. Each time the timer goes off, she stops wherever she is in the performance, the first time repeating, "And every thirteen minutes, someone else dies"; always she resets the timer. Park-Fuller writes about the way this timer comes to function in the piece:

> In retrospect, I can now say that it serves three purposes. First, as a social-medical critique, it sharpens our comprehension of how many people die from the disease and how little progress has been made against it.

Second, aesthetically, it symbolizes the themes of life's interruptions and improvisation, since I as performer cannot predict exactly when the timer will go off. Like the cancer that occurred so unexpectedly, forcing me to stop, reevaluate and revise my life, so the sounding of the timer forces me to stop and revise my performance. And, third, ethically, the timer evokes awareness of others whose stories do not end as fortunately as mine. Over the course of the play, it comes to represent them. By interrupting my narrative (the *survivor's* narrative), it symbolically gives the power to contradict my story to those who cannot tell their own. Their stories are not heard within the frame of my performance, but drawing attention to their absence reminds audiences that *someone had a different story that will never be told*. In this way, the piece attempts to transcend the "merely personal" in personal narrative—*to stand with*, not to *stand in for*, others' stories. (2003, pp. 218–219)

The educational and therapeutic objectives have a primacy in Park-Fuller's piece that shapes several of these performance choices. She assumes no knowledge of breast cancer experience among her audience and makes that acceptable by emphasizing her own ignorance of the disease prior to diagnosis, while making sure to include substantive factual information to contextualize her individual tale. She speaks simply and humbly about her journey, in a way that that sets her up, not as professor and expert, but as fellow traveler, using a simple colloquial language that invites the audience member to view her as a friend who has been there. Yet she manages to do a great deal of teaching along the way, as she consistently calls the audience to attend to the larger cultural context in which her individual story unfolds. It is interesting to compare the sophisticated and perceptive academic discourse Park-Fuller employs in writing about this performance to the everyday discourse of her performed narrative. In such a comparison, it becomes clear that Park-Fuller brings to the staged narrative a highly trained capacity for adapting her level of diction to target audience and rhetorical goals.

CONCLUSION

As we see in even this limited selection of staged personal narratives, the performer draws from a wide array of compositional and staging strategies, from the simplest retelling of an experience while seated or standing before the audience on a bare set to a much more highly dramatized narrative or collection of narratives. Some scripts are compilations of poetry, song, everyday life performance, improvisation, and more. Almost invariably, performers of their own story draw into the narrative the words of others, whether the remembered words of friends or family, imaginary scenes, or the literary works of others. While the consciousness with which performers acknowledge their privileged location onstage varies, most of the performances we have considered work to expose and complicate that assumption of power—often by directly calling attention to voices not represented. Most powerfully perhaps, the autobiographical performance calls out to us with the claim that a particular life matters, and matters in ways that the master narrative might well have obscured. The staged claim that one's life is worth the audience's attention seems to call forth a mirroring response, one in which the audience members reflect in turn on the value of their own lives, responding in kind with yet another story, if not a full-fledged performance, about the meaning they have struggled to make of the lives they are living.

In personal narrative performance and in auto/biographical performance, the audience occupies a pivotal role as witness and participant. As we have discussed, the formulation of context, the intimacy—and the community created by the presence—of the shared life, call forth a unique performance situation. Craig Gingrich-Philbrook (2000) says that this situation demonstrates "solo performance's status as a situated accomplishment of existential collaboration" (p. viii). In locating the strategies and characteristics of this genre of performance, we find the fabric woven between story and storyteller and performer and spectator to be direct descendents of the oral tradition and of the early literature in the performance history of the field of performance studies. Narrative remains paramount in performed autobiography, in all its complex permutations and inherent simplicity.

Auto/biography and personal narrative are flexible performance forms: they can be performed in spaces from theatres to classrooms to tents pitched out of doors (as in the original Chautauqua performances). Constructions of self, memory, and milieu constitute the central elements of autobiographical performance. A genre of great fluidity and possibility, autobiographical performance signifies through the act of natural conversation: to speak one's life in the presence of another is to claim a measure of consequence.

REFERENCES

Alexander, B. (2000). "Skin flint (or, the garbage man's kid)": A generative autobiographical performance based on Tami Spry's "Tattoo Stories." *Text and Performance Quarterly, 20,* 97–114.

Bell, E. (2003). "Orchids in the arctic": Women's autobiographical performances as mentoring. In L. C. Miller, J. Taylor, & M. H. Carver (Eds.), *Voices made flesh: Performing women's autobiography* (pp. 301–318). Madison: University of Wisconsin Press.

Bowman, M. S., & Bowman, R. L. (2002). Performing the mystory: A textshop in autoperformance. In N. Stucky & C. Wimmer (Eds.), *Teaching performance studies* (pp. 161–174). Carbondale: Southern Illinois University Press.

Bruner, J. (1993). The autobiographical process. In R. Folkenflik (Ed.), *The culture of autobiography: Constructions of self-representation* (pp. 38–56). Palo Alto, CA: Stanford University Press.

Capo, K. E. (1988). "I have been her kind": Anne Sexton's communal voice. In F. Bixler (Ed.), *Original essays on the poetry of Anne Sexton* (pp. 22–45). Conway: University of Central Arkansas Press.

Carver, M. H. (2003). Risky business: Exploring women's autobiography and performance. In L. C. Miller, J. Taylor, & M. H. Carver (Eds.),

Voices made flesh: Performing women's autobiography (pp. 15–29). Madison: University of Wisconsin Press.

Corey, F. C. (Ed.). (1993). *HIV education: Performing personal narratives.* Tempe: Arizona State University Press.

Dailey, S. J. (Ed.). (1998). *The future of performance studies: Visions and revisions.* Annandale, VA: National Communication Association.

Faires, R. (2000, February 25). Two generations, one art: Terry Galloway and the Rude Mechanicals make loud, messy theatre together. *The Austin Chronicle.* Retrieved June 14, 2004, from http://www.austinchronicle.com/issues/dispatch/2000-02-25/arts_feature.html

Gage, C. (2003). The last reading of Charlotte Cushman. In L. C. Miller, J. Taylor, & M. H. Carver (Eds.), *Voices made flesh: Performing women's autobiography* (pp. 125–151). Madison: University of Wisconsin Press.

Galloway, T. (1993). *Out all night and lost my shoes* (B. Hamby, Ed.). Tallahassee, FL: Apalachee Press.

Gentile, J. S. (1989). *Cast of one: One-person shows from the Chautauqua platform to the Broadway stage.* Champaign-Urbana: University of Illinois Press.

Gingrich-Philbrook, C. (1997). Refreshment. *Text and Performance Quarterly, 17,* 352–360.

Gingrich-Philbrook, C. (2000). Editor's introduction. *Text and Performance Quarterly, 20,* vii–x.

Jones, J. (2003). Sista docta. In L. C. Miller, J. Taylor, & M. H. Carver (Eds.), *Voices made flesh: Performing women's autobiography* (pp. 237–257). Madison: University of Wisconsin Press.

Langellier, K. (1986). Personal narratives and performance. In T. Colson (Ed.), *Renewal and revision: The future of interpretation* (pp. 132–144). Denton, TX: NB Omega.

Lee-Brown, E. (2004). *Autobiography, adaptation, and agency: Interpreting women's performance and writing strategies through a feminist lens.* Unpublished doctoral dissertation, University of Texas at Austin.

Luce, W. (1976). *The belle of Amherst: A play based on the life of Emily Dickinson.* Boston: Houghton Mifflin.

MacKay, C. H. (2003). Performing historical figures: The metadramatics of women's autobiographical performance. In L. C. Miller, J. Taylor, & M. H. Carver (Eds.), *Voices made flesh:*

Performing women's autobiography (pp. 152–164). Madison: University of Wisconsin Press.

Miller, L. C. (2001). Alice does and Alice doesn't. In L.C. Miller & R. Pelias (Eds.), *The green window: Proceedings of the giant city conference on performative writing* (pp. 44–51). Carbondale: Southern Illinois University.

Miller, L. C. (2003). Gertrude Stein never enough. In L. C. Miller, J. Taylor, & M. H. Carver (Eds.), *Voices made flesh: Performing women's autobiography* (pp. 47–65). Madison: University of Wisconsin Press.

Miller, L. C., & Taylor, J. (2003). Editors' introduction. In L. C. Miller, J. Taylor, & M. H. Carver (Eds.), *Voices made flesh: Performing women's autobiography* (pp. 3–14). Madison: University of Wisconsin Press.

Park-Fuller, L. (2000). Performing absence: The staged personal narrative as testimony. *Text and Performance Quarterly, 20,* 20–42.

Park-Fuller, L. (2003). A clean breast of it. In L. C. Miller, J. Taylor, & M. H. Carver (Eds.), *Voices made flesh: Performing women's autobiography* (pp. 215–236). Madison: University of Wisconsin Press.

Pineau, E. L. (2003). Intimate partners: A critical autobiography of performing Anais. In L. C. Miller, J. Taylor, & M. H. Carver (Eds.), *Voices made flesh: Performing women's autobiography* (pp. 33–46). Madison: University of Wisconsin Press.

Rogers, C. (2003). Georgia O'Keeffe x Catherine Rogers. In L. C. Miller, J. Taylor, & M. H. Carver (Eds.), *Voices made flesh: Performing women's autobiography* (pp. 103–124). Madison: University of Wisconsin Press.

Silko, L. M. (2000). Interview with Leslie Marmon Silko. In E. L. Arnold (Ed.), *Conversations with Leslie Marmon Silko* (pp. 29–36). Jackson: University Press of Mississippi.

Spry, T. (2003). Illustrated woman: Autoperformance in "Skins: A daughter's reconstruction of cancer" and "Tattoo stories: A postscript to 'Skins.'" In L. C. Miller, J. Taylor, & M. H. Carver (Eds.), *Voices made flesh: Performing women's autobiography* (pp. 167–191). Madison: University of Wisconsin Press.

Taylor, J. (2003). On being an exemplary lesbian: My life as a role model. In L. C. Miller, J. Taylor, & M. H. Carver (Eds.), *Voices made flesh: Performing women's autobiography* (pp. 192–214). Madison: University of Wisconsin Press.

11

The Strange Case of the Body in the Performance of Literature Classroom

An Enduring Mystery

BRUCE HENDERSON

AUTISM AS METAPHOR: FOUR PRELUDES ON PERFORMANCE AND THE BODY'S PEDAGOGY

Twenty years after receiving my first PhD in interpretation (now performance studies) from Northwestern University, I have returned to my home town (Oak Park, the western suburb of Chicago that produced such writers as Ernest Hemingway, Carol Shields, and my own high school classmate Jane Hamilton) to begin work as a graduate student again at one of Illinois' public universities, the University of Illinois at Chicago. Today I have entered an equally "blurry" field, disability studies. It is an exciting, if somewhat dizzying time to be a new student in this emergent field, one that has grown out of rehabilitation sciences into an area more concerned with cultural critiques of policies, practices, and representations of the disabled body, mind, and experience. My new

experience is not unlike entering performance studies when I did. I was part of the generation that saw the shift from "interpretation" or "oral interpretation" (with its fairly exclusive attention to the study of literature through performance) to "performance studies."

One of my fellow graduate students in the program is a woman trained in rehabilitation therapy, who is excited about performance studies and plans to make it one of her cognate areas. When I ask her whom she is reading and whom she has studied, she names Richard Schechner, whose recent textbook (2002) she has adopted as her founding text, and two scholars, Carrie Sandahl and Jim Ferris, whose work bridges disability studies and performance studies.

When I mention the rich tradition of performance studies at Northwestern, a 40-minute ride to the north, she seems only vaguely aware of it. Nor is she familiar with the earlier work done by William Rickert with "group performance of literature" by students with disabilities at Wright State University, even though it is her alma mater. And coursework in the "performance of literature" has long been absent from the theatre and communication curricula at the University of Illinois at Chicago. I agree—partly out of missionary zeal, partly out of the selfishness of wanting someone with whom to talk about performance—to help her with an independent study she plans to do on disability and performance theory. But I wonder where to begin. And of what use will the "performance of literature" be to someone whose primary interest is in the autobiographical work of performance artists with disabilities?

At the same that I volunteer to work with my fellow graduate student (whose own excitement is infectious and who has welcomed me as an older returning student) I hunt for a novel to read. For the first time as a student, I am taking a full load of classes and have only one work of literature assigned for any of them. So, amidst the somewhat alien corn of Foucault, Goffman, Darwin, Stephen Jay Gould, Ian Hacking, and Althusser through which I am wandering, I feel a hunger (and the metaphor of consuming is apt—reading is an activity I associate with eating, both in positive and negative ways) for fictional story.

Somewhere I read of a new British novel, *The Curious Incident of the Dog in the Night-Time* by Mark Haddon (2003), which is receiving enthusiastic reviews and which I can justify in my monastic reading existence because of its central premise. It is a novel told from the point of view of an autistic boy, a teenager who is a savant in math, but who can describe the world only through a perspective unencumbered by or disengaged from "normal" human processes of interpretation and from "normal" expressions of emotion. (I am learning to put "normal" in scare quotes, both in print and in speech.) It begins, in almost Orwellian numerical fashion, with a chapter marked "2" (we learn later that the narrator will assign only prime numbers to the chapter headings):

> It was 7 minutes after midnight. The dog was lying on the grass in the middle of the lawn in front of Mrs. Shears's house. Its eyes were closed. It looked as if it was running on its side, the way dogs run when they think they are chasing a cat in a dream. But the dog was not running or asleep. The dog was dead. There was a garden fork sticking out of the dog. The points of the fork must have gone all the way through the dog and into the ground because the fork had not fallen over. I decided that the dog was probably killed with the fork because I could not see any other wounds in the dog and I do not think you would stick a garden fork into a dog after it had died for some other reason, like cancer, for example, or a road accident. But I could not be certain about this. (p. 1)

With some impatience, I put the book aside. Yes, I think to myself, I see what the novelist is doing, and I note from the back cover that he has worked with autistic children. But I do not think I can go on this journey with Christopher, the narrator, for some two hundred pages, for much the same reason that Conan Doyle's Sherlock Holmes mysteries always left me cold: it feels more like a logic problem than a story. (The novel, in fact, takes its title from a line in the Sherlock Holmes story "Silver Blaze"; see Doyle, 1890/1963, p. 27.) Raised on the modern novel of Freudian (and post-Freudian) exploration of consciousness and unconsciousness, I cannot imagine myself caring enough about listening to this boy figure who killed his neighbor's dog to stay with him in this emotionless, distanced, utterly observational and unselfreflective voice. It is a gimmick, a writing-class exercise. I turn to something lighter and pulpier, a chatty novel of the gay world of NYC theatre.

Yet, a week or so later, I return to the autistic boy's story. I feel guilty—what kind of student of disability am I if I haven't the patience to sit with this individual? I have learned that it is "better" to view something like autism not as a deficit but as a difference—and to try to understand what an autistic may possess that may be viewed as strengths rather than weaknesses, presences rather than absences. And so I try again—perhaps it is because summer has turned to autumn, perhaps because the work load is such that I cannot bear the density of interior life my favorite novels provide, who knows? But this time I follow Christopher's journey to the solution of the mystery (and then some, as he takes the perilous journey to London to see his estranged mother). And I find myself experiencing both pain and overwhelming, sometimes tear-producing affection for him. It is not that at any point in the novel his own autistic style changes and he becomes an empathic, "cured" subject—this is not a novel of transformation in that sense. Nor do my tears come from a response based in pity or charity. I think I weep simply because I have learned more about what it means to be him and to have experienced the difficulty of his journey—just as a I recall a teenaged self years ago weeping as Sam carried Frodo up Mount Doom to fulfill his destiny.

While Christopher's way of knowing the world is not my own, I believe I have successfully learned how he knows the world—a thing autistics must themselves learn (and consciously so) about the way the "others" do. In a sense, I wonder, is this not what all literature demands of us—to relearn the world each time we read someone else's words?

The word "autistic" both scares me and attracts me, and I think I can locate the beginning of its shameful fascination for me. Twenty-five years ago, as a first-semester graduate student in interpretation at Northwestern University, I am struggling in the beginning graduate seminar, Studies in Performance,

taught by Professor Lilla Heston (sister of the famous actor Charlton). Heston dominates the class. I find myself so nervous in front of her that I give some of the most tentative, most ineptly self-conscious performances I will ever give. I cannot get beyond her piercing stare. My choices of texts seem to alienate her and my intellectual explanations of performance choices are unpersuasive to her. Finally, during a class performance critique, she describes my gestures as "autistic." I am so shocked by the use of the word that I essentially shut down for the rest of the course. I have received a message (to this day I do not know if it is the one she intended or not). I am a pathological performer—there is a sickness to my work. I have to look up "autistic" in the dictionary, and see it is a disease (today we refer to it as a syndrome or spectrum) of, among other things, an inability to communicate. I understand now (and did then, I suspect) that what she referred to was a lack of connection between my physicalization (gestures, posture, movements) and the text I was performing. To my instructor, this lack of connection appeared to be unconscious rather than chosen.

I realize now, over 25 years later, that Heston was using the word "autistic" (if the word was chosen with any conscious intent) to shock me into being more self-aware as a performer. Her own performances, while always a joy to witness, were lessons in self-presentation. One felt that every moment had been planned and revised meticulously, like the prose of her beloved Henry James: the pleasure was in her ability to behave in a controlled manner and yet be "in the moment" at the same time. I think that, in an odd way, she was trying to encourage me to be both more disciplined and less self-absorbed as a performer.

The word "autistic" today carries a wider spectrum of potentialities, both positive and negative, than in 1978 when I took the course. I have often wondered whether the late Dr. Heston would remember this "curious incident" and what she would have to say about the changing face of autism today. She was a gifted actress and reader, but my memories of her onstage are of her solitariness: as Mrs. Alving in the final moment of Ibsen's *Ghosts,* alone with her son who is no longer capable of communicating with her, or as Bernarda Alba, isolated in her tyrannical reign over her house of women (her daughters) and able to make brief, genuine contact with an other only in her few exchanges with her servant. Were Heston's performances, even in traditionally staged plays, variations on a kind of positive construction of the "selfness" of some kinds of autism—the sense of being isolated yet observant at the same time?

Having gathered my thoughts for this essay as an overview of one problem in the teaching of the performance of literature, I sit down to one last "read" for inspiration. I turn to a book I picked up earlier in the semester, Francis Spufford's memoir, *The Child That Books Built* (2002), in which he traces his development from infancy to adulthood through his reading habits and choices. He begins with a description of what the experience of reading was for him:

> "I can always tell when you're reading somewhere in the house," my mother used to say. "There's a special silence, a *reading* silence." I never heard it, this extra degree of hush that somehow traveled through walls and ceilings to announce that my seven-year-old self had become about as absent as a present person could be. The silence went both ways. As my concentration on the story in my hands took hold, all sounds faded away. (p. 1)

Spufford describes his reading behavior as "catatonic." For Spufford, the experience of reading silently has the degree of engagement we might associate with a performer in public. Yet at the same time it is a private engagement. The text's meaning is not unlike the meaning of the sounds the autistic makes when touched: we as a public witness something that can only

partially be made accessible to us. In his writing on performance, Wallace Bacon (1966, 1972) preferred the word "communion" to "communication": for him, performance, like literature itself, could never be simply a "transfer" of meaning. The autistic can participate in acts of communion, though what he or she makes of them will probably be different from the perceptions of the "normal" subject.

It is not entirely accurate to say that the autistic does not experience his or her body. But it may be accurate to say that the autistic has a different kind of cognitive access to the ways in which his or her body is one of many other bodies that share experiences, emotions, responses. Many autistics (there is a wide range of ways of being and knowing covered by the spectrum) are deeply gifted in ways not usually associated with stereotypes the public has learned from such films as *Rain Man.* For example, while some autistics have difficulty maintaining attention in ways that appear normative to most people, they can become focused to an extreme degree on a pattern, or on a category, or on a phenomenon. Similarly, while difficulty in communicating interpersonally is one of the usual impairments associated with autism, many autistics can learn how to perform social scripts and to understand what lies underneath the protocols and conventions of interaction.

Such memory work need not simply be rote or robotic. It can achieve depth and authenticity, through a learning process different from simply participating in society in a natural way. In her recent memoir *Songs of the Gorilla Nation,* Dawn Prince-Hughes (2004), a writer and primatologist, movingly describes her own journey to self-discovery through observation of and interaction with gorillas. She writes about her success in working at a zoo, after an isolated childhood and a part of her adulthood spent homeless on the streets. She notes: "The fact that I excelled at certain tasks—keeping records, making keen observations, descriptively communicating information, and memorizing events perfectly—not only saved me but deposited me exactly where I wanted to be" (pp. 103–104). Prince-Hughes now lives with a partner and has a son. She has learned how to perform in a way that provides her satisfaction and pleasure—through her autism, not in spite of it.

Autism is a condition I now study, in my second graduate career. It has also become a powerful metaphor for the body in performance, as I reflect upon the history of my field of study in my first graduate career. Is it worth asking whether part of what makes some performances valuable and worthwhile is a figuratively "autistic" element, which can be seen in the history of teaching and practicing the performance of literature? In saying this, I am thinking especially of the phenomenon of solo performance: the long tradition of the single reader, holding a book or standing at a lectern, who addresses a text to an audience.

In other words, do we have a history that both promotes and diminishes the connections between body-of-performer and body-of-text at different times, sometimes simultaneously? How does this always complex, overdetermined set of relations shift back and forth over time? What remains constant? And what does all this augur for the future of teaching the performance of literature?

BACK TO BEFORE: WHAT THE RHAPSODE "KNEW" (OR DIDN'T)

Textual evidence in the Homeric epics, along with comparatively recent research by Milman Parry (Parry, 1987) and Albert Lord (2000), suggests that there was a kind of performance that predated our contemporary notions of a fixed text: of a text that can be separated in a meaningful way from the moment of performance or from the body of the performer. The Homeric bard composed in performance, typically in a style that involved a musicality and rhythm perhaps not entirely unlike some of today's rap artists. For such a bard, who was

synonymous with the concept of "poet," the text was always fluid and protean: themes, motifs, and some formulaic (metrically regular) phrases were the anchors from one performance to another. Because written language did not yet exist (or, later, existed for very limited purposes, of which literary publication was not yet one) there was no sense in which verbatim repetition could be viewed as a mark of fidelity to a text. Thus, the art of performance was one in which the body (which included the voice and, by extension, all that the body could fill, including context, space, and even audience) was the medium for "publication." There was freedom and, in the terms of Foucault (1961/1977), discipline in such a performance aesthetic. While it is likely that habit led to certain passages becoming more and more fixed, only with the introduction of writing as a dominant verbal mode could we imagine a notion of a text as something that could be separated from the body of its composer and then reperformed by another performer.

With such a transition, a new kind of performer emerged: the *rhapsode,* literally "stitcher of lines." Eugene and Margaret Bahn (1970), who provided one of the earliest attempts to survey traditions in the performance of nondramatic literature, note the first reference to such performers in the sixth century BCE A particular group of rhapsodes, devoted to the preservation and recitation of the Homeric epics, were known as the Homeridai. Such performers were itinerant, traveling to different festivals and competitions, but also often attaching themselves to particular courts and noble houses. One such rhapsode was Ion, who was transformed into a somewhat fictional character in Plato's early dialogue that bears his name (trans. 2001b). This dialogue parallels another early dialogue, *Gorgias* (trans. 1998), which similarly interrogates the nature and office of the sophist, orator and teacher who claimed to be able to teach virtue through the teaching of rhetoric.

One of Plato's final dialogues, the *Phaedrus* (trans. 2001a), returns to the question of spoken versus written language, critiquing writing as the beginning of the loss of knowledge.

Plato's technique in each of the dialogues is similar. He has his version of Socrates (his own teacher) encounter a practitioner of one of the arts of spoken performance (or, in the case of *Phaedrus,* an audience member) and proceeds to question, as if from a naïve and uninformed position, the very definition and basis of the art. The performer always falls into the traps of logic and dialectic (which Plato believed to be the only true paths to knowledge). The opponents of Socrates inevitably concede the intellectual bankruptcy of their claims. Of course, Plato, true rhetorician that he is, never gives Socrates a worthy opponent: dialectic often seems more a veil for Socrates' own rhetorical demonstrations than a genuinely "dialogic" opportunity for investigation, in the sense pursued by Bakhtin (1981). Plato's Ion and Gorgias are always depicted as pleasant, entertaining, yet rather empty-headed men, proud of their public acclaim, but unable to defend an idea beyond a question or two.

In the *Ion,* Plato raises two important questions about the performance of literary texts that have recurred through history and remain relevant and open today for teachers and students. Plato (through Socrates) questions, first, what the rhapsode "knows" and, second, from what source the rhapsode derives his performance skills. He does this through a series of seemingly innocuous questions, each of which leads Ion down the primrose path to an admission of ignorance.

Concerning "knowledge," Socrates asks Ion questions designed to reveal the rhapsode's limits. On the subjects about which Homer speaks, the rhapsode possesses knowledge inferior to that of the actual practitioner of each activity. Ion must concede, finally, that diviners are better equipped to speak of divining, mathematicians of arithmetic,

and nutritionists of nutrition than is the rhapsode—even though the rhapsode, in his performance of Homeric epic, speaks of these fields through the words of Homer. Socrates gets Ion to concede even that he is ill-equipped as a critic of poetry, because he is able to speak only about Homer and not about all poets (a sobering thought in our own day of critical specialization). This series of reductions points out that the ability to perform poetry is not the same as possessing knowledge about the subjects it describes or narrates. Even Homer's "knowledge" as original composer of the poems is suspect, as Plato believes in a world of "ideals": original forms of which our own human knowledge and experience are a mere set of copies.

Ion's mistake, from a contemporary perspective, is his failure to challenge the terms of the debate itself: to ask whether he should "know" the "facts" of nutrition, divining, or arithmetic is to confuse the "mimetic" with the "original" (or "original copy," in Plato's sense). Ion is an expert on the art of "imitating," if you will—of using his body (including voice, intellect, and emotions) to (re)create the imagined world created in Homer's words. Similarly, Socrates and Ion conflate performance with criticism, "speaking Homer" with "speaking about Homer." It is possible to define performance as a form of literary criticism: this was the pedagogical mission of "interpretation" in twentieth century American schools. But Socrates and Ion (as imagined by Plato) do not describe performances. Rather, they discuss what would seem to be *lectures,* speeches given by the rhapsode on the texts he performs.

Socrates' second challenge to Ion, Plato's question of the source of "inspiration" (which we may make roughly synonymous with "ability," "accomplishment," or "talent," though none of these terms is a perfect fit) is inextricably tied to the first. The challenge Ion does not really make to Socrates is that performance is itself a field of knowledge. This then would raise the troubling question of the degree to which performance is an "art": an activity with rules and processes, which can be accessed through rational discourse, through analysis of its components, through the acquisition of skills, and through methodological steps and practices. Indeed, Socrates claims that performance is not such an art. (He makes the same claim about oratory, to which, it is often suggested, Aristotle's *Rhetoric* may be seen as a response; we have no such response from Aristotle about the performance of literature, as his *Poetics* is really about dramatic structure and theatrical production and not about solo performance.) In one of those characteristic speeches that combine flattery and insult, Socrates provides Ion with the following set of options:

> If you're really a master of your subject, and if, as I said earlier, you're cheating me of the demonstration you promised about Homer, then you're doing me wrong. But if you're not a master of your subject, if you're possessed by a divine gift from Homer, so that you make lovely speeches about the poet without knowing anything—as *I* said about you—then you're not doing me wrong. So choose, how do you want us to think of you—as a man who does something wrong, or as someone *divine*. (2001b, p. 48)

Ion, who is probably not the first and certainly not the last performer to prefer praise as a divinity to critical and moral argument, accedes to the "lovelier way." In doing so, he misses the opportunity to articulate for Socrates what goes into the training and education of a performer. Socrates' flattery convinces him to keep mysterious the processes by which the rhapsode creates his performance.

Questions of what constitutes the education and/or training (the two words suggest very different pedagogical and philosophical outlooks) of the performer of literature persist to the present day. How does the performer learn to "perform"? Can performance be taught?

(The same question, of course, arises with such arts as acting, music, painting, dance, and writing.) Or is all such teaching merely critical response to and refinement of given talents? In the performance classroom, what attention should be given to theory as opposed to practice—and how should teachers combine the two? Should such classrooms be dominated by textual study, with delivery skills and techniques viewed as always emergent from the demands of texts? Or should performance classrooms stress attainment of skills and techniques of performance ("delivery") and trust that students will learn about textual and critical analysis through courses in literature departments? Socrates' seemingly innocent question (similar to questions posed not only in the *Gorgias,* about public speaking, but also by such famous teachers of oratory as Isocrates) continues to provide the subject for debate.

FROM ELOCUTION TO EXPRESSION TO INTERPRETATION: THE DEBATE OVER THE BODY'S PERFORMATIVE DISCIPLINE

The research of Bahn and Bahn (1970) suggests that the performances of the rhapsodes and the teaching of interpretation in twentieth century American schools are early and late chapters in the same history. At the beginning of the century in which I studied the performance of literature, teachers turned away, like Plato's Ion, from the mission of explaining that performance is itself a field of knowledge. In acknowledging the mystery of performance, they preferred concepts like "suggestion" and later "communion" (which focused the student's attention on the thing performed, a literary text) to examinations and discussions of the performing body itself.

The reasons for this relate to a growing distaste among educators for the study of elocution, as it had developed in England and America during the eighteenth and nineteenth centuries. As taught in private studios and "schools," and as practiced in settings ranging from private salons to the public platforms of the Lyceum and tent Chautauqua circuits, elocution had acquired a bad name. At the end of the nineteenth century, a generation of charismatic teacher-performers—among them, Charles Wesley Emerson, S. S. Curry, Genevieve Stebbins, Leland Powers, and Anna Morgan—worked hard to give academic respectability to training in "speech arts," but largely failed to find a place for such training in colleges and universities. Curry (1896) advocated the name "expression" for what he saw as "The Advance Needed" beyond the "mechanical" and "imitative" practices of "histrionic art" on the elocutionary platform and the stage (pp. 121, 361–384). The teachers of expression emphasized the performer's responsiveness to literature's "suggestiveness," and de-emphasized the cultivation of vocal and bodily techniques. "In the typical lesson" of a Curry textbook,

> the performer should use the body to suggest a poetic speaker's reactions to a phenomenon in nature—as the embodiment of a moment of situated "impression" or total perception—rather than trying to imitate through voice and gesture the thing perceived (rolling waves, crashing surf, squawking gulls, and so forth). Audience members complete the chain-reaction of "suggestiveness" by kinesthetically performing the text in their own bodies. (Edwards, 1999, p. 21)

Although the study of expression was a short-lived cultural phenomenon, it provided the transition from nineteenth century elocution to the academic study of interpretation in the twentieth century.

Any discussion of interpretation or oral interpretation in American higher education must consider the role played by the National Communication Association (NCA). Founded in 1914 as the National Association of Academic Teachers of Public Speaking, the organization discouraged the membership of

elocutionists and platform entertainers "who were not educationally oriented," as early member Frank Rarig remembers (Rarig & Greaves, 1954, p. 499; Edwards, 1999, pp. 63–78). It is safe to say that, without the advocacy of the NCA (under its various names), the study of interpretation probably would have lacked the academic respectability to situate itself on a widespread basis in colleges and universities. As the study of interpretation receded in the decades following World War II, the NCA's Interpretation Division reinvented itself: in 1991, it became a Performance Studies Division, and resituated literary interpretation as one study among many in a rapidly expanding field. Through the history of the NCA, scholars can trace important connections between nineteenth century "elocution" and twenty-first century "performance," as theorized and practiced by generations of educators.

It is significant, therefore, that the elusive mystery of describing embodied performance should present itself at the NCA's first annual meeting in 1915. A paper delivered by Maud May Babcock, later published in the fledgling *Quarterly Journal of Public Speaking,* provoked a response by Rollo Anson Tallcott, which provoked a further response by Babcock. The "impersonation" versus "interpretation" debate of 1916—the "great debate," as David A. Williams (1975, p. 43) humorously dubs it—identified issues that remained alive for teachers of interpretation through most of the twentieth century.

The "great debate" centered around issues of both definition and appropriateness. Babcock, echoing the expression teachers, defined interpretation

> as the presentation of any form of literary material . . . without the aid of dress, furniture, stage settings, or literal characterizations in voice, action, or make-up. Such presentation must be content with suggesting the real thing to the imagination of the audience. (1916/1940c, p. 85)

Impersonation, by contrast, seeks "literal characterization" in "realistic surroundings." Readers interpret, whereas actors impersonate: "The reader is always himself, while the actor is always some one else" (1916/1940c, pp. 85–86). Babcock's examples support the view that suggestive interpretation appeals to "the cultured and the learned." She seeks "prophets and reformers who will raise the standards of entire communities by honest efforts at interpreting literature, for the sake of the message," and will not "exploit themselves" like "vaudeville" performers (p. 93). Performers who focus on the techniques of embodied practice, rather than the "message" of the literature itself, risk the charge of exploitation.

The pioneering Babcock established the Speech Department at the University of Utah. She staged dramatic productions, and was considered the "first lady" of "physical education" at Utah (Engar, n.d.). While it is tempting to read a kind of latter-day Victorianism surrounding the body, in the writings of Babcock (1916/1940a, 1930/1940b, 1916/1940c) and those who were in sympathy with her position, the situation is not quite so simple. Babcock deplored "impersonation" (under which we might group practices as disparate as the comic character monologue and the monodrama) as a breach of the aesthetic of what she saw as the "finer art" of interpretation. But she clearly was invested in the culture and disciplining of the body: she believed in the values of physical education, and participated in what her university claims was the first dramatic production done by an institution of higher learning. Hers was not a simple, stereotypically maidenly reticence regarding the indecency of bad behavior—though the body has never been an untroubled site of cultural meaning and anxiety, whatever the era.

Rather, her view of "interpretation" seems a complex nexus of social attitudes towards the body and the cultural position of popular entertainment and high art, in which the body becomes the vessel of meaning: the "symptom," in Foucault's sense, upon which a nation turned its gaze for expression of its own understanding of what certain language meant. While some vestiges of the antitheatrical bias that pervaded middle-class culture in the United States are surely part of Babcock's moral aesthetic, her views also reflect the growth of the Chautauqua circuit and its competitors: in professional platform entertainment, what began as a spiritually ennobling project devolved eventually into something more akin to the world of the circus, with its sawdust tricks and freak-show exhibitions. How legible was the line between the exhibition of the "Venus Hottentot," the African woman displayed because of her (to Caucasian eyes) outsized buttocks, and the young woman or man on an elocutionary platform, nearly a century later, doing birdcalls and childish imitations? In a sense, what was at stake in both was a loosening of the discipline of the body—hence, of the mind and spirit, which for many European and American followers of Delsarte in the late nineteenth century made performance a holy act (see, for example, Shaver, 1954).

While there was a place for theatrical "impersonation," then, in fully staged productions—particularly of the canonical, "secular scripture" as Northrop Frye (1978) terms it, the literary culture exemplified by Shakespeare—Babcock argued both for a return to the nobler texts of the lyrical poem (along with fine examples of the relatively new genre of the novel) and for an aesthetic that would appropriately discipline the body to meet its requirements. Babcock's call for "interpretation" over "impersonation" was a call for a return to the moral interpretation of literature. While the body itself has the capacity for elevation, when in harmony with the spiritual and the moral, it can be debased into mere sensation and easy pleasures of the flesh. So it is, Babcock argued, with literature: one must learn to discriminate between elevated and debased texts. Contemplation of literary classics, rather than training in impersonative techniques, produces the most valuable disciplining of the body.

It is important to resist a kind of historical "presentness" in which we place ourselves at too far a distance from what may feel like a bluestocking primness in Babcock's philosophy. Less than three decades ago, as a student of interpretation, I witnessed how questions of selection of material became sources of debate, even the grounds for some graduate students in my program being failed on their "recital" requirement. In some cases, the reason for failure was either the student's poor taste in selecting material, or the student's inability to observe the subtle nuances of language in favor of too robust (usually veiled as "shallow") an *actio*.

Rollo Tallcott (1916/1940), a faculty member and dean at Ithaca College during Babcock's years at Utah, responded to Babcock's initial paper with an attempt to distinguish more finely a spectrum of performance aesthetics. Tallcott would be best known for his book *The Art of Acting and Public Reading* (1922); the title of that text suggests a philosophy that, while keeping the two "arts" separate, nonetheless sees them as related, as part of the same general educational and aesthetic endeavor. In the "great debate" of 1916, he argued for four "degrees" of literary performance, from "interpretative reading" (which apparently would correspond to a straightforward reading, done with intelligence and feeling, in which the personality and the presence of the reader as such are never disguised), to "impersonative reading" (with its greater degree of "suggestive" characterization), "straight personation," and, finally, "acting" (1916/1940, p. 94). The line between "straight personation" and "acting" might best be seen in the difference between performing a one-person monologue (Julie Harris as Emily Dickinson alone onstage in *The Belle of Amherst*) and acting in a multi-character play (Julie Harris as Frankie Addams, interacting with other characters, in *The Member of the Wedding*).

Tallcott makes a sensible-sounding argument: that the kind of literature being performed should dictate which of his four approaches should be selected. Yet he cannot discard the moral imperative of such aesthetic debates, and concedes the following:

> If personation were something indecent, or positively harmful to education, there would be an excuse for staunchly refusing to adopt it; but, on the contrary, it is being shown every day to be not only harmless but a very powerful means for stimulation to the appreciation of interpretation. Taking it from a standpoint of true lyceum entertainment, it is a sort of preliminary course to work of higher cultural value. I believe it is just as noble to teach people to entertain well and cleanly as it is to teach literary interpretation, although, of course, the latter should always be the final goal; for who shall say that the primary teacher is doing any less noble work than the high-school teacher or the college professor? (1916/1940, p. 100)

This passage is fascinating in part because it turns back and forth on itself, sometimes within a single sentence. While Tallcott argues for the value of "personative" performance as "clean" entertainment (note the hygienic language that we find not only in other parts of speech pedagogy of the time, but also in other avenues of public education), he finally concedes that it has the same status, in a sense, as using nursery rhymes to introduce infants and young children to the notion of verse and poetry itself. There is a developmental and evolutionary rhetoric at work here.

Part of the disagreement between Babcock and Tallcott, as Williams points out, has to do with a lack of agreement about the meaning of the very terms themselves. How much of a performer's attempt to give voice and body to character "counted" as "impersonation"? How much "suggestion" was permitted for the performer still to remain in the domain of "interpretation"? What Babcock and Tallcott share is a belief in the superiority of suggestiveness to literalness as an aesthetic of performance, a philosophy passed down by Curry and the "expression" teachers. One can trace this view back to the ancients. In the *Ars Poetica,* Horace (trans. 2001) maintains that the representation of certain actions onstage should be discouraged both because such representations are unbelievable when literalized and because to perform them violates codes of decorum: an audience can visualize the blinding of Oedipus more vividly and profitably in the mind's eye than through any enactment of it onstage.

The American teachers who made "suggestion" one of the hallmarks of interpretation's aesthetics related the concept not only to issues of decorum and probability but to the comparatively new psychological approach to speech and communication advanced by such scholars as Charles Henry Woolbert. It was Woolbert's mission, during the first three decades of the twentieth century, to transform "public speaking" into "speech science," in professional settings like the forerunner organization of the present-day NCA. His "theory of delivery" drew upon "current academic psychology" rather than the training routines of nineteenth century elocutionists; the theory viewed suggestion as more psychologically "real," valuable, and satisfying to the interior life of the performer and audience than pantomime or impersonation (Cohen, 1994, pp. 49–53; Gray, 1954, pp. 436–440). As Williams (1975, pp. 52–53) notes in his essay on the "great debate," the aesthetic of suggestion continued to dominate the work of such major postwar teachers as Charlotte Lee. As revised by coauthor Tim Gura, the tenth edition of the well-known Lee textbook *Oral Interpretation* (2001) carries suggestion into the twenty-first century as one of the bedrocks of its aesthetic.

Careful and sympathetic readers of the textbook literature of interpretation, as this grew

during the mid-twentieth century, might view the pedagogical interest in suggestion and "non-impersonative" performance as anticipating the growth of reader-centered aesthetic and critical theories that emerged in the last quarter of the twentieth century. The call by Babcock and others for performers to remain fully and recognizably "themselves" is consonant with a more recent interest in featuring the dialogue between reader and text. Performance theorist Dwight Conquergood (1985) describes the possibility for such dialogues, for example, in his Bakhtinian approach to the literary experience. This interest also finds its place in the growth of hybrid forms of personal narrative performance. In memorable performances by John Anderson of Emerson College, a literary text becomes a kind of intertextual opportunity for the juxtaposition of personal experience and the expressive values that literary texts may serve in our lives. One performance by Anderson— a *bricolage* of sections of Faulkner's *As I Lay Dying,* an audiotape recording of a past family dinner, and his own narrated memories of his mother's death—extends and complicates some of the concerns Babcock and Tallcott articulate in their debate. Notably it presents a "reader" who "is always himself" (unlike Babcock's "actor" who "is always some one else")—but in ways that exceed what Babcock seems to have imagined.

In attempting to lead performers away from elocution's mechanical rules of voice and body training, the influential Babcock rejected even Tallcott's modest attempt to categorize and relate performance modes. The mystery of suggestive performance began and ended with contemplation of the literary text. Ironically, as the twentieth century progressed, the practical difficulty of cultivating a suggestive delivery led to a return of mechanical rules and regulations that often seem quite removed from either a clearly articulated rationale for their necessity or superiority over other rules, or the specific requirements of the text being performed. At national and regional conferences of communication educators, many of whom judge competitions at the secondary school and college levels, a lively debate continues from year to year about judging standards (although this kind of debate tends to take place in hallways and over dinner tables rather than at formal sessions). In competitive performance, a set of rules for judging "oral interpretation" and "readers theatre" still obtains. A physical script (sedimented into small black notebooks which are de rigueur) must be present; offstage focus (even in such events as the duet performance of dramatic literature) must be maintained; movement must be limited; and contestants receive reminders that a given event falls in an "interpretation" category and not an "acting" one. As recently as the 1990s, when I was a judge for such contests at both the secondary and college levels, such criteria for "suggestiveness" were stated on ballots. Rule violations constituted grounds for lowered evaluations or even disqualification.

Tallcott's approach to performance has the potential to be more open-ended and less rule-obsessed. A knowledgeable acting teacher should understand the need for different performance aesthetics for a chorus speech from a Greek tragedy and a character monologue from a play by Albee or Mamet. Such a teacher should be able to draw such distinctions among different kinds of literature, or at least between different specific texts: Eliot's dramatic lyrics "act" differently from Browning's "dramatic monologues," for example. With the growth of presentational aesthetics in professional theatre, the need for the actor to understand the demands of narrative and lyric texts becomes an imperative for flexibility.

Yet Babcock's championing of the suggestive delivery of quality literature, to appeal to the tastes of "the cultured and the learned," appears to have had a more lasting influence on the pedagogy of interpretation during the twentieth century (see, for example, Johnson, 1940). It survives in the "art" of interpretation

described by Wallace Bacon, whose influential textbook went through three editions between 1966 and 1979. Bacon takes the important step of largely eliminating discussions of physical and vocal technique: the student's preparation for performance consists chiefly of "communion" with a literary text. "Surely communication is important," Bacon writes, but communication need not take place between a performer and an audience:

> If it is true that the study of literature itself is valuable, and that literature gives forth its fullest secrets when it is articulately sounded, then the study of interpretation is valuable for the student because the literature which he sounds gives forth its secrets to *him*, whether or not others are listening. (1966, pp. 5–6)

For Bacon, interpretation is an art of the body, but the *performer's* body requires no discussion. Bacon achieves a canny shifting of the "locus" and identity of the body at the center of the study: he takes as his concern the *poem's* body, which the performer's body must "match." In later editions of the textbook, the concept of "matching" becomes the primary guide in the disciplining of the performer's body:

> It is perhaps not too much to suggest that there is a kind of love relationship between reader and poem, each reaching out to the other. The interpreter must not deny to the body of the poem its right to exist. (1972, p. 34)

Performance, like growth in nature, "is not a matter of information; it is in some final way a mystery to which we pay homage" (1972, p. 35). Like any mystery, there are things about performance that cannot be articulated in language.

It is misleading to speak only of Bacon's singular achievement, for other educators in the postwar era continued to teach and practice oral interpretation in more technique-oriented ways that favored public recital over literary study. (My example of secondary school contests suggests one place where the "platform art" has continued to thrive since the age of oratorical culture and the elocution studio.) But Bacon came to the teaching of interpretation at a time when training in technique was in decline. As Lynn Miller Rein (1981) has documented in her history of the Northwestern University School of Speech, the ebbing of support for technical training seems to have provoked the resignation of C. C. Cunningham as department chair of interpretation. During the nearly two-decade Cunningham era at Northwestern, two successive deans of Speech made deep cuts in the resources for Interpretation. Ralph Dennis had fired the "individual instruction" staff during the Great Depression; his successor James McBurney provoked Cunningham's protests by failing, among other things, to provide adequate studio space for student practice. In the age of radio and sound film, McBurney clearly saw the "platform art" of oral interpretation, which Cunningham practiced impressively, as a vanishing academic discipline in the postwar years; it had vanished already, since the demise of Chautauqua circuits, as a popular entertainment form. McBurney's choice for Cunningham's replacement was Bacon, a PhD in English from the University of Michigan with no "interpretation" experience whatsoever. It was part of Bacon's charge, as the new chair of Interpretation, to improve the academic respectability of a program that had clung too firmly to its roots in the "elocution and oratory" curriculum of the nineteenth century. Among Bacon's achievements were the exponential growth of Interpretation's PhD program and, within national and regional associations of speech educators, the increased visibility of Northwestern's interpretation department as a center for literary study. In the decades preceding his retirement in 1979, Bacon became the preeminent figure in interpretation scholarship

within the NCA (see Edwards, 1999, pp. 16–33, 85–93; Rein, 1981, pp. 53, 77–82, 154–155).

But as Bacon's career came to an end, the demise of interpretation as an academic study seemed not very far away. An important essay in the prestigious NCA journal *Communication Monographs* announced the need to reexamine the interpretation course, by challenging what might be considered a "text" available for, and legitimate for, study through performance. In "A New Look at Performance," Elizabeth C. Fine and Jean Haskell Speer (1977) threw down the gauntlet by stating: "For the greater part of the academic history of oral interpretation, performance has been acknowledged as one of the most effective ways to understand literature and treated as a means to that end, but seldom has it been examined in its own right" (p. 389). Their article, drawing on the work of such current folklorists and ethnographers as Richard Bauman, Roger Abrahams, and Dell Hymes, called for performers, teachers, and scholars to expand both their methodologies (to include the burgeoning work being done by social scientists in such fields as anthropology, sociology, and psychology) and the objects of their study (beyond those traditionally considered "literature"). Fine and Speer's article is best seen perhaps as an articulation of a shift of possibilities rather than as a prescription for (or proscription of) the performance of literature—an opening up of possibilities rather than yet another narrowing of the locus of study.

In the wake of the Fine and Speer essay, a growing number of interpretation teachers affiliated with the NCA saw the need to decenter literary study within the discipline. Ronald Pelias (1985) argued that "interpretation thought and performance criticism" can be divided into four schools, which intersect with each other and are often coexistent in the classroom. Performance is (1) performing art; (2) communicative act; (3) self-discovery; and (4) literary study. While acknowledging the dominance of literary study throughout the twentieth century, Pelias resituated it in a wider field of concerns. So did Jill Taft-Kaufman (1985) in her review of twentieth century theory and practice by scholars and teachers associated with the NCA's Interpretation Division: a wideranging interest in performance research had replaced the mid-century dominance of text-centered literary studies. As noted above, a Performance Studies Division emerged from the NCA's Interpretation Division a mere six years later.

The postwar era in American speech education, in short, witnessed a series of resituatings of the body within different conceptions of "text" and the different disciplines of embodiment they suggested. Contrasting disciplines were required by the literary study advocated by Bacon, and by the questioning of the very assumptions of such study called for by Fine and Speer—the kind of questioning that cleared the way for the paradigm shift from the study of textual interpretation to the study of performance in its own right.

At the beginning of the essay, I invoked autism as a powerful metaphor for the body in performance, and related this term to pedagogical approaches: the methods used to educate, train, or discipline that body. It seems to me that some important parts of the history of interpretation pedagogy have been characterized by teachers who, for a variety of reasons, were uncommunicative about their work to anyone but their own colleagues and students. Taft-Kaufman perceptively assessed the "dearth of published research" as a pragmatic concern for professional growth, and a contributing factor to "disciplinary isolation" (1985, pp. 179–181); at the heart of her concern, nearly twenty years ago, was a scholarly discipline of teacher-practitioners who borrowed their theory from other disciplines (notably literary studies) and "published" their applications of that theory in the constantly vanishing records of classroom performances and productions on campus stages.

Conquergood (1986) sounded a similar warning to members of the NCA's Interpretation Division:

> We cannot claim proprietary rights to "performance" simply because we have husbanded it as a well-kept secret for so long. Nor can we expect other disciplines to take seriously our claims about performance if we are not willing to have them tested in the public arena of disciplinary exchange. (p. 30)

Autism becomes a valuable metaphor for a phenomenon that my former teacher Lilla Heston never considered: the collective inability of "interpreters" to explain themselves to those not afflicted with their condition. The mystification and undertheorizing of performance by an Ion anticipates the unwillingness of interpretation teachers in the twentieth century to investigate and explain how the performing body *performs*. From Babcock's promotion of suggestive interpretation, before the first meeting of the future NCA, to Bacon's advocacy of audience-less "communion" with the poem, the pedagogy of interpretation has emphasized the mystery of its processes rather than the possibility of their explication.

I certainly do not wish to suggest that the history I have recounted is merely a pathological or self-defeating one. In a sense, this is the reason I invoke Mark Haddon's novel, with its autistic narrator/hero, in one of the preludes to this essay. The novel teaches us to live inside the autistic's experience—to value it for what it offers, and to understand how what it does *not* offer alters significantly what its narrator can and cannot know and tell us (and himself). The autistic's way of knowing the world can offer him or her strengths that other people do not possess, and can lead to certain kinds of discoveries and ways of knowing that add immeasurably to the world. Consider, for example, Temple Grandin's *Thinking in Pictures* (1996). Here the autistic professor of animal sciences eloquently articulates what it means to live inside her body and mind. Her condition has enabled her to help make the way she works with farm animals such as cattle more "humane," more centered on the experiences of animals, than it would have been without her autism; her work has guided nonautistic members of her profession. Like Ion's "autism," the metaphorical autism Babcock or Bacon—in needing to keep interpretation something somehow private, not contaminated by appeals to the masses—is a necessary and valuable, if troublesome, part of our history as teachers and students. Or so it seems, after the study of "interpretation" has vanished into the study of "performance."

THE ART OF LOSING—OR NOT?

As we continue to become more varied as teachers, students, and performers, there may be, for many, an inevitable sense of loss. Yet there is no reason to lose a sense of a shared culture and history. New performers and performances will continue to take on cultural and even canonical status. They may expand our sense of text to include such performances that cross borders, such as John Anderson's *As I Lay Dying* collage, which will remain etched in my memory and in my *body* as long as I breathe. They may be the folkloric storytelling performances of John Gentile and Penninah Schramm. They may be the performative writings performed by Amy Burt and Scott Dillard, to name just two individuals whose autobiographical work seems to me indistinguishable from any category of literature I know.

I struggle to emerge from my own literary-centered autism. A few years ago my department hired a new faculty member, whose teaching assignment would center around storytelling and other courses in performance studies, including the beginning course in the analysis and performance of literature. In conversation, I said to my colleague, "Well, as Elizabeth Bishop says, 'The art of losing isn't hard to master,'" to which my young colleague replied "Elizabeth Bishop? Where does

she teach?" After a moment of stunned silence (how could someone who teaches performance not know who Elizabeth Bishop is?), and after I explained, with a somewhat edgy tone to my voice, that she happened to be one of the five greatest postwar poets, she replied, with no defensiveness, "Well, I don't really know literature that well. My majors were communication and history."

And, the more I thought about it, the more I realized that I needed to rethink my own response. My colleague took her undergraduate degree at a small liberal arts college where there were no courses in the performance of literature, her masters in a general communication program, and her doctorate from a highly regarded program where performance studies is much more situated in ethnography, communication theory, and folkloric studies. There is absolutely no reason why I should have had the right to expect that she would know Bishop and this particular poem (1978)—though my own generation of students probably could have recited much of the poem by heart.

My colleague, however, is steeped in ethnographic theory and method and has a far more sophisticated understanding of what is at stake in such performance traditions than I have. Her work on the life stories of Holocaust survivors is every bit as detailed, specific, and textually sophisticated and insightful as my own might be on Bishop's texts. I also know, on the basis of three years of teaching with this colleague, that her study of the texts produced by people in interviews and everyday conversations has taught her what she needs to know in order to lead her students into a world of performing poetry, short stories, diaries, letters, plays, and other kinds of texts: a careful way of listening to and responding to the voices and bodies of others (not unlike the positive qualities associated with some forms of autism, as can be seen in the autobiographical writings of Prince-Hughes and Grandin). When I have her students in my advanced classes in the performance of literature, I have confidence that they know how to approach a text in performance. It no longer seems so important whether she brings them to that knowledge through Bishop's compressed lyrics, or through a dense description of one of her participants speaking of liberation from Auschwitz. The words of a poem, the words of an interview: they speak to each other, not in separate, isolated, "autistic" realms, but in a shared knowledge of loss. There is art in both, there is loss—but there is no loss of art.

REFERENCES

Babcock, M. M. (1940a). Impersonation versus interpretation. In G. E. Johnson (Ed.), *Studies in the art of interpretation* (pp. 102–105). New York: Appleton-Century-Crofts. (Original work published 1916)

Babcock, M. M. (1940b). Interpretation or impersonation. In G. E. Johnson (Ed.), *Studies in the art of interpretation* (pp. 106–111). New York: Appleton-Century-Crofts. (Original work published 1930)

Babcock, M. M. (1940c). Interpretative presentation versus impersonative presentation. In G. E. Johnson (Ed.), *Studies in the art of interpretation* (pp. 85–93). New York: Appleton-Century-Crofts. (Original work published 1916)

Bacon, W. A. (1966). *The art of interpretation.* New York: Holt, Rinehart and Winston.

Bacon, W. A. (1972). *The art of interpretation* (2nd ed.). New York: Holt, Rinehart and Winston.

Bacon, W. A., & Breen, R. S. (1959). *Literature as experience.* New York: McGraw-Hill.

Bahn, E., & Bahn, M. L. (1970). *A history of oral interpretation.* Minneapolis: Burgess.

Bakhtin, M. M. (1981). *The dialogic imagination: Four essays* (C. Emerson & M. Holquist, Trans.). Austin: University of Texas Press. (Original work published 1975)

Bishop, E. (1978). One art. In *Geography III* (pp. 40–41). New York: Farrar, Straus and Giroux.

Cohen, H. (1994). *The history of speech communication: The emergence of a discipline, 1914–1945.* Annandale, VA: Speech Communication Association.

Conquergood, D. (1985). Performing as a moral act: Ethical dimensions of the ethnography of performance. *Literature in Performance, 5*(2), 1–13.

Conquergood, D. (1986). Between experience and meaning: Performance as a paradigm for meaningful action. In T. Colson (Ed.), *Renewal and revision: The future of interpretation* (pp. 26–59). Denton, TX: NB Omega.

Cunningham, C. C. (1941). *Literature as a fine art.* New York: Nelson.

Curry, S. S. (1896). *Imagination and dramatic instinct.* Boston: School of Expression.

Doyle, A. C. (1963). Silver Blaze. *The memoirs of Sherlock Holmes* (pp. 7–33). New York: Berkley Medallion. (Original work published 1890)

Edwards. P. C. (1999). Unstoried: Teaching literature in the age of performance studies. *Theatre Annual, 52,* 1–147.

Engar, A. (n.d.). Maud May Babcock. Retrieved March 5, 2004, from http://www.media.utah.edu/UHE/b/BABCOCK,MAUDE.html

Fine, E. C., & Speer, J. H. (1977). A new look at performance. *Communication Monographs 44,* 374–389.

Foucault, M. (1973). *The birth of the clinic: An archeology of medical perception* (A. Sheridan, Trans.). New York: Pantheon. (Original work published 1963)

Foucault, M. (1977). *Discipline & punish: The birth of the prison* (A. Sheridan, Trans.). New York: Pantheon. (Original work published 1961)

Frye, N. (1988). *Northrop Frye on Shakespeare.* New Haven, CT: Yale University Press.

Frye, N. (1978). *The secular scripture.* Cambridge, MA: Harvard University Press.

Geiger, D. (1967). *The dramatic impulse in modern poetics.* Baton Rouge: Louisiana State University Press.

Gentile, J. S. (1989). *Cast of one: One-person shows from the Chautauqua platform to the Broadway stage.* Champaign-Urbana: University of Illinois Press.

Grandin, T. (1996). *Thinking in pictures.* New York: Vintage.

Gray, G. W. (1954). Some teachers and the transition to twentieth-century speech education. In K. R. Wallace (Ed.), *History of speech education in America: Background studies* (pp. 422–446). New York: Appleton-Century-Crofts.

Haddon, M. (2003). *The curious incident of the dog in the night-time.* New York: Doubleday.

Horace. (2001). *Ars poetica* (D. A. Russell, Trans.). In V. B. Leitch (Gen. Ed.), *The Norton anthology of theory and criticism* (pp. 124–135). New York: Norton.

Johnson, G. E. (Ed.). (1940). *Studies in the art of interpretation.* New York: Appleton-Century-Crofts.

Lee, C., & Gura., T. (2001). *Oral interpretation* (10th ed.). Boston: Houghton Mifflin.

Lord, A. B. (2000). *The singer of tales* (2nd ed.). Cambridge, MA: Harvard University Press.

Parry, A., (Ed.). (1987). *The making of Homeric verse: The collected papers of Milman Parry.* Cambridge, MA: Harvard University Press.

Pelias, R. J. (1985). Schools of interpretation thought and performance criticism. *Southern Speech Communication Journal, 50,* 348–365.

Plato. (1998). *Gorgias* (J. H. Nichols, Jr., Trans.). Ithaca, NY: Cornell University Press.

Plato. (2001a). From *Phaedrus* (A. Nehamas & P. Woodruff, Trans.). In V. B. Leitch (Gen. Ed.), *The Norton anthology of theory and criticism* (pp. 81–85). New York: Norton.

Plato. (2001b). *Ion* (P. Woodruff, Trans.). In V. B. Leitch (Gen. Ed.), *The Norton anthology of theory and criticism* (pp. 37–48). New York: Norton.

Prince-Hughes, D. (2004). *Songs of the gorilla nation: My journey through autism.* New York: Harmony Books.

Rarig, F. M., & Greaves, H. S. (1954). National speech organizations and speech education. In K. R. Wallace (Ed.), *History of speech education in America: Background studies* (pp. 490–517). New York: Appleton-Century-Crofts.

Rein, L. M. (1981). *Northwestern University School of Speech: A history.* Evanston, IL: Northwestern University School of Speech.

Robb, M. M. (1968). *Oral interpretation of literature in American colleges and universities* (Rev. ed.). New York: Johnson Reprint.

Schechner, R. (2002). *Performance studies: An introduction.* London: Routledge.

Shaver, C. L. (1954). Steele MacKaye and the Delsartian tradition. In K. R. Wallace (Ed.), *History of speech education in America: Background studies* (pp. 202–218). New York: Appleton-Century-Crofts.

Spufford, F. (2002). *The child that books built: A life in reading.* New York: Metropolitan.

Taft-Kaufman, J. (1985). Oral interpretation: Twentieth-century theory and practice. In T. W. Benson (Ed.), *Speech communication in the 20th century* (pp. 157–183). Carbondale: Southern Illinois University Press.

Tallcott, R. (1922). *The art of acting and public reading.* Indianapolis, IN: Bobbs-Merrill.

Tallcott, R. (1940). The place for personation. In G. E. Johnson (Ed.), *Studies in the art of interpretation* (pp. 102–105). New York: Appleton-Century-Crofts. (Original work published 1916)

Williams, D. A. (1975). Impersonation: The great debate. In R. Haas & D. A. Williams (Eds.), *The study of oral interpretation: Theory and comment* (pp. 43–57). Indianapolis, IN: Bobbs-Merrill.

12

On the Bias

From Performance of Literature to Performance Composition*

RUTH LAURION BOWMAN AND MICHAEL S. BOWMAN

Every pattern piece bears markings that together constitute a "sign language," indispensable to . . . every stage [of the process]. . . . Note all symbols carefully. . . . Some pertain to alteration.

—Reader's Digest Complete Guide to Sewing (1976, p. 57)

PREFACE: SEAM-STRESSES

[Blinds, a platform with stairs, and a bathtub. A seamstress is sewing as the audience enters. Lights fade to black. Lights rise on the seamstress and then the full stage as seven women enter from upstage with pieces of fabric. One woman, Girl Friday, has paper. The women position themselves across the stage, Girl Friday in the tub. In various rhythms, the women rip, tear, rend the fabric . . . and the paper. The women gather the torn remnants, place them in the tub and exit. Lights isolate the Seamstress and Girl Friday who, in the tub, tosses her paper bits into the air . . . like snow. A light rises on the "Veiled Lady," upstage behind blinds. X-fade of lights from Girl Friday and the Seamstress to Coverdale and Mrs. Moodie as they enter into isolated spots.

Possible inclusion: As the last few women place their remnants in the tub and exit and Girl Friday begins to make snow, a short excerpt from *Rear Window* is projected on a pair of half-opened blinds. In the excerpt, Lisa Fremont stares out of Jeffries' rear window and then says to him, "Tell me everything you saw. And what you think it means."] (R. Bowman, 2003, p. 1)

On June 29, 1854, the *Boston New Era* published an account concerning a woman who had "imparted energy to a machine" (Brandon, 1983, p. 8). "Through the instrumentality of J. M. Spear," a Universalist clergyman, philanthropist and, in all likelihood, the author of the reported incident,

> a request came . . . that on a certain day [Mrs. ___] would visit the tower at High Rock . . . . When there . . . she began to experience the peculiar and agonizing sensations of parturition, differing somewhat from the ordinary experience, in as much as the throes were *internal,* and of the *spirit* rather than of the physical nature, but nevertheless quite as uncontrollable, and not less severe than those pertaining to the latter. This extraordinary physical phenomenon continued for about the space of two hours . . . the most interior and refined elements of her spiritual being were imparted to, and absorbed by, the appropriate portions of the mechanism [which, by means of "superior direction" had appeared on High Rock]. . . .
>
> The result of this phenomenon was, that indications of life or pulsations became apparent in the mechanism; first to her own keenly sensitive touch, and soon after to the eyes of all beholders. These pulsations continued for some weeks, precisely analogous to that of nursing (for which preparation had previously been made in her own organization) until at times a very marked and surprising motion resulted. . . .
>
> Neither Mrs. ___ nor myself can profess to have, as yet, any definite conception as to what this "new born child," the so-called "Electrical Motor" is to be. . . . But the incalculable benefits which have already accrued to us in the unfoldings of the interior principles of physical and human science have overwhelmingly compensated us for all that it has cost us, whether in means or reputation. (quoted in Brandon, 1983, pp. 9–10; emphasis in original)

When ambling through the rooms of my mind-on-mesmerism, I always find this account firmly ensconced on the sofa in the living room, the weight of a large lap cat, smiling smugly,

obliquely, so (confound it) at ease in its ability to rise from the sofa and take its leave of me. I'm not ready for that to happen. I am in love. I am in love with my electric light bulb Eureka moment on mesmerism. It turns me on.

It turns me on, out the door, and into the street where the vendors of mesmerism display their varied goods. As I pick through the bits and pieces, the nubby wools and slick satins, I realize that I am not in love with mesmerism itself; I am in love with its remnants. I am in love with what people have made out of the always already leftovers of mesmerism and what I can make with them now. I want to make something, too. Actually, I want to make something that becomes a remnant. Disposable. Reusable—perhaps. For me, a memory that hangs out with my Eureka moment on the sofa at home.

I collect to make a remnant. It is a model, a pose, a figure—of a woman who gave birth to an electric babe.

TWO CLASSROOMS

> **warp** *n:* **1 a** (1): a series of yarns extended lengthwise in a loom and crossed by the woof **b:** FOUNDATION, BASE <the – of the economic structure is agriculture . . . **3 a:** a twist or curve that has developed in something orig. flat or straight . . . **b:** a mental twist or aberration. (*Webster's,* 1975, p. 1320)

Let us imagine two performance classrooms. Although they may be located in the same building, they are separated by a great distance. In the first classroom, by means of constant vigilance, conducted with great effort, a distinction between text and performance is maintained. In this classroom, if a student appears, one who specializes in that particular kind of performance that relies too heavily on improvisation, personality, or technique, he will be led to the classroom door and sent down the hall or across campus to some other place. In this classroom, the law holds that only the text may be performed. The teacher's business is to judge, first of all, whether the text was indeed performed but, more importantly, whether certain performances have crossed an invisible line and, by leaving out too much or by putting too much in, have left the protected zone of the text for the contraband zone beyond the text. Attempting to eliminate the need for this continual ad hoc adjudication, the teacher tries to draft rules from examples that would clearly distinguish, in principle, between the allowed and the forbidden, a performance of the text and a performance that goes beyond the text. When drafted, these rules allow teachers and students to detect improper performances, ones characterized by too much improvisation or imagination or invention. The teacher calls these rules "Interpretation."

weft *n:* **1 a:** WOOF **b:** yarn used for the woof . . . **1 woof** *n:* **1 a:** a filling thread or yarn in weaving . . . **2 woof** *n:* **1:** a low gruff sound typically produced by a dog . . . **3 woof** *vi:* to make the sound of a woof. (*Webster's,* 1975, pp. 1328, 1350)

In the second classroom, the opposition between text and performance has been abandoned. Here, the students and teacher attend only to the consequences resulting from what happens onstage. The air seems less clear in here, almost impossibly dense, as if the sounds and images were accumulating somehow, condensing, no longer cleansed by the freshening breeze of the text. It is difficult to get one's bearings in here, to locate any fixed, solid point by which to navigate. Yet, an odd liveliness has appeared in the classroom, a charge of sensations curiously different from those who were in the first classroom.

Because the warp has very little give or stretch, most garments are cut to fall vertically on the warp or lengthwise grain. In turn, the more giving weft or crosswise grain of the fabric runs horizontally across the garment, around the bulk of the body.

These two classrooms do not really exist, although they have names. The first one has

most recently been called "Oral Interpretation" or "Performance of Literature." Wallace Bacon, who was chair for many years of the Department of Interpretation at Northwestern University, wrote about the difficulty of life in the first classroom. He argued that the art of interpretation consisted in sailing between the "dangerous shores" of text and performance without steering too closely to either. But, at the end of the day, those of us who were trained in Interpretation knew from which shore the interpreter's craft had departed and to which shore it was to return. Oral interpretation was about the art of reading literature aloud—a special kind of literary appreciation, to be sure, but literary appreciation nonetheless. Its very identity as a practice hinged on the conviction that "[1]iterary appreciation for the silent reader and literary appreciation for the oral performer are in some respects vitally distinct" (Bacon, 1960/1975, p. 4).

Variations in the weave of fabrics arise from how the warp and weft are patterned to intersect. For instance, a common plain weave typically recites, "No give Woof No give Woof No give Woof No give Woof," while a jaunty twill riffs, "Woof Woof No give No give Woof Woof No give No give Woof No give No give Woof Woof."

Proof of that conviction came when a reader was able to demonstrate his or her understanding of the text in the performance itself. Reading aloud helps us participate in the life of the text—not just the lexical meanings of the words, but also its tensions, motives, ambiguities, ironies, and other complexities—in a way that silent reading often does not. Such participation enhances our knowledge of the text and what it is attempting to do or say. With such knowledge, we can begin to participate even more fully in the life of the text through ever more "lively" performances. Over time, this process of discovery and refinement should progress to a point where the inner life of the text and the inner life of the reader begin to coalesce or "match." And when that point comes, the liveliness of the reader's performance should be congruent with that of the text. If the performance displays too little life, the reader has misunderstood the lesson performance was meant to teach him or her; if the performance displays too much life, has become too showy or spectacular, then he or she has answered the siren's call of another sort of error, a kind of egotism, forgetting that the text is the interpreter's whole excuse for being (Bacon, 1960/1975, p. 5; Bacon, 1979, pp. 5–10, 35–40, 70–74).

> 1 bias *n:* a line diagonal to the grain of a fabric . . . 2 a: an inclination of temperament or outlook . . . : PREJUDICE <a–in favor of jolly fat men> b: BENT TENDENCY . . . 3 a: a peculiarity in the shape of a bowl that causes it to swerve when rolled on the green . . . syn see PREDILECTION—on the bias: ASKEW, OBLIQUELY
>
> 2 bias *adj:* DIAGONAL, SLANTING—used chiefly of fabrics and their cut . . .
>
> 4 bias *vt:* 1: to give a settled and often prejudiced outlook . . . 2: to apply a slight negative or positive voltage. (*Webster's*, 1975, p. 106)

We were trained primarily in classrooms resembling the first one, and we still venture into them on occasion. But we now spend most of our time trying to imagine the second. The second classroom seems newer to us than the first one, perhaps because the names we give it, "Performance Art" or "Performance Composition," are relatively new. It is tempting to say that the second classroom is evolving from the first in a process akin to natural selection or adaptation, but the more time we spend there, the less convinced we are of the accuracy of that kind of narrative. So let us tell another story.

When the warp and weft meet at a crooked intersection, they are off their grain and on the grain of the bias. They have become jolly fat men. They have become jolly fat men who swerve obliquely when rolled on a green. Perhaps this is why at least two people should

work together to realign crooked intersections. On the other hand, rolling with the distortion may well be worth the experience.

WHAT WAS ORAL INTERPRETATION?

[Audience talk erupts forth. Seamstress continues to plant weeds upstage left.]

AUD A:	By common consent, the whole nation has gone mad on the gaseous fumes of mesmerism!
AUD B:	And why not! For once there is a serious, scientific explanation of nature, her forces, and in turn those that govern society and politics.
AUD C:	It also proves the existence of a soul in mankind!
AUD A:	How convenient for you . . . that the fundamental truth, the power behind all things, is an invisible fluid that no one can see!
AUD C:	But you assume that sight is the arbiter of truth.
AUD A:	No, I'm saying the almighty buck is . . . and that's the *only* thing mesmerism proves. Why anyone who has a penny for a "do-it-yourself" guide to mesmerism has opened a shop, enlisted their daughters as mediums and paraded the product in connection with ads for seegars, pills, hair oil, and cough candies.
AUD C:	But your very argument is grounded in material matters whereas mesmerism not only addresses physical maladies but moral and spiritual ones too.

AUD A: Entire families, little magnetized troupes, strutting their stuff on the stage alongside striped pigs and laughing gas.

AUD D: It's the work of the devil!

AUD C: No, it's the one true religion: god's universal sunshine pouring its beams into the dungeon we've *made* of religion.

AUD A: What?!

AUD B: In scientific terms, mesmerism accounts for all the unexplained events that the miracle mongers of virtually every religion have used to shackle mankind to them.

AUD C: Yes, that's it! With mesmerism, anyone can contact god and enter heaven on their own accord without some select priesthood standing in the way. Mesmerism Democratizes Religion!

AUD A: Hogwash! It simply replaces one intermediary for another; the magnetizer for the priest.

AUD B: Initially, perhaps, but once we learn more each of us will be able to draw on the universal fluid as we will.

AUD C: A will derived from the will of God!

AUD A: . . . which will lead to the same old chaos. Your faith in some universal moral "Will" we each use as we "Will" is ludicrous. You've only to look around to see the perversions: Here we are having paid our buck to watch one man seduce another! There's universal morality for you!

AUD D: Black magic is what it is: Satan's way of claiming innocent souls!

AUD B: But it's been proven that subjects won't perform acts contrary to their normal behavior.

AUD A: And we all know what's "normal," right? We've all read "Confessions of a Magnetizer," correct? First hand testimony that mesmerism exploits our sexual drives.

AUD D: It's rape and debauchery is what it is! A villainous art where profligate men of depraved appetites take a disgusting delight in seducing half-witted girls whose parents have prostituted them to this wicked trade.

AUD B: Rehash! Rehash of the sensationalist press! You've bought their quackery hook, line and sinker!

AUD D: No, I've seen it. Zombies stretched beamlike between chairs! Fluid darting from the eye of the operator to penetrate the brain of the bewitched! A cloudy haze streaming from the mesmerist's fingers! Insects electrified in magnetized water! It's witchcraft, plain and simple.

AUD B: You've been brainwashed by the press!

AUD A: Exactly! And just as she's been brainwashed by the press, so too but to a far greater extent mesmerism can be used to induce the public body to mass hysteria, such as led to the witch-burnings in the old countries and in our own.

AUD B: But it also can be used to perfect mankind. Would you have us revert back to the brute force of muscle? Cast aside the discoveries of steam, and electricity, and now mankind's own telegraphic force of nature? Why it may allow us to perform surgeries without an anesthetic, address the vagaries of the nervous system, improve the concentration of industrial workers . . .

AUD C: Convert pagans to Christianity!

AUD B: In sum, it reveals the power of the mind over matter and thereby all discord can be cured and eliminated.

AUD A: Whose mind!? Whose matter!? Your simple equation ignores the very real horrors of urbanization, industrialization, slavery . . .

AUD B: Oh god, an abolitionist too!

AUD A: It's the hocus-pocus of utopian cant in the hocus-pocus of the side-show, which proves nothing at all!

GIRL FRIDAY: [To Coverdale.] . . . more or less than the extraordinary power of the imagination: a shift from common sense, as we know it anyway, to a willingness to imagine a situation and play within it.

COVERDALE: Which may well reveal the appalling emptiness

GIRL FRIDAY: or possibilities

COVERDALE: of the self.

(R. Bowman, 2003, pp. 68–71; see Brandon, 1983, p. 39; Coale, 1998, p. 4; Collyer, 1838, pp. 19, 25; Du Potet de Sennevoy, 1838, p. 341; Ewer, 1855; Fuller, 1982, pp. 29, 32; Hawthorne, 1852/1986, p. 198; Kaplan, 1975, p. 35; Marks, 1947, pp, 5, 53, 203–205; Poe, 1837/1928, pp. 46–47)

In the United States, the heyday of mesmerism ran from around 1835 through the 1840s, after which it ceded popular strength and its more sensational phenomena, such as table-turning and clairvoyance, to its big sister, spiritualism. Touted as a universal cure, mesmerism captivated the public because it cut across the predominant intellectual currents of the day, binding enlightened rationalism (soon to become pragmatism), transcendental romanticism, and burgeoning capitalism in the common cause and Victorian vision of progress. Moreover, its physiological, psychological, spiritual, social, and theatrical facets "could be embraced selectively. One could pick and choose what one wanted and needed" (Kaplan, 1975, p. 7). What John Priestley said of electricity could also be said of mesmerism: "As the agent is invisible, every philosopher is at liberty to make it whatever he pleases" (quoted in Darnton, 1968, p. 16).

We were fortunate enough to begin our careers at a moment when the discipline we trained for disappeared. We entered a graduate degree program in oral interpretation at Northwestern University in the early 1980s, and we spent the next few years studying the histories, theories, and practices of oral interpretation, with the aim of entering a profession where we could teach others how to read and perform literature. But by the time we finished graduate school, the degrees they gave us were in something else: performance studies. There are only a handful of us who hold master's degrees in interpretation and PhDs in performance studies. The disciplinary tensions and turmoil of the 1980s may not be written on our bodies, exactly, but they are always written there at the top of our CVs.

> In all electrical phenomena we observe currents coming and going. (Mesmer, 1785/1958, p. 29)

> We are many in the city
> Who the weary needles ply;
> None to aid and few to pity
> Tho' we sicken down and die;
> But 'tis work, work away

By night and by day
Oh, 'tis work, work away
We've no time to pray.

(Judson, 1849, p. 26)

The irony of our graduate education was in the way it prepared us to teach something that was about to disappear. On one level, training in oral interpretation was an intensive craft— a method, a *technē*, an art to some—designed to enhance one's understanding of and appreciation for texts, literary texts most especially. When anyone asked, "What is oral interpretation?" we recited the mantra of the day: The study of literature through performance, and the study of performance through literature. The first part of that formula made sense to us, because that is what we did nearly every day in our classes. No one really understood the second part of the statement, but none of us dared admit that, and so it always passed without elaboration or comment. But on another level—and this is the dark and dirty secret of interpretation, the thing that most outsiders never really appreciated—interpretation taught us to think irreverently about our subject matter, both literature and performance. Our professors in the English and theatre departments sensed this, judging by their schizophrenic reactions to us when we ventured into their classes—by turns horrified or bemused at how we read literature or how we thought about and practiced performance.

One reinforces the action of Magnetism by multiplying the currents upon the patient. . . . [T]o touch a patient with force, gather together as many people as possible in his apartment. Establish a chain of people which leads from the patient and ends at the magnetizer. One person leaning against the magnetizer, or with his hand upon his shoulder, increases his action. There is an infinity of additional ways I might relate, such as using sound, music, light, mirrors, etc. . . . In order to magnetize a tree . . . a bottle . . . a flower. . . . (Mesmer, 1785/ 1958, pp. 63, 66–68)

For the Vienna-trained physician, Franz Anton Mesmer, the principal benefit of mesmerism or, as he termed it, "animal magnetism" was physiological, although his discourse regarding it swerves obliquely toward the metaphysical. In his doctoral thesis of 1766, Mesmer drew on the scientific, philosophical and folk archives of the past to articulate the presence of an "extremely subtle 'universal fluid'" that surrounds and permeates all things. Influenced by the planets, this universal fluid, a fluidium, ebbs and flows in the human body as it does in tidal waters in a two-part magnetic manner. When the two flows are in magnetic disharmony, maladies result and, Mesmer theorized, if you "control the tidal waves entering the physiology from outside the body . . . you control the illnesses" (quoted in Buranelli, 1975, p. 114). To balance errant flows, Mesmer's treatments progressed from his fixing magnetic plates or "tractors" to the patient, to his administering repetitive downward "passes" of his hands a few inches away from the victim's body, to, in France, the mode of operation for which he became most famous, or infamous: the communal *baquet*.

Mesmer moved to Paris from Vienna in 1778. There, he applied to the Academy of Sciences and the Royal Society of Medicine for funding, but both institutions snubbed his efforts, leveling charges of "quackery" and immorality at Mesmer (*Report*, 1833, p. 77). However, aided by the popular press, Mesmer gained support among radical intellectuals, amateur scientist-philosophers, and the commercial upper class. One in particular, Nicolas Bergasse, a lawyer from a wealthy bourgeois family in Lyons, met Mesmer's financial needs by establishing the Société de l'Harmonie Universelle with an initiation fee of 100 louis-d'or. The society was a smashing success not only among the aristocrats and upper-class intellectuals who could afford the fee but also among the populace who learned of Mesmer's treatments through the letters, pamphlets, pictures, and "counterfeit tubs that were hawked on the streets" (Darnton, 1968, p. 52). While

Mesmer contrived to keep the key points of his theory a secret, the treatments, being communal and often administered before "the presence of a crowd of witnesses" (*Report*, 1833, p. 115), became a spectator sport (Miller, 1995, pp. 5–6).

GIRL FRIDAY (as tour guide): Bonjour and good day. As you are having paid your fee, I welcome you to "l'Harmonie," first established in 1778. We all knowing our history of la France and les Etats-Unis, oui? Bon. My name is Monique and if you are having a question, please be telling me.

First, we are entering the lovely drawing room of Franz Anton Mesmer's spacious home in Paris. As you see, the patients are sitting around a *baquet* or, how do you say . . . a . . . a vessel? A wooden vessel . . . which it is filled with water that has been mesmerizing with iron bits or shavings. The iron rods, or often we are using a rope, issue from the vessel and the patients, they apply the rod to the afflicted parts of their body. Many times they are holding hands and pressing their knee, their knees, together to make a mesmeric chain . . . like a . . . uh . . . circuit . . . a circuit magnetique. Oui? You understand? From the ante-chamber, soft musique is hearing, made by a pianoforte and, sometimes, we are having we . . . have a glass harmonica or an opera singer. The musique sending reinforcing waves of the fluid universal into the patient's body. We have many assistants who are young and strong so they can be pouring the magnetic water over the patients and applying also various techniques therapeutic.

Since la tête always is receiving universal fluid from the stars and the feet, they always receiving fluid from la terre, the assistants (it makes good sense) they concentrate on the midi, on the . . . ah . . . the middle, the equator of the body. They gently rub the patients' backs, or sides or, oui . . . upon the breasts. This makes the patients having convulsions or crises or, what do you call it? It is like a play, like in a play, a climax, I think it is called.

Sometimes, though, the patients, they just falling asleep. For violent convulsives, there are chambers with lovely pads or mattresses on the wall. Sometimes, Monsieur Mesmer he comes too, in a long robe of lilac silk embroidered with gold flowers and wearing a white magnetic wand or . . . rod that he is using to trace artistic figures on the body to make it calming.

In addition to what I showing you today, outdoor treatments are available, too. Here, Monsieur Mesmer usually magnetizing trees and attaching patients to the tree with a rope. We also providing, in the back room, tubs for the poor and, for a small fee, portable tubs for mesmeric baths at home in your privacy. I hope you enjoying the tour. Merci and thank you. And having . . . have you any questions? (R. Bowman, 2003, pp. 3–4; see Binet & Féré, 1901, p. 11; Darnton, 1968, pp. 6–8; Mackay, 1869, p. 279; Wagstaff, 1981, pp. 2–3)

It was an odd double-game we learned to play. On the one hand, oral interpretation did teach us to read well, and because most of what we read was literature from the western canon, we developed a healthy knowledge of and respect for it. On the other hand, we all knew that part of our delight in *performing* literature lay in what we could make the literature do that it could or would not do on its own. There is always something of a *tour de force* element at work in performance, after all, and the plain and simple truth of the matter is that for many of us performing literature was an irreverent, aggressively playful, and often erotic act, not the hand-holding tryst in the parlor between platonic lovers that most scholarship in our field made it out to be. Something unusual always happened when we added the voice and body to the text, adapting or translating materials from one medium to another, and though various disciplinary measures occasionally were used to try to make us behave, things regularly went awry.

Whether using plates, passes, or portable tubs, Mesmer's aim was to effect a convulsive or crisis state in the subject that would shock the magnetic fluid back into a harmonious pattern, to put him or her back on-grain, so to speak. Over the next sixty years or so, experiments by Mesmer's devotees and other physicians (largely in France, England, and Germany) yielded alternative theories and treatments. In 1784, the lucid state of sleep or "artificial somnambulism" was chanced upon by the Marquis de Puysegur. This hypnotic practice became known as "mesmerism," and thereafter practitioners advanced it as a more effective treatment than the crisis state Mesmer himself sought to induce. Magnetized objects were virtually discarded, replaced by the understanding that the somnambulistic state could be incited by the superior magnetic force or "will" of the skilled physician via his administering repetitive passes, commands, or a concentrated stare. As Poe speculated in 1837, mesmerists "possess an unusual abundance of the magnetic fluid; or else, owing to their peculiar constitutional temperament they distribute it more readily than others; or, which is perhaps more probable, they have the faculty of CONFINING THEIR WILL TO THE OBJECT OF THEIR ATTENTION WITHOUT DISTRACTION, and at the same time making it act with great power" (1837/1928, pp. 50–51; emphasis in original). Further experimentation in the medical community and elsewhere yielded the more spectacular or, as some might have it, "hocus-pocus" phenomena associated with mesmerism (Marks, 1947, p. 5), such as table-turning, catalepsy, unrestrained or "improper" behavior, clairvoyance, self- and other diagnosis, and amnesia.

Others who have told pieces of this story—what Northwestern's interpretation department was like "back in the day" (e.g., Edwards, 1999; Hamera, 1998; Henderson, 1998)—have let the cat out of the bag already: how we learned about double-voiced discourse and the carnivalesque pleasures of "awryness" not so much from Bakhtin—although he helped us articulate it—but from watching and listening to the professoriate in that department at work. The Department of Interpretation did not teach us to do what we do now. We learned to do other things there that we no longer do very often. Yet, the experience of moving through that difficult, eccentric, "interdisciplinary" program—the manner in which we did things there—has played an enduring role in whatever it is that we have become. As Hamera (1998) suggested, the performance studies of today is heir to the conversations and improvisations we learned in those classrooms, which on the surface were about something else. To forget that is a form of amnesia (p. 274).

THE KILLER BS

> [*The Seamstress sews in the shadows.*]
>
> —R. Bowman, 2003, p. 36

> *The only thing of interest in a refuted system is the personal element. It alone is what is forever irrefutable.*
>
> —Nietzsche, quoted in Ray, 1995, p. 76

While physicians concentrated on the physiological effects of the great fluidium and religious folks the metaphysical, social reformers drew on the conceptual premises of mesmerism to support antiestablishment and utopian philosophies, communities, and, in France, a revolution. In *Mesmerism and the End of the Enlightenment in France,* Darnton (1968) traces how mesmerism was used by radical intellectuals in pre- and postrevolutionary France, its fluid character able to adapt to and appear on the stages of both reason and romanticism.

Another important character in our story, of course, is theory. Edwards (1999) has called attention to the indebtedness of performance studies to a canon of theory, rather than the canon of literature that interpretation was meant to serve, and there is no question that he is right about that. Everyone was reading theory in the early 1980s, and its influence was everywhere in the criticism we were reading and in the performance art that seemed to have become all the rage. Yet, while theory seemed to be telling most everyone else at the time that they could think irreverently about literature, performance had already taught us to do that. For us, theory let us think irreverently about performance.

Prior to the revolution, scientific discoveries and marvels captured the imagination of the reading public and prevailed in its popular literature. Science was fashionable. And while the onslaught of popular scientific writings about invisible agencies and their corresponding cosmologies was confusing—e.g., what had been a primary element, water, became a "compound of inflammable and dephlogisticated air" (Darnton, 1968, p. 17)—the public was enthralled rather than discouraged.

As channeled through the popular press, the apolitical discourse of science was reader-friendly, as accessible to the common man as were the frequent demonstrations of scientific marvels. Both gave rise to fad commodities which the public could participate in or purchase for itself, as was the case with mesmeric tubs, lightning rods, and balloon rides, hats, and sweets. Of course, embedded within the "apolitical" discourse was a subversive ideology that, through reason, all men could understand and command the laws of nature. In the last two lines of a poem praising an early balloon flight in Lyons, such sentiments ring clear: "The eagle of Jupiter has lost his empire,/And the feeble mortal can approach the gods" (quoted in Darnton, 1968, p. 20). As Darnton summarizes, while few of the reading public had ever read Rousseau's Social Contract, they knew all about Mesmer's

universal flow, its "mysteries, scandals, and passionate polemics." Little wonder then that the radical elite should use "the popular and apolitical vogue of science," its discourse and modes of address, to disseminate their revolutionary ideas (Darnton, 1968, pp. 161–162).

As it happened, most of the theorists whose writing we gravitated toward had last names that began with the letter "B." Brecht and Burke were already somewhat known to us, but as time passed, more "Bs" kept showing up: Bakhtin, Barthes, Baudrillard, Benjamin, Berger, Boal. One day, one of us jokingly referred to them as "the Killer Bs," and the term has always stuck with us. Although no one used the term "performative writing" in those days, what was appealing about theory as it was practiced by the Killer Bs was its spectacular quality. It was dizzying, breathtaking, and often vastly entertaining. It seemed to fulfill Aristotle's definition of good theatre, and its relationship to literature was precisely the sort of relationship that performance held for us: irreverent, playful, aggressive, erotic. It helped us imagine the kinds of performances we desired to give, something that could break down or break away from the old text-vs.-performance dualism in which we felt trapped—and in which the discipline of performance studies is still largely trapped—in order to create some "third" kind of writing/performance.

> The surplus of movement excited by the friction of an elastic body which happens to be exposed to another body, so as to effect a discharge, forms *artificial electricity*. (Mesmer, 1785/1958, p. 29; emphasis in original)

Mesmerism was particularly appealing to radicals because its immense popularity during the 1780s was coupled with controversy. The controversy centered on the condemnation of Mesmer by the aristocratic academy. Mesmer's battle and battle tactics became a model or pose through which the radical intelligentsia expressed their own discontent with *les gens en place* (men in power) and their dogmatic conservation of aristocratic privilege. In short, "Mesmer's fight was their fight" (Darnton, 1968, p. 90).

Through much of the decade, the radical elite inundated the public with reader-friendly pamphlets that described and defended mesmerism as a science. In this way, mesmerism served as a rhetorical hook, appealing to the public's fascination with science and thereby implying every citizen's right to access it. Simultaneously, the social politics of mesmerism as a revolutionary praxis took shape in the letters, novels, memoirs, lectures, and textbooks that the proponents of mesmerism shared with each other and, by the decade's end, with the reading public.

Although we didn't stumble across it until later, Jean-Luc Godard's well-known characterization of his aims as a filmmaker captures perfectly the sense of what we wanted to accomplish and what we found modeled for us in the work of the Killer Bs: "research in the form of a spectacle" (Godard, 1968/1972, p. 181).

The "most energetic" and prolific advocate of mesmerism was Nicolas Bergasse who, "by injecting a Rousseauist bias into a mesmerist analysis of the . . . relations among men," envisioned "a way to revolutionize France" (Darnton, 1968, pp. 108, 124). Bergasse drew on two popular notions of the day—physical-moral causality and the aim of natural law—to argue that animal magnetism was the conservative agency of nature and hence was charged with maintaining "a constant and durable harmony" within and among all entities (quoted in Darnton, 1968, p. 114). When man was in flow with nature, à la Rousseau's primitive state, the fluid was enabled to produce healthy bodies, just minds and social relations. When man was out of flow, the reverse occurred. It was Bergasse's claim that in modern-day France, those least connected with the law of flow in nature were the aristocratic *gens en place* whose depraved lifestyle had affected their governance of French institutions which, in turn, had effected physical

and moral malaise throughout the state and its people. Like Rousseau, Bergasse advocated a return to a more primitive or natural and therefore more harmonious society, a like reformation of the arts, and a concentration on educating children so as to stem the top-down tide of corruptive (i.e., artificial) influences or, in the vernacular of the day, "sensations" or, in the vernacular of our day, "interpellations." Unlike Rousseau, Bergasse grounded the cause and cure of social malaise in scientific fact. In sum, the "more robust constitution" of the natural mesmerized man "would make us remember independence. When, with such a constitution, we necessarily would develop new morals, how could we possibly put up with the yoke of the institutions that govern us today?" (quoted in Darnton, 1968, p. 124).

[Coverdale dons a winter coat as two Blithedale members enter, also dressed in winter duds. The trio piles into the tub and sets off to Blithedale. As they deliver their little manifesto, Girl Friday performs "the snow" which becomes increasingly heavy. By the climax, the trio in the tub is spot lit as is the Seamstress who may help Girl Friday create the veil of snow falling on (occasionally pelted at) the folks in the tub.]

COVERDALE: There were three of us,

BL MEMBER A: Blithedale communitarians,

BL MEMBER B: Agrarian socialists,

COVERDALE: who rode together through the storm.

BL MEMBER B: Our destination was Blithedale,

BL MEMBER A: a rented tract of farmland

COVERDALE: with a house (thank god),

BL MEMBER A: that lay on the Charles River nine miles outside the city of Boston.

COVERDALE: As we threaded our way through the narrow streets of the city,

BL MEMBER B: the buildings on either side seemed to press too closely in upon us

BL MEMBER A: and the snowfall, too, looked inexpressibly dreary,

COVERDALE: (I would almost call it dingy),

BL MEMBER A: coming down through the city smoke and alighting on the sidewalk only to be molded into the impress of somebody's patched boot or overshoe.

BL MEMBER B: Thus, the track of old conventions was visible on what was freshest from the sky.

COVERDALE: But, when we left the pavements of the city and the muffled hoof of the team beat upon the country road, then there was better air to breathe.

BL MEMBER A: Air that had Not been Breathed Once and Again,

BL MEMBER B: Air that had Not heard Words of Falsehood and Formality,

BL A & B: like all the Air of the Dusky City!

BL MEMBER A: If ever Mankind might give Utterance to their Wildest Dreams,

BL A & B: yes,

BL MEMBER A: and Speak of Earthly Happiness as an Object to be Attained,

BL A & B: YES, We Were Those Men and Women!

BL MEMBER B: It was Our Purpose

COVERDALE: (generous and absurd as it was)

BL MEMBER B: to Cast Aside our Meager Materiality and Live a Life of Cooperation rather than Competition.

ALL: YES.

BL MEMBER B: To Refuse the Paltry Principles on which Societies have all along been Based.

ALL: YES.

BL MEMBER B: To Step Off the Tired Treadmill of the Established System!

BL MEMBER A: To Vacate the Rusty Relic of Society!

BL MEMBER B: To Shut Up the Ledger!

COVERDALE: Fling aside the Pen!

BL MEMBER A: Retire from the Pulpit!

COVERDALE: Abandon the Sweet Indolence of Life . . .

BL MEMBER B: To Lessen the Laborers' Great Burthen of Toil

ALL: By Performing our Due Share! YES! We had Left the Struggling Self Seeking World To Form an Equal Brotherhood and Sisterhood Of Earnest Toil and Shared Beneficence! [Freeze beat.]

COVERDALE: With such unflagging spirits, we made good companionship with the tempest and, at our journey's end, professed ourselves reluctant to bid the rude blusterer good-bye. To own the truth, however, I was little better than an icicle and began to be suspicious that I had caught a fearful cold.

(R. Bowman, 2003, pp. 8–10; see Hawthorne, 1852/1986, pp. 11, 19)

PERFORMING THEORY

In 1845, the *New York Daily Tribune* estimated that there were probably about twice as many women seeking work as seamstresses "as would find employment at fair wages." These 10,000 workers, the *Tribune* concluded, constituted an oversupply of workers who could not possibly earn enough to keep themselves alive. "One and a half to two dollars per week," it declared, "is represented as the average recompense of good workwomen engaged at plain sewing, and there are very many who cannot, by faith and diligence, earn more than a dollar a week." (Kessler-Harris, 1982, p. 65)

> *To convince is to conquer without conception.*
>
> —Benjamin, 1928/1996, p. 446

Many of us who helped invent performance studies but whose training was in oral interpretation worried about the status of literature in the emerging discipline, its possible disappearance into the abyss of textuality. Elsewhere, we have argued that the "semiotic misrule" seemingly authorized by theories of textuality does not mean abandoning literature, but instead developing a more "writerly" or "producerly" orientation to solo and group performances of literature (Bowman 1995, 1996; Bowman & Bowman, 2002; Bowman & Kistenberg, 1992). But that isn't what we want to talk about here. This is another story.

"We the undersigned, peaceable, industrious and hardworking men and women of Lowell [mills in Massachusetts], confined in unhealthy apartments, exposed to the poisonous contagion of air, vegetable, animal and mineral properties, debarred from proper Physical Exercise, Mental discipline, and Mastication cruelly limited, and thereby hastening us on through pain, disease and privation, down to a premature grave, pray the legislature to institute a ten-hour working day in all the factories of the state." . . . signed by 2,000 mostly female operatives. (*Voice of Industry*, 1845, quoted in Kessler-Harris, 1982, p. 62)

Are women to be born for this, to toil, shrivel, die and rot? . . . My very soul is roused with indignation. The women of France once rose in rebellion. Their cry was "bread for our babes"; will the women of our country ever utter this cry as they gather in crowds from the attics, cellars, by lanes, and dark dens of filth and squalor? Alas! Yes, if no change comes for the better, they too will thirst for the purple cup of revolution. (*Stray Leaves from a Seamstress's Journal*, 1853–54, quoted in Reynolds, 1989, p. 356)

In *Heuretics: The Logic of Invention*, Greg Ulmer (1995) argues that creative work is more systematic than popular mythology might have us believe, that it proceeds as much from imitation or emulation as it does from inspiration or imagination or genius or specialization. In reviewing a number of discourses on method, ranging from Plato's *Phaedrus* to Breton's surrealist manifesto, Ulmer found a common set of elements. Those elements, Ulmer suggests, can be mnemonically summarized by means of the acronym *CATTt*, representing the following operations:

C = Contrast

A = Analogy

T = Theory

T = Target

t = tale (or form in which the work will appear)

Performance studies, like all intellectual and artistic formations, developed by extrapolation in this same manner. Performance studies is heavily invested in the mythology of the "antidiscipline" and flaunts its eccentricities as if flaunting eccentricity were something peculiar, but if we take as performance studies' "manifesto" any of the representative texts by Schechner (1985, 1988, 1992) or Conquergood (1985, 1991, 1995) that are commonly cited as charting the direction of the field, we can detect the pattern of invention identified by Ulmer.

Contrast

For Schechner and Conquergood performance studies is imagined in contrast to the conservatory and professional training models of most academic theatre and performance programs; by extension, performance studies is projected as intervening in the entertainment and showbiz apparatus, as well as in the textualist paradigm of knowledge that relegates performance to an ancillary role of illustrating or disseminating whatever knowledge or truth is thought to be contained in texts.

Published in 1852, Nathaniel Hawthorne's *The Blithedale Romance* is in part based on the author's experiences at Brook Farm in the spring through autumn months of 1841. Like many reform communities of the period, The Brook Farm Institute of Agriculture and Education was envisioned by its founders as "a society of liberal, intelligent and cultivated persons, whose relations with each other would permit a more simple and wholesome life, than can be led amidst the pressures of our competitive institutions" (quoted in Delano, 2004, p. 34). Such sentiments were directly informed by the utopian socialism of Charles Fourier, whose ideas were popularized in the United States through Albert Brisbane's *The Social Destiny of Man; or Association and Reorganization of Industry* (1840).

Analogy

Schechner and Conquergood both rely on the analogy and example of the anthropologist/ethnographer, someone whose business is to observe and interpret culture, rather than to engage in the elaborate form of gossip known as theatre or performance criticism within the institutional framework of the western literary/theatrical tradition. "Participant-observation" is the investigative method of the anthropologist/ethnographer, where that method itself is refigured as a special kind of performance activity.

A postrevolutionary French mystic and outspoken opponent of capitalism, Fourier had a plan for a future utopia that was ruled by "his" discovery of the principle of Universal Harmony. While Fourier claimed the idea as his own, in substance and rhetoric, the influence of Mesmer and, particularly, Bergasse is "evident in many of his works" (Darnton, 1968, p. 143). Like Bergasse, Fourier believed in physical-moral causality as a law of nature and urged a return to more a primitive, natural society. Thereby the "SUDDEN TRANSITION FROM SOCIAL CHAOS" as wrought by civilization "TO UNIVERSAL HARMONY" would be enabled (quoted in Darnton, 1968, p. 143; emphasis in original). Specific to Fourier's plan was the reorganization of society into discrete communities or "phalanxes," where each member would engage in an industry of his or her choice and also be allowed to express his or her natural impulses, including sexual ones.

Theory

Schechner and Conquergood also rely on the metaphor of the trickster—a traditional anthropological subject—to imagine how performance studies might function within the institutional space of the academy, and the performance studies scholar is projected as a boundary-crossing inter-/antidisciplinarian. Thus, performance studies might borrow or "poach" its theory from anywhere as it tries to "make do" within the confines of academe (de Certeau, 1974/1984). Even so, anthropology/ethnography may be identified as one major source of theoretical and methodological borrowing, while another might be that amalgam of poststructuralist theories known at one time as critical theory but now more commonly called cultural studies.

In later documents, Fourier does lend some credit to mesmerism, claiming that "if it had been abused in 'civilization,' it would be 'in great fashion, of great utility, in the state of harmony,'" for somnambulists or mesmerists would be able to contact the other world and thereby further enable the flow of harmonic fluid between the material and spiritual worlds (quoted in Darnton, 1968, p. 144).

Target

The immediate targets of performance studies are the professional discourses of communication and theatre studies, but the wider target is the human sciences generally. The performance studies scholar might be found anywhere within a college of arts and sciences, for the field's "specialization," as Edwards (1999) notes, "*is* the general field of human experience, studied *as* and *by* performance" (p. 83).

While Fourier was never mesmerized himself, he apparently "communicated mesmerically with his disciples" after his death, as recounted in the following 1853 transcription from a Fourierist table-turning session:

> [MEDIUM] . . . Ask the table, that is, the spirit that is inside it; it will tell you that I have above my head an enormous pipe of fluid, which rises from my hair up to the stars. It's an aromatic pipe by which the voice of spirits on Saturn reaches my ear . . . THE TABLE (thumping strongly with its foot)— Yes, yes, yes. Aromatic pipe. Conduit. Aromatic pipe. Conduit. Conduit. Conduit. Conduit. Yes. (quoted in Darnton, 1968, pp. 144–145)

tale

In the early years of its formation (roughly, the 1980s), one of the missing pieces in performance studies' invention of itself was the CATT's "tale." The major dilemma was whether the form in which performance studies should appear would be a scholarly essay or a theatrical performance of some kind. Conquergood repeatedly advocated performance as a means of scholarly representation, although his own work always appeared as a conventional scholarly essay. Indeed, most of the influential work that passed for performance studies has taken the conventional essayistic form of the disciplines from which it has borrowed. More innovative forms of scholarly representation began to appear in the early 1990s as personal narrative, autobiography, and post-/autoethnography took hold, and scholars often used venues other than academic books and journals for presenting these experiments with media, genres, and styles. It wasn't until the mid-1990s that things began to crystallize around the terms "performative writing" or "performance writing" (Allsopp, 1999; Phelan, 1992; Pollock, 1998).

Of the fifty or so Fourierist communities attempted in the United States between 1840 and 1860, Brook Farm and the North American Phalanx in Red Bank, New Jersey, are, in popular and historical accounts, the most frequently mentioned. Although the Brook Farm group waited until 1844 to replicate Fourier's practical scheme, a journal dedicated to his ideas was published at the farm, and in writing *The Blithedale Romance* Hawthorne entertained two or three volumes of Fourier's works. For the most part, Brook Farm and cooperatives like it stressed Fourier's concepts of industrial reorganization, also known as Associationism in the United States. Hawthorne, on the other hand, directed his sights toward the more prurient and explicit connections between (Fourierist) social reform and mesmerism, as he saw them practiced in New England at the time.

As noted earlier, mesmerism flourished in the United States from the mid-1830s through the 1840s. Marketed to the U.S. public as a universal cure for physical, spiritual, and social ills, mesmerism becomes a multivalent metaphor in Hawthorne's hands to critique social reform practices of his day, the various ploys of the Blithedale characters, the narrator Miles Coverdale's voyeuristic inclinations, and Hawthorne's own craft of writing fiction. In large part, Hawthorne's view is negative, his distrust of mesmerism palpable.

In sum, performance studies invented itself by combining anthropology and critical theory/cultural studies whose lessons and strategies it translated onto another domain—literary theatre and oral interpretation. There, literature was translated most often into "verbal art" or "cultural performance" or "textuality," while critical theory/cultural studies' concern with the politics of textuality reappeared as the politics of performativity.

THE BODY ELECTRIC

> *"You can see them in those shops," said seamstress Aurora Phelps, "seated in long rows, crowded together in a hot close atmosphere, working at piece-work, 30, 40, 60, or 100 girls crowded together, working at 20 and 25 cents a day."*

> —Kessler-Harris, 1982, p. 78

> *"The especial genius of Woman, I believe to be electrical in movement, intuitive in function, spiritual in tendency." It is this electrical, magnetic nature, [Margaret] Fuller argues, that makes women especially useful as mesmeric mediums.*

> —Reynolds, 1989, p. 378

> *Everything now, in its own way, wants to be television.*

> —Ulmer, 1989, p. 11

As embedded in the reform discourse that influenced the making of Brook-Blithedale

Farm, mesmerism is used by Hawthorne to question the moral-physical (thought-enactment) ambiguities of the period generally and its reform movements in particular. One glaring irony that encapsulates both concerns the economic history of the times. In 1837, a financial panic brought on an economic depression that lasted well into the 1840s. Credit was tight and, as a result, many smaller farms in New England were abandoned or sold off. The rural dispossessed gravitated to the cities where they found they had to compete with European immigrants for industry jobs. The inflated and embattled labor base drove down wages and put a temporary end to trade union activity and the advancements gained in the 1830s. Insufferable working conditions, overcrowded tenements, and staggering increases in poverty and crime testified that living in the city as one of the "exploited 'lower million'" was a tough row to hoe. Meanwhile, the wealthy "'upper ten'" (Reynolds, 1989, p. 126)—the "industrialists from Boston and New York"—snapped up the cheap rural acreage and converted it into summer resorts for leisure and profit (Kolodny, 1986, p. xi). The travesty escalates when "social reformers" such as Hawthorne and his fellow social democrats vacated the cities in a romantic huff of antiindustrial protest and invested in the promise of Brook Farm for 500 bucks a share. Hawthorne apparently bought two shares, one for himself and another for his fiancée, Sophia Peabody, but a year later turned tail and sued the cooperative in an effort to reclaim his investment. Eleven years later, Hawthorne published *The Blithedale Romance.*

> It is not, I apprehend, a healthy kind of mental occupation, to devote ourselves too exclusively to the study of individual men and women. If the person under examination be one's self, the result is pretty certain to be diseased action of the heart, almost before we can snatch a second glance. Or, if we take the freedom to put a friend under our microscope, we thereby insulate him from many of his true relations, magnify his

peculiarities, inevitably tear him into parts, and, of course, patch him very clumsily together again. What wonder, then, should we be frightened by the aspect of a monster, which, after all . . . may be said to have been created mainly by ourselves!

. . . But I could not help it. (Hawthorne, 1852/1986, p. 69)

One of the most important courses in our graduate program at Northwestern, at least in terms of how it shaped our thinking, was the history seminar we were all required to take. And perhaps the most important part of that seminar was being introduced to orality-literacy theory through the work of scholars like Albert Lord, Eric Havelock, Jack Goody, Walter Ong, and Marshall McLuhan. The central idea of orality-literacy theory, of course, is that the technology by which we communicate affects the way we think. While we are the inventors of our media, as McLuhan was fond of saying, eventually our media turn around and reinvent us. The invention of the phonetic alphabet brought about a seismic shift in the way people thought by making possible for the first time practices of analysis, logic, and reason as we know and practice them today. In Ong's (1982) neat formulation, "writing restructures consciousness" (p. 78).

Orality-literacy theory was influential in shaping how the field of oral interpretation imagined itself. In the beginning—that is, in the old, preliterate days of Homer—the performer of literature was the Big Man of whatever tribe or community to which he belonged. Without writing to serve as an artificial memory system, a culture's history and, indeed, its very identity and existence depended on the living memory of those charged with keeping and reciting knowledge, which was always cast in the memorable forms of story, song, and dance. Literature did not exist in the strict sense of that term. Whatever verbal arts the culture produced were so intimately linked to performers and performances that their domains were identical: no performance, no poetry; no poetry, no culture.

The sewing machine, introduced in the 1850s, far from lightening the seamstresses' load, increased pressure to produce more. The machine encouraged centralization into small shops where work could be routinized and efficiently distributed. Seamstresses faced continual unemployment: cycles of harsh overwork followed by idleness. (Kessler-Harris, 1982, p. 66)

New York City Physician Claims Itinerant Mesmerists Bilking The Public Of Their Hard Earned Dollar.

Factory Girl Mediums Would Rather Sleep Than Do An Honest Day's Work. (R. Bowman, 2003, p. 25; see Fuller, 1982, p. 32)

With the invention of literacy, the relations between literature and performance changed. No longer was it necessary to trust the knowledge and stories of culture to the memory and display skills of the performer. Once knowledge became separable from performance, it also changed—and when knowledge changed, we changed as well. The history of performance that we studied was a story of the shifting fortunes of the performer as chirography and then typography altered the regimes of knowledge, information, and communication.

While an "equal brotherhood and sisterhood" is the stated aim of the reformers who assemble at Blithedale, each proves to be transfixed by his or her own reform agendas, such as women's rights, penal reform, and, in the case of Coverdale, enacting the "calm observer" so as to "distil . . . the whole morality of the performance" (Hawthorne, 1852/1986, p. 97). As the characters each pursue what they see as their "natural impulses," conflicts arise and, in an effort to survive, they reconfigure their reform desires in terms of sexual conquest and monetary gain. The key tactic for success is to discover and then disclose to others the intimate secrets of one's competitor or object of desire.

In one instance, the wealthy and exotic feminist, Zenobia, and the penniless city seamstress, Priscilla, are vying for the affections of the prophet of penal reform, Hollingsworth. When Zenobia discovers that Priscilla is also the renowned "Veiled Lady" of the mesmerist stage, Zenobia attempts to discredit her by performing the "legend" of "The Silvery Veil" at a Blithedale parlor theatrical (Hawthorne, 1852/1986, p. 108). Veiled itself as fantasy, Zenobia's tale of deception recounts how the "famous . . . creature" vanished from the public eye only to reappear "amid a knot of visionary people" (Hawthorne, 1852/1986, pp. 108, 114). There, she attaches herself to a particular "lady" (i.e., Zenobia), who learns from a "Magician" (i.e., Priscilla's former mesmerist-operator) that the girl "'is doomed to fling a blight over [the lady's] prospects.'" To thwart her efforts, the lady must take the Magician's veil, throw it over her foe, stamp her foot, and call for the Magician, and he will come and seize her (Hawthorne, 1852/1986, p. 115). In both the tale and the telling, the lady and Zenobia do just as the Magician-mesmerist bids. They fling a veil over Priscilla's head and thereby unveil her. In the next chapter, Coverdale enacts a similar performance when he "attempt[s] to come within [Priscilla's] maidenly mystery" by taking "just one peep beneath her folded petals" (Hawthorne, 1852/1986, p. 125).

Because such performances are commonplace among the Blithedale set, it takes but little time to realize that the great fluidium is greatly askew at Blithedale. The main reason for the errant flows, it appears, is that "social harmony" is being attempted by individuals who also embody the Jacksonian ethos of competitive individualism. The romance then is not about socialistic reform; it is about capitalism and the distortions (e.g., of social reform) that arise from its enactment. In the lurid parlance of the penny-press, a befitting byline of the period might report: *Sensationalist Reformers Wallow In The Very Sewers They Attempt To Scour Clean* (Bowman, 2003, p. 32)

Of course, by means of the narrative he uses to recount his Blithedale experiences, Coverdale wallows in these same sewers—and so does Hawthorne.

The implications of orality-literacy theory were especially fascinating to us, for if McLuhan, Ong and the others were correct in suggesting that communication technologies restructure consciousness, then the development of mechanical and electronic audiovisual media, beginning with photography and telegraphy in the early nineteenth century, marked the beginning of another shift in how humans would communicate, invent, and think. We were entering a postliterate age, the consequences of which we were only beginning to imagine.

> In a crisis one should observe three stages: perturbation, coction [literally "a cooking, or coming to the boiling point"], and evacuation. (Mesmer, 1785/1958, p. 43)

GIRL FRIDAY: In etymological terms, hysteria means "wandering womb." In Mesmer's time and thereafter, the prescribed treatments for female hysterics, or "wandering wombs," were bleeding, blistering, religious salvation, or marriage. The latter was based on the understanding that a woman's excessive behavior was due to her lack of sexual relations. As Hollingsworth might have it, the woman was a "petticoated monstrosity" because she had "missed out on woman's particular happiness." Of course, Mesmer's cure was to induce that very state of "happiness"—an orgasmic crisis or climax—while those mesmerists who followed quieted the wandering wombs by hypnosis or, as the wary press implied, by means of their penetrating will power. Since then, electric shock therapies and the clinical manipulation of the clitoris have been used in severe to middling cases, while those who suffer from mild displays of excess are becalmed by the flow of the great fluidium through a score of household appliances, exercise gizmos, sexual gadgets, and beauty parlor treatments. (R. Bowman, 2003, p. 81)

In the first flush of excitement over the possible implications of orality-literacy theory, as well as the energy surrounding the invention of performance studies, there was some understandable though misplaced euphoria. Ong's belief that the postliterate age would be characterized by a "secondary orality" seemed to augur a world where we would move "beyond" the text to a place where performance would achieve greater recognition and prominence. In the contemporary postliterate or postmodern age, some critics believed, performance would be where it's at (Benamou & Caramello, 1977). This sentiment has been echoed in a number ways in various publications over the last 25 years, and widespread dispersal of "performance" as a metaphor and critical tool for a variety of "studies" in virtually every discipline of the arts, humanities, and social and "hard" sciences is touted as further evidence that we have left the age of reason and discipline and entered the age of performance (McKenzie, 2001).

But if Ong and the others are correct in suggesting that alphabetic thinking is now giving way to cinematic/electronic thinking—that literacy is yielding to "electracy" (Ulmer, 2003)—then neither text nor performance will be quite what it was in the conditions of either literacy or orality. If we want to know what this new age of "electrate" performance will be, instead of looking back at what the old oral or preliterate world was like, we need to figure out what "cinematic/electronic thinking" might be. But to put the question in that way is to make it damnably difficult to answer. Perhaps, then, as Ulmer (1989, 1995) and others have argued (see Ray, 1995, 2001), the better approach would be to locate some examples of it—to assume that some of the newer forms of communication/"writing"/"performance" are instances of it—and then try to gain some experience of it by emulating or simulating those forms.

Like other literati of the period, Hawthorne was fully aware that in writing fiction he was not unlike a mesmerist in so far as both make use of the suggestive force of language to construct identities, disclose internal thoughts and feelings, and create imaginary worlds that persuade the reader or audience of their literal or figurative truth. In his construction of Coverdale's narrative, Hawthorne explores this aspect of mesmerism to such an extent that, in the end, the romance is about—as it always has been—Coverdale, and his self-entranced perspective. In the final chapter, appropriately titled "Miles Coverdale's Confession," Coverdale offers a brief critique of his narrative state before proceeding, in the remaining pages, to prove its truth. He asks, "What, after all, have I to tell?" In response he answers, "Nothing, nothing, nothing!" (Hawthorne, 1852/1986) p. 245). If concentered on Coverdale's narrative, the verdict of the novel is nihilistic and devastating. However, on the refracted level of the narrative, the "nothing" of language is countered by its ability to recall of what it consists—of what came before—and thereby it always interrupts the not-so-natural flow of itself, forward.

In teaching over the last few years, we have become increasingly aware that ideas, works, and issues that are difficult to discuss and understand abstractly can be approached through simulation exercises—mimicry, imitation—based on more or less concrete instructions. Extrapolating from Benjamin, we might say that for us to teach is to communicate without initial conceptualizations. So that, for example, if we want our students to understand something about texts and performances, asking them to think about abstract aesthetic or theoretical categories seems less effective than giving them instructions about how to practice different kinds of textual and performance activity. We can tell them, for instance, that different textual practices develop by extrapolating from models found in some other field or discipline or practice—about how a modern writer like Faulkner borrowed from philosophers like Bergson, as well as from the cinema, to help him conduct his narrative experiments; about how surrealism, which was an aesthetic/political movement, borrowed from Freudian psychoanalysis, a medical practice. We can give them things like N. Scott Momaday's *The Way to Rainy Mountain* or Laurie Anderson's *Nerve Bible* and tell them to use it as their model for producing a performance, letting them know that *imitation* is as important as *imagination* in both learning and the creative process. We can introduce them to Roland Barthes's ideas about the "writerly" text simply by telling them that Barthes believed that every text contains a set of "instructions" for producing another, similar composition. Finding the "instructions" implicit in the model is the key, of course, and that is where our reading and discussion are focused. We usually tend to do this with the class, primarily to check our tendency to produce an instruction like "write in such a way as to imbricate your authorial Self in a collective order, intertextually articulated in myth, history, and personal experience," an instruction that we could not give to an undergraduate class with a straight face. So, as a group, we come up with homelier things, such as: "write in very short anecdotes, none longer than a paragraph" or "use a story told to you by your parents or grandparents" or "include pictures from a family photo album."

In that spirit and in the spirit of our essay, we offer a simple do-it-yourself guide for sewing your own performance composition, for those moments when you cannot help but create something, however clumsy the result:

1. Select the kind of costume you would like to wear—e.g., social reformer, historian, mesmerist, cultural critic, cynic, performance theorist, seamstress, or all of them rolled into one, perhaps.

2. Collect lots of different fabrics, patterns, and notions associated with the costume you have chosen. Remnants are fine, as are nontextiles, such as an old bathtub or snow or plants or that odd piece of sheet metal you find out back. If the materials don't seem to go together, that's okay—collect them anyway.

3. Create your own fabrics and notions, too, by imitating or transforming some of those you've collected. For example, weave yourself into the threads of a Girl Friday and detail with detachable trims, such as Tour Guide or Media Theorist or Snow Illusionist or Graduate Student.

4. Stand back (or move in close) and take a look at your collection. Select a piece, notion, or remnant you particularly like. For you, at this time and this place, it is the metonym, the model, the pose, or the figure that best represents the costume you desire and also, perhaps, fear.

5. Use the figure to guide how you pattern your costume. Ask yourself what bits from your collection you desire to cut and stitch together to serve as the warp or foundation of your costume. Ask yourself whether the filler bits should woof loudly or softly through contrast or analogy. Ask yourself what bias bits you will inevitably have to include in the costume and how far askew you want to go.

6. After you are satisfied with the initial layout of what you have designed, assume that it is wrong and try again. Another option is to add in more bias bits that are just not "you," that you don't look or feel good in. Like a jolly fat man or woman, roll with the seeming distortions.

7. Put your costume together, realizing that the various media of assemblage (everything from safety pins to heavy, high-tech industrial machinery) will affect the pattern and, hence, the figure in the costume that you have made.

COVERDALE: And, so, after all is said and done, what have I to tell you?

[Lights fade to black. In silence/the sound of the seamstress planting her weeds, which now cover the stage, at Coverdale's feet.] (R. Bowman, 2003, p. 82)

NOTE

*Section editor's note: the essay employs techniques of "performative" or "performance" writing to address the challenge of documenting a theatrical production. Ruth Laurion Bowman staged her adaptation of Nathaniel Hawthorne's 1852 novel *The Blithedale Romance* in the HopKins Black Box Theatre, Louisiana State University; public performances took place on November 12–16, 2003. The essay juxtaposes strips of text: passages from Ruth Laurion Bowman's script, quotations from historical research for the script, narratives and syntheses of this research, and reflections on the history of the academic discipline in which the research took place. In the section introduction, above, I discuss in more detail the strategies that inform the essay's unconventional form.

REFERENCES

Allsopp, R. (1999). Performance writing. *Performing arts journal: A journal of performance and art, 21*(1), 76–80.

Bacon, W. A. (1975). The dangerous shores: From elocution to interpretation. In R. Haas & D. A. Williams (Eds.), *The study of oral interpretation: Theory and comment* (pp. 1–9). Indianapolis, IN: Bobbs-Merrill. (Original work published 1960)

Bacon, W. A. (1979). *The art of interpretation* (3rd ed.). New York: Holt, Rinehart and Winston.

Benamou, M., & Caramello, C. (Eds.). (1977). *Performance in postmodern culture.* Milwaukee, WI: Center for Twentieth Century Studies.

Benjamin, W. (1996). One-way street (E. Jephcott, Trans.). In M. Bullock & M. W. Jennings (Eds.), *Walter Benjamin: Selected writings, Vol. 1, 1913–1926* (pp. 444–488). Cambridge, MA: Belknap-Harvard University Press. (Original work published 1928)

Binet, A., & Féré, C. (1901). *Animal magnetism.* New York: Appleston.

Bowman, M. S. (1995). "Novelizing" the stage: Chamber theatre after Breen and Bakhtin. *Text and Performance Quarterly, 15*, 1–23.

Bowman, M. S. (1996). Performing literature in an age of textuality. *Communication Education, 45*, 97–101.

Bowman, M. S., & Bowman, R. L. (2002). Performing the mystory: A textshop in autoperformance. In N. Stucky & C. Wimmer (Eds.), *Teaching performance studies* (pp. 161–174). Carbondale: Southern Illinois University Press.

Bowman, M. S., & Kistenberg, C. J. (1992). "Textual power" and the subject of oral interpretation: An alternate approach to performing literature. *Communication Education, 41*, 287–299.

Bowman, R. L. (Adapter & Director). (2003). Nathaniel Hawthorne's *The Blithedale Romance* [performance script]. Baton Rouge: Louisiana State University.

Brandon, R. (1983). *The spiritualists: The passion for the occult in the nineteenth and twentieth centuries.* London: Weidenfeld and Nicolson.

Brisbane, A. (1840). *The social destiny of man; or association and reorganization of industry.* Philadelphia: Stollmeyer.

Buranelli, V. (1975). *The wizard from Vienna: Franz Anton Mesmer.* New York: Coward, McCann, and Geoghegan.

Coale, S. C. (1998). *Mesmerism and Hawthorne: Mediums of American romance.* Tuscaloosa: University of Alabama Press.

Collyer, R. H. (1838). *Lights and shadows of American life.* Boston: Brainard.

Conquergood, D. (1985). Performing as a moral act: Ethical dimensions of the ethnography of performance. *Literature in Performance, 5*(1), 1–13.

Conquergood, D. (1991). Rethinking ethnography: Toward a critical cultural politics. *Communication Monographs, 58*, 179–194.

Conquergood, D. (1995). Caravans and carnivals. *The Drama Review, 39*(4), 137–141.

Darnton, R. (1968). *Mesmerism and the end of the enlightenment in France.* Cambridge, MA: Harvard University Press.

de Certeau, M. (1984). *The practice of everyday life* (S. Rendall, Trans.). Berkeley: University of California Press. (Original work published 1974)

Delano, S. F. (2004). *Brook farm: The dark side of utopia*. Cambridge, MA: Belknap-Harvard University Press.

Du Potet de Sennevoy, B. (1838). *An introduction to the study of animal magnetism*. London: Churchill.

Edwards, P. (1999). Unstoried: Teaching literature in the age of performance studies. *Theatre Annual, 52*, 1–147.

Ewer, F. C. (1855). *The eventful nights of August 20th and 21st: And how Judge Edmonds was hocused*. New York: Samuel Hueston.

Fuller, R. C. (1982). *Mesmerism and the American cure of souls*. Philadelphia: University of Pennsylvania Press.

Godard, J. L. (1972). *Godard on Godard* (T. Milne, Trans.). New York: Viking Press. (Original work published 1968)

Judson, E. Z. C. (1849). *Mysteries and miseries of New York: A story of real life*. New York: Dick and Fitzgerald.

Hamera, J. (1998). Debts: In memory of Lilla Heston. In S. J. Dailey (Ed.), *The future of performance studies: Visions and revisions* (pp. 272–275). Annandale, VA: National Communication Association.

Hawthorne, N. (1986). *The Blithedale romance*. New York: Penguin Classics. (Original work published 1852)

Henderson, B. (1998). Studies in the history. In S. J. Dailey (Ed.), *The future of performance studies: Visions and revisions* (pp. 114–117). Annandale, VA: National Communication Association.

Kaplan, F. (1975). *Dickens and mesmerism: The hidden springs of fiction*. Princeton, NJ: Princeton University Press.

Kessler-Harris, A. (1982). *Out to work: A history of wage-earning women in the United States*. England: Oxford University Press.

Kolodny, A. (1986). Introduction. In N. Hawthorne, *The Blithedale romance* (pp. vii–xxx). New York: Penguin Classics.

Mackay, C. (1869). *Memoirs of extraordinary popular delusions and the madness of crowds*. London: Routledge.

Marks, R. W. (1947). *The story of hypnotism*. New York: Prentice-Hall.

McKenzie, J. (2001). *Perform or else: From discipline to performance*. New York: Routledge.

Mesmer, F. A. (1958). *Maxims on animal magnetism* (J. Eden, Trans.). Mt. Vernon, NY: Eden Press. (Original work published 1785)

Miller, J. (1995). Going unconscious. In R. B. Silvers (Ed.), *Hidden histories of science* (pp. 5–6). New York: New York Review of Books.

Ong, W. J. (1982). *Orality and literacy: The technologizing of the word*. London: Methuen.

Phelan, P. (1992). *Unmarked: The politics of performance*. New York: Routledge.

Poe, E. A. (1928). *The philosophy of animal magnetism*. Philadelphia: Patterson & White. (Original work published 1837)

Pollock, D. (1998). Performing writing. In P. Phelan & J. Lane (Eds.), *The ends of performance* (pp. 73–103). New York: New York University Press.

Ray, R. B. (1995). *The avant-garde finds Andy Hardy*. Cambridge, MA: Harvard University Press.

Ray, R. B. (2001). *How a film theory got lost, and other mysteries in cultural studies*. Bloomington: Indiana University Press.

Reader's Digest complete guide to sewing. (1976). Pleasantville, NY: The Reader's Digest Association.

Report of the experiments on animal magnetism made by a committee of the medical section of the French Royal Academy of Sciences (J. C. Colquhoun Esq., Trans.). (1833). London: Whittaker.

Reynolds, D. S. (1989). *Beneath the American renaissance: The subversive imagination in the age of Emerson and Melville*. Cambridge, MA: Harvard University Press.

Schechner, R. (1985). *Between theatre and anthropology*. Philadelphia: University of Pennsylvania Press.

Schechner, R. (1988). Performance studies: The broad spectrum approach. *The Drama Review, 32*(3), 4–6.

Schechner, R. (1992). A new paradigm for theater in the academy. *The Drama Review, 36*(4), 7–10.

Ulmer, G. (1989). *Teletheory: Grammatology in the age of video*. New York: Routledge.

Ulmer, G. L. (1995). *Heuretics: The logic of invention*. Baltimore, MD: Johns Hopkins University Press.

Ulmer, G. L. (2003). *Internet invention: From literacy to electracy*. New York: Longman-Pearson Education.

Wagstaff, G. F. (1981). *Hypnosis, compliance and belief*. New York: St. Martin's Press.

Webster's new collegiate dictionary. (1975). Springfield, MA: G. & C. Merriam.

13

Staging Paradox

The Local Art of Adaptation

PAUL EDWARDS

Over the past half-century, Chicago's diverse theatrical scene has provided a uniquely receptive setting for the work of directors who stage original adaptations of narrative texts, or develop extreme "rewrightings" (Dessen, 2002) of conventional dramas. Even the Joseph Jefferson Awards and Citations—Chicago's honors for Equity and non-Equity productions—have recognized the category "New Adaptation" alongside the older classification "New Work."[1] Contributing to Chicago's reputation as a center of theatrical "adaptation" is the tradition of staging "chamber theatre," begun in 1947 by Robert S. Breen in Northwestern's Interpretation (now Performance Studies) Department. Although no one working professionally in Chicago continues to stage chamber theatre before public audiences, many have learned techniques and approaches—styles of creatively addressing a source text—from contact with Breen and his students.

No artist, group, or community can lay claim to having invented adaptation as an art form. It is hard to imagine any play that has not adapted *something,* some kind of "pre-text" (as I explore this term below). But comments by some of Chicago's most celebrated adapter/directors suggest that the art of adaptation in the local context of a city's theatre scene has reaccentuated (often in very indirect, even accidental ways) important features of Breen's paradoxical experiments.

The first section of this essay, "Method and Margin," establishes the terms for my discussion of a triangulated relationship in an unique academic setting: at Northwestern, a wideranging sense of practice enjoys a complicated relationship not only to theory but to method. Here, practice cannot be discussed apart from its extension into the professional theatre community. I consider the case of the Lookingglass Theatre, which has devoted much of its creative energy over its decade and a half of existence to the development of original works and adaptations of nondramatic literature. The company began when David Schwimmer, prior to his successful television career, brought together a talented group of fellow Northwestern graduates; it has grown with the infusion of other Northwestern-trained artists like the Tony-Award-winning adapter and director Mary Zimmerman. The educational roots of this group lead me to examine the beginning of adaptation coursework at Northwestern: the next section, "Chamber Theatre," explores the career of Breen and the staging form he invented. In the following section, "Adapting Adaptation," I employ interview materials to discuss the accomplishments of three students who subsequently became teachers of adaptation in Northwestern's Department of Performance Studies: Zimmerman, Njoki McElroy, and Frank Galati.[2] The essay concludes with reflections on how the theory and practice of stage adaptation have changed at Northwestern, and in Chicago theatre, since Breen first experimented with staging short stories in the late 1940s.

METHOD AND MARGIN

Within the context of interpretation, the teaching of theatrical forms adopted several names in the second half of the twentieth century. "Interpreters theatre" and "group performance" were common labels for a pedagogical interest that embraced forms like "readers theatre" and "chamber theatre." The more familiar form, readers theatre, had deep roots in the verse-speaking choirs of oratorical culture (see Kleinau & McHughes, 1980, pp. 45–67; Williams, 1975) as well as the theatrical tradition of the staged reading. Coger and White (1967) somewhat fancifully trace readers theatre to the beginnings of western drama in ancient Greece, and annotate a list of well-known productions by professional actors in the postwar era that employed the form's techniques and conventions (pp. 10–15). But attempts like this to locate readers theatre in some kind of theatrical mainstream fail to convince. In its heyday, readers theatre was a teaching technique. It enjoyed its greatest

public visibility in campus playhouses, civic and church assemblies, and school competitions. Performers typically held manuscripts, faced the audience, and sat on chairs or high stools (hence the scatalogical epithet "stool theatre" employed by theatre professors who took a dismissive view of oral interpretation). Characters addressed each other in the convention of "offstage focus": actors seated side-by-side would see each other "out front," thereby diminishing the audience's expectation that the actors would fully embody the physical business suggested by the text (see Coger & White, 1967, pp. 46–58; Maclay, 1971, pp. 16–44). The aesthetic effect was that of an incomplete stage picture: a suggestive stimulus to the audience's imagination, rather like an elocutionary platform reading with the added variety of many actors' voices.

The goal of such performance was to deemphasize physical spectacle and direct the attention of actors and audience toward the experience of the text. During the period of interpretation's greatest influence, the teaching of readers theatre fully aligned itself with the desire to "cause" performers and viewers alike "to experience literature": readers theatre "differs from a conventional play in that it demands stricter attention to the aural elements of the literature" and "requires" its audience to "generate its own visualization of the scenery, the costumes, the action, the make-up, and the physical appearance of the characters" (Coger & White, 1967, pp. 8–9). As articulated by Robert Breen and elaborated by his student Joanna Hawkins Maclay (1971), the goal of readers theatre is to "feature the text" rather than the spectacle of actors' bodies in motion or the machinery of theatrical illusion (pp. 3–6).[3] Even in Breen's own writing about chamber theatre (the more fully theatricalized form that I discuss below) the "proposition" to which student performers should dedicate themselves is "the service of literature" (1978, p. 6).

The characterization of illusionistic spectacle as somehow antagonistic to the *appreciation*

and *study* of literature (even dramatic literature) is a backward-reaching view: it relates
such staging forms to the idealistic theories of
suggestion advanced in the late-nineteenth
century by "expression" teachers like S. S.
Curry (1891, 1896). The virtue of "suggested"
scenery and costuming recurs in Maclay's
advice to designers (1971, pp. 46–59). The
performing body should be similarly suggestive: actors' gestures and vocal inflections are
significant merely as continuations and ampli-
fications of literary figures and images (1971,
p. 68). In language reminiscent of Curry nearly
a century earlier, Maclay expresses the view
that the "presentational" simplicity of readers
theatre "tends to universalize" for an audience
the experience of a literary text, whereas the
"representational manner" of conventional
theatre "tends to particularize the experience"
in reductive ways (1971, p. 20). In the textbook literature that appeared from the 1960s
to the 1980s, the methodizers of interpreters
theatre often contrast the representational aesthetic of a putative "conventional" theatre
with a presentational aesthetic that more fully
engages audience members' imaginations.
Kleinau and McHughes (1980) go so far as to
associate representational forms with "pictorial space," and presentational forms (those
friendly to the projection of literary texts) with
"acoustic space" (pp. 5–14).[4]

If I tend to speak of readers theatre and
chamber theatre in the past tense, I do so
because both forms failed to find a receptive
setting in either academic or professional theatre. Their narrowed focus on embodied
performance in "the service of literature" con-
signed them to the same fate as the art of interpretation itself. The photographs of student
productions that illustrate some of the textbooks—guides to script-in-hand, presentational staging, in a bare-stage world of "stools,
benches, and ladders" (Maclay, 1971, p. 53)—
seem as quaint, and almost as distant in time,
as the ghostly reproductions of group "poses
plastiques" and "tableaux mouvants" that

filled the pages of *Werner's Magazine* during
the Delsarte craze of the late-nineteenth century. This is not to suggest that the textbook
literature is theoretically unsophisticated.
Theatres for Literature by Kleinau and
McHughes (1980) begins, for example, with a
functional distinction between "work," words
on the page, and "text," the constant remaking of the "work" by performers (p. 2), that is
largely consistent with the famous distinction
by Roland Barthes (1971/1986). Maclay's
Readers Theatre (1971) sets off from a similar
prying-open of "text" beyond the concept of
printed "words" (p. 4). Even the conservative *Handbook* by Coger and White (1967)
demonstrates a nuanced understanding of
modernist theatre after Brecht and Piscator.
Breen's belatedly published *Chamber Theatre*
(1978), written in the 1960s, is remarkable for
its interdisciplinary grasp of critical thought,
from perception studies to film theory. Maclay
(1971) is no less adept than her mentor Breen
at perceiving theatrical space and time through
the lenses of aestheticians and phenomenolo-
gists, from Rudoph Arnheim to Maurice
Merleau-Ponty.

"The choreographer who reads Merleau-
Ponty," however—as Shannon Jackson (2004)
reminds us—"is not a 'professional' to the
theory professor" (p. 28). While teachers of
interpreters theatre borrowed elaborately from
theory and criticism, they failed to gain respect
for the activity of stage performance itself
as an embodied form of theoretical or critical
inquiry. They failed to gain respect as well
from a different kind of professional across the
campus of many colleges and universities: the
theatre professor who trained students for
stage, television, and film careers, and mocked
the theatrical pretensions of "stool theatre."
Jackson is correct, it seems to me, in her
assessment of marginalization by literary theorists of those who "professed performance."
Not only did dramatic literature often find
itself "outside the literary canon" in this or
that scholar's estimation, but the teaching of

interpretation never succeeded in becoming more than a "marginal cultural expression": despite its alignment "with the dominant" and "canonical" in literary studies, it struggled unsuccessfully to find acceptance by literary "professionals" (2004, p. 24). In Jackson's narrative, which critiques the opposition of theory and practice in institutional settings across the twentieth century, theatre and interpretation find themselves equally outside the embrace of theory. Yet I would complicate this narrative by locating interpretation pedagogy outside the embrace of theatrical practice. Bound to both literary theory and theatrical practice, the group performance of literature found itself marginalized by both. The double bind of high-modernist interpretation studies produced a double rejection. If it is true that every academician functions "as the amateur to someone else's professional" (Jackson, 2004, p. 28) then the pedagogy of interpreters theatre was stigmatized as doubly amateurish.

Yet the twentieth century narrative is more complicated still, at least as it developed at Northwestern University. My interest in departmental and faculty "genealogy" at Northwestern (see Edwards, 1999) has led me to view with great suspicion any notion of inevitability or grand design in the growth of academic institutions. The grand design of Robert McLean Cumnock in the late-nineteenth century was to establish on Northwestern's young Evanston campus a course of study, and later a school, of elocution and oratory. While the twenty-first century School of Communication continues to celebrate Cumnock as its founder, almost nothing in that school looks back to Cumnock's design or pedagogical mission. That the school should have theatre professionals on the faculties of *two* departments—Theatre and Performance Studies—is the product of accident and unpredictable growth. No one, a century ago, would have planned such seeming redundancy—just as no one would have planned the seeming

redundancy of drama coursework in multiple locations across campus, both inside and outside the school.

The string of accidents that brought two highly visible, award-winning theatre professionals to a department of performance studies, rather than theatre, is the focus of the section "Adapting Adaptation" below. My focus here is the complicated relationship of those two professional artists to the interpreters theatre pedagogy that figured so significantly in the history of the department in which they now teach. Both Frank Galati and Mary Zimmerman studied with Robert Breen. Both teach courses descended from the readers theatre and chamber theatre courses developed by Breen, and both promote the value of textual study in the training of theatre artists. Yet in their professional work, as adapter/directors, both move far beyond "the service of literature" or "featuring the text." Creative artistry is not the product of pedagogical method, and cannot be constrained by it. Galati's adaptation of *The Grapes of Wrath* (1991) and Zimmerman's adaptation of *Metamorphoses* (2002) are not the products of studying group performance textbooks, however strong the influence of a messy, unmethodical tradition that produced such textbooks. And what they teach in a present-day "presentational aesthetics" classroom is creative artistry, not textbook method. Their distance from textbook method is complicated by their movement through, and beyond, a certain tradition—one that was never embraced at Northwestern, in the increasingly professional postwar decades, by either the critical theorist in English or the practicing artist in theatre.

Groups of talented students similarly have moved through and beyond this tradition, on their way to forming theatre companies that regularly stage original adaptations. Founders of such critically acclaimed companies as Arden in Philadelphia, and Lookingglass, Redmoon, Lifeline, and About Face in Chicago, took coursework in the Theatre and

Performance Studies Departments after Galati had joined the faculty, and during the years in which Zimmerman made the transition from student to professor.[5] Lookingglass presents a unique success story. In June 2003, the 15-year-old company opened an eight-million-dollar theatre in a Chicago landmark, the Water Tower Water Works building on Michigan Avenue. Formerly "a proud member of the itinerant theatre community, renting space where it could" (Houlihan, 2003), Lookingglass now invites comparisons to the venerable Goodman Theatre and more recent arrivals such as Steppenwolf and the Chicago Shakespeare Theatre—landed gentry in Chicago's theatre and entertainment districts. To launch the new space, founding members David Schwimmer and Joy Gregory adapted *Race*, the oral history of "the American obsession" by Chicagoan Studs Terkel (1992). The choice acknowledges several Lookingglass trademarks: the staging of original adaptations, the centrality of storytelling in theatrical forms, the potential of live theatre for activism and advocacy, and the company's identification with and commitment to a specific community.[6]

As Northwestern students drawn to the vision and, as they call it, "chutzpah" of Schwimmer, the founders staged avant-garde "classics" (the term seems apt) like the Andre Gregory-Manhattan Project *Alice in Wonderland* (Gregory, 1972, 1973) and new plays like Steven Berkoff's *West* (1985). Schwimmer and company, producing their work in student groups outside the Theatre Department, featured what company members described to me in 1994 as "a poor theatre aesthetic," in which "the body was *everything*." This approach had almost no place in orthodox Theatre Department coursework at the time. The company officially launched itself in 1988 with its own improvisational adaptation of Lewis Carroll's *Through the Looking-Glass:* "very physical and very raw," remembers founding member Larry Distasi, "and very much driven

by us in the moment of performing it." What distinguished the early Lookingglass work, as I remember it, from the example of Grotowski (which several company members invoke) was the sheer audience-directed exuberance, the circus acrobat's joy of being "in the moment of performing" before others.

Lookingglass members describe the company's founding as oppositional to, but not dismissive of, aspects of institutional structure and practice. Their collective origin myth exemplifies Derrida's "dangerous" supplement (1967/1976, p. 145) or, differently, the quality of "outsideness"—the "surplus of vision" that only an outside presence can supply, as a condition for "creative understanding" and true dialogue—that Bakhtin explored in various ways throughout his career (Bakhtin, 1986, pp. 1–7; Morson & Emerson, 1990, pp. 52–56). But the conceptual language I find most helpful, in tracking their story, is a spinning of the term *paradox* that I remember first encountering in my study with translator Richard Howard of certain Barthes texts (see 1971/1986, p. 58). It is conventional to contrast the terms *orthodox* (straight or right in opinion, doctrine, or *doxa*) and *heterodox* (of another opinion, not in accordance with *doxa*). An early meaning of paradox ("beyond" *doxa*) reflects the sense of heterodox expression—a "statement or tenet contrary to received opinion or belief"—but with the stronger suggestion of something "marvelous or incredible," "absurd or fantastic" (*OED*, 2005). If I contrast orthodox and paradoxical positions, this relates to the "marvelous" and "fantastic" ways in which theatre innovators often position themselves against or beyond the *doxa* of an academic discipline or what Brecht called the "apparatus" of a theatre community (Brecht, 1964, pp. 34–35).

Early in the professional life of Lookingglass, Mary Zimmerman arrived from a different corner of the Northwestern campus: the graduate program in Performance Studies. Her first collaboration with Lookingglass was the acclaimed 1990 production of *The Odyssey*. Zimmerman introduced a number of paradoxes into an already oppositional framework. Influenced by Zimmerman's work with performance art, the company shifted from a body-is-everything aesthetic to a focus on visual spectacle. With Zimmerman, Cox recalls, began the company's search for "the stunningly beautiful image" in show after show.[7]

Another innovation was Zimmerman's interest in the stage adaptation of fiction, which she had studied for over a decade at Northwestern with teachers like Galati. Zimmerman recalls that with Galati's Tony-Award-winning 1989 production of his script for Steinbeck's *The Grapes of Wrath* (Galati, 1991), adaptation "was just sort of in the air, I think," not just at Northwestern but in Chicago generally—and perhaps nationally, since the Broadway decade that ended with *The Grapes of Wrath* had begun with the tour of the Royal Shakespeare Company *Nicholas Nickleby* (Edgar, 1982/1992). Although the Lookingglass founders had participated in the culture of adaptation as Northwestern students—"they had their mind open to that," observes Zimmerman, through "the experience of having taking courses" with Performance Studies faculty—it was Zimmerman's arrival at Lookingglass that moved the company decisively toward a trademark interest in producing original adaptations. The production history on the company's current website features eighteen adaptations of narrative fiction and nonfiction, including six by Zimmerman (Homer's *Odyssey, The Arabian Nights,* the Sade fantasia *S/M,* the Grimm-inspired *Secret in the Wings, Metamorphoses,* and *Eleven Rooms of Proust*), two by Schwimmer (*Race* and Sinclair's *The Jungle*), and adaptations by other company members of narrative fiction by Hawthorne, Bulgakov, Dostoyevsky, Calvino, and Dickens. When augmented by about a dozen Lookingglass "original plays," the list of "world premieres" greatly overshadows the

handful of established playscripts produced by the company. Lookingglass "has *no interest* in the play that was hot in New York now," Zimmerman tells me in the late fall of 2003. "Even Steppenwolf and the Goodman do the play that won the Pulitzer. . . . They vie for who's gonna get to do the already done play that everyone already likes. I mean, Lookingglass is *phe-nom-e-nal-ly*" (she draw this out in the manner of Dickens's Mr. Tite Barnacle, giving it the air of a word of about five-and-twenty syllables) "risk-taking, because almost everything it does is new work." Zimmerman praises the company for a courage she helped to inspire.

The "adaptation" trademark had been firmly impressed upon Lookingglass by the critical wing of the Chicago apparatus (see for example Christiansen, 1990) when I interviewed ensemble members in 1994. Why has the group focused so heavily upon adaptations of narrative works? The question provokes a torrent of responses from the table. "There are *less rules,*" says Hara, with a book than with a play. One has the freedom to "*create* theatre," instead of merely "*doing* theatre." Cox describes the sheer thrill, the sense of challenge, in seeking a theatrical way to make an audience see the visions he saw while reading a novel. Staging a book "immediately asks the question, *How?* And the answer to that question is . . . " Hara interrupts him: "is what we," as a company, "are about, almost." Distasi adds, with a laugh, "And we got away with it." Laura Eason insists, moreover, that adaptation "allows us to *write,* too." It has become important for the company "to feel like we're creating not just physically with our bodies, but also that we're *contributing* to the text." Company adaptations are "loose" enough to accommodate expressive and rhetorical functions beyond "just *choosing*" and arranging "words from the pre-existing text."

This impassioned response leads me to ask a potentially tedious question. If not to the *letter* of the text, then to *what*, exactly, does the Lookingglass adapter remain faithful? It is not the author's intent, they agree. "The idea is to tell the same story," Hara suggests, "the way it *affected* you. I mean, the things about the novel or the story that resonate, that are still, like, banging off the walls of your ribcage" when you finish reading a novel or compelling work of nonfiction. "We want to be faithful to *that*." In translating a book to "the medium of theatre" one cannot "choose all the scenes. But we want to tell the same story."

The director/adapter/auteur as *storyteller:* this draws me back to the group's description of how it chooses projects. The ensemble listens annually to director proposals. Persuasiveness in this forum relates to passion. "Somebody who's on fire comes in with a project and puts it on the table," says Cox, "and then the rest of us go, Yeah, that's what I want, that *fire* is what I want. And then we vote and decide." Hara agrees: "Without the passion of the director for the project, there's nothing. . . . Why do you want to tell this story? Why now?" Zimmerman, nearly a decade later, calls Lookingglass "a company of directors," not of actors. The number of ensemble members, by her estimate, who have not yet "directed a play" constitutes a distinct, and shrinking, minority.

As I listen to this, I recall what I first discovered when studying with Robert Breen: that adaptation is not a timeless theory or set of techniques, but a succession of diverse embodied practices, driven by desire and even desperate neediness. The book I have just read—this book whose scenes have banged off the walls of my ribcage—*must* be told again to my world, in my age. I would tell the story myself, but my lone body is not adequate to supply the visions that the book has projected on my mindscreen. I must extend myself through ten, twelve, fifteen bodies. This, I confess, is my fantasy of "Shakespeare reading" (Froissart, Holinshed, Montaigne, Plutarch,

Cinthio, Lyly, Plautus, Seneca's *Thyestes,* Ovid's *Metamorphoses,* Lodge's *Rosalynde,* Harsnett's *Declaration of Egregious Popish Impostures,* plus whatever the Renaissance equivalent was for the magazine lying open in the dentist's office). The Shakespeare we have begun to reimagine, as a "highly collaborative" artist rather than early modernism's solitary genius (Masten, 1997, p. 4), might have been at home in a setting like Lookingglass: as a "good thief" bringing his passion for stories to the table with project after project, and unrestrained by a pedantic fidelity to how the story was told before. The "true apprentice knows how to steal," Jerzy Grotowski insisted, to *continue* someone else's earlier discoveries and "*not just repeat*" them (quoted in Richards, 1995, pp. 3, 105).

The good thieves who inaugurated the eight-million-dollar complex on Michigan Avenue were Schwimmer, who wanted to do a production of *Race,* according to Zimmerman, "basically since the day the book came out"; and Zimmerman herself, who revised *Secret in the Wings* for the new space's second production. The two productions suggest to her the *extremes* of the company's director/adapter/auteur sensibility. *Race,* based on personal narratives collected by Terkel, is "almost a hundred percent . . . a *real* person naturalistically speaking to the audience. . . . It's incredibly specific and direct." Whereas "*Secret in the Wings* is like, What the hell is going on? . . . It never, *ever* speaks what it is always saying." The content is "never in the language," but rather in the "structure, and gesture, and music, and the staging." What unites the two as Lookingglass productions, Zimmerman suggests, is the fact that they are both "very much ensemble pieces." But the ensemble members I interviewed identify a different connection: each was proposed by a *storyteller, on fire* with a project, who made the entire ensemble feel, *That fire* is what I want. (Why do you want to tell this story? Why now?)

A genealogical task I face is the tracing of a connection, from Breen through Galati to Zimmerman and the Lookingglass founders. The most readily available statements by Breen, the interpretation teacher and textbook author, admonish students to "feature" and "serve" the letter of the text. By the time the practice of adaptation reaches Lookingglass, the service of literature has given way to the service of storytelling, in one's own time and place, and the remaking of text. To pursue Jackson's amateur/professional distinction: does such a shift constitute a rejection of method by professional practice, located (in figures like Zimmerman and Galati) both inside and outside the university? Or does the professional adaptation of "adaptation" itself constitute a fresh telling of Breen's story, in new language?

CHAMBER THEATRE

"He was the *artist* of the department when I was there," remembers Katharine Loesch, emerita professor at the University of Illinois at Chicago, who completed her PhD in Interpretation at Northwestern in 1961. "He was *the* artist." Frank Galati, who began undergraduate study at Northwestern just as Loesch was departing, has similar memories of Robert Breen. Actors in Breen's campus productions and students in his staging classes were

> learning from the novel, and learning from narrative art, what the *stage* was—not just what the *novel* was, but what the *stage* is—when the assignment is to *let that story live,* and to give voice to every syllable of its musical score. . . . I think we found out more about how plastic and pliable and psychological *physical space* is, by virtue of Breen's assignments, than we did by trying to understand that Shakespeare's stage had just as much *plasticity,* and was just as much a psychological space.

What Galati calls the "plasticity" of the Shakespearean stage was very much a

twentieth century rediscovery, arising from such innovations as William Poel's revolt against the grand manner of Victorian production and E. K. Chambers's pioneering research on *The Elizabethan Stage* (1923). Peter Brook speaks of having once been "gripped by living theatre" when a postwar Hamburg company performed *Crime and Punishment* in the only available space, a garret; the sheer freedom of "the convention of a novel" in an empty space leads Brook to celebrate our fresh awareness

> that the absence of scenery in the Elizabethan theatre was one of its greatest freedoms. . . . The Elizabethan stage. . . just a place with some doors . . . enabled the dramatist effortlessly to whip the spectator through an unlimited succession of illusions. . . . So it is that in the second half of the twentieth century . . . we are faced with the infuriating fact that Shakespeare is still our model. (1968, pp. 72–73, 78, 87)

But Galati's point is that two decades of Breen students—encountering Brook's comments in 1968 or racing to see his brilliant demonstration of "plasticity" in the celebrated Royal Shakespeare Company *Midsummer Night's Dream* that toured Chicago in 1971—already had grasped a powerful working sense of all this. The professional achievements of Galati and Zimmerman, or in a more modest way the campus stagings of narrative by teachers like Njoki McElroy and myself, "have all been, in these very profound, almost mystical ways, informed by" Breen's achievements, Galati insists, and his "marvelous way of being in the world."

What I have called a culture of adaptation at Northwestern—Zimmerman's sense of adaptation being "in the air" when the Lookingglass founders passed through—can be traced to Breen, but perhaps through lines of influence more "mystical" (as Galati suggests) than direct. Zimmerman remembers taking only one course from Breen, called out of retirement, and gaining little from the "eccentric and sort of quiet" emeritus professor. His very presence at a midwestern university—inventing his "art form," as his obituaries styled it, in his theatrical laboratory—remains a puzzle. Zimmerman jokes with me, "Where *did* Bob Breen come from?"

When Breen (b. 1909) first studied theatre at Northwestern, the program was one of six areas of instruction in the School of Speech that Dean Ralph Dennis had reshaped from the old "elocution and oratory" curriculum. The others were public speaking and persuasion, interpretation (the "fine art"), voice and interpretation (personal studio instruction in platform skills), correction (the forerunner of the present-day Communication Sciences and Disorders Department), and physical education; a degree program in radio would not arrive for another decade. (The lines were more porous than they would be in the "departmental" decades after World War II: the local legend Alvina Krause, hired after the arrival of C. C. Cunningham as a voice and interpretation instructor, would transform herself over a long career from a teacher of the oral interpretation of drama to the school's best-known teacher of acting.) After graduating in 1933, Breen stayed on as an "assistant in dramatic production" while pursuing his MA degree (awarded in 1937); he also taught at another Illinois college before heading to New York in 1938. Breen enjoyed some success as a professional actor and dancer, before resuming a teaching career and then joining the infantry in the war. He received the Purple Heart for a wound that ended his dancing career (although dance would continue to shape his sense, as a director, of dynamic stage movement) and seems to have taken yet more steam out of his professional ambitions. (There were other Robert Breens in show business: he is not to be confused with the Broadway director who helped reshape ANTA in the late 1940s, or with Hollywood child star Bobby Breen.)

After his return to Chicago in the postwar years, Breen's involvement with the entertainment industry was sporadic. Galati, who is seven years older than I, remembers seeing Breen during his years as a popular panelist on the DuMont Network quiz show *Down You Go,* before it moved to New York: Northwestern's star faculty member Bergen Evans was the "pompous" moderator, who "would say, 'Now, Professor Breen, um, in the Oxford English Dictionary, the word . . . ,'" in response to which Breen performed "the fuddy-duddy professor, who was very funny and would make jokes." Galati describes as well the wry persona that Breen often brought into the classroom: the flip side of his other persona, a virtuoso actor-demonstrator who remains my model for what I understand to be the quotational style of Brecht's "Street Scene" (1964, pp. 121–129). Breen's other television outing, an NBC summer replacement in 1951 called *Short Story Playhouse,* began to good reviews but faded after two months. Breen blamed the producers for abandoning literature of "quality"—Tolstoy and Sinclair Lewis—in favor of "popular magazine stories" with no narrative interest, which "were frankly junk." After the mid-1950s, Breen restricted his creative life largely to another quarter-century of work with his brainchild chamber theatre on Northwestern's campus, and to occasional roles in campus plays directed by his colleagues.

So what did this brainchild look like?[8] Call to mind the image of someone performing a passage of narrative fiction. It does not matter if your image is an old-fashioned platform elocutionist, a parent reading a story to a child, Simon Callow or Anton Lesser imitating a Dickens public reading, Charlton Heston performing the Bible on cable television, or Toni Morrison reading a chapter from one of her novels to a class at Princeton. To stay with the last example: Mavis sits in a strange kitchen and begins to make contact with the presence of her two dead children.

Left alone Mavis expected the big kitchen to lose its comfort. It didn't. In fact she had an outer-rim sensation that the kitchen was crowded with children—laughing? singing?—two of whom were Merle and Pearl. Squeezing her eyes shut to dissipate the impression only strengthened it. When she opened her eyes, Connie was there, dragging a thirty-two-quart basket over the floor. "Come on," she said. "Make yourself useful." (Morrison, 1998, p. 41)

The reader performs all the voices, narrator and characters. She projects a kind of unity, that of the social storyteller: the confident image of full speech, emerging from a voice and body that seem to "match," in Wallace Bacon's specialized sense (1972, pp. 34, 133–137), the narrative omniscience.

Harder to imagine, for most readers, would be a chamber theatre scene using the same text, which begins with an act of subject-splitting. This approach does not dramatize the passage, in the manner of either realism (viewed through the conventionally invisible fourth wall) or epic drama. It does something much stranger, which many viewers in the past half-century have found intolerable; "untheatrical" is the dismissive adjective that I have heard most often. Chamber theatre puts onstage a narrator no longer in complete control of the story. The narrator's omniscient reports now seem mere suggestions that the characters must complete. Familiar devices like narrated interior monologue become interior "dialogue." The narrator often describes redundantly, highlighting gestures that characters also "act." And the characters also describe themselves, straying into the space of narrative perspective and third-person language.

NARRATOR:	Left alone Mavis expected the big kitchen to lose its comfort.
MAVIS:	[Aside to NARRATOR.] It didn't.
NARRATOR:	In fact she had an outer-rim sensation that the kitchen was crowded with children

MAVIS:	laughing? singing?
NARRATOR:	two of whom were Merle and Pearl. Squeezing her eyes shut to dissipate the impression
MAVIS:	only strengthened it.
NARRATOR:	When she opened her eyes,
CONNIE:	[Entering; to MAVIS.] Connie was there,
NARRATOR:	[Indicating to MAVIS.] dragging a thirty-two-quart basket over the floor.
CONNIE:	"Come on," she said. "Make yourself useful."

When Breen rejoined the Northwestern faculty after World War II, he began to experiment with this technique in the interpretation classroom. He had many students who would read passages of fiction formally similar to Morrison's first paragraph, and detect only a long block of narrative report, spoken by a single voice. To encourage them to hear multiple voices encoded in passages of free indirect discourse, or to respond to literary language as gesture and symbolic action, Breen would have students script and stage chamber theatre.[9] He would regard the script I offer above as only one possibility for bringing out the dialogues inhabiting language—even language that formally resembles monologue. Galati agrees that Breen as a teacher "in his heyday" was far more improvisatory and playful, more committed to the exploration of multiple options, than the rather inflexible persona who narrates his textbook *Chamber Theatre* (1978).

Breen remembers the first experiments with the form taking place "in the spring of 1947, in a little theatre belonging to the French department at Northwestern" (Forrest & Loesch, 1976, p. 3). He credits his student Gerald Freedman, who would go on to a distinguished career on Broadway and at the Great Lakes Theatre Festival, with adapting and directing the first full-length production in 1949.

Another Northwestern arrival in 1947 was Wallace Bacon (b. 1914), the new chair of the Interpretation Department where Breen was an instructor. With the phasing-out of the voice and interpretation staff and the threatened departure of a disgruntled C. C. Cunningham, School of Speech Dean James McBurney faced a tough choice: either eliminate the etiolated interpretation coursework (which had the closest ties to the school's mission at its founding) or find a leader who could elevate its academic respectability. Bacon, a PhD in English from the University of Michigan, inherited a program that had hovered uneasily during Cunningham's stewardship between a genteel "fine arts" emphasis and an undergraduate "teaching of skills" curriculum. Bacon succeeded in creating, among other things, a credible graduate program: where Cunningham had directed only two doctoral dissertations, he would direct over fifty, and his colleagues twenty more, before his retirement in 1979. The second dissertation he directed was Breen's (1950).

Here began a friendship that would result in a coauthored book, *Literature as Experience* (Bacon & Breen, 1959), and a cooperative but carefully negotiated pedagogical philosophy. Bacon's respectful, even devotional approach to textual study through performed "communion" (see Edwards, 1999, pp. 85–93) provided the department's *doxa* for three decades, and everyone on the teaching staff made orthodox pronouncements. "Chamber theatre is a *technique*, not an art," we read at the beginning of Breen's textbook on staging. There follows the language about "the service of literature": chamber theatre "makes manifest for an audience the structure, the theme, and the tone of literature" (1978, p. 6). The book wraps up with a long "list of 'don't's'":

> *don't* rewrite unless you absolutely have to . . . ; *don't* cut the descriptions just because they are descriptions; *don't* change the indirect discourse to direct discourse; *don't* alter the diction in the interest of

"clarifying," "modernizing," or "dramatizing" the style.

Breen concludes this "admonition" with the image of adapters "drunk with power," beginning "to think of the work of fiction as theirs rather than the author's" (1978, pp. 85–86). At odds with such pronouncements was Breen's own practice. Over the years, I reviewed with Breen a number of his scripts—ingenious two-hour reductions of thousand-page novels—and sometimes asked him how his method squared with the advice in his book. My favorite answer (in response to a question about his script for *Anna Karenina*): "Well, the first cut is the hardest. After that it gets easy." In fairness, the textbook told student adapters that if "their conscience will accept the aesthetic responsibility for the results," they "are free to do what they please" (1978, p. 86). Yet to our last conversations, he defended his position about the self-effacement of the performing body "in the service of literature."

Breen's artistic practice, in my view, created a long-running disturbance within the mission of Bacon's academic department. Despite his admonitions about "service" and textual fidelity, Breen handed the audience a paradox every time he adapted a book, or invited his students to stage a short story. Narratologist Seymour Chatman speaks of the "anthropomorphic trap" of imagining the narrating agencies in works of fiction (not merely their "implied authors" but even their narrative voices) as representations of human characters: he complains about critics who view *any* fictional narrator as a talking body, having "literally . . . crossed the line from discourse to story . . . to go strolling with the characters" (1990, pp. 88, 120). Yet the practice of chamber theatre on Breen's terms requires falling into such a trap every time out. Revisit my Toni Morrison example: when an omniscient, undramatized narrator, in the time-and-space "scene" of discourse, *literally* steps into the "scene" of story to mirror and prompt the thoughts of the character Mavis, this defies our commonsense experience of reading printed fictions. Mavis was *then,* the storyteller (or storytell*ing,* as Chatman might insist) is *now.* With a chamber theatre scene, however, two time-space relationships contaminate one another, in a weave or dance of actors' bodies. "Well, you ought to encourage the narrator to enter into the dialogue with the characters," Breen explains to interviewers in 1975, "even though it seems that the narrator is a disembodied figure who can not be seen by the characters" (Forrest & Loesch, 1976, p. 5).

However illogical this stage image might seem, there are real-life models for it. The image is familiar to anyone who has ever sat in an acting class with an engaged teacher. Two students labor to stay "in the moment" as Hamlet and Ophelia, or Elena and Astrov, while this talkative body hovers around their intimate scene and side-coaches. Such scene-work typically takes place before an audience. The acting coach inhabits the audience's time and place—a discourse "scene"—and in fact so do the two actors. But the actors strive to maintain the representation of their characters in another time and place—a "scene" of story—even while the acting coach buzzes instructions, over their shoulders or in their faces, on how to push and tweak their work-in-progress.[10] Far from being recondite or obscure, such an example is commonplace for the acting students in my classes. I introduce these students to the chamber theatre narrator by asking them to think about the paradoxical behavior of their acting teachers.

But Breen was interested in materializing more abstract psychological relationships. A favorite example was the experience of doubling and psychological mirroring at the heart of such dead metaphors as "talking to" oneself or "being beside" oneself. "Why not let the narrator," a nonidentical physical mirror, "stand in the locus of the self who is addressed?" Whether an utterance emerges from the lips of the character or her mirroring

narrator "doesn't really make a great deal of difference as long as we set up a dialogue relationship" within a private moment of self-awareness (Forrest & Loesch, 1976, p. 5). Does so far-fetched an embodiment of metaphor (even dead metaphor) have any verisimilar equivalents? When I interviewed Breen in 1989, we had not spoken for a while. In an attempt to frame my first question, I rehearsed a long list of concerns: the works of theory I had been reading, the staging problems my students had encountered. When my preamble reached fifteen minutes (I was there to tape-record *him,* after all) I caught myself and apologized. "No, no, no, no, no," he reassured me, "it's important for you to be listening to yourself." Breen "in his heyday" was loved and feared for withering his students with a deadpan sarcasm, usually apparent to everyone in the room except the witheree. Had the wearer of this patient face, mirroring my confusions, decided to leave me with one last demonstration? Or was this a demonstration of a different sort—the nonidentical face of the other, the narrator of a larger discourse, who stares back when we talk to ourselves?

The great disturbance to interpretation's orthodoxy was chamber theatre's splitting of the human subject. Elsewhere I have argued that the odd, mirror-filled mise-en-scène of chamber theatre, inspired by Breen's interest in the I/me dialogues of William James, bears striking resemblances to the revision of Freudian *Ichspaltung* that Jacques Lacan elaborated in the 1940s and early 1950s, and mapped out in schematic form in his 1954–55 seminar (see Edwards, 1999, pp. 95–98, 127). But a simpler image will serve. The image of the elocutionary platform reader, which Bacon's interpretation pedagogy updated and even rarified, was drawn and quartered by Breen's technique for staging literature. Solo performance of literature, as it was known, declined in coursework settings as the study of interpretation faded at Northwestern. Far more common today are courses that Breen inspired, featuring adaptation: the transformation of interpretation's literary text into a group performance text. Chamber theatre was the hybrid product, as Bacon (1972, p. 416) called it, of an insistently cross-disciplinary imagination. Bacon (1975) expressed a growing concern about the "widespread interest" in phenomena like chamber theatre that had moved the academic discipline toward "an increased emphasis upon performance" (one of the "dangerous shores" that the student of literature must navigate) and a "loosening of bonds" to the text (p. 223). And for good reason, as it turns out: chamber theatre helped to open the pedagogical space for a range of courses, from narrative stagings to image-based time-art and performance art. As seen in my Morrison script, chamber theatre transformed the storytelling subject from a unified body image into many bodies, exploded into relations of irreducible difference. Without intending to, perhaps, Breen uncorked the bottle. Michael Bowman (1995) aptly describes the genie that escaped: moving beyond Breen, we have begun to explore literary adaptation as a site of resistance, disobedience, performative authorship, "misrule," and reading "against the grain" (pp. 14–17). We have begun to celebrate the irresponsible reading, and we do it in groups, like the Lookingglass Theatre Company.

Bowman's critique suggested my own need for a performance vocabulary different than Breen's, to describe the *impact* of his staging method beyond his own prescriptions. "Bob *hated* to write," Bacon told me on several occasions: he struggled to find the simplest, most flexible terms possible to describe his own staging experiments. But even seemingly transparent terms are slippery. The etymology of "text" leads us to "woven thing," a composition that is closed and finished. After Barthes (1971/1986), of course, we must pause to clarify that we *mean* composition, "weave" of words, and *not* the sense obtained by spinning the term into the opposite of "work" (the finished

product, the book on a shelf). "Text," so reversed, becomes a readerly process, a "methodological field," a *"network"*; "the Text attempts to locate itself very specifically *behind* the limit of the *doxa* . . . ; taking the word literally, we might say that the Text is always *paradoxical*" (pp. 57–61). The literary text of the old Interpretation Department at Northwestern was the book on the shelf—but paradoxically the book that existed only when "matched" by a performer's living act. Breen pushed this paradox even farther.

In recent decades, perhaps no conceptualization of text has come under such assault as the view that a literary text (published or unpublished) precedes, and authorizes, all subsequent performances: every theatrical production, every reading at a lectern, will be an "instance" (version, variation, adaptation) of a text that will remain finished, stable, and in most cases available for future study. "One of the ways both literary and performance studies have misconceived dramatic performance," argues W. B. Worthen (1998), "is by taking it merely as a reiteration of texts, a citation that imports literary or textual authority into performance." What is needed is an expansion of the "sophisticated approach to performance" that considers "the interplay between the scripted drama and the (actual, implied, or imagined) practices of stage performance," as employed for example in "Shakespeare studies—one corner of literary study where performance has had an effect" (pp. 1094, 1098).

While taking exception to Worthen's broad-brush portrait of the antitextual bias in performance studies departments (I happen to teach in one) I appreciate both the need he perceives and some of the examples he employs to illustrate it. My own illustration of the interplay between literary text and dramatic performance is the one I first learned, if rather indirectly, from Breen. Moving beyond Bacon's paradox of text-as-body, Breen created a "performance text" that—however much it claimed to "serve" or repeat a literary work—could not be pushed back into that work once released. Rather than describing the performance as an instance of a literary text, I found it necessary to begin working interactively (if not entirely in reverse): my analytical description must set out from the performance text, which validates the search for "pretexts" including (but not limited to) the identified literary source.

Some readers will bristle at my reaccentuation of "performance text." I now use the term to describe the orchestrated, "woven" ensemble of materials and effects that an audience "reads" (see Edwards, 2003, pp. 43–44). In the case of a scripted play (as opposed to, say, long-form improvisation) these materials and effects *include* the "literary text," the words rehearsed and spoken by actors. But they include as well the distinctive qualities of the actors' voices and bodies, the live or recorded music underscoring the action, the style and condition of the furniture onstage, the paint treatment on the walls of the set—even the smell of the burning incense wafting from the stage to the house, or the taste of the wine or coffee that the actors invite the audience to share. The performance text is not static, but plastic and temporal. Its dialogue with an audience, as Patrice Pavis has suggested, reveals a certain openness and "play in the structure" (1982, pp. 138–139).

Richard Schechner has argued that performances are textual only in the narrowest and most restricted cases. "Simply put, the text is there," he declares in a 1997 interview,

> but performance is not. Or maybe one or two performances are—you take a class to the theatre, you look at a videotape. But these are only instances. . . . In performance studies, the text would be a performance everyone has seen together or a videotape of a particular performance. . . . But what is most interesting to me is to point out the variables possible. . . . (quoted in Harding, 2000, p. 206)

Yet what interests Joseph Roach (1985) in *The Player's Passion* is the history of an actor's art, as influenced by science's shifting conceptions of how the body works: the art consists not of the variables, but of the successful repetitions. Even concepts so seemingly familiar as "spontaneity" have been construed variously: to mean either "free improvisation" or its opposite, "habituated, automatic response." The paradox of acting, for Roach, relates to the interaction of these two meanings: "the actor's spontaneous vitality seems to depend on the extent to which . . . actions and thoughts have been automatized, made second nature." Although "every night the actor's experience . . . is somewhat different," nevertheless "the words, gestures, and movements that the actor embodies are so nearly the same as to be indistinguishable from those of the night before." Ballet dancers provide some of the most striking examples of this (pp. 15–18).

I suppose that my use of performance text most successfully addresses *this* kind of repetition—as well as the more mundane kinds of repetition, such as the set pieces or lighting cues that remain insensibly the same from performance to performance (except when altered by accidents or mistakes). In using the term, I tend to focus on the elements of a production that strike me as repeatable—or, more than this, as *designed* to be repeatable. Christopher Innes (2000) provides a striking example, from the wildly improvisational *Dionysus in 69* that Schechner developed with the Performance Group: "even if the colloquial tone" of the actors' line-delivery "gave a spontaneous effect, all the variants were fixed." So dependent was "the Performance Group on the script" that during one performance, when a female spectator "bonded with the actor playing Pentheus, . . . they left the performance space. The rest of the group were unable to continue, since no alternative had been rehearsed" (p. 71). Or to cast this in my own terms: the interesting variables caused so great a disruption that the performance text (in this case, a text with enormous play in the structure) could not repeat. Schechner's own anecdotes, such as an audience's "kidnapping" of Pentheus, suggest that the show could go on under extraordinary circumstances. But even Schechner (1973) admits that the company "began to resent participation especially when it broke the rhythms of what had been carefully rehearsed." By the time the production closed, "most of the performers had had it with participation" (pp. 40–46).

Innes (2000) traces a specialized use of "pretext" or "pre-text" to Artaud—"any preestablished dramatic 'situations are only a pretext' for performance"—and later Schechner, who would identify this or that literary text as merely "a source of 'scenarios' for improvisation" and appropriation (pp. 70–71). Susan Letzler Cole (1992) employs "pretexts" to describe the hodgepodge of sources, appropriations, and paraphrases in the work of Elizabeth LeCompte.[11] The term has led me to reverse some tenets of my former teachers. The stage—a "memory machine," as Marvin Carlson (2003) has recently suggested—is not merely "the sensory illustration of a text already written, thought, or lived outside the stage" (Derrida, 1966/1978, p. 237). What it remembers and repeats, however imperfectly, are its pretexts. Woven tightly or loosely (with more or less play) these pretexts are as various as identified literary sources, random quotations, recorded songs, and even actors' bodies that bear traces of our memories of them in other roles. Pretexts include as well our memories of social behavior: in my most faithful chamber theatre staging of a short story, the reverentially handled source text shares the stage with the "pretext" memory of an Alvina Krause side-coaching student actors, or myself in conversation with Breen.

Interpretation's stable object of study was the poem on the page. Its enduring paradox, the performance text, is harder to describe as a fixed work or product. "I find that the

greatest satisfaction in Chamber Theatre comes from process rather than product," Breen confessed. "I would rather do a series of scenes in different ways, trying this and trying that, than be concerned with some definitive or final way that must be fixed for the sake of performance" (quoted in Forrest & Loesch, 1976, p. 6). A few years before his retirement, Breen (1975) gave a melancholy assessment of his strange invention's failure to establish an identity in professional theatre, alongside better-known Chicago exports like Paul Sills's "story theatre."[12] Chamber theatre must "settle for its value" in the classroom: the form "may be and often is 'entertaining' and 'theatrically exciting,' but these are fringe benefits. If they are too directly pursued, the critical function of Chamber Theatre may lose its centrality and suffer the fate of most novelties" (p. 207). While the liberating potential of his experiments fired the imaginations of students, and students of students, Breen himself continued to tinker with the *rigorous* practice of his method before small audiences at Northwestern. Galati, in February 2003, remembered the theatrical excitement. He reeled off the names of Breen productions—"*Look* at his *As I Lay Dying, look* at his. . . "—before I interrupted him. "Well, nobody *did,* that was the problem." Galati laughed, a little ruefully. "That doesn't make it less great," he reminded me.

ADAPTING ADAPTATION

How do the careers of Galati, Zimmerman, and Njoki McElroy exemplify a movement beyond Breen and the "service of literature"? It is important to stress movement, because each first wandered into Bacon's Interpretation Department by accident. In the late 1960s, McElroy (b. 1925) was a public school teacher working with emotionally disturbed children. She had founded the Cultural Workshop of North Chicago, which involved teenagers in public performances designed to teach them (as the public schools, she felt, failed to do) about

African American history and culture. Richard Willis of Northwestern's Theatre faculty saw the group, encouraged McElroy to study directing with him, and later urged her to pursue a master's degree—but not in Theatre, McElroy remembers with a laugh. Her ambition to investigate performance as a community-based teaching tool "would be *accepted* better" in Interpretation. "The Theatre Department was *done*," McElroy remembers—in words that recall Augusto Boal's sense of the bourgeois theatre as "the finished theatre," reflecting the desired image of a "complete, finished world" (Boal 1974/1985, p. 142) rather than a world in process. "You came into that structure," she remarks, "you *fit* into that structure." She began her graduate work across the street, therefore, in an academic structure with more play in it. Here she would complete a doctoral dissertation, under Bacon's direction, and in 1970 inaugurate the pathbreaking Performance of Black Literature course that she would teach until 2003.[13]

One of McElroy's curricular innovations was an annual group performance, staged by her students in free-admission open classroom settings. Initially she used preexisting plays. But her self-styled "adventurous" work with teachers (later colleagues) Breen and Leland Roloff—experimenting with "new media" and avant-garde performance—inspired her to stage adaptations and original material.[14] McElroy would freely adapt texts of fiction and nonfiction—and then hand a script to groups in class, studying the source texts, with the invitation to shape and adapt the script even further. One goal was a lesson in empowerment: students who typically "didn't have authority in *any* situation" became directors, writers, and designers of a public event. During her last 15 years with the course, scripts included career retrospectives of major African American artists (Josephine Baker, Langston Hughes, Gwendolyn Brooks) and portraits of literary and cultural movements like the Harlem Renaissance.

As McElroy describes her desire to make students aware of their *own* voices, engaged in the public sounding-forth of another (literary) voice, I am reminded of the Lookingglass's desire in selecting *storytellers* as directors. Why tell this story? Why now? In her decades of teaching, McElroy appreciated "text" as Barthes reaccentuates the term: she wanted to show performers that a published book or finished script "is *plastic*, you know, it's plastic, and you can work with it. . . . In adapting, you have an opportunity to use your own creativity." Students can apply such creativity not only to literature but to the "adaptation of life." McElroy demonstrated this in 2000 with the compelling *Everyday People*: an imaginary journey inspired by the storytelling she heard among passengers on a bus trip through southern Indiana, and reset in the standstill of a terminal.[15] The production begins with the invocation of Sankofa, "an Akan word from Ghana, which literally means, Return and pick it up." The performance text "picks up" many pretexts, ranging from *a cappella* relyrics of popular songs, to borrowings and rehandlings of material from Pearl Cleage, James Baldwin, and filmmaker Haile Gerima.[16] It picks up as well the techniques of chamber theatre, employed loosely to stage a given storyteller's relationship to a scene of memory.

The progression of narrators is not casual or random—the kind of "any actor can narrate" strategy seen throughout a stage adaptation like *Nicholas Nickleby*. McElroy insists that we live in a world saturated with stories, of which only a few break through into our everyday communication. It takes a hothouse atmosphere like a bus station, from which the stranded cannot escape, for some storytellers to grab and hold our attention. (Actors do this more aggressively at the beginning of the performance; gradually we relax and accept being grabbed.) Travelers who might prefer to shrug off the passing stranger's story, and move away, are *compelled* to listen—just as we in the audience (extending that crowded room) are compelled by the conventions of theatre to sit and listen to the homeless man, the prisoner's sister, the sullen runaway. Like the spirit Sankofa, we do not fly off: we "return and pick up" the story that, in other circumstances, we might ignore.

More than this: *no one,* we learn, has the *whole* story. We encounter character B in character A's recollection—but character B's story *exceeds* its narrowed life there, and continues for our ears, outside character A's earshot. None of the characters, McElroy insists, is one-dimensional: "you think that you've got this character all checked out, and that character comes up with something that says, No, I'm too complex for you to figure me out in that way, it's not that simple." So it is that character A discovers she does not truly know *her own* story, until it acquires the "outsideness" of an attentive stranger, or the "talking book" that the stranger reads aloud. The text of this performance is not a work, as Barthes suggests, but a network. It not only unfolds, but folds back. It is a weave of pretexts. It is very much a production, moreover, of the polymorphous culture of adaptation that Breen set in motion.

Frank Galati (b. 1943) discovered this culture when he transferred to Northwestern's Theatre Department from Western Illinois University. Alvina Krause took notice of his talent, and he began "to sit in on her class every now and then." But the faculty "rivalry and competition" in the Theatre Department which trickled down to student "camps" and a "kind of guruism," drove the literature-loving actor to seek another major. "I never took an acting course, and I never took a directing course," remembers the award-winning actor and director. Preparing to transfer into English, he ran into an Interpretation student who knew he was an actor. "'You know, Dr. Breen is having auditions for *Anna Karenina,* why don't you go over there?' . . . The next thing I knew, I was Levin in *Anna Karenina,*" and a major in Bacon's department. Camps of students in

Theatre, as Galati observes, thought themselves "cool kids" for aligning with this or that teacher. The presence of a small department—*supplementary* in Derrida's sense, practicing performance *outside* Theatre—created a fully credentialized space for a whole new camp of "cool kids," bookish acting students "getting hip to" phenomena like "chamber theatre" and "media performance." Zimmerman remembers that the "tag line" for the undergraduate Interpretation student, twenty years later, "was the Theatre major with a briefcase." The perception of "cool" is relative, of course; by the early 1960s, in any case, a small academic department had developed its own theory of theatrical relativity.

Galati credits this in large part to Bacon's openness to faculty innovation. "I think one of the things that we all learned from him, directly, or indirectly, was his advice to all of us as teachers to *be ourselves,* you know, to teach to our strengths": not every teacher's "genius," or "ability to ignite and inspire," is "right for every student." McElroy praises Bacon for the same qualities. The "unintimidated" chairman "made me feel that I could really *go* without being all bound up in tradition"—even when some "way-out," "break-the-boundaries" activity went against the grain of Interpretation Department doxa. The paradox of Bacon's leadership is that, despite his commitment to the rigorous discipline he elaborated in the several editions of his performance textbook, he recruited teachers and students who would test the very limits he seemed to impose. This made the old department an exciting place to study, if not always a harmonious one.

These stories remind me of Sofiya Gubaidulina's anecdote about the encouragement of Dmitri Shostakovich, in a far more charged political context. Having taught himself to be creative during decades of "correction" by Stalin's cultural ministers, the composer would praise his most original students with irony: "Don't be afraid of being yourself. My wish for you is that you should continue on your own, *incorrect* way." Continue, with my blessing, down your own wrong path: "I am infinitely grateful to Shostakovich for those words. I . . . felt fortified by them to such an extent that I feared nothing, any failure or criticism just ran off my back" (quoted in Wilson, 1994, p. 306).

The wrong path of chamber theatre, then—brushing one of Bacon's "dangerous shores"—led Galati to direct his first department-sponsored production in 1970, an adaptation of Joyce's *Dubliners* story "The Dead." Acting in that production gave me my own first taste of chamber theatre. "I was a purist," Galati recalls,

> back when we did "The Dead," you know, I absolutely refused to cut a single word. And I maintained that discipline even in some of the longer works that I cut, with regard to internal sections that it seemed to me needed to be preserved as they were crafted by the writer.

Attempts to employ a Breen-like rigor came to an end with an adaptation of Anne Tyler's *Earthly Possessions* staged at Steppenwolf Theatre in 1991. Galati's last return to "the 'old way' . . . split the 'first person' between two actresses, and it just didn't work. . . . There wasn't the sort of zest of simplicity, you know?" By that point, Galati had learned a different kind of simplicity in abundantly complicated projects like *The Grapes of Wrath*. In reducing the four-hour running time of Steppenwolf's original production, Galati made a "watershed" discovery about his "job" as adapter-director. He had to steer a middle way between the temptation to dramatize—to "find the play" in a novel by "winding it up more tightly"—and "Breen's invitation to let the novel *play*, to let it wander on its own way and let us follow after it." What he faced, while reshaping the production for its long journey to Broadway, was the need to find the *theatre's* story:

I knew I had to get the Joads to California before the intermission. And that's not *Steinbeck's* job. And that's not the Joads' job. They're struggling. . . . They're doing *their* job. *My* job was to somehow cross that distance from the very opening to . . . "It's California."

If the *study* of adaptation had sharpened Galati's "perception of story," the *job* of adaptation required him to unlearn the rigor of his teacher, who insisted on repeating all the devices of novelistic narrative.

Mary Zimmerman (b. 1960) speaks similarly about the evolution of storytelling devices in her original adaptations. As a Theatre student at Northwestern, she took many Interpretation classes (although she was never a major until her graduate study) and learned the chamber theatre method by acting in numerous faculty-directed productions. She remembers being "very chamber-theatre-y and very preserve-all-the-narrative" when starting out as a director. But both creative growth and considerations of audience have led her to a style that features "less frequent and lengthy appearances" of onstage narrators. "I found other ways *to hide the narrative in there?*" she says to me in a faux-nervous rising inflection—as if her bad faith had summoned the ghost of Robert Breen, doom'd for a certain term to walk the night.

Our conversations in 2003 cover the various ways in which she has reaccentuated the practice of Breen and his students. Like Galati, Zimmerman claims to have grasped a clearer sense of *story* in the theatre through her practice of adaptation. In shaping texts far "larger than can be done . . . in an evening," Zimmerman seeks those episodes and elements that will interact productively with other pretexts: "what my actors are going to be really good at, and what the space is going to accommodate, and what the set suggests." In much of her work she gravitates toward "ancient literature . . . because I think performance is *embedded* in it—they were *oral* texts, they were *performed* texts." Stories from oral cultures "may be codified into an accepted print text," but "old things that survive have proved their vitality and their immediacy and their relevance by the fact of their survival." More than this, the contemporary artist feels "the security of joining a big chorus instead of feeling, *I'm* the maker of this." The old story that might have received its first performances by a singer of tales must now speak in the hybrid language of a technologically sophisticated theatre. Zimmerman speaks of how she first came to appreciate this in adaptation classes, even though she might have moved beyond most of the *specific* techniques advanced there: "When the assignment is to take a work of art that was not constructed for space and time, you find out what 'the theatrical' is. Because that is the ingredient you're adding, or coaxing out of it, you know?" The experience is "*everything* about performance," because the source text "wasn't written with a *convenience*, the *accommodations*, of the way a play accommodates its venue." Her words recall Galati's appreciation of learning in Breen's classroom exercises about the stage's *plasticity*.

If not to the *letter* of the text, then to *what*, exactly, does the adapter remain faithful? The question I posed to Lookingglass artists, in 1994, receives a revealing answer from Zimmerman in November 2003. She rehearses fidelity in a series of ratios. In her 2003 staging of Seneca's *Trojan Women* at the Goodman Theatre, the only writerly signature she added to David Slavitt's translation (1992) was the lyric to a song composed for the production by her friend Philip Glass. In a very different way, the arrangement of quotations in *The Notebooks of Leonardo da Vinci* (in various productions from 1989 to 2003)—"no matter how kind of crazy my staging is"—presents "one hundred percent Leonardo's language, zero percent my own." By contrast, the script of the celebrated *Metamorphoses* production (Zimmerman, 2002) is "fifty-fifty in terms of my text and David Slavitt's" translation of Ovid (1994). And the much-revised *Secret in the Wings,* inspired by a list of Grimm tales and Italo Calvino's retelling of "The Three Blind Queens" (1980),

> really shouldn't even say "adapted by." It should say "written by," because . . . there's not a word of deliberately copied language from any particular text. It's my own *memory*, and a jumbling-together of stories from childhood.

Of Zimmerman's two Chicago productions in 2003, then, which was the more personal?

> That's a really good question. . . . *Trojan Women* was personal to me in terms of my political convictions at the time, and I felt that the language of Seneca and David Slavitt . . . was much stronger than anything *I* could ever write.

Daniel Ostling's set for the modern-dress production cruelly invoked the ruins of the World Trade Center towers; staring almost straight down from the theatre's highest gallery, I experienced some of the vertigo and sheer faintness described by my friend Kameron Steele, who watched unbelievingly and helplessly from a nearby building in Manhattan as the jumpers on 9/11 hit the street. And although the actors, faithfully speaking the Seneca translation, said nothing about America's current adventure in Iraq, one could not ignore such details as the white noise of helicopters, or Zimmerman's casting choice of Fredric Stone—a ringer for Dick Cheney—in the role of Agamemnon. The *adaptation* of multiple pretexts produced a personal statement by Zimmerman that not all the performing bodies onstage necessarily needed to share. In more direct ways, *Secret in the Wings* is "the most personal of my plays," Zimmerman concedes, "because the language is most my own."

Then perhaps the better way to ask the question is this: which of the two very personal adaptations is more faithful? Zimmerman returns several times to the image of student painters,

> those people that you see making those exact copies in the Louvre. There's something about that practice of your hand literally going through that motion that teaches you something *general* about representation or painting. . . . I think that's how you learn to write, just like the painter in the Louvre, or whatever. By having to, you know . . .

She starts to say "memorize," but reconsiders. "By, you know, just *dealing, dealing, dealing* with the body of the text." She invokes her experience in "jillions" of undergraduate Interpretation Department classes, where the rigors of a typical assignment required the student to memorize and embody a literary text in ways that were "not against-the-grain or not fractured or not interwoven with other texts" (three moves that characterize much of Zimmerman's most distinctive work). Such precise engagement with "great literature" (Zimmerman trills her voice like an elocutionary lady, on her way to making a serious point) "imprints in you internally a kind of deep structure of narrative and of storytelling" that prepares you to take your own path. Galati agrees, when I mention this a few days later: "We paid our dues." Such "disciplines of the text," as Worthen (1995) expressed the matter, were not the dead end of oratorical culture at Northwestern: they were the springboard for two artists who have moved compellingly *beyond* literature in their best-known public work.

In taking their own "incorrect" ways—in moving beyond literature, interpretation, chamber theatre—Galati and Zimmerman have helped shape the "local" art of adaptation in Chicago, and have taken it to international stages. For their work as adapter/directors, both have won multiple Joseph Jefferson Awards, as well as Tony Awards. Notable among Zimmerman's many achievements is the prestigious MacArthur Fellowship,

which she received in 1998. At the top of Galati's equally impressive list of honors is his election, in 2001, to the American Academy of Arts and Sciences. McElroy, spinning the culture of adaptation toward community activism, has been recognized for performance-based work in education going back to the 1960s; the honor she mentions with greatest pride is an NAACP Living Legend Award in 2001.

WITHOUT THE WORDS

The double movement within a local context that I have tried to describe—from textbook method to professional practice, and from featuring to fissuring a text—can be seen in the ambitious *Chekhov Cycle* by Redmoon Theatre's Jim Lasko. The first installment, *Nina*, which inspired my admiring report in another essay (see Edwards, 2003, pp. 38–40, 52–53), reinvented Chekhov's *The Seagull* as an almost wordless clownscape in a Chicago public park during the summer of 2002. The following spring, Lasko took many of the same artists indoors at the Steppenwolf Studio to develop and stage *Seagull*, a second "rewrighting" of the play. While installment two restored free translations of much of Chekhov's text, the most memorable "language" was visual and gestural.

The *Cycle*'s Kostya, like Lasko himself, is a puppeteer as well as a "theatre-maker." Much of *Seagull*'s surprising spectacle, therefore, invokes contrasts of scale. Human actors often behave like large-scale versions of Kostya's puppets. The physical environment provides many of them with boxes to inhabit, when they are "put away" after a scene, and elements of the set permit transformation into *mise-en-abîme* structures that echo the larger dramatic world. Like the earlier *Nina*, *Seagull* expands the role of Masha. The production's final image dramatizes her yearning, beyond the moment of Kostya's death, by transforming her box into a life-size doll house: as she addresses the empty chair (presumably the one in which the Kostya "doll" would sit) she bursts into tears. The production's most moving images, as well as its most comic ones (Medvedenko accompanying his tuba recital on a toy piano, which he plays with his free hand), are not in Chekhov's play. In many cases they develop further possibilities of images from the *Nina* production. *Nina*, like Chekhov's *The Seagull,* is a pretext for installment two. The text as network or methodological field: Lasko's *Chekhov Cycle* presents its various texts, from literary source text to performance text, as constantly in motion and capable of transformation. Installment three promises to reinvent everything once more, beyond the plot, in a nontheatrical site.[17]

As a PhD student in Northwestern's Theatre and Drama Program, Lasko found the most gratifying coursework at two institutional extremes: the performance studies adaptation classes and the undergraduate acting courses in theatre. This gifted artist, who left his academic program to devote his full energies to creative work, shares these thoughts: "The culture at Northwestern promoted the belief that you can adapt anything to the stage and, from there, that almost anything, literary or other, can be made to feel alive and present" in performance. He remembers the "fearless" risk-taking of students, and the ability of teachers "at their best" to encourage this fearlessness. "The work I make now," he says, owes much to "a permissive and critical culture" that encouraged "exploration":

> I've moved toward objects, toward an intensely physical style. Neither physical performance nor object work was being much explored at Northwestern when I was there. Most of the work was heavily text-based.

But his current "success with this image-based style" has deep roots in the "intelligence" promoted by close textual study. "It is as though I'm doing the adaptations we were trained to do" at Northwestern, "but without the words."

The same work "but without the words": this expresses the paradox of my title. The dues-paying student of text traces the hand of a master like Chekhov before embarking on three panels of abstract expressionism. Toward the end of the session I conducted in 1994 with Lookingglass ensemble members, Christine Dunford offered her own views about books and actors' bodies—competing pretexts—on stage:

> One of the things that I've observed in watching adaptations . . . is that they seem to get *stripped down* from the book. The *richness* of the book seems to get stripped down. But then when I see actors bring that stripped-down version to life, all the blood washes back into it. And it might not be the *same* blood . . . as the book had, but it's now a full experience again.

One kind of "richness," or "blood," is literary language. Another is the theatre's array of material languages, including actors' expressive bodies. If the storytellers of Lookingglass are correct, the retelling of a book in one's own medium, in one's own time and place, is a kind of aesthetic transfusion: the "blood" is new, but it courses through the same narrative veins.

NOTES

1. For information about Chicago's "Jeff" Awards, see http://www.jeffawards.org/.

2. The essay cites transcripts of several personal interviews: with Frank Galati on February 10, 2003, and November 25, 2003 (both conducted in Evanston, Illinois); with Njoki McElroy on July 17, 2003 (conducted in Evanston); with Mary Zimmerman on February 10, 2003, August 20, 2003, and November 19, 2003 (all conducted in Evanston); and with six members of the Lookingglass Theatre Company, Tom Cox, Larry Distasi, Andy White, Doug Hara, Laura Eason, and Christine Dunford, on October 4, 1994 (conducted in Chicago). When useful, I have distinguished between transcripts of two interviews with Robert Breen: one conducted by David Wohl

on June 6, 1973 (in Evanston), and another by me on October 16, 1989 (in Evanston). Additionally, I have cited personal communications by e-mail or telephone from Jim Lasko on December 4, 2003; Katharine Loesch on February 3, 2004; Kameron Steele on September 11, 2001; and Mary Zimmerman on December 15, 2003. Unless otherwise noted, quotations from these individuals are drawn from this list of unpublished sources.

3. The theme of Breen's course in readers theatre at Northwestern, as it developed during the 1960s, was "featuring the text." As part of curricular revisions in the mid-1980s, the readers theatre and chamber theatre courses once taught by Breen became a two-part course in "presentational aesthetics," taught most frequently during the past two decades by Galati and Zimmerman.

4. Other representative textbooks include Haas (1976), Long, Hudson, and Jeffrey (1977), and Pickering (1975). Although the popular *Handbook* by Coger and White (1967) went through two subsequent editions (in 1973 and 1982) the approach of the textbook's first edition (which I cite) remained substantially unchanged. Among the various bibliographies of books and essays, the most helpful is Peterson (1985).

5. For information about these theatres, see the following websites: Arden Theatre, http://www.ardentheatre.org/; Lookingglass Theatre, http://www.lookingglasstheatre.org/; Redmoon Theater, http://www.redmoon.org/; Lifeline Theatre, http://www.lifelinetheatre.com/; and About Face Theatre, http://www.aboutfacetheatre.com/.

6. Few Chicago companies have taken more seriously their responsibility as members of a larger community, composed of theatregoers and nontheatregoers alike. Throughout the company's history, the multifaceted Lookingglass outreach program has been one of Chicago's most distinguished, and has inspired the full-time commitment of several ensemble members. For information, see the education page on the company's website.

7. Zimmerman provides a valuable contrasting perspective on her early work with Lookingglass in her doctoral dissertation (1994).

8. An earlier version of several paragraphs describing chamber theatre appeared in *Unstoried* (Edwards, 1999). I am grateful to the editors of *Theatre Annual: A Journal of Performance Studies,* published by the College of William and Mary in Virginia, for permission to include a selection of unmarked quotations.

9. For Breen's clearest description of how he began to demonstrate to his students the critical

usefulness of chamber theatre, see Forrest and Loesch (1976, pp. 2–3).

10. For many years now, in my staging classes, I have discussed how the narratologist's "story" and "discourse" might be understood as *scenes* when applied to the work of adapters. I have not seen this usage elsewhere.

11. "Pretext" appears in Cole's complicated account of the Wooster Group's *Frank Dell's The Temptation of Saint Antony,* directed (and to a large extent devised and composed) by LeCompte. Cole borrowed the term, as she explains, from David Savran (1986, p. 40), the author of a book-length study of the Wooster Group's early productions (1988). Her use of it often seems interchangeable with "source text."

12. Sills comments that the "narrative technique developed by Robert Breen" was "very similar to story theater where the actor could speak about his character in the third person. Except they used a narrator. So I just cut out the narrator twenty years later and that was story theater" (quoted in Sweet, 1996, p. 15). Breen remembers that Sills became aware of chamber theatre after seeing episodes of *Short Story Playhouse;* later, during his years at Second City, he met Breen when he came to Northwestern to lecture. "Story Theater is a theatrical tour de force," Breen observed to Wohl in 1973, "and is very successful, but it's got nothing to do with the critical analysis of literature. . . . My entertainment of audiences," by contrast, "is kind of a secondary thing."

13. See McElroy (1975). Following McElroy's departure from Northwestern, the black literature course continues to be taught by associate professor E. Patrick Johnson.

14. McElroy cites the example of George C. Wolfe's 1989 adaptation "Spunk: Three Tales by Zora Neale Hurston" (Wolfe, 1991) as a liberating experience in her growth as both writer and adapter.

15. In May, 2000, the black literature class produced two scripts, for which two student directors made different selections from McElroy's *Everyday People* stories. I have chosen to discuss the performance text (preserved on my own videotape record) directed by Jean Garrison, as performed in Northwestern's Theatre and Interpretation Center on May 20, 2000.

16. Songs range from the 1969 Sly and the Family Stone hit that suggests the play's title, and "Big Brother" from Stevie Wonder's 1972 album *Talking Book,* to Dionne Farris's 1995 "Don't Ever Touch Me (again)." The content of one scene echoes Gerima's film *Sankofa* (1993); a racist

father's tirade paraphrases moments from the horrific lynching scene in Baldwin's "Going to Meet the Man" (1965/1995); and a character educates another about "the brothers" with an extended quotation from Pearl Cleage's *Deals with the Devil* (1993, pp. 44–49).

17. The program for *Seagull*, which opened at the Steppenwolf Studio on March 20, 2003, announces "another outdoor production, a site-specific work, that activates a public space with the life of Chekhov's characters"; in installment three, the characters will "leave Chekhov's story behind" (Lasko, 2003, p. 12). Other Redmoon productions have intervened. As of June 29, 2004, installment three of *The Chekhov Cycle* has not been announced for production. In "Drift" (Edwards, 2003, p. 39) I incorrectly identify the actress playing Masha as Vanessa Stalling, who played Nina in Lasko's productions of *Nina* and *Seagull;* in both productions, Sharon Lanza played Masha.

REFERENCES

Bacon, W. A. (1972). *The art of interpretation* (2nd ed.). New York: Holt, Rinehart and Winston.

Bacon, W. A. (1975). The dangerous shores a decade later. In R. Haas & D. A. Williams (Eds.), *The study of oral interpretation: Theory and comment* (pp. 221–228). Indianapolis, IN: Bobbs-Merrill.

Bacon, W. A., & Breen, R. S. (1959). *Literature as experience*. New York: McGraw-Hill.

Bakhtin, M. M. (1986). *Speech genres and other late essays* (V. W. McGee, Trans.). Austin: University of Texas Press.

Baldwin, J. (1995). Going to meet the man. In *Going to meet the man* (pp. 227–249). New York: Vintage International. (Original work published 1965)

Barthes, R. (1986). From work to text. In *The rustle of language* (R. Howard, Trans., pp. 56–64). New York: Hill and Wang. (Original work published 1971)

Berkoff, S. (1985). *West, Lunch, and Harry's Christmas: Three plays*. New York: Grove Press.

Boal, A. (1985). *Theatre of the oppressed* (C. A. & M. O. L. McBride, Trans.). New York: Theatre Communications Group. (Original work published 1974)

Bowman, M. S. (1995). "Novelizing" the stage: Chamber theatre after Breen and Bakhtin. *Text and Performance Quarterly, 15*, 1–23.

Brecht, B. (1964). *Brecht on theatre: The development of an aesthetic* (J. Willett, Trans.). New York: Hill and Wang.

Breen, R. S. (1950). *Symbolic action in the oral interpretation of Robinson Jeffers' "Roan stallion."* Unpublished doctoral dissertation, Northwestern University, Evanston, IL.

Breen, R. S. (1975). Chamber theatre. In R. Haas & D. A. Williams (Eds.), *The study of oral interpretation: Theory and comment* (pp. 207–211). Indianapolis, IN: Bobbs-Merrill.

Breen, R. S. (1978). *Chamber theatre*. Englewood Cliffs, NJ: Prentice-Hall.

Brook, P. (1968). *The empty space*. New York: Avon.

Calvino, I. (1980). The three blind queens. In *Italian folktales* (G. Martin, Trans., pp. 407–409). New York: Harcourt Brace Jovanovich. (Original work published 1956)

Carlson, M. (2003). *The haunted stage: The theatre as memory machine*. Ann Arbor: University of Michigan Press.

Chambers, E. K. (1923). *The Elizabethan stage* (4 vols.). Oxford, England: Clarendon Press.

Chatman, S. (1990). *Coming to terms: The rhetoric of narrative in fiction and film*. Ithaca, NY: Cornell University Press.

Christiansen, R. (1990, December 2). A fearless new breed of directors hits town. *Chicago Tribune*, sec. 13, pp. 4–5.

Cleage, P. (1993). *Deals with the devil and other reasons to riot*. New York: Ballantine Books.

Coger, L. I., & White, M. R. (1967). *Readers theatre handbook: A dramatic approach to literature*. Glenview, IL: Scott, Foresman.

Cole, S. L. (1992). Elizabeth LeCompte directs *Frank Dell's The temptation of Saint Antony*. In *Directors in rehearsal: A hidden world* (pp. 90–123). New York: Routledge.

Curry, S. S. (1891). *The province of expression*. Boston: School of Expression.

Curry, S. S. (1896). *Imagination and dramatic instinct*. Boston: School of Expression.

Derrida, J. (1976). *Of grammatology* (G. C. Spivak, Trans.). Baltimore, MD: Johns Hopkins University Press. (Original work published 1967)

Derrida, J. (1978). The theatre of cruelty and the closure of representation. In *Writing and difference* (A. Bass, Trans., pp. 232–250). Chicago: University of Chicago Press. (Original work published in 1966)

Dessen, A. C. (2002). *Rescripting Shakespeare: The text, the director, and modern productions*. England: Cambridge University Press.

Edgar, D. (Adapter). (1992). *The life and adventures of Nicholas Nickleby*. In B. McNamara (Ed.), *Plays from the contemporary British theater* (pp. 317–628). New York: Mentor-New American Library. (Original work published in 1982)

Edwards, P. (1999). "Unstoried: Teaching literature in the age of performance studies." *Theatre Annual, 52,* 1–147.

Edwards, P. (2003). Drift: Performing the relics of intention. *Theatre Annual, 56,* 1–53.

Forrest, W., & Loesch, K. (1976). Chamber theatre and the dramatization of narrative: An interview with Robert Breen. *Oral English, 2*(4), 1–12.

Galati, F. (1991). *John Steinbeck's The grapes of wrath*. New York: Penguin.

Gerima, H. (Director/Writer). (1993). *Sankofa* [Motion picture]. (Available from Mypheduh Films, Inc., P.O. Box 10035, Washington, DC 20018-0035)

Gregory, A. (1972). *Alice in Wonderland*. New York: Dramatist's Play Service.

Gregory, A. (1973). *Alice in Wonderland: The forming of a company and the making of a play*. New York: Rabbit Hole–Merlin Press.

Haas, R. (1976). *Theatres of interpretation*. Ann Arbor, MI: Roberts-Burton.

Harding, J. M. (2000). An interview with Richard Schechner. In J. M. Harding (Ed.), *Contours of the theatrical avant-garde: Performance and textuality* (pp. 202–214). Ann Arbor: University of Michigan Press.

Houlihan, M. (2003, June 8). A landmark move. *Chicago Sun-Times*. Retrieved January 5, 2004, from http://www.lookingglasstheatre .org/news/index.html

Innes, C. (2000). Text/pre-text/pretext: The language of avant-garde experiment. In J. M. Harding (Ed.), *Contours of the theatrical avant-garde: Performance and textuality* (pp. 58–75). Ann Arbor: University of Michigan Press.

Jackson, S. (2004). *Professing performance: Theatre in the academy from philology to performativity*. England: Cambridge University Press.

Kleinau, M. L., & McHughes, J. L. (1980). *Theatres for literature: A practical aesthetics for group interpretation*. Sherman Oaks, CA: Alfred.

Lasko, J. (2003). Notes on the play. *Chicago Playbill, 119*(4), 12.

Long, B. W., Hudson, L., & Jeffrey, P. R. (1977). *Group performance of literature*. Englewood Cliffs, NJ: Prentice-Hall.

Maclay, J. H. (1971). *Readers theatre: Toward a grammar of practice*. New York: Random House.

Masten, J. (1997). *Textual intercourse: Collaboration, authorship, and sexualities in Renaissance drama*. England: Cambridge University Press.

McElroy, N. (1975). Problems in developing and teaching an interpretation of black drama course. *Speech Teacher, 24,* 211–217.

Morrison, T. (1998). *Paradise*. New York: Alfred A. Knopf.

Morson, G. S., & Emerson, C. (1990). *Mikhail Bakhtin: Creation of a prosaics*. Palo Alto, CA: Stanford University Press.

OED Online. (2005). Retrieved June 3, 2005, from http://dictionary.oed.com.turing.library.north western.edu/cgi/entry/50170980?query_type= word&queryword=paradox&first=1&max_ to_show=10&sort_type=alpha&result_place= 1&search_id=01yn-vDWLvm-1185&hilite= 50170980

Pavis, P. (1982). *Languages of the stage: Essays in the semiology of theatre* (S. Melrose et al., Trans.). New York: PAJ Publications.

Peterson, E. E. (1985). *Readers theatre: An annotated bibliography*. Annandale, VA: Speech Communication Association. (ERIC Document Reproduction Service No. ED 289207)

Pickering, J. V. (1975). *Readers theatre*. Encino, CA: Dickenson.

Richards, T. (1995). *At work with Grotowski on physical actions*. London: Routledge.

Roach, J. R. (1985). *The player's passion: Studies in the science of acting*. Newark: University of Delaware Press; London: Associated University Presses.

Savran, D. (1986). Adaptation as clairvoyance: The Wooster Group's *Saint Anthony*. *Theater, 18*(1), 36–41.

Savran, D. (1988). *Breaking the rules: The Wooster Group*. New York: Theatre Communications Group.

Schechner, R. (1973). *Environmental theater*. New York: Hawthorn Books.

Slavitt, D. R. (Trans.). (1992). *Trojan women*. In *Seneca: The tragedies* (Vol. 1, pp. 1–42). Baltimore, MD: Johns Hopkins University Press.

Slavitt, D. R. (Trans.). (1994). *The metamorphoses of Ovid*. Baltimore, MD: Johns Hopkins University Press.

Sweet, J. (1996). *Something wonderful right away* (Rev. ed.). New York: Limelight Editions.

Terkel, S. (1992). *Race: How blacks and whites think and feel about the American obsession.* New York: Anchor-Doubleday.

Williams, D. A. (1975). Whatever happened to choral reading? In R. Haas & D. A. Williams (Eds.), *The study of oral interpretation: Theory and comment* (pp. 58–70). Indianapolis, IN: Bobbs-Merrill.

Willis, R. A., & McElroy, H. (1971). Published works of black playwrights in the United States, 1960–1970. *Bulletin of Black Theatre, 1,* 8–15.

Wilson, E. (1994). *Shostakovich: A life remembered.* Princeton, NJ: Princeton University Press.

Wolfe, George C. (1991). Spunk: Three tales by Zora Neale Hurston. In *Two by George C. Wolfe* (pp. 65–132). Garden City, NY: Fireside Theatre.

Worthen, W. B. (1995). Disciplines of the text/sites of performance. *The Drama Review, 39,* 13–28.

Worthen, W. B. (1998). Drama, performativity and performance. *PMLA, 113,* 1093–1107.

Zimmerman, M. A. (1994). *The archaeology of performance: A study of ensemble process and development in the Lookingglass Theatre production of The Arabian nights.* Unpublished doctoral dissertation, Northwestern University, Evanston, IL.

Zimmerman, M. A. (2002). *Metamorphoses: A Play.* Evanston, IL: Northwestern University Press.

PART IV

Performance and Pedagogy

BRYANT KEITH ALEXANDER

In *Teaching Against the Grain: Texts for a Pedagogy of Possibility,* Roger Simon (1992) offers a germinal construct that underscores the meaningful connection between pedagogy and performance. He writes that the nature of pedagogy asks a series of questions: "'What should be taught and why?' with considerations as to how that teaching should take place" (pp. 55–57). His orientation to the nature of pedagogy questions issues of content and purpose. Yet the accomplishment of pedagogy, the cornerstone of it's meaning, is made manifest in performance; in *how teaching should take place.* Highly steeped in the possibilities and politics of critical pedagogy, his approach to describing teaching signals an understanding of education as a cultural and embodied practice, a doing. It is the what, why, and how of teaching that establishes the links between self and society, between culture and identity, between perpetuating the status quo and empowering a radical transformation of knowing that can have material consequences as we strive towards a more democratic society.

"Critical theorists see school as a form of cultural politics; schooling always represents an introduction to, preparation for, and legitimatization of particular forms of social life. It has always been implicated in relations of power, social practices and the favoring of forms and knowledge that support a specific vision of past,

present and future" (McLaren, 1998, p. 164). A *performance studies paradigm of pedagogy* capitalizes and situates these concerns by revealing, interrogating, and challenging legitimated social forms of teaching, learning, and knowing while working toward transforming social systems to liberate the human spirit. Performance studies scholars understand that the processes of socialization and enculturation are acts of instruction, internalizing cultural scripts, and embodied performances.

Performance pedagogy as a theoretical construct focuses both on the pedagogy of teaching performance in performance studies, and on engaging performance as a strategic pedagogy: performance as a way of knowing, performance as a strategic analytic; performance as a way of seeing and understanding the nuanced nomenclature of human social dynamics. In this sense performance pedagogy also includes the nature of performativity in/as pedagogy. In *Articulate Bodies,* Elyse Pineau (2004) offers a good template on which to tease at the notion of performativity and its link to educational processes when she writes,

> In the performative dynamic, history and the ideological meanings it bears, operates along three temporal axes: it precedes and creates the condition for action; it is instantiated anew in each moment, and it is carried forward through each repetition. In other words, if "performance" is the situated

253

instantiation of historical meanings, "performativity" is the sociocultural dynamic that lends it longevity, power, and the appearance of inevitability. Thus, one might attend to discreet performances within educational life while investigating the performative trajectories in which they are embedded. (pp. 1–2)

Pineau draws on the definitional heritage of performativity from J. L. Austin's (1962) speech-act theory as politicized in Judith Butler's (1995) phenomenology of gender to emphasize the ritualized repetition of communicative acts that have historical consequences. Thus, to look simply at the link between performance and pedagogy as a singular activity within the confines of the classroom situation is problematic. It is problematic if performance is reductively constructed as enacted behavior or aesthetic entertainment in the moment of its engagement without an accompanying recognition of its historical, social, or cultural antecedents. It is problematic if performance pedagogy coalesces into a *methods fetish* in educational discourse and not into a more *humanizing pedagogical framework* that helps teachers and students interrogate their collusion in the social construction of meaning (Bartolome, 1996). It is problematic if the performance-pedagogy link is only used to examine the reductive *metaphor of teachers as performers* and not *teaching as an interpretive act,* a performative process that excavates new conditions of knowledge meaning (Edgerton, 1993, p. 220; Pineau, 1994).

Further, it is problematic if the utility of performance as pedagogical method overlooks the larger structures and ways in which the repetition of historical norms and enacted behaviors are translated through particular teaching practices. It is problematic if the performance-pedagogy link is not also seen as a complex and productive site of possibility that both disrupts and transforms the processes of knowing in the reified location of the classroom and, maybe more importantly, in the broader social, cultural, and political contexts of everyday

living. The performance-pedagogy link is also problematic and reductive if we resist seeing performance and pedagogy as they "relate to cultural practice and the materiality of bodies— hence a displayed enactment of ideology and enfleshed knowledge—influenced and motivated by the politics of race, gender, power, and class in the forms of folklore, ritual, spectacle, resistance, and protest" (Alexander, Anderson, & Gallegos, 2005, p. 2).

With this in mind, I press Roger Simon's interrogative approach to discussing pedagogy against Lawrence Grossberg's (1994) query of cultural studies. He writes that "the question of cultural studies is not so much who we are speaking to (audience) or even for (representation), but whom we are speaking against. And consequently, the resources we need, the strategies we adopt, and the politics we attempt to define must always take into account the particular context in which we are struggling"; struggling to teach, struggling to inform, and struggling to transform the world (p. 9). Performance pedagogy as constructed in performance studies is poised at a productive intersection with cultural studies, where performance is viewed not only as discursive human behavior and methodology, as a set of critical tools, and as a paradigm of knowing; but also as a strategic illumination and intervention in human social processes.

Performance in the classroom is both a behavior and a theoretical position. The behavior involves enacted practices of cultural and intercultural contact magnified in the materiality of lived experiences. These behaviors always come into contact and conflict with the often privatized theoretical logics that guide the specific processes of teaching, nestled within the larger social constructs of schooling and education. As a corrective Henry Giroux (2001) calls for a *performative pedagogy* or a *public pedagogy,* one that "opens a space for disputing conventional academic borders" and that reconfigures classroom space to all practiced places where the dynamism of human social commerce effects knowing and living (p. 8). Such a pedagogy raises questions "beyond the institutional boundaries of the disciplinary organization of question and answers" and gets at the core of *how we know what we know* (Grossberg, 1996, p. 145).[1]

Here, issues of authority, of who asks the questions, is based in a system of survival, and the answers are acts of liberation. Defined in and through its performative functions, public pedagogy is marked by its attentiveness to the interconnections and struggles that take place over knowledge, language, spatial relations, and history.

In *Teachers as Cultural Workers: Letters to Those Who Dare to Teach,* Paulo Freire (1998) has outlined the need for teachers to be cultural workers: public intellectuals who work towards social change, not the remanifestation of the *status quo*. Giroux (1996) captures this sentiment well when he charges teachers to work "pedagogically and theoretically to ensure the development of a socially responsible citizenry and a critical, multicultural, democracy" (p. 96). To center this project within the context of educative processes (in the classroom and in everyday life) is to engage in an insurgent critical pedagogy that begins to empower voice at the core level of social indoctrination and cultural practice. And to engage performance as a strategic mechanism is to also center such transformative processes and ways of knowing the world through and in the body: the body as conduit of being, the body as the materiality of presence, the body as the nexus of need, and the body as a site of knowing.

Outlining a more concrete link between performance and pedagogy Giroux (2001) writes, "The performative nature of the pedagogical recognizes the partial breakdown, renegotiation, and reposition of boundaries as fundamental to understanding how pluralization is linked to the shifting nature of knowledge, identities, and the process of globalization" (p. 9). Performative pedagogy as public

pedagogy acknowledges that performance has always been used as procreative, protective, and pedagogical agent beyond the confines of the classroom and in the broader constructions of human social engagement in the form of ritual practices, pop cultural influences, and in the arenas of politics and religion, among others.

In the introduction to their book, *Education and Cultural Studies: Toward a Performative Practice,* Henry A. Giroux and Patrick Shannon (1997) offer a construction of performative pedagogy that I use to expand the notion of performance from a tool of performing theory to performance as an embodied methodology: a mechanism that facilitates a theoretical dialogue between students and curriculum, students and teachers, students and audience, and students and society. They state,

> The concept of the performative in this text provides an articulating principle that signals the importance of translating theory into practice while reclaiming cultural texts as an important site in which theory is used to "think" politics in the face of a pedagogy of representation that has implications for how to strategize and engage broader public issues. Pedagogy in this context becomes performative through the ways in which various authors engage diverse cultural texts as a context for theorizing about social issues and wider political considerations. (p. 2)

This *articulating principle* does not merely *translate theory into practice,* because practice and experience are always sites of complex ways of knowing. In fact, bell hooks (1994) says, "No gap exists between theory and practice. Indeed, what experience makes more evident is the bond between the two—that ultimately reciprocal process wherein one enables the other" (p. 61). And, while pedagogy may turn to performance as a strategy of seeing and being seen, of calling attention to, and magnifying that which is microscopic or so habituated as to go unnoticed, performance offers much more to pedagogy. As an embodied epistemology performance is both the act of doing and the act of knowing. Performance becomes a core register of pedagogical discourse.

In positing *performance as a form of pedagogical discourse,* I am suggesting that performance is a critical process of sense making which meets and exceeds the pedagogical challenges between teachers and students: to teach and learn in meaningful, critical, yet creative ways. Instead of teachers solely constructing traditional examinations in which students match their knowledge to expected standards of expressions, in performance students are required to synthesize their understanding through *enfleshed knowledge,* what Peter McLaren (1993) describes as "the building of discursive positionalities and economies of affect from the discourses and material practices available and the histories and regulatory practices of their operations" (p. 275).

Performance as pedagogical discourse signals students to engage both their critical and creative skills as well as their enfleshed knowledge in order to display and present their understanding of complex concepts grounded in social, cultural, and political issues through the body—and maybe more importantly through their experience. Their performances serve as products that evidence their understanding and their resistance. These performances also serve as demonstrations of how they came to their understanding, as well as critical dialogic engagements with those who witness the performance. In constructing the notion of *performance as a pedagogical discourse,* I am suggesting that it offers the opportunity for a critical engagement of issues that go beyond pedestrian notions of *experiential learning* to a form of *critical performative pedagogy.* In her article "Performance Studies Across the Curriculum: Problems, Possibilities, and Projections" (1998), Elyse Pineau comments on *critical performative pedagogy* in this way:

> Critical performative pedagogy combines acute physical awareness of one's kinetic and kinesthetic sense with candid and thoughtful consideration of the implications of those bodily sensations. Every time that we ask students to perform across gender, ethnic, or generational lines we have the opportunity to unpack their resistance to the unfamiliar, their stereotypic assumptions about how others move through the world, as well as to confront their own habituated responses and experiences. (p. 133)

And while I fully agree with Pineau, I also see that critical performative pedagogy *should not* be limited to teachers "unpacking" and deconstructing student responses. This traditional element of the educational equation, laden with power and dominance, risks reducing the act of performance and Pineau's rich contribution to just another opportunity to critique. Far too often teachers, caught up in the power of their own positionality, overlook what they can learn in the process of engaging student performances as a lesson in their own pedagogy, and in their own *dense particularity* (Mohanty, 1989).

A critical performative pedagogy also offers teachers and other students in the class (the audience), the opportunity to see themselves again through the performances of others; performance as a barometer of truth or reality. The performance can serve as critical reflexive lens in order for teachers and students to see and realize their own *resistances, stereotypic assumptions, habituated responses, and experiences* relative to particular issues related to the *theoretical arguments that frame* the assignment and the person in performance. This is especially important when teachers and students explore the complex intersections of race, sex, class, gender, and privilege; and how the politics of these embodied practices blend and bleed the borders between school and society.

CHAPTER OVERVIEWS

The chapters in this section explore the productive relationships between critical pedagogy and performance in diverse ways. Each demonstrates that the production, consumption, and dissemination of knowledge are critical performances intimately linked to activism as well as to the formation of institutional practices and identities. While the authors of these chapters "do their own thing," they are consistent in their enunciation of the necessarily tensive elements of politics, possibilities, practices, and punctuations that mark the unique relationship between pedagogy, performance, and performativity in the specific context of the classroom, and in larger processes of schooling, education, culture, and society.

In general ways, the two chapters that frame this section, offered by Nathan Stucky and Norman Denzin, offer historical and theoretical discussions of the current trends *in* performance pedagogy, and the ethics *of* performance pedagogy that extend beyond the narrow confines of the classroom. The three interceding chapters by Mady Schutzman, Greg Dimitriadis, and Kristin Valentine serve as very specific case studies of the ways performance pedagogy enlivens the pedagogical enterprise; how pop cultural phenomenon such as hip hop can serve as artistic, political, and educative medium; and the ways performance pedagogy might intervene in particular social conditions. These authors extend and deepen theoretical logics that undergird the performance/pedagogy link, while signaling the reader to critique reductive ways of seeing the power and efficacy of performance.

In his chapter, "Fieldwork in the Performance Studies Classroom: Learning Objectives and the Activist Curriculum," Nathan Stucky takes on the challenge of articulating, reinforcing, and delineating what we know about the potency and efficacy of performance as/in/with pedagogy and/or curriculum. His chapter is based on addressing a series of interrelated queries: What are the learning objectives in the performance studies curriculum? What are the ideologies that

are engaged in the performance studies classroom? What are the values of performance studies in the university and in liberal education? How is it that, when we ask questions about the efficacy, effectiveness, viability, value, or importance of performance studies, we raise questions of class and privilege that have particular implications for university education? What values and for whom? Most importantly, how is it that as an educational enterprise performance studies, especially as it is practiced in many institutions in the United States, participates in an ongoing experiment in social change? What is the transformative capacity of performance studies to adjust to needs, to new circumstances, to expand or contract, as conditions require? And how are those adjustments reflected in performance studies pedagogy?

In her chapter, "Ambulant Pedagogy," Mady Schutzman employs and deploys performativity as pedagogical tool, as a methodological critique that enhances radical pedagogical goals. Through a metaphorical use of "ambulant pedagogy," Schutzman weaves, dances, and choreographs an intricate and sophisticated logic about a *transitive pedagogy,* one that crosses the borders of staid teacher-student interactions and the classroom as purely intellectual work space; one that crosses students into new realms of knowing through an embodied epistemology of serious play; one, she writes, where "a kin(a)esthetic sensibility advocates for a deeply implicated pedagogical organ, accountable and answerable to powerful political agendas" that must be critiqued on the level of the human and the humane—thereby challenging the threats to keep students and learning as immobile structures of social indoctrination; one where teachers and students challenge their knowledge of the known with the immediacy of the altogether real.

In "Pedagogy on the Move: New Intersections In (Between) the Educative and the Performative," Greg Dimitriadis charts his own understanding of the efficacy of performance pedagogy through the shifting terrains of his academic training, leading him from the technocratic logics of the ivory tower back to the more embodied politics of hip hop culture. Through his unique survey of literature, he reinforces and extends views of performance as a key site where texts are put into motion, where social, cultural, and material constructions are articulated and rearticulated in new and (often) powerful ways. The "performative turn," for Dimitriadis, gestures toward an "interactionist epistemology" where context replaces text, verbs replace nouns, and structures become processes. The emphasis is on change, contingency, locality, motion, improvisation, struggle, and how these are implicated and interrogated at the intersections between race, cultural practice, performance, and pedagogy. In the chapter Dimitriadis confirms that *there are no safe spaces here, no alibis for our effectivities. The world is always already performative, always already in motion.*

This interactionist turn has critical implications for pedagogy, decentering the privileged and delimited role of the teacher in the classroom. It forces us to look towards the new "in between" spaces where culture is being "performed" in the everyday. This means taking seriously the work done in and by nontraditional educational curricula (e.g., popular culture), programs (e.g., arts-based initiatives), and institutions (e.g., community centers). It means looking towards *artists as educators*. It means looking at *educators as artists*. Above all else, it means seeing pedagogy always in motion. This chapter looks towards these and other phenomena as it explores new intersections in (between) the educative and the performative.

In "Unlocking the Doors for Incarcerated Women Through Performance and Creative Writing," Kristin Valentine outlines and details the specific application of performance as pedagogical strategy and political engagement in her work with women in Arizona's Perryville

State Prison. Her hypothesis is that "mind-liberating activities generated by performance and creative writing programs . . . increase effective communication skills that help women avoid actions harmful to themselves and others." In her project she offers a detailed description of her own syllabus and pedagogical practices in working with, teaching, and empowering incarcerated women, while also including a survey of other approaches. The chapter ends with the particular hope "that other performance scholars will help develop and improve prison programs for incarcerated people in their communities." She grounds her optimism in the work of Dwight Conquergood (1998), who suggests "that the performance paradigm involves 'immediacy, involvement, and intimacy as modes of understanding'" (p. 26).

In the final chapter in this section, "The Politics and Ethics of Performance Pedagogy: Toward a Pedagogy of Hope," Norman Denzin works outward from a series of assumptions embedded in a radical critical performance pedagogy. He argues that the call to performance in performance studies and in the human sciences requires a commitment to a politics, ethics, and aesthetics of performance, one that moves from critical race theory to a radical critical performance pedagogy; one that works towards new models of democracy. In his chapter, the *ethics of performance* and *the performance of ethics* are framed through a post-9/11 world in which a radical critical performance pedagogy might help us recuperate from the devastation of physical destruction, as well as the psychic devastation always present and only laid bare through terrorist acts. He advocates for the empowering links between critical pedagogy and a critical pedagogical theatre, borrowing from and building on the discourses of indigenous peoples, whose theories of ritual performance blend and blur with performative acts that critique, transgress, transform, and bring dignity to human practices.

Such a performance ethic refuses commodification as it draws upon indigenous, feminist, queer, and communitarian ethical formulations within this radical pedagogical hermeneutic. Denzin argues for the intersection of the performative and the political on the terrain of a praxis-based ethic. *This ethic performs pedagogies for the oppressed, and enacts a politics of possibility grounded in pedagogies (performative practices) of love, care and compassion.* It is rearticulated and redefined every time it is reimagined; every time it is possibilized; and every time it is performed. While Denzin works to *retheorize the grounds of performance studies, redefining the political and the cultural in performative and pedagogical terms,* his work reconfirms Conquergood's (2002) description of performance studies as an interventionist strategy; an embodied form of radical research; a culture-centered epistemology that "struggles to open the space between analysis and action, and to pull the pin on the binary opposites between theory and practice" (pp. 145–46). *Performance is a methodology that is radical because it cuts to the root of how knowledge is organized,* both in the academy as an institutional and cultural construct, and in the ways pedagogy reflects a particular set of performances that can help to reimagine the world.

NOTE

1. Giroux cites Grossberg in building his larger argument for "performing public pedagogy as engaged social citizenship."

REFERENCES

Alexander, B. K., Anderson, G., & Gallegos, B. P. (2005). Introduction. In *Performance theories in education: Power, pedagogy, and the politics of identity* (pp. 1–11). Mahwah, NJ: Erlbaum.

Austin, J. L. (1962). *How to do things with words.* Cambridge, MA: Harvard University Press.

Bartolome, L. I. (1996). Beyond the methods fetish: Toward a humanizing pedagogy. In P. Leistyna, A. Woodrum, & S. A. Sherblom (Eds.) *Breaking free: The transformative power of critical pedagogy* (pp. 229–252) (Reprint Series No. 7, Harvard Education Review). Cambridge: MA: Harvard Graduate School of Education.

Boal, A. (1985). *Theatre of the oppressed.* New York: Theatre Communication Group.

Butler, J. (1995). *Gender trouble: Feminism and the subversion of identity.* New York: Routledge.

Conquergood, D. (1998). Beyond the text: Toward a performative cultural politics. In S. J. Dailey (Ed.), *The future of performance studies: Visions and revisions* (pp. 25–36). Annandale, VA: National Communication Association.

Conquergood, D. (2002). Performance studies: Interventions and radical research. *The Drama Review, 46*(2), 145–156.

Edgerton, S. H. (1993). Toni Morrison teaching the interminable. In C. McCarthy & W. Crichlow (Eds.), *Race identity and representation in education* (pp. 220–250). New York: Routledge.

Freire, P. (1998). *Teachers as cultural workers: Letters to those who dare to teach.* Boulder, CO: Westview.

Giroux, H. A. (1996). Doing cultural studies: Youth and the challenge of pedagogy. In P. Leistyna, A. Woodrum, & S. A. Sherblom (Eds.), *Breaking free: The transformative power of critical pedagogy* (pp. 83–107) (Reprint Series No. 7, Harvard Education Review). Cambridge: MA: Harvard Graduate School of Education.

Giroux, H. A. (2001). Cultural studies as performative politics. *Cultural Studies ↔ Critical Methodologies, 1*(1), 5–23.

Giroux, H. A., & Shannon, P. (Eds.). (1997). *Education and cultural studies: Toward a performative practice.* New York: Routledge.

Grossberg, L. (1994). Introduction: Bringin' it all back home—Pedagogy and cultural studies. In H. Giroux & P. McLaren (Eds.), *Between borders: Pedagogy and the politics of cultural studies* (pp. 1–25). New York: Routledge.

Grossberg, L. (1996). Toward a genealogy of the state of cultural studies. In C. Nelson & D. D. Parameshwar Gaonkar (Eds.), *Disciplinarity and dissent in cultural studies* (pp. 87–107). New York: Routledge.

hooks, b. (1994). *Teaching to transgress: Education as the practice of freedom.* New York: Routledge.

McLaren, P. (1993). *Schooling as a ritual performance: Towards a political economy of educational symbols and gestures.* New York: Routledge.

McLaren, P. (1998). *Life in schools: An introduction to critical pedagogy in the foundations of education* (3rd ed.). New York: Longman.

Mohanty, S. P. (1989). Us and them: On the philosophical bases of political criticism. *Yale Journal of Criticism, 2*(2), 1–31.

Pineau, E. L. (1994). Teaching is performance: Reconstructing a problematic metaphor. *American Educational Research Journal, 31,* 3–25.

Pineau, E. L. (1998). Performance studies across the curriculum: Problems, possibilities and projections. In S. J. Dailey (Ed.), *The Future of performance studies: Visions and revisions* (pp. 128–135). Annandale, VA: National Communication Association.

Pineau, E. L. (2004.) *Articulate bodies: Under/mining the trope of performance in pedagogical praxis.* Unpublished manuscript.

Simon, R. I. (1992). *Teaching against the grain: Texts for a pedagogy of possibility.* New York: Bergin & Garvey.

14

Fieldwork in the Performance Studies Classroom

Learning Objectives and the Activist Curriculum

NATHAN STUCKY

I remember a childhood rhyme from my primary school days, "We're all in our places with bright shining faces." Looking back now, I see this as an implied directive pointing children to create particular performances of classroom order—to join in a uniform group activity, to be properly seated at our desks, to hold our facial expressions in demonstrations of willing attention, and to internalize these directives into attitudes of compliant enthusiasm. Such directives participate in the dominant culture's regulation of performances linked in this case to an ideology that disciplines the bodies of students in the classroom (Dolan, 2001; Hamera, 2004). The elemental function of the classroom involves behavioral change, whether from an era of regulated bodies or from a more recent one informed by critical pedagogy in which "the body is conceived as the interface of the individual and society" (McLaren, 1995, p. 64). As a teacher I enter my classroom with the expectation of change or at least assuming the potential that both my students and I can explore new possibilities. In the performance studies classroom, expectations of change are often framed with concern for personal and political issues, as well as social issues related to gender, race, class, and ethnicity linked to the potential for individual growth and learning.

What I discuss as exploring new possibilities with the expectation of change is similar to ways Joni Jones describes the performance studies classroom as a space of resistance within the academy where she hopes to effect social change (2002, p. 175). It also recalls what Soyini Madison has termed "the performance of possibilities." Madison writes: "In a performance of possibilities, I see the 'possible' as suggesting a movement culminating in creation and change" (1998, p. 277). I think I sometimes back away from the "profess" part of "professor" because it can be confused with dominating authority and with institutional hegemony. If I don't want to tell my students what to think, but rather engage them with possibilities, the classroom dynamic requires my own flexibility. If I hope for performances of possibilities in my students I must start with myself. As Madison puts it, this work must begin by examining our purpose and assumptions; those forces that motivate and undergird what we do as teachers, as well as the role and function of pedagogy (p. 278).

In this chapter I consider some of the broad purposes and uses of performance studies within university education by examining its place in the curriculum, and the pedagogy of performance beyond the classroom. I begin with a set of questions that I hope to address both directly and indirectly in the following pages:

- What does performance studies teach?
- What do students learn?
- What are the goals and objectives in the performance studies curriculum?
- What ideologies are engaged in the performance studies classroom?
- What are the values of performance studies in the university and in liberal education?

Perhaps because performance studies is a field substantially engaged with personal and social discovery, with theory as well as artistic practice, it inspires greater formal discussion of its efficacy. When we ask questions about the efficacy, effectiveness, viability, value, or importance of performance studies, we are raising questions that are connected to issues of class and privilege in ways that have particular implications for university education. What values do we teach and for whom? As an educational enterprise, especially as it is practiced in many institutions in the United States, performance studies participates in an ongoing experiment in social awareness and illuminates possibilities for social change. The metamorphic capacity of performance studies

adjusts to needs, to new circumstances; it expands or contract as conditions require. How are those adjustments reflected in performance studies pedagogy? Without presuming that all teachers of performance studies or all institutions are alike, the articulated purposes (and assumptions) in performance studies curricula may provide some insight.

As a preliminary exploration of these and other questions I provide examples from representative performance studies syllabi, performances, and other activities from universities across the United States. Through these examples, I describe performance studies coursework and examine the performance work of scholar/artists whose teaching extends beyond the formal construct of the classroom. In writing and producing works on and through performance, many teachers/scholars of performance studies carry their influence from the classroom directly to the public. In the final section I examine how performance studies does the work of social engagement in the classroom and especially in public performances in traditional and nontraditional performance spaces, including those staged in college and university venues.

The final section of this chapter theorizes the work of performance studies through what I call "The Performance Studies Toolbox" by introducing a theoretical frame, identifying a set of practices, and enumerating performance studies' pedagogical engagement in a list of learning objectives. This preliminary study is limited by four interrelated variables: the sample size of syllabi examined, number of performances, the selection process (initial judgment about diverse program scope, geographic distribution, availability, and institutional variety) and the parameters of the literature review. My provisional conclusions, therefore, derive from empirically generated data as well as my years of experience as a teacher, as a performance studies scholar, and as the chair of a department that hosts a performance studies program.

Because different university structures place performance studies in diverse administrative units, the discussion of courses and curricula here should be read as indicative, not exhaustive. Performance studies may be housed in such departments as theatre, communication, English, speech communication, or anthropology; it may exist as a stand-alone department; as an undergraduate, masters, or doctoral specialization or as an interdisciplinary program; it may be administered in colleges of fine arts, communication, liberal arts, humanities, or arts and sciences. My objective here is not to conduct a census, but rather to point toward the territory where performance studies practices are located. I hope to show something of how *the performance of possibilities* is already "reaching toward light, justice, and enlivening possibilities" wherever it is located (Madison, 1998, p. 284).

CHANGING SOCIETY ONE STUDENT (AND ONE TEACHER) AT A TIME

Much of performance studies pedagogy over the past few decades (and, in various forms, over centuries) can be viewed as balancing the goals of enlightening individual students on one side, and influencing society on the other. Performance is *"revelatory to the performer . . . [and] to the listeners"* (Long & HopKins, 1982, p. xiii), and it may also participate in emancipatory political discourse in the service of furthering progressive utopian ideals (Denzin, 2003). Some teachers, perhaps most, move toward reforming society by starting with change of the individual. As Joni L. Jones puts it in the description of one of her courses at the University of Texas: "The course rests on the basic assumption that performance changes the performer, thereby changing the world" (2002, p. 176).

When we talk about change, or *the performance of possibilities* in the performance studies curriculum, it might be helpful to take a page from communication scholarship about

persuasion. We don't expect to turn people 180 degrees in a single speech, an evening's performance, or a class lecture (although let's not discount those possibilities). In persuasion we'd measure success in increments. *Possibilities are realized.* How do you measure that moment? I remember once in a theatre history seminar many years back, the venerable Oscar Brockett discounted the prevailing idea that the medieval European church gradually developed a revised western theatre incrementally moving from within the church to without to larger and more elaborate script, notions that are still widely held by many historians. Dr. Brockett simply stated, "All it takes is for somebody to have an idea." Once you have the idea you can jump from two actors to twenty instead of stepping up to three, then four, then five. You can skip from simple to elaborate scenery. And in the performance studies classroom you can act on possibilities in that moment because there are no other moments. *All moments are now.* Teachers can help create possibilities for themselves and their students, but they cannot control change. Change, when it happens, always happens in the moment of its engagement, the now.

One of the more provocative advocates of performance as a means of affecting change in the social world has been Augusto Boal. His adherents, now scattered widely, have adopted and adapted his work, promulgated these variants in diverse circumstances, and found multiple successes. Boal is *de rigeur* in many performance studies curricula these days. In his course "Empowerment Through Theatre," at the College of William and Mary, Bruce McConachie named the following goal in the syllabus: "By exploring the political and theatrical ideas and techniques of Augusto Boal, students will learn ways of empowering themselves and others" (McConachie, 2002, p. 247). McConachie found that "modest progressive work centered on the goals and strategies of Boal can occur in academic settings if one can negotiate the immense gap between Boal's Marxist assumptions about oppression and the student's lack of experience of oppressive situations" (p. 247).[1] The course objectives included empowering the students and also helping "students learn ways of empowering others" (p. 249). Here one can clearly see the dual interests of performance studies courses as socially involved on two levels: change of the individual student and change in the larger social context.

Some courses take an oblique approach to social change in which the articulated focus centers on exploring the self. Others take a more direct approach in which the underlying assumption is that critical and reflexive awareness is the intended purpose. For example, the description of "Topics in Critical Theory: Critical Race Theory" at New York University states: "This course will offer students methodologies to think critically about race and ethnicity. Fundamental phenomenological questions about the relationship between 'self' and 'other' will launch our inquiry" (Muñoz, 2003). The expectation that students will "think critically about race and ethnicity," projects a shift in the kind of critical thinking students presumably bring with them into the classroom. It is also a direct intervention in the types of traditional curricular and instructional processes that often avoid critical thinking about race and ethnicity. The activity implied by the offer to "think critically" implicates possibilities. In this case a particular kind of thinking is itself a site of performance, the pedagogical center.

Performance studies courses routinely address critical thinking, as well as oral and written communication skills, along with objectives oriented to the specific course. The following course objectives from "Women & Theatre: The Politics of Representation" at Miami University, can serve as a typical example. While the topic centers around a feminist approach to theatre, the objectives include broad individual development goals

(e.g., writing and critical thinking) consonant with expectations in many university classes. The instructors articulate the following course goals:

By the end of the semester . . . we hope students will have

1. increased their familiarity with a variety of dramatic forms;

2. learned to integrate theoretical materials into various forms of expression;

3. enriched their understanding of the relationship between artistic products and cultural agenda;

4. examined societal patterns of power and assumptions about suitable roles and behavior for women;

5. increased their ability to read and critique a visual text;

6. developed their skills as critical thinkers and "resistant readers";

7. strengthened their skills as seminar participants; and

8. expanded and improved their writing skills.

(Howard & Harrison-Pepper, 2003).

The course begins by asking how women have been presented on stage. In questioning the quality of those representations, it proposes to

prompt examinations of the ways in which gender is a performed cultural construct, made up of learned values and beliefs. The course also introduces ideas about race, ethnicity, and sexuality, and the ways in which these contribute to the cultural construction of identity.

Similar goals can be found in performance studies classes across the country. A course at

Arizona State University announces that it is "about communication, performance, and sexuality. Its goal is to challenge our understanding of human communication and sexuality through the examination of aesthetic performance texts" (Linde and Zukic, 2001).

Performance as Subject and as Method

Many performance studies classes involve *performance as a way of knowing;* they further the objective "to understand performance as a method of inquiry" (Pelias, 2001, p.1). While some performance scholars focus on *performances as a subject of study,* others view *performance as epistemological.* "Performance epistemology locates performance itself as a site and a method of study. In practice these two approaches 'interanimate' each other" (Stucky & Wimmer, 2002, p. 12). Descriptions of course expectations, for example, may bring together embodied immediate performances with writing and reflecting on the performances of self or others. A range of classroom behaviors may be specified as learning objectives that operationalize and clarify performance epistemology. In a course in "Performance as Cultural Criticism" for example, students were expected to: "Begin composing and linking their own emerging performance art sensibility to both social science and philosophical perspectives on communication theory and culture" (Gingrich-Philbrook, 1996). In some cases the link between subject and performance may be stated even more directly. Pineau's "Performance of Gender" class syllabus advises that,

> We will explore . . . through the act of performance. That means using embodied rehearsal as a method of discovery and aesthetic performance as a means of communicating what we've learned. By experimenting bodily with our own and others' gendered performances, we will work to gain experiential understanding about the process, the

patterns, and the implications of gender socialization. (Pineau, 2002b)

During the semester students learn what it means to "act like a man" or "act like a woman" through critical readings and discussion, as well as through performance. As is clear from Pineau's directive in coming to know through embodiment, performance itself is the means of discovery.

Performance studies teachers routinely ask critical questions to articulate course objectives and to further the students' engagement with the material. Howard and Harrison-Pepper, for instance, explore ways in which gender, race, and ethnicity are performative cultural constructs. They question whether theatre is really a "mirror held up to nature" and if so, how representative are the images of women that the theatre holds. Madison (2002) organizes her course, "African American Literature and Performance," around a cluster of related questions:

- What is the cultural and literary significance of autobiography?

- What does autobiography tell us about history and social context?

- What is revealed about African American life and culture in the four autobiographies assigned for the class?

- What are the unique contributions that these five autobiographies, in particular, add to our understanding of African American and American life, art, politics, and culture.

In this case the objectives of the course are implied by the questions asked. The context and course objectives are realized in the collaborative process of instruction. At the end of the term, one would expect students' ability to provide answers would have developed. The pattern of using questions to establish course goals can also be seen in Pollock's "Problems in Contemporary Performance Theory: Excess" class. Pollock first establishes a background for her class through an introductory description of issues that revolve around surplus value and normative identity practices (Pollock, 2003). The implied learning objectives in Pollock's class emerge from a series of additional questions in her syllabus:

- Beyond discourses of transgression and subversion, is it possible to exceed without reproducing and consolidating norms of identity and practice?

- When is excess good fun, hysterical pleasure, superfluity, and loss beyond measure, unheralded desire, the premise and supplement of disciplinary constraints?

- How does excess figure in economies of consumption articulated in the performing body (when shopping becomes eating becomes fat becomes "the fat lady" becomes waste and wasting away)?

- To what extent is excess the surplus value of a kind of intellectual production, what Barthes considered the need to speak "excessively" about reality? How do we evaluate the "excess" of any given practice?

The questions performance studies scholars frequently ask in teaching a course point toward broad issues in complex ways. The pursuit of answers inevitably reaches across disciplinary lines. Pollock's reading list, for instance includes literary theorists, philosophers, performance studies scholars, sociologists, anthropologists, and an array of cultural theorists.

This strategy of laying out what a student will learn (or is expected to encounter) implies a set of pedagogical procedures that, while ultimately centering attention on the student's relation to the course material, begins with invocations of ongoing scholarship. The overarching questions drive the course, provide the central focus, and become the measure of what the professor expects of students in the class.

The pedagogical practice of asking questions is a time-honored technique one that is not limited to performance studies classes. Asking a question makes relevant a response—that is, it invites a performance (whether that is an internal thought or culminates in some outward expression). Perhaps performance studies teachers sow many questions in order to harvest abundant possibilities in the form of performances or cultural critiques of social enactments.

Disciplining Classroom Performances in Performance Classes

Performance studies teachers in the present study often specified ways in which students were expected to encounter the material; in this form they described particular desired behaviors. To the extent that performance epistemology centers especially on experiential learning, the performance studies curriculum places weight on classroom behavior. Challenges to the mind/body split have practical classroom realizations. This may not differ from other disciplines in kind, but it is likely a shift in degree. Unlike some university courses that are structured around lectures and exams (e.g., large lecture hall classes and electronically scanned objective tests), performance studies classes typically involve an array of required in-class behaviors.

Linda Park-Fuller (2003) provides specific descriptions of three categories of behavior that garner credit for participation in her narrative performance class: cooperation and consideration, responsibility, and creativity and intellectual ideas. Park-Fuller explains likely behaviors in each category. For example,

> For creativity and intellectual ideas points are earned by coming up with good ideas as discussion participant, performer, audience member, or workshop member, by acting on those ideas, watching for opportunities to improve something, taking risks as a

performer, sharing insights about the readings, making intellectually strong contributions in discussion and written exercises.

It is worth noting that Park-Fuller gives special attention to particular kinds of enactment: not just "coming up with good ideas" but acting on them. She privileges doing. She goes to some length to describe a host of proactive behaviors she especially values. Park-Fuller specifies "taking risks as a performer" as an example of a valued behavior. Risk-taking in performance may involve personal vulnerability and it may raise the stakes of both success and failure. Helping students learn to monitor a group's activity and to assume an active response points toward an additional, though only implicit, objective: the classroom provides a model for students to carry outside the classroom. It says in effect, "When you see something that needs to be done, take action! It is your responsibility." What that may mean when translated into other arenas is impossible to predict, but the value clearly honors action, "making contributions," not sitting idly by.

Expectations of specific classroom performances are found throughout the course materials of performance studies classes; students are instructed to wait for applause to enter when arriving late on a performance day, to pay attention to other students' presentations, and even such explicit admonishments as: "Do not eat, drink, smoke, or chew in class. Turn off all cell phones and beepers" (Eckhard and Corey, 2003). Such rules, though apparently deriving from practical experience (problems in previous semesters result in rules appearing on subsequent syllabi), reflect the institutionalized disciplining of bodies implied by "We're all in our places with bright shining faces." In essence, part of the learning in any class is about the nature of learning itself in a given culture (e.g., this university classroom, this academic field). What can appear to be merely trivial issues of classroom etiquette may indicate substantial methodological processes.

Far from being trivial, requirements such as asking students to turn off cell phones says in effect, this academic discipline values performances, including those of other students—pay attention! Because many performance studies courses are theoretically oriented to an epistemology of embodied performance, the performance behaviors envisioned in classes can be central to the course objectives. My high school government teacher explained that, in teaching how the United States government worked, his course was intended to make us better citizens. We might ask what sort of citizens, or what expectations for future social behaviors, are fostered in performance studies classrooms. These expectations go beyond knowledge of particular subject matter. What Park-Fuller is teaching, when she expects students to *take action*, has more to do with particular kinds of socially performed engagement than with the content of a given text. Take risks and watch for opportunities to improve something—these are life skills that extend beyond the classroom.

Radical Pedagogy and Traditional Expectations

The relation of radical pedagogy to the traditional operation of a class can result in specific determinations of class performance regardless of course material. I am using the term "radical pedagogy" to suggest a pedagogy dedicated to widespread change and reform. Without wishing to assume the same territory, my sense of radical pedagogy borrows heavily from the critical pedagogy of Augusto Boal, Paolo Freire, and Peter McLaren. As McLaren explains: "Developed by progressive educators and researchers attempting to eliminate inequalities on the basis of social class, [critical pedagogy] has sparked up to the present a wide array of anti-sexist, anti-racist, and anti-homophobic, classroom-based curricula and policy initiatives" (2000, p. 35). The need to transform the educational apparatus is frequently connected to issues of social change to which educational processes are always reflexive and projective. Catherine Walsh contends, "issues of democracy, justice, and social vision are at the base of our work as educators, and, as such, provide a contextual framework for educational and pedagogical reform" (1996, p. 228).

No matter the subject, few professors appear to disregard the institutional constraint of assigning grades as a validation of knowledge and learning. These are extrinsic valuations of social process that are somatically felt and known, and are not always validation of what students know, and how they know it. Elyse Pineau offers insight on how one might negotiate this difficult terrain: "only through means of performance . . . can liberating pedagogies be developed that will enable students to construct meanings that are lived in the body, felt in the bones, and situated within the larger body politic" (Pineau, 2002a, p. 53). Admittedly, the outline of a course expressed in a syllabus does not always speak to the daily possibilities of transgressive pedagogical strategies. It can and does identify overarching expectations that serve as direction for experience, criteria for experience, and the ground on which both intrinsic and extrinsic evaluations might occur.

Performance studies courses typically (although not necessarily) assume humanistic and pluralistic values in identifying their objectives. The changes expected from students range from shifts in intellectual and critical understanding to felt bodily knowledge to demonstrable behavior differences as students move through the world. A number of performance studies courses address issues specifically related to understanding sexuality or gender. At Arizona State University, for example, a course entitled "Communication and the Performance of Sexuality" was designed to "challenge our understanding of human communication and sexuality through the examination of aesthetic performance texts." During the spring 2001 term, sections

of the course taught "how the enactment (performance) of personal sexual identity shapes societal and cultural norms of sexuality" (Linde and Zukic, 2001).

Performance studies courses frequently address particular social, political, or cultural concerns through the lens of performance. For example, the course description for Diana Taylor's "Topics in Latin American Performance: Performance and Conquest," at New York University includes this statement: "Performance was fundamental to both indigenous and European colonial epistemology, and was a primary means through which both cultures maintained or contested social authority . . . we will try to gain an appreciation of the complex function of performance in the political drama of new world conquest and colonization" (Taylor, 2003). Performance studies pedagogy frequently links performance outside the classroom with the classroom as a cultural performative arena. Given the understanding that "Global events and transnational movements such as colonialism and contemporary evangelism have uniquely *local* consequences that are often manifested, and sometimes transformed, through performance" (Kisliuk, 2002, p. 108)—it is not surprising that performance studies teachers conceptualize the classroom as a site where consequential issues can be explored, and the classroom as a space where issues are already manifested as regimes of social and cultural practice can be manifested in curriculum. The enormous ambition of many performance studies courses raises questions about how to assess their success.

Measuring efficacy and effectiveness in the university classroom conjures a host of questions. *Effectiveness for whom? Who is measuring and for what purposes? What values are involved?* Jon McKenzie discusses efficacy in the dominant paradigms in performance studies by tracing the "transformation of efficacy from transgression to resistance, the shifts in models from theater to theory and from ritual to performance art" (McKenzie, 2001,

p. 44). In a description of performance studies' shifting value systems, McKenzie contrasts the "valorization of theory" that has "displaced theater as a guiding model of performance studies; theory is what scholars produce, not theater, etc." (p. 45). In order to resolve these differences McKenzie argues that we need not select one over the other:

> Rather than choose between these two readings, we might instead draw them together and understand the paradigm's reevaluation of efficacy and its own institutionalization as two mutually reinforcing developments. That is, performance scholars have responded simultaneously to changes in the performances they study and in their own performances *of* study. Again, both of these developments must be situated within a broader sociopolitical context. Let us recall Blau's memory of the late 1960s' libidinal thinking which "subverted the repressive text and disrupted, along with the universities, the institutions of literature and theatre." Performance scholars' suspicion of institutions and discursively based methods and their theorization of embodied transgression were responses to normative forces at work both outside and inside the halls of the academy. (p. 45)

The core tension McKenzie identifies lies between a performance studies that creates institutional legitimization professionally and within the academy, and a performance studies that challenges "the Establishment, the Ivory Tower, the university lecture machine, and all the paradigms that shift about in them" (p. 48). The ultimate success of a given performance studies curriculum thus must be framed by larger questions of disciplinary definition and purpose, and those in turn may be framed in relation to institutions.

One finds varied responses of performance studies educators within particular institutional contexts. For the most part the paradigms or value systems of the curricula (and the teachers who teach within them) are implied, not specified, and must be deduced from various statements of purpose, goals,

objectives, and occasional theoretical writings. For some, the performance studies classroom "becomes a borderland, a liminal space capable of disrupting the social order" (Jones, 2002, p. 175). Others assume a more benign relationship among institutions. William Beeman describes the effectiveness of his performance studies class in relation to the disciplinary affiliations of his students: "Students from the performing arts regularly come to see the interconnection of performance activity with 'real life,' and students from the social sciences and humanities gain an appreciation of the power of performance to transform society and culture" (2002, p. 96). A number of critical self-reports of performance studies classroom efforts provide some descriptions of efficacy (Bowman and Bowman, 2002; McConachie, 2002; Jones, 2002). Many universities have assessment procedures in place that are designed to provide some helpful measures usually at the end of a given term. But it is not so easy to know the long-term effects of a given class or experience.

TEACHING BEYOND THE CLASSROOM

The university performance studies enterprise frequently extends beyond the traditional classroom to additional performance venues. Formal college-credit instruction and research occurs in developing, directing, and producing theatrical productions on university stages and in community locales. An essay by Linda Park-Fuller and Ronald Pelias surveys alternative and experimental performances, noting that many classroom performances derive from personal or autobiographical sources (Park-Fuller & Pelias, 1995, p. 126). In these performances one often sees the student's personal negotiation with social issues and pressures. Stories of coming out as gay, lesbian, or transgendered; stories in response to societal expectations of beauty (too fat, too thin, too blonde, too bland); stories of ageism and racism, stories in which the performer deals with personal loss—these and similar experiences fill performance studies classrooms and public performances.

In many university settings the classroom's permeable borders extend into productions staged for the public. Whether formal credit is assigned for working on these performances, and regardless of whether faculty members get course releases or other acknowledgment for their work, these venues often provide the most intense and involved instruction. When performance studies work moves from the classroom *per se* to more public venues—social critique, challenges to action, and calls for change may become more explicit. These performances are typically written (or scripted) locally and designed for specific community audiences. In these instances the potential "classroom" extends to different publics. Instead of students enrolled in a college course, the production, whether radical street theatre or a more traditional form, may more directly impact the community. Indeed, some practitioners design their productions specifically to address local concerns for local citizens.

In 1993 at the University of North Carolina at Chapel Hill, for instance, Soyini Madison staged a production about the cafeteria workers' strike that happened on the UNC campus in 1963 (Madison, 1998). Madison's production, based on the personal narratives of strike leaders and other workers, found many of those workers and their friends and family members as special guests of honor in attendance on opening night. Madison writes that the performance was "revolutionary in enlightening citizens to the possibilities that grate against injustice" (1998, p. 280).

Performance studies scholar/artists have addressed such subjects as: Hmong refugee concerns (Conquergood, 1992), breast cancer survival and the woman's body (Jenkins, 2002; Park-Fuller, 1995), the McCarthy era communist witch hunts (Jeffrey, 1977), farm crisis narratives (Carlin, 1992) and many others. Linda Park-Fuller (2003) catalogues a broad range of socially engaged performances under the rubric of Playback Theatre. The

exploits of the Mickee Faust Club, a cabaret performance troupe in Tallahassee, Florida, help to illustrate performance's potential range. The group "performs an eclectic mix of low-brow humor, literary and cinematic parodies, political and musical satire" that poke fun at liberal and conservative groups alike (Schriver & Nudd, 2002, p. 196).

One can find examples of engaged social performance at universities across the nation. Indeed, performances crafted to address specific local issues, as well as those that may also have broader implications, mark a major vein of performance studies work in many programs. By way of illustration, I will note just some of those from one university—The Kleinau Theatre at Southern Illinois University where I teach. I use these examples here because I am well acquainted with them, and I know how they address social issues. I expect that similar examples could be found at other universities.

- *Walking on Our Knees* (Bragg, 1989) collected oral histories and personal narratives of coal miners in southern Illinois and Kentucky, then crafted them into a formal performance. Drawing on her own family history and her understanding of this group of workers, Bragg's production spoke directly to issues of class for audiences that included miners as well as the university community.
- *Do You Sleep in That Thing?* was created by Jim Ferris (1992) about his experiences and those of other self-identified "differently abled" students, who presented their own stories as well as excerpts from literature to a mostly "temporarily abled" audience. The bipeds who attended had to duck under crutches, braces, and wheel chairs suspended from the ceiling to find their seats in the auditorium while those on wheels rolled right through, easily clearing the various devices dangling above their heads. The show specifically critiqued university and community awareness and resources devoted to accessibility issues as outmoded and inadequate—a particularly pointed criticism for a campus that had for many years identified itself as in the vanguard for its disability services.
- *Breaking the Cycle* (Montalbano, 1993), built on the experiences of women in a

domestic violence shelter, dealt with the power of personal narrative in helping abused women escape the cycle of victimization and become survivors.

- *Promises in Pink* (Ford-Brown & Glaspie, 1994) addressed issues related to breast cancer awareness; it was developed out of the personal narratives of breast cancer survivors, their friends, and family members. Staged in part as a public service, a professional health counselor was on hand to provide pre- and post-show information and contact and to help with the potential responses of audience members.
- *Get Up, Stand Up* (Rich, 1994) used techniques derived from Augusto Boal to deal with a variety of local student concerns: discrimination, campus safety (especially for women), date rape, and other topics.
- *Putting your Body on the Line* (Alexander, 1995) was a one-person show that explored various images and representations of black male identity through use of narrative, poetry, song, and movement.
- *Nursing Mother* (Pineau, 1998) developed in performance a response to the death of Pineau's mother and the birth of a child concretized in critique of the medical establishment for its treatment of people at both ends of life.
- *The Menstrual Show* (Charlesworth, 1999) explored the commercialization and commodification of cultural values relating to women's bodies, especially the proscriptions regarding the dominant culture's response to women's reproductive cycles.
- *Beautiful Body: My Journey as a Fatty* (Howell, 2002) critiqued the dominant culture's obsession with the "perfect body," and in so doing invited the audience to reevaluate their own conceptions and prejudices.
- *On Becoming Japerican* (Tankei, 2004), developed from stories told by trans-national students and Tankei's own autoethnographic work, grappled with questions of prejudice, misunderstanding, and identity for those no longer completely Japanese, nor completely American.

Perhaps this listing of just a few representative examples from one university can serve to indicate a range of productions with the university as a site of performance. I've only noted some of the productions in one venue that

seemed to me, as an interested party, among the most directly connected to clearly identifiable social issues. No less significant are those that speak to issues perhaps more obliquely, that address circumstances important to the human situation without explicitly naming the condition addressed. In this category one might find many adaptations of literary work, or thematic performances that seek to change attitudes or address questions of deep importance. Theatrical approaches to social concerns may be more or less direct. For example, *Angels in America* speaks directly to the HIV/AIDS pandemic, to witch hunts of communists and homosexuals, and to other specific issues, while the contextual relevance of a production of *Hamlet* may be less obvious but equally relevant.

Performance studies practitioners also move beyond university settings to other sites: community gatherings, theatres, nightclubs, schools, houses of worship, businesses, shopping malls, and city streets. By taking her performance of *A Clean Breast of It* to women's groups, hospitals, conferences, and schools, Linda Park-Fuller (1995) enacts a committed social engagement performance adapted to local needs. She marshals the resources of performance to serve particular groups by taking performance to the people. By enacting her own resistance Park-Fuller furthers dialogue that brings people together and serves as a catalyst for others who need to tell their own stories. I conceptualize the classroom as social and cultural space both inside and outside of the literal parameters of the university and in the community, and, thus, a practiced place, where the pedagogy of engaging social issues becomes classroom space.

Although it is commonplace for some to separate the university from "the real world," that type of valuing buys into a problematic distinction. What impacts students in my classroom does not happen in an ivory tower vacuum; it happens in our real world. Just as the scientific work of professors in university laboratories may be highly regarded, the performance work of university professors should not automatically be considered less significant than work in nonacademic venues. (Some academic theatre journals, for example, will not accept essays that address university productions.) Craig Gingrich-Philbrook, whose one-person performances frequently deal with an array of social issues often centering on gay identity in a dominant heterosexist culture, has toured to audiences across the country. He negotiates complex theoretical perspectives within very accessible frames of human experience. As he reflects on the performer-audience relationship he writes,

> Having performed in smaller, 'name' spaces and at universities, I began to wonder about the politics involved in maintaining that performing for 40 people in Manhattan was somehow more important or valuable than for a hundred in St. Peter, MN or Canton, NY. Such a perspective highlights the performance as a product that's made it into a "good market" rather than as a process of social engagement. (C. Gingrich-Philbrook, personal communication, January 6, 2004)

Such a concern for performance as social engagement characterizes much of the work of performance studies artists who are scattered around the globe, this whether within or beyond the narrow confines of New York.

Over the past several decades in hundreds of other college and university productions across the United States, teachers and students have engaged the resources of performance studies pedagogy in pursuit of personal as well as progressive social change. Whether modestly or radically envisioned, performance studies pedagogy is characterized by an ethical social conscience, an active search for better ways to think and live, an objective to change the world. Even as these productions vary widely in subject matter, style, relation to their audiences, connection to the formal classroom, and performance situation, they share

a common interest in pedagogy, in teaching performers and audiences something of value, in encouraging social change.

PRAGMATICS, POSSIBILITIES, AND PEDAGOGICAL APPROACHES TO PERFORMANCE PEDAGOGY: THE PERFORMANCE STUDIES TOOLBOX AND AN EXTENDED CONCLUSION

In the following section I organize some of my findings and discuss ways that socially engaged performance studies links the conditions of theorizing with artistic and scholarly praxis and with pedagogy. The categories below revisit an argument I initially developed for an audience of Japanese educators. At that time I developed a case for a pragmatics of performance studies as "equipment for living," a phrase evoking Kenneth Burke's *literature as equipment for living* (Stucky, 2003). In what follows I want to revisit what I called "the Performance Studies Toolbox" in order to extend the discussion in the context of a socially situated performance studies. I address performance studies pedagogy by, first, outlining a two-part description of a theory of socially engaged performance studies involving its characteristics as theoretical inquiry and disciplinary praxis, and second, by introducing a list of learning objectives compiled from a selection of university courses.

I imagine there are two main compartments in the Performance Studies Toolbox. For convenience I will label these *Characteristics of Theoretical Inquiry*, and *A Set of Practices*. Of course I recognize that any particular set of practices might also belong in the theoretical compartment and I understand that theoretical inquiry itself can be a practice. These categories, though, should help to keep this toolbox organized even if the division is somewhat arbitrary. What do we find if we take a look at these tools? The following is an initial naming of some *equipment for living* observed in performance studies practice.

Performance Studies Toolbox

Characteristics of Theoretical Inquiry in Performance Studies

Performance Epistemology. Performance studies is interested in what we know through performance and how we come to know it.

Diversity. Performance studies is interested in the phenomena of performance in any setting; it encourages multicultural perspectives; it participates in cultural and intercultural studies.

Interdisciplinarity. Performance studies draws strength from cross-disciplinary work and the use of multiple methodologies.

Metamorphosis. Performance studies adjusts, adapts, develops, and changes; the field continuously redefines and transforms itself.

Self-reflexivity. Performance studies is self-aware; it theorizes its own theories and processes.

Practices in Performance Studies: A Preliminary Set

Performance as a Way of Knowing. Performance itself is both the subject of knowledge and a core method of discovery.

Embodiment. Performance knowledge is located in the body whether that is specific artistic skill or everyday behavior (e.g., dance, movement, gesture, habit, routine, play).

Critical Observation. Among the more familiar practices are ethnographic and artistic methods.

Theoretical Frames. Performance studies involves new ways of organizing information and perceptions.

Citation. Performance practice includes description and special vocabulary to develop terminology and ways of naming what is learned through and about performance.

Social Engagement. Performance studies fosters certain kinds of interaction among individuals and with institutions. There is often an overt sense of values and social responsibility in performance studies practices.

Theatrical Resources. Performance studies and performance practice utilize theatrical techniques and knowledge from diverse cultures.

Ritual Practices. Religious, social, and personal rituals are honored both as subjects for study and for their transformative potential.

Intercultural and Cross-cultural Communication. Performance typically requires an engagement with "the other," frequently involving communication among multiple cultures. Such engagements may problematize the subject/object relationship; and they may be intra- as well as interpersonal, intra- as well as intercultural.

Imagination and Invention. The creative and critical processes of performance studies rely on and develop imagination.

Written Communication. Writing and reading are both utilized as modes of performance.

Oral Communication. From singing and formal speaking to spoken poetry and ordinary conversation, orality is a fundamental performance phenomenon.

Interdisciplinary Practices. Performance studies encourages free borrowing across performing arts, sociology, anthropology, ethnography, cultural studies, history, music, communication, psychology, literary studies, philosophy, and other disciplines. Through its intentional interdisciplinarity performance studies vigorously blurs the boundaries.

One can see in these two broad lists some of the basic equipment in the performance studies toolbox. Performance studies teacher/scholar/artists carry some version of this toolbox when they enter the classroom. Individual teachers may have packed their own specialized tools as well, or left some others behind since flexibility is a hallmark of this work.

Just as Kenneth Burke felt that poetry had practical real world value, we can also see that performance studies tools foster specific behaviors. The following list is an initial organizing of some of the uses of the tools of performance studies when employed in education. It is not an exhaustive list nor given in order of importance. We might think of these as some ways the Performance Studies Toolbox is made operational. The eighteen items below are "performance studies learning objectives" that could be found in typical classrooms.

Performance Studies Learning Objectives

After completing performance studies courses, students should be better able to demonstrate understanding of or engage in the following activities within the context of the particular course.

1. Engaged in critical observation of self and others.

2. Increased openness to self and others.

3. Learned subject knowledge (related to the discipline or course).

4. Gained theoretical and critical knowledge.

5. Increased humility and respect for difference.

6. Improved abilities in teamwork.

7. Improved abilities in problem solving.

8. Experienced project completion.

9. Engaged in performance (including procedures and kinesthetic knowledge).

10. Developed interpersonal communication skills.

11. Improved public presentation skills (speaking, discussing, performing).

12. Gained analytical and critical thinking skills (including performance analysis, evaluation, and critique).

13. Enhanced writing skills.

14. Strengthened oral communication skills (including empathy and listening skills.

15. Enhanced intercultural awareness and intercultural communication skills.

16. Examined social and cultural values.

17. Discovered interdisciplinary practices (including research skills and methodologies).

18. Developed adaptability, flexibility, and creativity.

Of course I am not suggesting that every course in performance studies does each of these things all of the time. Because the performance studies program that I am affiliated with is located in a speech communication department, my list may emphasize the communicative aspects of performance more than a list that might be developed by a colleague located in a different academic unit. However, this listing of eighteen learning objectives indicates actual practice in existing curricula housed in various academic structures.

In order to clarify the range of possibilities in the list of learning objectives, I will expand one example. Let us consider number twelve, writing skills. As evidence for the writing skills developed in performance studies courses, one can turn to the first collection of essays on performance studies pedagogy, *Teaching Performance Studies* edited by Stucky and Wimmer (2002). Contributors to that volume describe eighteen different kinds of writing they teach in their courses, and that number is only indicative of the possible range:

> formal paper writing; research paper writing; analytical essay writing; script writing from research on current issues; script writing through sampling auto/biographical and/or historical material; script writing for performance of self (stories to be told, sermons, speeches, presentations, reports); script (re)writing from literary texts; script writing without words, or image scripts; scenario writing; book writing; more formal performance autobiography writing; lesson-plan writing; journalistic writing; poetry writing; narrative writing that is poetically crafted; and ethnographic writing. (Stucky & Wimmer, 2002, pp. 9–10)

Although writing clearly can be an integral part of the performance studies classroom, it generally supports a more fundamental skill set that is unique to performance studies education: "the most crucial skill set students have an opportunity to discover is a way of embodied thinking that encourages self-reflection and critical distance as well as empathy, concern with cultural contexts, values, and issues, and confidence in their own opinions" (Stucky & Wimmer, 2002, pp. 9–10). Although performance studies pedagogy cannot be limited to teaching skill sets alone, these are abundant in the curricula and may develop even in the more theoretical and critically oriented courses.

The power of performance (and its disciplinary subject area performance studies) derives from its breadth, variety, elasticity, and its fundamental significance. Annette Martin catalogues some of the elements that compose performance: the importance of relationships, and curiosity, the way performance challenges and problematizes the assumed "fixity of our identities," the way performance encourages growth through risk and personal discovery (1993, pp. xii–xiv). One challenge for performance studies in the academy lies in articulating its value, a value that exists in the tension between its immensity and the intensely personal and private scope of its potential subject. We can talk about skill sets and subject knowledge more easily perhaps than personal growth, deepening values, empathy, risk, and curiosity; which both challenges and limits traditional curricular and pedagogical methods.

I conceptualize my own performance studies classroom as a site for fieldwork. I am a participant, an observer, an active agent, both performer and audience. As an educational enterprise, performance studies, especially as it is practiced in many institutions in the United States, invokes possibilities and encourages responsible change in individuals and society. The objectives address issues of nationalism, postcolonialism, race, class, gender, and ethnicity in ways designed to shift the social order. Performance studies teaches flexibility and innovation. It supports increased global understanding, it enhances cross-cultural education, it provides theoretical insights, artistic experience, and practical knowledge. The Performance Studies Toolbox provides equipment for those seeking individual transformation, social change, and expanding possibilities.

NOTE

1. Cited in Stucky & Wimmer (2002).

REFERENCES

Alexander, B. (Creator/Director). (1995). *Putting your body on the line* [Performance]. Carbondale: Kleinau Theatre, Southern Illinois University.

Beeman, W. O. (2002). Performance theory in an anthropology program. In N. Stucky & C. Wimmer (Eds.), *Teaching performance studies* (pp. 85–97). Carbondale: Southern Illinois University Press.

Bowman, M., & Bowman, R. L. (2002). Performing the mystory: A textshop in autoperformance. In N. Stucky & C. Wimmer (Eds.), *Teaching performance studies* (pp. 161–174). Carbondale: Southern Illinois University Press.

Bragg, S. (Creator/Director). (1989). *Walking on our knees* [Performance]. Carbondale: Calipre Stage, Southern Illinois University.

Carlin, P. S. (1992) "That black fall": Farm crisis narratives. In E. C. Fine & J. H. Speer (Eds.), *Performance, culture, and identity* (pp. 135–156). Westport, CT: Praeger.

Charlesworth, D. (Creator/Director). (1999). *The menstrual show* [Performance]. Carbondale: Kleinau Theatre, Southern Illinois University.

Conquergood, D. (1992). Fabricating culture: The textile art of Hmong refugee women. In E. C. Fine & J. H. Speer (Eds.), *Performance, culture, and identity* (pp. 207–248). Westport, CT: Praeger.

Denzin, N. (2003). *Performance ethnography: Critical pedagogy and the politics of culture.* Thousand Oaks, CA: Sage.

Dolan, J. (2001). *Geographies of learning: Theory and practice, activism and performance.* Middleton, CT: Wesleyan University Press.

Eckhard, B., & Corey, F. (2003). *Performance technologies* [Unpublished course syllabus]. Tempe: Arizona State University.

Ferris, J. (Director). (1992). *Do you sleep in that thing?* [Performance]. Carbondale: Kleinau Theatre, Southern Illinois University.

Ford-Brown, L., & Glaspie, T. (Creators/Directors). (1994). *Promises in pink* [Performance]. Carbondale: Kleinau Theatre, Southern Illinois University.

Gingrich-Philbrook, C. (1996). *Performance as cultural criticism* [Unpublished course syllabus]. Hempstead, NY: Hofstra University.

Hamera, J. (2004). Exposing the pedagogical body: Protocols and tactics. In B. K. Alexander, G. L. Anderson, & B. P. Gallegos (Eds.) *Performance theories in education: Power, pedagogy, and the politics of identity* (pp. 63–81). Mahwah, NJ: Erlbaum.

Howard, R., & Harrison-Pepper, S. (2003). *Women & theatre: The politics of representation* [Unpublished course syllabus]. Miami, OH: Miami University.

Howell, S. (Creator/Director). (2002). *Beautiful body: My journey as a fatty* [Performance]. Carbondale: Kleinau Theatre, Southern Illinois University.

Jeffrey, P. R. (1977). No sense of decency: The army-McCarthy hearings. In B. W. Long, L. Hudson, & P. R. Jeffrey (Eds.), *Group performance of literature* (pp. 125–154). Englewood Cliffs, NJ: Prentice-Hall.

Jenkins, M. (2002, September 12–14). *Menopause and desire* [Performance]. San Francisco, CA: The Marsh Theatre.

Jones, J. (2002). Teaching in the borderlands. In N. Stucky & C. Wimmer (Eds.), *Teaching performance studies* (pp. 175–190). Carbondale: Southern Illinois University Press.

Kisliuk, M. (2002). The poetics and politics of practice: Experience, embodiment, and the engagement of scholarship. In N. Stucky & C. Wimmer (Eds.), *Teaching performance studies* (pp. 99–117). Carbondale: Southern Illinois University Press.

Linde J., & Zukic, N. (2001). *Communication and the performance of sexuality* [Unpublished course syllabus]. Tempe: Arizona State University.

Long, B. W., & HopKins, M. F. (1982). *Performing literature: An introduction to oral interpretation.* Englewood Cliffs, NJ: Prentice-Hall.

Madison, S. D. (1998). Performances, personal narratives, and the politics of possibility. In Dailey, S. J. (Ed.), *The future of performance studies: Visions and revisions* (pp. 276–286). Annandale: VA: National Communication Association.

Madison, S. D. (2002). *African American literature and performance.* [Unpublished course syllabus]. Chapel Hill: University of North Carolina.

Martin, A. (1993). The power of performance. In C. Corey (Ed.), *HIV education: Performing personal narratives* (pp. xii–xviii). Tempe: Arizona State University Press.

McConachie, B. (2002). Theatre of the oppressed with students of privilege: Practicing Boal in the American college classroom. In N. Stucky & C. Wimmer (Eds.), *Teaching performance studies* (pp. 247–260). Carbondale: Southern Illinois University Press.

McKenzie, J. (2001). *Perform or else: From discipline to performance.* London: Routledge.

McLaren, P. (1995). *Critical pedagogy and predatory culture: Oppositional politics in a postmodern era.* London: Routlege.

McLaren, P. (2000). *Che Guevara, Paulo Freire, and the pedagogy of revolution.* New York: Rowman & Littlefield.

Montalbano, L. (Adaptor/Director). (1993). *Breaking the cycle* [Performance]. Carbondale: Kleinau Theatre, Southern Illinois University.

Muñoz, J. (2003). Topics in critical theory: Critical race theory [Course description]. In *Performance studies course bulletin.* New York: Tisch School of the Arts, New York University. Retrieved December 8, 2003, from www.nyu.edu/tisch/performance

Park-Fuller, L. (1995). Narration and narratization of a cancer story: Composing and performing "A Clean Breast of It." *Text and Performance Quarterly, 15*(1), 60–67.

Park-Fuller, L. (2003). *Narrative performance* [Unpublished course syllabus]. Tempe: Arizona State University.

Park-Fuller, L., & Pelias, R. (1995). Charting alternative performance and evaluative practices. *Communication Education, 44,* 126–139.

Pelias, R. (2001). *Performance studies II* [Unpublished course syllabus]. Carbondale: Southern Illinois University.

Pineau, E. (Creator/Director). (1998). *Nursing mother* [Performance]. Carbondale: Kleinau Theatre, Southern Illinois University.

Pineau, E. (2002a). Critical performative pedagogy: Fleshing out the politics of liberatory education. In N. Stucky & C. Wimmer (Eds.), *Teaching performance studies* (pp. 41–54). Carbondale: Southern Illinois University Press.

Pineau, E. (2002b). *Performance of gender* [Unpublished course syllabus]. Carbondale: Southern Illinois University.

Pollock, D. (2003). *Problems in contemporary performance theory: Excess* [Unpublished course syllabus]. Chapel Hill: University of North Carolina.

Rich, M. (Creator/Director). (1994). *Get up, stand up* [Performance]. Carbondale: Kleinau Theatre, Southern Illinois University.

Schriver, K., & Nudd, D. (2002). Mickee Faust Club's performative protest events. *Text and Performance Quarterly, 22*(3), 196–216.

Stucky, N. (2003). Performance studies as equipment for living. *Dokkyo International Review, 16,* 57–68.

Stucky, N., & Wimmer, C. (2002). Introduction: The power of transformation in performance studies. In N. Stucky & C. Wimmer (Eds.), *Teaching performance studies* (pp. 1–29). Carbondale: Southern Illinois University Press.

Tankei, S. (Creator/Director). (2004). *On becoming Japerican* [Performance]. Carbondale: Kleinau Theatre, Southern Illinois University.

Taylor, D. (2003). Topics in Latin American performance: Performance and conquest [Course description]. In *Performance studies course bulletin.* New York: Tisch School of the Arts, New York University. Retrieved December 8, 2003, from www.nyu.edu/tisch/performance

Walsh, C. (1996). Making a difference: Social vision, pedagogy, and real life. In C. Walsh (Ed.), *Educational reform and social change: Multicultural voices, struggles, and visions* (pp. 223–240). Mahwah, NJ: Erlbaum.

15

Ambulant Pedagogy

MADY SCHUTZMAN

When performance studies reached disciplinary status, the notion of performativity as an analytic, as a way of reading cultural phenomena, began to permeate discourses in cultural studies, the humanities and social sciences. Students enthralled by performance theories and practices were not limited to investigations of traditionally defined staged events. Instead, the very components and tropes of performance—embodiment, play, rehearsing and scripting, improvisation, masquerade, illusion, liveness—to name just a few—became lenses through which to interrogate, document, and theorize cultural production. Innumerable arenas became subject to such performative scholarship—from courtrooms to street protests, from initiation rites to gender passing. Gender itself, along with identity, has subsequently been deconstructed and rewritten *vis-à-vis* performance research.

The classroom itself as site of institutionalized power dynamics has been one of many cultural spaces revised through a performative analytic. Regardless of the strategies and structures employed in a classroom (i.e., whether designed to foster conservative or radical ideology, whether abiding by traditional or alternative teaching models), there is always a performative dynamic at work. But I am not interested here so much in an analysis of the classroom per se—that is, in classroom as stage—as in how performativity as critique enhances radical pedagogical goals. By "radical pedagogical goals," I am presuming a critique of intransitive learning and "narration sickness" that characterize "schooling" (Freire, 1986, p. 57);[1] according to Augusto Boal (1992), a colleague of Paulo Freire, "Pedagogy is transitive. Or it isn't pedagogy" (p. 238).

Within progressive formats that foster dialogue, peer critique and assessment, student-driven syllabi, interdisciplinary agendas, and praxis, learning happens within the ever-shifting terrain between social markers of race, gender, and class and their various manifestations in embodied voices, interpretations, and languages. Pedagogy itself is revealed as the ever mutable and dynamic mystery that it is—an array of nonreproducible (always different) performances, the meaning of which occurs in elusive spaces between all partici-pants who are subject not only to information per se but also to *how* information, ideas, texts, personal stories, etc. are rendered aes-thetically.

Just as audiences leave the theatre recuper-ating different meanings from the inescapable collision of form and content in any staged performance, digesting the content *vis-à-vis* the representational style in which it was con-veyed (melodrama, musical comedy, natural-ism), students learn subject matter from *how* lectures, presentations, and discussions are aesthetically performed (ironically, tragically, indifferently). Education is the unquantifiable outcome of different people assembling differ-ent meanings from these pedagogical perfor-mances but also from a mess of unruly intentions, unconscious performances, endless mis-takes and mis-readings. It is impossible to map or predict the pedagogical enterprise, though of course we enter pedagogical space with a set of tools, goals, data, methodologies, and expectations; we come prepared only to recognize that preparedness launches but does not constitute meaning, effect, or affect. We would all be genuinely humbled to acknowl-edge that teaching and learning do not happen codependently or contiguously: what I think I am teaching is not necessarily what students are learning.[2]

But within this already dynamic landscape of pedagogy, performativity provides yet another tool, one that proffers a uniquely "*ambu*latory" approach to the *ambi*guous interactions we call teaching and learning. I borrow the term 'ambulatory' from Susan Foster's (1995) discussion of "ambulatory scholarship" (pp.11–17). Foster coins the term to critique how canonical scholarship neglects the language of the body as a means of marginalizing those discourses that intervene in patriarchal and logocentric value systems. The body as a discursive category invites inquiry not only into stigmatized social bodies (racialized and/or eroticized groups, queers, women) but also into the bodies of historical subjects that we write/teach about and the bodies of those who write. Through ambulant scholarship, Foster seeks to animate written discourse with an embodied sense of agency; she wants writing to do what human bodies do—to move, to perform.

The etymological root *ambi* means to wan-der. Performance studies—as a growing field of thought—provides an ambling, wandering analytic from which to read cultural phenom-ena. It couples the exploratory curiosity of wandering with a focused intentionality of dis-covering the unknown through bodily experi-ence. Put another way, performance studies has affected the very way in which we theorize by foregrounding kin(a)esthetics. In harness-ing motion as a *way* to perceive, we discover motion in what we study; in allowing thought to stray, we discover invaluable deviations and digressions. Kin(a)esthetics marries kinet-ics (action, transition, force) with aesthetics (strategy, style, perception). Employed as a critical tool, it provides a way to discern the unrecognized aesthetics of performances of everyday life (whether they be material, emo-tional, or ideological) as well as the movement hidden in seemingly static aesthetic representa-tions of the real.

In my discussion of movement through-out this chapter, I am not speaking exclusively of physical movement. However, I would like to cite here the work of Rudolf Laban (founder of *choreutics*, the art dealing with the analysis of movement) who *does* focus on bodies moving through space and time, pre-cisely as ground from which to speculate on kin(a)esthetics as a dialectic. Laban (1974) tells us that we must overcome the illusion of standstill, of snapshot-like perceptions of mind. Movement, he says, is in a continuous flow within the locality itself; the illusion of standstills creates an artificial separation of space and movement (p. 3). "Bodies moving in space" is reconceived as visible aspects of space (movement) interacting with invisible features of movement (space). (Empty) space authorizes bodily movement; bodily movement reconfigures space. Laban also devised a system of notation, a highly encoded written language to register the effort and shape of bodies moving in space. The hieroglyphic and gestural language is a kind of bridge between word and performance. It is an unstable in-between text that is a moving writing as well a writing of movement. Albeit metaphysical and positivist, it provides a readable map of bodies in space that defies snapshot cognition.

This chapter is a reflection on motion. I have chosen a handful of performance tropes through which to explore kin(a)esthetics as an orientation to our pedagogical endeavors. I do not provide exercises or models, though I do suggest that we reinvigorate the classroom, any classroom, with the performance theories and practices we study.[3] I am not providing here a linear argument but rather a movement through a series of thinkers, thinkers whose writings speak to kin(a)esthetics in some fashion and which, together, constitute a survey of sorts in performance theory. In each section, I pair two theorists to foster a more dialogic approach. I invite readers to imagine the possible relationships between the various texts cited and the pedagogical approaches they suggest.[4]

IDENTITY AND THE
EQUIVOCAL GIFT OF THE SIGN

"One does one's body."

—Butler, 1990, p. 272

With good reason postmodernism has relentlessly instructed us that reality is artifice, yet . . . we nevertheless go on living, pretending that we live facts, not fictions. . . . Some force impels us to keep the show on the road.

—Taussig, 1999, p. 14

We have learned from Judith Butler (1990) that "the body is not merely matter but a continual and incessant materializing of possibilities" (p. 272). Under her influence, I imagine my corporeal life awash in the effects of "unlived" experiences, the ephemeral stuff of dreams and imagination. Much of that unmanifested stuff, however unnameable, inscribes my bodily pronouncements with significance all the same. How and where does the body express personal memories, family legacies, and historical stories turned mythical from constant retelling? How and where does my body express the provocative characters I have consumed from books and popular culture? And then, so many of these characters consumed have bodies marked so differently from my own. Yet, they too inscribe my being significantly, even if by way of a reaction against, a fear of, a desire for, or a power with.

To counteract the stress on my very organs, muscles, and bones that are moved by these presences, both the physically proximate and the hypermediated ones, that I cannot help but encounter, I keep my "identities" porous, open to that intimate otherness that borders me. I assume that by manipulating, reconstructing, the nature of identity—something consequential and authoritative yet far more malleable than my physique—I can literally keep myself bending and not breaking. I keep the notions of mutation and ambling pulsing through the very skin of the characters and scripts to which I (often unwittingly) cathect, trying to ward off fixity and habit, trying to keep at bay the forgetfulness that eases the burden of critical awareness and its incessant bid to be accountable to changing circumstances. Meanwhile, practicing routine and indulging the comforts of its limits, orders, and security are seductive, even necessary. "We act and have to act," says Michael Taussig, "as if mischief were not afoot in the kingdom of the real and that all around the ground lay firm" (1999, p. 15). After all, the world turns on wheels that we simply can't afford to reinvent; no matter how strong our penchant for deconstruction, we too, need to ride the bus.

The fundamental precept of performance as an unstable ground upon which all actors are subjects and objects at once sets the pedagogical stage. We assume scripted positions but we play them knowing that we are not what that position denotes. As we study Butler, the markers of identity—expressed in gesture, speech, ideology, argument, action, gender, race—are riddled by the crooked nature of signs. Signs lie but they are all we have to work with. We rely upon them as defenses and as weapons. For instance, feminist writers Gayatri Spivak (1996) and Chéla Sandoval (2000), speaking of the performances of gender that signify sanctioned femininity, recommend "strategic essentialism" (p. 214) and "tactical subjectivity" (p. 58), respectively.[5] Identities-as-signs can be embodied and paraded for politically activist purposes without submitting to the potential tyranny of those signs. We play the fabrication critically. As we become more literate about the nature of signification, the "lie" is retrieved from its censure as betrayer of truth and becomes, instead, the new paradigm for understanding precisely what truth is made of. We use "fictions" as provisional platforms upon which to exercise agency.

Signs are the constructions we build our lives on, the social facts that postmodernism tries to deconstruct but cannot make disappear. It is in "this silly if not desperate place between the real and the really made-up" that we function as creative beings (Taussig, 1999, p. 15). It is also where we function as critical beings. One lesson of kin(a)esthetic awareness is that it points to where this conjoined creativity and criticality resides and vibrates. We act and watch ourselves act; we are subject and object at once; we look in two directions and write the difference. The constantly shifting change of perspective—doing, thinking about doing, redoing, rethinking, on and on—recasts notions of authority. That is, authority becomes founded not on a constancy of power and control and knowledge but on the ability to navigate a complex terrain of equivocal signs. The author—from autour, enlarger—critically deciphers and creatively recodes on the spot, improvises, in the act of commanding meaning.

> Claude Levi Strauss (1963) tells the story of Quesalid, a Kwakiutl Indian, who did not believe in the power of shamans. Desiring to expose them for their deceptive tricks, Quesalid first begins to associate with them, to learn their curious techniques of prestidigitation, simulation, the art of nervous fits, how to induce vomiting, and the use of spies. After working many months as an apprentice for an experienced shaman, all his suspicions confirmed, he himself was called upon to treat an ailing person. Knowing all the tricks, he performed a treatment and successfully "cured" his patient. Quesalid never abandoned his critical faculties and yet he became more and more intrigued about the "false supernatural" (p. 176)—those techniques that were, performatively speaking, much less convincing than his own, in which he spits out the illness in the form of a "bloody worm." Fully aware of the really made-up, Quesalid fights for and perfects a more real magic, and the word spreads of his remarkable style. People come to him sick and leave cured. And so Quesalid becomes a great shaman, seemingly "[losing] sight of the fallaciousness of the technique which he had so disparaged at the beginning" (p. 178). Levi Strauss concludes his tale saying, "Quesalid did not become a great shaman because he cured his patients; he cured his patients because he had become a great shaman." (Taussig, 1997, p. 180)

In spite of Quesalid's critical agenda founded on clear evidence of the legerdemain of Kwakiutl "healers," he became a living sign of what he was determined to debunk. Once he took on the body of the sham-man, albeit only (at first) as a disengaged substitute, the aesthetic power of the performance he mimicked transformed him into a shaman. The actual effect he had on patients—i.e., healing them—attests to an inescapable kin(a)esthetic interplay between Quesalid's physical body, the convincing performance Quesalid gave as he perfected the (artful) techniques, the longing of the patients, and the physical bodies of the patients. Facts and fictions dance, so to speak, through the ambivalent terrain we so glibly call cause and effect, recasting the seemingly linear relationship as a multidirectional and itinerant one. Everyone involved is well aware of magic, of the representational container being used to perform healing, and there is finally no reason to replace it with something more "real." Everyone seems to know it is a construct which, as Taussig tells us, "cannot be name-called out of (or into) existence, ridiculed or shamed into yielding up its powers . . . For in construction's place—what?" (Taussig, 1999, p. 15).

I would be remiss to not point out how those in the business of propaganda—corporate advertisers, the state, ideologues—employ the very same aesthetic tools to magically endow certain self-serving fictions with truth functions. Any content, any story, any image, any fact is prone to a shape-shifting existence in the hands of signifying strategists. What was yesterday's absolute is tomorrow's mistake, what had been denied is suddenly avowed, what was stolen is refabricated as an original, what teaches you you're deficient then sells you the cure. The gifts of performativity are always prone to abuse in ethical terms— that is, its tropes can be engaged to lie away others' very existence. As marginalized people perform (false) essentialism to fight the erasure, it is important to remember that such performances can and will be used as a weapon to magically demonize the group all the more. The exchange is slippery. Standing one's ground is a performance often worth staging.

JOINT WORK, THE TRICKSTER, AND THE JOKE(R)

Before a body can come to life, every separation, every boundary, must be breached in some way . . . Unless [bodily organs] can incorporate internal forces of

transgression, organic structures are in danger of dying from their own articulation.

—Hyde, 1998, p. 258

Jokes occur because society is structured in contradiction; there are no jokes in paradise.

—English, 1994, p. 9

Lewis Hyde (1998), writing about the trickster character in mythology and literature, asks the question of "how to stay in motion when the world puts barriers in your path" (p. 266). His answer is through joint work, translation, and rearticulation. The etymological root of "articulation" is from articulus, ar, to join, to fit, and arthron, a connecting word in language, a joint. Tricksters are boundary dwellers: they move boundaries, make boundaries porous, point to boundaries just at the moment of violating them. They engage these strategies, in large part, in order to redistribute power from those who have to those who do not, announcing their political goals through indirect means (lying and deception are their trademarks). The very nature of the new boundary constitution is transience; it is not intended to withstand time but rather to respond to its vicissitudes. By embracing and harnessing the virtues and tactics of nomadism—of refusing any one identity but playing all, and employing motion as a way of life and a mode of interaction—they reshape and respace the social terrain. The way to keep moving when the world puts obstacles in your path is, for Hyde, to shape-shift, to play the wild card, or joker, assuming whatever value is called for in order to trump the challenger. In this way, one "slips the trap of culture."

The genius of the trickster character—the anti-archetype archetype—derives from a belief that designs of all sorts are revitalized by contact with all that they normally exclude

(p. 266). This contact is a humored rather than a rigid one. Humors of the body keep the body fluid, keep the joints oiled. Similarly, humor itself as a performative trope, while it frees us from sobriety and preciousness, also provides a "joint space," a common space for those who would normally refuse company together. Literary theorist James F. English (1994) says, "Humor often makes us laugh with those whose psychical organization is radically irreconcilable with our own" (p. 14). Another way to understand this displacing and yet conjoining value of humor is to consider, briefly, jokes *per se* and how they offer an ambulant way to act and to theorize.

There are many kinds of jokes. The ones I am interested in here author a unique and disquieting space between common sense and uncommon sense, between assumed values and transgressive behavior.[6] They oscillate in the uncharted territory between them, demand that we, as listeners, reconsider our own boundaries of propriety, question our long held moral codes, and discover, in spite of ourselves, a new and unstable relationship between what is safe and what is offensive.

> An elderly man was at home, dying in bed. He smelled the aroma of his favorite chocolate chip cookies baking. He wanted one last cookie before he died. He fell out of bed, crawled to the landing, rolled down the stairs, and crawled into the kitchen where his wife was baking cookies. He crawled to the table and was just barely able to lift his arm to the cookie sheet. As he grasped a warm, moist, chocolate chip cookie, his wife suddenly whacked his hand with a spatula.
>
> "Why?" he whispered. "Why did you do that?"
>
> She replied, "They're for the funeral."

This kind of joke keeps us on the edge of our comfort zones; it makes our comfort zones uncomfortable; it wakes us up to our definitions of "us" (vs. them), and in the best scenario, keeps us vigilant regarding the hardening of our positions. English contends that when we laugh at jokes "we do not know what we are laughing at . . . While humor seeks to shore up identifications and solidarities, it does so by working on those very contradictions of 'society' which assure that all such identifications and solidarities will be provisional, negotiable, unsettled" (1994, p. 10). Jokes, he continues, would cease to exist if we could clearly delineate lines of identity and difference. It's the combined pleasure and discomfort of something being unresolvable that makes us laugh. Through the performative event of a joke, the framework of inside/outside, antagonist/protagonist, oppressor/oppressed is refused for its oversimplification and its stagnancy.

Certain jokes demand listeners to reposition themselves in relation to the issues raised. In the joke about the elderly man, we are summoned to laugh at the blatant refusal of a dying man's wish, something we would otherwise treat with deference. Other jokes require listeners to navigate ambivalent space created by a play with language itself. This punnish format characterized many of Groucho Marx's quips: "Outside of a dog, a book is man's best friend. Inside of a dog, it's too dark to read." Or, "Time flies like an arrow. Fruit flies like a banana." Television's ditsy darling of the 1950s, Gracie Allen, employed this same ludic sensibility in a more politicized context—that is, as a woman wriggling out of any responsibility and befuddling just about everyone she encountered.[7]

Gracie Allen's entirely unselfconscious comments function as delinquent pointers, aberrant signs. In the space of her jokes, the audience must attend to the uncomfortable disparity between the obvious and the odd—to the very lapse created by a verbal approximation. It is a speculative space, a place of instability. But it is also a place of challenge and dissent. In refusing predictability—that is, in missing the point— Gracie forces us to wonder, what is the point anyway? Is it deserving of our trust? How did it come to be taken as fact? Who benefits from our complicity with it? Her joking is a compelling albeit subtle way of questioning the reliability of evidence and the apparatus of belief itself by interjecting tension, a stirring, in proximity to a previously held value. While she is never on target, neither does she make shots in the dark; she takes listeners always within range of the intended response—the "right" answer—and offers instead a critique of "rightness."

> It was the final exam for an English course at the local university. The professor was very strict and told the class that any exam that was not on his desk in exactly two hours would not be accepted and the student would fail. A half hour into the exam, a student came rushing in and asked the professor for an exam booklet.
>
> "You're not going to have time to finish this," the professor said as he handed her a booklet.
>
> "Yes I will," she replied. Then she took a seat and began writing.
>
> After two hours, the professor called for the exams, and the students filed up and handed them in. All except the late student, who continued writing. A half hour later, she came up to the professor who was sitting at his desk preparing for his next class. She attempted to put her exam on the stack of exam booklets already there.
>
> "No you don't, I'm not going to accept that. It's late."
>
> She stared at the professor looking incredulous and angry. "Do you know who I am?"
>
> "No, as a matter of fact I don't," replied the professor.
>
> "DO YOU KNOW WHO I AM?" she asked again.
>
> "No, and I don't care," replied the professor with an air of superiority.
>
> "Good," she said as she lifted the stack of completed exams, placed hers in the middle, and walked out of the room.

Tricksters capitalize on slipperiness to reconfigure a power relationship. In the above anecdote, a student jokes her way out of a hierarchical trap that threatens her autonomy, her desire to bypass the rules. While this particular

story may not make evident an abuse of authorial power—he is strict but not necessarily oppressive—it nevertheless renders vividly how the nomadic quality of trickster can rewrite ambiguous territory (language, representation, symbols) for potentially liberatory agendas. Brazilian theatre director and social activist Augusto Boal (1979) designed an entire theatrical language known as the Joker System (a precedent to Theatre of the Oppressed for which he is well known) that enacts many of the principles of joking and trickery for activist and pedagogical purposes.

The original Joker in Boal's system was a director who intervened in all performances and played everyone's part at different moments, offering commentary and critique on the story and the performances, giving lectures and rousing the audience to action, interviewing the characters, and serving as general master of ceremonies. The Joker belongs nowhere in particular and yet oversees everything, he or she moves into and out of the action, reveals the spaces between characters and actors, and never takes on any one role or position. Similar to the joker in a deck of cards, Boal's Joker is a wild card with no identity of its own and yet able to loan its value to whatever it chooses. The Joker System privileges polyphony, non-linearity, carnivalesque ruptures and reversals in time and space, resonance, and ambiguity over identity and precision, all in the service of destabilizing institutions that dam up the flow of human and natural resources and that aggregate power in highly fortressed ideological and literal enclaves. It seeks to create an alternative order in which boundaries are called upon as temporary signatures or endorsements that maximize rather than delimit access to agency.[8]

PRESENCE AND ITS TRACE

> *I propose then a theater in which violent physical images crush and hypnotize the sensibility of*

the spectator seized...by a whirlwind of higher forces.

—Artaud, 1958, p. 83

The shadow of writing falls across the illusion of presence.

—Fuchs, 1996, p. 75

When mainstream theatre practitioners (but also Joseph Chaikin, Julian Beck, and others among the experimental avant garde) speak of the concept of presence their language tends to wax somewhat quixotic and yet positivist, as if describing a condition whereby some ineffable denizen has arrived, like a divinity, to occupy an otherwise abandoned body. Whether this presence oozes from the cells or alights from the spirit, the body thus possessed is ascribed a kind of libidinous glow—afire, wild, and untouchable. Artaud's (1958) mystical theories and their influence on western theatre incarnate this visage of artists "like victims burnt at the stake, signalling through the flames" (p. 13), his ideal of the performing body a prelinguistic or postlinguistic total signifier of the refusal of death and dualism between matter and mind, idea and form, action and reflection, concrete and abstract. In a fashion, the Artaudian sign is a sign utterly liberated from its representational chains and transmuted into pure revelation, released into a superabundant wholeness, or presence. "Everything in this theater," says Artaud "is immersed in a profound intoxication which restores to us the very elements of ecstasy" (p. 65).

The kind of presence that characterizes Artaudian aesthetics invites surrender from audiences more than it does agency; it overwhelms the mind's penchant for critical reflection in favor of an empathic bonding and cathartic purging. In contemporary performance and popular culture, such techniques of "presence" have been harnessed as a kind of emotional sorcery, casting audiences into a dumbfounded reactivity. In the pursuit of entertainment, a Spielberg-like manipulation of the senses liberates viewers from unresolved conflicts, fears, and a sense of social and political impotence. Brecht (1964), of course, taught us to precisely exploit this alienation, to disengage from the roles we play (on and off the stage) as socialized beings, to live in the fertile terrain between thought and action, reality and illusion, actor and character, the familiar and the strange. Presence can be experienced with pleasure but it must serve, not nullify, agency.[9]

In the 1970s, deconstruction ruptured the metaphysical, the aura of presence. Under the influence of Derrida's *differánce* (from defer—to put off), the wholeness of presence cracks in space and time: hovering around and within presence are trace-structures—that which presence displaces, everything that is not itself. Theatre practitioners began to stage not presence but the trace. One way in which the trace was staged, explains Fuchs (1996), was to introduce writing per se into performance.[10] Written words—visually legible text—destroyed the illusion that the drama being consumed was composed of spontaneous speech (p. 74). Audiences were forced to remember that there was a rehearsed text, that presence as an absolute truth in present time obfuscated a far more complex way of seeing and reading and making meaning of the performing self. Writing on the stage destroyed the ideal of pure self-presence (p. 73).

How does conventional theatrical presence and its subsequent displacement into disembodied spaces (the space of writing on stage, in this case) relate to kin(a)esthetic ways of thinking? Ironically, both formats challenge the western duality between body and mind and in so doing undo the rigid and overdetermined tension between them. On the one hand, citing Balinese theatre as an ideal, Artaud (1958) imagines a theatre in which the actor is "a moving hieroglyph" (p. 61), a body so encoded with cultural writing and thought that every symbolic gesture is a physical abstract. Through the body, culture and mind are not reduced but exalted. In place of a polarity, Artaud does not posit an easy fusion between body and mind but rather a complex intimacy that vibrates and screams meaning.

On the other end of the continuum, the visible moving presence of words/written text in performance (Fuchs cites Foreman, The Wooster Group, and Stuart Sherman among others), forces us to *see* the "body of the text." Text becomes an actor; like all other aspects of performance, it happens now (Fuchs, 1996, p. 89). But as it acts, it creates a new kind of presence characterized by interruptions, lapses, memories, tellings and retellings; it is a presence devoid of absolutes. This text-character reveals traditional character to be "an error" (Foreman, as cited in Fuchs, 1996, p. 84). While Artaud condemned the western stage for productions that "seem like so much stuttering," this vision of "presentable writing" gives stuttering itself a presence that can be recognized as the undulating tissue between language and body.

In her play, *Información para extranjeros* (*Information for Foreigners*), Argentine playwright Griselda Gambaro invites audience members to enter into a collage of vignettes, episodes, and spectacles in twenty-one scenes. They are led by two actors through a labyrinth of compartments, offices, storage rooms, bathrooms, and narrow hallways. The guides are incompetent; they repeatedly confuse audience members, abruptly change directions, and walk people into dark and obstructed spaces. There is no plot development and no character development: in the tradition of fellow Argentine playwright Osvaldo Dragún, there is, rather, a presentation of *character underdevelopment*—characters have no names, roles are ill defined—which dissuades audience identification. One eventually becomes oriented to disorientation. In the last scene, everyone gathers in a large room and several prisoners are brought in and beaten. Suddenly the lights come up, all actors disperse except for those playing prisoners, and the set starts to be dismantled. A guide announces: "Señoras y señores, qué esperan? La función ha terminado" (Ladies and gentleman, what are you waiting for? The show is over). The audience members linger briefly watching the continuing action, then most head haltingly toward the door. As they exit, police sirens wail and other actors rush in and interact with the prisoners. Most audience members turn back toward the stage to watch the action. Most stand restlessly, shuffling, confused. (Postma, 1980, pp. 35–45)

In *Información,* Gambaro stages the "traces" of authorial leadership in Argentina in 1972, and audiences unaccustomed to noticing them, no less experiencing them, as embodied realities, struggle to move through the disorienting space. Throughout the piece, spectators are made uncomfortable, their movement through the sets made purposefully difficult, frightening, and unsafe. Spectators become actors in a sense, stumbling and faltering through the script. At the end of the piece, they are left with the responsibility of interpreting a confused message: "the performance is over" communicated in voice over, "the performance is not over" conveyed by bodies continuing to act on stage. They are not only unsure of their role (to leave or not to leave) but, more importantly, unsure of how to define a role for themselves in the absence of clear direction. The play's game is to immerse spectators into the action, but then in the hands of untrustworthy leaders, recognize their ill-fated dependence and the need to become not just witnesses but also writers, critics, and evaluators of their own destiny. They are forced to ask themselves who and what they believe in, on what criteria they make choices, and how they reconcile conflicting desires. By staging the stuttering and the traces that haunt a more conventional presence, the performance, although a pretense, makes reality more real, more pronounced physically than audience members had perhaps previously allowed themselves to experience it.

The practice of pedagogy is also always located in real space. While learning is happening on multiple and complex levels and informed by many unnameable kin(a)esthetic processes, the classroom itself is a well rehearsed text. How a teacher performs knowledge is inextricably linked with how she performs authority. And in spite of attempts to work against authority's lustrous presence, instructors contend with students' often unwitting projections as if authority belonged, inevitably, to the instructor. The enactment of authorial presence as a hierarchical privilege is predicated on an ongoing dialogue, often unspoken, between teacher and students. As Laura Mulvey (1975) made evident in her exploration of the pleasures derived from narrative cinema, critical audiences take delight in constructs that under scrutiny might betray their better critical judgment; students and instructors too, in spite of apparent aspirations for a more radical pedagogy, chose a comforting (re: culturally sanctioned) presence over a challenging trace. Locating ourselves in less stable terrain requires renunciation of what traditional presence as an aesthetic performance makes easier for everyone; such relocation casts a shadow on the seductive illusions we have come to enjoy and forces an uneasy engagement with ignorance.

PEDAGOGY AS WRITING, AND THE PERFORMATIVE LESSON

> *To speak the body, the writing itself must move.*
>
> —Foster, 1995, p. 9

> *Writing becomes itself, becomes its own means and ends, recovering to itself the force of action.*
>
> —Pollock, 1998, p. 75

Susan Foster (1995) and Della Pollock (1998) take on the question of writing the body ("ambulatory scholarship") and writing as performance ("performative writing"), respectively. Foster reminds us that the historian, the theorist, has a body and that that body is involved in writing. Once we are alerted to the value and meaning in kinesthesia, she says, we cannot dis-animate how the bodies we sense (including those we study) effect us, create meaning in us. Our physicality affects how we think and how we write, and the page is a stage upon which those physical meanings are put into motion. Pollock is interested in making *writing* perform (p. 75). She argues for a writing that makes things happen, materializes possibilities, cites and re-cites, follows the body's restlessness and transience, articulates the not-me, presents and disappears, encounters the reader, moves "as if," and is aware of itself as a practice that displaces rather than makes meaning. Reading Pollock, I am inspired to *enter* writing, to bring my inconstant body and mind—a veritable force field of subjectivities, tensions, consequences, recollections, materialities, images, and indecipherable other stuff—to the page. I become a writer performing which subsequently manifests as a writing that performs.

As a teacher of performance studies there is an implicit bidding, certainly a justification, to transmute the written texts we read and explore into "performance texts." Actually, we do this all the time without necessarily being aware of it. We bring texts onto the classroom stage, though we are not always conscious of or accountable to the aesthetic choices that come to bear on those texts as they "act." What are the default aesthetics of our unrehearsed performative lessons? And once we recognize the importance of aesthetic choices, how might we choose to teach Brecht compared to Foucault? Might we designate an interloper to alienate our Brecht lesson and rearrange the seats panoptically when discussing Foucault? Perhaps. More to the point is to reflect upon the movement that happens in and around and through the text as it moves off the page and becomes a writing performed in time and space. Pedagogy itself is a writing; performance studies suggests that it is a bodily writing. Texts already written are rewritten with our bodies, made active in space. The lesson—that odd container that pretends to hold teaching and learning—becomes, for our purposes here, a kin(a)esthetic terrain, an active casting of a written text into performative space.

First, of course, we must note that the text already lives off the page by what we bring to it as we read. Perhaps we read through the sadness of a loss, the excitement of an interaction with a loved one, the frustration of a project unfulfilled, the distractions of past memories or future projections. Then, we might consider how the written texts themselves perform on the page: what bodies wrote those texts? How were those bodies made visible in the texts? What does the text's "presence" (in style as well as content) tend to displace, make invisible? How did our bodies, as readers, partake in rendering meaning to the text?

Second, how does the text take on new meaning when cited by others? It is precisely through this embodiment that new information, even new paradigms, are uncovered.[11] We bring our own authorship to it; we re-authorize aspects of it and discredit others, revealing the way texts come to live as *intra*personal dialogues—as sites within us. As we re-cite it now we also expose how texts made performative move through time—that is, through citing comes a negotiation of text read then and text cited now. This re-iteration puts the text in motion. The text can also be understood as a kind of mask that can be taken on and off like a role, an action that articulates the very space between itself and the one who speaks it. Finally, the text functions as a medium of sorts that channels the exchange of bodies in space and time, a context for (and not an end in itself of) whatever is to be learned. And because this exchange is riddled with interruptions, digressions, quotations, and constant reauthorizations, it loses any

singular authority—it becomes public, a public body.

If the lesson is conceived as a collaborative dialectical writing in time, it suggests improvisation, with the shared text as the melody or structure from which an unpredictable rewriting will happen. Benjamin (1966) says of improvisation: "The task here is not to decide once and for all, but to decide at every moment" (p. 425). Randy Martin (1999) addresses how improvisation (in the classroom in particular) makes not only the text, but the context renegotiable. He refers to improvisation as the moment when a response to a text (or content) restructures the very field in which that response takes place. "Obviously in these incidental changes," Martin suggests, "the rules, the relations of authority as such do not disappear . . . but their appearance becomes noticeably contingent on the very activity that the students engage in" (p. 199).

Casting the text as a kin(a)esthetic performer is an opportunity to revise on the spot the over-rehearsed script of pedagogical traditions. The performative lesson foregrounds and exploits the very paradoxes of pedagogical space by indulging in play—an incessant rewriting not only of ideas, bodies, and information but of the very frame, or structure, within which they are happening. Play, as compared to games, as compared to *dis*play, allows and encourages change at any time in the rules of the game being played—creating both a pleasure and a tension.

Every spring Jews around the world celebrate Passover with a ritual dinner, or seder. The Passover story, which commemorates the Jews' freedom from the Egyptians, is read aloud in both Hebrew and English from the Haggadah before dinner is served. In my extended family, the reading, replete with prayer and song, is done with only a modicum of formality and earnestness; amidst the ceremonious atmosphere, there is the typical fare of joking, arguing, acting-out, boredom, and frustration that marks all of our family gatherings. One particularly memorable seder occurred in 1990. It started out with the usual bantering: my father wanting to explain (in depth) the meaning of seder (again) and to read every section of the Haggadah; my mom anxious to move the service along quickly so that the food wouldn't be overcooked. Approximately 20 minutes into the ritual, it was time for the recitation of The Four Questions, an oral exchange of questions and answers performed traditionally between the youngest son at the table and his father. The task that year fell to my nephew, Russell, who was 13 at the time. But when asked to read the first question he refused. After some laughter and gentle mockery, most of us merely amused by his adolescent defiance, he was asked again to read. But Russell would have nothing of it. The tension around the table increased, the usual frivolity and indifference now infused with some anger and exasperation. But when the third request was refused, there was no hiding the agitation, particularly from my brother who felt publicly embarrassed by his son's obstinacy. "What will it take Russell," asked my brother with controlled rage in his voice, "for you to read the Four Questions?" And for the first time that night, Russell's face lit up in an impish smile as he answered, "If I can do them in rap." And so he did. And, as it turned out, seder 1990 kept that thirteen year old coming back for many years hence.

Russell's performance is interesting in a few registers. He demonstrated how tradition withstands time only by changing, and how performance serves as a bridge between the antiquated and the contemporary. Tradition—as a set of rules, expectations, structures, and written doctrine—survives the cultural vicissitudes of new generations by, in fact, being performed, lived, and thus reclaimed, albeit altered in the process. Ironically, performance with all its quintessential variability and immediacy becomes a vehicle for strengthening and disseminating conventions. Russell's innovative improvisation kept an anachronous custom honest and relevant, not only for him but for everyone around the table. However much they whined and rolled their eyes, they were in

fact, recipients of a *mitzvah*—an act of giving dictated by Jewish law.

Second, while Russell may have been embodying his cultural values as a way of claiming some autonomy and visibility within an already overdetermined family spectacle, he was also reflecting back to his elders their own performance of ambivalence about the holiday proceedings and its meaning. My mother's anxiety about her culinary role and my constant correcting of the gender biased language of the Haggadah had inflected every Passover for more than a decade; these interventions were now part of what Passover was for all of us. Russell, in a rather ingenious performative move, played back to us our own cultural practice: rewriting, renaming, redirecting, and even a degree of disrespecting were already always par for the course.

PLAYING IN/AS PEDAGOGY

There is no possible reason for climbing except the climbing itself; it is a self-communication

—Csikszentmihalyi, 1990, p. 54

This phenomenon, play, could only occur if the participant organisms were capable of some degree of metacommunication, i.e., of exchanging signals that carry the message "this is play."

—Bateson, 1972, p. 179

When Gregory Bateson (1972) declares, "human beings have evolved the metaphor that is meant" (p. 183), he is referring to humans' granting a truth function to representations—the primary process in which map and territory (representation and the thing being represented) are equated. In secondary processes of the mind, people can discriminate between the two. In play, a third-order functioning, they are both equated and discriminated (p. 185). For Bateson, awareness and active exploitation of this cohabitation is what he calls play. Augusto Boal (1995) describes a similar phenomenon of play as *metaxis*: "the state of belonging completely and simultaneously to two different, autonomous worlds: the image of reality and the reality of the image" (p. 43).

The kin(a)esthetic value of play and metaxis derives from its very paradoxical nature. We live our representations as if they are real and knowing they are not. In fact, play's metacommunicative message ("this is play") articulates the very space in which we *can* act "as if" and reap its experiential values. For example, we can be aggressive in play without suffering the consequences of what such aggression would mean if acted outside the play frame: the playful nip is not the bite, as Bateson reminds us. The performative frame allows the actions that happen within them to be real forces of change in dimensions of communication, perception, structure, and ideology. Ironically, the change is potent precisely because when we know conceptually "this is play," when engaged in it we don't know it.

Mihaly Csikszentmihalyi calls this phenomenon "flow," an autotelic experience which is an end it itself. He describes it as an immersion into a "field of force" in which there is an active role for self and a loss of consciousness of self simultaneously; the self expands its boundaries precisely by losing consciousness of itself.[12] This immersion into "enjoyment" is active, not passive; it is characterized by forward movement and the delicate balance between challenge and skill. It is only when the risk of play itself becomes too difficult (beyond the player's ability to meet the challenge) that self-consciousness breaks "flow" and saves us from an experience of failure. The paradox of "flow" experiences lies in providing a complex pleasure that derives from effortless movement just on the brink of a breakdown.

Four New York University students headed to the Staten Island ferry in New York City to do invisible theatre on littering. Their goal was to engage ferry riders on the environmental hazards of discarding their trash on the open-air deck. After purchasing hot dogs, pretzels, popcorn, and various other fast foods from the concession, one of the four proceeded to eat and litter, casting wrappers and Styrofoam cups, napkins, and food-remains recklessly onto the deck. Several passengers sitting nearby watched in disbelief, one of them in particular, growing more and more irate. Eventually, unable to contain himself, he confronted the litterer. A debate ensued, the other students chiming in either pro or con, along with other passengers drawn into the arguments being presented (some highly researched and informative, others incredulous but perhaps popular), e.g., littering is environmentally corrupt vs. littering provides jobs for people on the janitorial staff. The "performance" was successful in that it created a site, a public event—fabricated and yet real—through which to furnish environmental data and social hypotheses. But this one irate man would have nothing of it. As the conversation proceeded, he disappeared temporarily only to return with Security. Seeing the litter on the floor, the policeman asked who was responsible. Several passengers pointed to the culpable student. "Did you do this?" the policeman asked. "Yes, but no," the student muttered, anxiously miming a time-out to the other students to indicate that the performance was now over. "You see, officer, we are NYU students doing an invisible theatre performance. I did throw this stuff on the deck but it's not real litter, it's make-believe litter." Staring at the trash on the floor, the Security guard looked incredulously at the student, and wrote out a ticket, a real $100 ticket, for littering.

The experiment on the ferry was an application of Augusto Boal's invisible theatre, a format he advanced in Argentina in the early 1970s during the reign of a brutal military regime. As an activist and director, Boal wanted to raise vital political issues with audiences through theatre but realized that overt, staged drama—that is, acting that clearly announced itself as such—would have been politically inopportune if not downright dangerous. The goal of invisible theatre was to stimulate a discussion and to educate others about issues affecting their lives by capturing the attention of people who did not know they were watching a planned performance. At the time of its inception, performers were trying to stay out of jail; in being invisible, they escaped being "disappeared." In the case above, NYU students as well made invisible the frame, "this is play," and exploited the fusion of theatre and real life that invisible theatre allows.

Of course, the stakes were far less serious in 1990s New York City than in 1970s Argentina. Rather than avoiding disappearance, they were merely protecting themselves from being dismissed as "actors" and, accordingly, freeing the audience from the safety of being theatrical spectators. Within the manifest frame of a play, audiences are more prone to say, "It's just theatre" (re: not real) and assume a more passive role as observer only. While the manipulation that characterizes invisible theatre has been challenged on ethical grounds—the students live in "aesthetic space" (they are acting) while the unassuming spectators (who are *not* acting) are taken unawares—perhaps one of the important conceptual lessons of invisible theatre is that acting off the stage happens constantly in every day life, every time we chose to speak, not speak, act, not act. And, obviously, there is always an element of the real in such play—it is inescapable. It is amusing to consider how the students sought to use "play" to trump the reality of "the real trash" to avoid the very real $100 ticket, all within their understanding of the efficacy of the invisible theatre performance, and all to the utter incredulity of the security guard.

While invisible theatre avoids the final reveal (the ferry case is an exception), it is interesting to note that only when students had to face the real consequences of their "staged" actions did the audience have to face the impact of being played. Everyone got a glimpse (appreciated or not) into the complexities of invisible theatre's pedagogical profundity. Students acted as unmarked teachers of sorts, provoking a "real" dialogue and raising consciousness in a way that disallowed ferry goers to find refuge in structures—i.e., theatre and classroom—that ordinarily sanction passivity for nonactors. The students engaged play *as* pedagogy, a radical pedagogy at that.

There is always a dimension of performance (alongside the real) in play, and performance creates a particular spatial tension, a transitive space. The term "transitive" is defined as "of showing, or characterized by transition." In showing, in the act of requiring a space in which something can be shown, transitional space is created. Augusto Boal (1995) calls the space created by performance "aesthetic space." He defines aesthetic space as "a space within a space, a superposition of spaces" (p. 18). It is created by the interpenetration of the platform or stage and the space of the spectator, whether present or imagined—that is, the space created between actor and spectator can occur, thanks to our imagination, within the same person. Boal's aesthetic space is transitional space, it is kin(a)esthetic.[13]

While the actual classroom is always a kin(a)esthetic space, kin(a)esthetic space also exists between representation and thing, map and territory, play frame and play itself. Pedagogy is situated at the borders where these pairings meet and therein lies its radical potential. We look both ways and play in the difference. We act within the frame "as if," we notice ourselves acting, we alter the frame (sometimes unwittingly) and we act within the frame "as if" again differently. This ambulant pedagogy—kin(a)esthetic pedagogy—keeps transfiguring itself and the content it holds, and in so doing highlights the ethical and political dimensions of cultural performances of all kinds. Fake and real are forever wed in a political dance, discernible and negotiable only through another complex dance—that of analysis and critical thinking which has the power to rematerialize.

The more astute we become to the nervous, paradoxical, morphing dimensions that characterize aesthetic spaces, the more we learn to act according to their wisdom. They become not merely dimensions we negotiate or spaces we inhabit, but the modes in which we think. Rather than conceiving of our bodies moving through kin(a)esthetic space we come to experience kin(a)esthesis moving bodies, identities, ideas, boundaries, and representations of all kinds.

AFTERTHOUGHTS: THE AESTHETICS AND POLITICS OF AMBLING

While the term *ambulant* is associated with wandering, the term *ambulatory*—sharing the root "ambi," to amble—is associated with recuperation. Recuperation means to get or bring back, recovery, restoration. To be ambulatory is to be "back on one's feet" which implies a return to justice as well as to health; losses and damages are recovered as well as strength. One is now able to hold his or her own, is solvent, poised and ready to go. Just as the concept of *ambulant* has provided a lens to recognize and reassess how pedagogy moves, so might the concept of *ambulatory*. Through its lens, pedagogy might be understood as a confluence of efforts, forces, styles, signs, histories, languages, and bodies whose interactions are defined by the desire to recuperate knowledge one from another, i.e., to recuperate bodies from history, efforts from signs, histories from styles, languages from bodies, etc., in various and complex affinities and reverberations. Pedagogy is ambulant because it is always and endlessly improvising—improving upon itself and functioning within a landscape without clear horizons; perhaps it is ambulatory because it merges the notion of solvency—stability and balance—with the predication of moving again, being back on

one's feet, recovering enough balance only to risk losing it once again. In imagining this risky ambling—setting forth with both promise and ambivalence—I can't help but to see clowns with their awkward and precarious gait. The incessant tripping and slipping seems to cast into question prevailing values of stability, depicted as two feet planted firmly on the ground. Pedagogy might learn something from a study of how clowns move on their feet.

But this begs a bigger question. There are different ways to move, motivated by different goals, while passing through different landscapes. Being ambulant itself demands aesthetic qualification. How do we amble and why? My initial attempt to answer this question provoked a roster of kinds of travelers: the *flaneur* strolls aimlessly in covert search of adventure; the *nomad* relocates as cultural practice; the *explorer* travels with deliberation to discover something new; the *tourist* goes elsewhere to validate his or her own identity; the *trekker* moves laboriously on foot, intimate with the changing landscape; the *hiker* moves for pleasure and to overcome her physical limitations; the *commuter* crosses back and forth to bridge physical or economic needs; the *vagrant* ambles out of destitution, the *refugee* to flee, the *pilgrim* in search of an answer, the *passenger* not necessarily of her own will, and the *fugitive* to avoid responsibility.

And yet this panoply of movers begs yet another question. How, aesthetically speaking, do we embrace the ambulant spirit in relation to social and historical circumstances? What political investments drive our ambling and what kinds of movement forward our agendas? The very same questions inflect ambulant pedagogy per se. How does our pedagogy change in pace, weight, vibration, urgency, direction, style, and effort on the first day of teaching after September 11, 2001, on subsequent 9/11s, when our government attacks Iraq, or on Election Day? We shift more than just the content of our classroom discussions on such occasions (and on many others of perhaps less dramatic import). The entire pedagogical "theatre" has been transformed whether we choose to pay attention to it or not; the field of play has been littered with new obstacles, reconfigured by new rules, consequences, and responsibilities. And the classroom, as an organ of the social body, participates necessarily in the new show. To speak of pedagogy we must speak of its placement and function within the *social body* and its *social movements;* pedagogy is both an inscription of and a risk to the body politic. A kin(a)esthetic sensibility advocates for a deeply implicated pedagogical organ, accountable and answerable to powerful political agendas whose classic plays have been overrehearsed, well-endowed, pervasively distributed, and far too readily consumed. If our pedagogy remains dutifully ambulant and ambulatory— socially agile and recuperative—the classroom may survive the immobility and superfluity that threatens it.

And amidst all the complex movement that may characterize ambulant pedagogy—of shifting frames of play, between performed and real, in endless re-citations of texts, of slippery signs, and in the very active joints of our bodies—there are also limits and hazards and high stakes. An acknowledgement of kin(a)esthetic processes is not an acquiescence to unbounded relativism. Rather, it bespeaks the aesthetic dimensions of *all* critical, political, and material performances of which taking hard and fast positions are options—strategic immobility is a kin(a)esthetic choice. It warns against subscribing to habituated, seemingly harmless, performances as if they too were not marked aesthetically, often with blind and contemptuous privilege.

NOTES

1. Freire is often cited for his critique of the "banking" concept of education whereby knowledge is deposited, so to speak, by self-proclaimed experts (teachers) into the heads of those who know nothing (students). In lieu of this concept,

Freire proposes dialogue which grants pedagogy its subversive force. Seeking a revolutionary leadership, he proposes "co-intentional education. Teachers and students (leadership and people), co-intent on reality, are both Subjects, not only in the task of unveiling that reality, and thereby coming to know it critically, but in the task of re-creating that knowledge" (p. 56). Freire's radical pedagogy is transitive rather than intransitive; students are active participants in their education by teaching what they know.

2. See Schutzman (2002) for an essay that interweaves a description of a course taught at CalArts, excerpts from student papers, performative writing, and a self-reflexive analysis of the class experience that brought the author to these pedagogical speculations.

3. While the discipline of performance studies inspires the pedagogical speculations of this essay, the notion of kin(a)esthetics as a way to approach the classroom is by no means restricted to the performance studies classroom. Whether teaching European history, semiotics, or calculus, the interactivity that constitutes and dynamizes the classroom transcends (and, as suggested, transforms) the subject matter per se.

4. The sources cited in the following pages constitute approximately one half of the readings I assign for a year-long course I teach at California Institute of the Arts, entitled Performance Theory and Practice. I employ them here as a textual remapping of the class and as the basis of the performative agenda of the in-class lessons. This class is the most current "data" from which I theorize and speculate on the subjects of this essay.

5. These concepts recognize the temporal aspect of identity-based methods employed as subversive acts without falling into a generalized essentialism that denies the internal differences in a group.

6. Jokes function on many levels and some clearly reinforce prescribed cultural boundaries— insult jokes, for example, that intensify or humiliate our allegiances.

7. The format of the television series on which Gracie performed with her real-life husband George Burns contained Gracie linguistically in an ineffectual domestic space; her verbal antics, no matter how "liberating," were framed at beginning and end by George's denigrating narration of Gracie as a hopelessly stupid woman. Nonetheless, her verbal trickery illustrates a performative strategy of escape, a way to "slip the trap of culture" that Hyde speaks of. The following is an

excerpt from the film *A Damsel in Distress* written by P. G. Wodehouse (1937) and produced by RKO Radio Pictures. (GB is George Burns, GA is Gracie Allen):

GB: (on phone). You'll have to talk to my secretary. She's not in yet. You better call about 12 o'clock, she'll be in then to go out to lunch.

GA: (entering office). Hello.

GB: You should have been in two hours ago.

GA: Why, what happened?

GB: What happened? If you're not here on time I'll have to get myself another stenographer.

GA: Another stenographer? Do you think there's enough work for the two of us?

GB: Look, I mean I'm gonna fire you!

GA: Fire me? Why if it wasn't for my father . . . you wouldn't be here in London now.

GB: If it wasn't for your father, you wouldn't be working for me for two weeks. You wouldn't even be working for me for two days. Not even two minutes.

GA: Well, a girl couldn't ask for shorter hours than that.

GB: Did you type that letter I dictated last night?

GA: Well, no, I didn't have time so I mailed him my notebook. I hope he can read my shorthand.

GB: You mailed your notebook? You know Gracie, I'm beginning to think that there's nothing up here. (He points to his head.)

GA: Oh, George, you're self-conscious. (phone rings).

GB: I'm not in.

GA: He's not in.

GB: Find out who it is.

GA: (to George). It's a Hawaiian.

GB: A Hawaiian?

GA: Well, he must be. He says he's brown from the morning sun.

GB: Look, the man's name is Brown. The *Morning Sun* is the newspaper he's working on. But tell him I'm not here.

GA: He's not here (pause). I tell you he's not here (pause). Ah, you don't do you, well you can ask him yourself if you don't believe me. (to George). George, will you tell him you're not here, he doesn't believe me.

8. Boal discusses the Joker System in his book *Theatre of the Oppressed* (1979, pp. 159–194). This system was developed when Boal worked with the Arena Theater of Sao Paulo and precedes the joker of Theatre of the Oppressed (TO) as

understood in contemporary practice. Many of the roles of the original Joker now belong to the spect-actors, the audience members who take part in the action of TO.

9. It is interesting to note that much of the inspiration for Artaud's concept of presence came from Balinese theatre, while Brecht, far more aligned aesthetically with a deconstructive and Derridian impulse, was inspired by a study of Chinese theatre. The allure of nonwestern systems provided, perhaps, a conceptual crystallization of their respective critiques of western theatre, each seeing in these highly coded and ultimately strange aesthetics what they needed to see—Artaud, a highly volatile presence characterized by heightened ritualistic unity, and Brecht, a highly referential presence characterized by alienated social tension.

10. I owe much of the following discussion about the inclusion of writing into experimental performance of the 1970s to E. Fuchs (1996).

11. Students in my Performance Theory and Practice class at CalArts select particular readings that they "perform" in class. For example, on the day that we will be discussing Foucault's (1979) article "Panopticism" in *Discipline and Punish*, one or two students do a five-minute performance of the article as they understand it. Students find that the attempt itself is almost always a way of giving interiority to the theories being read. One student put it this way: "Theory resides in a kind of outer space and embodiment of the theory gives it an inner space as well" (Milly Sanders, 2003).

12. Susan Foster (1995), cited in the previous section, sees the corporeal dimension of this immersion experience when she says, "The author loses identity as the guiding authority and finds him or herself immersed in the process of the project getting made. This is not mystical, it's really quite bodily" (p. 83).

13. Boal (1995) describes the characteristics and properties of aesthetic space in his book *The Rainbow of Desire*: (1) plasticity ("time and space can be condensed or stretched at will, and the same flexibility operates with people and objects, which can coalesce or dissolve, divide or multiply," p. 20); (2) it is dichotomic and it creates dichotomy ("the people and the things which are in this place will be in two spaces" p. 23); (3) it is telemicroscopic ("like a powerful telescope, the stage brings things closer" p. 27).

REFERENCES

Artaud, A. (1958). *The theater and its double.* New York: Grove Press.

Bateson, G. (1972). *Steps to an ecology of mind.* New York: Ballantine Books.

Benjamin, W. (1966). *Briefe.* Frankfurt, Germany: Suhrkamp.

Boal, A. (1979). *Theater of the oppressed* (C. A. McBride & M. Leal McBride, Trans.). New York: Urizen Books. (Original work published 1974)

Boal, A. (1992). *Games for actors and non-actors* (A. Jackson, Trans.). London: Routledge.

Boal, A. (1995). *The rainbow of desire: the Boal method of theatre and therapy* (A. Jackson, Trans.). London: Routledge.

Brecht, B. (1964). *Brecht on theatre: The development of an aesthetic* (J. Willett, Trans.). New York: Hill and Wang. (Original work published 1957)

Butler, J. (1990). Performative acts and gender constitution: An essay in phenomenology and feminist theory. In S. E. Case (Ed.), *Performing feminisms: Feminist critical theory and theatre* (pp. 270–282). Baltimore: Johns Hopkins University Press.

Csikszentmihalyi, M. (1990). *Flow: The psychology of optimal experience.* New York: Harper and Row.

English, J. F. (1994). *Comic transactions: Literature, humor and the politics of community in twentieth-century Britain.* Ithaca, NY: Cornell University Press.

Foster, S. L. (1995). Choreographing history. In S. L. Foster (Ed.), *Choreographing history* (pp. 3–21). Bloomington: Indiana University Press.

Foucault, M. (1979). *Discipline and punish: The birth of the prison* (A. Sheridan, Trans.). New York: Vintage Books. (Original work published 1975)

Freire, P. (1986). *Pedagogy of the oppressed* (M. B. Ramos, Trans.). New York: Continuum. (Original work published 1970)

Fuchs, E. (1996). *The death of character: Perspectives on theater after modernism.* Bloomington: Indiana University Press.

Hyde, L. (1998). *Trickster makes this world: Mischief, myth, and art.* New York: North Point Press.

Laban, R. (1974). *The language of movement: A guidebook to choreutics.* Boston: Plays, Inc.

Levi-Strauss, C. (1963). *Structural anthropology* (C. Jacobson & B. G. Schoepf, Trans.). New York: Basic Books.

Martin, R. (1999). Leaping into the dialectic: Etudes in materializing the social. In A. Kumar (Ed.), *Poetics/politics: Radical aesthetics for the classroom* (pp. 191–200). New York: St. Martin's Press.

Mulvey, L. (1975). Visual pleasure and narrative cinema. *Screen, 16*(3), 412–428.

Pollock, D. (1998). Performing writing. In P. Phelan & J. Lane (Eds.), *The ends of performance* (pp. 73–103). New York: New York University Press.

Postma, R. (1980, Fall). Space and spectator in the theatre of Griselda Gambaro: "Información para extranjeros," *Latin American Theatre Review, 35–45.*

Sandoval, C. (2000). *Methodology of the oppressed.* Minneapolis: University of Minnesota Press.

Schutzman, M. (2002). Guru clown, or pedagogy of the carnivalesque. *Theatre Topics, 12*(1), 63–84.

Spivak, G. C. (1996). Subaltern studies: Deconstructing historiography (1985). In D. Landry & G. MacLean (Eds.), *The Spivak reader: Selected works of Gayatri Chakravorty Spivak* (pp. 203–236). New York: Routledge.

Taussig, M. (1999). A report to the academy. In A. Kumar (Ed.), *Poetics/politics: Radical aesthetics for the classroom* (pp. 13–16). New York: St. Martin's Press.

16

Pedagogy on the Move

New Intersections in (Between) the Educative and the Performative

GREG DIMITRIADIS

I took my first academic position in fall of 1999 as an assistant professor of educational foundations. The move was only the latest in a long line of disciplinary transgressions. I had BA degrees in economics and English, MA degrees in English and American studies, and a PhD in speech communication. Like many my story was uneven, emergent, driven by personal circumstance and accident as much as intellectual planning and foresight. Nevertheless, there seemed a particular logic to this latest move. I had spent the better part of the decade interrogating the cultural phenomenon of *hip-hop music* and culture. While my object of inquiry remained largely the same, my approaches were disparate, moving between the textual and the ethnographic (Dimitriadis, 2001a; 2001b; 2003).

I had spent the four years previous to 1999 working at a community center in the urban Midwest, trying to understand how young people understood the texts I had worked with and through for most of my adult life. In the end, I came to see popular culture (such as hip-hop) as an alternative curriculum and community-based organizations (such as the one I worked at) as alternative learning settings. I found a disciplinary and intellectual home in education, though I had to remove these constructs from their more familiar traditional moorings to do so. I found myself in a complex space, one that forced me again and again beyond the prescriptive confines of schools walls. Indeed, though I found a home in education, it was only opened up through the "performative."

As Dwight Conquergood (1998), Della Pollock (1998), and most recently Norman Denzin (2003) have made so very clear, performance is a key site where social, cultural, and material constructions are put into motion, are articulated and rearticulated in new and (often) powerful ways. The "performative turn" looks towards an "interactionist epistemology," one where "context replaces text, verbs replace nouns, structures become processes. The emphasis is on change, contingency, locality, motion, improvisation, struggle, situationally specific practices and articulations, the performance of con/texts" (Denzin, 2003. p. 16). There are no safe spaces here and no alibis for our effectivities, both in their enabling and constraining dimensions (Lee, 1999). The world is always already performative, always already in motion. This interactionist turn has critical implications for pedagogy, decentering the privileged and delimited role of the teacher in the classroom, forcing us to look towards the new "in between" spaces where culture is being "performed" in the everyday.

This chapter looks towards these and other phenomena as it explores new intersections in (between) the educative and the performative. More specifically, I focus here on key moments when the performative forced me to decenter my own interpretive parameters and open myself up to new ways of thinking about texts and practices. More broadly, I will argue that these new, perhaps more unstable understandings of texts and practices necessitated new ways of thinking about the ethics and politics of pedagogy and educational inquiry. This chapter, then, will be necessarily personal and autobiographical, an effort to think through my own interpretive trajectory by way of the performative, highlighting its ethical and political demands and responsibilities.

TEXTS

My fascination with hip-hop took hold during my college years and quickly became an academic project. As with many other scholars, my interest in popular culture seemed to find a natural home in the humanities (in general) and English departments (more specifically). My impulse was to examine hip-hop recordings as "texts," as a modern-day poetics. This meant, of course, looking past the cultural distinctions that had buttressed my formal education—distinctions between what I had to study in school (so-called "high" culture) versus what I consumed for leisure (so-called "popular" culture). For me the burgeoning hip-hop world suddenly seemed as important as any social or political movement which had been enshrined in the academy. The hip-hop recordings I was newly exposed to suddenly seemed educative and serious—profoundly so. In many respects, this interest spoke to the moment in hip-hop when I first began to engage it—the mid- to late eighties.

The mid- to late eighties was a moment when rap artists like KRS-One and Rakim rejected their roles as popular icons, drawing on a new density in language and word play and, perhaps most importantly, foregrounding a self-defined tradition, concerned with, among other things, the origins of the art form (Dimitriadis, 2001a). This was a key moment of critical validation for hip-hop—the moment when it moved from being "just" a party music to a music with seeming depth and complexity. It was a moment when rap articulated with the deep embodied sense of "artistry" so enmeshed in the academic imagination. The self-professed trappings of artistic and pedagogic complexity came hand in hand with a focus on the individual artist. I recall here Rakim rapping on "I Know You Got Soul" (Eric B. and Rakim, 1987), "I start to think and then I sink into the paper, like I was ink / When I'm writing, I'm trapped in between the lines / I escape, when I finish the rhyme." This stress on language, on the textual, on the creative process, stood in some distinction to the earlier rap texts that tended to be party oriented.

Judged from my own interpretive criteria, the music of Rakim and KRS-One seemed intensely complex and worthy of study. Suddenly music, which had always been there for me, seemed more serious and important, more worthy of academic study and inquiry. In many respects, I took the cue from the artists themselves who took on these trappings. Rappers were no longer only entertainers but self-professed poets, artists, and intellectuals (in ways I will discuss below). We see a key parallel here with the move from swing to bop in jazz. As Amiri Baraka (LeRoi Jones) noted in his still classic discussion of the shift, early swing music was a dance music and a "functional" music propelled by the immediate demands and needs of ever-changing audiences (1963). The birth of bebop signaled a shift in music and style. Denser and more intricate arrangements became the norm, while symbols of seeming sophistication, the "goatee, beret, and window-pane glasses" all became part of evidencing the jazz artist's "fluency with some of the canons of formal Western nonconformity" (p. 201).

As opposed to swing artists, bebop artists turned their backs on their role as entertainers; a kind of cool distance was effected by Charlie Parker, Miles Davis, and others. This was not a dance music first and foremost. Artists like Parker and Davis mined and reworked classic standards of the era, giving the music a self-conscious intellectual feel and dimension. According to Baraka (1963), this was very much about moving from a functional art form to one that was more of a self-defined and directed "art" music. Indeed, Ralph Ellison, among others, would mourn this passing. He writes that with bop, jazz "has become separated from the ritual form of the dance . . . the response of the audience is more intellectual . . . and thus its participation is less immediate" (2001, p. xxix). It was at precisely this moment that the field of jazz criticism exploded.

Similar to early jazz, hip-hop began as a live practice, dependent upon the moment-to-moment responses of the audience. The earliest hip-hop singles evidence this indissoluble focus on the occasion or event in a number of ways. First and foremost, the prevailing theme throughout these singles is partying, getting crowds involved in the unfolding event. Lines like "Come alive y'all and give me what you got" abound throughout, flowing in and out of the more structured narrative sequences, as in a live show. Concurrently, the pronoun "you"—i.e., the live hip-hop crowd—reveals a familiar and friendly relationship between artist and audience. This holds true for "Rapper's Delight" by The Sugar Hill Gang (1979) as well as for nearly all early singles, including "Spoonin' Rap" (1980) by Spoonie Gee, "Money (Dollar Bill Y'all)" (1981) by Jimmy Spicer, and "Supperrappin'" (1980) by Grandmaster Flash and the Furious Five. In all these examples, the "you" indexes the participants necessary to sustain the event, active agents who engage and sustain the culture in complex and multiple ways in particular sites.

This sense of the event, of the recursive nature of interaction and communication, is evidenced, as well, in the use of call-and-response routines. These routines were ubiquitous in live hip-hop shows and are also featured on nearly all the earliest rap singles. For example, Jimmy Spicer raps on "Adventures of Super Rhymes" (1979), "When I say 'rock,' you say 'roll,' when I say 'ice,' then you say 'cold' / Then when I say 'disco,' you say 'the beat,' I say it's 'like honey,' then you say 'it's sweet.'" The audience responds in turn. In addition, the Funky Four rap on "That's the Joint" (1979), "Before you hear the party people yell 'Sugarhill' / So what's the deal?" to which the audience responds, "Sugarhill!!" These call-and-response routines give clear testimony to the intimacy of the club or party situation with which these performers were perhaps most familiar. Rap grew out of a dialogic and interactive tradition, one that linked artists and audiences in some concrete fashion.

As noted, artists in the mid-eighties moved away from hip-hop as only a dance or party music. Artists like Rakim and KRS-One increasingly defined themselves as poets, artists, and pedagogues. Rap artists during the mid-eighties brought a greater degree of vocal sophistication to this art as well as an increased awareness of the role of rappers as poets and pedagogues. This move was not so clearly about forwarding a specific political or educative agenda, at least initially. More important, it seems, was an awareness of hip-hop as its own complex and nuanced cultural field, with real stakes and consequences. More than anything, artists like KRS-One and Rakim acknowledged the kind of creative depth and play that could be brought to the art form—particularly as set against a dominant, popular American culture. In this sense, rap artists came to function as critical pedagogues—self-consciously attempting to "re-engage a social world" that often seemed constituted at a distance, wholly *a priori* (McLaren, 1997, p. 13). Rap artists, here, were committed to the role and importance of hip-hop as an emerging vehicle for creative activity—indeed, "to the practical realization of self-determination and creativity on a social scale" (p. 13).

Key here was a loose collective of artists, Boogie Down Productions. KRS-One—the group's front man and lead vocalist—stressed a more overtly pedagogical, more lyric-intense music with the release of their first singles in 1986 and their first album in 1987, *Criminal Minded*. The opening cut on the album is aptly titled "Poetry," while the last is the title cut. The feel of this track, "Criminal Minded," is definitely conversational. Gone are clipped shouts and instead long lines begin with "see" and "I mean,"—lines delivered above, below, as well as on, the beat. KRS-One evoked the feel and flow of an educated and conversant poet here. The term "b-boy" originally connoted one who participated in all the facets of hip-hop culture. KRS-One, however, rejects all this when he raps that he is not a "king" or a "b-boy," but a "teacher" and a "scholar."

In addition, an explicit focus on the political emerged with time as well. Boogie Down Productions' second album was entitled *By All Means Necessary* and featured KRS-One on the cover, mimicking the famous photo of Malcolm X standing by a window with his rifle drawn. Artists like Public Enemy extended this political and nationalist trend. Specifically a kind of black nationalist identity politics became apparent in rap during the late eighties as its community stretched irretrievably beyond local boundaries. For example, Public Enemy's second album, *It Takes a Nation of Millions to Hold Us Back* (1988) stressed a political agenda as evinced by titles such as "Rebel Without a Pause" and "Prophets of Rage." Indeed, Chuck D and Flavor Flav wed a problack stance with Nation of Islam ideology on these tracks as well as on others, including "Bring the Noise." Terms such as "devil" and "black Asiatic man" abound throughout, referencing the intricate genesis beliefs preached by Nation founders W.D. Fard and Elijah Muhammad. The Nation of Islam became a pronounced force in rap at this time, its blend of militancy and problack ideology finding enthusiastic support among many young African Americans.

It was a heady time for rap music. It was the moment in which the art evolved into an explicitly artistic and politically educative medium. It was the moment that rap appeared to be a serious art from—worthy of criticism and attention. Personally, it meant a more intense engagement with these hip-hop texts. It was around this time, my senior year of college, that I began looking at hip-hop as an art form. Like many however, I had a textual bias. As I understood it the import of these texts was to be located and understood through deep textual engagement. I was doing this work from within an English department and my unit of analysis was rap recordings. In many respects, my work betrayed the kind of textual bias that Dwight Conquergood and Norman Denzin, among others, have discussed. As Conquergood (1998) has written, there is an "almost total domination of textualism in the academy" (p. 25).

Importantly, this stress on textualism, on recorded lyric content, occluded the transactional dimensions of rap performance, which had been so important initially. I recall here seeing Public Enemy in concert in 1987 (near New York City) and again in 1994 (in Buffalo). The shows seemed less like small-scale community performances and more like major-label rock extravaganzas. Elaborate props and rigid codification all gave their performances a kind of large-scale grandiosity foreign to most early—clearly less formal—hip-hop music. The group, for example, was flanked on stage by the Security of the First World (or the S1Ws), a paramilitary outfit that carried fake Uzi submachine guns, dressed in camouflage, and did an elaborate stage show behind band leaders Chuck D and Flavor Flav. Perhaps most importantly, the group "performed" their previously recorded material for the audience. Unlike early rap performances, the music was not continually negotiated and processed in live practice and performance. This would become the norm for rap artists, as the "text" or recording emerged as the centerpiece of this activity.

As I moved away from the text-based discipline of English to the interdisciplinary space of American studies, however, I was exposed to important work at the margins of ethnomusicology and performance studies, work concerned with documenting and understanding performance in context. Christopher Small's performance-centered approach in *Music of the Common Tongue: Survival and Celebration in Afro-American Music* (1987) proved extraordinarily useful. Small notes here that "music is not primarily a thing or a collection of things, but an activity in which we engage." He continues to characterize the social engagement of music as a performative collaboration that not only includes "performing and composing . . . but also listening and even dancing to music; all those involved in any way in a musical performance can be thought of as *musicking*" (emphasis added,

p. 50). As Small and others have stressed, many nonelite western forms of music cannot be understood outside of their relationship with, and connections to, dance, something that can be said for early hip-hop as well.

Ethnomusicologist John Chernoff (1979) writes that African music is, quite literally, only realized through the participation of dancers. "In African music, it is largely the listener or dancer who has to supply the beat: the listener must be *actively engaged* in making sense of the music; the music itself does not become the concentrated focus of an event, as at a concert. It is for this fundamental reason that African music should not be studied out of its context or as "music": the African orchestra is not complete without a participant on the other side" (p. 50). Dancers do not simply accompany drummers as they perform. Rather, dancers become integral parts of the event, supplying an additional rhythm, through the pounding of their feet, to the polyrhythmic event. Rhythms play off of each other, dancers interacting with drummers and drummers interacting with dancers in entirely recursive ways. All are responsible for sustaining the event.

Work in performance studies has concretized the social collaboration of meaning making in performance. Pelias and Van-Oosting's (1987) work, in suggesting a "paradigm for performance studies," distinguishes it from earlier forms of oral interpretation. The authors discuss how new iterations of performance studies dislodge canonical and rigid understandings of texts, events, performers, and audiences. As they argue, performance studies is ecumenical in disposition, "including all members of a speech community as potential artists, all utterances as potentially aesthetic, all events as potentially theatrical, and all audiences as potentially active participants who can authorize artistic experience" (p. 221). Like certain strands of ethnomusicology noted above, this work has decentered the assumed role and importance of the "text," opening up a broader and less rigid understanding of what constitutes a performance and aesthetic transaction.

For me, what I will call a "performance-centered approach" represented a fundamentally different way to look at hip-hop—from text to context, noun to verb. This meant understanding that all texts circulate in multiple contexts, allowing me to see the limits of referential work on self-contained recorded texts. Politics or artistic worth did not and could not be calibrated only from song lyrics taken out of context. Rather, the entire event needed to be looked at. This meant decentering my own investments in the humanities and opening up to a range of influences, including work in ethnomusicology and performance studies. Indeed, decentering texts through the performative became a key way to open up new spaces for interrogating their roles and functions.

PRACTICES

Decentering my relationship with rap texts allowed me to think about their uses in new ways. More specifically, the empirical impulse behind ethnomusicology took me more squarely to the social sciences (generally) and the discipline of speech communication (specifically). Speech communication is an applied and varied field, running the gamut from classical rhetoric to experimental research. I took up concerns at the intersection of ethnography of communication and sociocultural linguistics. Ethnography became my method of choice, though my understanding of its role and importance would change over time. Here, too, my evolving understanding of the performative would prove critical.

There is a long history of interest in the performative in ethnography, particularly in linguistic anthropology. Perhaps the most common distinction in this regard is the distinction between "unmarked" and "marked" performance. The classic linguistic distinction, established by de Saussure (1900/1959), was between "langue" and "parole," or language structure and performance. One the one hand, early scholars in ethnography of communication (EOC), including Richard Bauman and Dennis Tedlock, were interested in marked performance, performance that marks itself as unique or special, such as storytelling. According to folklorist and ethnographer Richard Bauman (1992a), "while the term may be employed in an aesthetically neutral sense to designate the actual conduct of communication . . . performance usually suggests an aesthetically marked and heightened mode of communication, framed in a special way and put on display for an audience" (p. 41).

On the other hand, Dell Hymes and others asked us to focus on unmarked performance or "parole." For Hymes and others, the unit of analysis for linguistics was not idealized grammars taken out of context, but performance— what people were able to do with language in real, everyday situations. Hymes and others shifted focus to the variability of communication in particular cultural settings. He wrote, "We shall not be able to have a theory that accounts for the meaning of language in different lives and cultures . . . until we examine . . . the actual functioning of language" (1974, p. 126). Hymes, thus, insisted that one could not study language as realized in grammar alone. "Grammar" is merely one more abstraction that can be removed from concrete and unfolding speaking situations. Language needs to be explored in socially situated activity as realized in stable speaking patterns.

Popular cultural texts like rap music took on new meaning for me in this regard. They were the "langue" from which young people would perform everyday speech, a kind of dialogic fodder for young people to pick up, use, and mobilize. I thus set out to study the communicative processes that young people used to position themselves and others *vis-à-vis* key rap texts (Dimitriadis, 2001b). I began conducting focus groups and interviews about rap music in the spring of 1996 at a local community center in a small Midwest city that served an almost wholly black and poor population. The results were more surprising than I expected. While young people certainly "performed selves" around these texts, the performances were more jarring that I expected. It was difficult, if not impossible, I found, to read practices off of texts—texts (broadly defined) such as the work of Tupac Shakur and the filmic history *Panther* as well as the Southern rap scene. Media effects, I found, became more unpredictable as I moved from texts to social networks to individual biographies. I saw these texts put to myriad uses by these young people in their daily lives, in ways that wholly exceeded my predictive powers.

I recall here the dramatic events surrounding the death of rapper Tupac Shakur in Las Vegas late in 1996: his shooting on September 13, his death five days later, and the work these young people did in resurrecting him, through myth, over the next year or so—when such talk was most common. These young people were devastated by the loss of Tupac (or 2Pac or Pac as he was most often referred to). I was at the community center (or "club") the night he finally expired from his mortal wounds (September 18) and was witness to the feelings of outrage and grief, devastation and loss that many immediately felt. Young children cried, older teens were enraged, virtually all stayed glued to BET (Black Entertainment Television) to watch the unfolding updates. This grief, however, soon changed in the days and weeks following, to elaborately constructed rumors and stories about Tupac's complicity in faking his death. These stories, circulating across the nation and around the world on the Internet, television, and in daily talk, differed in their details but were similar in constructing Tupac as the prime mover in his situation and in succeeding events. One young person commented: "I think Tupac got set up. They shot him but he survived. But then nobody knew he survived, 'cause I think he

probably, say like during the night he, he had snuck out . . . he, he had started feeling better and snuck out." He continued, noting how he was caught and was now in jail: "They got him on some top security. They know . . . Tupac's smart, he can deal some schemes, try to get out and stuff, but they got him on top security." The stress on both Tupac's physical invulnerability ("they shot him but he survived") as well as his mental acumen ("Tupac's smart, he can deal some schemes") marked many such stories.

The uses to which these texts were put never ceased to surprise me, a fact of course underscored by my position as a white person in a nearly all-black setting. During my weekly discussion groups, I drew on a broad range of material, including hip-hop recordings, music videos, and films, to help frame discussion. Often, these "texts" became part of how young people talked about unfolding events at the club and in the community. I recall here the fall of 1997, when the Ku Klux Klan, fresh from a march in a nearby city, proposed a controversial rally in the city where I was conducting this research. Though I knew the Klan more than capable of horrific acts of violence, I certainly did not think any of the younger people at the club were in any immediate danger, and I was not, strictly speaking, afraid of the group. However, the intense fears and anxieties of these young people (especially young children and adolescents) soon became apparent. I remember sitting at the front desk of this community center with the unit director signing young people in, the day the news hit. It soon became clear, these young people were literally unsure whether the Klan would come to their houses, attack them in the streets, or follow them home to hurt their families. All the ways that violence (or the threat of violence) can completely overtake and disorient us became exceedingly apparent quite quickly.

In the immediacies of this moment, my adolescent participants turned to *Panther* (1995), a film about the Black Panther Party for Self

Defense, which we had been watching and discussing in my weekly groups. Indeed, it became clear to me that these young people resonated with this film in specific ways. I introduced several films including *Malcolm X* (1992) (a true story about the killed Nation of Islam leader) and *Rosewood* (1997) (about the violent extermination of an all-black town early in the twentieth century). Yet it became evident in several focus groups devoted to these films about black history that the highly charged Black Panther film spoke to these young people and their very compelling fears, in ways that others did not. *Panther,* a Hollywood endeavor, was "real" to these young people—even more "real" than the PBS *Eyes on the Prize* documentary about the group, which I showed as well. This film conjured up a useful kind of reality in ways mediated and complicated by a whole host of specific factors and forces that I could not have predicted *a priori.*

In particular, these young people made intertextual, if not interstitial, links between this film and others (nonhistorical ones) that featured the same actors—films like *Menace II Society* (1993), *Friday* (1995), and *Jason's Lyric* (1994). They made connections between the Black Panthers, their own friendship networks (or "cliques"), modern-day gangs like Black P-Stone, and such wildly successful professional wrestling associations as the New World Order (or NWO). They coalesced around the movie's violent scenes while they ignored those with a lot of talking (i.e., "the boring parts"!) and, finally they drew upon their own local knowledge and experiences to connect with and comment on the film's antipolice subtext. These were the situated contextual factors that mediated their understanding of black history, that made *Panther* real, that allowed them to deal in specific ways with events that unfolded in 1997 in this city. More particularly, comments like, "We need the Panthers! We need some Black Panthers! Really, I need some Black Panthers by my

house" became common in and out of group talk.

The research described above was conducted by way of small focus groups most often composed of friends. This research highlighted the unpredictability and specificity of how young people in local social networks used such texts. Even more revealing, however, was the more intensive one-on-one work that took me more directly to the lives of teens in less circumscribed ways. Indeed, of all my work over that four-year period, no part of it was more revealing than the story of Tony and Rufus and their uses of southern rap (the music of Master P, Eightball and MJG, and others). In the popular imagination about black teenagers, Tony and Rufus followed the only two available paths—one (Rufus) was "good" while the other (Tony) was "bad." Over the years I knew them, Rufus by and large stayed out of trouble and stuck close to the community center and its staff members. He was well liked by everyone with whom he came into contact and received a number of awards at this center. Tony, however, had a less sanguine life. He had numerous discipline problems at school and with the law, and he was a member of a local chapter of a national gang. When I first met the pair, however, they referred to each other as "cousins" though they were in fact best friends. Tony and Rufus both grew up in the same small Mississippi town and both had made the move to the city where I conducted this research about a decade earlier. These teens recreated notions of the South—specifically, a sense of community—in this city, by using popular cultural resources which linked them to important familial networks in their new home as well as "down South." Hip-hop, here, was used to create notions of community and place that transcended easy stereotypes about good and bad youth.

As noted, media effects became increasingly unpredictable as I moved from popular texts to social networks to individual biographies.

The "performances" became increasingly open to articulation and rearticulation, across selves, histories, and traditions. These tendencies towards the performative have been highlighted and even exacerbated in this particular social, cultural, and material moment, I found—the distinction between marked and unmarked performance collapsing, in this more radical and even unpredictable understanding of performance. In some sense, all our actions now have always-already been "put on display, objectified . . . and opened to scrutiny by an audience" due to the proliferation of interpretive frameworks circulating in media culture today (Bauman, 1992a, p, 44). As Denzin notes, "We inhabit a dramaturgical culture. The dividing line between performer and audience blurs, and culture itself becomes a dramatic performance" (2003, p. x). Performance, here, is a "transgression, a force which crashes and breaks through sedimented meanings and normative traditions and plunges us back into the vortices of political struggle" (Conquergood, 1998, p. 32). Indeed, my evolving understandings of "performance" challenged me to rethink the extent to which young people "performed" selves and social relations in and through popular culture—as well as how unpredictable those performances truly were. Young people used these texts to talk about privileged selves (e.g., the talk about Tupac's life and death), histories (e.g., the talk about *Panther* and the KKK), and traditions (e.g., the talk about southern rap)—none of which I could have predicted beforehand. This was, clearly, an educative process if a counterintuitive one.

In sum, the performative allowed me to decenter my own relationship to hip-hop. First, it forced me to rethink my own interpretive criteria around popular recordings or "texts," now seeing them as enmeshed in live activities. I had, with time, to decenter my privileging of rap recordings and their displays of verbal virtuosity to account for the multilayered nature of performance. Second, it

forced me to rethink the connection between texts and practices, enabling me to see the ways in which people's relationship to these texts were always performative, always exceeding my own interpretive horizons. I had, again with time, to acknowledge how lived practices surprised me more and more as I moved from social networks to individual biographies.

PEDAGOGY

However, decentering texts and practices, I maintain, does not mean simply discarding them—it means rearticulating them as well (Conquergood, 1998, p. 26). The "pedagogical," I argue here, is a key space where this recentering takes place. Indeed, I want to argue here that a performative understanding of texts and practices opens up new spaces to see pedagogy as a radical and ethical activity. Just as texts and practices can only be seen in performative contexts, pedagogy gives us the ability—or the imperative—to rearticulate those intersections, and to take responsibility for them.

By *performance as pedagogy,* I mean to take the discussion beyond the perhaps familiar—if still useful—conceit of "teaching as a performance art" (Sarason, 1999). In a well known iteration of this discussion, noted educational psychologist Seymour Sarason writes, "A teacher is more than a conduit of subject matter. A teacher literally creates the ambience on the stage of learning and that teacher is the chief actor, the 'star,' the actor who gets top billing" (p. 3). He continues, comparing the curriculum to a script:

> The written script is like a curriculum, the task of the actor and the director is to make it come alive for an audience and the obligation is not discharged by knowing the script, by regurgitating it. Becoming and sustaining a role is an artistic process of identification and imagination about which our comprehension is far from clear. (p. 4)

Indeed, just as an actor makes a "script" come alive for an audience, the role of the educator here is to make the curriculum come alive for the student.

Again, this is a useful conceit, but betrays the kind of textual bias Conquergood and others have interrogated—it reifies "the script" of curriculum as a text of origin. Elyse Pineau's (1994) work on the metaphorical links between teaching and performance is germinal here. She cautions against the dangers of treating performance as a simple way to "enhanc[e] educational communication," arguing instead for performance as a "generative metaphor for examining educational experience" (p. 8). The challenge of the performative, for Denzin (2003), Pineau and others, takes us into new radical spaces, where "educators and students engage not in the 'pursuit of truths,' but in collaborative fictions—perpetually making and remaking world views and their tenuous positions within them" (Pineau, 1994, p. 10). Indeed, while I found "performance" a useful way to reframe my interest in the textual and the ethnographic, it has pushed me in more fundamental ways to rethink the pedagogical. A performative epistemology encourages us to think of culture as always in motion, always on display, always open to invention and reinvention.

Decentering texts and practices takes us to new pedagogical terrain. Pedagogy, here, is emergent, each encounter different from the next. Ethics and morals become central. Here I recall Freire's (1970) *Pedagogy of the Oppressed,* in which the author argues, among other things, that the pedagogical encounter is grounded in the ethical imperative *to become more fully human.* We give ourselves over to each other—the lines between "teacher" and "student" blurring—in a collaborative effort to "name" the world, to become subjects in our own stories and narratives. For Freire, this is a radically unpredictable endeavor, an emergent collective experience girded by a faith in the emancipation of all peoples, oppressors and oppressed alike. He writes,

> To surmount the situation of oppression, people must first critically recognize its causes, so that through transforming action they can create a new situation, one that makes possible the pursuit of a fuller humanity. But the struggle to be more fully human has already begun in the authentic struggle to transform the situation. (p. 29)

He continues,

> The task of the dialogical teacher in an interdisciplinary team working on the thematic universe revealed by their investigation is to "re-present" that universe to the people from whom she or he first received it—and "re-present" it not as a lecture, but as a problem. (p. 90)

This means entering in authentic dialogue, without *a priori* conclusions about the nature of oppression or its transformation.

As these discussions underscore, a performative epistemology makes us responsible for how we inhabit the world. There is no recourse to foundational claims. The world, here, is always-already pedagogical, always being articulated and rearticulated. How we choose to enter this back-and-forth is the key to the ethical dimension of performance. In particular, the performative decenters our taken-for-granted assumptions about pedagogy—where it happens and with what texts. As Giroux writes, "Pedagogy in this context becomes public and performative, in part because it opens a space for disputing conventional academic borders" (2000, p. 130). Such an approach invites us to look for education in unsuspecting places. In the multiple environs of social influence where faith, law, and cultural performance confirm or confine the nature of human possibility—in community centers and churches; in alternative in-school initiatives; in popular culture; in prisons; and in the work of poets, novelists, visual artists, and playwrights.

I would like to highlight three—albeit partial, contingent, and open to rearticulation—areas of research where I have begun to interrogate these concerns, points where I have entered these conversations and engaged these issues. They are the role of popular culture as an alternative curriculum, the importance of non-traditional school learning sites for disenfranchised youth, and new possible roles for art and aesthetics in the rethinking of school life today.

First, as several recent ethnographies have demonstrated, we can not understand popular culture and young people's identities in predictable ways (Dimitriadis, 2001b; Dolby, 2001; Perry, 2002; Yon, 2000). More and more, as this work makes clear, we must ask ourselves what kinds of curricula—broadly defined—young people draw on to understand, explain, and live through the world around them. Young people in the United States and around the world are elaborating complex kinds of social and cultural identifications through music like hip-hop and techno in ways that challenge predictive notions about texts, practices, and identities. I recall here Nadine Dolby's (2001) ethnography of South African students in a post-Apartheid moment. As Dolby shows, these students use popular (American) culture to navigate new racial and ethnic identities precisely as these categories are called into question by progressive political upheaval.

Next, recent work on community-based organizations and "safe spaces" raises important questions as to where "education" is happening today. For Weis, Fine, and others, this has meant looking at how a variety of young people "homestead" or claim authentic and meaningful spaces and identities within a variety of sites, both in school and out of school (Dimitriadis, 2003; Fine and Weis, 1998; Fine, Weis, Centrie, and Roberts, 2000; Weis and Fine, 2000). In a series of articles and books, for example, Weis and Fine take us to a community-based art program named "Molly Olga," an "Orisha" house of spirit worship,

and an abstinence-only school-based sex education program, among many others sites. My own recent work has looked at how local arts and education programs in Buffalo, New York, coordinate the work of practicing artists and teachers in schools and community centers throughout the city. Often methodologically reflective, this work takes us to the terrain of young people's lives in ways that challenge normative assumptions about young people and the ways we understand them.

Finally, in the face of these realities—which have largely outstripped the delimited field of traditional educational theory and practice—recent work has struggled with art and aesthetics as a realm for interrogating new models, new theories, new intellectual ancestors, and new ways of thinking, acting, and being as transformative intellectuals and pedagogues. This work has taken us away from the increasingly circumscribed field of expert research and theory to the overlapping spaces of postcolonial art, music, novels, poetry, and criticism (as in my recent work with Cameron McCarthy). This extends to the work of authors such as Wilson Harris and Toni Morrison, painters like Jean-Michel Basquiat, Gordon Bennett, and Arnaldo Roche-Rabell, and public intellectuals such as CLR James and James Baldwin (Dimitriadis and McCarthy, 2001). This work echoes and extends a now reconceptualized curriculum studies field, the work of William Pinar, Madeline Grumet, and others, into the whole area of "difference" in an age of globalization (Crichlow, 2003; Dimitriadis and McCarthy, 2001; Low, 2001; McCarthy, 1998).

Taken together, a performance-centered approach to pedagogy means decentering and rethinking our object of analysis, moving us into a space where pedagogy is on the move, always in motion.

In closing, as I argued throughout, my initial understandings of hip-hop texts and practices were called inextricably into question as I moved towards the performative. My ability to read meaning of off these cultural articulations was decentered again and again. Yet, this is no excuse or alibi for cynicism or despair. By seeing culture always already in motion, we are encouraged to ever attempt to recenter our meanings and understandings of it. This is the space of pedagogy. On one level, a performance-centered approach to pedagogy means ever questioning where education takes place today and with what texts. On another level, it means taking responsibility for the questions we ask and the kinds of pedagogy we enact. This is the space of hope and possibility—again, the space of pedagogy and performance *tout court*—one which demands we redefine the realm of intellectual and educative activity today.

REFERENCES

Baraka, A. (1963). *Blues people.* New York: Quill.

Bauman, R. (1992a). Performance. In R. Bauman (Ed.), *Folklore, cultural performance, and popular entertainments: A communications-centered handbook* (pp. 41–49). Oxford, England: Oxford University Press.

Bauman, R. (1992b). Contextualization, tradition, and the dialogue of genres: Icelandic legends of *kraftaskald.* In A. Duranti & C. Goodwin (Eds.), *Rethinking context: Language as an interactive phenomenon* (pp. 125–145). Cambridge, England: Cambridge University Press.

Chernoff, J. (1979). *African rhythm and African sensibility: Aesthetics and social action in African musical idioms.* Chicago: University of Chicago Press.

Conquergood, D. (1998). Beyond the text: Toward a performative cultural politics. In S. Dailey (Ed.), *The future of performance studies: Visions and revisions* (pp. 25–36). Washington, DC: NCA.

Crichlow, W. (2003). Stan Douglas and the aesthetic critique of urban decline. In G. Dimitriadis & D. Carlson (Eds.), *Promises to keep: Cultural studies, democratic education, and public life* (pp. 155–165). New York: RoutledgeFalmer.

de Saussure, F. (1959). *Course in general linguistics* (W. Baskin, Trans.). New York: Philosophical Library. (Original work published 1900)

Denzin, N. (2003). *Performance ethnography: Critical pedagogy and the politics of culture.* Thousand Oaks, CA: Sage.

Dimitriadis, G. (2001a). Pedagogy and performance in black popular culture. *Cultural Studies/Critical Methodologies, 1*(1), 24–35.

Dimitriadis, G. (2001b). *Performing identity/performing culture: Hip hop as text, pedagogy, and lived practice.* New York: Peter Lang.

Dimitriadis, G. (2003). *Friendship, cliques, and gangs: Young black men coming of age in urban America.* New York: Teachers College Press.

Dimitriadis, G., & McCarthy, C. (2001). *Reading and teaching the postcolonial: From Baldwin to Basquiat and beyond.* New York: Teachers College Press.

Dolby, N. (2001). *Constructing race: Youth, identity, and popular culture in South Africa.* Albany: SUNY Press.

Ellison, R. (2001). *Living with music.* New York: Vintage.

Eric B. & Rakim. (1987). *I know you got soul* [Audio recording]. New York: Fourth and Broadway Records.

Fine, M., & Weis, L. (1998). *The unknown city: Lives of poor and working-class young adults.* Boston: Beacon Press.

Fine, M., Weis, L., Centrie, C., & Roberts, R. (2000). Educating beyond the borders of schooling. *Anthropology & Education Quarterly, 31*(2), 131–151.

Freire, P. (1970). *Pedagogy of the oppressed.* New York: Continuum.

Funky Four. (1979). *That's the joint* [Audio recording]. Englewood, NJ: Sugar Hill Records.

Giroux, H. (2000). *Impure acts: The practical politics of cultural studies.* New York: Routledge.

hooks, b. (1992). *Black looks: Race and representation.* Boston: South End Press.

Hymes, D. (1974). *Foundations in sociolinguistics: An ethnographic approach.* Philadelphia: University of Pennsylvania Press.

Lee, J. (1999). Disciplining theater and drama in the English department: Some reflections on 'performance' and institutional history. *Text and Performance Quarterly, 19*(2), 145–158.

Low, B. (2001). "Bakardi slang" and the language and poetics of T Dot hip hop. *Taboo: A Journal of Culture and Education, 5*(2), 15–32.

McCarthy, C. (1998). *The uses of culture.* New York: Routledge.

McLaren, P. (1997). *Revolutionary multiculturalism: Pedagogies of dissent fore the new millennium.* Boulder, CO: Westview Press.

Pelias, R., & VanOosting, J. (1987). A paradigm for performance studies. *Quarterly Journal of Speech, 73,* 219–231.

Perry, P. (2002). *Shades of white: White kids and racial identity in high school.* Durham, NC: Duke University Press.

Pineau, E. (1994). Teaching is performance: Reconceptualizing a problematic metaphor. *American Educational Research Journal, 31*(1), 3–25.

Pollock, D. (1998). Introduction: Making history go. In D. Pollock (Ed.), *Exceptional spaces: Essays in performance & history* (pp. 1–45). Chapel Hill: University of North Carolina Press.

Sarason, S. (1999). *Teaching as a performance art.* New York: Teachers College Press.

Small, C. (1987). *Music of the common tongue: Survival and celebration in Afro-American music.* London: John Calder.

Spicer, J. (1979). *Adventures of super rhymes* [Audio recording]. Camden, NJ: Jazz Records.

Weis, L., & Fine, M. (2000). *Construction sites: Excavating race, class, and gender among urban youth.* New York: Teachers College Press.

Yon, D. (2000). *Elusive culture: Schooling, race, and identity in global times.* Albany: SUNY Press.

17

Unlocking the Doors for Incarcerated Women Through Performance and Creative Writing

KRISTIN BERVIG VALENTINE

Performance studies, feminist, and other critical scholars are often active in struggles for social justice. "Over the years, theories and practices have moved steadily toward the social and political goals of employing performance as an instrument of social awareness and change" Park-Fuller (2003, p. 288; see other public-issue research published by Capo, 1983; Conquergood, 1992, 1995, 1998; Langellier, 1986; Kistenberg, 1995; Mann, Hecht, and Valentine, 1989; and Valentine, 1986). As communication scholar Stephen Hartnett (2003) argued in *Incarceration Nation,* we academics "need to approach issues of social justice not only as sites of research, but also as sites of engagement with disadvantaged communities" (p. 5). I invite readers of this chapter to look carefully at the realities surrounding incarceration in their own communities.

My research engagement is concentrated on and for incarcerated women whose numbers, at the end of 2002 in the United States, had reached 96,099 (6.8 percent of the total imprisoned population) according to the statistical website managed by Ann Pastore (2003). Greenfeld and Snell (1999) report that recidivism rates in 1999 were as high as 50 percent. Meda Chesney-Lind, a prolific and impassioned advocate of prison reform for women, noted despairingly,

> The number of women incarcerated in prisons and jails in the United States is now about ten times greater than the number of women incarcerated in all of Western Europe. This despite the fact that Western Europe and the United States are roughly equivalent in terms of population. (Chesney-Lind, 2002, p. 81)

Possession of illegal drugs, petty theft, forgery, and fraud head the list of reasons for female incarceration. The vast number of incarcerated women in America noted above

(96,099) is due largely to the fact that finding even small amounts of drugs on a person is now defined as a criminal act, leading to criminalization of a whole new population that never would have gone to prison before.

Sharon Cohen wrote about a young woman incarcerated in a Michigan prison because her boyfriend, unbeknownst to her, had stashed a plastic bag of heroin in the car she was driving. The law was set up to put drug kingpins away with mandatory life sentences but it caught DeDonna Young. Young who, at age 43, has "celebrated—if that's the right word—18 birthdays in a shared cell not much bigger than a walk-in closet" was sentenced to spend the rest of her life there unless the law is changed (Cohen, 1997, p. A35). Richie (2002) points out the corollary problem of the children for whom women were responsible before incarceration:

> One of the most significant consequences of mass incarceration for women is the almost irreparable damage done to their role as mothers and their status as parents when they are removed from their communities and detained in correctional facilities. Conservative estimates suggest that 75 percent of women in prison are mothers, and two-thirds have children under the age of eighteen. (p. 139)

Thus, these children must have alternate caregivers, usually a grandmother, or the woman's sister or aunt, compounding the problem by affecting the incarcerated woman's family and wider community.

As a social activist in several of my communities (e.g., academic women, politics, prison reform), I find that it is the experiences within this practice that often drive my scholarship. Rather than thinking "How can I make this piece of scholarship relevant and practical to the community?", I often ask "How can I create scholarship on behalf of these communities from my activist practice?" And further, "How do I make it jargon-free

and accessible?" Currently, this orientation to teaching and writing is called "service-learning." Yet, at least since 1978, many of us performance studies teachers have been helping students enhance the greater good of communities, both close at hand and globally, through performance skills and knowledge.

In *Theatre of the Oppressed,* Augusto Boal (1998) writes, "a theatre that attempts to change the changers of society cannot lead to repose, cannot re-establish equilibrium" (p. 105). We need to use our knowledge, experience, and resources to aid communities who need to *change the changers of society.* A notable example of this type of social justice work is that of Linda Park-Fuller, who has taken the Performance in Social Contexts class at Arizona State University to a new level with her Playback Theatre work (Park-Fuller, 2003). She has refined the teaching of Playback Theatre to feature full participation of audience members with cast members on topics relevant to actions benefiting the community. Park-Fuller, like many other performance activists, is indebted to Augusto Boal.

Stringer (1999) characterizes the results of community-based action research as "democratic, enabling the participation of all people, equitable, acknowledging people's equality of worth, liberating, providing freedom from oppressive, debilitating conditions, and is life-enhancing, enabling the expression of peoples' full human potential" (p. 10). Those life-enhancing goals are consistent with recently published scholarship on behalf of incarcerated people (see Burke, 1992; Chevigney, 1999; Corey, 1996; Hartnett, 2003; Holton, 1995; Lamb and Women of York Correctional Institution, 2003; O'Brien, 2001; Owen, 1998; Valentine, 1998).

My reasons for volunteering to teach in prisons were based on my long-term interest in the conditions of imprisoned women around the world. More specifically, my concerns with prisoners began in the 1970s when I taught at the University of Kentucky. There, one of the intelligent, but risk-taking, communication majors was caught with marijuana and given a one- to five-year sentence at a federal prison near Lexington. I asked myself: "If I were to be incarcerated, how would I avoid despair? How would I exist with no intellectual work to do?" As a result, I joined with Maureen Donovan, then a University of Kentucky graduate student, to conduct a performance-based communication class at that federal prison. After I moved to Arizona State University in 1976 and for the following twenty years, I continued to volunteer at correctional facilities for women. Once inside the prison fences, I used performance studies pedagogy to teach communication skills because I've been witness to the positive results of this pedagogy in broader constructions of my social pedagogical practice.

GOING TO PRISON

The routine was similar each time I traveled to the women's prison. With students from my undergraduate Performance in Social Contexts class, or with graduate students, at Arizona State University, I left downtown Phoenix and drove west on the freeway that heads toward Los Angeles. Forty-five minutes later, I exited and drove the short way to the parking lot at Perryville, site of Arizona's largest state prison facility for women. We locked our backpacks, purses, and other personal items in the truck of the car, as requested by prison security, and then walked to the guard station to receive our temporary permits.

The guard, sitting behind bulletproof glass, slid out a metal drawer into which we placed our driver licenses. The drawer slid in and we watched for several minutes while the guard checked the approved visitor list. Finally, the drawer slid back out with our entry permits. After waiting at the first of the security doors we heard the lock click open, and we entered a holding area to wait for the second metal door to open into the reception area. Here we

went through a metal detector and were often halted by an alarm because one or more of the students wore shoes with metal shanks.

Often, after examining the items we had brought with us, the reception guard refused us permission to bring writing paper inside because, we were told, "they just sell writing paper that volunteers bring in." However, when we explained we were there, as in former visits, to teach the performance and creative writing class authorized by the prison's General Educational Development (GED) diploma teachers, the guard always relented.[1] We then went through a third set of security doors and were finally in. Through the glass windows of the visiting area, where we taught, we could see an expanse of yard, with some grass but mostly gravel, situated between rows of closed-door cell-dwellings leading away from the reception building.

The women inmates had painted cheerful child-oriented scenes on the white walls of the visitors' room because this is where the women are allowed to see their children and preapproved family members during visiting hours.

Although the metal chairs were already arranged in rows, we quickly moved the chairs into a circle as we waited for our students to arrive. Alone, in couples, or in small groups, they entered, some hesitantly, even though our inside contact, Theresa Meyette, had advertised and talked up the class. They sat, talking quietly at first, some smoking, some cracking open sunflower seeds, and some chewing gum. They ranged in age between 20 and 50, and were neatly dressed in prison garb, which used to be blue jeans and blue denim shirts but is now bright orange.

Unless it was the first class of a new semester, I started by asking what writing they brought with them and who might like to read aloud first.[2] On one memorable day, Theresa brought "Darkland," a poem she wrote while in "the hole" (solitary confinement) for organizing a protest against the administration's decision not to allow a sweat lodge to be built for Native American inmates. Reading with intensity, she began:

> It's been a long time since I sat in total darkness. Once again, I feel back in the womb, protected. I want to crawl into a fetal position; go back before the time I came screaming and kicking out of the womb, before floodlights dashed my little eyes, shocking me into existence. It seems like an eternity since the floodlights here went out. In prison you never seem to be in darkness. There is always the image of razor wire and the perimeter lights, gawking light-monsters, invading my little cell. Now it's completely dark and I hope the sun takes its time coming around.

Before she was paroled, Theresa Meyette was a leader in the series of voluntary college-level courses in performance and creative writing that I either taught or supervised. Like her, the women inside the prison miss being in the "free world"—the world where they are able to control such everyday actions as opening the fridge for a snack or the bathroom cabinet for an aspirin. In addition to the loss of such freedoms, they have lost intelligent play, curiosity, unfettered affection, choice of friends, and free expression. They especially miss being able to communicate without constant supervision. The current state of the penal system in the United States helps contextualize these women's writings, and it also contextualizes a larger approach to performance-based activist curriculum within the system.

CURRENT SITUATION IN PENOLOGY

Forty-seven million U.S. citizens have federal or state criminal records; this is roughly one-fourth of the adult population, and a disproportionate percentage are people of color. Adopted as part of the "get tough on criminals" attitude that prevailed in the 1980s and 1990s, a range of strategies including "three strikes," mandatory sentences, and the "war on drugs" has resulted in this mass incarceration (Mauer and Chesney-Lind, 2002, p. 1).[3]

Writing on the necessity for changing how the United States deals with convicted persons, Elaine Lord, superintendent of Bedford Hills, a New York prison for women, declared,

> The United States sentences people to prison for far longer terms than are rendered in many other countries of the world. We seem to have a need to destroy hope right now, whereas other countries see hope as critical to prisoners and prison systems. We need to begin to look at how punitive we really are and come to some decisions as a society in terms of what we want. The cost of our current actions is extremely high and will weigh down not only this generation but many generations to come. (Lord, 1995, p. 265)

The good news is that the prison pendulum is swinging away from adding punitive measures toward exploring alternatives to prisons. It is more than ironic that the swing toward prison alternatives is being accelerated by right-wing fiscal conservatives who, even though they decry "coddling criminals," are beginning to recognize that closing prisons' exit doors, while pushing more and more people into their entrances, results in greater budget deficits.[4]

My experience and direct observation during more than twenty years in teaching communication in women's prisons validates contentions that we need to change the way we deal with convicted persons. As evidence of this growing problem that affects us as citizens in general, and as college/university teachers in particular, the newsletter of the National Communication Association (NCA) reported that from 1987 to 1995 spending on prisons increased by 30 percent while spending on higher education decreased by 18 percent (Morreale, 1997, p. 10). As of January 2000, according to the *Washington Post*, the United States has two million incarcerated persons and the cost of housing those inmates currently exceeds $40 billion a year ("U.S. Imprisoned Population," 2000). In Arizona, between 1977 and 2003, the number of prison inmates increased nearly 1000 percent, from 3,229 to 30,083 (Nelson, 2003, p. 17).

PERFORMANCE AND CREATIVE WRITING CLASSES FOR INCARCERATED WOMEN

During our experiences teaching in a prison, Donovan and I asked inmates what prison represents; the replies included loneliness, depression, fear, hostility, but most of all utter boredom (Valentine and Donovan, 1978, p. 5). Although prison regulations require inmates to work, one of the women in my class wryly told me that when yard duty is assigned to a hundred women, the work can be finished in a couple of hours, leaving six hours of boredom to endure while they try to look busy.

At each of the correctional facilities in which I have volunteered, every permissible function other than the basic ones of eating, drinking, and being sheltered is considered a privilege that can be rescinded following even the slightest infraction. The performance and creative writing class I supervised was considered an inmate privilege subject to revocation.

My course goals were different from, yet not at odds with, the institution's mission to control behavior. As stated in my proposal document, the goals for the communication (performance studies) and English (creative writing) classes were to improve skills in writing creative essays, personal narratives, poetry, prose, and/or drama; and, concurrently, to increase communication skills through the performance of creative artistic texts. This program offered inmates opportunities to exercise decision-making and take ownership and responsibility for what they produced.

We never turned away anyone and we usually attracted 10–15 students, with a median age of 30, who said they had an interest in communication and creative writing. I can guess that the reason there were no more than 10–15 out of the total population is that, after a mandatory 40-hour work week, the women

had limited spare time. Some engaged in athletic events, but most sat on benches in the yard and talked with one another, watched censored TV, or slept. Those with intellectual or self-help interests had the options of consulting law books or reading the few general-topic books and magazines in the library, attending meetings of religious groups, twelve-step and Alcoholics Anonymous sessions, or our creative writing and performance classes.

There is growing evidence that postsecondary education is helpful to both the inmate and the smooth functioning of the prison system. In their 1995 survey of prison research, Gerber and Fritsch (1995) found that "adult academic and vocational correctional education programs lead to fewer disciplinary violations during incarceration, to reductions in recidivism, to increases in employment opportunities, and to increases in participation in education upon release" (p. 119). Stevens and Ward (1997) carried out further research with student-inmates who earned either an associate or baccalaureate degree while incarcerated in North Carolina. Their results confirmed earlier research demonstrating that inmates who earned associate and baccalaureate degrees while incarcerated tend to become law-abiding individuals significantly more often after their release from prison than inmates who had not advanced their education while incarcerated. An important conclusion drawn from these findings is that it is less expensive to educate inmates than to reincarcerate them (p. 106).

Continuing along this path toward positive outcomes through education and with the help of graduate students from the university's creative writing program and students in communication studies, I provided instruction and support through performance and writing activities. We relaxed some of the prison rules as we did so. Bending strict prison rules, we urged them to speak out, to socialize in class, and to criticize, albeit respectfully, each other's work. We didn't call students "Inmate Jones" or "Inmate Smith" as we were verbally instructed to do; we called them by the names they preferred, usually their first names. "As a volunteer, be mellow," a prison-employed teacher once told me. "Mellow volunteers," she told us, "are always professional and know when to bend rules and when to follow them to the letter." She contrasted "mellow" volunteers with "soft" volunteers who are too trusting, or overly familiar and naïve, and with "hard" employees who go strictly by the detailed rule booklet and give no leeway. Of course, I recognize that security takes precedence over education as the prison's primary function. Were any of us to violate security, we would not be allowed to continue providing the women's weekly mental survival break.

Because of the complexity of webs of inmate relationships, we kept private the students' assignments and our written comments to them unless individuals wished to share them. Often they were eager to read their work aloud to their classmates. Most of the time they also requested an even wider dissemination of their work. Thus, we frequently produced, with their permission, photocopied booklets containing their creative works from that semester. At times, we managed to get permission for a semiopen performance for staff and selected inmates.

Although some new students arrived and others left (when their sentences were up, when they were paroled, had class privileges taken away, or acquired other interests), some were with us for years. One of our tasks, therefore, was to carry out our goals with constantly changing activities.

One of our activities was scripting poems to be read aloud by dividing the nuanced voices in the poems among the students. Performing poetry enabled them to understand performance as both product and a way of knowing through their voices and bodies. We focused on more effective vocal variety and nonverbal expressions, as well as on understanding ideas, ourselves, and our communities through the processes of reading, writing, and performing literature written by the students and recognized authors. One semester, we were lucky enough to get the authorities to allow the poet Adrienne Rich, visiting Tempe as the university's scholar-in-residence, to read her poetry aloud and talk to invited inmates. She charmed everyone with her honesty, directness, and creativity. The encouragement she gave to the audience was just the spark some of them needed to write creatively.

We adapted some of the ideas from Julia Cameron's *The Artist's Way* (1992), including these prompts:

1. *Imaginary Lives.* If you had five other lives to lead, what would you do in each of them? Whatever occurs to you, jot it down. Do not overthink this exercise. The point of these lives is to have fun in them.

2. *Color Schemes.* Pick a color and write a few sentences describing yourself in the first person. For example, if you chose silver you might write "I am silver, high-tech and smooth, the color of half-light; I feel serene."

3. *A Letter.* Write an encouraging letter to your own inner artist. The artist in you loves praise and encouragement.

They wrote about experiences inside prison and their internal search for purpose. As a mental escape from confinement, they often wrote about being in the "free world" doing everyday activities such as visiting with a beloved grandmother, going to the grocery store, or taking their children to the park. I have reprinted a few of their creative works in the section below titled "Women and Their Artistic Texts."

Some of the other activities we used successfully for and with the incarcerated women students were creative and spontaneous. For example, we all shouted together: "I am SUPERWOMAN! I'm faster than a speeding train! I can leap tall buildings in a single bound! I can do anything!" And while seemingly simple, these engagements gave action to voice, and voice to dreams in the ways in which only performance can.

We also liked using our nonverbal synecdochical actions to react to the following situations:

We are standing in the snow.

We are stranded in the desert.

A heavy object is falling out of the sky.

We are sitting in a small boat. The boat begins to rock.

Our feet hurt.

Mail we've been waiting for just arrived.

We found a flowering weed in the prison yard.

Our favorite person just blew us a kiss.

Each simplistic act magnified the complex relationship between human thought and social action, between intention and reaction, between the ways in which individual desire is made manifest in social systems with varying levels of impact and effect. Each simple act directed the participants to see and understand that their agency is an act of being, an act of knowing, and an act of doing—each of which undergirds all of our responsibilities as social creatures living in the company of others. Through performance-based improvisational work and their writing we believe that we helped to empower these women. Lord (1995) writes that this foregrounds "their life histories in a safe setting in which they could sort out the pathways that took them to prison, come to be aware of themselves in terms of those life histories, and finally accept and examine their own responsibility for their own actions" (p. 261).

We took ideas from poetry therapy books (e.g., Leedy, 1973, and Mazza, 1999). One project that worked especially well is what Mazza called "poetic stems." These are phrases designed to stimulate thinking by starting a poem with one of the following thoughts: *If you knew me . . . I believe . . . I feel loved when . . . When I am alone . . . When I am in a crowd . . . Yesterday I was . . . Today I am . . . Tomorrow I . . . Hope is . . . Fear is . . . Anger is . . . Despair is . . . Happiness is . . . Love is . . . I keep on because . . . What matters most is . . . My greatest strength is . . .* (Mazza, 1999, p. 165)

One semester, we assigned students to write and perform an epistle entitled "To the Golden Country." The letter was to be addressed as follows: *"To a time when _____, from a time when _____"* and to begin with the word "Greetings" followed by narration written to help the reader imagine the smell, sound, touch, and other sensory images of the authors' created worlds. With some of the women, this "Golden Country" letter helped lead them closer to a sense of hopefulness critical to surviving their bitter situations.

Creative play can be liberating for the inmates while, ironically, also serving the prison system by allowing "an emotional outlet and a societally accepted manner of expressing whatever is on the inside," as Steiner explained in her maximum security prison theatre project (1974, pp. 22–23). In a poem an inmate can write "fuck the guards," but if these same words were uttered in a guard's hearing, she'd get a fast trip to the isolation unit. In class, she can be free to laugh, and to be "outta here" in her mind.

Because a character or narrator can act as a reflector of current feelings and as a mask for different ones, a performance and creative writing communication program in the prisons inspires imagination and liberating discourses of normally concealed emotions, motives, dreams, and desires. Writing and then performing their texts gave incarcerated women a measure of mental control over their regimentation. With these personal motivations (taking control, getting encouragement, enjoying laughter, substituting purpose for resentment, learning about self, feeling safe, mentally escaping), the inmate-students willingly came to class. And, despite the difficulties, some of the women came out from behind their protective numbness, went deep inside themselves to make sense out of institutional retribution, and used written and spoken avenues to communicate eloquently.

We observed some cautions, however, in our creative work with inmates. We performance teachers know how personal our work becomes to our students and to us. As we teach, we create activities encouraging students to open up, to write, and to perform personal narratives; and we introduce texts that may unsettle them (and us). But walking through those doors can sometimes put us, and the students, in a place into which we should not venture without help from psychologists, social workers, and others who have guiding expertise. Those of us who volunteer to teach behind bars caution ourselves to make connections with prison staff psychologists and social workers who are better equipped than we are to find help for an inmate-student with an emotional or spiritual problem.

When they learned that I was going to be talking and writing about them and their achievements to people in the "free world," some of the women gave me permission to include their work in print. It is time now to open the cell doors and listen to their words.

WOMEN AND
THEIR ARTISTIC TEXTS

In response to an activity to create similes for the concept "life," class members, with rare playfulness, wrote the following answers to an assignment to complete the sentence: "Life is like. . . ."

Life is a like a bagel. It's delicious when it's fresh and warm, but often it's just hard. The hole in the middle is its great mystery, and yet it wouldn't be a bagel without it.

Life is like eating grapefruit. First you have to break through the skin; then it takes a couple of bites to get used to the taste, and just as you begin to enjoy it, it squirts you in the eye.

Life is like a jigsaw puzzle, but you don't have the picture on the front of the box to know what it's supposed to look like. Sometimes, you're not even sure if you have all the pieces.

Life is like riding an elevator. It has a lot of ups and downs and someone is always pushing your buttons. Sometimes you get the shaft, but what really bothers you are the jerks.

Life is like a poker game. You deal or are dealt to. It includes skill and luck. You bet, check, bluff, and raise. You learn from those you play with. Sometimes you win with a pair or lose with a full house. Whatever happens, it's best to keep on shuffling along because the game never ends if your life depends on the deal of a friendly card.

Life is like a maze in which you try to avoid the exit.

Theresa Meyette (1986, 1987), one of the most accomplished poets I've ever met, was once an inmate in the Arizona Correctional Facility for Women. She wrote a poem titled "Brown Skin People" in April 1986. Shortly before she wrote this impassioned poem, men and women from Mexico seeking migrant work in U.S. farms were found dead, stuffed into the trunk of a car, a recurring tragedy in the American Southwest. In a letter to me, accompanying permission to reproduce it, Meyette wrote, "I would hope it has its impact on others as it did on me when I was struggling to write it. I feel BROWN SKIN PEOPLE has a soul of its own. . . . Being incarcerated has had its benefits when it comes to perceiving human nature and life in general. And I have the time to do these things."

BROWN SKIN PEOPLE

BY THERESA MEYETTE

I.

Brown sweaty faces/supporting fearful eyes/

peer through cracks of a/condemned building in some river bed./

The taste of freedom/popping in stale mouths/that have not had water/

for two days./

Hearts beat a psychotic drum rhythm/while fear overpowers hunger./

Illegal aliens/stacked like empty barrels/on a warehouse dock/

waiting the pick up/at midnight./

Anticipation soars/as the hours drag on./ Questions blossom and/die with fear./

"The pick up is here."/Deposited in vans and cars/crammed into tight spaces/

like trash in a Hefty Bag/the journey begins./

Los Angeles, Salinas Valley,/California, Arizona/out into the night they crawl.

Green light go for the/ freedom seekers/whose fate lies within.

II.

Red Light! Red Light!/Flashing, Flashing./

Ten bodies lie twisted/within the Chevy coffin/

enveloped in the last/ounce of life's breath./

Explosions of white light/pierce eye sockets,/penetrate brains./

Mother Mary, Jesus, save our souls./

Flaco opens his eyes./Slowly his dream is/

butchered by the shiny golden badge which/meets his gaze head on./

Out! Out!/ bark the shiny badges./Action, reactions, hands/

grab the blouse of Nina/dragging her from the/trunk of the car./

Metal bites cold./Dreams of freedom/send hot searing pain/

to a heart/ that does not feel/through the numbness/seized by the moment./

Crammed, shoved and/kicked into vans/sirens sound the Victory/

announcing the capture of the harmless./

Mug shots, finger prints,/ bodies stripped, and money; /what money?/

The Captain gave orders/to keep the money.

III.

Nina sits in stillness./A young girl lies crying/in the corner of her cell./

Nina thinks of her/little ones crying/from hunger, cold and disease./

The last rain washed away/cardboard dwellings down the/

river, and now Manuel and Estra/sit cold by the fire and beg morsels of food,/while Nina sits warm,/with belly full, resting/

against the bars, watching/this young child cry./

Nina lies awake in darkness,/chants low, over and over/

chants the old songs her/grandmother taught her./

A woman crawls from her sleep,/passes Nina,/kicks her./

"Shut up you old bitch/no one hears your stupid prayers./

Shut up so I can sleep/peaceful for once."/

Prayers escape with the hours/for others who lie in torment./

Flaco sits/knees drawn tight to/his tired body,/

eyes closed, he falls into/a dream state./

Chained to a mountain top,/he looks down./

Lupe, his wife, holds to her breast/Jorge, and baby Theresa,/

what will they do now?/Starved and homeless they wait.

IV.

Felipe finds himself/surrounded by men of two hearts./

There is a game played, the strongest steal from the weak./

Felipe does not understand./He smells the rancid odor of evil/

that reeks from the breathing pores./

Felipe is blind,/but in his darkness/he smells strawberry blossoms/

from the fields,/

feels the textured skin of the/avocado fruit he came to pick./

All Felipe will pick now/is his tattered soul/from the concrete floor,/

when Sam and Billy/get done picking him.

V.

Brown skin people/flee El Salvador, Guatemala,/all regions of sister Mexico,/

into a country with closed eyes/and empty hearts./

The Junta stalks them,/White Government hunts them,/

and they continue to struggle/for their birthright—life./

Victims without passports/pay heavily to enter a country/

unsympathetic to their survival./

Robbed and beaten,/then left to die,/consumed by Arizona desert,/

over unfamiliar mountains/crawling through wilderness/

fingers digging into earth/every inch of the way,/they go on./

Then, there are those/who paid the price./

$800, $1,500, $2,500 each,/to travel/

in the trunk of a car.

VI.
Wind blows cold/howls the death chant/sends its vibration/into the night./

Frozen raindrops/beat torturous minutes/into hours,/

ruthlessly drives/hours into Monday,/Tuesday, and finally/Wednesday. . . . /

The journey continues,/for those who paid the price/

North, San Clemente, then/Salinas Valley./

How much longer/would half frozen/bodies lay stacked/in horizontal position?/

Lay waiting for/signs of life,/or worse yet,/feel quietly stop/as gun barrels/

click off safeties./

Already life has ceased to move/underneath the bottom layer./

Maybe they are asleep,/or dreaming about the future ahead./

Soon they will be there,/stretching starved bodies./

Tomorrow at sunrise picking begins/then money sent home./

More families will attempt/The Great Escape/from poverty, disease and the/

fear of death,/attempt the escape from a country/

torn between destitution and political strife./

Tomorrow the dream becomes a REALITY.

VII.
An engine shuts off./A car door slams,/Voices can be heard outside./

Footsteps come closer./Another car door slams./

Bodies bounce to the forward motion,/another journey begins./

Wheels thump/horns honk/brakes grab/speed picks up/faster, faster,/

sailing toward lettuce fields/soaring toward a dream./

Brakes grab,/slower,/slower,/stop./

Loud voices of authority bark,/rattling penetrates the back seat./

Footsteps all around,/a kick to the tires,/a car door slams./

Footsteps/closer,/closer,/stopped./

Horizontal bodies/lay frozen in fear/lay breathless./

Metal meets metal/turns left,/turns right,/turns reality into a nightmare/

as the trunk door springs open,/

exposing horizontal bodies/for the world to see./

Look World!/NBC!/ABC!/CBS!/

Ten brown bodies/lie frozen in death, lie face down/

like lettuce heads/they will never pick.

Poem courtesy of Theresa Meyette

"WHAT I WANT MY WORDS TO DO TO YOU": MORE WORK WITH WRITING AND PERFORMANCE IN PRISONS

"What I Want My Words To Do To You" is a documentary about creative writing and performance in a women's prison that premiered nationally on PBS's series P.O.V. (Point of View) in December 2003 (Gavin, Katz, and Sunshine, 2003).[5] This documentary interspersed footage of a writing workshop at the Bedford Hills (New York) Women's Correctional Facility with performances of the inmates' efforts. Playwright Eve Ensler was the workshop facilitator. The camera crew filmed the workshop inside the prison, as well as the rehearsals with professional actors, including Glenn Close, outside of the prison, and finally the live performance of the inmates' writings as spoken by these professional actors inside the prison. The audience members were incarcerated women and prison officials. Often the camera focused on the emotionally engaged faces of the writers whose words were being spoken on stage.

In this documentary, Judith Clark, one of the inmate-writers, told viewers that she wanted her words to "leave you dissatisfied with simple explanations and rote assumptions, thirsty for complexity and the deep discomfort of ambiguity. . . . I want to make you wonder about your own prisons. I want to make you ask why." In response to her work with the poetry project Glenn Close offered the following reflection:

> For the last five years, a core of us have performed pieces from the workshop for the prison population, and then in a public venue in order to raise money for Bedford's educational programs. It is an experience that is disturbing, painful, funny, touching, and ultimately profoundly inspiring. (Close, 2003, p. 1)

More creative writing from the Bedford Hills project is published in Bell Gail Chevigny's *Doing Time: 25 Years of Prison* (1999). Another useful volume of inmate creative writing is *Couldn't Keep It To Myself: Testimonies from Our Imprisoned Sisters* (Lamb, 2003). Many of the stories in Lamb's edition detail horrific actions, and the worst kind of abuse, yet often reveal both hope and humor. As a follow-up to this publication, CBS's *60 Minutes* aired, on May 7, 2004, a story about Lamb's program at York Correctional Institution in Connecticut. In this broadcast, Steve Kroft reported that, after finding out about the *Testimonies* book, prison authorities closed down Lamb's creative writing course—that is, until *60 Minutes* and the writers' organization PEN protested, at which point Governor Blumenthal intervened to have the writing program reinstated (Fager, 2004).

Jean Trounstine's *Shakespeare Behind Bars: The Power of Drama in a Women's Prison* (2001) is a detailed description of her ten years as a drama teacher-coach-director in a women's prison in Massachusetts. Of her inspiration to record merged experiences and insights of the inmates she wrote,

> What started as an experiment—creating theatre behind bars—had gradually grown into a program. Eventually, the program took on a philosophy: art has the power to redeem lives. That philosophy, often challenged and at odds with Corrections, was in part, what drove me to write this book. (2001, p. 2)

Trounstine's compelling descriptions of the women who studied Shakespeare take the reader from the first meetings with her inmate-actors through to their public performances. In an early rehearsal for *The Merchant of Venice*, Trounstine told of Gloria's surprising response: "I never would've guessed *The Merchant of Venice* was this down to earth . . ." (p. 48). The women learned—often to their own surprise—that they could both understand and perform Shakespeare's words. Another theatre-related publication (part biography, part interview, part script), is Rena Fraden's

Imagining Medea: Rhodessa Jones and Theater for Incarcerated Women (2001). Fraden describes Rhodessa Jones, a performance artist who works primarily with African American inmates. Jonathan Shailor's production of Shakespeare's *King Lear* in the Racine, Wisconsin, correctional institution for men was reported on by Jodi Wilgoren in *The New York Times* (2005, April 29). Shailor is a communication professor at the University of Wisconsin-Parkside.

Newly released women inmates in North Carolina formed a drama group called C.H.A.I.N.S. This drama group has helped inmates reconnect to their communities in reconciliation. Their self-generated performance texts are performed largely for community churches. When a report on the activities of this group was aired by National Public Radio in November of 2003 (Hansen and Biewen, 2003), listeners heard Marsha (no last name given) describe her monologue, "A Song of Lament," as a public acknowledgment of the pain she caused her two sons by leaving them with their grandmother when she was incarcerated.

Volunteering in an institution focused on rehabilitation, H. C. Davis and his helpers organized a program to help women inmates keep closer connections to children by asking the women to choose books for the children, audiorecord them, and then talk, on tape, about these books. In "Educating the Incarcerated Female: An Holistic Approach" (Davis, 2001), Davis describes how volunteers mail these books and the audiotapes to the children.

More of these encouraging developments include C. Lewis Holton's "Once Upon a Time Served: Therapeutic Application of Fairy Tales Within a Correctional Environment" (1995); Marjorie Melnick's "The Use of Professional Theater Techniques in the Treatment and Education of Prison and Ex-Offender Populations" (1984); Barbara Owen's *"In the Mix": Struggle and Survival in a Women's Prison* (1998); Carol Burke's

Vision Narratives of Women in Prison (1992); and especially Patricia O'Brien's *Making It in the "Free World": Women in Transition from Prison* (2000). O'Brien presents stories of women who have been successful in staying out of prison after incarceration in hopes that their stories will benefit others currently in the transition from prison. Also noteworthy is the work of communication scholar Stephen Hartnett (2003). Poetry written by men in Indiana and California prisons where he taught is found in his *Incarceration Nation: Investigative Poems of Hope and Terror.*

Based on my 20 years of teaching inside prisons, coupled with extensive reading of pertinent literature, my hypothesis is that mind-liberating activities generated by performance and creative writing programs (such as the ones described in these pages) increase effective communication skills that help women avoid actions harmful to themselves and others. By acquiring these skills they increase their abilities to avoid reincarceration when they are released from prison, thereby benefiting themselves, their families, and their communities. Reading and listening to the personal creative writing of inmates is a productive way to open up a dialogue with the public and their legislators. Such dialogues could encourage policies emphasizing rehabilitation and reintegration of incarcerated persons, and suggest alternatives to the current criminal justice system that will have more positive outcomes for all.

EPILOGUE

I am optimistic that other performance scholars will help develop and improve prison programs for incarcerated people in their own communities and will join in the public debates about alternatives to prisons. We should be encouraged by the prison-related programs sponsored by the National Communication Association (Seattle in 2000, Atlanta in 2001, New Orleans in 2002, and Boston in 2005), and by a growing number of people subscribing to the listserv maintained by Jennifer Wood.[6] Conquergood insists that the performance paradigm involves "immediacy, involvement, and intimacy as modes of understanding" (1998, p. 26). Following that paradigm, we can work on alternatives to incarceration. We can also volunteer, teach, and do research with and for men and women whose bodies and minds are locked up. They are waiting for us.

In solitary confinement, Theresa Meyette (1987) finished her "Darkland" essay with these words:

> The darkness is beautiful, as are my memories. I will wait for the light to come again, for the grey wolf, the yellow wolf, the sunrise. I will wait with memories of a dark night in my prison cell. I will wait in Darkland.

Researchers must always ask the question: which community is their work designed to benefit? Is it the academic, the not-for-profit, the for-profit, the government, a social agency, or some other? Let us continue to engage in pedagogy, performance, and scholarship that actively seeks change; that has the immediacy of affecting lives and the lived conditions of others; and that establishes attachment and affinity with and for communities that would most benefit from our knowledges, skills, and resources.

NOTES

1. Some university students who taught with me use the experience as part of their graduate research; others volunteered out of a desire to improve the debilitating conditions of confinement for women in prison. I thank especially Marianne Botos-Radcliffe, Kris Coggins Kulchin, Kim Christoff, Laura Frick Galloway, Jim Franco, Lita Henderson, Jennifer Linde, John Magni, Crystal Malloy, Terri McCartney, Christine Muldoon, Cheryl McKibben Najafi, Rachel Rognrud Sacco, James Scoles, and Jason Watkins-Brock.

2. Inmates whose creative work is presented here have given me permission to use their words. I thank them all and wish them well.

3. For more information about current conditions in women's prisons, see Meda Chesney-Lind's "Imprisoning Women" (2002), as well as her book *Female Offender: Girls, Women and Crime* (1997); Catherine Fisher Collins' *Imprisonment of African American Women: Causes, Conditions and Future Implications* (1998); and Kathleen O'Shea's *Women on the Row: Reflections from Both Sides of the Bar* (2000).

4. Specific and persuasive practical alternatives and ideas are being published in many recent books and articles. The most useful is *Penal Abolition: The Practical Choice* by Canadian activist Ruth Morris (1995), who presents practical alternatives to warehouse prisons. I also recommend Amnesty International's *Not Part of My Sentence* (1999), Pat Carlen's *Alternatives to Women's Imprisonment* (1990), and Henry Ruth and Kevin P. Reitz's *The Challenge of Crime* (2003). Of particular relevance to members of the National Communication Association are the websites www.prisoncare.org and that maintained by Jennifer Wood (as of 2005). Further work is being done by volunteers in an Arizona project titled "Women Living Free." Volunteers "teach life skills to and with women starting a year before their release and continuing up to two years after their release. Volunteers teach everything from grooming and yoga to employment readiness and financial literacy. The women are urged to keep journals and envision what they want their lives to be in three years. For many, it's the first time they've planned their own future" (Villa, 2004, p. B-2). Women Living Free is administered by the not-for-profit organization Arizona Women's Education & Employment, Inc. (AWEE). Their website is www.awee.org.

5. Related information about this documentary can be found at http://www.pbs.org/pov/pov2003/whatiwant/update/html.

6. Email listserv maintained by Jennifer Wood for NCA members who are prison activists: <L-Prison-care@Lists.psu.edu>

REFERENCES

Amnesty International. (1999). *Not part of my sentence: Violations of the human rights of women in custody*. Washington, DC: Author.

Boal, A. (1998). *Theatre of the oppressed*. (C. A. McBride & M. O. L. McBride, Trans.). London: Pluto Press.

Burke, C. (1992). *Vision narratives of women in prison*. Knoxville: University of Tennessee Press.

Cameron, J. (1992). *The artist's way: A spiritual path to higher creativity.* New York: Jeremy P. Tarcher/Putnam.

Capo, K. E. (1983). From academic to social-political uses of performance. In D. W. Thompson (Ed.), *Performance of literature in historical perspectives* (pp. 437–457). Lanham, MD: University Press of America.

Carlen, P. (1990). *Alternatives to women's imprisonment.* Buckingham, England: Open University Press.

Chesney-Lind, M. (1997). *The female offender: Girls, women and crime.* Thousand Oaks, CA: Sage.

Chesney-Lind, M. (2002). Imprisoning women: The unintended victims of mass imprisonment. In M. Mauer & M. Chesney-Lind (Eds.), *Invisible punishment: The collateral consequences of mass imprisonment* (pp. 79–94). New York: New Press.

Chevigny, B. G. (1999). *Doing time: 25 years of prison writing—a PEN-Aspen American Center prize anthology.* New York: Arcade.

Close, G. (2003). *What I want my words to do to you: A letter from Glenn Close.* Retrieved May 30, 2005, from www.pbs.org/pov/pov2003/whatiwant/about_glenn.html

Cohen, S. (1997, September 7). One short ride turns into a lifetime. *Los Angeles Times,* p. A35.

Collins, C. F. (1998). *The imprisonment of African American women: Causes, conditions and future implications.* Jefferson, NC: McFarland.

Conquergood, D. (1992). Performance theory, Hmong shamans, and cultural politics. In J. Reinelt & J. R. Roach (Eds.), *Critical theory and performance* (pp. 41–64). Ann Arbor: University of Michigan Press.

Conquergood, D. (1995). Between rigor and relevance: Rethinking applied communication. In D. Cissna (Ed.), *Applied communication in the 21st century* (pp. 79–96). Hillsdale, NJ: Erlbaum.

Conquergood, D. (1998). Beyond the text: Toward a performative cultural politics. In S. Dailey (Ed.), *The future of performance studies: Visions and revisions* (pp. 25–36). Annandale, VA: National Communication Association.

Corey, F. C. (1996). Personal narratives and young men in prison: Labeling the outside inside. *Western Journal of Communication, 60,* 57–75.

Davis, H. C. (2001). Educating the incarcerated female: An holistic approach. *Journal of Correctional Education, 52*(2), 79–83.

Fager, J. (Executive Producer). (2004, May 7). Couldn't keep it to myself. *60 minutes* [Television series]. New York: CBS News. Retrieved May 15, 2004, from www.cbsnews.com/stories/2004/05/07/60minutes/main6161203.shtml.

Fraden, R. (2001). *Imagining Medea: Rhodessa Jones and theatre for incarcerated women.* Chapel Hill: University of North Carolina Press.

Gavin, M., Katz, J., & Sunshine, G. (2003, December 16). What I want my words to do to you. *P.O.V.* [Television series]. Washington, DC: Public Broadcasting System. Retrieved December 16, 2003 from www.pbs.org/pov/pov2003/whatiwant/update/html

Gerber, J., & Fritsch, E. J. (1995). Adult academic and vocational correctional education programs: A review of recent research. *Journal of Offender Rehabilitation, 22,* 119–142.

Greenfeld, L. A., & Snell, T. L. (1999, December). *Women offenders* (NCJ #175688). Washington, DC: U.S. Department of Justice, Bureau of Justice Statistics.

Hansen, L. (Producer/Host), & Biewen, J. (Interviewer). (2003, November 16). Profile: Life after prison for Marsha, a single mother in North Carolina. *Weekend edition* [Radio broadcast]. Washington, DC: National Public Radio.

Hartnett, S. (2003). *Incarceration nation: Investigative prison poems of hope and terror.* Walnut Creek, CA: AltaMira/Rowman & Littlefield.

Holton, C. L. (1995). Once upon a time served: Therapeutic application of fairy tales within a correctional environment. *International Journal of Offender Therapy and Comparative Criminology, 39,* 210–221.

Kistenberg, C. J. (1995). *AIDS, social change and theatre: Performance as protest.* New York: Garland.

Lamb, W., & Women of York Correctional Institution (2003). *Couldn't keep it to myself: Testimonies from our imprisoned sisters.* New York: Regan Books/HarperCollins.

Langellier, K. M. (1986). From text to social context. *Literature in Performance, 6,* 60–70.

Leedy, J. J. (Ed.). (1973). *Poetry the healer.* Philadelphia: Lippincott.

Lord, E. (1995). A prison superintendent's perspective on women in prison. *The Prison Journal, 75,* 257–269.

Mann, C., Hecht, M., & Valentine, K. (1989). Performance in a social context: Date rape versus date right. *Central States Speech Journal, 39,* 269–280.

Mauer, M., & Chesney-Lind, M. (Eds.). (2002). *Invisible punishment: The collateral consequences of mass imprisonment.* New York: New Press.

Mazza, N. (1999). *Poetry therapy: Interface of the arts and psychology.* Boca Raton, FL: CRC Press.

Melnick, M. (1984). The use of professional theater techniques in the treatment and education of prison and ex-offender populations. *Journal of Group Psychotherapy, Psychodrama and Sociometry, 37,* 104–116.

Meyette, T. (1986). *Brown skin people.* Unpublished poem.

Meyette, T. (1987). *Darkland.* Unpublished poem.

Morreale, S. (1997, June). Morreale's mailbag. *Spectra: A newsletter of the National Communication Association,* p. 10.

Morris, R. (1995). *Penal abolition: The practical choice.* Toronto: ON: Canadian Scholars Press.

Nelson, R. (2003, April 3–9). Big House Inc. *Phoenix New Times,* pp. 3ff.

O'Brien, P. (2001). *Making it in the "free world": Women in transition from prison.* Albany: SUNY Press.

O'Shea, K. A. (2000). *Women on the row: Reflections from both sides of the bars.* Ann Arbor, MI: Firebrand.

Owen, B. (1998). *"In the mix": Struggle and survival in a women's prison.* Albany: SUNY Press.

Park-Fuller, L. (2003). Audiencing the audience: Playback theatre, performative writing, and social activism. *Text and Performance Quarterly, 23,* 288–310.

Pastore, A. L. (2003). *Sourcebook of criminal justice statistics* (NCJ #198877). Albany, NY: Hindelang Criminal Justice Research Center. Retrieved April 6 from www.ojp.usdoj.gov/bjs/abstract/pjim02.htm.

Richie, B. E. (2002). The social impact of mass incarceration on women. In M. Mauer & M. Chesney-Lind (Eds.), *Invisible punishment: The collateral consequences of mass imprisonment* (pp. 136–149). New York: New Press.

Ruth, H., & Reitz, K. P. (2003). *The challenge of crime: Rethinking our response.* Cambridge, MA: Harvard University Press.

Steiner, L. (1974). Poetic self-actualization: Creative stimulation for rehabilitation and reintegration. *Journal of the Illinois Speech Association, 28,* 21–27.

Stevens, D. J., & Ward, C. S. (1997). College education and recidivism: Educating criminals is meritorious. *Journal of Correctional Education, 48*(3), 106–111.

Stringer, E. T. (1999). *Action research* (2nd ed.). Thousand Oaks, CA: Sage.

Trounstine, J. (2001). *Shakespeare behind bars: The power of drama in a women's prison.* New York: St. Martin's.

U.S. imprisoned population may hit 2 million in 2000. (2000, January 1). *The Washington Post,* p. A1.

Valentine, K. B. (1986). A social contexts component for interpretation education. *Communication Education, 35,* 399–405.

Valentine, K. B. (1998). If the guards only knew: Communication education for women in prison. *Women's Studies in Communication, 21*(2), 238–243.

Valentine, K. B., & Donovan, M. (1978). Rationale for communication arts in correctional institutions. *Journal of the Arizona Communication and Theatre Association, 9,* 2–6.

Villa, J. (2004, January 16). Outreach program gives boost for the long term. *The Arizona Republic,* pp. B1–B2.

Wilgoren, J. (2005, April 29). In one prison, murder, betrayal and high prose: Lear behind bars. *New York Times,* p. A13.

Women Living Free. (2005). Volunteer organization for helping women inmates reenter society more successfully—a not-for-profit program administered by Arizona Women's Education & Employment, Inc.

18

The Politics and Ethics of Performance Pedagogy

Toward a Pedagogy of Hope

NORMAN K. DENZIN

To invoke and paraphrase William Kittridge (1987, p. 87) today in post–9/11 America with Patriot Acts, Homeland Security Administrations, and a president who performs scripts of fear written by others, we are struggling to revise our dominant mythology . . . to find a new story to inhabit, to find new laws to control our lives, laws designed to preserve a model of a free democratic society based on values learned from a shared mythology. Kittridge is clear, only after reimagining our myths can we coherently remodel our laws, and hope to keep our society in a realistic relationship to what is actual and what is ideal. The ground upon which we stand has dramatically shifted. The neoconservatives have put into place a new set of myths, performances, narratives, and story, and a new set of laws that threatens to destroy what we mean by freedom and democracy (Giroux, 2004).

Scholars in performance studies must ask a series of questions. "How can we use the aftermath of the crisis of 9/11 as a platform for rethinking what is meant by democracy and freedom in America today?" "Can we revise our dominant mythologies about who we are?" "Can we fashion a post–9/11 narrative that allows us to reinvent and reimagine our laws in ways that express a critical pedagogy of hope, liberation, freedom and love?" "Can performance studies help us chart our way into this new space?" "Can we take back what has been lost?"

War is peace; Freedom is slavery; Ignorance is strength

—Orwell, 1949, p. 17

In this chapter I seek a politics and an ethics fitted to *a radical critical performance pedagogy*. I seek *a pedagogy of hope* crafted for life after 9/11. I want to contribute to a conversation that seeks to preserve a model of a free democratic society. In outlining this democratic pedagogy, I draw selectively from a series of performance texts written since 9/11/01.[1] In so doing I join four discourses, merging the performance turn in the human disciplines (Alexander, 2005; Conquergood, 1998), with theories of critical pedagogy (Giroux & Giroux, in press) and critical race theory (Darder & Torres, 2004; Ladson-Billings & Donnor, 2005), connecting these formations to the call by indigenous scholars for a new ethics of inquiry (Smith, 2005), new pedagogies of hope, new models of democracy.

The "democratic character of critical pedagogy is defined largely through a set of basic assumptions" (Giroux & Giroux, in press, p. 1): Pedagogical practices are always moral and political. The political is always performative. The performative is always pedagogical. Through performances, critical pedagogy disrupts those hegemonic cultural and educational practices that reproduce the logics of neoliberal conservatism (Giroux & Giroux, 2005). Critical pedagogy subjects structures of power, knowledge, and practice to critical scrutiny, demanding that they be evaluated "in terms of how they might open up or close down democratic experiences" (Giroux & Giroux, 2005, p. 1). Critical pedagogy and critical pedagogical theatre hold systems of authority accountable through the critical reading of texts, the creation of radical educational practices, and the promotion of critical literacy (Giroux & Giroux, 2005, p. 2). In turn critical pedagogy encourages resistance to the "discourses of privatization, consumerism, the methodologies of standardization and accountability, and the new disciplinary techniques of surveillance" (Giroux & Giroux, 2005, p. 3). Critical pedagogy provides the tools for understanding how cultural and educational practices contribute to the construction of neoliberal conceptions of identity, citizenship, and agency.

The call to performance in the human disciplines requires a commitment to a progressive democratic politics, an ethics and aesthetics of performance (Pollock, 1998) that moves from critical race theory (Darder & Torres, 2004; Ladson-Billings & Donnor, 2005) to the radical pedagogical formulations of Paulo Freire (1998, 1999, 2001), as his work is reformulated and reinvented by Antonio Darder (2002), Kincheloe and McLaren (2005), Fischman and McLaren (in press), Giroux (2001, 2003), and Giroux and Giroux (in press) and others.

This performance ethic borrows from and is grounded in the discourses of indigenous peoples (Mutua & Swadener, 2004). Indigenous theories of ritual performance blend and blur with performative acts that critique, transgress, and bring dignity to human practices. This performance ethic honors difference and refuses commodification, as it draws from indigenous, feminist, queer, and communitarian formulations.

Within this radical pedagogical space, the performative and the political intersect on the terrain of a praxis-based ethic. This is the space of critical pedagogical theatre, which draws its inspirations from Boal's (1995) Theatre of the Oppressed. This ethic performs pedagogies that resist oppression. It enacts a politics of possibility (Madison, 1998) grounded in performative practices that embody love, hope, care and compassion.

A postcolonial, indigenous participatory theatre is central to this discourse (Balme & Carstensen, 2001; Greenwood, 2001).[2] Contemporary indigenous playwrights & performers revisit and make a mockery of nineteenth century racist practices. They interrogate and turn the tables on blackface minstrelsy and the global colonial theatre that reproduced racist politics through specific cross-race and cross-gender performances. They show how colonial performers used whiteface and blackface to construct oppressive models of whiteness, blackness, gender, and national identity (Kondo, 2000, p. 83; Gilbert, 2003).

Indigenous theatre nurtures a critical transnational, yet historically specific, critical race [and class] consciousness. It uses indigenous performance as a means of political representation and critique (Magowan, 2000, p. 311). Indigenous theatre reflexively uses historical restagings, masquerade, ventriloquism, and doubly inverted performances involving male and female impersonators to create a subversive theatre that undermines colonial racial representations (Bean, 2001, pp. 187–188). This theatre incorporates traditional indigenous and nonindigenous cultural texts into frameworks that disrupt colonial models of race and class relations. This theatre takes up key diasporic concerns, including those of memory, cultural loss, disorientation, violence, and exploitation (Balme and Carstensen, 2001, p. 45). This is a utopian theatre that addresses issues of equity, healing, and social justice.[3]

Consider the following:

In *House Arrest* (2003) Anna Deavere Smith offers "an epic view of slavery, sexual misconduct, and the American presidency." Twelve actors, some in blackface, "play across lines of race, age and gender to 'become' Bill Clinton, Thomas Jefferson, Sally Hemings . . . and a vast array of historical and contemporary figures." (Kondo, 2000, p. 81)

In Native Canadian Bill Moses' play *Almighty Voice and His Wife* (1993), Native performers, wearing whiteface minstrel masks, mock such historical figures as Wild Bill Cody, Sitting Bull, and young Indian maidens called Sweet Sioux (Gilbert, 2003, p. 692)

In Sidney, Australia, aboriginal theatre groups perform statements of their indigenous rights demanding that politicians participate in these performance events "as co-producers of meaning rather than as tacit consumers." (Magowan, 2000, pp. 317–318)

Thus do indigenous performances function as strategies of critique and empowerment.

The Decade of the World's Indigenous Peoples (1994–2004; Henderson, 2000, p. 168) has ended. Nonindigenous scholars have yet to learn from it, to learn that it is time to dismantle, deconstruct, and decolonize western epistemologies from within, to learn that research does not have to be a dirty word, to learn that research is always already political and at least sometimes (even for postpositivists) moral.

Shaped by the sociological imagination (Mills, 1959), building on George Herbert Mead's discursive, performative model of the act (1938, p. 460), critical pedagogy imagines and explores the multiple ways in which performance can be understood, including as imitation, or mimesis; as poiesis, or construction; or as kinesis, movement, gendered bodies in motion (Conquergood, 1998, p. 31; Pollock, 1998, p. 43). The researcher-as-performer moves from a view of performance as imitation, or dramaturgical staging (Goffman, 1959), to an emphasis on performance as liminality, construction, (McLaren, 1999), to a view of performance as embodied struggle, as an intervention, as a breaking and remaking, as kinesis, as a sociopolitical act, as a sensuous, material production that erupts in the moment of performativity "across the intersecting planes of identity, community, culture and politics" (Conquergood, 1998, p. 32; Pollock, 1998, p. 43).

Viewed as struggles and interventions, performances and performance events become gendered transgressive achievements, political accomplishments that break through "sedimented meanings and normative traditions" (Conquergood, 1998, p. 32). It is this performative model of emancipatory decolonized indigenous research, that I develop here (Garoian, 1999; Gilbert, 2003; Kondo, 2000; Madison, 1998). Drawing on Garoian (1999), DuBois (1926), Gilbert (2003), Madison (1998), Magowan (2000), Pollock (1998), and Anna Deavere Smith (2003), this model proposes a utopian performative politics of resistance (see below). Extending indigenous initiatives, this model is committed to a form of revolutionary, catalytic political theatre, a project that provokes and enacts pedagogies of dissent for the new millennium. This is a variant of forum theatre, Boal's Theatre of the Oppressed, his Rainbow of Desire, Legislative Theatre used within a political system to produce a truer form of democracy (Jackson 1995, p. xviii).

LIFE IN AMERICA AFTER SEPTEMBER 11, 2001

After the bombing of the World Trade Center and the Pentagon on September 11, 2001, a number of interpretive social scientists wrote about this event and its meanings in their lives. These personal narratives could be performed within the mystory format.

Michelle Fine's (2002, p. 137) narratives text opens thus:

"The mourning after"

> 12 September 2001
> You can tell who's dead or missing by their smiles. Their photos dot the subways, ferries, trains and Port Authority Terminal, shockingly alive with joy, comfort and pleasure . . .
> The air in the City chokes with smoke, flesh, fear, memories, clouds and creeping nationalism . . . Now a flood of flags, talk of God, military and patriotism chase us all . . .

Two days later Fine writes,

> The Path train stopped. In a tunnel. No apparent reason. I couldn't breath. Anxiety . . . Is this an ok way to die? . . .

Lives and politics; grief and analysis

> Those of us in New York seem to be having trouble writing . . . U.S. politics then and now, racial profiling and anxious worries about what's coming next . . . Death, ghosts, orphans, analyses of U.S. imperialism, Middle East politics, and the terrors of terrorism sit in the same room. . . .

Two years have passed since Fine wrote these lines. They could have been written yesterday. "U.S. imperialism, Middle East politics, and the terrors of terrorism sit in the same room." How do you write and perform the meaning of the present, when the nightmares and terror that define the present have never been experienced before? How do you write about an unending terror when each day starts with a new crisis, when lies are held up as truths, and black has become white, and yes means no?

Turning to Annie Dillard, I seek my own meaning in these events. Dillard says that divinity is not playful, that the universe was not made in jest, but in "solemn incomprehensible earnest. By a power that is unfathomably secret, and holy and fleet" (1974, p. 270), and violent, I choose to believe this.

ETHICS FOR PERFORMANCE STUDIES

Any consideration of performance ethics must move in three directions at the same time, addressing three interrelated issues: ethical pitfalls, traditional ethical models, and indigenous performance ethics connected to political theatre (Boal, 1995). Conquergood (1985, p. 4) has identified four ethical pitfalls that performance ethnographers must avoid. He terms them "The Custodian's Rip-Off," "The Enthusiast's Infatuation," "The Skeptic's Cop-Out," and "The Curator's Exhibitionism."

Cultural custodians, or cultural imperialists, ransack their biographical past looking for good texts to perform and then perform them for a fee often denigrating a family member or a cultural group who regard such experiences as sacred. The enthusiast's infatuation, or superficial stance, occurs when the writer (and the performer) fail to become deeply involved in the cultural setting which they re-perform. Conquergood (1985, p. 6) says this trivializes the other because their experiences are neither contextualized, nor well understood. Modifying Conquergood, the skeptic or cynic values detachment and being cynical. This position refuses to face up to the "ethical tensions and moral ambiguities of performing culturally sensitive materials" (Conquergood, 1985, p. 8). Finally the curator or sensationalist, like the custodian, is a performer who sensationalizes the cultural differences that supposedly define the world of the other. He or she stages performances for the voyeur's gaze, perhaps telling stories about an abusive, hurtful other (Conquergood, 1985, p. 7).

These four stances make problematic the question "How far into the other's world can the performer and the audience go?" Of course we can never know the mind of an other, only the other's performances. We can only know our own minds, and sometimes not well. This means that the differences that define the other's world must always be respected. There is no null point in the moral universe (Conquergood, 1985, pp. 8–9).

The second issue is implicit in Conquergood's four ethical pitfalls. He presumes a researcher who is held accountable to a set of universal ethical principles that are both duty-based and utilitarian. Duty-based ethics assume researchers and performers who are virtuous, have good intentions, and are committed to values like justice, honesty, and respect. This is Conquergood's ideal performer. However, Conquergood is concerned with more than good intentions; he is concerned with the effects, or consequences, of a performance on a person or a community. Thus he appears to implicitly endorse a utilitarian ethics based on consequences and pragmatic effects, not good intentions. This is the cost-benefit utilitarian model used by Human Subject Review Boards when they ask how this research will benefit society.

Both of these models have deficiencies. Carried to the extreme the duty position can result in a moral absolutism, requiring that persons live up to an absolute standard, regardless of its human consequences (Edwards & Mauthner, 2002, p. 20; Kale, 1996, pp. 121–122). But who holds these values; whose values are they? The utilitarian model is predicated on the belief that the ends justify the means (Kale, 1996, p. 122), thus the "wrongness or rightness of actions are judged by their consequences, not their intent" (Edwards & Mauthner, 2002, p. 20). Whose consequences are being considered, whose means are being used, best for whom?

It is necessary to contrast these two universalist models with feminist and critical pedagogically informed ethical models (Edwards & Mauthner, 2002, p. 21). Contingent feminist ethical models work outward from personal experience, and from local systems of meaning and truth, to social contexts where experience is shaped by nurturing social relationships based on care, respect, and love. The researcher is an insider to the group, not an outsider (Smith, 1999, p. 139). The desire is to enact a locally situated, contingent, feminist, communitarian ethic that respects and protects the rights, interests, and sensitivities of those one is working with, including ideas specific to the cultural context (Denzin, 1997, p. 275; Smith, 1999, p. 119). Contingent ethical models have been adopted by social science professionals associations that often navigate between universal normative models and contingent ethical directives (Edwards & Mauthner, 2002, p. 21). Such guidelines are then meant to guide the researcher when the kinds of pitfalls and dilemmas Conquergood identifies are encountered.

These professional guidelines do not include a space for culturally specific ethical ideas and values (Smith, 1999, p. 120). Within specific contexts, for instance the Maori, specific ethical values and rules are prescribed in cultural terms. These understandings include showing respect for others, listening, sharing, and being generous, cautious, and humble. Smith is quite explicit. "From indigenous perspectives ethical codes of conduct serve partly the same purposes as the protocols which govern our relationships with each other and with the environment" (p. 120).

In contrast to social science codes of ethics and the protocols used by human subject review boards, critical pedagogy seeks to enact a situationally contingent ethic that is compatible with indigenous values. This ethic is predicated on *a pedagogy of hope*. It is based on values shared in the group. It blends intentions with consequences. It presumes that well-intended, trusting, honest, virtuous persons engage in moral acts that have positive consequences for others. This is a communitarian dialogical *ethic of care* and responsibility. It presumes that performances occur within sacred aesthetic spaces where research does not operate as a dirty word. It presumes that performers treat persons, their cares, and their concerns with dignity and respect. Indeed, the values that structure the performance are those shared by the community and its members. These values include care, trust, and reciprocity. Because of these shared understandings this model assumes that there will be few ethical dilemmas requiring negotiation.

A feminist, communitarian performance ethic is utopian in vision. While criticizing systems of injustice and oppression, it imagines how things could be different. It enacts a *performance pedagogy of radical democratic hope*. "What African American minstrels created was a new form of theater based in the skills of the performers, not their ability to conform to stereotypes" (Bean, 2001, pp. 187–188).

An empowering performance pedagogy frames the third issue that must be addressed.

The multivoiced performance text enacts *a pedagogy of hope*. A critical consciousness is invoked. The performance event engenders moral discernment that guides social transformation (Christians, 2000; Denzin, 2003, p. 112). The performance text is grounded in the cruelties and injustices of daily life. Like Boal's radical theatre, a documentary-drama format may be used, drawing on current events and media accounts of these events. A radical performance ethic is grounded in a politics of resistance. The performance must be ethically honest. It must be dialogical, seeking to locate dialogue and meaningful exchange in the *radical center*.

The other always exists, as Trinh (1989) would argue, in the spaces on each side of the hyphen (Conquergood, 1985, p. 9). The performance text can only be dialogic, a text that does not speak about or for the other, but which "speaks to and with them" (Conquergood, 1985, p. 10). It is a text that reengages the past, and brings it alive in the present. The dialogic text attempts to keep the dialogue, the conversation—between text, the past, the present, performer and audience—ongoing and open-ended (p. 9). This text does more than invoke empathy, it interrogates, criticizes, and empowers. This is dialogical criticism. The dialogical performance is the means for "honest intercultural understanding" (Conquergood, 1985, p. 10).

If this understanding is to be created, the following elements need to be present. Scholars must have the energy, imagination, courage, and commitment to create these texts (see Conquergood, 1985, p. 10). Audiences must be drawn to the sites where these performances take place, and they must be willing to suspend normal aesthetic frameworks, so that coparticipatory performances can be produced. Boal is clear on this, "In the Theatre of the Oppressed we try to . . . make the dialogue between stage and audience totally transitive" (1995, p. 42). In these sites a shared field of emotional experience is created, and in these moments of sharing, critical cultural awareness is awakened.

Critical pedagogical theatre creates dialogical performances that follow these directives from Augusto Boal (1995, p. 42):

Directives from Boal: Show how

1. Every oppressed person is a subjugated subversive.

2. The Cop in our Head represents our submission to this oppression.

3. Each person possesses the ability to be subversive.

4. Critical Pedagogical Theatre can empower persons to be subversive, while making their submission to oppression disappear.

The co-performed text aims to enact a *feminist communitarian moral ethic*. This ethic presumes a dialogical view of the self and its performances. It seeks narratives that ennoble human experience, performances that facilitate civic transformations in the public and private spheres. This ethic ratifies the dignities of the self and honors personal struggle. It understands cultural criticism to be a form of empowerment, arguing that empowerment begins in that ethical moment when individuals are lead into the troubling spaces occupied by others. In the moment of co-performance, lives are joined and struggle begins anew.

Ethical Injunctions: Does this Performance

1. Nurture critical race consciousness?

2. Use historical restagings and traditional texts to subvert and critique official ideology?

3. Heal? Empower?

4. Avoid Conquergood's four pitfalls?

5. Enact a feminist, communitarian, socially contingent ethic?

6. Present *a pedagogy of hope*?

HOPE, PEDAGOGY, AND THE CRITICAL IMAGINATION

The critical imagination is radically democratic, pedagogical, and interventionist. Building on Freire (1998, p. 91) this imagination dialogically inserts itself into the world, provoking conflict, curiosity, criticism, and reflection. Extending Freire (1998), performance auto-ethnography contributes to a conception of education and democracy as pedagogies of freedom. As praxis, performance ethnography is a way of acting on the world in order to change it. Dialogic performances, enacting a performance-centered ethic, provide materials for critical reflection on radical democratic educational practices. In so doing, performance ethnography enacts a theory of selfhood and being. This is an ethical, relational, and moral theory. The purpose of "the particular type of relationality we call research ought to be enhancing ... moral agency" (Christians, 2002, p. 409), moral discernment, critical consciousness, and a radical politics of resistance.

Indeed performance ethnography enters the service of freedom by showing how in concrete situations persons produce history and culture, "even as history and culture produce them" (Glass, 2001, p. 17). Performance texts provide the grounds for liberation practice by opening up concrete situations that are being transformed through acts of resistance. In this way, performance ethnography advances the causes of liberation.

As an interventionist ideology the critical imagination is hopeful of change. It seeks and promotes an ideology of hope that challenges and confronts hopelessness (Freire, 1999, p. 8). It understands that hope, like freedom, is "an ontological need" (p. 8). Hope is the desire to dream, the desire to change, the desire to improve human existence. Hopelessness is "but hope that has lost its bearings" (p. 8).

Hope is ethical. Hope is moral. Hope is peaceful and nonviolent. Hope seeks the truth of life's sufferings. Hope gives meaning to the struggles to change the world. Hope is grounded in concrete performative practices, in struggles and interventions that espouse the sacred values of love, care, community, trust, and well-being (Freire, 1999, p. 9). Hope, as a form of pedagogy, confronts and interrogates cynicism, the belief that change is not possible, or is too costly. Hope works from rage to love. It articulates a progressive politics that rejects "conservative, neoliberal postmodernity" (Freire, 1999, p. 10). Hope rejects terrorism. Hope rejects the claim that peace comes at any cost.

The critical democratic imagination is pedagogical, and this in four ways. First, as a form of instruction, it helps persons think critically, historically, sociologically. Second, as critical pedagogy, it exposes the pedagogies of oppression that produce and reproduce oppression and injustice (see Freire, 2001, p. 54). Third, it contributes to an ethical self-consciousness that is critical and reflexive. It gives people a language and a set of pedagogical practices that turn oppression into freedom, despair into hope, hatred into love, doubt into trust. Fourth, in turn, this self-consciousness shapes a critical racial self-awareness. This awareness contributes to utopian dreams of racial equality and racial justice.

The use of this imagination by persons who have previously lost their way in this complex world is akin to being "suddenly awakened in a house with which they had only supposed themselves to be familiar" (Mills, 1959, p. 8). They now feel that they can provide themselves with critical understandings that undermine and challenge "older decisions that once appeared sound" (p. 8). Their critical imagination enlivened, persons "acquire a new way of thinking . . . in a word by their reflection and their sensibility, they realize the cultural meaning of the social sciences" (p. 8). They realize how to make and perform changes in their own lives, to become active agents in shaping the history that shapes them.

A PERFORMATIVE PERFORMANCE STUDIES

Following Conquergood (1998), Pollock (1998), Madison (1998), and Giroux (2000a, p. 127) I am attempting to (re)theorize the grounds of performance studies, redefining the political and the cultural in performative and pedagogical terms. The discourses of postmodern (auto)ethnography provide a framework against which all other forms of writing about the politics of the popular under the regimes of global capitalism are judged.

In this model, a performative, pedagogical cultural studies becomes autoethnographic. The autoethnographer becomes a version of McLaren's (1997a, 1997b) reflexive *flaneur/flaneuse* and Kincheloe's (2001) critical *bricoleur,* the "primordial ethnographer" (McLaren, 1997a, p. 144), who lives "within postmodern, postorganized, late capitalist culture" (McClaren, 1997a, p. 144; 1997b, p. 295), and functions as a critical theorist, an urban ethnographer, an ethnographic agent, a Marxist social theorist (McClaren, 1997a, pp. 164, 167; 2001, pp. 121–122).

The radical, performance (auto)ethnographer functions as a cultural critic, a version of the modern antihero "reflecting an extreme external situation through his [her] own extremity. His [her] . . . [autoethnography] becomes diagnosis, not just of him [her] self, but of a phase of history" (Spender, 1984, p. ix). As a reflexive flaneur/flaneuse or bricoleur the critical autoethnographer's conduct is justified because it is no longer just one individual's case history or life story. Within the context of history the autoethnography becomes the "dial of the instrument that records the effects of a particular stage of civilization upon a civilized individual" (Spender, 1984, p. ix). The autoethnography is both dial and instrument.

The autoethnographer functions as a universal singular, a single instance of more universal social experiences. This subject is "summed up and for this reason universalized by his [her] epoch, he [she] resumes it by reproducing him [her] self in it as a singularity" (Sartre, 1981, p. ix). Every person is like every other person, but like no other person. The autoethnographer inscribes the experiences of a historical moment, universalizing these experiences in their singular effects on a particular life. Using a critical imagination, the autoethnographer is theoretically informed in poststructural and postmodern ways. There is a commitment to connect critical ethnography to issues surrounding cultural policy, cultural politics, and procedural policy work (Willis and Trondman, 2000, pp. 10–11).

The commitment, as McLaren argues, is to a theory of praxis that is purposeful, "guided by critical reflection and a commitment to revolutionary praxis" (1997a, p. 170). This commitment involves a rejection of the historical and cultural logics and narratives that exclude those who have been previously marginalized. This is a reflexive performative ethnography. It privileges multiple subject positions, questions its own authority, and doubts those narratives that privilege one set of historical processes and sequences over another (McLaren, 1997a, p. 168; 1997b, p. 290).

CRITICAL PERFORMANCE PEDAGOGY

A commitment to critical performance pedagogy and critical race theory (CRT) gives performance studies a valuable lever for militant, utopian cultural criticism. In *Impure Acts* (2000) Giroux calls for a practical, performative view of pedagogy, politics, and cultural studies. He seeks an interdisciplinary project that would enable theorists and educators to form a progressive alliance "connected to a broader notion of cultural politics designed to further racial, economic, and political

democracy" (p. 128). This project anchors itself in the worlds of pain and lived experience, and is accountable to these worlds. It enacts an ethic of respect. It rejects the traditional denial by the West and western scholars of respect, humanity, self-determination, citizenship, and human rights to indigenous peoples (Smith, 1999, p. 120).

Critical Race Theory

Such a project engages a militant utopianism, a provisional Marxism without guarantees, a cultural studies that is anticipatory, interventionist, and provisional. Such a project does not back away from the contemporary world, in its multiple global versions, including the West; the third world; the moral, political and geographic spaces occupied by First Nations and Fourth World persons; and persons in marginal or liminal positions (Ladson-Billings, 2000, p. 263; Ladson-Billings & Donnor, 2005). Rather it strategically engages this world in those liminal spaces where lives are bent and changed by the repressive structures of the new conservatism. This project pays particular attention to the dramatic increases around the world in domestic violence, rape, child abuse, hates of crime, and violence directed toward persons of color (Comaroff & Comaroff, 2001, pp. 1–2).

Extending critical legal theory, critical race theory theorizes life in these liminal spaces, offering "pragmatic strategies for material and social transformation" (Ladson-Billings, 2000, p. 264). Critical race theory assumes that racism and white supremacy are the norms in American society. Critical race scholars use performative, story-telling autoethnographic methods to uncover the ways in which racism operates in daily life. Critical race theory challenges those neoliberals who argue that civil rights have been attained for persons of color. Those who argue that the civil rights crusade is a long, slow struggle are also criticized

(Ladson-Billings, 2000, p. 264). Advocates of CRT argue that racism requires radical social change. Neoliberalism and liberalism lack the mechanisms and imaginations to achieve such change (Ladson-Billings, 2000, p. 264). Critical race theorists contend that whites have been the main beneficiaries of civil rights legislation.

Strategically, CRT examines the ways in which race is performed including the cultural logics and performative acts that inscribe and create whiteness and nonwhiteness (McLaren 1997b, p. 278; Roediger, 2002, p. 17). In an age of globalization and diasporic postnational identities, the color line should no longer be an issue, but sadly it is (McLaren, 1997b, p. 278.)

PARTICIPATORY PERFORMANCE ACTION INQUIRY

Drawing on the complex traditions embedded in participatory action research (Fine, Torre, Boudin, Bowen, Clark, Hylton, et al., 2003; Kemmis & McTaggert, 2000), as well as the critical turn in feminist discourse, and the growing literature for and by indigenous peoples (Smith, 1999, 2005), critical performance pedagogy implements a commitment to participation and performance *with*, not *for*, community members. Amplifying Fine, et al. (2003, pp. 176–177), this project builds on local knowledge and experience developed at the bottom of social hierarchies. Following Smith's (1999) lead, participatory performance work honors and respects local knowledge and customs and practices and incorporates those values and beliefs into participatory performance action inquiry (Fine, et al. 2003, p. 176).

Work in this participatory, activist performance tradition gives back to the community, "creating a legacy of inquiry, a process of change, and material resources to enable transformations in social practices" (Fine, et al. 2003, p. 177). Through performance and participation, the scholar develops a "participatory mode of consciousness" (Bishop, 1998, p. 208), and understanding. This helps shape the participant-driven nature of inquiry and folds the researcher as performer into the narrative and moral accountability structures of the group.

This project works outward from the university and its classrooms, treating the spaces of the academy as critical public spheres, as sites of resistance and empowerment (Giroux, 2000, p. 134). Critical pedagogy resists the increasing commercialization and commodification of higher education. It contests the penetration of neoliberal values into research parks, classrooms, and the curriculum. It is critical of institutional review boards who pass ever-more restrictive judgment on human subject research.

A commitment to critical pedagogy in the classroom can be an empowering dialogical experience. The instructional spaces become sacred spaces. In them students take risks and speak from the heart, using their own experiences as tools for forging critical race consciousness. The critical discourse created in this public sphere is then taken into other classrooms, into other pedagogical spaces where a militant utopianism is imagined and experienced.

As a performative practice this project interrogates and criticizes those cultural narratives that make victims responsible for the cultural and interpersonal violence they experience. These narratives blame and victimize the victim. But performance narratives do more than celebrate the lives and struggles of persons who have lived through violence and abuse. These narratives must always be directed back to the structures that shape and produce the violence in question. Pedagogically, the performative is political and focused on power. Performances are located within their historical moment, with attention given to the play of power and ideology. The performative becomes a way of critiquing the political, a way of analyzing how culture operates pedagogically to produce and reproduce victims.

Pedagogically and ideologically the performative becomes an act of doing (Giroux, 2000, p. 135), a dialogical way of being in the world, a way of grounding performances in the concrete situations of the present. The performative becomes a way of interrogating how "objects, discourses, and practices construct possibilities for and constraints on citizenship" (Nelson & Gaonkar, 1996, p. 7; also quoted in Giroux, 2000, p. 134). This stance connects the biographical and the personal to the pedagogical and the performative. It casts the cultural critic in the identity of a critical citizen, a person who collaborates with others in participatory action projects that enact militant democratic visions of public life and community and moral responsibility (Giroux, 2000, p. 141). This public intellectual practices critical performance pedagogy. As a concerned citizen working with others, he or she takes positions on the critical issues of the day, understanding that there can be no genuine democracy without genuine opposition and criticism (Giroux, 2000, p. 136).

In turn radical democratic pedagogy requires citizens and citizen-scholars committed to taking risks, persons willing to act in situations where the outcome cannot be predicted in advance. In such situations a politics of new possibilities can be imagined and made to happen. Yet in these pedagogical spaces there are not leaders and followers; there are only coparticipants, persons jointly working together to develop new lines of action, new stories, new narratives in a collaborative effort (Bishop, 1998, p. 207).

> *We must find a new story to perform . . . we must preserve a model of a free democratic society.*
>
> —Kittridge, 1987, p. 87

A radical performance pedagogy politically and ethically means putting the critical sociological imagination to work. This work involves pedagogies of hope and freedom. A performative cultural studies reflexively and ethically enacts these pedagogies. These practices require a performance ethics, which I have discussed in some detail.

NOTES

1. I call these war diaries, reports from the homeland and its battlefields. This essay extends arguments in Denzin (2005, 2003).

2. This theatre often uses verbatim accounts of injustice and violence in daily life. See Mienczakowski (1995, p. 5; 2001; also Chessman, 1971) for a history of "verbatim theater" and Mienczakowski's extensions of this approach, using oral history, participant observation, and the methods of ethnodrama. A contemporary use of verbatim theatre is the play *Guantanamo: Honor Bound to Defend Freedom* (Riding, 2004). This anti–Iraq war play addresses the plight of British citizens imprisoned at Guantanamo. The "power of Guantanamo is that it is not really a play but a re-enactment of views expressed in interviews, letters, news conferences, and speeches by various players in the post–September 11 Iraq war drama, from British Muslim detainees, to lawyers, from U. S. Defense Secretary Donald H. Rumsfeld, to Jack Straw, Britain's foreign secretary" (Riding, 2004). Nicolas Kent, the play's director, says he believes "political theater works here because the British have an innate sense of justice. When we do stories about injustice . . . there is a groundswell of sympathy . . . people are furious that there isn't due process. With Islamophobia growing around the world I wanted to show that we, too, think there is an injustice" (Riding, 2004).

3. At another level indigenous participatory theatre extends the project connected to third world popular theatre. This is political "theatre used by oppressed Third World people to achieve justice and development for themselves" (Etherton, 1988, p. 991). The International Popular Theatre Alliance, organized in the 1980s, uses existing forms of cultural expression to fashion improvised dramatic productions which analyze situations of poverty and oppression. This grass-roots approach uses agitprop and sloganizing theatre (theatre pieces devised to ferment political action) to create collective awareness and collective action at the local level. This form of theatre has been popular in Latin America, in Africa, in parts of Asia, in India, and among Native populations in the Americas (Etherton, 1988, p. 992).

REFERENCES

Alexander, B. (2005). Performance ethnography: The reenacting and inciting of culture. In N. K. Denzin & Y. S. Lincoln (Eds.), *Handbook of qualitative research* (3rd ed.) (pp. 411–442). Thousand Oaks, CA: Sage.

Anand, B., Fine, M., Perkins, T., Surrey, D. S., & Renaissance School Class of 2000. (2002). *Keeping the struggle alive: Studying desegregation in our town: A guide to doing oral history.* New York: Teachers College Press.

Balme, C., & Carstensen, A. (2001). Home fires: Creating a pacific theatre in the diaspora. *Theatre Research International, 26*(1), 35–46.

Bean, A. (2001). Black minstrelsy and double inversion, circa 1890. In H. J. Elam, Jr., & D. Krasner (Eds.), *African American performance and theater history* (pp. 171–191). New York: Oxford University Press.

Bishop, R. (1998). Freeing ourselves from neocolonial domination in research: A Maori approach to creating knowledge. *International Journal of Qualitative Studies in Education, 11*(2), 199–219.

Boal, A. (1995). *The rainbow of desire: The Boal method of theatre and therapy.* London: Routledge.

Chessman, P. (1971). Production casebook. *New Theatre Quarterly, 1*(1), 1–6.

Christians, C. (2000). Ethics and politics in qualitative research. In N. K. Denzin & Y. S. Lincoln (Eds.), *Handbook of qualitative research* (2nd ed.) (pp. 133–155). Thousand Oaks, CA: Sage.

Comaroff, J., & Comaroff, J. (2001). Millennial capitalism: First thoughts on a second coming. In J. Comaroff & J. Comaroff (Eds.), *Millennial capitalism and the culture of neoliberalism* (pp. 1–56). Durham, NC: Duke University Press.

Conquergood, D. (1985). Performing as a moral act: Ethical dimensions of the ethnography of performance. *Literature in Performance, 5*(1), 1–13.

Conquergood, D. (1998). Beyond the text: Toward a performative cultural politics. In S. J. Dailey (Ed.), *The future of performance studies: Visions and revisions* (pp. 25–36). Annandale, VA: National Communication Association.

Darder, A. (2002). *Reinventing Paulo Freire: A pedagogy of love.* Boulder, CO: Westview.

Darder, A., & Torres, R. D. (2004). *After race: Racism after multiculturalism.* New York: New York University Press.

Denzin, N. K. (2003). *Performance ethnography.* Thousand Oaks, CA: Sage.

Denzin, N. K. (2005). Emancipatory discourses, and the ethics and politics of interpretation. In N. K. Denzin & Y. S. Lincoln (Eds.), *Handbook of qualitative research* (3rd ed.) (pp. 933–958). Thousand Oaks, CA: Sage.

Dillard, A. (1974). *Pilgrim at Tinker Creek.* New York: Harper & Row.

DuBois, W. E. B. (1926). Krigwa Players Little Negro Theatre: The story of a little theatre movement. *Crisis, 32*(1), 134–136.

Edwards, R., & Mauthner, M. (2002). Ethics and feminist research: Theory and practice. In M. Mauthner, M. Birch, J. Jessop, & T. Miller (Eds.), *Ethics in qualitative research* (pp. 14–31). Thousand Oaks, CA: Sage.

Etherton, M. (1988). Third world popular theatre. In M. Banham (Ed.), *The Cambridge guide to theatre* (pp. 991–992). Cambridge, England: Cambridge University Press.

Fine, M. (2002). The mourning after. *Qualitative Inquiry, 8*(1), 137–145.

Fine, M., Torre, M. E., Boudin, K., Bowen, I., Clark, J., Hylton, et al. (2003). Participatory action research: From within and beyond prison walls. In P. M. Camic, J. E. Rhodes, & L. Yardley, (Eds.), *Qualitative research in psychology: Expanding perspectives in methodology and design* (pp. 173–198). Washington, DC: American Psychological Association.

Fischman, G. E., & McLaren, P. (in press). Rethinking critical pedagogy and the gramscian legacy: From organic to committed intellectuals. *Cultural Studies—Critical Methodologies, 5*(1).

Freire, P. (1998). *Pedagogy of freedom: Ethics, democracy, and civic courage* (P. Clarke, Trans.). Boulder, CO: Rowman & Littlefield. (Original work published 1992)

Freire, P. (1999). *Pedagogy of hope* (R. B. Barr, Trans.). New York: Continuum. (Original work published 1992)

Freire, P. (2001). *Pedagogy of the oppressed* (30th anniversary ed., M. B. Ramos, Trans.). New York: Continuum. (Original work published 1971)

Garoian, C. R. (1999). *Performing pedagogy: Toward an art of politics.* Albany: SUNY Press.

Gilbert, H. (2003). Black and white and re(a)d all over again: Indigenous minstrelsy in contemporary Canadian and Australian theatre. *Theatre Journal, 55,* 679–698.

Giroux, H. (2000). *Impure acts: The practical politics of cultural studies.* New York: Routledge.

Giroux, H. (2001). Cultural studies as performative politics. *Cultural Studies—Critical Methodologies, 1*(1), 5–23.

Giroux, H. (2003). *The abandoned generation: Democracy beyond the culture of fear.* New York: Palgrave.

Giroux, H. (2004). *The terror of neoliberalism: Authoritarianism and the eclipse of democracy.* Boulder, CO: Paradigm.

Giroux, H., & Giroux, S. S. (in press). Challenging neoliberalism's new world order: The promise of critical pedagogy. *Cultural Studies—Critical Methodologies, 5*(1).

Glass, R. D. (2001). On Paulo Freire's philosophy of praxis and the foundations of liberation education. *Educational Researcher, 30*(1), 15–25.

Goffman, E. (1959). *The presentation of self in everyday life.* New York: Doubleday.

Greenwood, J. (2001). Within a third space. *Research in Drama Education, 6*(2) 193–205.

Henderson, J. Y. (2000). Postcolonial ledger drawing: Legal reform. In M. Battiste (Ed.), *Reclaiming indigenous voice and vision* (pp. 161–171). Vancouver, Canada: University of British Columbia Press.

Jackson, A. (1995). Translator's introduction. In A. Boal, *The rainbow of desire: The Boal method of theatre and therapy* (pp. xviii–xxvi). London: Routledge.

Kemmis, S., & McTaggert, R. (2000). Participatory action research. In N. K. Denzin & Y. S. Lincoln (Eds.), *Handbook of qualitative research* (2nd ed.) (pp. 567–606). Thousand Oaks, CA: Sage.

Kincheloe, J. L. (2001). Describing the bricolage: Conceptualizing a new rigor in qualitative research. *Qualitative Inquiry, 7*(6), 679–692.

Kincheloe, J. L., & McLaren, P. (2005). Rethinking critical theory and qualitative research. In N. K. Denzin & Y. S. Lincoln (Eds.), *Handbook of qualitative research* (3rd ed.) (pp. 303–342). Thousand Oaks, CA: Sage.

Kittridge, W. (1987). *Owning it all.* San Francisco: Murray House.

Kondo, D. (2000). (Re)visions of race: Contemporary race theory and the cultural politics of racial crossover in documentary theatre. *Theatre Journal, 52*(1), 81–107.

Kvale, S. (1996). *InterViews: An introduction to qualitative research interviewing.* London: Sage.

Ladson-Billings, G. (2000). Racialized discourses and ethnic epistemologies. In N. K. Denzin & Y. S. Lincoln (Eds.), *Handbook of qualitative research* (2nd ed.) (pp. 257–277). Thousand Oaks, CA: Sage.

Ladson-Billings, G., & Donnor, J. (2005). Racialized discourses and ethnic epistemologies. In N. K. Denzin & Y. S. Lincoln (Eds.), *Handbook of qualitative research* (3rd ed.) (pp. 279–302). Thousand Oaks, CA: Sage.

Madison, D. S. (1998). Performances, personal narratives, and the politics of possibility. In S. J. Dailey (Ed.), *The future of performance studies: Visions and revisions* (pp. 276–286). Annandale, VA: National Communication Association.

Magowan, F. (2000). Dancing with a difference: Reconfiguring the poetic politics of aboriginal ritual as national spectacle. *Australian Journal of Anthropology, 11*(3), 308–321.

McLaren, P. (1997a). The ethnographer as postmodern flaneur: Critical reflexivity and posthybridity as narrative engagement. In W. G. Tierney & Y. S. Lincoln (Eds.), *Representation and the text: Re-framing the narrative voice* (pp. 143–177). Albany: SUNY Press.

McLaren, P. (1997b). *Revolutionary multiculturalism: Pedagogies of dissent for the new millennium.* Boulder, CO: Westview.

McLaren, P. (1999). *Schooling as ritual performance* (3rd ed.). Lanham, MD: Roman & Littlefield.

McLaren, P. (2001). Che Guevara, Paulo Freire, and the politics of hope: Reclaiming critical pedagogy. *Cultural Studies—Critical Methodologies, 1*(1), 108–131.

Mienczakowski, J. (1995). The theatre of ethnography: The reconstruction of ethnography into theatre with emancipatory potential. *Qualitative Inquiry, 1*(2), 360–375.

Mienczakowski, J. (2001). Ethnodrama: Performed research—limitations and potential. In P. Atkinson, S. Delamont, & A. Coffey (Eds.), *Handbook of ethnography* (pp. 468–476). London: Sage.

Mills, C. W. (1959). *The sociological imagination.* New York: Oxford University Press.

Mutua, K., & Swadener, B. B. (Eds.). (2004). *Decolonizing research in cross-cultural contexts: Critical personal narratives.* Albany: SUNY Press.

Nelson, C., & Gaonkar, D. P. (1996). Cultural studies and the politics of disciplinarity. In C. Nelson & D. P. Gaonkar (Eds.), *Disciplinarity and dissent in cultural studies* (pp. 1–22). New York: Routledge.

Orwell, G. (1949). *Nineteen eighty-four.* New York: Harcourt, Brace and Company.

Pollock, D. (1998). A response to Dwight Conquergood's essay: 'Beyond the text: towards a performative cultural politics.' In S. J. Dailey (Ed.), *The future of performance studies: Visions and revisions* (pp. 37–46). Annandale, VA: National Communication Association.

Riding, A. (2004, June 15). On a London stage, a hearing for Guantanamo detainees. *New York Times,* p. B2.

Roediger, D. (2002). *Colored white: Transcending the racial past.* Berkeley: University of California Press.

Sartre, J. P. (1981). *The family idiot: Gustave Flaubert, 1821–1857* (Vol. 1) (C. Cosman, Trans.). Chicago: University of Chicago Press. (Original work published 1971)

Smith, A. D. (2003). *House Arrest and Piano.* New York: Anchor.

Smith, L. T. (1999). *Decolonizing methodologies: Research and indigenous peoples.* London: Zed Books.

Smith, L. T. (2005). On tricky ground: Researching the native in the age of uncertainty. In N. K. Denzin & Y. S. Lincoln (Eds.), *Handbook of qualitative research* (3rd ed.) (pp. 85–108). Thousand Oaks, CA: Sage.

Spender, S. (1984). Introduction. In M. Lowry, *Under the volcano* (pp. xii–xxiii). New York: New American Library. (Original work published 1947)

Trinh, T. M. (1989). *Woman, native, other.* Bloomington: Indiana University Press.

Willis, P., & Trondman, M. (2000). Manifesto for ethnography. *Ethnography, 1*(1) 5–16.

Wilson, A. (1996). The ground on which I stand. *American Theatre, 13*(7), 14–16, 71–74.

PART V

Performance and Ethnography, Performing Ethnography, Performance Ethnography

OLORISA OMI OSUN OLOMO (JONI L. JONES)

Performance and ethnography meaningfully come together as performance ethnography, which is ethnographic research embodied by the ethnographer, the fieldwork community, an audience, or any combination of these participants. Performance ethnography rests on the idea that bodies harbor knowledge about culture, and that performance allows for the exchange of that knowledge across bodies. The dense exploration of culture suggested by Clifford Geertz's "thick description"—that sensuous detailing of ethnographic experiences—is given flesh with performance ethnography as the ethnographer, the fieldwork community members, and the audience collaboratively exchange their understandings and experiences through performance.

This embodied knowledge, which had long been the hallmark of oral interpretation and theatre prior to the formation of the discipline now known as performance studies, joined with anthropological and sociological theories of culture to develop the intellectual frameworks for performance ethnography. The longstanding collaboration between Richard

Schechner as a theatre director and theorist and Victor Turner as an anthropologist led to a distinctive mapping of the contours of performance ethnography. In *From Ritual to Theatre,* Turner declares "There must be a dialectic between performing and learning. One learns through performing, then performs the understanding so gained." (1982, p. 94) This assertion directly relates to Turner's "social drama/stage drama" diagram in which the events of the real world meld into those on stage, and the activities on stage shape our understanding and experience of our real worlds. Turner further indicates the relationship between theatrical performance and everyday life when he acknowledges, in a forward to Schechner's *Between Theater and Anthropology* (1985), how his work was influenced by Erving Goffman's explication of everyday life performance. Both Turner and Goffman drew upon an understanding of the intelligence in the body to postulate theories about how humans manipulate, respond to, and interact in the worlds in which we live. In this way, performance is not merely a metaphor for everyday life, but instead everyday life is a series of performances, many of which are what Schechner calls "restored behaviors." According to Schechner,

> Restored behavior is used in all kinds of performances from shamanism and exorcism to trance, from ritual to aesthetic dance and theater, from initiation rites to social dramas, from psychoanalysis to psychodrama and transactional analysis. In fact, restored behavior is the main characteristic of performance. (1985, p. 35)

This definition situates the body as the primary site of information, transmission, and transformation, thus underscoring the primacy of body knowledge as performance ethnography evolved into a distinctive methodology.

Much of Schechner and Turner's work examined nonwestern cultural rituals such as the deer dances of the Arizona Yaqui, Korean shamans, or marriage practices among the Ndembu of Zambia, and many of the performances they created centered around the ethnographer's ability to understand these cultures by taking on roles from these communities. Embodiment in ethnography took on new contours as performance studies scholar Dwight Conquergood pushed the practice toward a Bakhtinian sense of dialogue, thereby including the fieldwork community members among the bodies that must be thoroughly considered in the performance work. While Turner was most concerned with strengthening the anthropologist's understandings of culture through performance, and Schechner focused on the complexities of how culture bearers enacted rituals, Conquergood was equally concerned with the ethical performance practices of the ethnographer *and* the participation of fieldwork community members in shaping the representations performed of them.

Conquergood's "Performing as a Moral Act: Ethical Dimensions of the Ethnography of Performance" (1985) and "Rethinking Ethnography: Towards a Critical Cultural Politics" (1991, reprinted in this volume) are foundational essays in the development of performance ethnography largely because of the centrality that Conquergood gives to the body in each work. In "Performing as a Moral Act," Conquergood writes,

> Dialogic performance is a way of having intimate conversation with other people and cultures. Instead of speaking about them, one speaks to and with them. The sensuous immediacy and empathic leap demanded by performance is an occasion for orchestrating two voices, for bringing together two sensibilities. At the same time, the conspicuous artifice of performance is a vivid reminder that each voice has its own integrity. (p. 10)

Conquergood used documentary film as a space for dialogic performance with "Heart Broken in Half" (1990). In this examination of Chicago street gangs, street gang members across neighborhoods and generations talk of their experiences, explain their use of symbols, and guide the viewer on a tour of key locations, thereby actively constructing the self-representations that contribute to Conquergood's film. While performance ethnography has typically been fashioned as a live event, this film by an esteemed performance ethnographer serves as an example of how embodiment manifests as dialogue in performance. It is important to note that Conquergood later came to challenge his own use of dialogue as he recognized that true dialogic performance cannot be achieved without a balance of power between the participants. In "Lethal Theatre: Performance, Punishment, and the Death Penalty" (2002), Conquergood suggested "co-performative witness" as an alternative stance to dialogue. And it will be interesting to see where this concept might take performance ethnography.

In "Ethnography and the Politics of Adaptation" in this handbook, Derek Goldman acknowledges the multilayered reality of the dialogue developed between him and author Leon Forrest as Goldman adapts Forrest's *Divine Days* (1992) for a stage performance. For Goldman, the process of adaptation became an ethnographic exploration into the specifics of the novel, into Goldman's own identity as a white artist/scholar, and into Forrest's ultimately unsuccessful battle with prostate cancer. Goldman writes that these intertwined realties "focused for me the implications of adaptation as a dialogic process made in this case more urgent, intense and vital by the complex dynamics of race and by the immediate claims of mortality." This work crystallizes Conquergood's point that "performance is a vivid reminder that each voice has its own integrity." (1985, p. 10)

The body-to-bodyness implied by Conquergood's sensuous intimate conversation is a requirement for the dialogue that Conquergood recommends. His works moves away from studying culture to inhabiting culture, with all of the messiness and vulnerability and aliveness that such inhabiting demands.

Conquergood is more explicit about the emphasis on the body as a site of knowledge in "Rethinking Ethnography." Here, he offers five ways of "rethinking the 'world as text' to the 'world as performance':

1. Performance and Cultural Process. What are the conceptual consequences of thinking about culture as a verb instead of a noun, process instead of product?

2. Performance and Ethnographic Praxis. What are the methodological implications of thinking about fieldwork as the collaborative performance of an enabling fiction between observer and observed, knower and known?

3. Performance and Hermeneutics. What kinds of knowledge are privileged or displaced when performance experience becomes a way of knowing, a method of critical inquiry, a mode of understanding?

4. Performance and Scholarly Representation. What are the rhetorical problematics of performance as a complementary or alternative form of "publishing" research?

5. The Politics of Performance. . . . How does performance reproduce, enable, sustain, challenge, subvert, critique, and naturalize ideology? How do performances simultaneously reproduce and resist hegemony?

These questions are provocatively explored in this volume in D. Soyini Madison's "The Performance Script." In her examination of the controversial Ghanaian practice of *Trokosi,* in which "young girls and women are committed to religious shrines to live and work in order to appease the wrath of God against their village, as reparation, for a crime committed against God by a male member of her family," Madison insists on fashioning "culture as a verb" by creating "a collaborative performance of an enabling fiction between observer and observed" as she devised a performance of competing ideologies performed by herself and the Ghanaians with the most at stake in the cultural political debate. In a note to herself during fieldwork, Madison wrote, "This performance will not engage the Trokosi practice itself, but the debate and the discursive and historical formations that create it and sustain it, as well as those indigenous voices that are out to change it." (p) This inclusion of fieldwork community members is a far cry from the traditional image of the solo white, male, western ethnographer recording lives as if they are commodities or disembodied artifacts. bell hooks challenges this bodiless ethnography in her critique of the cover image to James Clifford and George Marcus's *Writing Culture: The Poetics and Politics of Ethnography* (1986) when she writes

One sees in this image a white male sitting at a distance from darker-skinned people, located behind him; he is writing . . . I fix my attention on the piece of cloth that is attached to the writer's glasses, presumably to block out the sun; it also blocks out a particular field of vision. This "blindspot," artificially created, is a powerful visual metaphor for the ethnographic enterprise as it has been in the past and as it is being written. As a script, this cover does not present any radical challenge to past constructions. It blatantly calls attention to two ideas that are quite fresh in the racist imagination: the notion of the white male as writer/authority, presented in the photograph actively producing, and the idea of the passive brown/black man who is doing nothing, merely looking on. (pp. 126–127)

Rather than creating with an artificially constructed blind spot, Madison embraces the rigorous process of generating work that is multivocalic, that shares ethnographic authority, and that relies on performance to bring forward the intricacies and competing truths that are inherent to Trokosi. Madison's work goes beyond envisioning fieldwork community members as consultants to scripts, to casting those community members as central figures in the performances. Her essay offers an instructive map for moving through reams of field notes and hours of personal interrogation to the creation of a dense and fruitfully ambivalent performance. This is quite a different exercise than, say, "The Laramie Project," Moises Kaufman's theatrical collaboration centered on the murder of Matthew Shepard or "Fires in the Mirror," Anna Deavere Smith's solo performance based on the killing of Gavin Cato and Yankel Rosenbaum in Crown Heights, New York both of which use ethnographic stories that are then performed by professional actors.

Performance studies scholars have also created ethnographic performances that were then performed by actors rather than by the fieldwork community members. Della Pollock's production of coal miners' narratives collected by cast members and Shannon Jackson's productions taken from fieldwork on theatrical auditions were not performed by members of the fieldwork community, but they were often attended by members of those communities, thereby making the members of those communities active collaborators as participating spectators. In each of these examples, the sense of accountability and ideological authenticity is shifted when those who lived the stories are not also performing in those stories or acting as witnesses to the performances.

This full inclusion of fieldwork community members into the development and performance of ethnographic texts coincides with the rise of cultural studies in the United States. By the time *Cultural Studies* (1992) edited by Lawrence Grossberg, Cary Nelson, and Paula Treichler and *The Cultural Studies Reader* (1993) edited by Simon During appeared, Turner and Schechner had published major works on the intersections of performance and anthropology, Conquergood had offered solo performances of Laotian refugees and produced a documentary film of Chicago street gangs. Performance studies was evolving from a primarily literature-based discipline and a theatre/dance discipline to one deeply enmeshed in the construction of culture. Cultural studies seeks to reveal the political ideologies wrapped around everyday human behavior and cultural production, giving particular attention to the way race, gender, sexuality, geography, and class shape our understandings of behavior and culture. In "Ethnography, Rhetoric, and Performance," Conquergood notes that the word "performance" has "emerged with increasing prominence in cultural studies" (p. 84) and that "the new ethnography of performance scholarship . . . pushes towards a performative cultural politics" (p. 95). Through his critical review of three ethnographic monographs, Conquergood valorizes the power of bodily held understandings as he applauds the ethnographers for humble compassionate negotiations in the field, and he encourages all ethnographers to respect the "politically loaded" positions they inevitably occupy. This situates ethnography as an overtly politicized activist enterprise that is "committed to action in the world" (p. 95). These actions are played out on the bodies of the ethnographers and the community members in a series of intricate and delicate power plays.

When the fieldwork community members are incorporated into the performance, the potential for politicization and advocacy becomes apparent. Unlike conceptions of ethnography that espouse neutrality and objectivity, performance ethnography's attention to embodiment (and the attendant politics of embodiment) situate the practice deeply in a political frame. Embodiment is political; a stance is already implied through the sociopolitical narratives embedded in bodies. Norman Denzin stresses the politics of embodiment in his discussion of performance ethnography as he calls for a "sixth moment" in which performance ethnography exists not merely to describe or even explain culture, but instead exists to advocate for specific people, positions or ideas. In this way the embodiment of performance ethnography is literally about saving, honoring, rejecting, and critiquing particular bodies. Performance ethnography performed by the community makes it clear that specific bodies are at stake. Denzin describes the "sixth moment" as, "a socially responsible ethnographic journalism that advocates democracy by creating a space for and giving a civic (public) voice to the biographically meaningful, epiphanal experiences that occur within the confines of the local moral community" (1997, p. 281). Because ethnography is done with and on bodies, it cannot be neutral, and for Denzin, must be envisioned as advocacy.

In D. Soyini Madison's book, *Critical Ethnography: Method, Ethics, and Performance,* she expands the "critical" by emphasizing the significance of ethics and performance in the art and politics of fieldwork. Madison also troubles autoethnography and deepens what it means to examine our own subjectivity as ethnographers:

But critical ethnography—or what some have called the "new ethnography" (Goodall 2000)—must not only critique the notion of objectivity, but must also critique the notion of subjectivity as well. . . . This "new" or postcritical ethnography is the move to contextualize our own positionality, thereby making it accessible, transparent, and vulnerable to judgment and evaluation. In this way, we take ethical responsibility for our own subjectivity and political perspective, resisting the trap of gratuitous self-centeredness or of presenting an interpretation as though it has no "self," as though it is not accountable for its consequences and effects. Doing fieldwork is a personal experience. Our intuition, senses, and emotions—or what Wallace Bacon (1979) refers to as "felt-sensing"—are powerfully woven into and inseparable from the process. We are inviting an ethics of accountability by taking the chance of being proven wrong. (2005, p. 6)

Performance ethnography can function as critical ethnography by serving as an agent of social change. Madison was determined to keep the socially efficacious aims of her work at the forefront of the production as she explains,

This performance must not only inform and enlighten. It must not only be beautifully beautiful, but it must have palpable effects for structural change and policy. Indeed, I felt the weight of purpose, which was also the weight of representation. I remembered Stuart Hall's warning that how a people are represented are how they are treated, and Dwight Conquergood's assertion that images and symbolic representations drive public policy. (**p**)

The script she shares demonstrates the democratic potential in presenting with equal respect competing sides of the issue.

Performance ethnography has the greatest democratic thrust as a constructed live exploration of the culture the ethnographer has experienced. As Conquergood explains in "Ethnography, Rhetoric, Performance,"

Performance—powerfully conceptualized— is the borderlands terrain between rhetoric and ethnography that is being vigorously explored and developed from both perspectives. Performance studies is the new frontier for staking joint claims to poetics and persuasion, pleasure and power, in the interests of community and critique, solidarity and resistance. In the topography of contemporary cultural studies, performance is now the commonplace, the nexus between the playful and the political. (1992, p. 80)

In this way, performance is the crucible for forging new visceral understandings of culture. "Community and critique, solidarity and resistance" are where performance and democracy come together.

In establishing the goals of a radical democracy, political scientist Chantal Mouffe writes,

The notions of citizenship and community have been stripped of much of their content by liberal individualism, and we need to recover the dimension of active participation that they hold in the classical republican tradition. Now this tradition needs to be made compatible with the pluralism that is central to modern democracy. (1992, p. 3)

The key ideas here for performance ethnography are citizenship, community, active participation, and pluralism. Theorizing culture and democracy can surely help us to shape these realities, but the doing of culture and democracy has an immediate impact on our lives. When an audience collaborates in performance ethnography, they are enacting the rights of citizenship. To join in, to have your position heard, is to participate in society as a fully endowed citizen with both social and political rights.

Note that the democratic potential in performance ethnography seems to disregard the decidedly nondemocratic world of ancient Athens on which ideals of U.S. democracy are said to be based. Women and slaves were not fully enfranchised citizens, and while Denzin and I are clearly calling for a democracy in

which all members fully participate, it is vital to note which bodies have traditionally been omitted from authority positions in ethnography. A wave of incisive feminist critiques of or alternatives to traditional ethnography— including Trinh T. Minh-ha's *Woman, Native, Other*; Kamala Viswesreran's *Fictions of Feminist Ethnography*; *Black Feminist Anthropology: Theory, Politics, Praxis, Poetics* edited by Irma McClaurin, and *Women Writing Culture* edited by Ruth Behar and Deborah A. Gordon—suggest that women and people of color have been relegated to the object position in ethnography rather than occupying the space of contributing subjects who shape their own representations. Performance ethnography makes visible who the players are, and gives room for multiple truths to exist simultaneously.

In this volume, Barbara Browning explores the complexities of representation and agency as she examines the various ways in which ethnography about dance can serve to reinscribe cultural and national stereotypes that shape how we actually experience dance performances themselves. Her contrast of Maya Deren and Katherine Dunham allows for a fruitful understanding of how "movement aesthetics can be convincingly related to their larger sociopolitical context" (**p**). Browning, like Madison, Goldman, and Conquergood, is interested in the way in which performance and ethnography are politically engaged acts that reveal much about the ethnographers, the aesthetic and everyday life performers, and the intertwined worlds they create together.

Performance ethnography embraces the muddiness of multiple perspectives, idiosyncrasy, and competing truths, and pushes everyone present into an immediate confrontation with our beliefs and behavior. Body-to-body, we are less able to retreat into the privacy of our own limited self-serving thinking, our stereotypes and biases. We have to acknowledge the validity of another viewpoint, because it is living right there in front of us. In this way the embodiment and action that is inherent in performance ethnography makes this a methodology that reflects, in Conquergood's visionary phrasing, a "critical genealogy" that can be "traced from performance as *mimesis*, to *poesis*, to *kinesis*, performance as imitation, construction, dynamism" (1992, p. 84).

REFERENCES

Behar, R., & Gordon, D. A. (Eds.). (1996). *Women writing culture*. Berkeley: University of California Press.

Clifford, J., & Marcus, J. (Eds.). (1986). *Writing culture: The poetics and politics of ethnography*. Berkeley: University of California Press.

Conquergood, D. (1985). Performing as a moral act: Ethical dimensions of the ethnography of performance. *The Performance Quarterly, 5*(2), 1–13.

Conquergood, D. (1991). Rethinking ethnography: Towards a critical cultural politics. *Communication Monographs, 58*, 179–194.

Conquergood, D. (1992). Ethnography, rhetoric, and performance. *Quarterly Journal of Speech, 78*, 80–123.

Conquergood, D. (2002). Lethal theatre: Performance, punishment, and the death penalty. *Theatre Journal, 54*, 339–367.

Conquergood, D., & Siegel, T. (Producers). (1990). *Heart broken in half* [Motion picture]. (Available from Filmmakers Library, 124 East 40th Street, New York, NY 10016)

Denzin, N. (1997). *Interpretive ethnography: Ethnographic practices for the 21st century*. Thousand Oaks, CA: Sage.

During, S. (Ed.). (1993). *The cultural studies reader*. London: Routledge.

Forrest, L. (1992). *Divine days*. New York: Norton.

Grossberg, G., Nelson, C., & Treichler, P. (1992). *Cultural studies*. London: Routledge.

hooks, b. (1990). *Yearning: Race, gender, and cultural politics*. Boston: South End Press.

Jackson, S. (1993). Audition and ethnography: Performance as ideological critique. *The Performance Quarterly, 13*, 21–43.

Madison, D. S. (2005). *Critical ethnography: Method, ethics, and performance*. Thousand Oaks, CA: Sage.

McClaurin, I. (2001). *Black feminist anthropology: Theory, politics, praxis, poetics*. Piscataway, NJ: Rutgers University Press.

Mouffe, C. (1992). *Dimensions of radical democracy*. New York: Verso.

Pollock, D. (1990). Telling the told: Performing "Like a Family." *Oral History Review, 18*(2), 1–36.

Schechner, R. (1985). *Between theater and anthropology*. Philadelphia: University of Pennsylvania Press.

Trinh, T. M. (1989). *Woman, native, other*. Bloomington: Indiana University Press.

Viswesreran, K. (1994). *Fictions of feminist ethnography*. Minneapolis: University of Minnesota Press.

Turner, V. (1982). *From ritual to theatre: The human seriousness of play*. New York: PAJ Publications.

19

Dwight Conquergood's "Rethinking Ethnography"

D. SOYINI MADISON

The ethnographer must be a co-performer in order to understand those embodied meanings.

—Dwight Conquergood, "Rethinking Ethnography"

Dwight Conquergood's essay, "Rethinking Ethnography: Towards A Critical Cultural Politics," was first published in 1991 in *Communication Monographs* and arguably remains the foundational essay that charts a critical performance ethnography and the performative politics of embodied enquiry. For Conquergood the labor of "rethinking ethnography" is a labor of incorporating performance and the performative in the high stakes of naming a particular space, time, and desire in order to make change possible. The essay laid the groundwork for reframing ethnography as purposefully excavating "the political underpinnings of all modes of representation, including science," through a specific triad:

Bodies, Borders, and Performance (p. 351). For Conquergood, ethnography, through a performance lens, is particularly suited to unveil the oft hidden and convoluted processes of power, discourse, and materiality because of the consequences that emerge on the sites and interstices of bodies performing on the borders. Conquergood's triad is not simply three very powerful domains but three domains multiplied by infinity, that is, bodies, borders, and performances are happening in countless combinations of symbolic forms, innumerable locations of global and local trespassing, and never ending intentions that drive alterity.

Conquergood's call to rethink ethnography is to revision, reinvent, and recommit to an

347

ethnography that must engage a postcolonial, post–civil rights, post–cold war, postfeminist, and postmodern world. The essay reminds us that positivist claims and objective science as the rule of the day can no longer fit the complexity and flux of this struggling new world order. The imperial gaze of crass brands of positivism and objective science began to break at the "same time as the collapse of colonialism" (p. 351). Darker bodies were not only speaking truth to power but were now— for better and worse—members of the powerful. Conquergood's project was to unravel the iron thread of the imperial gaze that lacked embodied engagement, stagnated by impenetrable categories, and impervious to generative subaltern performances.

This essay was the harbinger of an oncoming cascade of work advocating an "alternative project" that examined with radical intention the "unfolding human condition" that critical, performance ethnography would illuminate (p. 352). Always the generous teacher and scholar, Conquergood served his readers by providing conceptual frameworks that were all at once clear, relevant, and inspiring. We are called to attend in the most deep and abiding way to an ethnographic encounter with Otherness that demands our whole body. Bodily attending means "shared time and space" in the feeling and sensing contact of flesh to flesh and face to face cotemporality:

> The performance paradigm privileges particular, participatory, dynamic, intimate, precarious, embodied experience grounded in historical process, contingency, and ideology. Another way of saying it is that performance-centered research takes as both subject matter and method the experiencing body situated in time, place, and history. The performance paradigm insists on face-to-face encounters instead of abstractions and reductions. It situates ethnographers within the delicately negotiated and fragile "face-work" that is part of the intricate and nuanced dramaturgy of everyday life. (pp. 358, 359)

Conquergood implores us to recognize what it means to "return to the body" as an ethnographic enterprise: we speak Other names, not just our own categories; we hear Other sounds, not just our own speech; we touch and smell and taste with our body in the co-performance of doing daily what Others do; and, we risk being foolish, or sick, or wrong. The body breathes and listens inside the temporal space with affect and emotion as theory and polemic conjoin to deepen these feelings even more.

If we are willing to understand that subjugated knowledges are always already embodied knowledges, then we can begin to accept the fact that the discourses of history, science, and empiricism that name them are not exclusively held in the written word, but on the very bodies themselves that move symbolically, traditionally, and inventively in the social and cultural performances of their daily lives. Bodies on the borders that dare to traverse the threat of their boundaries necessarily carry their knowledges with them in song, gesture, story, dance, adornments, secrets, etc., that writing can not capture or contain in the breath of a living moment. These performances manifest the alterity of knowledge performed through and located on and in the body. For Conquergood these were utterances of different kinds and categories within subaltern locations that performance ethnography labors to enter:

> For more than three years I have been conducting ethnographic research in one . . . polyglot immigrant neighborhood in inner-city Chicago. More than 50 languages and dialects are spoken by students at the local high school. The "Bilingual Student Roster" displays an exotic [list of names:] Assyrian, Tagalog, Vietnamese, Khmer, Hmong, Malayalam, Gujarati, Lao, Urdu, Cantonese, Greek, Pashto, Thai, Punjabi, Italian, Armenian, Dutch, Turkish, Ibo, Amharic, Slovenian, Farsi, and others. For the first 20 months of fieldwork I lived in an apartment alongside refugees and

immigrant neighbors from Mexico, Puerto Rico, Iraq, Laos, Cambodia, Poland, [and] Lebanon, as well as African-American, Appalachian White, and elderly Jew all living cheek-by-jowl in the same crowded, dilapidated tenement building. (p. 358)

If embodied practices and borderlands are the hallmarks of ethnographic inquiry then performance becomes both a method and an ethical principle. Performance demands that the researcher's body must be cotemporally present and active in a dialogical meeting with the Other—this is *co-performance*. In the last years of his life, Dwight was adamant that we displace the notion of participant-observation with the more precise, body invested, and riskier term co-performance. He regarded participant-observation as a shallow presence that lacked the depth of an invested, heartfelt self with the Other. For Conquergood, "observation" connotes an arrogance of seeing and judgment that co-performance refutes in its being and doing *with* the Other in a more intersubjective and interpersonal engagement:

> The bodily image of learning something "on the pulses" captures the distinctive method of performance-sensitive ethnography. The power dynamic of the research situation changes when the ethnographer moves from the gaze of the distanced and detached observer to the intimate involvement and engagement of "coactivity" or co-performance

with historically situated, named, "unique individuals." (p. 359)

The rise of performance for Dwight was also the rise of a critical, cultural politics of radical empiricism. This "intimate connection" of a fuller embodied engagement with feeling-sensing empirical knowledge was not only what Conquergood argued for but it was the way he lived his life. His ethnographic work was on the ground of being, flesh to flesh, in co-performances that led him to the Ban Vinai Refugee Camp in Thailand, to the Middle East of Palestinian refugees in the Gaza Strip, to the sites of inner city Chicago and urban street gangs, and, finally, to all night vigils and protest gatherings through out this country in opposition to the death penalty.

Dwight Conquergood passed away four months before this writing. In our last conversation over a transatlantic phone call (Dwight was in the hospital in Chicago and I was in West Africa) with clarity and grace he talked about the importance of doing "good work that matters in the world." He felt the world deeply in his strong desire, always, to make it just. The following essay is only one of the many, many legacies Dwight left in his hope for us to do "good work." Dwight loved performance in the way it both simply and complexly draws us into difficult and necessary spaces for the sake of a just world.

Dwight Conquergood conducting field research at Ban Vinai Refugee Camp in Thailand. He is performing with "Mother Clean" of the Ban Vinai Performing Company. The photo is by Lw Vang, 1985.

20

Rethinking Ethnography

Towards a Critical Cultural Politics *

DWIGHT CONQUERGOOD

Critical theory is not a unitary concept. It resembles a loose coalition of interests more than a united front. But whatever it is or is not, one thing seems clear: Critical theory is committed to unveiling the political stakes that anchor cultural practices—research and scholarly practices no less than the everyday. On this point the participants in this forum agree. Yes, critical theory politicizes science and knowledge. Our disagreements arise from how we view (and value) the tension between science/knowledge and politics. Logical empiricists are dedicated to the *eviction* of politics from science. Critical theorists, on the other hand, are committed to the *excavation* of the political underpinnings of all modes of representation, including the scientific.

Ethnography, with its ambivalent meanings as both a method of social science research and a genre of social science text (see Clifford and Marcus, 1986; Van Maanen, 1988), has been the most amenable of the social sciences to post-structuralist critique. It presents a particularly sensitive site for registering the aftershocks of critical theory. No group of scholars is struggling more acutely and productively with the political tensions of research than ethnographers. For ethnography, the undermining of objectivist science came roughly at the same time as the collapse of colonialism. Since then, post-colonial critics have set about unmasking the imperialist underpinnings of anthropology (Asad, 1973; Ashcroft, Griffiths, & Tiffin, 1989; Miller, 1990), the discipline with which ethnography has been closely but not exclusively associated. Clifford Geertz explains (1988, pp. 131–132):

The end of colonialism altered radically the nature of the social relationship between

Conquergood, Dwight. "Rethinking Ethnography." *Communication Monographs* 58.2 (1991): 179–194. Reprinted with permission of National Communication Association.

those who ask and look and those who are asked and looked at. The decline of faith in brute fact, set procedures, and unsituated knowledge in the human sciences, and indeed in scholarship generally, altered no less radically the askers' and lookers' conception of what it was they were trying to do. Imperialism in its classical form, metropoles and possessions, and Scientism in its, impulsions and billiard balls, fell at more or less the same time.

The double fall of scientism and imperialism has been, for progressive ethnographers, a *felix culpa*, a fortunate fall. The ensuing "crisis of representation" (Marcus & Fischer, 1986, p. 7) has induced deep epistemological, methodological, and ethical self-questioning.

Though some assume defensive or nostalgic postures, most ethnographers would agree with Renato Rosaldo's current assessment of the field (1989, p. 37): "The once dominant ideal of a detached observer using neutral language to explain 'raw' data has been displaced by an alternative project that attempts to understand human conduct as it unfolds through time and in relation to its meanings for the actors." Moreover, a vanguard of critical and socially committed ethnographers argues that there is no way out short of a radical rethinking of the research enterprise. I will chart four intersecting themes in the critical rethinking of ethnography: (1) The Return of the Body, (2) Boundaries and Borderlands, (3) The Rise of Performance, and (4) Rhetorical Reflexivity.

RETURN OF THE BODY

Ethnography's distinctive research method, participant-observation fieldwork, privileges the body as a site of knowing. In contrast, most academic disciplines, following Augustine and the Church Fathers, have constructed a Mind/Body hierarchy of knowledge corresponding to the Spirit/Flesh opposition so that mental abstractions and rational thought are

taken as both epistemologically and morally superior to sensual experience, bodily sensations, and the passions. Indeed, the body and the flesh are linked with the irrational, unruly, and dangerous—certainly an inferior realm of experience to be controlled by the higher powers of reason and logic. Further, patriarchal constructions that align women with the body, and men with mental faculties, help keep the mind-body, reason-emotion, objective-subjective, as well as masculine-feminine hierarchies stable.

Nevertheless, the obligatory rite-of-passage for all ethnographers—doing fieldwork—requires getting one's body immersed in the field for a period of time sufficient to enable one to participate inside that culture. Ethnography is an *embodied practice;* it is an intensely sensuous way of knowing. The embodied researcher is the instrument. James Clifford acknowledges (1988, p. 24): "Participant-observation obliges its practitioners to experience, at a bodily as well as an intellectual level, the vicissitudes of translation." In a posthumously published essay, "On Fieldwork," the late Erving Goffman emphasized the corporeal nature of fieldwork (1989, p. 125):

> It's one of getting data, it seems to me, by subjecting yourself, your own body and your own personality, and your own social situation, to the set of contingencies that play upon a set of individuals, . . . so that you are close to them while they are responding to what life does to them.

This active, participatory nature of fieldwork is celebrated by ethnographers when they contrast their "open air" research with the "arm chair" research of more sedentary and cerebral methods.

Ethnographic rigor, disciplinary authority, and professional reputation are established by the length of time, depth of commitment, and risks (bodily, physical, emotional) taken in order to acquire cultural understanding.

Letters of recommendation often refer approvingly to bodily hardships suffered by the dedicated ethnographer—malarial fevers, scarcity of food, long periods of isolation, material discomforts, and so forth, endured in the field.

Bronislaw Malinowski, credited with establishing modern standards of ethnographic fieldwork—whose own practice remains unsurpassed—recommended bodily participation, in addition to observation, as a mode of intensifying cultural understanding (1922/ 1961, pp. 21–22):

> [I]t is good for the Ethnographer sometimes to put aside camera, note book and pencil, and to join in himself in what is going on. He can take part in the natives' games, he can follow them on their visits and walks, sit down and listen and share in their conversations.

Fifty years later, Geertz still affirms the corporeal nature and necessity of fieldwork (1973, p. 23):

> It is with the kind of material produced by long-term, mainly (though not exclusively) qualitative, highly participative, and almost obsessively fine-comb field study in confined contexts that the mega-concepts with which contemporary social science is afflicted . . . can be given the sort of sensible actuality that makes it possible to think not only realistically and concretely *about* them, but, what is more important, creatively and imaginatively *with* them.

Although ethnographic fieldwork privileges the body, published ethnographies typically have repressed bodily experience in favor of abstracted theory and analysis. In the shift from ethnographic method (fieldwork) to ethnographic rhetoric (published monograph), named individuals with distinct personalities and complex life histories are inscribed as "the Bororo" or "the Tikopia." Finely detailed speech and nuanced gesture are summarized flatly: "All the voices of the field have been smoothed into the expository prose of more-or-less interchangeable 'informants' (Clifford, 1988, p. 49). The interpersonal contingencies and experiential give-and-take of fieldwork process congeal on the page into authoritative statement, table, and graph. According to post-colonial feminist critic Trinh T. Minh-ha (1989, p. 56): "It is as if, unvaryingly, every single look, gesture, or utterance has been stained with anthropological discourse. . . ."

Recognition of the bodily nature of fieldwork privileges the processes of communication that constitute the "doing" of ethnography: speaking, listening, and acting together. According to Stephen Tyler (1987, p. 172), the postmodern recovery of the body in fieldwork means the return of speaking, communicating bodies, a "return to the commonsense, plurivocal world of the speaking subject." He pushes this point (1987, p. 171): "Postmodern anthropology is the study of [wo]man—'talking.' Discourse is its object and means." Trinh reminds us that interpersonal communication is grounded in sensual experience (1989, p. 121): "[S]peaking and listening refer to realities that do not involve just the imagination. The speech is seen, heard, smelled, tasted, and touched." When modernist ethnographers systematically record their *observations,* they forget that "seeing is mediated by saying" (Tyler, 1987, p. 171).

Michael Jackson wants to recuperate the body in ethnographic discourse (1989, p. 18), to reestablish "the intimate connection between our bodily experience in the everyday world and our conceptual life." He argues (1989, p. 11): "If we are to find common ground with them [the people we study], we have to open ourselves to modes of sensory and bodily life which, while meaningful to us in our personal lives, tend to get suppressed in our academic discourse." Jackson wants to restore the epistemological and methodological, as well as etymological, connection between experience and empiricism. He names his project "radical empiricism" and positions it within and against "traditional empiricism." What traditional empiricism attempts to control, suspend, or bracket out—"the empirical reality of our personal engagement with and attitude to those others" (1989, p. 34)—radical empiricism privileges as "the intersubjective grounds on which our understanding is constituted" (1989, p. 34):

> The importance of this view for anthropology is that it stresses the ethnographer's *interactions* with those he or she lives with and studies, while urging us to clarify the ways in which our knowledge is grounded in our practical, personal, and participatory experience in the field as much as our detached observations. Unlike traditional empiricism, which draws a definite boundary between observer and observed, between method and object, radical empiricism denies the validity of such cuts and makes the *interplay* between these domains the focus of its interest. (1989, p. 3)

The project of radical empiricism changes ethnography's traditional approach from Other-as-theme to Other-as-interlocutor (Theunissen, 1984), and represents a shift from monologue to dialogue, from information to communication.

Jackson provocatively argues that traditional ethnographic "pretenses" about detached observation and scientific method reveal anxiety about the uncontrollable messiness of any truly interesting fieldwork situation (1989, p. 3):

> Indeed, given the arduous conditions of fieldwork, the ambiguity of conversations in a foreign tongue, differences of temperament, age, and gender between ourselves and our informants, and the changing theoretical models we are heir to, it is likely that "objectivity" serves more as a magical token, bolstering our sense of self in disorienting situations, than as a scientific method for describing those situations as they really are.

The radical empiricist's response to the vulnerabilities and vicissitudes of fieldwork is honesty, humility, self-reflexivity, and an acknowledgement of the interdependence and reciprocal role-playing between knower and known:

> In this process we put ourselves on the line; we run the risk of having our sense of ourselves as different and distanced from the people we study dissolve, and with it all our pretensions to a supraempirical position, a knowledge that gets us above and beyond the temporality of human existence. (Jackson, 1989, p. 4)

Johannes Fabian focuses on temporality as a strategy for bringing back the body-in-time in ethnographic discourse, and with it the body politic. In a trenchant rhetorical critique of ethnographic texts (1983, p. 148), he identifies the "denial of coevalness" as a strategy for "keeping Anthropology's Other in another time" and thereby keeping "others" in their marginal place. Coevalness is the experience of cotemporality, the recognition of actively sharing the same time, the acknowledgement of others as contemporaries. Fabian argues forcefully that ethnography manifests "schizochronic tendencies" (1983, p. 37). On the one hand, the discipline insists on the coeval experience of fieldwork as the source of ethnographic knowledge, and on the other hand, this coevalness is denied in professional discourse that temporally distances others through labels such as "tribal," "traditional," "ancient," "animistic," "primitive," "preliterate," "neolithic," "underdeveloped," or the slightly more polite, "developing," and so forth. Clifford (1988, p. 16) calls this tactic a "temporal setup." In a deeply contradictory way, ethnographers go to great lengths to become cotemporal with others during fieldwork but then deny in writing that these others with whom they lived are their contemporaries. Fabian warns (1983, p. 33): "These disjunctions between experience and science, research and writing, will continue to be a festering epistemological sore."

More problematically, he reveals (Fabian, 1983, p. 144) how the expansionist campaigns of colonialist-imperialist policies "required Time to accommodate the schemes of a one-way history: progress, development, modernity (and their negative mirror images: stagnation, underdevelopment, tradition). In short, *geopolitics* has its ideological foundations in *chronopolitics.*" Anthropology is complicit with imperialism and the ideology of progress when it rhetorically distances the Other in Time.

For Fabian, the way to prevent temporal reifications of other cultures is for ethnographers to rethink themselves as communicators, not scientists. He states this fundamental point in strong terms (1983, p. 71): "Only as communicative praxis does ethnography carry the promise of yielding new knowledge about another culture." Ethnographers must recognize "that fieldwork is a form of communicative interaction with an Other, one that must be carried out coevally, on the basis of shared intersubjective Time and intersocietal contemporaneity" (1983, p. 148). He privileges communication because "for human communication to occur, coevalness has to be *created*. Communication is, ultimately, about creating shared Time" (1983, pp. 30–31). Whereas Paul Ricoeur (1971) wanted to fix the temporal flow and leakage of speaking, to rescue "the said" from "the saying," contemporary ethnographers struggle to recuperate "the saying from the said," to shift their enterprise from nouns to verbs, from mimesis to kinesis, from textualized space to co-experienced time.

This rethinking of ethnography as primarily about speaking and listening, instead of observing, has challenged the visualist bias of positivism with talk about voices, utterances, intonations, multivocality. Sight and observation go with space, and the spatial practices of division, separation, compartmentalization, and surveillance. According to Rosaldo (1989, p. 41), "the eye of ethnography" is connected to "the I of imperialism." Sight and surveillance depend on detachment and distance. Getting perspective on something entails withdrawal from intimacy. Everyday parlance equates objectivity with aloofness. Being "too close" is akin to losing perspective and lacking judgement.

Metaphors of sound, on the other hand, privilege temporal process, proximity, and incorporation. Listening is an interiorizing experience, a gathering together, a drawing in, whereas observation sizes up exteriors. The communicative praxis of speaking and listening, conversation, demands copresence even as it decenters the categories of knower and known. Vulnerability and self-disclosure are enabled through conversations. Closure, on the other hand, is constituted by the gaze. The return of the body as a recognized method for attaining "vividly felt insight into the life of other people" (Trinh, 1989, p. 123) shifts the emphasis from space to time, from sight and vision to sound and voice, from text to performance, from authority to vulnerability.

BOUNDARIES AND BORDERLANDS

Geertz's well-known "Blurred Genres" essay (1983, pp. 19–35) charts ethnography's ambivalent participation in the postmodern redistribution of analytical foci from center to periphery, delimitation to dispersal, whole to fragment, metropole to margin. To be sure, ethnographers for a long time have been situated more characteristically in the peripheral village than in the metropolitan center. They have been predisposed professionally to seek out the frontier and hinterlands, the colony rather than the capital. But this preoccupation with marginal cultures that obliged them figuratively and literally to live on the boundary did not prevent them from still seeing identity and culture, self and other, as discrete, singular, integral, and stable concepts. Once they crossed the border and pitched their tent on the edge of the encampment, they confidently set about describing "the Trobrianders," or "the Nuer," or "the ghetto," interpreting these cultures as distinct, coherent, whole ways of life. In so doing, they centralized the peripheral instead of de-centering the "metropolitan typifications" that they carried inside their heads (Rosaldo, 1989, p. 207).

All that confidence in continuous traditions and innocent encounters with pristine cultures has been shattered in our post-colonial epoch. Borders bleed, as much as they contain. Instead of dividing lines to be patrolled or transgressed, boundaries are now understood as criss-crossing sites inside the post-modern subject. Difference is resituated within, instead of beyond, the self. Inside and outside distinctions, like genres, blur and wobble. Nothing seems truer now than Trinh's pithy insight (1989, p. 94): "Despite our desperate, eternal attempt to separate, contain, and mend, categories always leak."

Rosaldo believes that contemporary geopolitics, including decolonization and multinational corporations, requires thinking about boundaries not simply as barriers but as bridges and membranes (1989, p. 217): "All of us inhabit an interdependent late-twentieth-century world marked by borrowing and lending across porous national and cultural boundaries that are saturated with inequality, power, and domination." Further, the border-crossings emblematic of our postmodern world challenge ethnography to rethink its project: "If ethnography once imagined it could describe discrete cultures, it now contends with boundaries that crisscross over a field at once fluid and saturated with power. In a world where 'open borders' appear more salient than 'closed communities,' one wonders how to define a project for cultural studies" (Rosaldo, 1989, p. 45). Rosaldo argues that the research agenda needs to move from centers to "borderlands," "zones of difference," and "busy intersections" where many identities and interests articulate with multiple others (1989, pp. 17, 28).

The major epistemological consequence of displacing the idea of solid centers and unified wholes with borderlands and zones of contest is a rethinking of identity and culture as constructed and relational, instead of ontologically given and essential. This rethinking privileges metonym, "reasoning part-to-part" over synecdoche, "reasoning part-to-whole" (Tyler, 1987, p. 151); it features syntax over semantics. Meaning is contested and struggled for in the interstices, *in between* structures. Identity is invented and contingent, not autonomous: "'I' is, therefore, not a unified subject, a fixed identity, or that solid mass covered with layers of superficialities one has gradually to peel off before one can see its true face. 'I' is, itself, *infinite layers*" (Trinh, 1989, p. 94).

Clifford argues (1988, p. 10) that much of non-western historical experience has been "hemmed in by concepts of continuous tradition and the unified self." The presuppositions of pattern, continuity, coherence, and unity characteristic of classic ethnography may have had more to do with the West's ideological commitment to individualism than with on-the-ground cultural practices. "I argue," says Clifford (1988, p. 10), "that identity, ethnographically considered, must always be mixed, relational, and inventive." The idea of the person shifts from that of a fixed, autonomous self to a polysemic site of articulation for multiple identities and voices.

From the boundary perspective, identity is more like a performance in process than a postulate, premise, or originary principle. From his historical study of the "colonial assault" on Melanesia, and his 1977 fieldwork study of a courtroom trial in Massachusetts where land ownership by Mashpee Native Americans was contingent upon "proof" of tribal identity, Clifford (1988, p. 9) came to understand identity as provisional, "not as an archaic survival but as an ongoing process, politically contested and historically unfinished." In our postmodern world the refugee, exile, has become an increasingly visible sign of geopolitical turbulence as well as the emblematic figure for a more general feeling of displacement, dispersal, what Clifford describes

(1988, p. 9) as "a pervasive condition of off-centeredness. . . ."

Betwixt and between worlds, suspended between a shattered past and insecure future, refugees and other displaced people must create an "inventive poetics of reality" (Clifford, 1988, p. 6) for recollecting, recontextualizing, and refashioning their identities. The refugee condition epitomizes a postmodern existence of border-crossings and life on the margins. With displacement, upheaval, unmooring, come the terror and potentiality of flux, improvisation, and creative recombinations. Refugees, exiles, homeless people, and other nomads enact the post-structuralist idea of "putting culture into motion" (Rosaldo, 1989, p. 91) through experiences that are both violent and regenerative. Taking the Caribbean as an illuminating example, Clifford notes (1988, p. 15) that its history is one of "degradation, mimicry, violence, and blocked possibilities," but it is also "rebellious, syncretic, and creative."

In *The Practice of Everyday Life*, Michel de Certeau (1984, p. 30) celebrates the interventions of marginal people whose creativity, "the art of making do," gets finely honed from living on the edge, a borderlands life:

> Thus a North African living in Paris or Boubaix (France) insinuates *into* the system imposed on him by the construction of a low-income housing development or of the French language the ways of 'dwelling' (in a house or a language) peculiar to his native Kabylia. He superimposes them and, by that combination, creates for himself a space in which he can find *ways of using* the constraining order of the place or of the language. Without leaving the place where he has no choice but to live and which lays down its law for him, he establishes within it a degree of *plurality* and creativity. By an art of being in between, he draws unexpected results from his situation.

My own fieldwork with refugees and migrants in Thailand, the Gaza Strip, and inner-city Chicago resonates deeply with Clifford's observations (1988, p. 16): "Many traditions, languages, cosmologies, and values are lost, some literally murdered; but much has simultaneously been invented and revived in complex, oppositional contexts. If the victims of progress and empire are weak, they are seldom passive."

There are implications for rhetoric and communication studies from ethnography's current interest in boundary phenomena and border negotiations. Communication becomes even more urgent and necessary in situations of displacement, exile, and erasure. Trinh, a Vietnamese-American woman, speaking as an exile to other exiles, articulates the difficulty and urgency of expression for all refugees and displaced people (1989, p. 80):

> You who understand the dehumanization of forced removal-relocation-reeducation-redefinition, the humiliation of having to falsify your own reality, your voice—you know. And often cannot *say* it. You try and keep on trying to unsay it, for if you don't, they will not fail to fill in the blanks on your behalf, and you will be said.

The *discourse of displacement* is a project that beckons rhetorical and communication scholars.

And if the increasingly pervasive feeling of discontinuity and finding oneself "off center among scattered traditions" (Clifford, 1988, p. 3) incites us to speak, then we must draw on *topoi* from among multiple discursive styles and traditions. Jackson notes the intertextual and heteroglossic nature of discourse (1989, p. 176): "Reviewing the historical mutability of discourse, I am also mindful that no one episteme ever completely supercedes another. The historical matrix in which our present discourse is embedded contains other discursive styles and strategies, and makes use of them." Never has the rhetorical canon of *inventio* taken on more emphatic meaning than in the current rethinking of culture and ethos (see Wagner, 1980).

Cities throughout the United States have become sites of extraordinary diversity as refugees and immigrants, increasingly from the hemispheres of the South and the East, pour into inner-city neighborhoods. Rosaldo makes the point that one does not have to go to the "Third World" to encounter culture in the borderlands (1989, p. 28): "Cities throughout the world today increasingly include minorities defined by race, ethnicity, language, class, religion, and sexual orientation. Encounters with 'difference' now pervade modern everyday life in urban settings." For more than three years I have been conducting ethnographic research in one of these polyglot immigrant neighborhoods in inner-city Chicago. More than 50 languages and dialects are spoken by students at the local high school. The "Bilingual Student Roster" displays an exotic array of languages that in addition to Spanish, Korean, and Arabic, includes Assyrian, Tagalog, Vietnamese, Khmer, Hmong, Malayalam, Gujarati, Lao, Urdu, Cantonese, Greek, Pashto, Thai, Punjabi, Italian, Armenian, Dutch, Turkish, Ibo, Amharic, Slovenian, Farsi, and others. For the first 20 months of fieldwork I lived in an apartment alongside refugee and immigrant neighbors from Mexico, Puerto Rico, Iraq, Laos, Cambodia, Poland, Lebanon, as well as African-American, Appalachian White, and elderly Jew all living cheek-by-jowl in the same crowded, dilapidated tenement building. The local street gang with which I work reflects the same polyglot texture of the neighborhood. It is called the Latin Kings, originally a Puerto Rican gang, but the current members include Assyrian, African-American, Puerto Rican, Guatemalan, Salvadoran, Vietnamese, Lao, Korean, Palestinian, Filipino, Mexican, White, and others (Conquergood, Friesma, Hunter, & Mansbridge, 1990).

Few phrases have more resonance in contemporary ethnography—and with my own fieldwork—than Bakhtin's powerful affirmation (1986, p. 2) that "the most intense and productive life of culture takes place on the boundaries. . . ."

THE RISE OF PERFORMANCE

With renewed appreciation for boundaries, border-crossings, process, improvisation, contingency, multiplex identities, and the embodied nature of fieldwork practice, many ethnographers have turned to a performance-inflected vocabulary. "In the social sciences," Geertz observes (1983, p. 22), "the analogies are coming more and more from the contrivances of cultural performance than from those of physical manipulation." No one has done more than Victor Turner to open up space in ethnography for performance, to move the field away from preoccupations with universal system, structure, form, and towards particular practices, people, and performances. A dedicated ethnographer, Turner wanted the professional discourse of cultural studies to capture the struggle, passion, and praxis of village life that he so relished in the field. The language of drama and performance gave him a way of thinking and talking about people as actors who creatively play, improvise, interpret, and re-present roles and scripts. In a rhetorical masterstroke, Turner (1986, p. 81) subversively redefined the fundamental terms of discussion in ethnography by defining humankind as *homo performans*, humanity as performer, a culture-inventing, social-performing, self-making and self-transforming creature. Turner was drawn to the conceptual lens of performance because it focused on humankind alive, the creative, playful, provisional, imaginative, articulate expressions of ordinary people grounded in the challenge of making a life in this village, that valley, and inspired by the struggle for meaning.

Distinguishing characteristics of performance-sensitive research emerge from Turner's detailed and elaborated work on social drama and cultural performance. The performance paradigm privileges particular, participatory, dynamic, intimate, precarious, embodied experience grounded in historical process, contingency, and ideology. Another way of saying it is that performance-centered research takes as both its subject matter and method the experiencing body situated in time, place, and history. The performance paradigm insists on face-to-face encounters instead of abstractions and reductions. It situates ethnographers within the delicately negotiated and fragile "face-work" that is part of the intricate and nuanced dramaturgy of everyday life (see Goffman, 1967).

Turner appreciated the heuristics of embodied experience because he understood how social dramas must be acted out and rituals performed in order to be meaningful, *and* he realized how the ethnographer must be a co-performer in order to understand those embodied meanings. In one of his earlier works (1975, pp. 28–29) he enunciated the role of the performing body as a hermeneutical agency both for the researcher as well as the researched:

> The religious ideas and processes I have just mentioned belong to the domain of performance, their power derived from the participation of the living people who use them. My counsel, therefore, to investigators of ritual processes would be to learn them in the first place "on their pulses," in coactivity with their enactors, having beforehand shared for a considerable time much of the people's daily life and gotten to know them not only as players of social roles, but as unique individuals, each with a style and a soul of his or her own. Only by these means will the investigator become aware. . . .

The bodily image of learning something "on the pulses" captures the distinctive method of performance-sensitive ethnography. The power dynamic of the research situation changes when the ethnographer moves from the gaze of the distanced and detached observer to the intimate involvement and engagement of "coactivity" or co-performance

with historically situated, named, "unique individuals."

The performance paradigm can help ethnographers recognize "the limitations of literacy" and critique the textualist bias of western civilization (Jackson, 1989). Geertz (1973, p. 452) enunciates the textual paradigm in his famous phrase: "The culture of a people is an ensemble of texts, themselves ensembles, which the anthropologist strains to read over the shoulders of those to whom they properly belong." In other words, the ethnographer is construed as a displaced, somewhat awkward reader of texts. Jackson vigorously critiques this ethnographic textualism (1989, p. 184):

> By fetishizing texts, it divides—as the advent of literacy itself did—readers from authors, and separates both from the world. The idea that "there is nothing outside the text" may be congenial to someone whose life is confined to academe, but it sounds absurd in the village worlds where anthropologists carry out their work, where people negotiate meaning in face-to-face interactions, not as individual minds but as embodied social beings. In other words, textualism tends to ignore the flux of human relationships, the ways meanings are created intersubjectively as well as "intertextually," embodied in gestures as well as in words, and connected to political, moral, and aesthetic interests.

Though possessed of a long historical commitment to the spoken word, rhetoric and communication suffer from this same valorizing of inscribed texts. A recent essay in the *Quarterly Journal of Speech* (Brummett, 1990, p. 71; emphasis mine) provides a stunning example of the field's extreme textualism: "Such a [disciplinary] grounding can only come about in the moment of methodological commitment *when someone sits down with a transcript of discourse* and attempts to explain it to students or colleagues—*in that moment we become scholars of communication.*" In the quest for intellectual respectability through disciplinary rigor, some communication and rhetorical scholars have narrowed their focus to language, particularly those aspects of language that can be spatialized on the page, or measured and counted, to the exclusion of embodied meanings that are accessible through ethnographic methods of "radical empiricism" (Jackson, 1989).

The linguistic and textualist bias of speech communication has blinded many scholars to the preeminently rhetorical nature of cultural performance—ritual, ceremony, celebration, festival, parade, pageant, feast, and so forth. It is not just in non-western cultures, but in many so-called "modern" communities that cultural performance functions as a special form of public address, rhetorical agency:

> [C]ultural performances are not simple reflectors or expressions of culture or even of changing culture but may themselves be active agencies of change, representing the eye by which culture sees itself and the drawing board on which creative actors sketch out what they believe to be more apt or interesting "designs for living.". . . Performative reflexivity is a condition in which a sociocultural group, or its most perceptive members acting representatively, turn, bend or reflect back upon themselves, upon the relations, actions, symbols, meanings, codes, roles, statuses, social structures, ethical and legal rules, and other sociocultural components which make up their public "selves." (Turner, 1986, p. 24)

Through cultural performances many people both construct and participate in "public" life. Particularly for poor and marginalized people denied access to middle-class "public" forums, cultural performance becomes the venue for "public discussion" of vital issues central to their communities, as well as an arena for gaining visibility and staging their identity. Nancy Fraser's (1990, p. 67) concept of "subaltern counterpublics" is very useful: " . . . arenas where members of subordinated social groups invent and circulate counterdiscourses, which in turn permit them to formulate oppositional interpretations of their identities, interests, and needs."

What every ethnographer understands, however, is that the mode of "discussion," the discourse, is not always and exclusively verbal: Issues and attitudes are expressed and contested in dance, music, gesture, food, ritual artifact, symbolic action, as well as words. Cultural performances are not simply epideictic spectacles: Investigated historically within their political contexts, they are profoundly deliberative occasions (see Fernandez, 1986).

Although cultural performances often frame a great deal of speech-making—formal oratory, stylized recitation and chant, as well as backstage talk and informal conversation—it would be a great mistake for a communication researcher simply "to sit down with a transcript of discourse" and privilege words over other channels of meaning. Turner (1986, p. 23) emphatically resists valorizing language or studying any of the multiple codes of performed meaning extricated from their complex interactions: "This is an important point—rituals, dramas, and other performative genres are often orchestrations of media, not expressions in a single medium." There is a complex interplay, for example, between song, gesture, facial expressions, and the burning of incense, and even incense has different meanings when it is burned at different times, and there are different kinds of incense. "The master-of-ceremonies, priest, producer, director creates art from the ensemble of media and codes, just as a conductor in the single genre of classical music blends and opposes the sounds of the different instruments to produce an often unrepeatable effect" (Turner, 1986, p. 23).

Turner encourages ethnographers to study the interplay of performance codes, focusing on their syntactic relationships rather than their semantics (1986, pp. 23–24):

> It is worth pointing out, too, that it is not, as some structuralists have argued, a matter of emitting the *same* message in different media and codes, the better to underline it by redundancy. The "same" message in different media is really a set of subtly variant

messages, each medium contributing its own generic message to the message conveyed through it. The result is something like a hall of mirrors—magic mirrors, each interpreting as well as reflecting the images beamed to it, and flashed from one to the others.

The polysemic nature of cultural performances "makes of these genres flexible and nuanced instruments capable of carrying and communicating many messages at once, even of subverting on one level what it appears to be "saying" on another" (Turner, 1986, p. 24). The performance paradigm is an alternative to the atemporal, decontextualized, flattering approach of text-positivism.

Rethinking the "world as text" to the "world as performance" opens up new questions that can be clustered around five intersecting planes of analyses:

1. *Performance and Cultural Process.* What are the conceptual consequences of thinking about culture as a *verb* instead of a *noun,* process instead of product? Culture as unfolding performative invention instead of reified system, structure, or variable? What happens to our thinking about performance when we move it outside of Aesthetics and situate it at the center of lived experience?

2. *Performance and Ethnographic Praxis.* What are the methodological implications of thinking about fieldwork as the collaborative performance of an enabling fiction between observer and observed, knower and known? How does thinking about fieldwork as performance differ from thinking about fieldwork as the collection of data? Reading of texts? How does the performance model shape the conduct of fieldwork? Relationship with the people? Choices made in the field? Positionality of the researcher?

3. *Performance and Hermeneutics.* What kinds of knowledge are privileged or displaced when performed experience becomes a way of knowing, a method of critical inquiry, a mode of understanding? What are the epistemological and ethical entailments of performing ethnographic texts and fieldnotes? What are the range and varieties of performance modes and styles that can enable interpretation and understanding?

4. *Performance and Scholarly Representation.* What are the rhetorical problematics of performance as a complementary or alternative form of "publishing" research? What are the differences between reading an analysis of fieldwork data, and hearing the voices from the field interpretively filtered through the voice of the researcher? For the listening audience of peers? For the performing ethnographer? For the people whose lived experience is the subject matter of the ethnography? What about enabling the people themselves to perform their own experience? What are the epistemological underpinnings and institutional practices that would legitimate performance as a complementary form of research publication?

5. *The Politics of Performance.* What is the relationship between performance and power? How does performance reproduce, enable, sustain, challenge, subvert, critique, and naturalize ideology? How do performances simultaneously reproduce and resist hegemony? How does performance accommodate and contest domination?

The most work has been done in Numbers One, Two, and Five, particularly One. Although we still need to think more deeply and radically about the performative nature of culture, Erving Goffman, Kenneth Burke, Dell Hymes, and a host of other social theorists have already set the stage. The expansive reach of conceptualizing performance as the agency for constituting and reconstituting culture, leads from performance as Agency to performance as ultimate Scene: "All the world's a stage." The popularity of Shakespeare's adage notwithstanding, we scarcely have begun to unpack and understand the radical potential of that idea.

Numbers Three and especially Four are the most deeply subversive and threatening to the text-bound structure of the academy. It is one thing to talk about performance as a model for cultural process, as a heuristic for understanding social life, as long as that performance-sensitive talk eventually gets "written up." The intensely performative and bodily experience of fieldwork is redeemed through writing. The hegemony of inscribed texts is never challenged by fieldwork because, after all is said and done, the final word is on paper. Print publication is the telos of fieldwork. It is interesting to note that even the most radical deconstructions still take place on the page. "Performance as a Form of Scholarly Representation" challenges the domination of textualism.

Turner (1986, pp. 139–155) advocated, practiced, and wrote about performance as a critical method for interpreting and intensifying fieldwork data. It is quite another thing, politically, to move performance from hermeneutics to a form of scholarly representation. That move strikes at the heart of academic politics and issues of scholarly authority. Talal Asad points in this direction (1986, p. 159):

> If Benjamin was right in proposing that translation may require not a mechanical reproduction of the original but a harmonization with its *intentio*, it follows that there is no reason why this should be done only in the same mode. Indeed, it could be argued that "translating" an alien form of life, another culture, is not always done best through the representational discourse of ethnography, that under certain conditions a dramatic performance, the execution of a dance, or the playing of a piece of music might be more apt.

If post-structuralist thought and the post-modern moment continue to open up received categories and established canons, more of this experimentation with scholarly form might happen. If the Performance Paradigm simply is pitted against the Textual Paradigm, then its radical force will be coopted by yet another either/or binary construction that ultimately reproduces modernist thinking. The Performance Paradigm will be most useful if it decenters, without discarding, texts. I do not imagine life in a university without books, nor do I have any wish to stop writing myself. But I do want to keep thinking about what gets lost and muted in texts. And I want to think about performance as a complement, alternative, supplement, and critique of inscribed texts. Following Turner and others, I want to keep opening up space for nondiscursive forms, and encouraging research and writing practices that are performance-sensitive.

RHETORICAL REFLEXIVITY

Far from displacing texts, contemporary ethnography is extremely interested in and self-conscious about its own text-making practices. There is widespread recognition of "the fact that ethnography is, from beginning to end, enmeshed in writing" (Clifford, 1988, p. 25). These writings are not innocent descriptions through which the other is transparently revealed. "It is more than ever crucial for different peoples to form complex concrete images of one another," Clifford affirms (1988, p. 23), "as well as of the relationships of knowledge and power that connect them; but no sovereign scientific method or ethical stance can guarantee the truth of such images. They are constituted—the critique of colonial modes of representation has shown at least this much—in specific historical relations of dominance and dialogue." Geertz (1988, p. 141) argues that even "the pretense of looking at the world directly, as though through a one-way screen, seeing others as they really are when only God is looking . . . is itself a rhetorical strategy, a mode of persuasion."

Ethnography is being rethought in fundamentally rhetorical terms. Many of the most influential books recently published in ethnography are meta-rhetorical critiques. It seems that everyone in ethnography nowadays is a rhetorical critic. Many ethnographers now believe that disciplinary authority is a matter of rhetorical strategy not scientific method. Geertz is perhaps most blunt about the essentially rhetorical nature of ethnography (1988, pp. 143–144):

> The capacity to persuade readers . . . that what they are reading is an authentic account by someone personally acquainted with how life proceeds in some place, at some time, among some group, is the basis upon which anything else ethnography seeks to do . . . finally rests. The textual connection of the Being Here and the Being There sides of anthropology, the imaginative construction of a common ground between the Written At and the Written About . . . is the *fons et origo* of whatever power anthropology has to convince anyone of anything—not theory, not method, not even the aura of the professorial chair, consequential as these last may be.

Much of the current rethinking of ethnography has been sobered and empowered by vigorous rhetorical critique of anthropological discourse.

Geertz is foremost among ethnography's practicing rhetorical critics. His rhetorical criticism of E.E. Evans-Pritchard's (E-P) ethnographic texts is exemplary (1988). He identifies E-P's stylistic token as "drastic clarity" (1988, p. 68) that translates onto the page as "a string of clean, well-lighted judgements, unconditional statements so perspicuously presented that only the invincibly uninformed will think to resist them," a sort of "first-strike assertiveness" (1988, p. 63). The rhetorical questions Geertz (1988, p. 64) puts to E-P's texts are: "How (why? in what way? of what?) does all this resolute informing inform?" His "deep reading" of E-P yields these insights (1988, p. 64):

> *How he does it:* The outstanding characteristic of E-P's approach to ethnographic exposition and the main source of his persuasive power is his enormous capacity to construct visualizable representations of cultural phenomena—anthropological transparencies. *What he does:* The main effect, and the main intent, of this magic lantern ethnography is to demonstrate that the established frames of social perception, those upon which we ourselves instinctively rely, are fully adequate to whatever oddities the transparencies may turn out to picture.

According to Geertz (1988, p. 66) E-P produces a "see-er's rhetoric." With E-P's texts, like all rhetorical practice, "the way of saying is the what of saying" (1988, p. 68).

At a deep level, Geertz insightfully notes (1988, p. 70), E-P's discussion of the Nuer and the Azande underwrite his own cultural ethos as much as they illuminate the other:

> . . . it validates the ethnographer's form of life at the same time as it justifies those of his subjects—and that it does the one by doing the other. The adequacy of the cultural categories of, in this case, university England, to provide a frame of intelligible reasonings, creditable values, and familiar motivations for such oddities as poison oracles, ghost marriages, blood feuds, and cucumber sacrifices recommends those categories as of somehow more than parochial importance. Whatever personal reasons, E-P may have had for being so extraordinarily anxious to picture Africa as a logical and prudential place—orderly, straightforward and level-headed, firmly modeled and open to view—in doing so he constructed a forceful argument for the general authority of a certain conception of life. If it could undarken Africa, it could undarken anything.

By bringing "Africans into a world conceived is deeply English terms" he thereby confirmed "the dominion of those terms" (1988, p. 70).

Geertz as rhetorical critic moves beyond formalist analysis and situates ethnographic texts within their distinctive institutional constraints and engendering professional practices (1988, pp. 129–130):

However far from the groves of academe anthropologists seek out their subjects—a shelved beach in Polynesia, a charred plateau in Amazonia; Akobo, Meknes, Panther Burn—they write their accounts with the world of lecterns, libraries, blackboards, and seminars all about them. This is the world that produces anthropologists, that licenses them to do the kind of work they do, and within which the kind of work they do must find a place if it is to count as worth attention. In itself, Being There is a postcard experience ('I've been to Katmandu—have you?'). It is Being Here, a scholar among scholars, that gets your anthropology read . . . published, reviewed, cited, taught.

Geertz weights the Being Here writing it down side of the axis. To be sure, ethnography on the page constrains and shapes performance in the field. But it is also true, I believe, that experiential performance sometimes resists, exceeds, and overwhelms the constraints and strictures of writing. It is the task of rhetorical critics to seek out these sites of tension, displacement, and contradiction between the Being There of performed experience and the Being Here of written texts.

This rhetorical self-reflexivity has helped politicize ethnography: "The gap between engaging others where they are and representing them where they aren't, always immense but not much noticed, has suddenly become extremely visible. What once seemed only technically difficult, getting "their" lives into "our" works, has turned morally, politically, even epistemologically, delicate" (Geertz, 1988, p. 130). Ethnographic authority is the empowering alignment between rhetorical strategy and political ideology. Once shielded by the mask of science, ethnographers now have become acutely aware of the sources of their persuasive power (Geertz, 1988, pp. 148–149):

What it hasn't been, and, propelled by the moral and intellectual self-confidence of Western Civilization, hasn't so much had to be, is aware of the sources of its power. If it is

now to prosper, with that confidence shaken, it must become aware. Attention to how it gets its effects and what those are, to anthropology on the page, is no longer a side issue, dwarfed by problems of method and issues of theory. It . . . is rather close to the heart of the matter.

Trinh (1989, p. 43) enacts this struggle towards self-reflexive awareness of textual power in her book subtitled "Writing Postcoloniality and Feminism": " . . . what is exposed in this text is the inscription and de-scription of a non-unitary female subject of color through her engagement, therefore also disengagement, with master discourses."

It is ironic that the discipline of communication has been relatively unreflexive about the rhetorical construction of its own disciplinary authority. It would be illuminating to critique the rhetorical expectations and constraints on articles published in the *Quarterly Journal of Speech,* or *Communication Monographs.* What kinds of knowledge, and their attendant discursive styles, get privileged, legitimated, or displaced? How does knowledge about communication get constructed? What counts as an interesting question about human communication? What are the tacitly observed boundaries—the range of appropriateness—regarding the substance, methods, and discursive styles of communication scholarship? And, most importantly for critical theorists, what configuration of socio-political interests does communication scholarship serve? How does professionally authorized knowledge about communication articulate with relations of power? About the connection between a field of knowledge and relations of power, Michel Foucault (1979, p. 27) offers this sobering insight: " . . . power produces knowledge . . . ; power and knowledge directly imply one another; . . . there is no power relation without the correlative constitution of a field of knowledge, nor any knowledge that does not presuppose and constitute at the same time power relations."

NOTE

*I borrow the term "critical cultural politics" from James Clifford (1988, p. 147).

REFERENCES

Asad, T. (Ed.). (1973). *Anthropology and the colonial encounter*. London: Ithaca Press.

Asad, T. (1986). The concept of cultural translation in British social anthropology. In J. Clifford & G. Marcus (Eds.), *Writing culture: The poetics and politics of ethnography* (pp. 141–164). Berkeley: University of California Press.

Ashcroft, B., Griffiths, G., & Tiffin, H. (1989). *The empire writes back: Theory and practice in post-colonial literatures*. New York: Routledge.

Bakhtin, M. (1986). *Speech genres* (C. Emerson & M. Holquist, Eds.; V. McGee, Trans.). Austin: University of Texas Press.

Brummett, B. (1990). A eulogy for epistemic rhetoric. *Quarterly Journal of Speech, 76,* 69–72.

Clifford, J. (1988). *Predicament of culture*. Cambridge, MA: Harvard University Press.

Clifford, J., & Marcus, G. (Eds.). (1986). *Writing culture: The poetics and politics of ethnography*. Berkeley: University of California Press.

Conquergood, D., Friesma, P., Hunter, A., & Mansbridge, J. (1990). *Dispersed ethnicity and community integration: Newcomers and established residents in the Albany Park area of Chicago*. Evanston, IL: Center for Urban Affairs and Policy Research, Northwestern University.

de Certeau, M. (1984). *The practice of everyday life* (S. Rendall, Trans.). Berkeley: University of California Press. (Original work published 1974)

Fabian, J. (1983). *Time and the other: How anthropology makes its object*. New York: Columbia University Press.

Fernandez, J. (1986). *Persuasions and performances: The play of tropes in culture*. Bloomington: Indiana University Press.

Fraser, N. (1990). Rethinking the public sphere: A contribution to the critique of actually existing democracy. *Social Text, 25/26,* 56–80.

Foucault, M. (1979). *Discipline and punish: The birth of the prison* (A. Sheridan, Trans.). New York: Vintage Books. (Original work published 1975)

Geertz, C. (1973). *Interpretation of cultures*. New York: Basic Books.

Geertz, C. (1983). *Local knowledge: Further essays in interpretive anthropology*. New York: Basic Books.

Geertz, C. (1988). *Works and lives: The anthropologist as author*. Palo Alto, CA: Stanford University Press.

Goffman, E. (1967). *Interaction ritual: Essays on face-to-face behavior*. New York: Anchor Books.

Goffman, E. (1989). On fieldwork. *Journal of Contemporary Ethnography, 18,* 123–132.

Jackson, M. (1989). *Paths toward a clearing: Radical empiricism and ethnographic inquiry*. Bloomington: Indiana University Press.

Malinowski, B. (1961). *Argonauts of the western Pacific*. New York: E. P. Dutton. (Original work published 1922).

Marcus, G., & Fischer, M. (1986). *Anthropology as cultural critique: An experimental moment in the human sciences*. Chicago: University of Chicago Press.

Miller, C. (1990). *Theories of Africans: Francophone literature and anthropology in Africa*. Chicago: University of Chicago Press.

Ricoeur, P. (1971). The model of the text: Meaningful action considered as a text. *Social Research, 38,* 529–562.

Rosaldo, R. (1989). *Culture and truth: The remaking of social analysis*. Boston: Beacon.

Theunissen, M. (1984). *The other: Studies in the social ontology of Husserl, Heidegger, Sartre, and Buber*. Cambridge, MA: MIT Press.

Trinh, T. M. (1989). *Woman, native, other: Writing postcoloniality and feminism*. Bloomington: Indiana University Press.

Turner, V. (1975). *Revelation and divination in Ndembu ritual*. Ithaca, NY: Cornell University Press.

Turner, V. (1986). *The anthropology of performance*. New York: PAJ Publications.

Tyler, S. (1987). *The unspeakable: Discourse, dialogue, and rhetoric in the postmodern world*. Madison: University of Wisconsin Press.

Van Maanen, J. (1988). *Tales from the field: On writing ethnography*. Chicago: University of Chicago Press.

Wagner, R. (1980). *The invention of culture* (Rev. ed.). Chicago: University of Chicago Press.

21

Ethnography and the Politics of Adaptation

Leon Forrest's Divine Days

DEREK GOLDMAN

To live means to participate in dialogue: to ask questions, to heed, to respond, to agree, and so forth. In this dialogue a person participates wholly and throughout his whole life: with his eyes, lips, hands, soul, spirit, with his whole body and deeds.

—Mikhail Bakhtin (1984, p. 293)

The things that I loved in life and wanted to convert and transform into literature were themselves filled with the yeast of chaos. There was a tension between discipline and chaos. My battles were between the flesh and the spirit; they were about the question of race, about the question of how to write out of a sensibility of oppressed people, about the fact that so many of the heroes of that drama were people filled with rage and chaos who eventually lost their lives in the struggle.

—Leon Forrest (as quoted in McQuade, 1995, p. 45)

In 1998 at Northwestern University, I directed a group of 25 performers, 21 of whom were African American, in the premiere of *Divine Days,* my stage adaptation of Leon Forrest's epic novel of African American life. The work was presented in the Barber Theatre as part of Northwestern's "mainstage" season. I had the privilege of working closely with Forrest over the last year of his life to develop the script, and much of the richness of this project was rooted in the uncanny ways the content and themes of the production were embedded in the process. In positioning the *Divine Days* project as a field site for the multilayered processes of adaptation, especially as they involve the politics of identity and race in the context of cultural production within and among an overwhelmingly white institutional apparatus, this essay explores convergences between ethnography and theatrical practice (in particular the adaptation of literature for the stage), endeavors that are often reductively miscast as separate wings of performance studies.

Dwight Conquergood has noted that scholars in performance studies are "committed to the *excavation* of the political underpinnings of all modes of representation" (1991, p. 179), and this essay posits that adaptation is a particularly fertile *site of* and *methodology for* this process of cultural and political excavation. As Norman Denzin emphasizes in his recent book *Performance Ethnography: Critical Pedagogy and the Politics of Culture* (2003), these issues become particularly vexed in the context of performed practices of race, whether in everyday life, textual representation, or staged production. To the extent that adaptation has at times been ghettoized as a formalist practice rather than a worldly and politicized one, adapters and directors have not always been able to deploy the full range of its resources for the understanding, celebration, and transformation of, for example, complex raced identities. Building on the contributions of Henry Giroux, Denzin envisions a project that "will connect reflexive autoethnography with critical pedagogy and critical race theory [and] . . . will necessarily treat political acts as pedagogical and performative, as acts that open new spaces for social citizenship and democratic dialogue, as acts that create critical race consciousness" (p. 5).

In her performative ethnography *Tango and the Political Economy of Passion* (1995), Marta Savigliano argues that "Origins should not be gotten out of the way at the beginning so the interpretation can proceed. Rather, problems of originating belong in the middle because they are central to the interpretation" (p. 32). Often we conceptualize the processes of both literary adaptation and ethnography as having "origins" that can be traced back to a source which preexists the adapter or ethnographer's transformation of them into a new form. Forrest's work underscores the disparate nature of origins as well as how this theme acquires particularly complex, tragic meanings in relationship to African American expressive culture. The *Divine Days* process was a living reminder that origins are not fixed, singular points of departure but are rather like veins, bloodlines that run through bodies, spinning out from the center to produce sweat, blood, and motion.

The dictionary defines adapt as "to make fit (as for a specific or new use or situation) often by modification," and also as "to bring one into correspondence with another." I am conceptualizing adaptation as both a transformational activity central to how performance operates as an "embodied practice of making meaning" (Pollock, 1998, p. 20), and as a critical trope for a large range of encounters, of efforts "to make fit," and "correspondences with one another" that emerge within what ethnographer Roger Lancaster has evocatively called "the density of real-life experience" (1992, p. 282). Throughout our journey to bring *Divine Days* to the stage, I developed an ever-deepening appreciation of adaptation, not only as an artistic practice but as a life process, as an extension of and corollary to ethnographic practice, as a fundamental dimension of performance pedagogy, as an embodied mode of critical engagement, and as a laboratory for exploring questions of identity and race, textual fidelity and authority, and the operations of power—both within and beyond a given text.

Among other things, the *Divine Days* project provided me with a critical lens into the culture of privilege I was inhabiting at a private, expensive, predominantly white, Eurocentric, "Research 1" university. As I attempt here a kind of autoethnographic restaging of a few of the salient features of this project, my own positionality is a source of discomfort and contradiction. On the one hand I fear that I unwittingly minimize my own sense of complicity in aspects of Eurocentric privilege that this project has, I think, helped me to begin to view differently. At worst, I risk depicting myself as a kind of gunslinging lone cultural hero, a solitary cowboy who rides into a border town and kicks up dust as he toils to expose the ignorance (or blind privilege) of its inhabitants. In fact nothing could be further from my actual experience of the *Divine Days* project, in which I was constantly astounded, not by own role as an agent of transformation but, on the contrary, by the sense that its most profound meanings were either "happening to me," or were embedded in scenes in which my role felt like that of an attentive bystander, especially as more and more of the social dramas the project engendered were being played out outside of my orbit. As I attempt to write about the project, I find myself walking a tightrope familiar to others who engage in intercultural work from positions of power and relative privilege (e.g., most ethnographers and stage directors), one that has been evocatively summed up by Donna Landry and Gerald Maclean, in their introduction to *The Spivak Reader*:

> Whenever we set about reading "our" texts and find them leading us obsessively back to ourselves, it is a good idea not to stop there, with ourselves as centers of meaning, but rather to go on and to think through the possibility that the personal might necessarily lead us outside "ourselves" to the political. (Spivak, 1996, p. 12)

In *Fictions of Feminist Ethnography* (1994), Kamala Visweswaran discusses the deep connections between fiction and ethnography, calling to mind analogous projects linking history and fiction such as Hayden White's *Metahistory* (1975) and Michel de Certeau's *The Writing of History* (1988): "There are demonstrable fictions of ethnography in the constitution of knowledge, power and authority in anthropological texts, and . . . we may also consider fiction as ethnography" (p. 16). Visweswaran argues that while the disciplines of fiction and ethnography each set out to construct "a believable world," they differ in that readers are meant to reject the factual quality of fiction, while they are meant to accept ethnography's "factual" claims. However, Visweswaran goes on to state that,

> Even this distinction breaks down if we consider that ethnography, like fiction, constructs existing or possible worlds, all the while retaining the idea of an alternate "made" world. Ethnography, like fiction, no matter its pretense to present a self-contained narrative or cultural whole, remains incomplete and detached from the realms to which it points." (1994, p. 1)

In treating the *Divine Days* process as an ethnographic field site, I am triangulating the relationship between fiction and ethnography investigated by Visweswaran by adding the practice of adapting literature for the stage (including both the scripting and staging processes). Clearly the dynamics I discuss as characteristic of the adaptation process overlap significantly with dimensions of theatrical practice more generally (the staging of plays), just as, of course, not all texts one would adapt for the stage would open up the kinds of questions around politics and power I am describing here. Still it troubles me that as surveys of the field of performance studies are written, adaptation as an interpretive artistic practice is usually omitted, suggesting a lack of recognition of a significant current in performance studies with a long historical and professional trajectory. For example, Marvin Carlson's *Performance: A Critical Introduction* (1996) and Richard Schechner's *Performance Studies: An Introduction* (2003) ignore the practices of performing and adapting literature in their respective surveys of the field, and the annual conferences held by Performance Studies international have featured essentially no engagement with the subject of adaptation.

By contrast, Paul Edwards' monograph "Unstoried: Teaching Literature in the Age of Performance Studies" (1999) offers a richly detailed institutional history of the performance of literature and its evolution out of the elocutionary movement, through oral interpretation's transformation into performance studies, and into a fraught present featuring what Judith Hamera has characterized as "the now irrevocable loss of a commitment" by the field "to the oral interpretation of literature" (1998, p. 273). Mary Strine suggests that the "cultural turn" which precipitated a "virtual eclipse of interest in literature" has within it the potential to offer a return to literature "now as always a politically inflected cultural form and potentially empowering practice" (1998, p. 4). Many performance studies students come to know adaptation and the performance of literature as what Edwards calls a "core interdisciplinary activity" (1999, p. 15) that directly engages the kinds of questions around power and politics central to courses in performance theory, cultural studies, and ethnography. Conquergood speaks to this when he urges performance scholars "to embrace a both/and complexity, instead of an either/or polarization" (1989, p. 84).

Through the *Divine Days* project, I came to see adaptations as more than theatricalized versions of the text but as dialogic and full-fledged cultural performances, described by Della Pollock as "performances on the edge of everyday life . . . that combine special roles, rules and structures in the process of defining cultural experience" (1990, p. 4). As the process unfolded, the adaptation and the source text each appeared to flicker between states of self-centeredness and of selflessness, much like two people in intimate conversation, who alternatively assert, listen, make eye contact, avert each other's gaze, reassert

and reconfigure their ideas, and become transformed. Indeed adaptation seemed to swirl around and through all aspects of the *Divine Days* project—as a craft, an image, a defining trope, a pedagogical practice, a survival mechanism, and as a way of being in the world.

ADAPTATION AND THE CRAFT OF ETHNOGRAPHY: "SENSUOUS FIDELITY"

Divine Days can be at once read as a literary ethnography, as a social and cultural history, as a jazz oratorio, as an homage to orality, as an autobiography, and as a kind of "critical race study." Published in 1992, its 1,135 pages draw heavily upon the rhythms and cadences of jazz to depict one transformative week in 1966 in the life of the narrating hero, the young playwright Joubert Antoine Jones. During this week Joubert makes many interrelated discoveries about his own identity and cultural legacy, which together mark a turning point in his development as an African American artist. Central among these is his epiphany about the complex meanings of the death of the legendary and mythic figure of Sugar-Groove, a shape-shifting mentor who dies on a mountaintop seeking the meaning of life. It is Joubert's developing understanding of the significance of his inheritance of Sugar-Groove's legacy that will ultimately lead to his coming of age as a man and as a writer. Joubert's quest is to "adapt" the voices and stories of his people into plays, and thus to foster a "Black literary revival" through performance.

The range of characters and situations with which Joubert comes into contact reflects the tremendous diversity of black life. He moves between members of the black middle class and those in artistic and intellectual circles, from the most impoverished citizens to preachers, healers, tricksters, criminals, derelicts, soldiers, and political zealots. As John Cawelti points out: "It is surely no exaggeration to say that *Divine Days* is the most encyclopedic account

yet created of the whole range of contemporary African-American urban culture" (1997,
p. 58). The novel is *about* adaptation, and
Joubert takes a profoundly ethnographic
approach in his efforts to sculpt a vast array of
cultural experiences into performance.

Leon frequently pointed out during our
collaboration that our relationship had pronounced parallels to that between Joubert and
Sugar-Groove in *Divine Days*. At many levels,
he observed, I was Joubert, the young playwright "trying to listen to those voices wherever they take me," and he was the mythic
mentor Sugar-Groove, ultimately dying on the
mountaintop, and imparting the wisdom from
the song "Nature Boy" that haunts the novel:
"The greatest thing you'll ever learn is just to
love and be loved in return." Leon's passion for
performance, the fact that his grandson was a
student at Northwestern whom I had mentored
and who had appeared in several productions
that I directed (and ultimately in *Divine Days*),
and the reality that Leon was very ill with
prostate cancer throughout our relationship all
contributed to deepening and complicating the
intimacy between us. It also focused for me the
implications of adaptation as a dialogic process
made in this case more urgent, intense, and
vital by the complex dynamics of race and by
the immediate claims of mortality. As Joubert
tries to come to terms with the death of Sugar-
Groove, he is visited and haunted by the many
voices that make up his heritage, and that
inform his work as a playwright:

> But why and how do these voices select me
> to do their talking and their bidding? To tell
> their troubles to? Why do they talk to me?
> Their returning and revolving presence spins
> me into re-creation as they transform them-
> selves through me; and I through their ever-
> expanding presence in my life, am racked
> forevermore. They are determined simply
> and cunningly to live. (Forrest, 1992, p. 12)

Renato Rosaldo (1989) points out that the
spatial paradigm which epistemologically

undergirds the primacy of objectivity is the
false notion that we acquire perspective by
stepping away. Rosaldo suggests that culture's
richest meanings emerge when we are in
motion, operating dynamically and often
messily from inside the fray of culture.
Joubert's apprehension about his own inextricable and radically subjective ties to the culture and history he wants to address in his
plays is central to what he learns and comes to
accept through the process of *Divine Days*:

> Out of my burden with the bones I can
> reshape a new kind of theater. To write not
> so much about the characters, but rather out
> of their fabulous sagas and tales, in an imag-
> inative, and honest manner, so that they
> finally, merely supply my imagination with
> the yeast, the spirit for a creative, zealous,
> thriving and throbbing theater. (Forrest,
> 1992, p. 977)

Joubert's artistic mission "to reshape out of
[his] burden with the bones" carries with it the
recognition that these voices come simultaneously from within and from outside, and that
his writing cannot be separated from his active
participation in his own life and culture. What
Joubert articulates and struggles with throughout the novel is his own vision of the
playwright/adapter as a kind of critical ethnographer, attuned to the ethical dimensions of
his work, and sensitive to the problems of
appropriation. His distinction between writing
"*about*" the characters, and finding an honest
way to communicate "*out of*" the reality of
their worlds parallels the distinction ethnographer Johannes Fabian draws when he calls
for doing ethnography *with* a group of
people rather than *of* them (1990, p. 259),
transforming the traditional relationship
between observer and observed into a form of
partnership.

For Fabian and for Joubert, as for performance ethnographers ranging from Conquergood to Anna Deavere Smith, the process
becomes about an embodied form of active

listening, akin to what Conquergood has called *dialogical performance:* "This performative stance struggles to bring together different voices, world views, value systems and beliefs so that they can have a conversation with one another. The aim of dialogical performance is to bring self and other together so that they can question, debate and challenge one another." (1985, p. 9). The "conversation" that Conquergood champions requires an exceptional kind of listening, one that is foundational to the craft of the ethnographer, the fiction writer, the adapter, and the stage director.

Michael Taussig has asserted that "the wonder of mimesis lies in the copy drawing on the character and power of the original, to the point whereby the representation may even assume that character and power" (1993, p. xiii). Thus the process of mimetically "making over" becomes an act of full-fledged originality, of remaking, or of imaginative remembering. Applying Taussig's concept of "sensuous fidelity" to the adaptation process suggests that the adapted work, in its simultaneous endeavor to honor the polyphonic richness of its source and to remake this source in a new form, can derive "magical, soulful power" from it through the very process of undertaking to represent it. The craft of adaptation is suffused with this highly charged relationship "between fidelity and fantasy," about which Taussig pleads with us to "please remember how high the stakes are here, insinuated with the struggle for life" (p. 17). Joubert Jones is deeply attuned to these "stakes" when he asks searchingly in *Divine Days,* "What must I do to produce a Black literary revival, in order to be saved? First of all shut up my mouth! And listen to those voices wherever they take me" (Forrest, 1992, p. 12).

The concept of "sensuous fidelity" suggests a fully corporeal, dialogical commitment to *listening* to the source in a manner that is neither overly self-effacing nor overly self-serving. For Taussig, as for Joubert Jones, this is not just an issue of artistic representation, but an ethical, political, and ethnographic concern as well. The kind of embodied listening that Taussig and Joubert Jones describe is "sensuous" in that the ears are not all that one needs to carry it out, but rather, as described by Mikhail Bakhtin, it is a process one engages "with his eyes, lips, hands, soul, spirit, with his whole body and deeds" (1984, p. 293).

The Adaptation of
Institutional Spaces and Contexts

> *The new space . . . is formed by the inwardness of the outside, the interiority of the "othered," the personal that is always embedded in the public. In this new space one can imagine safety without walls, can iterate difference that is prized but unprivileged, and can conceive of a . . . world "already made for me, both snug and wide open, with a doorway never needing to be closed." Home.*
>
> —Toni Morrison (1998, p. 4)

Many of the black students involved in *Divine Days* indicated that they had previously seen themselves as the unnamed antagonists to what Joseph Roach has termed the performances of "gendered whiteness" (1996, p. 31) that dominated the campus mainstream. The adaptation and staging of the novel was, among other things, an attempt to create a new space. The rhetorical power of this space emerged largely from the fact that the space carved out by the project was simultaneously operating in each of the three terrains Henri Lefebvre names in *The Production of Space*— the physical, the mental, and the social (1991, pp. 11–12).

Perhaps the most radical problematic that contributed to the project being resistant and threatening was its status as part of the campus mainstream. So many of its meanings were negotiated, not on the fringe, but "in the same place as power" (Foucault, 1980, p. 142). Several African American students whom I knew well had expressed to me in confidence their own and their friends' ambivalence or hostility toward the Theatre and Interpretation Center at Northwestern, and the institution of the "mainstage" season that resides there, of which the production of *Divine Days* would be a part. These students articulated their sense that this had heretofore been a place from which they were excluded, and that they had developed their own vibrant artistic and community forums in other spaces where they felt more at home.

During the period in which I was beginning work on *Divine Days,* Khalid Abdul Muhammad visited the Northwestern campus, amidst much protest from the campus Hillel organization and other student groups. In his preceding visit to Kean College Muhammad had said: "Jews are hook-nosed, bagel-eatin,' lox-eatin' impostors. . . . Everybody always talks about Hitler eliminating six million Jews. But nobody ever asks what did they do to Hitler?" (Austen, 1994, p. 67). During the same period, Northwestern had been on the national news for incidents of racial hatred on campus. Muhammad's visit to campus was adamantly supported by many of the very students and student groups I was approaching to talk with about *Divine Days* (and vehemently criticized by other groups with which I was allied). It was certainly more than peculiar one evening to walk directly through a protest organized by the campus Hillel to attend a meeting in an attempt to recruit and build connections with the African American community for our project. But this crossing soon became for me emblematic of the threshold work of the production: the innumerable crossings and adaptations that brought multiple worlds into creative collision.

As I embarked on the *Divine Days* project, I was conscious of entering what Rosaldo has called a "borderlands" existence. Within these borders and border crossings reside tense intersections of power and difference, as well as heightened opportunities for "creative cultural production" (1989, p. 208). I occupied this borderlands turf anxiously. I felt keenly aware that I was not always welcome, and that not everybody assumed I had good intentions. The mainstage production season at Northwestern is made up of more than ten productions annually, of which *Divine Days* was the only one produced by the performance studies department (the others were produced by the theatre department). As soon as I proposed *Divine Days* as a mainstage project, there was controversy and hesitation from members of the theatre department, most notably because of the number of African American performers I was seeking. In the ten years since I had begun as an undergraduate student at Northwestern, there had been very few roles for African Americans on the mainstage, and even fewer projects that featured this community in any substantive way. Taken together, the theatre and performance studies departments had an extremely small number of African American majors, and quite naturally people wondered where I would find the black actors. Predictably, some also wondered aloud about the appropriateness of me directing such a large-scale "black" production. The chair of performance studies tried to deflect these objections by underscoring the fact that I had worked extensively creating performance in inner city environments and intercultural contexts, as well as developing and directing numerous multicultural productions through my professional theatre company StreetSigns. Others commented in my defense that the fact that Forrest, the chair of African American studies, had entrusted his work to me and was so supportive of the project should be "good enough."

While I was gratified by their responses, I worried about the paradoxical nature of my own motivations. As I worked to subvert the claims that the project was impossible, was I guilty of espousing a romanticized and self-serving notion of how the project would transform the community, while suppressing the ways it might be motivated by my own personal goals and desire for prestige? During this time I found it hard to separate the "artistic" unease I felt, largely rooted in my desire to do justice to Leon and his text, from vexation about my fraught positionality in terms of the project's implications around power and representation. In each context, the force of adaptation seemed to be manifesting less in its capacity to effect benign or eloquent transformations than in its potential to be transgressive, and even to inflict violence. I found myself increasingly apprehensive about who or what might be on the other end of this unwitting violence (e.g., Forrest's text, my own authority or reputation, the health of the larger community, the good-faith commitments of others who invested in the process).

I had developed relationships with a number of African American students who had become involved with the African-American Theatre Ensemble (AATE), a group that functioned as an alternative space for African American performance work on campus, and whose student productions I had admired. A handful of these students had been in courses I had taught, or had participated in other smaller productions I had staged. AATE had used Shanley Pavilion as its performance space, a charming, somewhat ramshackle site outside the institutional confines of the theatre building and the department. From my discussions with students, it was clear that most of them felt extremely ambivalent (and several were downright hostile) towards the "mainstage" apparatus, and even towards the building where the mainstage theatres and all the theatre classrooms were housed.

It was apparent to me from the outset of our work on *Divine Days* that I would have to operate outside the standard paradigm of how a mainstage production is cast. Putting up the standard flyers and sign-up sheets in the theatre building was not going to suffice. The fact that there were so few African American majors in theatre and performance studies made this recruitment process especially difficult (and crucial), because students would have to be sold on the fact that this extracurricular activity was worthy of an immense investment of their time away from their other commitments; my friends at AATE had commented that it was hard to draw African American students even to their projects, because so many of them were, for example, pre-med students, and did not have the luxury of compromising their academic commitments or risking grade slippage to commit to extracurricular work.

The Theatre and Interpretation Center is only yards away from areas that African American students populate comfortably and habitually (the Norris Student Center, for example), but there was an abyss to overcome. During the recruitment process, Leon and I arranged an information session and reading from the evolving script, with both of us present, to be held at the Norris Student Center. The selection of this space was itself the result of much strategizing. Initially it had been planned in the Theatre and Interpretation Center, and an African American student of mine suggested that there would be black people who might not attend if we held it there. In this sense the spatial values of campus places became pointed and dramatically heightened, creating both additional possibilities and challenges for adaptation across literal and figurative thresholds.

At this time Leon's health was very precarious. He was being shuttled in and out of the hospital numerous times each week, and he had not had the strength to be on campus, or anywhere else in public, for some time. Nonetheless we were talking daily at this point, and I was paying regular visits to his home and to Evanston Hospital. He suggested that we go ahead and plan a date for this event and he would do the best he could to make it, but that it was unlikely. On each day that we spoke he would bring this meeting up and reassure himself about the date, the time, and the space. It was clear to me how desperately he wanted to attend, in order to signal to the community his personal investment in the project. His wife Marianne later told me that Leon had worried aloud a great deal about this session, repeatedly stating his concern that members of the community might try to "chew Derek up and spit him out for his audacity."

Very early on the morning of the event he phoned me, sounding extremely weak, and said that his attendance did not look promising. I reassured him that it would be productive even without him, and encouraged him to rest and take care. Internally, though, I worried about his absence, especially since he himself had seemed so concerned about the community's response. I knew that a number of people were planning to attend just to see Leon, as he had not been on campus much for several months, and I wondered about the mood in the room when I explained that he would not be there.

Leon not only showed up that afternoon, but he spoke with eloquence and read forcefully from the script, his voice quaking with intensity, to the assembled students, faculty members, and campus administrators. As depleted as he was, he remained a very fine performer of his own writing. Bruce Rosenberg has described his reading of his own work as characterized by "a preacher's histrionic skill: intonation, gesture, expression, and eye contact are all active" (1997, p. 125), and this afternoon was no exception.

The reading seemed the perfect enactment of all the claims about the project I had felt myself straining to make. The attendees went away energized and the project now felt infinitely more possible; we were underway. Through his own determination, Leon brought the great weight of his tenuous presence to bear on the space of my interaction with potential performers and representatives from campus organizations. As he walked in the room in Norris and crossed the threshold from private to public space, from absence to presence, he seemed to enact the mortal stakes in the project, putting his own health literally on the line to underscore and mitigate the raced identity issues that essentially defined the project. In this way we began the long process of adapting the novel to the space and the space to the novel, conjoining their respective politics in a way that amplified each in relation to the other and began to bring both *home*.

It was clear that the event that afternoon took an enormous amount out of Leon, and, when I drove him home, he was visibly weak. When I dropped him off, he sighed deeply, kissed me, and added, "Well, that went exactly the way I hoped it would." It was equally clear to me that while the project might now occupy a more powerful and viable position on campus, from the perspective of many potential participants my authority was absolutely borrowed from Leon, and would remain provisional and subject to continual negotiation.

ADAPTATION AS CRITICAL PEDAGOGY

Many of the performers in the *Divine Days* production had the opportunity to take an advanced course, developed around Forrest's novel and related issues of performance and adaptation, which I taught immediately prior to the rehearsal process. I defined the course as "a scholarly performance workshop," in which the focus would be the adaptation and staging of *Divine Days*. I also saw it as a vital opportunity to rehearse the processes of ensemble-making and community-building that I felt were crucial to the success of the production. My greatest hope was that the sense of community engendered in this forum would not only establish a strong foundation for the rehearsal process, but would create a space where race relations and issues of power could be discussed and performatively explored within what for some was the previously unfamiliar (or inhospitable) territory of Northwestern's Theatre and Interpretation Center. The students created an expansive range of often intertextual performances throughout the course, and there were myriad ways in which adaptation became a tool for negotiating the text through and in relation to their own diverse identities, institutional relationships, and life histories. In this way adaptation became a methodology for pursuing what Giroux has termed "border pedagogy," in which knowledge and power come together "not to merely reaffirm difference but to interrogate it, to open up broader theoretical considerations, to tease out its limitations, and to engage a vision of community in which student voices define themselves in terms of their distinct social formations and their broader collective hopes" (1992, p. 29).

To my surprise, 26 students enrolled, 17 of whom were African American. These students constituted a cross-section of undergraduates and graduate students, as well as representing a wide variety of majors and areas of interest. On the first day of the course, as we went around the circle introducing ourselves, one of the three African American theatre majors in the room—indulging in a moment of deliberate parody and carnivalization which seemed to broadcast explosively the subtext of the moment—stood, shrieked, shook, fell over, and cried out: "Yes, black people! I never thought I'd see so many black people in this place! *They*'re never going to believe this!" to a chorus of laughter and applause from the other students.

As the student continued to play the scene, mining it for all its mimetic excess, lying flat on her back in slapstick ecstasy and letting her repeated cries of "Black people! Black people!" resolve into a kind of ceaseless, fervent whisper, the rest of us seemed to celebrate too, though a bit more timidly, as our eyes met

across the circle. There was something joyously *bad* about what she was saying that seemed, at least for the moment, to connect and to liberate us. In that apparently cathartic release, she was uttering a kind of secret. Her speech acted to create not only a "they," but to posit a "we," to generate a collective "us" already bonded even if in a tentative and fragile way. Her cry seemed to acknowledge that our project might forge what Darlene Clark Hine and others have called a "culture of dissemblance" (2000, p. 20), replete with opportunities for "talking back" and for signifying. In so doing she performed community by effectively citing the terms of our mutual identification.

As we proceeded to talk that day, the "they" that the student had invoked so vividly continued to be dramatized. "They" grew in stature, and it became clear that this "they," however elusive to define, was an important character in our community—one of the main ingredients out of which our project might forge a meaningful "we." As we spoke of this "they" on that first day, an African American student who had never previously taken a performance class aligned his feelings about being black at Northwestern with W. E. B. DuBois's notion of "double consciousness," which DuBois defines as a "contradiction of double aims" felt by those "striving to be . . . co-worker[s] in the kingdom of culture" (1989, p. 51). As described by David Lionel Smith, the black intellectual becomes implicated in white culture through education, and in black culture through social, political, and emotional ties, "thereby representing both and neither" (1998, p. 186). Several of the white students also offered that they felt they were experiencing a new sensation of "double-consciousness" in a class dominated by African Americans. One student said, "It's strange to have walked into this theatre hundreds of times, and to walk in today and, for the first time feel like an outsider."[1] Her comments suggest the ways in which the context of this course racialized whiteness in a way that felt new for many of the students.

Throughout the course, students would build on and deepen the precedent they established the first day, which Giroux argues is a central feature of border pedagogy, as students are given the opportunity "to air their feelings about race from the perspective of the subject positions they experience as constitutive of their own identities" (1992, p. 137). They would also replay these identities through the sensuous, affective work of performance, shifting from a constitutive to a performative sense of identity. It was through that trickster-shift that we began to explore and to define the many facets of the adaptation process together.

One of the first assignments for the class was to develop performances from the first sections of the *Divine Days* text, where they found the theme of "double-consciousness" that was so central to our first discussion reflected through the figure of the "lost-found" mulatto orphan Hans Henson, who haunts the narrating hero Joubert. The figure of Hans Henson embodies the split between whiteness and blackness, a split many of the students, black and white, connected to and about which many students chose to create introductory performances.

> Yes, I am a black orphan nigger child of the world—with a German mother and a black G.I. American father—that's what I see and hear about me and that's that. Half of me is black and the other half is white. That's like a joke too at the circus, where a clown is outfitted in a suit of two colors. But the world in my case can't see the white half looking for the black half, when actually I'm yellow. So be it. (Forrest, 1992, p. 20)

The performances the students in the course created about Hans Henson were at once adaptations of Forrest's text and of the students' own polysemic identities, predicaments, personal investments in the project, and reactions to the material. Without being directed to, more than half of the students began to physicalize Hans's (and their own)

double-consciousness, taking on Hans's "split-ness," his "lost-found-ness," in bodily terms. For some students, this splitness manifested as the constricted dance of a tightrope-walker, while for others it evoked more violent kinesthetic sensations, such as bodies being pulled apart to the persistent sounds of diabolically loud sawing. These performances engaged the doubleness of self and literary Other to address the complexities of being torn by twin identifications with whiteness and blackness. In so doing, they performed the function of finding and communicating the echoes of raced binarisms in our immediate context.

As several of the students who participated in the course but were not in the cast of the production pointed out to me, the ghosts of the Hans Henson performances were visible six months later in the production onstage, manifesting both as specific choices about, for example, character movement and gesture, but, more profoundly, as a kind of stylistic foundation for many aspects of the overall work, including elements of its choreography, design, musicality, choral work, and acting style. In this and other performance rounds, students also built on Forrest's and Joubert's extensive use of intertextuality by juxtaposing and riffing between Forrest's text and any number of other critical, literary, and musical texts. These embodied, critical "stagings" posited adaptation as not only a technique we might use *on* a text, but as a richly dialogic way of engaging *with*, *against*, and *across* texts.

As the course progressed and we moved deeper into the book, the students' eventually found W. E. B. DuBois's notion of double-consciousness directly alluded to, and in fact critiqued, by the character of the fair-skinned Negro reporter Warren Wilkerson, whom Joubert encounters at the end of his journey to uncover the mystery of the death of his mentor Sugar-Groove. Sitting up in bed in the nursing home sucking on a bottle of Old Forester whiskey "like an ancient white monkey," the 87-year-old Wilkerson pontificates:

That will to synthesize was what DuBois never understood . . . to absorb and reinvent; to take it all in and to masticate it, and process it, and spew it back out, as lyrical and soaring as a riff by Father Louie. . . . DuBois never understood that with his double consciousness theories. (Forrest, 1992, p. 889)

In one of the final class sessions, the same student who had referred to DuBois on the first day pointed us to this Wilkerson passage. He spoke of how right Wilkerson/Forrest was, how the process and the text had actually transformed his initial sense of "double-consciousness":

I really get what Wilkerson is saying. It's more like layers on top of one another than a "this is over here—that is over there" type of thing. Now that we've chewed all this text up and spewed it out, as he says, I see how it can all be one thing, how it's not black here and white there . . . but how it's more like riffs and streaks . . . like all these really great jazz riffs in here. I feel like that split I talked about on the first day, which was both inside me and outside me, isn't really a split now. It's riffs.[2]

Just as Forrest's novel itself defies double-consciousness with its riffs on literally hundreds of cited intertexts from Joyce to Dostoevsky to Ellison to Billie Holiday and Bessie Smith, so the staging itself was informed by a jazz logic, an aesthetic of "riffing." For the student performers, their commitment to exploring this unfamiliar style was in the end rooted largely in their understanding of its political meanings and the more individuated personal resonances they explored in the course. I believe that when the student performers later commented on the agency they felt in performing *Divine Days,* much of this feeling can be attributed to these moments in which the text and the process of performing appeared to become inseparable from the context and processes by which they were made, understood, and deployed.

The *Divine Days* course left me with the conviction that to teach adaptation is to *riff* on any number of the binary divisions that have characterized double-consciousness in the American cultural imagination, such as those between the teacher who knows and the student who learns, artistic and intellectual production, oral interpretation and performance studies, cultural politics and aesthetic practice. Understood in this way, adaptation may be a crucial means of dismantling and reinventing power structures that those binaries have held in place. To teach adaptation is to conceptualize literature as a space out of which to make meanings rather than as merely a place to find them. It is to accentuate the students' intellectual, political, and artistic agency to build on the texts, to learn from each other in an embodied, performance-centered way, not only to learn the course material but to produce it and transform it, to adapt it.

Adaptive Processes of Casting and Production Design

At an early production meeting for *Divine Days,* the concern was raised by a faculty member in the design program that "every time we have tried to light black faces here, they have come out in very strange, frightening tints of green." Our lighting designer confessed that he was nervous about the challenge of illuminating black faces and would look to faculty members with more experience in that area for support. The costume designer then expressed particular concern about make-up, since she had "never made up dark faces." This led to a conversation about whether the cast would be buying make-up kits, which is normally demanded of actors in mainstage productions. Two of the cast members had already expressed to me their concern about having to pay for these, which they, as biology majors, might never use again. In quotidian dialogues like these throughout the process, we frequently found ourselves in uncharted and delicate terrain.

The process of casting the production was itself a site of complex negotiation. Like most academic theatres, the Northwestern main-stage season had typically engaged in racially restrictive casting. Students of color almost never appeared in what were perceived as "white" roles unless these roles were very small, and over time a vicious cycle had evolved, in which most of these students did not bother to audition for or attend these productions. Part of the problem, as Ellen Donkin points out, is the critical lack of directors of color in academic institutions. Additionally, Donkin argues,

> Students of color in these same institutions, many of whom are already under pressure to bypass the arts for preprofessional programs of study, are often doubly reluctant to undertake a storming of the barricade. In the meantime the campus theaters continue to generate representations on the stage that reinforce the public perception of *student* as white and *minority* as minor. Faculty directors respond to a situation that is in good part their own making by declaring that there are no minority actors and that, as a consequence this year, again, there can be no minority show. The campus theater becomes a locus for erasure of the minority student presence and for that reason carries a special burden of responsibility for figuring out a way forward. (1993, p. 79)

In the end, 187 people auditioned for *Divine Days*, of whom 71 were black females, 18 were black males, 86 were nonblack females, and 12 were nonblack males. Whereas Leon and I had once wondered whether we could find the African American performers we needed, we were, in the end, faced with an embarrassment of riches. By the time the auditions were posted, two false rumors had spread: first, that there were no good roles for non–African American performers, and, second, that participants in the course had an inside track or were precast. It took significant localized efforts to

change this perception, through announcements in acting classes and pointed notes on the callboard. It seemed ironic that, having been told this project was impossible because of the number and quality of African American performers I sought, that my biggest concern was finding strong white performers. Throughout this period I worried that these parts of the process could not help but reify the separation between the African American and non–African American communities.

Casting always involves painful and difficult decisions, especially in academic environments where the auditioners are often one's own students, whose development one has had the joy of witnessing over months and years. But this process was particularly wrenching because so many of the students had become so invested in the project, whether through the seminar, their own relationship to Leon and his work, or simply their sense of the meanings this project was starting to accrue on campus, which by now seemed to be resonating outside the orbit of my own day-to-day encounters. Over the weeks in which I labored over casting decisions, I felt cruel that, with Leon's help, we had succeeded in generating desire, commitment, and even a sense of agency within students around this project, and now I was in the position of selecting the small percentage of these students who would really get to participate in the main event.

While most students were publicly understanding about these decisions, and some even continued to participate in the project in other substantive ways, the irony of the power I was wielding was not lost on me. Whereas normally during and immediately after casting I do not actively seek out contact with those who were not cast, in this case there were many students with whom I felt compelled to meet individually in order to attempt to signal my continued appreciation and gratitude for their work. I was rarely more aware during the entire process of my status as a white male than in these meetings; some of the meetings were quite emotional, and some were awkward, but in the end I felt that these meetings were crucial sites of adaptation, where the conditions of power foundational to the meanings that mattered most in this project were negotiated.

Adaptive Processes of Rehearsal and Performance

In discussing the production of Femi Osofisan's Yoruba play *Farewell to a Cannibal Rage* which she staged at Stanford, Sandra Richards says: "My twenty-year experience in working with student productions had taught me that—feeling embattled, guilty, or confused—African American students often used a theatrical production as an arena in which to confront their relationships to elite white institutions and to impoverished black communities" (1996, p. 179). Rehearsal is largely a pragmatic space, characterized by familiar structures of modification and repetition, as well as a politics of authority that is usually unspoken but inherently understood. There is a kind of silent contract about how the actors, director, stage manager, choreographer, and designers all relate to each other. Paradoxically, these central relationships seem to function a little differently in every project, and yet the understandings about these relationships, which are suffused with implications of authority and are so central to the health and coherence of the creative process, usually remain unspoken. If they are ever discussed overtly it is most often because there is conflict or disagreement. Everyone who worked on the *Divine Days* process found that these normally implicit presumptions and silent mutual understandings became sites of active, explicit negotiation and adaptation.

After a long rehearsal about two weeks into the rehearsal process, one of our guest artists, Ernest Perry, an accomplished veteran actor who, as a guest artist, was performing the role of Sugar-Groove, made a passionate speech to the entire company in which he repeated the refrain "30 years" several times. His message was that in 30 years of professional acting all over the world, it was Forrest's material that had spoken to him the most deeply—the one that most powerfully intersected with his own identity and history. "Take it from Sugar-Groove," he went on to say, "You won't have another opportunity like this for at least 30 years." From then on, whenever Ernest would sense things getting off-track, or when he felt the cast just needed a reminder of the stakes, he would simply say "30 years." Shortly before we opened the production, after a late rehearsal in which we all felt depleted and worn down, Ernest posted a large sign on the callboard and distributed copies to the company. Under the word "URGENT" in large capitalized letters he had written the following, in verse form:

> WE SAT IN THE CIRCLE
> VERBALLY COMMITTED,
> DEDICATED
> SO WE SAID
> LEON'S WORDS ARE VITALLY
> IMPORTANT THIS OPPORTUNITY
> THINK IN TERMS OF THIRTY YEARS
> WE MUST RESPECT THE WORK
> WE MUST COMMIT SERIOUSLY
> WE MUST BE ON TIME
> READY, PREPARED
> WE MUST BE HELPFUL
> WITHOUT THREATENING
> WE MUST WORK TOGETHER
> HARMONIOUSLY, CREATIVELY
> SLAVES, BLOOD, SACRIFICE
> LEGACY
> WE OWE IT TO OURSELVES
> WE OWE LEON FORREST
> WE OWE DEREK GOLDMAN
> SO FAR WE ARE GOOD
> SHOULD WE SETTLE? OR
> SHOULD WE BE GREAT!

> *—SUGAR-GROOVE '98*

Consistently throughout the process, Perry's outward contextualization of the project in historical terms ("Slaves, Blood, Sacrifice/ Legacy") rhetorically emphasized for the students the magnitude of the work in which they were participating. This form of spiritual leadership had both an ideological and a more practical function. The vast majority of the students working on the show had never been asked to give this amount of time to any project before, particularly one for which they were not receiving credit and which in most cases was not part of their chosen course of study. Not only was the rehearsal schedule necessarily intensive, but the demands of learning Forrest's text, with its precise musicality, as well as mastering the demanding physical choreography, far exceeded the students' expectations. In addition, most of the students had meaningful other commitments—Northwestern Community Ensemble gospel choir, a cappella groups, science lab sessions, campus organizations— that had in the past been at least as important as any theatre work they had done. For the artistic team this meant walking a difficult line between enforcing the special demands of this project by asking these students to make a profound shift in their priorities, and being sensitive to the grueling balancing act the students had to perform in their lives in order to be part of this project. Perry's capacity to get the students to invest in their crucial role in the making of what he insisted was a culturally historic event inspired all of our adaptive capacities as we negotiated a seemingly infinite array of divergent personal, cultural, and artistic investments and perspectives.

Through dozens of collaborations, choreographer Peter Carpenter and I had worked to develop and hone a style and performance aesthetic built upon a foundation that came from the performers' own creative, kinetic response to the material. Carpenter describes how important this approach to developing material was to the collaborative community making *Divine Days*:

One of the reasons that race seemed to be less of an issue than it might have been was that in the work we always do to build ensemble, and the work I do with them just to develop my material, I get so much from them. I use a lot of their movement material—and you had had this whole class where they had generated very specific, often personal material which clearly influenced your thinking about the piece, and they saw this. So I really believe the performers felt like they were in deep dialogue with the two white guys staging the show, as opposed to them feeling like we had it all figured out—and this made a big difference in all aspects of the process.[3]

In his work as a choreographer, Carpenter is concerned with tapping into the ensemble's "kinesthetic imagination." Thus the body and its history and sensuality are incorporated into processes of memory that move fluidly between highly individuated, unique manifestations and shared, collective, and communal material. While the work is very physical, it has never been central to our theatre-making aesthetic that the performers consider themselves dancers before the process begins. In fact, much of what I believe makes Carpenter's choreography so moving to watch is our awareness of the vast range of "training" among the performers within a style that both highlights their individuality and their capacity to work together as an ensemble. There is normally some initial resistance from the performers to this way of working, which Carpenter says stems from the fact that "so many of them have not used their bodies that way before, and there's some fear of the style." One of the participants in the project described Carpenter's process as follows:

We move how we can, and then he pushes that to dance. At first he lets you stay totally within the comfort zone, and then he gives you options to push that and stages a version with you "pushing," but by then it feels organically connected to your own comfort zone. Your own expressive capacities are the foundation, and yet we all feel truly like dancers.[4]

Over time, the performers start to see that what Carpenter builds is a layering process, that the foundation of material they are developing, which might at first seem too abstract or too facile, will go through many organic transformations, expansions, and distillations before it is sculpted into the ultimate production. As such they are engaged in a continuous, embodied process of adapting material they themselves have generated. As a result they are physically invested in the layers of meaning their material contributes to the production. An important part of this process happens when their own material is taught to and absorbed and transformed by other ensemble members. Through the dialogic, embodied nature of this work, they experience themselves as engaged in a kind of coauthorship of the staged work.

In response to the production, we noticed that many white audience members focused on the virtuosity of the performance, in particular the athleticism of the dancing and the extraordinary gospel singing, while African Americans tended not to comment on this at all, but to talk in much more depth about the content of the piece, especially around Forrest's nonstereotypical characters, such as the complexity of the women represented, and the very rare portrayal of black homosexuality in the character of LaSalle. One white professor from the theatre department who had voiced some concern about the project physically grabbed me in the hallway after seeing it and, shutting his office door behind him, whispered with extreme intensity "Where on earth did you dig them all up?" In our ensuing conversation, his praise was fervent but entirely fixated on one issue: "How had I ever gotten them to speak so clearly?" Another faculty member kept his feedback on the production to four words: "They sure can sing."

Presenting a notoriously demanding African American novel in the context of a subscription season attended primarily by older, white audiences meant we were conscious of fashioning a production that would be "multivocal" in its capacity to be read and appreciated by audiences with different kinds of cultural awareness and experience. Much of this multivocal quality was already a part of *Divine Days* as both form and subject. Consequently, the material seemed disposed toward a multivocal production—that is, through its exhilarating but demanding centrifugal force it spun out in many directions, and thus aspired to offer audience members multiple points of entry. This is not to say that the novel adapted itself to the stage in the sense of either pouring forth an appropriate script or of accommodating the social conditions of the Barber Theater and Northwestern. Rather, the production generated a heightened awareness of the possibility of various kinds and points of engagement. Through it we positioned ourselves to meet with different, even contradictory, audience perspectives. As a result "adaptation" began to describe that meeting place, that contact zone, as coursing and unpredictable as it was. Adaptation was as much about the moments and reckonings to which we rose—embodied in the afterwards of the production—as it was embedded in the process of the production per se.

Adaptation and Remembrance: The Fragile Body

In his essay "From Speech to Writing," Roland Barthes articulates the immeasurable loss of all the "scraps of language" that dissolve away in the move from the embodied, interpersonal encounter to the written representation of that encounter:

When we speak, we want our interlocutor to listen to us; we revive his attention with meaningless interpellation (of the type "Hello, hello, can you hear me?"); unassuming as they are, these words and expressions are in some way discreetly dramatic: they are appeals, modulations—should I say, thinking of birds: songs?—through which a body seeks another body. It is this song—gauche, flat, ridiculous when written down—which is extinguished in our writing. (1985, p. 4)

Barthes' subsequent discussion of how the "fragile (or frantic) body . . . flings itself toward another body" (p. 5) in dialogue is suggestive of several layers of meaning as I try to write about the *Divine Days* project. It evokes both the fear of what will inevitably be lost in the writing, as well as an acute, distinctly separate awareness of what is already lost to me as I work to remember it, as in some moments I listen to a Dictaphone recording of a meeting with Leon, and in others ponder coffee-stained pages of notes—all faint, distant traces of his actual bodily presence. Nor is this loss entirely the product of memory's failings and the passage of time, for I can connect Barthes's description to a very strong physical sensation I often had during these meetings—a conscious awareness that many of these meetings' richest meanings were happening in an unrepresentable "now." This awareness is also at the heart of the text of *Divine Days* itself, haunting Joubert's consciousness as he sits with Sugar-Groove and hears the troubled, profound stories of his origin, wondering with private intensity, "How do I write this?"

The sensation of loss Barthes describes, in which ideas are "constantly overwhelmed by the body," is heightened in a context such as my later meetings with Leon, scenes in which body and spirit seem to be held at arm's length from one another. It is heightened first because we are involved together in envisioning and mapping a new, embodied event for the theatre, a place that Barthes himself calls "a celebration of the body" and, even more profoundly, it is heightened because one of the bodies in this generative space is not well. Here the very circumstances of the meeting, its location, duration, the energy it demands, even the physical sensations of sight and smell, all conspire to foreground the body in all of its vulnerability. The very nature of my collaborative relationship with Forrest was

radically transformed by his ever-increasing vulnerability to the cancer that was ravaging his body. While our early meetings had taken place in his campus office and at local restaurants, possessing the veneer of polite formality characteristic of people who are just getting to know each other, our later encounters were filled with bedpans, blood clots, bags of urine, and scenes of me lifting Forrest's diminished body every two or three minutes, in a fond yet vain attempt to ease the painful pressure on his enormous tumor.

Often I would try, in the frantic fragility Barthes describes, to "write" those sensations, but as field notes viewed from the unavoidable distance of critical reflection, many of them fall into cliché or sentimentality. At several points throughout my notes, in the midst of furious scrawls on themes of artistic reinvention, chaos, and polyphonic jazz structures, can be found little sentences and fragments like "so generous of spirit today," and "he seems weaker," and "I'm grieving his loss and he's still here," and "blood count low, transfusion tomorrow," and simply, "I love him." These are moments of narration innocent of the distance of critical perspective. They read as miniature enactments of that state which is engendered, above all, by proximity to death (and to birth): a state in which one feels more known by what is real than knowing of it.

As I sit three and a half years after the production in that same apartment in Evanston visiting Marianne Forrest, Leon's widow, my eyes wander again over the familiar terrain of his bookshelves—where copies of his own his own works sit aside those of his personal friends Ellison, Wideman, and Morrison, as well as hundreds of authors who inspired him, from Faulkner to Joyce to Marquez.

There is one book on the shelf that was not there when Leon and I were working in that room together. In a bright white sleeve with a vibrant, multicolored image from Romare Bearden on it, there sits a hardcover copy of *Meteor in the Madhouse*, Leon's just published posthumous work of novellas, a sequel to

Divine Days. Leon had shared pieces of this writing with me during our time together, and near the end of his life finally felt that the work had taken on a shape. Marianne quietly tells the story of how, after he could no longer write, Leon dictated the end of the book to her in the hospital. Leon's final words as a writer were spoken, not written, "songs" that flung themselves towards all the surviving bodies that might someday hear. In the final passages Leon spoke to Marianne, Joubert is dying, but in this death there are seeds of ferocious reinvention. The swirling voices of Shakespeare, Jesus, Coltrane, and the "tear-drenched" nurses all gather to lift him off to another world where he will encounter still more voices:

> No wonder I had to go down dead in this madhouse—in order to breathe upon the righteous and rowdy riffs of existence again. Oh, yes, and now to wail with a horn full of plenty: LET THERE BE LIGHT, Baby, LET THERE BE LIGHT.
>
> LET THERE BE LIGHT, Baby, LET THERE BE LIGHT. But then as I let my eyes filter across the room, they fell upon the tear-drenched eyes of my nurses. I could feel no evil for the Lord is with me, His staff is with me, and then I could feel a swoop of angelic voices beneath my gown as I sailed out to other voices and other democratic chambers and other spheres into the distances of time. (Forrest, 2001, p. 254)

As Joubert departs, there is no divide or clear threshold between this world and the next. There is music, and dancing, and flight, but no resolutions, endings, or conclusions are in sight. There are only new "voices," "chambers," and "spheres"—spaces where the processes of adaptation that have consumed his life will carry on in forms that are, as yet, unimagined.

NOTES

1. Holly Frank, from class transcript, September 23, 1997.

2. Glenn Jeffers, from class transcript, December 8, 1997.

3. Peter Carpenter, from personal interview, November 8, 2000.

4. Lynn Johnson, from personal interview, October 10, 1999.

REFERENCES

Austen, R. (1994). The uncomfortable relationship: African enslavement in the common history of blacks and Jews. *Tikkun, 9*(2), 65–69.

Bakhtin, M. (1994). *Problems of Dostoevsky's poetics* (C. Emerson, Ed. & Trans.) Minneapolis: University of Minnesota Press. (Original work published 1973)

Barthes, R. (1985). *The grain of the voice: Interviews 1962–1980* (L. Coverdale, Trans.). New York: Hill and Wang. (Original work published 1984)

Breen, R. S. (1986). *Chamber theatre.* Evanston, IL: William Caxton.

Carlson, M. (1996). *Performance: A critical introduction.* New York: Routledge.

Cawelti, J. G. (Ed.). (1997). *Leon Forrest: Introductions and interpretations.* Bowling Green, KY: Bowling Green State University Press.

Conquergood, D. (1985). Performing as a moral act: Ethical dimensions of the ethnography of performance. *Literature in Performance, 5,* 1–13.

Conquergood, D. (1989). Poetics, play, process, and power: The performative turn in anthropology. *Text and Performance Quarterly, 9,* 82–88.

Conquergood, D. (1991). Rethinking ethnography: Towards a critical cultural politics. *Communication Monographs, 58,* 179–194.

de Certeau, M. (1988). *The writing of history.* (T. Conley, Trans.). New York: Columbia University Press. (Original work published 1975)

Denzin, N. K. (2003). *Performance ethnography: Critical pedagogy and the politics of culture.* Thousand Oaks, CA: Sage.

Donkin, E., & Clement, S. (Eds.). (1993). *Upstaging big daddy: Directing theater as if gender and race matter.* Ann Arbor: University of Michigan Press.

DuBois, W. E. B. (1989). *The souls of black folk.* New York: Bantam.

Edwards, P. (1999). Unstoried: Teaching literature in the age of performance studies. *Theatre Annual, 52,*1–147.

Fabian, J. (1990). *Power and performance: Ethnographic explorations through proverbial wisdom and theater in Shaba, Zaire.* Madison: University of Wisconsin Press.

Forrest, L. (1992). *Divine Days.* New York: Norton.

Forrest, L. (2001). *Meteor in the madhouse* (J. G. Cawelti & M. Drown, Eds.). Evanston, IL: Northwestern University Press.

Foucault, M. (1980). *Power/knowledge: Selected interviews and other writings*. New York: Pantheon.

Giroux, H. (1992). *Border crossings: Cultural workers and the politics of education*. New York: Routledge.

Hamera, J. (1998). Debts: In memory of Lilla Heston. In S. J. Dailey (Ed.), *The future of performance studies: Visions and revisions* (pp. 211–216). Annandale, VA: National Communication Association.

Hine, D. C. (2000). Rape and the inner lives of women. In V. Ruiz & E. C. DuBois (Eds.), *Unequal sisters: A multicultural reader in U.S. women's history*. New York: Routledge.

hooks, b. (1989). *Talking back: Thinking feminist, thinking black*. Boston: South End Press.

Lancaster, R. (1992). *Life is hard: Machismo, danger, and the intimacy of power in Nicaragua*. Berkeley: University of California Press.

Lefebvre, H. (1991). *The production of space* (D. Nicholson-Smith, Trans.). Oxford, England: Blackwell. (Original work published 1974)

McQuade, M. (1995). The yeast of chaos: An interview with Leon Forrest." *Chicago Review, 41*(2–3), 43–52.

Morrison, T. (1998). Home. In W. Lubiano (Ed.), *The house that race built* (pp. 3–12). New York: Vintage.

Pollock, D. (1990). Telling the told: Performing *Like a family*. *Oral History Review, 18*, 1–36.

Pollock, D. (Ed.). (1998). *Exceptional spaces: Essays on performance and history*. Chapel Hill: University of North Carolina Press.

Richards, S. L. (1996). *Ancient songs set ablaze: The theatre of Femi Osofisan*. Washington DC: Howard University Press.

Roach, J. (1996). *Cities of the dead: Circum-Atlantic performance*. New York: Columbia University Press.

Rosaldo, R. (1989). *Culture and truth: The remaking of social analysis*. Boston: Beacon.

Rosenberg, B. A. (1997). Leon Forrest and the African American folk sermon. In J. G. Cawelti (Ed.), *Leon Forrest: Introductions and interpretations* (pp. 114–127). Bowling Green, KY: Bowling Green State University Press.

Savigliano, M. E. (1995). *Tango and the political economy of passion*. Boulder, CO: Westview.

Schechner, R. (2003). *Performance studies: An introduction*. New York: Routledge.

Smith, D. L. (1998). What is black culture? In W. Lubiano (Ed.), *The house that race built* (pp. 178–193). New York: Vintage.

Spivak, G. C. (1996). *The Spivak reader: Selected works of Gayatri Chakravorty Spivak* (D. Landry & G. Maclean, Eds.). New York: Routledge.

Strine, M. S. (1998). Mapping the "cultural turn" in performance studies. In S. J. Dailey (Ed.), *The future of performance studies: Visions and revisions* (pp. 3–9). Annandale, VA: National Communication Association.

Taussig, M. (1993). *Mimesis and alterity: A particular history of the senses*. New York: Routledge.

Visweswaran, K. (1994). *Fictions of feminist ethnography*. Minneapolis: University of Minnesota Press.

White, H. K. (1975). *Metahistory: The historical imagination in nineteenth-century Europe*. Baltimore: Johns Hopkins University Press.

22

"She Attempted to Take Over the Choreography of the Sex Act"

Dance Ethnography and the
Movement Vocabulary of Sex and Labor

BARBARA BROWNING

The ethnographic analysis of dance is most meaningful, of course, when movement aesthetics can be convincingly related to their larger sociopolitical context. In this essay I want to survey briefly two protodance ethnographic texts which suggested possible strategies for making these links; two deeply influential texts which would help to establish this area of scholarship; several of the more recent and interesting books in the field; and finally my own reading of the transformation of the movements of the body politic into particular cultural dance forms, ultimately into politically engaged and aesthetically challenging experimental choreography.

TECHNIQUES OF THE BODY: WORK AND SEX IN MAUSS AND BOAS

Marcel Mauss (1872–1950) published the essay "Techniques of the Body" in 1935, in the *Journal de Psychologie Normale et Pathologique*. It's a seminal text—pithy, funny, but profound. It raises, for me, some of the most salient questions in dance scholarship—and, for that matter, in dance production. These are questions plumbed by some of the most incisive works in the field of dance ethnography, but also in the choreographic experimentation that we broadly construe as "postmodern," both here in the United States and abroad. In the essay, Mauss bemoans the fact that so much of what interests him in human behavior tends to be relegated to the category of "miscellany" in sociological and anthropological studies. He refers to the underexamined banal activities we tend to naturalize, and hence ignore. Mauss argues that acts of quotidian movement—walking, squatting, sitting—are by no means "natural," but are in fact highly culturally specific: "A young Frenchman has no idea how to sit up straight;

his elbows stick out sideways; he puts them on the table and so on" (Mauss, 1992, p. 458). While Mauss emphasizes the cultural context of body techniques, he cites yet another primary category in any given culture that differentiates the ways in which people accrue movement techniques: "Sexual division of body techniques (and not just sexual division of labor)" (p. 460). That is, while it goes without saying that a society's sexual division of labor will lead many men and women to accrue a different set of techniques, even non-functional gestures, such as making a (non-pugilistic) fist, might be learned differently by the different genders.

So will sexual techniques themselves. Mauss's "Biographical List of Body Techniques" begins and ends (or nearly ends) with gender-specific activities related to sex and reproduction: He starts with *"Techniques of birth and obstetrics"* (Buddha's mother, he tells us, gave birth in a standing position, clinging to the branch of a tree) and ends, almost,[1] with *"Techniques of reproduction."* Of the latter, Mauss notes matter-of-factly: "Nothing is more technical than sexual positions" (p. 473) (he cites specifically a position in which a woman's knees are suspended from a man's elbows—a technique he insists enjoys popularity throughout "the whole Pacific").

Labor and sex are, doubtless, highly choreographed activities. Mauss's occasionally comical suggestions regarding the cultural specificity of certain techniques don't undermine the force of his call for more serious consideration of these seemingly banal body techniques as significant elements of culture. And one might—in fact should—extend his observations on the importance of the intracultural choreographic differentiation of normative gender body techniques to comprehend class as well. That is, again, it's not simply a matter of *class* division of labor, but of the ways in which individuals are choreographed *into* their class through a variety of naturalized quotidian movements.

Mauss's near-contemporary, Franz Boas (1858–1942), also expressed an interest in the choreographic aspects of quotidian movement. Boas, like Mauss, is not remembered primarily as a dance ethnographer, and yet he promoted and participated in the foundation-laying work of his daughter, Franziska Boas, and a number of his students and protégés who would establish the emerging field of dance ethnography. In 1972, Franziska Boas would publish a series of papers presented by her father and several others some 30 years earlier in a seminar on the function of dance in human society. Franz Boas, while not positing himself as a dance specialist, pays close attention to the relationship between quotidian gestures and more recognizably choreographic movement among the Kwakiutl. In the question-and-answer period, someone asks: "What is the relation of ordinary movement in everyday activity to the movements of the dance?" (p. 18) Boas goes on to reflect, like Mauss, on the cultural specificity of walking, and then, prompted by another question, of the habits of sitting provoked by the use of a canoe. He ponders the aesthetics of "movements having to do with work" (p. 19) and their relationship to choreographic patterns in cultural dances.

While, as I said, Boas isn't typically categorized as a dance scholar,[2] he actively encouraged the development of the field, urging his students (among them Margaret Mead and Claire Holt—both contributors to his daughter's 1972 volume—as well as his daughter[3]) to examine seriously movement and gesture. And Boas's sensitivity to gender and race politics in the field of anthropology[4] seems to me directly related to his inclination to link cultural aesthetics to movements of labor, which, following Mauss's argument, cannot be extricated from sex, class, and ethnicity.

In other words, I'm suggesting that seeing the connections between the quotidian movements of sex and work and that movement more easily construed as "dance" is an inherently politicized project.

DEREN, DUNHAM, AND THE
GRACE OF THE BODIES' BEARING

There is a passage in Maya Deren's *Divine Horsemen* which might, and should, give one pause:

> If a visitor to Haiti were to spend most of his time on a country roadside, he would have the sense of being spectator at some theater-in-the-round, where a lyric dance drama of prodigious grace and infinite variety is in continuous performance. One could say that the beginning is an overture in the pre-dawn dark, when small groups of "voyageurs," making their way market-ward from the distant mountains, pass unseen along the road, trailing a melodic line. . . . The bodies of the market-bound women are like fine dark stalks, at once supple and steady, bearing tremendous blooms of egg-plant purple, tomato red, carrot orange, greens of all shades, on their heads. . . . Whether here, or in the men walking toward the fields, the grace of the bodies' bearing is so manifest that it imparts elegance to even the most poorly cut dress and the most patched and baggy overalls. In the backyard, the women cooking, tending the children, carrying water, forever doing laundry or braiding each other's hair, possess, also this same grace of the body, which, since so much is demanded of it, has discovered how to achieve by balance what might otherwise require muscular force. (Deren, 1953, p. 226)

Deren calls this technical prowess a "natural grace," but also a "stylization," learned through habit and necessity. Stylization, one might also note, is inherent in the description itself, which effectively choreographs a context for thinking about Haitian movement aesthetics. The passage itself is highly theatricalizing, even as it attributes theatricality to the landscape and the culture of Haiti.

Of course what is disconcerting about the passage is the aestheticizing of the labor of a peasant class working under brutal conditions, such that the very trappings of their poverty (the poorly cut dress, the patched overalls) acquire an air of elegance, becoming mere costumes in the "lyric dance drama" of their daily struggles.

Interestingly, long before she became interested in Haitian dance, Deren (1917–1961) was a committed labor activist. She spent her college years at Syracuse University and NYU working for the Young People's Socialist League, and later participated in the Trotskyist movement in New York. How is it that a woman with such an interest in class politics could slip into such an apparent romanticization of the choreography of exploitative labor? *Divine Horsemen*, in fact, is a book rife with such awkward moments, where issues of class and aesthetics seem at odds. The "Author's Preface" presents an even more vexing maneuver, when Deren suggests that her "own ordeal as an 'artist-native' in an industrial culture" lent her an insider's vantage point in addressing Haitian peasant culture:

> Of all persons from a modern culture, it is the artist who, looking at a native looking at a "white" man—whether tourist, industrialist or anthropologist—would mutter the heart-felt phrase: "Brother, I sure know what you're thinking and you can think that thought again!" (Deren, 1953, p. 8)

One can sympathize with Deren's observation about the lack of support for artists (an observation certainly valid today) and still cringe at the suggestion that the underfunded and misunderstood North American experimental filmmaker suffers parallel indignities to those of an impoverished Haitian laborer.

And yet if one reads Deren with some indulgence, taking on good faith her longstanding commitment to thinking seriously about labor politics, there might be reason to want to recuperate something from the description of the "grace of the [workers'] bodies' bearing."

That "lyric dance drama" that Deren describes is a well-worn cliché among many so-called ethnic dance companies, who are often pressed by funders, venues, and audiences to give a sense of the larger social contexts from which their "cultural" dances emerge. How many African, Caribbean, and Latin American companies have initiated their programs with graceful women bearing baskets or jars on their heads, sashaying onto the stage with dignified grace, as muscular men rhythmically haul in fishing nets, drag hoes, or wield machetes? Is there a way to read through the romanticization of the scene, and think deeply about how labor's movement *is* choreographic, but not ever *merely* aesthetic? Could that observation help us to understand how even more obviously aesthetic dance performances bear resonances which should make us reflect on labor and class issues?

And what of sex? Again, in the case of Deren, one is tempted to suggest that certain aspects of her sexual politics which preceded her research in Haiti might have inflected her manner of reading sexual choreography in Haitian dance. The section where she considers most closely the erotics of Haitian dance, not surprisingly, is the section dealing with Erzulie, the "Goddess of Love." Erzulie possesses, Deren writes, "a fecundity which minor men would call promiscuity. But her several lovers among the [deities], who are major men, and the serviteurs, who have learned to see her through their eyes, have never called it that." (1953, pp. 141–42)

Deren describes not only Erzulie's dancing, but also her ritual obligations which fall outside of what would typically be understood as dance: "Her first act is to perform an elaborate toilette. . . . It is the elaborate formalism of her every gesture which transforms this toilette from a simple functional activity to a ritual statement." (1953, p. 141) The quotidian act of Erzulie's sexual toilette becomes, for Deren, the very essence of aesthetic refinement, exemplary of "the painstaking process by which a work of man—be it art or myth—is created" (p. 142).

It strikes me as by no means insignificant that it is Erzulie that Deren will claim to receive, spiritually, into her own body. And it also strikes me as by no means insignificant

that Deren herself, in developing her public and artistic persona, cultivated "a fecundity which minor men would call promiscuity."

The first volume of the massive documentary biography, *The Legend of Maya Deren,* compiled by VèVè A. Clark, Millicent Hodson, and Catrina Neiman, contains materials relating to Deren's activities up until the period when Deren began working for Katherine Dunham, prior to the flourishing of her film experiments and the research travels to Haiti which would eventually lead to the publication of *Divine Horsemen.* There are various colorful anecdotes regarding Deren's personal life in the late '30s, when she was living in Greenwich Village and was active in the Trotskyist movement. An old acquaintance, Louis Zwerling, provides a couple of interviews on the Bohemian political and social scene in which Deren circulated. And in a decidedly *minor* and yet amusing passage, Zwerling remembers,

> She had an apartment in the Village. She was one of the few people around who had an income of her own and an apartment of her own. It was a very small apartment—all I can remember is the bedroom *(Laughs)*. The memory is kaleidoscopic. She was never at rest. She was constantly involved in something—either writing, packing things or putting things away. Whatever she was doing always had a sense of energetic need about it. . . . I think I spent about two or three nights there at the most. The thing that I remember most is that she attempted to take over the choreography of the sex act *(Laughs)*. (Clark, Hodson, & Neiman, 1984, p. 319)

The Legend of Maya Deren is an interesting project precisely because of the editors' disinclination to editorialize—or to prioritize the Deren archive. Clark, Hodson, and Neiman refrain from deleting or commenting explicitly on some of the more questionable or even tasteless reminiscences (Zwerling goes on to remember: "She was very hairy *[Laughs]*." Clark et al., 1984, p. 322).

But the very "miscellany" of Deren's own persona—the choreography of her sexual and political being—are intensely meaningful. As are Erzulie's. *"Do you remember how she walked?"* they ask Zwerling. And he answers,

> Yes. I remember how she walked. She had a very masculine walk, very straight, shoulders pulled back. I danced with her a few times. And I dance with great abandon. That's the only time she loosened up, the first night we were dancing at the Village Vanguard. I used to go there often. She was there that night. We danced and were seduced while dancing. She did have abandon when she danced, otherwise she was very uptight. (Clark et al., 1984, p. 322)

But when *wasn't* she dancing? Her "energetic," incessant activity around her apartment, her "masculine" walk, her choreographic assertiveness in the sex act—these were as much a part of her dance with Zwerling as what happened at the Village Vanguard. It's *all* choreographic—and all deeply meaningful.

When Deren first contacted Katherine Dunham in 1941, she professed herself to have "a very deep feeling for the dance with some uncultivated talent in that direction." (Clark et al., 1984, p. 431) And although Dunham would take her on as an assistant on the basis of her obvious intelligence and passionate interest in ethnological research, she was never convinced that Deren really had a gift, uncultivated or otherwise, for dance. No one ever questioned Dunham's movement sensibility, or virtuosity. Dunham (b. 1909) conducted research on dance and religion in Haiti long before Deren, but her best-known book on the subject, *Island Possessed,* was published years later than *Divine Horsemen*—and in fact eight years after Deren's untimely death.

Her research was encouraged by her anthropological mentor, Melville Herskovits, who was a student of Boas, and she had also had contact with others of his protégés, including Margaret Mead. In fact, Dunham recounts, "The last handshake was with the father of them all, Franz Boas, just before I left New York for the Caribbean" (Dunham, 1969, p. 66). Dunham represented, for Herskovits as well as another mentor, Robert Redfield, and Boas, the hope of an "insider's perspective," at least relative to their own, in Haiti: this, on the basis of her race, as well as her dance training.

Dunham's kinetic sensitivity is evident in the detailed descriptions of movement sequences in the dances of Vodou. She had earlier documented these dances in even greater detail in academic publications. *Island Possessed* isn't, strictly speaking, a dance ethnography: it combines ethnographic accounts of various rituals with observations on Haiti's political history (including a scathing assessment of the remnants of the U.S. military occupation there) and a significant amount of personal narrative. Political history is inextricable in the book from personal memoir, as one of Dunham's most intense relationships in Haiti was with Dumarsais Estimé, who would go on to serve, briefly and under tremendous pressure, as Haiti's president. One of Estimé's primary concerns was the exploitative child labor practice known as "'ti moune," or "little people." Dunham writes,

> The "ti moune" system was one of the preoccupations of the Estimé whom I knew—and education for the masses, and shoes for everyone, and sanitation in market places, which were the disseminating points of disease, and recognition of Haiti on an equal level in the rest of the world. . . . Gradually I began to see the things around me with his eyes, with his evaluations, though never losing the intense preoccupation with what I had come to Haiti for, the vaudun and the complex surrounding it. (Dunham, 1969, p. 42)

Dunham *does* record the rituals, and their aesthetic principles as revealed through the dance. But she sees this choreography as part of a larger political dance. When she recounts her instruction in the dances of the deities, she also recounts the various body techniques she had to acquire in living under the deprivations of the Vodou community. She describes learning among her fellow initiates to squat over a calabash in order to pee—a far piece from the elegant amenities offered by the luxury hotel where she would receive the visits of the future president. These gestures are part of the movement pedagogy which will allow her, ultimately, to dance among Vodou *serviteurs*.

Island Possessed trains its eye not only on the aesthetic choreographies of Haitian Vodou practitioners, but also on their daily lives. Dunham reflects, as well, on her own social status moving through that world. She also reflects on her sexual traversal of that space. While her reminiscences of Estimé are relatively discreet (certainly more discreet than those of Louis Zwerling), Dunham makes it clear that she, too, exercised a certain "fecundity" which "minor men" might construe as promiscuous. She owns that way of moving through the world with a combination of dignity, self-possession, and grace.

And ultimately, all of these techniques of the body—from the seemingly banal but immensely significant act of squatting over a calabash to lying down beside Dumarsais Estimé to learning the incredibly challenging spine-undulation of Vodou's ritual choreographies—*all* of these techniques of the body inform one another. They also, without a doubt, went on to inform her choreographic practice as one of the great movement innovators and experimentalists of twentieth century dance.

FOLDING THE TOWEL: "A-DEE, A-DAH, A-DEEEEEE . . . DAH"

The connections between the movement techniques of labor, sex, and dance are implicit in Deren and Dunham. In some of the more provocative dance ethnography of the last fifteen years or so, these connections have become explicit. Sally Ann Ness's *Body, Movement and Culture: Kinesthetic and Visual Symbolism in a Philippine Community* (1992)

contains some marked moments where a Maussian reading of the techniques of quotidian movement are directly related to Philippine dance aesthetics. In fact, her theoretical introduction on "Ethnography and Choreography" argues that dance training sensitizes one to quotidian choreographies within one's own culture, as well as another's. Ness recollects learning a modern choreography, "For Betty," from a company member of the Bill Evans Dance Company—a movement phrase which involved a scooping arm movement echoed by a circling of the hips.

The very stylization and specificity of the phrase lead her to consider her body techniques outside of the studio:

> Who was this "I" that learned the dance? Initially, the person learning "For Betty" was the "I" of ordinary life, a being that rode the city buses daily up and down Seattle's steep hills and lived in a run-down college dormitory in its marginally safe Central District. This "I" performed such everyday actions as folding bathroom towels and straightening bed sheets, buying groceries at local health food coops, and drinking innumerable cups of Seattle's famous everyday coffee from the heavy mugs and cups of its many coffeehouses. This person who entered the studio of the repertory class was an "I" that had emerged from a certain habitual posture, a daily "Seattlite" posture so well practiced that it no longer needed to be mindful of the relationships between its major bodily members. This was an "I" that lived mainly in its visual and aural imagination and memory, up "inside" its head. It possessed an arm, which served "me" throughout the ordinary courses of the day, lifting mugs, holding books, clutching bags, and so forth. However, in the process of acquiring the choreography, this normal "I" that had started out to learn the movement turned out to be inappropriate for the task." (Ness, 1992, p. 4)

The acquisition of an unfamiliar movement pattern through choreography, that is, brings one into awareness of one's existing body techniques in a way that makes them strange. "There is something," Ness says, "essentially anthropological about choreographic phenomena" (1992, p. 4). The making-strange parallels the inherent destabilization of naturalized movement techniques which occurs in ethnographic fieldwork.

Ness goes on to explore everyday activities in which one might suddenly become aware of "dancelike moments":

> Sometimes, when I am performing ordinary daily tasks—folding up a bath towel, moving a potted plant from a table to the floor, or walking to the corner store—I feel almost as though I am doing someone's dance. It happens when the rhythm of the action is especially clear, clear enough to vocalize as a sound phrase. In the case of folding a towel, holding it by both corners, one in each hand, and pressing the center of the top edge to my sternum with my chin to hold it steady, the phrase might emerge as:
>
> "a-*dee*, a-dah, a-deeeeee . . . dah"
>
> (one fold, another fold, holding center/releasing chin and letting top half fall over bottom . . . folding finished). (1992, p. 7)

While Ness quite self-consciously situates her movement world within a relatively comfortable middle-class life of U.S. privilege, it strikes me as not inconsequential that the exemplary quotidian movement in which she understands herself to be always, on some level, dancing is an act of domestic labor which tends to be understood as predominantly women's work: the folding of laundry. She will go on to remark on certain "resilient" aspects of quotidian movement among the people of Cebu City, such as the manipulation of chess pieces,[5] performed with a certain agility and precision. These quotidian movements will inform her reading of the Cebuanos' dances. But in keeping with Mauss's observations, it isn't merely national or local culture which choreographs our body techniques. Class and gender inflect them as well.

Appearing three years after Ness's book, Marta Savigliano's *Tango and the Political Economy of Passion* (1995) conjoined issues of political economy with libidinal economy. In an ambitious if at times unwieldy effort to demonstrate dance's imbrication in the power struggles of ethnicity, labor, and sex, Savigliano argues that dance's aesthetic and "affective" qualities cannot be abstracted from their political context: "A trackable trafficking in emotions and affects has paralleled the process by which the core countries of the capitalist world system have extracted material goods and labor from, and imposed colonial state bureaucratic apparatuses and ideological devices on, the Third World periphery" (pp. 1–2). Tango is, itself, a "Spectacle of Sex, Race and Class" (p. 30) in which these related power struggles are given choreographic form.

While Savigliano doesn't perform movement analysis on specific, embodied aspects of these struggles, she does suggest that an initiation into the dance form is an initiation into larger dances of sex and labor. In two accounts of her own pedagogical experiences of the tango, "First Steps in Tango" and "Latest Tango Steps: Postmodern Uses of Passion," Savigliano indicates that her uncle's choreographic instruction was meant not only to steer her across the dance floor, but into the world of sexual conflict, and her theoretical inculcation into postmodern cultural theory was meant to choreograph her understanding of the politics of intellectual labor. Further, she suggests that the very stylization of her writing about these dances, literal and figurative, takes on both the aesthetic and the political strategies of the dance itself. She proposes a *partnering* with her reader—one which is agile, tricky, and not infrequently antagonistic. This is, precisely, her manifestation of intellectual labor *as* a dance:

> Poststructuralism refreshed my memories of tango and provided me with a scholarly discourse to write about it; at the same time, tango allowed me to perform poststructuralist strategies quite "comfortably"—with the

sense of ownership, of dancing the tango—
and it pushed me into a critique of the multivocal, multilayered game. "Latest Tango
Steps: Postmodern Uses of Passion" is actually a tango about postmodernism—a tango
in prose, melodramatic like the tango. It is a
tango account of postmodernism, as the
First Steps are a poststructuralist, feminist
account of tango (caricatures, representations suited to what I wish to emphasize,
both ways). Postmodernism is a universalizing, naturalizing and totalizing version of
the cynicism and fatalism displayed by the
tango. This is what I have tried to express
in the "Latest Tango Steps." (Savigliano,
1995, p. 223)

In a somewhat less formally complex manner, Julie Taylor's *Paper Tangos* (1998) also
attempts to find in the tango itself a model for
a kind of psychic labor which might allow
Taylor to break through and discover the
deeper political ramifications of the disciplining of the body through choreographic pedagogy. "In Argentina, the tango," she writes,

> can create a space to reflect on power and
> on terror. The tango can talk about how to
> think about these things, how to carry them
> with dignity and grace, and how to demon-
> strate the nobility of the human spirit by
> learning to bear such suffering and never-
> theless to dance." (Taylor, 1998, p. 72)

Paper Tangos, as its title implies, replicates
structurally some of the strategies of the
dance's partnering, drawing the reader into a
complicit and intimate political and psychic
tango. She convincingly lays bare the memories of political violence that Argentines both
exercise and exorcize through the dance; and
she confessionally bares her own history of
sexual trauma which likewise surfaces in
choreographic maneuvers. The political disciplining of bodies during the Dirty War, and
the terror of Taylor's childhood sexual abuse,
are read as choreographic phenomena which
are merely rendered visible in the dance.

While the language of gracefulness under the
pressures of suffering may seem to echo Deren's

observations of "the grace of the bodies'
bearing," Taylor insists that the suffering is also
what is manifested in the dance—the dance
insists that we not forget it, that we look at it.

Alma Guillermoprieto's *Samba* (1990) also
considered a dance form which is often characterized as manifesting outward ebullience
and grace in the face of desperate social conditions, and this narrative is certainly a part
of that book's stance. But her more recent
*Dancing with Cuba: A Memoir of the
Revolution* (2004) presents a more nuanced
and ambivalent account of the relationship
between dance and the politics of labor and
sex. In some ways, *Dancing with Cuba* echoes
Dunham's *Island Possessed*: it looks back on
the author's experiences, years before the
penning of the book, in an unfamiliar but
politically compelling culture, replete with
interwoven sexual relationships and aesthetic
revelations. Guillermoprieto spent six months
in Cuba in 1970 as a modern dance instructor
in the National Art Schools. She arrived a relatively unpoliticized aesthete, and gradually
absorbed some of the political idealism of the
followers of the revolution. Her class politicization was thoroughly intertwined with her
developing sense of her sexual self, and her
views of dance couldn't be extricated from
either of those things. She leaves, however,
ambivalent about it all, and the retrospective
stance of the book, reflecting on Cuba's political trajectory since then, remains ambivalent.
The "Epilogue" compresses Guillermoprieto's own trajectory:

> In the early months of my return I lost a
> good number of my dance-world friends,
> who couldn't understand the new vocabu-
> lary I'd brought back from Havana or my
> reproaches for their lack of solidarity with
> the world's sufferings. I made new friends
> who shared my concerns. I protested against
> the Vietnam War in New York and in
> Washington, and I dedicated long hours of
> work to Latin America's struggles for liber-
> ation. I stopped dancing. . . . (2004, p. 283)

But did she stop dancing? Or had the understanding of the choreographic complexity of labor and sex become ingrained in her way of looking at the world?

Guillermoprieto documents both the utopianism of the revolution and its missteps. The emphasis on the *zafra,* the collective participation of all members of society in the sugar harvest, regardless of individuals' mastery of the body techniques of agricultural labor, begins to look like an unstrategic choreographic choice on Castro's part. The dance of the state is shown to be at times as awkward as Guillermoprieto's efforts to teach modern dances which seem, even to her, woefully out of place.

The most evocative dance description in *Dancing with Cuba* is not in the passages recounting either the awkwardness or the agility of her students as they learned both the "folkloric" dances of their country or the Cunningham technique Guillermoprieto had been contracted to teach them. Rather, it is a description of a cosmic ballet spontaneously danced by Guillermoprieto on the eve of her departure. She is out with a small group of friends, some politically committed but vulnerable gay nondancer intellectuals who have become her most intimate and elucidating companions in Cuba. They are trying to explain to Guillermoprieto the mechanics of a lunar eclipse, and finally decide to demonstrate it to her by choreographing themselves into the alignment of the heavenly bodies. They cast Guillermoprieto as the earth, as they embody sun and moon, and each takes on his or her appropriate orbital pattern and speed of revolution: "And we laughed and spun and laughed and spun, until the eclipse occurred" (Guillermoprieto, 2004, p. 282).

The cosmic choreography, of course, is an extreme figure of a naturalized understanding of how we dance together. But the eclipse configured by Guillermoprieto in this passage is a very worldly one: the political ambivalence she experienced in watching both the successes and the failures of communism. Encroachment on

sexual freedom, as well as aesthetic freedom, would ultimately complicate Guillermoprieto's enthusiastic embrace of the revolution's politics of labor. Whether or not one agrees with the conclusions she drew, one can see that these are inextricable choreographies.

"RAW SELF . . . SOCIAL BODY . . . STEREOTYPES . . . ALL AT THE SAME TIME . . ."

My own work in the field of dance ethnography has concentrated on Brazilian dance—including religious, martial, and secular movement arts. My first book, *Samba: Resistance in Motion* (1995) examined samba, the divine choreographies of Candomblé, capoeira, and the various, constantly evolving popular dances of the carnaval and other popular festivals in Salvador, Bahia. I later published *Infectious Rhythm: Metaphors of Contagion and the Spread of African Culture* (1998) in an effort to place the African diasporic cultural forms of Brazil in a larger sociopolitical context. That political contextualization was in *Samba* in a somewhat embryonic form. *Infectious Rhythm* had little direct analysis of dance or movement arts, but many of its insights regarding the global dance of the exploitation of black labor and sexuality were derived from my experiences with dance.

In *Samba,* I documented the process of my initiation into Brazilian movement culture under the instruction of a number of individuals, including the Candomblé priestess Mãe Aildes, the capoeira master Mestre Boa Gente, and the charismatic and versatile movement artist Loremil Machado. I also studied at the Federal University of Bahia under the extremely talented Rosângela Silvestre, who would go on to establish a bicontinental career as an innovative choreographer merging "traditional" forms with other movement techniques. Silvestre has developed a movement pedagogy and a choreographic system (which she formerly described as "contemporary

Afro-Brazilian dance" but now more specifically labels the "Silvestre technique"). One of the marked aspects of her training process is that it draws on the movements typical of black women's labor in Brazil. That is, many of her preparatory exercises are recognizably mimetic of certain forms of domestic labor: the muscular stirring of an enormous bowl of *acarajé* or bean batter for frying; the full-bodied, undulating rubbing of laundry in the waters of a lagoon; and the more minute but equally choreographic gestures of the toilette.

The acknowledgement of the technical and even athletic aspects of quotidian movement occurs in other areas of Brazilian movement pedagogy. My capoeira master, for example, used to scoff at the idea of a "warm-up." One's entire day, he argued, should be considered an opportunity to attend to one's strength, balance, and flexibility. He would tell a student working as "boy" in an office (tellingly, this denigrating term was used in English) that any time he dropped a pencil on the floor, he had the opportunity to lunge, stretch, and reach for the pencil in a way that would prepare him for his evening movement classes. Silvestre also draws to some extent on capoeira in both her technique and choreographies. But women's movement vies with men's in its physicality, force, and dramatic power. While she herself derives many movements from the religious dances of Candomblé, and while her own mother is a priestess who performs "folkloric" dances regularly, Silvestre abstracts these movements, as well as the movements of labor exercised by her mother and so many other working class women, in a way which doesn't romanticize the challenges they face, but rather manifests the literal strength they need to face them.

In some ways, Silvestre's efforts to develop a technique and a choreographic style blurring the boundary between the traditional and the experimental obviously parallels Katherine Dunham's development of her own technique. Silvestre's insistence on highlighting the body

techniques of women's labor is a powerfully meaningful emphasis with deep political ramifications.

Rosane Chamecki and Andrea Lerner, two New York–based Brazilian choreographers, have a somewhat more attenuated relationship to "traditional" forms, and yet their choreographic rendering of sexual body techniques also speaks volumes to the relationship between dance and sexual expressivity in Brazil—and the ways that relationship is seen throughout the world. Recently, their company, chameckilerner, staged "Costumes by God" at the Dance Theater Workshop in New York. Chamecki and Lerner's program notes state: "In our latest pieces we've been breaking up from our polished and complex physical structures—we allow the body to be its raw self, the social body, full of references and stereotypes, all at the same time." (chameckilerner) What does this mean, to allow the body to be "raw," "social," and "stereotyped" at the same time?

As the audience took their seats at the opening of "Costumes by God," a naked man and woman, Levi Gonzalez and Jennifer Kjos, assumed a variety of tableaux vivants, not explicitly sexual in nature—yet their nudity evoked the title of the piece, and seemed to gesture simultaneously toward nature (they were both *au naturel,* of course, but also not particularly "dancerly" in body type—in other words, however technical their training history might have been, their bodies didn't bear its visible trace) and stylization (their gestures were oddly formal, frozen—and of course, there they were on a proscenium stage). After they exited the stage, the four principal dancers (Luciana Achugar, Maria Hassabi, Michael Portnoy, and Jeremy Wade) came on, dressed (one of the male dancers wore merely a twisted bed sheet, but the rest wore vaguely professional street clothing). For the rest of the evening, to Beco Dranoff's electronic/samba mixed score, these four dancers assumed an assortment of very explicitly sexual poses—usually in pairs, but in constantly changing configurations. Many of the poses were nearly still, yet evolving, and some involved the kind of awkward, humping, inelegantly convulsive movement one would tend to attribute to the most "natural," unself-conscious moments of sexual activity. But of course even these gestures were entirely chore-ographed. And in between segments, a virtu-osic Brazilian samba dancer, Fernanda Meyer, entered, in feathered headdress and white jeans and tank top, rhythmically and grace-fully gliding across the stage.

Was this "Brazilian dance"? What did this layered choreography, in which the categories of "raw," "social" and "stereotyped" sexual-ity overlapped, mean? The program notes cited Bataille on eroticism ("Human sexual activity . . . is . . . erotic . . . whenever it is not rudimentary and purely animal"—but then again, the piece seemed to ask, when is it?), and Marguerite Duras on an ideal theatricality which would create "the smell of sex." They also cited, to my surprise, my own *Samba:* "When I say that there are both internal and external stereotypes of Brazilian sexuality which get played out in dance, I should add that these stereotypes are sometimes difficult to distinguish and always difficult to disentan-gle from one another." Fortunately, the sen-tence still made sense to me when I read it. In fact, it made significantly *more* sense to me after watching "Costumes by God."

In a global context, Brazilian dance contin-ues to circulate with "the smell of sex." That is to say, it carries with it an international stereotype of sexual excess promulgated not only by tourism and cultural export, but by the reabsorption of the stereotype itself into a story the nation narrates to itself about its cul-tural identity. "Costumes by God" expressed a similarly ironic appraisal of the notion of Brazilians as "naturally sexually expressive" to Marta Savigliano's appraisal of the notion of Argentines as "inherently passionate." Samba and tango are indeed infinitely expressive

forms, but their inscriptions of sexuality are by no means evidence of a "natural" state. As Mauss so succinctly argued, "Nothing is more technical than sexual positions."

Except, possibly, the choreography of labor. Sally Ann Ness said that learning chore-ography taught her about the defamiliarizing and denaturalizing possibilities of ethnogra-phy. Ethnography might likewise teach dancers about the denaturalizing possibilities of dance. Experimental choreography which deals with naturalized notions of "culture" does much of the same work as the most rig-orous dance ethnography. Dunham knew this. And maybe if we keep writing it, and dancing it, we'll eventually be able to remember it.

NOTES

1. Here's the brief line that follows the section on sexual technique: "*Techniques of the care of the abnormal:* Massages and so on. But let us move on" (Mauss, 1992, p. 473).

2. In fact, this volume (Boas, 1972) documents a charmingly inarticulate response on Boas's part to a question about Kwakiutl dance aesthetics as demonstrated in a particular "light" kind of stamp-ing movement: "Lightness! . . . Very compli-cated . . ." (Boas, p. 19). Sally Ann Ness cites this passage as an exemplary moment illustrating the challenges of dance description: "Franz Boas's exclamation, "Lightness!," reveals the problematic nature of describing the quality of even a familiar movement, such as a stamp." (Ness, 1992, p. 238) Whether the suspended description of a gesture's "Lightness!" should be attributed to Boas's own lack of descriptive language or to the inherent diffi-culties in movement analysis is perhaps not so important as his own repeated insistence on the importance of ethnographic analysis being pro-duced by those with personal familiarity with the cultural material in question, whether on the basis of ethnicity, gender, or a history of dance training.

3. Franziska Boas (1902–1988) established her reputation as a dance therapist, but she was also the founder of the Boas School of Dance, which offered intercultural, or what today would probably be termed "multicultural," dance train-ing. A surprising number of future experimental-ists worked under her, including, notably, John Cage and Merce Cunningham.

4. Boas's explicit embrace of an antiracist politics in framing the goals of U.S. anthropology is surely his most significant, if controversial, intellectual intervention.

5. Interestingly, Maya Deren also abstracted and stylized the manipulation of chess pieces in her experimental film, *At Land* (Deren, 1944).

REFERENCES

Boas, F. (Ed.). (1972). *The function of dance in human society*. New York: Dance Horizons.

Browning, B. (1995). *Samba: Resistance in motion.* Bloomington: Indiana University Press.

Browning, B. (1998). *Infectious rhythm: Metaphors of contagion and the spread of African culture.* New York: Routledge.

Clark, V. A. (1984). *The legend of Maya Deren: A documentary biography and collected works* (Vol. I). New York: Anthology Film Archives.

Deren, M. (1944). At Land [Motion picture]. In *Maya Deren: Experimental Films (1943-58)* [Digital video disc]. (Available from Mystic Fire Video, 19 Gregory Drive, S. Burlington, VT 05403).

Deren, M. (1953). *Divine horsemen: The living gods of Haiti.* New York: Thames and Hudson.

Dunham, K. (1969). *Island possessed.* Chicago: University of Chicago Press.

Guillermoprieto, A. (1990). *Samba.* New York: Random House.

Guillermoprieto, A. (2004). *Dancing with Cuba: A memoir of the revolution.* New York: Random House.

Mauss, M. (1992). Techniques of the body. In J. Crary & S. Kwinter (Eds.), *Incorporations.* Cambridge, MA: Zone Books.

Ness, S. A. (1992). *Body, movement, and culture: Kinesthetic and visual symbolism in a Philippine community.* Philadelphia: University of Pennsylvania Press.

Savigliano, M. (1995). *Tango and the political economy of passion.* Boulder, CO: Westview Press.

Taylor, J. (1998). *Paper tangos.* Durham, NC: Duke University Press.

23

Staging Fieldwork/Performing Human Rights

D. SOYINI MADISON

To recreate for the stage the living performances of everyday remembrances, imaginings, and deeply felt encounters of ethnographic fieldwork is a radical act of translation. The substance of such a translation is only surpassed in its significance by the overwhelming necessity of purpose and ethical obligation.

This essay examines specific scenes from a public performance based on fieldwork in Ghana, West Africa. I lived in Ghana for nearly three years conducting field research with local human rights activists working in rural areas who were making courageous interventions on traditional religious practices with the specific purpose of protecting the rights of woman and girls. At the beginning of my third year, I began the process of adapting my field research into a performance to represent their work and the volatile debates that erupted from their work. These debates ignited tensions between believers in human rights on one side and believers in traditional cultural practices on the other, as well as those who were criticized by the

polarizing sides for believing in the value of both rights and tradition.

My fieldwork culminated in a performance in June 2000 in Ghana entitled: *Is It a Human Being or a Girl?*[1] The performance dramatized the range of voices and contentions from varied strands within and across human rights, traditional cultural practices, and corporate globalization. The performance was also an enactment of the implications in representing Otherness, blackness, and constructions of race and gender relative to my position as an African American and as a woman doing ethnography in Africa. And, finally, the performance embodied selections from the current literature on human rights and globalization, thereby illustrating the connections between poverty, corporate globalization, and human rights violations.

I hoped by adapting my fieldwork into a public performance before an audience of Ghanaians the performance (a) would help to assist local activists by inspiring more of an awareness among Ghanaians of human rights advocacy within their own indigenous context; (b) would disentangle and clarify the pertinent issues of the debate, as well as illuminate the connections between the global economy, poverty, and human rights abuses in the global South;[2] and (c) moreover, it would support the efforts of local activists in their struggles for social change and for public policy initiatives relative to women and children's rights.

THE PERFORMANCE QUESTION(S)

Civic debate holds a beautiful and compelling alchemy. When citizens of a society can transform their restless disturbances into public discourse by taking a stand and choosing sides; they un-nestle the expected and the possibility for alterity is born. For the ethnographer, such debates are the structures of feeling[3] put to the test and dramatized writ large.

The debates centered upon a remote and ancient religious practice known as *Trokosi* by human rights activists and *Troxovi* by traditional religious practitioners. According to rights activists, the Trokosi practice involves a child, usually a young girl below the age of twelve, being sent to a village shrine for a period of years or for the duration of her life. She is sent to the shrine for a crime or transgression committed by a family member (usually a male) in atonement or reparation for a violation that is deemed against the community and God. The girl is sent to the shrine to avert the wrathful punishment of God upon her family and village. Rights activists refer to these females as Trokosi. They describe the Trokosi practice as human bondage where girls and women labor mercilessly in the shrines as slaves without compensation or access to education and where they eventually become forced concubines of the shrine priests.

The traditionalists, however, refer to the practice as Troxovi where women and girls, referred to as *Faishidi,* are NOT sent to the shrines as slaves or concubines but are sent for moral training and cultural education. The traditionalists also claim the shrine protects the Faishidi (the females) from the amorality and the disgrace of their family's transgression. Traditionalists vehemently deny there is abuse because the Faishidi, as a result of their education in the shrine, are esteemed as "queens" with special powers. Traditionalists contend that Faishidi are taught and nurtured in the shrine in their role to become symbolic wives of the god Mawu.

The performance event was a montage of images, sounds, movements, and voices intended to disentangle and clarify both sides of the debate. In addition, the performance aimed to assist with the interventions of Ghanaian human rights activists working to reform the practice and who also wanted to preserve the more humane elements of tradition. Moreover, the performance captured the added challenge of these activists as they found themselves, for better and for worse, under the forces of the global economy, an economy that affects poverty and village life and, in turn, affects human rights.

The very notion of rights is fraught with fundamental disagreement: individual rights or collective rights; universal rights or indigenous rights; civil rights as/or against human rights. As some describe, we are living in the midst of a "human rights revolution."[4] What I know is that here on the flesh-and-blood ground of my fieldwork is the urgency for collective rights that are inseparable from human rights; and, there are indigenous rights that are universally imperative—certain things ought not to be done to any human being and certain other things ought to be done for every human being.[5] The more complex conundrum of civil rights and human rights comes down to the question: Do my civil rights infringe upon your human rights or vice verse? The freedom of movement, the freedom to acquire wealth, and the freedom to pursue happiness are rights in the global North that are putting human rights in the global South in jeopardy. This debate is more than a two-sided argument between traditionalists and rights activists. There is a third side. This side must be unraveled from its hidden abode[6] and seen in plain sight. This third side of corporate globality and its forceful machinations links poverty to the abuse of human rights.

After "being there" in the various villages in the Volta region where Trokosi/Troxovi was established and practiced; after spending a great deal of time getting to know and co-performing[7] with rights activists; after accompanying rights activists into the areas where the Trokosi/Faishidi women and girls live; after conducting several in-depth interviews with practitioners of traditional religion who supported the practice; after talking with others who were vehemently against it; after witnessing several Trokosi/Faishidi tell their stories; after meeting with chiefs and shrine priests; and, after continuously returning to the spaces where Trokosi/Troxovi was practiced, I was convinced that Trokosi/Troxovi was not *ONE* thing. It was not one homogeneous cultural practice. Some shrines were radically different from other shrines. The women and girls living as Trokosi/Troxovi in one area could not be neatly compared to those living in other areas. Trokosi/Troxovi as a religious and cultural practice *varied* depending upon where the shrine was located. *This variation of the practice was largely determined by economic circumstances.*

The areas where human rights violations were more severe were also areas where poverty was more severe. There was a stark correlation between human rights abuses and economic deprivation. As a result, several questions came to mind: How can I support the rights activists I have come to know, admire, and respect without examining how poverty impacts their work? How do I represent the dignity of tradition and honor the beliefs of traditionalists without condoning abusive cultural practices? How can I examine poverty in the developing world without implicating corporate globalization? And the most challenging

question: How do I persuasively interrogate corporate globality without interrogating local corruption and rights abuses?

THE PERFORMANCE PURPOSE

Scattered throughout my small apartment on the campus of the University of Ghana were stacks of fieldwork journals; piles of newspapers and assorted clippings; what seemed like a mountain of audio tapes; an assortment of journals and articles on African literature, politics, and philosophy; and, of course, the stockpile of books on human rights and globalization. The time had finally come; I had to stop and sort it all out. The fieldwork must end. The first questions—the red, hot, burning questions—had been answered or at least encountered. And this, for me, is the signal to move on. Next. It was time to write. Write, that is, for the body and for performance—writing that will see, hear, and move. Not such a long distance from the field yet so differently placed. I would take two years of fieldwork and make a performance. It was a matter of translating those layers and layers of witnessing—written, spoken, lived, and remembered—that surrounded me and then make them into art that mattered in *this* locale. Where do I begin? The moment that holds the very beginning is at once an end and a beginning: the end of the fieldwork and the beginning of a journey toward distinctions for art and politics. I must decide—pick and choose—from two years of living and listening in the field moments too loved and feared, too amorphous and concrete for writing, even for writing that honors the body.

Moving from the field to the script felt like I was about to cross the Sahara on foot or, even more overwhelming, compress epoch yearnings into one time-bound moment. Not impossible, just monumental. There were high stakes involved. I was about to stage a debate raging between a community of Ghanaians that held truth, dignity, and tradition at its core. Ghanaians are strongly invested in this debate. The debate constitutes implications for how they define themselves and are defined by others as a country and as a people in the twenty-first century: the battle over culture, African morality, and the process and evolution of human development. Moreover, the debate was also about something at the register of an even broader cultural politics. The performance would confront consequences of globality and globalization on local life. This performance must not only inform and enlighten, it must not only be beautifully beautiful, but it must have palpable effects for structural change and policy. Indeed, I felt the weight of purpose, which was also the weight of representation. I remembered Stuart Hall's warning that how a people are represented are how they are treated, and Dwight Conquergood's assertion that images and symbolic representations drive public policy (Hall 1992, Conquergood 1997).

I wanted to join the band of believers that illuminate politics through passion, to do what Johannes Fabian suggests and proceed from the informative to the performative (1983). And, for me, this meant a combination of natural intuition, performance technique, rhetorical strategy, and beautiful art. I was about to cross the Sahara and journey into epochs. And so, I began to enter with classic expectation— grand, nervous, and dreaming. But, the motions did not come with the necessary confidence. Something was missing. In moving from the field to the script, into more discoveries and more hard work, I needed to reassert, name, know, and embrace the guiding hand of *clarity of purpose* in this next stage. I must write it down, sing it, or repeat it like a mantra—whatever it takes for me to call it up when I veer off into too much or too little thinking, writing, and dreaming. On a the back of a postcard from the Kwame Nkrumah monument I wrote,

> The purpose is to honor the work of indigenous human rights activists and to show

that human rights is not an exclusive invention or concern of the West. The purpose is to represent the courage and intelligence of Ghanaians themselves who are working in their own country for human rights and justice. And, finally the purpose is to clarify the impact of corporate globalization on poverty and development in the global South and show the links between globalization, poverty, and human rights abuses.

As I looked about the apartment at the mass of information surrounding me, it was this clarity of purpose that provided the direction in choosing what to take with me into performance and what to leave behind. The focus on purpose lessens the weight of wallowing in the thickness of too much data to the point that I am stifled by so many choices. Choosing brought about its own brand of worries. There were narratives that were eloquent and deeply poignant, yet beyond my purpose. There were other narratives that powerfully enhanced the purpose but if made public would leave the narrator vulnerable. These were definitional ceremonies[8] performed for the narrators themselves, for me, and for the tape recorder with the trust they would not be publicly staged. These stories were the most difficult to relinquish because (from the village to the city) at varying levels of wisdom and poetry they recounted enormous acts of courage and sacrifice. The process of elimination was about meeting the goals of the project but it was also about trust. There were too many stories I had to file away still wishing the tellers could be acclaimed and appreciated through the performance, while also knowing their stories would make a strong and powerful impact on the show's purpose, but I could not use them.

And, there was another challenge that surfaced. As much as I fought against any one of the narrators appearing as a fool or a villain, and as much as I fought against blatantly promoting one side of the debate over the other, there were narratives and points of view that were privileged over others, primarily due to positioning and emphasis in the script. Objectivity was not my aspiration in scripting the performance, but equity in presenting both sides of the debate for my stated *purpose* was. I DID have a "side" in this debate and I did not wish to enact what felt like feigned objectivity, postmodern ambiguity, or safe and meaningless fairness. What I did try to keep in mind was that my side was synonymous with my recognized and transparent intentions and those intentions were best articulated first by *Ghanaians themselves* whose purpose and goals I shared. Also, my side was not without its own struggles and ambivalences about having a side in the first place, which would necessarily be part of this performance.

Moving from the field to the script, it is purpose that energizes will; then, it is politics and beauty that energizes performance.

THE PERFORMANCE SCRIPT

If ethnography is about anything it is about putting your body on the line. It is about being in a particular space for a particular period of time. You can't always change your address and live in the space (schools, police stations, cabarets, barber shops, etc.) but you must embrace the power of habitual and accustomed visitation in rituals of return and in co-performance. You can't do ethnography without embodied attention to the symbols and practices of a lived space. In-depth interviewing is a component of ethnography, but it is not ethnography, it is qualitative research. Something happens differently when your body must move and adjust to the rhythms, structures, rules, dangers, joys, and secrets of a unique location. Ethnography is as much, or more, about bodily attention—performing in and against a circumscribed space—as it is about what is told to you in an interview.

Ethnography elicits everyday ceremonies of engagement. Interviews often result in performed narratives as the proverbial knower and known move between impressions of knowledge and come together in dialogic co-performance. It is during the scripting process that these performed narratives must now be positioned for the stage.

After the rather painstaking process of deciding which narratives to leave in and which I must leave out, the narratives were finally selected. The next step was then ordering and juxtaposing them for the stage. It is at this point in the scripting process where it feels like you are both a social critic, building an argument of logic and persuasion, and an artist creating an object of imagination and beauty. But, no longer feeling like I'm walking the distance of the Sahara, I looked forward to rereading and relistening to the interview narratives a second time for the express intent of placing them in relationship between, against, and among each other: relationships of contrast, comparison, extension, and completion for the purpose of persuasion and advocacy as well as relationships of texture, intonation, tone, and lyricism for the purpose of linguistic style and aesthetic imagery. After reading and rereading—listening and relistening—to both the transcripts and live interviews, I took the timeworn and necessary next step: I grouped them. The grouping, like most methods of classification, developed organically out of the internal elements of the narratives: (1) Human Rights and Traditional Cultural Practices, (2) Corporate Globalization and Poverty, (3) Positionality and The Ethnographic Gaze.

In the *Human Rights and Traditional Cultural Practices* section, the focus was specifically on the debate itself, therefore the performance must reflect a style of contestation and rebuttal: pro-Trokosi was to embrace the voice of tradition and anti-Trokosi was to embrace the voice of human rights. To place the narratives in opposition reflected the tensions and volatility of the actual debate. As the point-counterpoint format demonstrated the disputes on each side of the argument, it was also intended to position the audience to ask the question, Where am I in this debate?

The theme of *Corporate Globalization and Poverty* would come after the first theme of rights and tradition, not only to amplify the critics of corporate globalization as respondents to the debate, but to assert that the Trokosi practice is not simply all good or all bad but that it is also a consequence of dubious globality and wretched poverty. It was in this section where I needed to ask a specific question: How do I expand the good/bad deadlock in order to get at what I believe to be a fundamental cause of human rights violations? Critiques of corporate globalization were not always an explicit part of the public debate carried out by the human rights activists and traditionalists I interviewed. However, criticism was explicit in the discussions among intellectuals, journalists, certain politicians, and other local activists I came to know when the subject of the Trokosi/Troxovi and human rights were mentioned. This was also the theme where I felt most implicated. The narrators in this section were clearly those of us who benefited most from processes of globalization, yet we were ironically the most critical of its consequences.

Positionality and the Ethnographic Gaze raised the question of my own subject positioning in the geographic space of West Africa, local rights, and the cultural practices of Others. Therefore, this theme demanded that I confront my privilege as a U.S. academic and a beneficiary of the global economy. My field notes, interview data, and the implications of my role as researcher interpreter and advocate raised questions regarding the strategic staging of my own subjectivity. Do I bring my own point of view toward globalization and consequently my own "Americanism" onto the stage? If I do this I risk the common charge of navel gazing, making myself the subject, telling my story at the expense of the Other. If I do not, I risk the charge of not making my own biases clear—of being unreflexive, of false

objectivity, of being the omnipotent observer without taking risks. If I enter the performance space or if I do not, it would be a problem. Will bringing my own story change the subject of inquiry and interest from the Other to ME? Does it make the Other's story more believable by exposing the subjectivity of the teller? These questions are certainly not a perfect measure against falling into ethnographic solipsism, but they are always the questions that help me keep in mind that I am not the subject for subject's sake, but my subjectivity is a vehicle—it is of "use value" to contextualize and historicize the Other.

THE PERFORMANCE REHEARSAL

The rehearsal process for staging ethnographic data demands a discreetly yet powerfully different set of considerations than staging a play or a literary text. The play is already written. The ethnography is not. It is always writing and rewriting itself through the rehearsal process. Therefore, the ethnographic performance not only constitutes an ethics of representation, it not only illuminates field experiences, but it is an act of data making. This means the ethnographic rehearsal must elaborate and clarify for *truth's* sake the ambiguities and risks of a people's nonfiction worlds. This is paramount because sometimes fiction is not always truer than fact.

The performance consisted of five cast members; all of whom were from the University of Ghana at Legon where I taught.[9] The first days of rehearsal were filled with an intriguing manner of cerebral evocation: thinking and talking about the meanings of Trokosi/Troxovi and how to manifest meanings through a performance that must always already pick and choose the very meanings it will display. The first days consisted of deeply relevant combinations of conversation and improvisation. I described the project in detail, my fieldwork, and the purpose of the performance. The cast thoughtfully discussed the practice and what side (if any) they stood on in the debate, as well as how they felt about the project and its purpose. The rehearsal process consisted of three dimensions: (1) Thematic Conceptualizations/ Reflective Enactment, (2) Movement Formations, and (3) Symbolic Reality.

Thematic Conceptualizations/ Reflective Enactment

The rehearsal method requires *reflective enactment* (Bacon, 1979; Conquergood, 1982; Pineau, 1994; Schechner, 1998). Reflective enactment is to match and embody a text, i.e., when the performance body and a body of knowledge palpably join in a new textual formation, sometimes with ease and sometimes with struggle. The performer enters the world of a text, and her own history, ideology, meanings, and values must now meet the history, ideology, meanings, and values of the knowledges presented before her in the text. She performs these knowledges: she feels their meanings, senses their implications, and she embodies their world. The text and context of her difference, her ideological and symbolizing body is actively cohered with the literal text and context under examination for performance. Through the performance and rehearsal process the performers get to know the stories and become them. The performer is in the moment of the "not me" and the "not not me," that is, she is herself within the self of the text. She enters into an affective and cognitive dialectic and coupling: Elyse Pineau states,

> The active body *learns* in ways that are eminently more personal, applicable, critical, and long-lasting than any other teaching method. Although this method bears resemblance to such practices as role-playing or drama therapy, genuine performance means probing beyond the surface of observable behaviors. Performance combines full body engagement with critical reflexivity, information must be engaged somatically as well as intellectually. It is the dialectical process of doing and reflecting, experiencing and

interpreting that distinguishes performance methodology from simply "acting out." (1994, p. 17)

The "doing and reflecting" that a performance methodology requires is an active intellectual, emotional, and empathic process. We grasp these textual and performative worlds and reflectively hold on to them; we relish the various ways we as performers are continuously interpreting what these worlds mean and do, and how they feel to us.

As a cast we read and reread the script, we talked, we played, we improvised, we moved, we questioned, and we imagined in our evocation of reflective enactment. From this point, it was at the level of *movement formation* when reflective enactment extended from our bodies and minds and began to shape the outer domains of the stage with a feeling of wonder, apprehension, and surprise.

Movement Formation

To create movement for the stage, we begin by forming small groups of two and three. We would then come up with a concept from our discussions and the narratives. *I asked them to name the concept—idea or conflict—in the form of a word or phrase, verb or adjective, that describes the reflective enactment of a particular moment in the script.* Examples of the words and phrases included: "suffering," "the matrix of human meanings," "poverty," "to furiously disagree, " freedom," "to observe with intensity" "strength and dignity," and "translation." The performance groups were then given time to create a *stage picture or stage image* of the concepts. The amount of time depended on how complex or detailed the image of the concept needed to be. In creating the image, the groups were often given various options depending on what kind of movement and how much movement was needed for a particular narrative, transition between narratives, or mood we wanted to depict on stage at a particular moment. The movements varied for each stage picture, including "still images" like a photograph, moving images, or moving images entailing a limited number of movements with a specific number of transitions. For example: I might ask for three distinct stage pictures or still images depicting "suffering" with two transitions between each movement, or I might ask a group to create one moving image of "translation."

After the completion of each group's image, the other cast members "read" the image, discussing what they saw and how it illuminates the text—extends, interrogates, interprets, and offers other possibilities. After the cast had sufficiently commented in an open exchange, then the group discussed how they interpreted the concept and developed their image. After each group created their movement formations and after the cast discussed them—what they represented, what questions and further meanings they raised, and how they could be improved—the stage pictures were then set to the words and text of the script. Matching the movement formations to fieldwork data opened a range of choices: we may decide to place a complete narrative within one movement formation, or only a word or phrase, or we may include several various movement formations for one narrative, or several narratives for one formation. In terms of matching voices with both the script and movement formations the choices were also endless: we sometimes included several different voices for one narrative—breaking up words and sentences with a different voice for emphasis—we sometimes formed a chorus of voices for a particular passage or punctuated a word or phrase by creating a repetition of voices—like a barely inaudible cacophony of sound. In matching and arranging voices, movements, words, and script, the possibilities become endless.

Adrian Jackson describes Augusto Boal's Image Theatre as

a series of exercises and games designed to uncover essential truths about societies and culture without resort, in the first instance, to spoken language—though this may be added in the various "dynamisations" of the images. The participants in Image Theatre make still images of their lives, feelings, experience, oppressions; groups suggest titles of themes, and then individuals "sculpt" three-dimensional images under these titles, using their own and others' "bodies as clay." However, the image work never remains static—as with all the Theatre of the Oppressed, the frozen image is simply the starting point for the prelude to the action, which is revealed in the dynamisation process, the bringing to life of the images and the discovery of whatever direction or intention is innate in them. (1992, pp. xix)

Symbolic Reality

This is the final image—what the audience will see—the movement that is kept for the stage. These symbolic forms that evolve from the rehearsal process are the images that *refer,* like a compelling photograph, to a specific reality. Symbolic reality *refers* and *re-presents* moments in the field that are now, in their very representation, evoking for the audience expanded meanings, implications, and consequences beyond that original moment of field experience. The symbolic reality can be "read" by an audience; it has its own performance syntax[10]—enactments to be comprehended—that tells the ethnographic story through performance. Translating ethnographic data to the stage is obviously a different kind of "reading" of ethnographic data that the written page cannot hold, it is to "rehydrate" the written word through embodied techniques (Jackson, 1993).

How the performing body on stage creates and extends meanings and images is the "thing" that is ultimately witnessed and consumed by the audience. The rehearsal process in the particular stage of reflexive enactment reforms and performatively "rewrites" ethnographic data that are then given over to movement formation in order to manifest their performative rewriting through sound, motion, and flesh. In rehearsal, symbolic reality now emerges from the dynamics of reflection and movement to culminate in a "product" that both represents reality and represents representations of a people's reality that must now be set to stage. Symbolic reality becomes the staged ethnographic performance that is a metaphor and metonym for the deeply lived experiences of fieldwork. The symbolic reality made through a performance of ethnography metaphorically recreates a particular world as a double performance— performing in *likeness* the performances of that world for interpretation. Symbolic reality metonymically embellishes the fragments and interstices of field experience for metaexperience in order to make the familiar, unfamiliar. Symbolic reality is the culminating creation that celebrates, truly, the inseparability of fiction and nonfiction.

THE PERFORMANCE EVENT

Excerpts from the Prologue

The Prologue was to become the first image, the portal of imaginary action, staged and replicated, where real, living voices defend the righteousness and necessity of tradition against those Other living voices who defend the dignity and self-determination of human rights. It would signal the flurry of intentions and the unheard truths on both sides. And, the prologue was to be something more; it was to be my own entry. It would open in plain sight *my* intentions and *my* unheard truths uncovering the ambivalences of my translations, my biases, and my privilege. It would mark the "why" of my presence in Ghana and the "who" of my assumed authority to write about it. It would introduce the politics of my restive double-consciousness in being African

and being American, because (in this instance) consciousness preceded doing. Therefore, the theme I wanted to embody in the prologue was *the polarizing nature of the debate and the ethnographer's dilemma in respectfully representing both sides, yet being considerately partial to one.*

The polarizing sides of the debate are deep, volatile, and absolute: Two actors fill the stage, each alternating the words: *Trokosi / Troxovi / Faishidi.* These words are repeated with force and indignation to represent the controversy over naming, the power of a name, and the human need to be honorably named.

(The actors "fill the stage" chanting the various names for the Trokosi practice)

Trokosi / Troxovi / Faishidi (repeated)

Trokosi–Wife! / Trokosi–Slave! / Trokosi- Wife! / Trokosi–Slave! / Slave/Wife

(In alternation, the words are repeated by the cast with anger and force. Actor 1 and Actor 2 stand at a distance with their backs to each other. As the words above are repeated they take steps away from each other until they are on opposite ends of the stage.)

Actor 1:[11]

The Trokosi system demands that a young girl be sent to a shrine by force

As reparation

As atonement

For a crime committed by a member of her family

Many of whom she does not even know

She is sent to the shrine where she must serve the priest

She must serve his every need

She labors in the shrine

She labors on the farm

She must have sexual intercourse with the priest

She is a virtual slave to the shrine and the priest in atonement for

An offence committed by someone else!

She must be sent to the shrine to satisfy God

Or / tragedy will befall her family and befall the community

If a Trokosi dies / she must be replaced by another young / virgin / girl from her family.

The Trokosi are in bondage

The Trokosi have no freedom

The Trokosi are denied an education

The Trokosi are denied the fruits of their own hard labor

They are denied the protection and dignity of their own bodies

They are denied the freedom to choose their own destiny

The Trokosi girl has committed no offence, no crime

(All performers from their positions upstage of Actors 1 and 2 repeat the word "lies" turning in all directions with focus on each other, off-stage, and the audience. Throughout the performance "lies" is spoken chaotically.)

LIES / LIES/ LIES (repeat)

(The performers upstage quiet down and repeat "lies" in a whisper.)

Actor 2

The Trokosi system is a system of training and education

Young women are sent to the shrines to learn valuable lessons of

Social / cultural / spiritual / and moral behavior

The young girls are honored and distinguished

For they are trained to be wives of the god

Their children are most ennobled and glorified

For they are children of the god

They are NOT sent to the shrine in atonement

But sent for training to lead a righteous path because

Their families can no longer teach them and lead them

To serve as role models in the society.

These queens will lead us!

"If you educate a man / you educate an individual

If you educate a woman / you educate a whole nation."

There are breakaway shrines—quack shrines

These shrines do NOT adhere to the proper training

These shrines do NOT honor and protect the girls

These shrines do no NOT practice traditional African religion

Genuine Troxovi shrines are *Afegame* (great houses)

To train these girls as leaders—to be great women of

Moral and spiritual character

The Trokosi are honored

The Trokosi are protected

The Trokosi are trained

The Trokosi are loved

(Performers begin moving in a weavelike pattern in and out and between one another. They raise their voices and repeat "lies" again in every direction.)

LIES/ LIES/ LIES/ (repeat)

(Performers now repeat the following lines walking in a frenzied pace filling the stage space.)

Christian chauvinists!

Human rights activist!

Traditionalist!

Offenders of human rights!

Religion!

Bondage!

Training!

Slavery!

Training!

Slavery!

Religion!

Bondage!

(Performers stop on the word "Bondage." In place, but not in a freeze, they repeat "lies" until it builds to peak volume and then they will bring it down to a whisper, then silence.)

LIESLIESLIESLIESLIESLIES (repeat)

(Performers form a small circle downstage center. Their palms are touching in various patterns to resemble a matrix of connections or levels. They will change positions periodically but they maintain the motif of the "matrix." Another performer, referred to as the Recorder,[12] has been in the background, hardly noticeable, comes forward to observe the ball of human connections.)

These voices that constitute the debate are physicalized on stage as a human matrix and the Recorder's encounter with this human matrix. The Recorder represents the researcher (me) and her role as "writer" and keeper of "written" knowledges. The label of Recorder is also used ironically to trouble the notion of writing and its entry toward orality and the embodied experiences that ethnographers are called upon to embrace.

I asked the performers to form a human matrix by moving into a tightly enclosed circle and from that point they "connected" to one another with the palms of their hands, their feet, and various points of their bodies touching

in differing positions at shoulders, knees, hips etc. They were to form a connecting bond where their bodies were contorted to conjoin one another in an intricate pattern of linkages. Within this matrix they were to change positions four times. One position moved to the next in slow motion, never letting the conjoining bond unravel, but changing into different combinations of connections. The Recorder was to walk very, very slowly toward the matrix, encircling it in cautious curiosity, and then back away from it in apprehension and ambivalent fearfulness. She was to create a slow, deliberate rhythm of moving towards the matrix and then away from it as if she dared to enter into its dense entanglements but could not transgress its complexity.

The next formation symbolized the Recorder's dilemma. She is trying to decipher this human ball of entanglements—to analyze and interpret means to disentangle and to decipher, then to order, and, finally, to name—but it is not easy to approach or enter into complex webs of human meaning. The Recorder moves closer to the matrix and in this nearness she begins to observe and trace some of the connecting links, but then the matrix changes form. She moves closer to this different configuration from another angle, but the matrix changes form again, and then again. Finally the Recorder, not really able to capture the complexity of the human connections and disconnections, spoke:

Truth is elusive

It is becoming too difficult to disentangle

I cannot find it

It is not neat and clear / not anymore

Not as I travel further / look deeper / and hear more

Am I looking in the wrong places?

I am only stumbling past a million half-truths

Yet, all of them are partial and powerful

I've met so many people here who are telling
their side of the truth—

The women and girls known as Trokosi do
live in servitude

Yes / I've seen them / I've listened to their
stories

I've been to those places . . . servitude / it is
true

But there is another truth

There are women who are called Trokosi who
live honorably within the rituals of an
ancient tradition

There is a truth somewhere between servitude
and honor

I need to ask more questions

This movement symbolized the elusiveness
of "truth" in the field when confronted with
the ambiguity of human expression, the contexts of contestation, and the unknowing of
outsiderhood. This formation also signified
the duality and reciprocity between inner self-
reflection and outer observation, as well as
literally demonstrating when the focus must
cease from self-reflection and move back into
the outer world of the subjects. This shift from
inner reflection to outer observation is trig-
gered by two performers moving downstage—
the Recorder's "subjects" taking hold of her
and guiding her attention away from reflections of herself to a seat upstage (a space
designed for her by them) where she may
watch them and listen to them more closely. In
this formation, we are reminded of the power
of the Other to translate *us* when we are in
caught in the dilemma of translating our translations of *them.*

Excerpts From Scene One

The debate constituted more than counter
stances that took hold in oppositional speech

and rhetoric of pure rebuttal; it was also about
dignity—the dignity of believing that what you
stand for is right and true, but more importantly that it is a divine calling. Each side was
taking up arms for "God's truth." It has been
known since the first prophets as a "cause."
That compelling force, reverently inspired yet
unalterably demanding, grabs hold of the matters of the world and seizes them—sometimes
with brute force, sometimes with love—until
they are, for good or bad, forever changed. It
was this force of a "true cause" that activated
both sides of the debate.

*(Actor 3 is stage right as the other performers
mime a scene upstage. Two other actors are
bending down as the Recorder takes notes and
"writes" on their backs. Another actor guides
the Recorder's hand as she writes.)*

Traditionalist–Actor 3

Before you can respect the human rights of
others you have to undergo certain tortures

Certain pains—as when you are sent to school

It is painful to receive an education

You must perform certain labors

After that your raw nature is developed into a
useful human being which can be used to
improve society

So the place of reform and rebirth is always a
place of suffering and pain

*(Actor 4 is center stage as the Recorder listens
and the other actors mime a scene that represents the concept of "freedom.")*

Rights Activist–Actor 4

My dream. . . .

I wish these slaves were free enough to own
property for themselves

To have resources to determine their future
for themselves and their children

To leave the shrines because they can take care of themselves

Money to buy a piece of plot and provide capitol big enough to start life

They can do it

I want them to become women with their destiny in their own hands free to think for themselves

I have another dream . . .

This dream is to enlighten Ghanaian culture about the role of women

And I must relate this to our religious practice

The Trokosi practice is just one of the many practices that hinder women from developing

I see the role of women as lighting two candles together

The two bright lights will give both of us a brighter life—we can enjoy our lives together

All these women who are kept illiterate and subjugated . . .

Imagine what they could contribute to our social economy / our politics and culture

Imagine what free men and women can do together

Imagine what type of development we would have in this country

---

Each narrative held its own particular and engaging truth. This excerpt from Scene One, in contrast to the prologue excerpt, inversely conceptualized the theme of chaos into a theme of clarity. This scene would reflect the skillful articulations of both traditionalists and rights activists as they wrapped their language in rhetorical strategies and poetic maneuvers that captured the logic and the passion of their cause, while each also skillfully legitimized and justified specific accusations cast against the opposing side.

(Actor 2 comes center stage as other actors look on and the Recorder takes notes upstage left.)

Traditionalist–Actor 2

I get very disgusted about the way these opportunists, disguised as human rights activists are using

The system to discredit the Ghanaian society especially my society—the Ewes

I get very upset about it

I see that these people are using the system to get money from the outside funders in Europe and the United States

To make themselves rich while defaming our tradition!

Those who are making the most noise about traditional religion are the people who claim they are Christians

They think that because they are Christians that anything to do with our traditional religion

Is dirty / is bad

So those who are making the most noise are those who don't want anything to do with

Our traditional religion

Our traditional practices are our own way of getting people to behave properly

(Actor 4 gently takes a "book" from Actor 2 and speaks to the audience as the other actors assume positions upstage and listen.)

Rights Activist–Actor 4

Africans believe in god / they feel god.

This is reflected in the tradition of their religion

The Trokosi is part of the religion

We like their religion

We admire it because like all religion, traditional religion practices morality

But we must say to them—

If your religion practices morality then don't be wicked!

We are interested in communal life / in the village everyone helps out

The problem of one person is the problem of all

The Trokosi is not good for the people

We respect the village and the religion

We only want to change the Trokosi practice

It is wrong

We don't want to break the shrines

We do not want to abolish the worship system

But what they do with the girls is wrong and it is going against progress / development

And our modern society

Why can't they release the girls and let them go to school?

If someone commits a crime that person must pay for his own crime

They should punish the offender / not the innocent girl!

Why?

If a boy-child insults his father / the father should not punish the sister

The father should punish the boy-child who insulted him!

Some people think that if we punish the direct offender the whole religion will be destroyed

We understand they must have a judicial system for order / peace and morality

This is good—lets keep that!

But do not sacrifice innocent girls by sending them inside the shrines

It is wrong

They have the interpretation that we want to abolish the shrines and ruin their worship

We do not

We only want to help the girls and women

The shrines should and must remain / yes

People go there for healing

The shrines help correct people

We recognize and respect the freedom of religion

We come to tackle the Trokosi practice on the basis of human rights

And not on the basis of religion

We don't come out to say your religion is bad

We see there is an aspect we respect / but there is an aspect that is against the law.

Continue to live your religion but without this violation of human rights

We don't say accept Jesus Christ and the god you worship is bad

No we do not impose Christianity / not in any of our literature / not anywhere.

But we do oppose the violation of human rights

This acknowledgement of *understanding* both sides of a debate then awakens an age-old question: Which side do I take? Or, perhaps the more important question becomes: Can I afford NOT to take a side?

Respecting the articulations on both sides of the debate and embodying the ethnographer's process in representing both sides while guided by the tensions of empathy on one hand and advocacy on the other, the thematic conceptualization that evolved became: *the persuasive force articulated, with passion and logic, by both traditionalists and rights activists under the ethnographic gaze AND the ethnographer's ruminations on ethics relative to taking a stand.*

(*After listening to both sides of the debate and several monologues that raise questions beyond Trokosi, the Recorder writes in her journal as she speaks out to the audience.*)

Recorder:

October 12, 1999, Dear Journal—

I am in a dilemma in the fieldwork

Throughout the interviews I am led down other paths—beyond Trokosi

The implications

Trokosi has greater implications

Rural life / The witch camps / The North / Nkrumah

Implications

These are subjects for another time . . . yet

These are subjects that are inside Ghanaian life

Witches, the first president of Ghana, Northerners, life in the villages

Why do they keep coming up / again and again?

Experience is never neat

Culture is never narrow

They say that Context is everything

Rural life / The witch camps / The North / Kwame Nkrumah

I am listening

They say that context is everything

I have been listening

I hope for good purposes

Excerpts From Scene Three

It was in this scene where the performance was to take a considerable turn and enter into the dubious domain of corporate globalization. This turn would land the performance in a different territory from the inner tensions of the debate. The new direction had to make sense and the territorial shift had to be enacted with justified authority and elegant polemics, or else it would quickly flatten into trendy "globalization speak" or recede into the abysmally incoherent. The influences of globalization on the Trokosi practice are sometimes obvious and sometimes not. When these influences do appear obvious—influences such as fair trade, third world debt, and agricultural dumping—they are obvious only in their presence around us; however the details of their consequences aren't always clearly *linked* to local poverty and human rights practices. The purpose of this scene was to establish that link. The purpose of the scene was also to bring to light the stories that are not Trokosi stories but surround Trokosi history. Context is not overdetermined here but necessarily evoked in the larger cause and effects of the Trokosi practice—both the specific practice and the larger cultural tradition. The theme would reflect how the dialectic, in theory and practice, between the global and the local become the context that profoundly determines the level of human rights, from one location to another, under the Trokosi system. Finally, Scene Three would offer the possibility for a progressive and radical resolution to the Trokosi debate. The thematic conceptualization must inhere contextual influences and global effects, but it must also unapologetically culminate in the possibility for a clear and attainable option. The performance intended to work against the notion of leaving the audience conscientiously disturbed while embracing ambiguous solutions that would activate them toward creating and determining their own course of action.

This is a noble intent, one that I admire and one that I often teach and practice relative to performance for social change. But this performance, in this time and for this space, required a more definite option or *possible* solution. The thematic conceptualization that evolved for Scene Three was: *The link between global forces and local life and the possibility for an inseparable coexistence between human rights and traditional African religion.*

The challenge now was to create the formations that would flow between globality, context, and resolution.

In this movement the Recorder moves from the role of interviewer and comes downstage and speaks directly to the audience. She poses a question to the audience regarding African debt and development. She moves closer to the audience to seek their response; however, before she can anticipate an answer, the interviewees (actors) still sitting upstage on the platforms ring out in alternating voices varying points of view on the global economy. After the interviewees have spoken their minds on globality, the Recorder returns downstage to speak out to the audience, and in a self-interrogating stance, she confesses her own ambivalences about being a privileged American while acknowledging that self-reflexivity withstanding, she must stop the ruminations upon her own angst and return to the field and the debate.

The movement illuminates the intersections between human rights and the economy under the backdrop of the IMF and the World Bank. It positions local voices as being both critics and inquisitors of economic policies that have proven to be ineffectual at best and regressive at worst. This leap from the local debate surrounding the Trokosi practice to that of the world economy is linked by a pivotal transition the Recorder enacts as she deliberates upon her double identity as an American woman of privilege and a woman of African descent living in an African country to which she "belongs" and for which she must ultimately commit (and commit to) the political act of representation.

(The Recorder comes downstage as actors look on.)

Recorder:

I am in the middle of my fieldwork

And there are so many questions still

Unanswered

I just wanted to understand the truth behind the Trokosi system

Just the Trokosi system

But now there are other stories

Other connections

Other surfaces that go so deep

The dilemma of listening for good purposes

What do I do with what I have heard

With what I have seen

A distant country

A distant people

But this country / these people / are not so distant anymore

They are part of me now

Like an inseparable friend

Like an unforgettable lover

This land / These people

Can these notes capture the poignancy of their lives?

The everyday moments of their laughter and

Their suffering

I cannot indulge in sentiment without politics

I cannot indulge in sentiment without politics

Development

Democracy

Wealth / poverty

I can not indulge in aesthetic spectatorship without political engagement[13]

What does Trokosi have to do with Development

What does Trokosi have to do with Democracy

What does Trokosi have to do with wealth and poverty

America

American

African

African American

Advanced

Advanced country

Black

American

Living

In

An

Advanced country

What do I have to do with Trokosi

BlackAmericanLivingInAnAdvancedCountry

What do I have to do with Trokosi?

I live in the richest country in the world

I will not give up my citizenship

I will not give up my privilege

I will not give up my citizenship?

I will not give up my privilege?

What does all this have to do with Trokosi / The witch camps / The North

The legacy of Kwame Nkrumah?

I live in the richest country in the world

What do I do with what I've learned here

I live in the richest country in the world

What have I learned here?

(The Recorder has acknowledged her ambivalent and ambiguous position as a recorder who is of two worlds, both worlds reaching beyond the limits of the Trokosi practice, yet also reaching into that practice and complexifying it through an economic dialectic that threatens freedom and enlightenment. It is at this point when the relationship between human development and economic development must be interrogated. The Recorder turns to the audience and asks:)

Could you clarify for me the problems some Africans are having with the World Bank, The International Monetary Fund, and Structural Adjustment Programs?

(The Recorder looks out to the audience for the answers. The Subjects seated behind her on the platforms represent both her consultants and her audience. They all answer her question in a symbolic intervention to give voice and critical agency to indigenous people who are affected by the programs and policies of the IMF and World Bank but who are not heard and whose philosophical and political awareness of these institutions is grossly underestimated.)

[The actors are presented here as "voices"—V# 1, 2, 3, 4, 5]

V#1: First of all the IMF and the WB need to listen!

V#3: People who put up an intellectual defense for the IMF and WB / I wonder if they actually read the letters of intent or conditionalities.

V#4: One thing we must recognize is that the only way that we can extricate ourselves is by developing technology— getting our own technologies and embarking on an industrial revolution. We must produce the products to meet our own most basic needs—

V#5: We are not talking about going to space. We are just talking about industrialization so we can meet our most basic needs.

V#1: So no child will go to bed hungry, and so that anyone who wants to work is given the opportunity to work.

V#2: It is not too much to ask for?

V#3: In northern Ghana, where I come from, it is the breadbasket of the country. The soil is productive for rice and agriculture, but this import liberalization program hurts the local farmer.

V#4: The big agricultural businesses dump their imports like rice and so the people suffer. How? You don't expect my uncle who is a rice farmer about 50 miles from Tamale and who has just about two acres and who doesn't have a tractor—just a hoe—to compete with these big agro businesses. My uncle produces about 15 bags of rice. He doesn't have the technology to produce a lot of rice. He goes to the market to sell his rice. Now, because he doesn't enjoy the economies of scale and production, his rice will be slightly more expensive than the imported one. So, you can't expect that peasant farmer to compete with that big agro business.

V#5: The IMF and WB don't factor that in, in terms of economic stability. Yes, the situation is better than it was some 18 or 20 years ago. But it is not where it could be or should be. It is aid-driven and the social cost is enormous—

V#1: Plus, the indebtedness. . . . There is no way we can ever pay back the loans—

V#2: Close to 7 billion dollars.

ALL: There is no way!

The performers turn their backs to the audience and the Recorder after the line: *There is no way.* The Recorder has been looking out to the audience, actively listening, with gestures of interest, alarm, and agreement, as though all that has been said is coming from the people who are watching the performance. The Recorder "listens" to the audience who represent the Ghanaian public to mark that it is they who speak these lines. The Recorder responds to these voices by acknowledging a tension that is both far and near between the global and the local, but also a tension that is both helpful and harmful.

(The Recorder speaks from her position on stage.)

The rich and the poor are at distances beyond comprehension

Yet

The rich and the poor are strangers up close and personal like opposing twins

One holds the other by global strings

Global and enormous

Global

Together and apart!

(On the line, together and apart*, each of the Actors picks up from the platform a journal— what is meant to be the Recorder's Journal. The Recorder turns and speaks to them:)*

The UN Development Report documents how globalization has dramatically increased inequality between and within nations, but at the same time it has brought people together like never before!

(Motivated by the dubious fact of globalization, the Actors begin reading passages from the Recorder's journal. They read each passage loudly but without emotion, as if they were reading information from a book, taking care to almost over-pronounce every word, but without emotion. This technique of punctuated reading without feeling results in dramatizing the "facts" of globalization:)

V#1:   We live in a world where the financial assets of just 200 of the richest people in the world are greater than the combined income of the more than 2 billion people!

V#2: The majority of trade and investments takes place between industrial nations.

V#4: Global corporations control a third of world exports

V#1: Of the 100 largest economies in the world, 51 are corporations

Recorder: What does this have to do with Trokosi?

V#2: The global economy disrupts traditional economies and weakens their governments to help them.

V#1: They are left to fend for themselves against failed states

V#2: Against destitution

V#4: Famine and plagues

V#1: They are forced to migrate

V#2: They are forced to offer their labor at wages below what it takes for them to live

V#4: They are forced to sacrifice their children

V#1: They are forced to cash in their physical environments

V#2: They are forced to neglect their personal health

V#3: They are forced to just survive?

Recorder: What does this have to do with Trokosi?

V#1: Education and health budgets are slashed to pay off debts

V#2: The total wealth of the 358 global billionaires equals the combined income of 45 percent of the world's population.

V#3: The recent transformation of the world economy[14]

V#2: Has not been matched by

V#1: Changes in our political institutions.

V#4: By changes in our political institutions

V#1: By changes in our political institutions

The Recorder then asks the question again: What has this got have do with Trokosi? This is a rhetorical question with the purpose of underscoring an obvious answer that will affirm the link between the local and the global, a link that has been dramatized up to this point in the performance. This section, in amplifying the voices of Ghanaians themselves in speaking to the dubious effects of globalization, rather than having those effects always told TO them, now turns in a reversal back to contemplations of Recorder.

(The Recorder comes down to center stage.)

Recorder:

It is time to go back in the field

It is time to go back to Trokosi

There are more questions

It is time to get back to the debate

Why is the debate about Trokosi so heated

Why is everyone so angry?

Trokosi is not the subject

The subject is the debate

It has got to be about the Debate

Can I shut up and listen for good purposes!

Anthropologist on board? Oh! BEWARE

Another westerner charges human rights abuses in Africa against an oblique paradigm?

Against her performance?

Westerners . . . ah / here we come to save
   Africa from herself

We have the answers . . . we have the A-I-D
   Listen while we show and tell you

To yourselves

Here we come, giddi yup / giddi yup / the
   wild, wild / West will show you and tell you

There are more questions

It's time to go back to Trokosi . . .

There IS such a thing as a good purpose

The Recorder enacts her own resentments
relative to western knowledge, arrogance, and
power as it relates to Africa and African people.
She employs the cowboy as a patriarchal trope
for imperialist practices and arrogant perception toward African people. She implicates her
own intentions and methods against the often
inept benevolence of her country as well as her
western academic training. Having interrogated
her subject position, she must reconcile the tensions within her own ambivalent reflections
regarding her own positionality and go back to
the field, ever mindful, again, of purpose.[15]

~ ~ ~

Ethnographic performance can do the labor of
making local work a global issue. It hopes to
re-imagine Otherness. It hopes to disturb and
invoke. It hopes to always and already make
Others known, real, and memorable, not only
in what they say, but in what they do.[16]

NOTES

1. The title, "Is it a Human Being or a Girl?"
came from and interview during my fieldwork.
My respondent informed me that when a baby is
born, instead of asking is it a girl or boy, in certain
areas of Ghana some may ask, "Is it a human
being or a girl?"

2. Instead of the primary use of the term
"third world" (a term coined in 1952, after World
War II, by the French demographer, Alfred Sauvy,
to refer to the economic tiers monde or the world
of "poor countries") in the global justice movement. Other terms have been added: "developing
nations," Majority World, and South or global
South. Generally, activists and scholars employ
the terms North and South to refer to the division
between wealthy first world countries largely concentrated in the North and impoverished third
world countries concentrated in the South, and to
the historical legacy of centuries of imperialism.

3. Raymond William's notion of structure of
feeling is the idea that there are shared emotions,
beliefs, and ideologies by members of specific
groups, classes, and cultures based on common
values, practices, structures, etc.

4. The idea of a "human rights revolution"
is discussed eloquently in Brian Orend's book
Human Rights: Concepts and Context (2002) and
Judith Blau and Alberto Moncada's book *Human
Rights: Beyond the Liberal Vision (2005).*

5. From Michael Perry's book *The Idea Of
Human Rights: Four Inquires* (1998), p. 6.

6. *Hidden abode* in its original conception
refers to the Marxist idea of the circuit and the
capitalist production that is hidden in the everyday. Here I refer to how the workings of power
are hidden from view, yet present in their effects.

7. *Co-performance* or co-performing is the
term Dwight Conquergood employs to replace
the idea of "participant-observation" to describe
the deeper and more complex ways ethnographers
interact and engage the more deeply felt and
sensed dimensions in which they "live" in and
with the cultures they study.

8. *Definitional ceremony* is based on the
work of anthropologist Barbara Myerhoff and the
notion that the sharing of a story is an act of defining history and identity—it is a needed performance of self that is not necessarily meant to be
shared beyond the moment of the interview.

9. Two of the performers, Christine Naa
Norley Lokko and S. O. H Afriyie-Vidza, were
students who were enrolled in several classes
I taught at the university; two others, Florence
Akosua Abea and Ekua Ekumah, were friends that
were experienced performers—Florence was a
dancer and Ekua an actor and director; the fifth
performer, Jacqueline "Jackie" Afodemo Dowetin,
was introduced to me by Ekua. Jackie was also an
experienced performer and was working with
Trokosi women on a theatre project in the Klikor
region of Ghana. The cast was committed to the
performance under the duress of final exams, the

usual end of the year frenzy, and a limited and rather rushed rehearsal time period. The cast varied in their knowledge and perspectives on the debate and the Trokosi/Troxovi practice. The one male performer, S.O.H, was Ewe. He was adamantly opposed to the Trokosi/Troxovi practice because of experiences with family relations who were victimized by the system. Ekua—whose parents were Ghanaian, but who lived in London, England where Ekua was raised—was sensitive to human rights issues but also felt it important to honor traditional religious practices and not demonize Trokosi without reference to its history and context. For Florence, who was Ashanti, the practice was basically unknown, yet she was curious about and attentive to what was constantly being revealed about the practice throughout our performance process. Christine, who was Ga, was active in a Christian based performance group on campus. She had heard of Trokosi but was not familiar with the details of the debate and indicated that she was against cultural practices where women were subjugated. Jackie, who was Ewe, came in during the third day of rehearsal. Based on her work with Trokosi women in the Klikor region, Jackie knew as much, if not more, than I did about the Trokosi system. She was a great source of information and inspiration during rehearsals.

10. *Performance syntax* is used to refer to the juxtapositions, linkages, and formations that performatively make meaning.

11. The monologues are all written in poetic form (sometimes referred to as poetic transcription) to capture the rhythm of the voice and to emphasize particular words and phrases that the prose form in its blocked text can not acknowledge.

12. The Recorder is the term used to describe the act of "textuality" that the ethnographer must both embrace and resist in the art and craft of fieldwork.

13. This was taken from Bruce Robbins in his book *Feeling Global: Internationalism in Distress.*

14. These lines, "The recent transformation of the world economy has not been matched by changes in our political institutions" are a direct reflection of the work of Bruce Robbins and Zygmunt Bauman.

15. On June 23, 2000, I attended a meeting called by the traditional rulers of the Tongu Region with two friends who led the campaign to transform the practice, Wisdom Mensah and Walter Pimpong. At the gathering, the traditional rulers of this region came forth with a statement denouncing the "dehumanizing" aspects of the tradition and stated the practice "should be transformed." The following is an excerpt from the larger statement of resolution:

> We also wish to state that, we the Traditional Rulers and people of the Tongu invited the Commission of Human Rights and Administrative Justice, and gave the mandate to the Non-governmental organizations such as International Needs Ghana to help us with the transformation process. . . . We also wish to call on the Government to enforce the law that they passed against ritual servitude in Ghana. (Resolution of Tongu Rulers, 2000)

The transformation of the Trokosi practice has been generally successful due to the work of several NGOs, particularly International Needs Ghana under the direction of Walter Pimpong and Wisdom Mensah. However, when I was in Ghana in December 2004 on a visit with some of my friends in the human rights community, they stated, even with the success of reforming the practice, they believed there were still a few shrines in operation that have been driven underground.

16. The public response to the performance was a mixture of gratitude, appreciation, and surprise. Each show received a standing ovation and audiences commented on how much they learned about the Trokosi/Troxovi practice and how inspired they were by the work of rights activists. Stakeholders on both sides of the debate had a range of responses. Some felt angry that the performance did not more forcefully support their position on the debate, others felt that it did support them, and there were others that especially appreciated the economic dimension. One of the more interesting responses, as well as the most common among audiences, was regarding the form. The idea that interview data, field notes, and critical commentary could be performed on stage was surprising to many. The performance was presented in June 2000, and at that time not very many people were staging qualitative research data at home or abroad. The activists I worked with felt that the form of staging fieldwork data was successful in representing their work and the pertinent issues surrounding Trokosi/Troxovi. We decided we would plan to use the performance as a means to raise funds in the United States.

REFERENCES

Bacon, A. W. (1979). *The art of interpretation.* New York: Holt, Rinehart & Winston.

Blau, J., & Moncada, A. (2005). *Human rights: Beyond the liberal vision.* New York: Rowman & Littlefield.

Conquergood, D. (1982). Communication as performance: Dramaturgical dimensions of everyday life. In J. I. Sisco (Ed.), *The Jensin lectures: Contemporary communication studies* (pp. 24–43). Tampa: University of South Florida Press.

Conquergood, D. (1997). Street literacy. In J. Flood, S. B. Heath, & D. Lapp (Eds.), *Handbook of research on teaching literacy through the communication and visual arts* (pp. 334–375). New York: Macmillan.

Fabian, J. (1983). *Time and the Other: How anthropology makes its object.* New York: Columbia University Press.

Hall, S. (1992). What is this "black" in black popular culture? In G. Dent (Ed.), *Black popular culture* (pp. 21–33). Seattle, WA: Bay Press.

Jackson, A. (1992). Introduction. In A. Boal, *Games for actors and non-actors* (pp. xxii–xxvii). New York: Routledge.

Jackson, S. (1993). Ethnography and the audition: Performance as ideological critique. *Text and Performance Quarterly, 13,* 21–43.

Pineau, E . (1994). Teaching is performance: Reconceptualizing a problematic metaphor. *American Educational Research Journal, 31*(1), 3–25.

Perry, M. (1998). *The idea of human rights: Four inquiries.* Oxford, England: Oxford University Press.

Robbins, B. (1999). *Feeling global: Internationalism in distress.* New York: NYU Press.

Schechner, R. (1998). What is performance studies anyway? In P. Phelan & J. Lane (Eds.), *The ends of performance* (pp. 357–362). New York: NYU Press.

PART VI

Performance and Politics

Themes and Arguments[1]

JUDITH HAMERA AND DWIGHT CONQUERGOOD

Politics and performance are intimately linked historically, conceptually, and pragmatically. This link is foundational; as Victor Turner (1982) explains, ritual elements of performance generate *communitas,* a sense of solidarity that has conservative or revolutionary consequences for the life of the *polis.* *Communitas* may be "spontaneous" and magical; "ideological," that is, theoretical, enmeshed in language and culture which may or may not be utopian; or "normative," which could be "ongoing, relatively repetitive," "transformative," or both (p. 49). In "Ion," Plato (1998) presents his concern about the solo performer's potential to create *communitas* in his audience. He charges the rhapsode Ion with spreading a contagious irrationality to his listeners, and the rhetorical overkill of his attack betrays a deeper anxiety about the social force of performance.

Richard Schechner (1985) defines performance as "restored behavior" (p. 33). Elin Diamond reminds us of the political implications of this:

> terminology of "re" in discussions of performance, as in *re*embody, *re*inscribe, *re*configure, *re*signify. "Re" acknowledges the preexisting discursive field, the repetition—and the desire to repeat—within the performative present, while "embody," "configure," "inscribe," "signify," assert the possibility of materializing something that exceeds our knowledge, that alters the shape of sites and imagines other as yet unsuspected modes of being.
>
> Of course, what alters the shape of sites and imagines into existence other modes of being is anathema to those who would police social borders and identities. (p. 2)

May Joseph (1999) observes that "[t]he idea of citizenship" is itself "a performing sphere that transforms the abstraction 'the people' into individuated political subjects and participating citizens" (p. 15). Jon McKenzie (2003) adds: "From annual performance reviews to high-performance missile systems—and yes, even to ritual and theatre—performance now gathers together a vast array of [sociopolitical] phenomena" (p. 118).

McKenzie's statement signals an important point: relations between performance and politics partake of the same multifaceted approaches to performance itself within the

419

field of performance studies. As Diana Taylor (2003) states in *The Archive and the Repertoire*:

> "Performance," on the one level, constitutes the object/process of analysis in performance studies, that is, the many practices and events—dance, theatre, ritual, political rallies, funerals—that involve theatrical, rehearsed, or conventional/event appropriate behaviors.
>
> On another level, performance also constitutes the methodological lens that enables scholars to analyze events *as* performance. Civic obedience, resistance, citizenship, gender, ethnicity, and sexual identity, for example, are rehearsed and performed daily in the public sphere. (p. 3)

Both approaches to performance—as subject of, and method of, analysis—emerge in four overarching and interrelated themes taken up by scholarship about performance and politics, including the essays in this section. They are

- Performance in/as the production of history
- Performance in/as the deployment of institutional power
- Performance in/as the production of identity and
- Performance in/as technologies of resistance

It bears repeating that these themes are not mutually exclusive, and that they overlap and reinforce one another, as in the five essays to follow.

PERFORMANCE IN/AS THE PRODUCTION OF HISTORY

Della Pollock (1998) gets to the heart of intersections between performance, politics, and history when she observes,

> Boundaries that have for so long kept the "facts" in and the "fiction" out of history are now crossed over and traced through with such supra-disciplinary questions as: What does it mean to represent the past? How have politics shaped traditions of representation? (p. 3)

While these questions are fully engaged in the "Performance and History" section of this volume, the political dimensions of Pollock's questions are also important here. Performance studies scholars have been instrumental in restoring excluded or marginalized histories to larger disciplinary conversations and, in so doing, they call for increased disciplinary self-reflexivity. In "Rethinking Elocution: The Trope of the Talking Book and other Figures of Speech" (2000), Dwight Conquergood rewrites the history of elocution over against its excluded others: African American and working-class speakers whose bodies and voices became signifiers of the "coarse and uncouth features" to be "refined" (p. 327). Lisa Merrill's (1999) critical examination of the life and work of actress Charlotte Cushman speaks back to the "invisibility" of women's same-sex erotic relationships in history generally, and in the history of performance in particular. Tracy Davis (1991) addresses the sociopolitical and economic dimensions of acting as gendered labor. Shannon Jackson's (2000) *Lines of Activity* reads Hull House "reformance" (p. 8) as the embodied consequences of Progressive Era social policy.

PERFORMANCE IN/AS THE DEPLOYMENT OF INSTITUTIONAL POWER

The performative dimensions of institutional power emerge in historical and contemporary analyses by performance studies scholars. Dwight Conquergood (2002) has been particularly eloquent in identifying and challenging institutional, including academic, biases that favor the written and the textual. He argues,

> Only middle-class academics could blithely assume that all the world is a text because reading and writing are central to their everyday lives and occupational security. For many people throughout the world, however, particularly subaltern groups, texts are often inaccessible, or threatening,

charged with the regulatory power of the state. . . .

The hegemony of textualism needs to be exposed and undermined. Transcription is not a transparent or politically innocent model for conceptualizing or engaging the world. (p. 147)

Likewise, Peggy Phelan poses an epistemological challenge to institutional regimes of visibility and reproduction. In *Unmarked* (1993), she challenges undertheorized testaments to the "power" of visibility as it is conventionally understood.

Currently, . . . there is a dismaying similarity in the beliefs generated about the political efficacy of visible representation. The dangerous complicity between progressives dedicated to visibility politics and conservatives patroling the borders of museums, movie houses, and mainstream broadcasting is based on their mutual belief that representations can be treated as "real truths" and guarded or championed accordingly. Both sides believe that greater visibility of the hitherto under-represented leads to enhanced political power. . . . Insufficient understanding of the relationship between visibility, power, identity, and liberation has led both groups to mistake the relation between the real and the representational. (p. 2)

Moreover, performance offers unique and important alternatives to institutional understandings of visibility, the real, and representation.

Performance studies scholars use these conceptual descriptions of, and challenges to, institutional power to engage the macro and micro practices of power at the level of state and extra-state actors. For example, Jon McKenzie (2003) examines intersections of performance and politics in the technocratic micro practices of, in, and beyond the state as he explores possibilities for reinventing democracy. He writes,

One thing we know for sure: with government performance, we are witnessing the emergence of a global yet fragmented network for testing and monitoring democracy's performance. More directly than performance studies, performance management, or techno-performance, government performance channels sovereignty machines and juridical orders. Right now, this network contains national governments, trans- and supranational entities, nation states, NGOs, academic researchers, and most importantly, dissatisfied democrats: that is, disaffected people. To what use this network will be put, and by whom or what: that is the question. (p. 126; see also McKenzie, 2001)

The intimate workings of institutional power are also examined by performance studies scholars. Kristin Langellier and Eric Peterson (2004) argue that families are performed into being, created and perpetuated by norms and genres of family stories. They argue:

Storytelling participates in family as institution and as agency. As an institutional practice, performing family stories is part of a frame-up which takes up, circulates, and renews models of acceptable identity in society according to local norms: good mothers and fathers, good children, good families. . . . Simultaneously, performing family stories engages a possibility for agency to build personal and communal identities that resist major narratives of the family. Resistance may take forms of struggle, refusal, repudiation, or contestation. (p. 113)

Langellier and Peterson's discussion of performance as a tool that both perpetuates institutional formations and offers agency within or against them leads to the third theme in scholarship dealing with performance and politics.

PERFORMANCE IN/AS THE PRODUCTION OF IDENTITY

Here, it is useful to reexamine the link between performance and performativity. Elin Diamond (1996) characterizes performance as "a doing and a thing done" (p. 1). "Performativity" is a particular linguistic method of making and doing. The term finds its roots in J. L. Austin's

(1975) *How to Do Things with Words*. A "performative" is a type of utterance that does something; its effect coincides with its use. Judith Butler (1993) extended the possibilities of performativity beyond the simply linguistic. For Butler, performativity is a way to explore the enunciation and apparent stability of identity categories, particularly sexuality and gender. Briefly put, a performative is both an agent of, and a product of, the social and political surround in which it circulates. Its effects are reinforced through repetition. Gender and sexuality were the identity categories initially theorized as performatives; they were engaged as "made" and not "natural" or inevitable, and therefore as available for intervention and un- or remaking. Butler and other critical scholars have also extended the notion of the performative to include race, class, and other dimensions of identity.

Performance studies scholars have applied the idea of the performative in a variety of compelling analyses. Two examples are illustrative of the political dimensions of identity construction and intervention. In *Disidentifications* (1999), José Esteban Muñoz gets to the heart of complex constructions of identity by minoritarian subjects.

> Minoritarian subjects need to interface with different subcultural fields to activate their own senses of self. This is not to say that majoritarian subjects have no recourse to disidentification or that their own formation as subjects is not structured through multiple and conflicting sites of identification . . . Yet, the story of identity formation predicated on "hybrid transformations" that this text is interested in telling concerns subjects whose identities are formed in response to the cultural logics of heternormativity, white supremacy, and misogyny— cultural logics that I will suggest work to undergird state power. (p. 5)

Muñoz explores a variety of disidentificatory performances that "make and do" hybrid identities. Among them are pieces by Cuban American lesbian performance artist Alina Troyano, aka Carmelita Tropicana. Troyano's work exposes "the ambivalent, complicated, mixed up, and jumbled nature of the hybrid self" (Muñoz, 1999, p. 138) and, in so doing, refuses the stability of simple performative repetitions of majoritarian identity categories. E. Patrick Johnson also uses performativity to critique presumptions of simple, stable, discrete categories of identity. In his book *Appropriating Blackness* (2003), he identifies performativity at work in Marlon Riggs's film *Black Is . . . Black Ain't*. Johnson writes,

> Riggs's film implicitly employs performativity to suggest that we dismantle hierarchies that privilege particular black positionalities at the expense of others; that we recognize that darker hue does not give us any more cultural capital or claim to blackness than do a dashiki, braids, or a southern accent. Masculinity is no more a signifier of blackness than femininity; heterosexuality is no blacker than gayness; and poverty makes one no more authentically black than a house in the suburbs. (p. 40)

Though he explores the critical potential of both performance and performativity, Johnson is quick to point out that

> although useful in deconstructing essentialist notions of selfhood, performance must also provide a space for meaningful resistance of oppressive systems. (p. 5)

While these two examples expose the play with, and critique of, identity formations as potentially liberatory, political intersections of performance and identity are not always so. Judith Hamera (2002) examines a family of Cambodian refugees whose attempts to reproduce "pure" Khmer classical dance seem to hold the promise of shoring up stable, productive identities in the face of trauma and dislocation. Instead, their efforts performatively reproduce their own deep social isolation and personal loss.

PERFORMANCE IN/AS TECHNOLOGIES OF RESISTANCE

In *Durov's Pig* (1985), Joel Schechter offers a small but telling example of performance as a technology of resistance. In 1907 in Germany, the eponymous Durov, a Russian satirist and clown,

> placed a German officer's cap, or "helm" as he called it, in the circus ring, and his trained pig ran to retrieve it. Using ventriloquism, Durov made the pig appear to be saying "Ich will helm," meaning "I want the helmet." But the phrase could also be translated "I am Wilhelm," thereby equating Germany's Emperor, Wilhelm II, with a trained pig. (p. 2)

The audience thought this was hilarious. The police and the Kaiser did not. Durov was arrested, charged with treason, and expelled from the country. Schechter explains,

> "The stage is one of my arms of government," the Kaiser had told actors at the Royal Theatre in Berlin. Durov's democratization of power reduced the Emperor's authority over his arms of government, and his army, by sharing it with a pig. One small circus act could hardly overthrow a government, and yet it represented a freedom from state control which the Kaiser could not countenance. (p. 3)

Key elements of performance in/as a technology of resistance emerge from this small example. First, such performances are, in some sense, improvisatory and tactical. They "boldly juxtapose diverse elements in order to suddenly produce a flash shedding a different light on the language of a place and to strike the hearer" (de Certeau, 1974/1984, pp. 37–38). Second, they often redeploy techniques of the conventional theatre to their own ends: mimicry, mise en scene, humor, props. Third, speaking back to power through performance may be confrontational and overt, or subtle and covert, what Zora

Neale Hurston (1935/1990) called "featherbed resistance":

> The theory behind our tactics: "The white man is always trying to know into somebody else's business. All right, I'll set something outside the door of my mind for him to play with and handle. He can read my writing but he sho' can't read my mind. I'll put this play toy in his hand, and he will seize it and go away. Then I'll say my say and sing my song." (p. 3)

Performance in/as a technology of resistance emerges in now-canonical texts of theatre studies, like the writings and stagings of Bertolt Brecht (see Willetts, 1964). It appears in practices of everyday life, both public and private, and in challenges to conventional modes of scholarly representation. A complete survey of performance in/as technologies of resistance is as impossible as one of all the relationships between performance and politics, so I will focus on only three examples here.

In her discussion of the daily practices of the Madres de Plaza de Mayo in Argentina, Diana Taylor (2003) develops the formulation "the DNA of performance." From 1977 on, the Madres protested the disappearance, the literal erasure, of their children by Argentina's right wing military government during their Dirty War. When a democratic government returned to power in 1983, they protested the lack of official resolve to prosecute those responsible for the disappearances. The women used photos of their missing children as core components of their protests. They produced proof of their children's lives against their official erasure. Taylor states, "This representational practice of linking the scientific and performatic claim is what I call the DNA of performance" (p. 171). Here, performatic proof supplies the visibility and the social force that scientific proof alone cannot.

Augusto Boal also developed techniques to speak back, to perform back, to oppressive regimes. His Theatre of the Oppressed (see

Boal, 1979) and Forum Theatre are living, evolving approaches to performance for social change. Boal writes:

> Our mandate's project is to bring into the centre of political action—the centre of decisions—by making theatre as politics rather than merely making political theatre. In the latter case, the theatre makes comments on politics; in the former, the theatre is, in itself, one of the ways in which political activity can be conducted. (1998, p. 20)

Boal's methods include confronting external oppression—"cops-on-the-streets," and the internalized workings of hegemony—"cops-in-the-head" (see Schutzman, 1994).

Finally, performance can resist sedimented conventions of scholarly representation by "braiding together disparate and stratified ways of knowing" (Conquergood, 2002, p. 152). For Dwight Conquergood, performance studies as radical research

> should revitalize the connections between artistic accomplishment, analysis, and articulations with communities; between practical knowledge (knowing how), propositional knowledge (knowing that), and political savvy (knowing who, when, and where). This epistemological connection between creativity, critique, and civic engagement is mutually replenishing, and pedagogically powerful. (p. 153)

Conquergood looks for "text-performance entanglements" that capture what Ngugi wa Thiong'o calls "orature," the recognition and representation of the fact that "channels of communication constantly overlap, penetrate, and mutually produce one another" (p. 154) to radically change what appears on the stage and on the page.

The five essays that make up this section address relationships between performance and politics across these four themes. Jan Cohen-Cruz's essay, "'The Problem Democracy is Supposed to Solve': The Politics of Community-based Performance," explores the intersections of community-based and activist performance. It begins with an overview of important historical markers in both genres, explores the idea of cultural democracy, and details the social aesthetic principles that animate these modes of performance.

E. Patrick Johnson is also concerned with issues of community in "Black Performance Studies: Genealogies, Politics, Futures." Here he examines the subjugated knowledges intrinsic to black expressive culture, knowledges further subjugated by that culture's invisibility within the field of performance studies itself. He goes on to demonstrate that, despite misogyny and homophobia, black women's, gays' and lesbians' creative work has resisted marginalization and maintained blackness as an open signifier.

In his award-winning essay, "Lethal Theatre: Performance, Punishment, and the Death Penalty," reprinted here, Dwight Conquergood reads the signifiers in this site of state-sanctioned killing as a fraught dramaturgy whose contradictions are never fully resolved. In so doing, he charts Americans' changing attitudes to the "magical realism" of capital punishment, and sets current practices in the context of responses to domestic and foreign terrorism.

Sandra Richards uses the form of a performance meditation to engage the complexities and contradictions in/of memory and trauma. In "Who is this Ancestor? Performing Memory in Ghana's Slave Castles," she enacts and interrogates her own attraction to, and revulsion of, eighteenth century Anglican priest Philip Quaque, whose religious practice facilitated European penetration of the coast of Ghana.

Finally, Jill Dolan concludes this section with a discussion of theatre and performance studies as laboratories for reimagining social relations. In "The Polemics and Potential of Theatre Studies and Performance," she offers an institutional history of these disciplines in the form of a personal genealogy, and reinvigorates Turner's notion of *communitas* with her theorizing of the utopian performative.

Conquergood (2002) insistently reminds us of the potential performance studies offers for politically engaged, productive, radical research that spans arbitrary divides between theory and artistic practice, and between academic and everyday knowledges. These five essays demonstrate this potential and point the way to new and generative connections between performance and politics.

NOTE

1. Judith Hamera and Dwight Conquergood were coeditors of this section of the *Handbook*. Unfortunately, Dwight did not live to complete this work. His spirit, and his work, inform and inspire this section and its introduction.

REFERENCES

Austin, J. L. (1975). *How to do things with words.* Cambridge, MA: Harvard University Press.

Boal, A. (1979). *Theatre of the oppressed.* New York: TCG.

Boal, A. (1998). *Legislative theatre.* (A. Jackson, Trans.). London: Routledge.

Butler, J. (1993). *Bodies that matter: On the discursive limits of sex.* New York: Routledge.

Conquergood, D. (2000). Rethinking elocution: The trope of the talking book and other figures of speech. *Text and Performance Quarterly, 20*(4), 325–341.

Conquergood, D. (2002). Performance studies: Interventions and radical research. *The Drama Review, 46*(2), 145–156.

de Certeau, M. (1984). *The practice of everyday life* (Vol. 1). (S. Rendall, Trans.). Berkeley: University of California Press. (Original work published 1974)

Davis, T. (1991). *Actresses as working women.* London: Routledge.

Diamond, E. (1996). Introduction. In E. Diamond (Ed.) *Performance and cultural politics* (pp. 1–12). New York: Routledge, 1996.

Hamera, J. (2002). An answerability of memory: "Saving" Khmer classical dance. *The Drama Review, 46*(4), 65–85.

Hurston, Z. N. (1990). *Mules and men.* New York: Harper. (Original work published 1935)

Jackson, S. (2000). *Lines of activity: Performance, historiography, Hull-House domesticity.* Ann Arbor: University of Michigan Press.

Johnson, E. P. (2003). *Appropriating blackness: Performance and the politics of authenticity.* Durham, NC: Duke University Press.

Joseph, M. (1999). *Nomadic identities: The performance of citizenship.* Minneapolis: University of Minnesota Press.

Langellier, K. M., & Peterson, E. E. (2004). *Storytelling in daily life: Performing narrative.* Philadelphia: Temple University Press.

McKenzie, J. (2001). *Perform or else: From discipline to performance.* London: Routledge.

McKenzie, J. (2003). Democracy's performance. *The Drama Review, 47*(2), 117–128.

Merrill, L. (1999). *When Romeo was a woman: Charlotte Cushman and her circle of female spectators.* Ann Arbor: University of Michigan Press.

Muñoz, J. E. (1999). *Disidentifications: Queers of color and the performance of politics.* Minneapolis: University of Minnesota Press.

Phelan, P. (1993). *Unmarked: The politics of performance.* New York: Routledge.

Plato (1998). Ion. In D. H. Richter (Ed.), *The critical tradition: Classical texts and contemporary trends* (pp. 29–37). Boston: Bedford.

Pollock, D. (1998). Introduction: Making history go. In D. Pollock (Ed.), *Exceptional spaces: Essays in performance & history* (pp. 1–45). Chapel Hill: University of North Carolina Press.

Riggs, M. (Director). (1995). *Black is . . . black ain't* [Film]. United States: Independent Television Service. (Available from California Newsreel, P.O. Box 2284, South Burlington, VT 05407)

Schechner, R. (1985). *Between theatre and anthropology.* Philadelphia: University of Pennsylvania Press.

Schechter, J. (1985). *Durov's pig: Clowns, politics and theatre.* New York: TCG.

Schutzman, M. (1994). Brechtian shamanism: The political therapy of Augusto Boal. In M. Schutzman & J. Cohen-Cruz (Eds.), *Playing Boal: Theatre, therapy, activism.* London: Routledge.

Taylor, D. (2003). *The archive and the repertoire: Performing cultural memory in the Americas.* Durham, NC: Duke University Press.

Turner, V. (1982). *From ritual to theatre.* New York: PAJ.

Willetts, J. (Ed. & Trans.). (1964). *Brecht on theatre.* London: Methuen/Hill and Wang.

24

The Problem Democracy Is Supposed to Solve

The Politics of Community-Based Performance

JAN COHEN-CRUZ

Getting communities involved in imagining their future is the problem that democracy is supposed to solve.

—Law theorists Lani Guinier and Gerald Torres (2002, p. 219)

The subject of this essay is the politics of community-based performance, expressed both directly by way of efforts to impact the status quo—i.e., activist performance—and indirectly by the very inclusive and participatory nature of its form, whatever the content of particular projects. Let me begin by clarifying my terms.

Community-based performance is characterized by deep interaction between artists and constituents grounded in a shared aspect of identity or circumstances. Professional artists, informed in some way by community participants, explore collectively meaningful themes and then develop and stage a piece that is by, for, and about a larger group of which those participants are a part. The goals of these partnerships include and exceed the creation of art. That is, community-based performance is hyphenated not just grammatically but also as a practice. Community-based art is situated between entertainment and efficacy, art for pleasure and art that concretely *does* something, be it in the realm of education, therapy, counter-historymaking, community-organizing, or social change.

Activist art is aesthetic production as part of a struggle for social change, such as seeking more rights for people who are being exploited, or resistance to changes that are deemed detrimental, e.g., fighting school budget cuts. Community-based activist art is as much about the process of involving local people in articulating their points-of-view as in a finished art object itself. Whereas *activist* and *community-based* emphasize process and participation, *political* art refers to an aesthetic object that an artist or ensemble creates as a response to a controversial public issue or action or to challenge the status quo. Think of superb individual artists and great anti-war oeuvres like Picasso's *Guernica* or Brecht's *Mother Courage,* viewable in art institutions (museums, theatres) and extolled for their universality and artistic virtuosity as much as for their message. Political artists and ensembles may also value processes and collective, non-hierarchical practices but the public face of their work is the art object.

Not all community-based performance is activist. It is as likely to celebrate cultural traditions or provide a space for a community to reflect as to participate in local struggles. But whether activist or not, community-based performance is committed to collective, not strictly individual, representation. The centrality of open participation is particularly important in these scary times, characterized by national measures such as the Patriot Act that control participation. And whatever the typical content of their work, community-based artists live in the same environment as their constituents, and are thus likely to be personally affected by the same nuclear power plants, epidemics, and economic ups and downs. Thus can they build on an experiential connection should activism *become* a goal of a particular project.

An example of an activist community-based production is *Wild Card* (2002), written and directed by Michael Fields, managing artistic director of the Dell'Arte Players. Dell'Arte is a physical theatre that established itself in the small town of Blue Lake, California, in 1974. When local Native Americans decided to build a casino in town, ensemble members raised money for dialogue specialists to convene town meetings. People on all sides of the issue envisioned the future of their small hamlet in the face of the

possibility of the casino, likely to attract large, noisy crowds. Having lived in the community nearly 30 years, Dell'Arte members were sensitive to the complexity of issues represented by the casino, especially given the obscene treatment of Native Americans throughout U.S. history and limited economic opportunities in the present. Nevertheless, the majority of the community feared the effects of the casino for everyone. Fields wrote *Wild Card* to continue the dialogue, in the spirit of "What now?"

A flaw in the production, despite Fields's efforts, was the absence of Native Americans performing in *Wild Card*. Indeed, soon after the first production, Fields remounted the project as *Wild Card 1.5* with 50 percent new material, including a Native American in a central role in the cast. *Wild Card* ends on this note:

> What makes a home? Is it comfort, time, a building, a landscape, a state of mind or all of the above? I think that home is character formed over years of use. . . . What worries me the most . . . [is that] where you arrive looks like just where you left. It's a sameness—as if everything is approved by the same universal building code. And I think it kills as surely as not. Blue Lake has always has its streak of difference; sometimes nasty, sometimes celebratory, sometimes conflictual, but so necessary . . . I don't like the spread of lights in the hills either. . . . But whatever the landscape be inscribed with— be it gold, timber, gambling or the next "new thing," we know that the river may very well sweep it all away tomorrow. Until it does it is in our keeping; but only if we make it so. There is such a thing as the "commons"—but to make it we all have to be there. (Fields, 2002)

The play can not unmake the casino but rather encourages local political involvement so that by the time an issue comes up, a more engaged community is ready to respond. A member of Dell'Arte, in fact, is running for city council as a result of the casino.

SELECTED HISTORICAL ANTECEDENTS OF U.S. ACTIVIST COMMUNITY-BASED PERFORMANCE

Community-based performance is a field with a genealogy rather than a cause-and-effect history. Although activist performance has frequently been associated with progressive causes, the power of heightened imagery and text, and broad participation, have been used to further agendas on all points of the political spectrum. The pageant is a case in point. Structured around a series of tableaux or moving pictures, early twentieth century pageants in the United States typically represented moments in the economic or social history of a town, using verse and prose embellished by choruses, songs, dances, and marches at a beautiful site, and cast with local citizens. According to historian David Glassberg, "civic officials sought to define local community identity, cohesion, and sense of common purpose through elaborate civic historical celebrations and commemorations" (1990, p. 282). Pageantry was radical for its time, an attempt to democratize performance by opening it to greater participation, broader audiences, and a more public role in civic life.

But at the same time, the pageant was an instrument to reenforce the status quo. While the American Pageant Association encouraged inclusion of diverse local groups, they also generally reinforced the distinctions between and social roles of each. People generally played roles similar to their actual occupations or statuses. People of the same background rehearsed their parts of the pageant separately from other groups, with a pageant master coordinating the whole. Pageants typically presented idealized versions of local social relations, free of class, ethnic, gender, and race conflict (Glassberg, 1990, p. 126). Blacks and Asians were rarely portrayed at all, and when they were, representations mirrored racist portrayals from the popular theatre of the day that "displayed an idealized view of race relations in the Old South and blacks as comic buffoons" (p. 132).

New immigrants were similarly given short shrift. Some pageants intended to introduce newcomers to American history through the opportunity to enact it in a visual form not dependent on fluency in English. But typically, tableaux of immigrant masses in native costume performed native songs and dances in the first act, and reappeared in "American" garb by the end, singing the national anthem. Though rhetorically about "civic uplift," pageants, in historian Linda Nochlin's view, were grounded as much in an unspoken fear as a "wish to do good for the vast, unprecedented waves of immigrants arriving on our shores" (1985, p. 92). This was perhaps the first artistic expression in the United States of the notorious erasing effect of "melting pot" philosophy.

On the other end of the spectrum, the Paterson Strike Pageant of 1913 represented immigrant workers contributing much more than picturesque and disposable costumes and food traditions. Created in the aftermath of a strike for decent working conditions that resulted in numerous workers' deaths, this pageant represented the battle between labor and capitalism at the same time as it helped participants to ritually deal with grief over their slain comrades. Fifteen-hundred Paterson workers represented images of their original mass actions in juxtaposition with passionate speeches redelivered by the original speakers from the strike. Nochlin theorizes, "In participating in the pageant, they became conscious of their experience as a meaningful force in history and of themselves as self-determining members of a class that shaped history" (1985, p. 91). This pageant is an example of a highly democratic community-based performance providing people with a platform, a context for reflection, and a process for meaningful participation in public life.

Activist performance has often been rooted in collective identification. In the 1930s, the United States experienced its only grass-roots amateur *movement* of workers creating theatre for workers, inspired by popular, participatory art events before and after the Russian Revolution of 1917[1] and catalyzed by the economic and political polarization of the Great Depression. The concept of class culture "presupposed that the conflicting economic and political interests between workers and their employers necessitated a different cultural expression by the conflicting classes" (Friedman, 1985, p. 112). Mass recitation, a popular aesthetic form, usually "pitted a chorus of workers against a capitalist or a representative of the capitalist class, such as a foreman or policeman" (p. 116). Plays were frequently in verse with choreography, archetypal characters, a presentational acting style, and a minimal, mobile set. This activist performance was one part agit-prop, riling up the audience and directing them towards a particular, propagandistic (i.e., one sided) agenda, another part communal ritual for the already converted, and a third piece education, such as representing activist strategies onstage that workers later tried in their lives.

The groundwork for the contemporary community-based performance field was laid in the 1950s, when despite U.S. prosperity, there was growing recognition that the American dream was not equally accessible to all Americans. The lid blew off in the tumultuous 1960s, when broad questioning of the status quo once again found expression in the arts. Much activist performance was organized around identity politics—under- or misrepresented groups bonded by ethnicity, class, sexual preference, or race. In 1968, Larry Neal published a virtual manifesto of one such project, the Black Arts Movement. Neal declared the existence of two Americas, one black, one white. He identified the black artist's work as addressing the spiritual and cultural needs of black people and creating a black aesthetic. He stated that the focus of the work would be "to confront the contradictions arising out of Black people's experience in the racist West" (p. 29). He acknowledged the leadership of

Amiri Baraka (formerly LeRoi Jones), in the 1964 creation of the Black Arts Repertory Theatre School, spawning black arts groups all across the United States.

Similarly, El Teatro Campesino, created in the 1960s as an organizing tool to consolidate farmworkers politically, gave rise to a multitude of Chicano theatre groups. Like the nineteenth century Mexican *carpa* or tent show, El Teatro was an example of popular performance that favors the underdog to create a vehicle of expression by the powerless. Chicano union organizer Cesar Chavez was aware of the power of humor, as manifested in the carpa, to critique and mobilize. Not just company director Luis Valdez—despite the "great man" theory of artistic excellence—but all the Chicano actors in El Teatro knew those traditions, and thus contributed greatly to *la causa* of union organizing (Broyles-Gonzales, 1994).

There's a saying that goes, "It's not the size of the ship that makes the waves, it's the motion of the ocean" (used by O'Neal, 1968, p. 70). In other words, political art relies on an agitated context for efficacy. Radicalness can not be willed—different historical moments offer different possibilities. In the mid-1970s, with a heightened consciousness to think globally but act locally, activist art practitioners looked to local contexts in which their work could play a role. For mass attention had shifted away from the national stage, and erstwhile national movements—against the war, for civil rights—had diminished. I date the beginning of the contemporary community arts movement to just this time.

THEORIZING THE POLITICAL IN COMMUNITY-BASED PERFORMANCE

Cultural Democracy

Law theorists Lani Guinier and Gerald Torres provide a starting point for theorizing the political in community-based performance by shifting the focus of democracy from the individual to the collective. They assert that democracy is less about the "right of individuals to choose individual candidates" than "about the value of groups that form around common concerns and participate in an ongoing democratic conversation" (2002, p. 170). They explain that whereas in representational democracy, people vote every few years for a professional politician to "stand in" for them, in participatory democracy people are directly involved in discussions, at least, concerning policies that affect them.[2]

Guinier and Torres connect political and aesthetic notions of representation. They give the example of Augusto Boal's Forum Theatre as a rich terrain for participatory democracy, as spectators intervene in scenarios to act out their own ideas for solving them. Guinier and Torres' understanding of participatory democracy is similar to policy consultants Don Adams and Arlene Goldbard's notion of cultural democracy, which they define as "a philosophy or policy emphasizing pluralism, participation, and equity within and between cultures" (2001, p. 108). Community-based performance typically manifests values conducive to cultural democracy, involving whole communities around common concerns and defying the tendency to professionalize civic engagement. In a world of lobbyists and electoral politics, where we rely on representational, not participatory, democracy, such an art project is particularly useful.

I do not mean to suggest that a participatory democratic mode of performance is uncomplicated. For example, many community-based productions rely on collaborations with local institutions. Take *Steelbound*, instigated by local ensemble Touchstone Theater in Bethlehem, Pennsylvania, in collaboration with director Bill Rauch and playwright Alison Carey of Cornerstone Theater and some 63 local people, many of them former steel workers. The play was a response to the closing of Bethlehem Steel, which threw the town into economic and emotional turmoil. Yet that corporation supplied some of the project's funding as well the space in which they performed, a former iron foundry. Critic Sara Brady avows the production was thus compromised, unable to critique the powerful institution providing support (2000).

Brady was inaccurate in subtitling her essay "Non-Radicality in Community-Based Theater." While Brady was right to raise the possibility of compromise as a result of collaboration with Bethlehem Steel, that company had already closed the majority of local plants; no stance vis-à-vis the corporation would bring the jobs back. *Steelbound was* radical in its degree of grass-roots participation, if not David-like and in this case futile in its taking on of the Beth Steel Goliath. The participants in *Steelbound* were focused on celebrating their material accomplishments (one refrain in the show is workers declaring, "We built America"); giving local people an opportunity to publicly express a range of feelings about working at "The Steel," from comparing it to hell to extolling the sheer power of the steelmaking process; and creating a public ritual of closure, a funeral for a way of life in a town where nearly everyone had family or friends employed by the company and people literally planned shopping around the changes of shifts to avoid the inevitable traffic. These are worthwhile goals and not acquiescence to the power of the corporation. *Steelbound* did not undertake an activist agenda vis-à-vis workers' rights. It is counterproductive to critique a production for something it was not trying to do.

Brady's limited conception of "radical" is not unlike that of some activists with preconceptions of what partnering with a theatre "should" entail. Whereas some activists tend to privilege message and outcome, community-based artists equally value the exchange and communion between artists and those who participate as actors and audience. Longtime community-based art journalist Linda Burnham writes, "Activist art includes in its goals the process of getting people to think and feel, to discover, empathize, or get angry. It's a partner to activism but their valorization of process is different" (personal communication, June 15, 2003).

At issue is how one measures political activity. Community-based performance offers its constituents the opportunity for participatory rather than representative cultural democracy. This is rarer than it may seem. Democracy as a political system rarely provides ways for people to come together and imagine their collective future. Very few communities hold town meetings that provide the basis for decision-making. Cultural processes that can funnel community points of view to representative decision-makers are crucial for a participatory democracy.

Principles

By looking at four principles on which community-based performance relies—communal context, reciprocity, hyphenation, and active culture—we can further identify the nature of its politics. Community-based performance emerges from a *communal context;* the artists' craft and vision are at the service of a specific group desire. It may be to further the goals of the civil rights movement, as with the Free Southern Theater. Its goal may be to affirm an under- or misrepresented culture, as with Roadside Theater in Appalachia. Artists committed to collective meaning-making use their aesthetic tools in concert with a group of people with lived experience of the subject and with whom they work to shape a collective vision.

Theatre and dance are, of course, already collaborative forms. The difference is that the hierarchical structure of the profession gives the bulk of the power to the producer, playwright, choreographer, and director, whereas community-based performance asserts a model of power shared among the various artists and community partners. As in ritual, community-based artists are inspired to make

beautiful art because of the socially meaningful role it plays. Aesthetics do not matter *less* in a ritual context but they serve a collective purpose rather than primarily reflecting on the individual maker.

Communal context also refers to the audience's experience in the actual time, place, and circumstances of the performance. Composer and activist Bernice Johnson Reagon describes how, during a march, the sound of protestors' singing preceded them as they walked, "so that by the time they reached their destination their voices had already occupied the space in a way the police could not reclaim. It wasn't just the message of the music that was important, but its ability to give physical presence and visceral force, to the movement" (quoted in Peeps, 2000, p. 271). The significance of the performance space is itself a political issue, because the "where" determines "who" the audience will be. Community-based performance is frequently performed at churches and schools, in parks and neighborhood community centers, and in particular theatres; indeed, at any venue where the people that performance is addressing gather.

Reciprocity describes the desired relationship between community-based artists and community participants. Community members receive such satisfactions as imaging and imagining, that is, translating ideas into forms and dreaming about what life could be; deep reflection, a natural outgrowth of play-building; critical distance on their lives; and public visibility, strategically important for the activist wing of community-based performance but meaningful to nearly everyone. That is, the fact that such art gathers a public to its performances can serve a political agenda in broadcasting a point of view. But no matter what the subject matter, a frequent refrain from people who have participated in community-based performances is how appreciative they were to have a moment in the spotlight. Treated with respect by people interested in their viewpoints, participants learn how to talk about their future in a collective setting, a skill that rarely comes without practice.

Artists are stretched by learning what people know and feel through the authority of their experience. Cornerstone Theater's Bill Rauch describes a sense of being groomed, as a young director at Harvard, to eventually become artistic director of a professional regional theatre (personal communication, 2003). Yet he was disappointed that most regional theatres were not, in fact, expressive of their particular place. He sensed there were stories out in the world that never got heard. Indeed, the structures of professional theatre rely on agents and script submissions, auditions and particular training methods not accessible to everyone. As an artist, Rauch believed he would grow by learning about what he didn't know, from people all across the United States who had different experiences than he did. He imagined a theatre that was as eclectic as the country itself, and set out to make such a troupe, with a handful of like-minded colleagues. Approaching people as partners in the creative process, the company Rauch et al. formed in 1986, Cornerstone, supplies the technique and people in a vast range of circumstances provide the content.

Reciprocity in community-based performance is rooted in an assets-based model of community-building which "insists on beginning with a clear commitment to discovering a community's capacities and assets" (Kretzman and McKnight, 1993, p. 1). In contrast to focusing on a community's deficiencies and problems, community-based artists as well as organizers need to also build on a community's strengths. This philosophy is manifested in the way the dancer/facilitators of the ensemble Urban Bush Women enter communities and co-create stories. They don't go in and say, "This is your story." Rather, inspired by Howard Zinn's *A People's History of the United States* (2003), they look at undertold stories. They call the story-gathering component of their work "When the lions tell history," which, as the African proverb suggests, is very different from the hunter's version (J. W. J. Zollar, personal interview, September, 2003). In contrast to top-down experts who assume what will be of interest to people, this process draws on the skills of trained artist/ facilitators to tease out what a range of people want to express and help them to do so.

Reciprocity is in distinct contrast to the all too familiar idea of "community service," bringing to mind a soup kitchen with the well-fed on one side, ladling out soup to the hungry who receive it on the other side. This one-directional model is not in the spirit of community-based performance, being neither dialogic nor reciprocal. Dialogue refers to "two or more parties with differing viewpoints working toward common understanding in an open-ended, face-to-face discussion" (Bacon, Yuen, & Korza, 1999, p. 12). Artists must be as sensitive to their differences from community participants as to the common ground they share. All involved must genuinely appreciate what the others bring to the collaboration, or why do it? Radical literary theorist Mikhail Bakhtin refers to dialogism as the quintessential mode of knowing. Dialogism, to Bakhtin, means that everything must be understood as part of a greater whole. There is a constant interaction between meanings, all of which have the potential of conditioning other meanings (1981, pp. 426–427). Bakhtin saw the goal of dialogue not as a specific solution but rather co-understanding.

Reciprocity is reflected in joint ownership of work created by the community whence it came *and* the artist/facilitator. That is, the contribution of both must be recognized or the result is either cooption of community material or underrepresentation of the artist. Just as community-based art fails to fulfill its potential when artists impose their own aesthetics and ideology, so is the work weakened by underinvolvement of the artist. Community-based performance artist Suzanne Lacy keeps a tight rein on the pageants that she creates with hundreds of people. I see that as a methodological choice, not an imposition. Within Lacy's process, people have great opportunity to explore their issues, bond with others, and become more public. Artists can equally be seemingly noncommittal, which may result in work that contradicts their own political stand. The piece may represent everyone involved but the artist/facilitator, and risk falling into a one-directional, artist-helping–the-people model.

Hyphenation is another principle of this field. Artists frequently experience art in relation to something in addition to aesthetics. The desired experience may be the intersection of, or dialogue between, art and religion, or therapy, or education. Art may also be a site for the articulation and expression of a political point of view or vision. Community-based performance is even more intrinsically hyphenated. Poet Muriel Rukeyser expresses the difference between art that is about something and art that does something when she writes, "Because you have imagined love, you have not loved; merely because you have imagined brotherhood, you have not made brotherhood" (1974, pp. 23–24). For community-based artists, symbolic expression is not enough; they want their art to have some concrete social implication, and they want a life in art that interacts with other realms (therapy, community organizing, etc.). This field challenges the philosophy of art-for-art's-sake, whereby an art work is complete unto itself, without reference or relationship beyond its own boundaries. The concreteness that Rukeyser evokes positions community-based performance to serve efficacious goals even as it continues art's traditional engagement of the viewer's senses.

As a hyphenated field, community-based performance has been shaped by theories from disciplines in addition to theatre. For example, Paulo Freire's ideas about liberatory pedagogy have been highly influential. Freire contrasts "the banking method" of education with dialogic, or problem-solving education

(1987). The former looks at teachers as experts whose job is to deposit their information into the heads of passive students who are mere receptacles. Dialogic education involves students asking questions and teachers and students together seeking answers, in a partnership. The quest to solve real problems energizes the process of education. Community-based performance follows this model in foregrounding community participants in a dialogic relationship with artist/facilitators, not merely audience/receivers, but co-creators in one way or another.

The principle of *active culture* expresses the insight that people frequently get more out of making art than seeing the fruits of other people's labors. The experience of making art causes people to plumb their hearts and minds, experiences and conceptions. Having tried to make art oneself, one can better appreciate other art. A core axiom of community-based performance is that everyone has artistic potential. Finding the aesthetic strengths of each first-time actor is one of the major challenges for community-based artists. Bill Rauch is a master at casting people in parts that are enhanced by the actor's real experience. Seeing the chief of the Walker River Paiute Tribe play the king in *The House on Walker River,* adapted from Aeschylus's *Oresteia,* added a layer of real power in performance that more than compensated for the actor's lack of theatrical training. In other words, just as the field draws on multiple disciplines, so can it draw on people's multiple capacities and apply them in performance.

Unlike pageants, in which participants also portray characters similar to themselves, Cornerstone community plays advocate diversity as one of their four key principles. (The others are listening, respect, and flexibility.) Germane to Cornerstone's process, diverse people interact in workshops, rehearsals, and performances. In a report on the company's methodology, researcher Ferdinand Lewis writes,

Experience has shown that no community is so monolithic that it does not contain a great deal of diversity. . . . A collaboration's successful outcome will literally depend upon its including participants who represent not only a wide range of economic and social backgrounds, ages and ethnicities, but also the diversity of the larger community of which the local community is a part. . . . As a framework for creativity, the concept of diversity can free the imagination from monolithic ideas, and encourage unexpected collaborations. . . . Whenever possible, the production team should represent a diversity of experience with Cornerstone collaborations, including participants who may be doing their first such project alongside those who have previously collaborated with the company. (2003, p. 6)

For Cornerstone then, active culture, inclusion, and diversity are both aesthetic and political pillars of the work.

METHODOLOGIES

Whereas the four principles explain *why* community-based performance can involve people in imagining their collective future, this section describes *how* it achieves this goal. The field's politics are a cultural manifestation of democracy that depends on particular ways of working: (1) It is an *elongated process*, not only a product, so there are multiple opportunities, over time, to participate. (2) Its *aesthetic forms*, especially storytelling (on which I elaborate in what follows), invite a broad cross section of participants. (3) It assumes an *expanded notion of art*. Specifically, community-based artists work at the overlap of art and other disciplines, both by stretching what they do as artists and through collaborations with nonartists, such as educators and activists, towards a common goal.

Elongated Process

Like performance generally, community-based art is not just the show but all the processes leading up to and following after it. Examination of these processes provides a way to unpack such work beyond the transaction between actors and spectators in the closed space and limited time of the show itself. The high value placed on preliminary and postperformance phases—the play, in and of itself, is *not* the (only) thing—corresponds to the structure of rites of passage, that category of ritual about change and transformation. Rites of passage provide a process for not just the person going through the change but for their community to recognize it and adapt accordingly as well. Given the proven success of rites of passage to dramatize and facilitate change for whole communities, it's instructive for activist community-based art makers to investigate how rites of passage accomplish this task.

According to anthropologist Arnold van Gennep, rites of passage have three-part structures: separation, liminality, and reintegration (1960). In the first stage, the persons going through the change are taken from their ordinary life to be specially prepared for the change. The middle phase is a period of "betwixt and between," no longer the old category but not yet the new. The third stage, often marked by a performance, is the moment of reincorporating the persons back into the community in the new status. An example of a rite of passage is marriage. The separation phase corresponds to the period of growing commitment during which the couple stops dating other people. Once engaged, the couple is betwixt and between—no longer single but not quite married. The wedding ceremony is the performance that marks the couple's new status in the community as married, not only for them but for their parents and friends, with the change in behavior they are expected to exhibit as well.

Influenced by anthropologist Victor Turner, performance theorist Richard Schechner identified seven phases of performance in a "pattern analogous to initiation rites" and harkening back to van Gennep (Schechner, 1985, pp. 20–21). Schechner's first four phases— training, workshop, rehearsal, and warm-up— correspond to van Gennep's first ritual stage, separation. They are the processes the actors go through before contact with the audience, during which they prepare for the performance. The middle stage of a rite of passage, liminality, corresponds to Schechner's fifth phase, performance, during which the transformation is symbolically represented but has not yet been effectuated in everyday life. Van Gennep's notion of reintegration, the point at which the people who have gone through the rite of passage rejoin their society with new roles and responsibilities, corresponds to Schechner's final two stages, cool-down and aftermath.

Noticing what phases are emphasized is instructive concerning a hyphenated project's goals; for example, the performance itself is not the be-all and end-all and may not even be at the center. In what follows I explain how these phases facilitate community-based performance principles—communal context, reciprocity, hyphenation, and active culture—on which its participatory democratic nature rests. I contend that it is precisely in its participatory process rather than in its subject matter that the politics of this field are most manifest. The experience of community ownership and decision-making is at the heart of the work, no matter what the theme of a production.

As concerns *training,* given this field's interdisciplinary nature, learning multiple skills in addition to the artistic is necessary. This expectation prepares artists to facilitate participatory processes of imagining a community's future. Dudley Cocke, for example, emphasizes the need for grass-roots artists to learn community organizing (personal communication, June, 2002). Community-based writer Alice Lovelace believes artists working for social change need training in conflict resolution (Lovelace, 2002). Particular performance skills are also invaluable. Touchstone artistic director Mark McKenna reflects on

Dell'Arte's school, which teaches popular theatre techniques such as commedia, an inherently interactive mode: "Students come to understand the performer's responsibility to the audience" (2002b). The school's focus is on creating one's own work, a critical skill for community-based performers. Dell'Arte teaches a sense of the artist's ownership of their work; Steve Bisher, associate school director, says that before he did workshops with Michael Fields, he "didn't know that as an actor you could have your own thoughts" (quoted in McKenna, 2002a).

The next phase, *workshop,* is the period of building the performance and invariably incorporates communal input. Research is one means of generating material, typically through extensive interviewing of local people connected to the project's theme. Participating artists need to develop a sense of the collaborating community and uncover both oral and written source materials, leading to developing the script. Each Cornerstone community show involves an average of 20 meetings with local focus groups and leaders. The company begins by finding one local person "making the leap of faith and becoming an advocate for the project," helping find appropriate people for an advisory board (Bill Rauch, quoted in Lewis, 2002). Cornerstone tells the board how they build a project and the board advises the company how to do so there. In the development of the art work, integration of local stories is one way that different points of view are put into conversation with each other. Dell'Arte audience member Kit Zettler emphasizes the cross-pollination this accomplishes: "You are not necessarily going to get a logger who comes to see this play and walks away saying I'm never doing that again. But a logger comes to the play because their friend got interviewed or was talked to" (quoted in McKenna 2002a). He thus ends up hearing other points of view, so essential in a democracy. In other projects, the community has a united point of view and creates the play as a form of advocacy.

A variation on the workshop phase is what Suzanne Lacy calls *embedding*, for example, focusing on people and institutions outside of art contexts that the creators want to reach (personal communication, 2003). At an early stage in the process, Lacy trains participants to contextualize the work in community organizations and the media. For example, while creating *Code 33*, which focused on improving police relations with Oakland teenagers, Lacy sent teenage participants out to talk with reporters and politicians about community policing. Laying the ground work for *Code 33*'s public components paralleled work on its internal aesthetic development.

Warm-up is the process immediately preceding a show. In plays meant to maximize audience participation, spectators are often given a way to prepare, too, perhaps through actual warm-up exercises. The community potluck dinner is another popular format. Cocke recounts that "often the Roadside actors move directly from the social mixing to the stage and begin the performance" (personal communication, June, 2002).

Next, the **performance** itself offers various dynamic opportunities for actor-spectator exchange and illustrates the hyphenation of the field. Carpetbag Theatre, a Knoxville ensemble that brings underrepresented voices to public attention, based *Red Summer* on historical documentation of local activists from the civil-rights era. Director Linda Parris-Bailey saw it as a way to tell residents that their belief nothing could change was historically incorrect: "Maybe if we just remind you of what has been here before, you can see some possibility for the future. We talk about people who take control" (quoted in Watkins, 2002). Parris-Bailey also sees a fundamentally celebratory component in the company's historical pieces. It is satisfying for actors and spectators to return stories to the communities from whence they came. The text of Los Angeles Poverty Department (LAPD)'s *Agents and Assets* is a transcript of a congressional hearing on CIA involvement in crack cocaine sales in California that indicts the War on Drugs. LAPD is composed largely of homeless people. There's an irony in hearing the words of educated, skilled politicians spoken by actors who at some point were casualties of the War on Drugs. Having an LAPD actor portray a politician creates a built-in critique. Teatro Pregones, a Puerto Rican ensemble based in the Bronx, used Boal's Forum Theatre with their production of *The Embrace* to engage audience dialogue on the spot. Forum invites spectators to replace a protagonist struggling with a social issue, in this case as a result of having AIDS. Spectators enact different possible ways of handling those struggles as part of the performance.

The **cool-down** phase immediately follows performance and may take the form of discussion. Though often very effective, postshow discussions also have their drawbacks. Sometimes spectators aren't ready to talk about a play so soon; sometimes artists bring in discussion leaders but audiences really only want to hear from artists. Pregones usually saves postshow discussion for new shows that they ask audiences to evaluate. Reflecting the field's emphasis on reciprocity, postshow panels may be as valuable for expert participants as for spectators and artists. At *Agents and Assets,* experts on the CIA reported being educated by their outspoken and eloquent LAPD copanelists from skid row. In *Steelbound,* cool-down took the form of postshow gatherings over dessert and drinks where spectators enjoyed unmediated conversation with each other. The artists of Alternate ROOTS often use the Critical Response Process[3] developed by choreographer Liz Lerman with her company, the Dance Exchange, after showing a work-in-progress. Lerman developed the process to put the artist herself in charge of the feedback session. Sometimes artists invite stories from the audience about the play's theme which in Cocke's experience have become a powerful subtext for the actors' next performance (personal communication, June, 2002).

Aftermath/ long term activities not immediately following the artwork take the initiative further. Aftermath is the stage following the run of the performance during which local participants and spectators, possibly facilitated by the artists, might act on what they have imagined together. One of community-based art's mantras is sustainability: artists must leave something behind. After the project has ended, are there local people with the skills to facilitate ongoing work? Is there a support network, any kind of ongoing program for people whose appetites have been whetted? Have people with the power to make the changes an activist community-based production expresses been engaged in such a way as to implement desired policies? During the years that Cornerstone did residencies in towns across the United States, they donated money for each community to start a theatre. LAPD partners with SRO Housing, which has renovated 30 former slum hotels into single-room occupancy hotels. They share the overall mission of helping people get off the street. LAPD adds a creative dimension to SRO which in turn lends an infrastructure that nurtures LAPD. Sometimes seeing a community-based performance influences an individual's later decision to become actively involved in political/civic life.

Aesthetic Forms Inviting Broad Participation

Whereas the aesthetics of community-based performance vary, some forms have proven especially conducive to activist goals. Such art is often a balance of "conventions and inventions" (John Cawelti, quoted in Berger, 1992, p. vii); that is, it combines elements familiar to particular communities with new and surprising aspects. The three most frequently used structures into which community material is integrated are collectively grounded popular forms, often-adapted literary texts, and original compositions shaped by the core participating artist(s)' particular creative process(es). Space constraints only allow me to elaborate on one, the method using collectively grounded popular forms.

Roadside Theater members build on forms familiar to their intended community, including the native ballad tradition and other story-based forms. From the Appalachian region themselves, ensemble members grew up surrounded by these traditions. Dell'Arte and Pregones are grounded in traditional forms as well, respectively a great range of European and Latino popular theatre. Popular theatre has historically relied on techniques accessible to people no matter what their education, such as the physical, archetypal Italian commedia dell'arte and the Mexican carpa, or tent show. The popular is often linked with democratization of theatre, extending beyond class boundaries by virtue of content, form, and venue. The French tradition of the popular was articulated by Romain Rolland in his book, *Le theater du peuple* (1903), described by theatre historian Marvin Carlson as "a theater accessible to the workers without being condescending, and educative without being pompous or exclusive. [Rolland] proposed for it three basic concerns: to provide relaxation for its patrons after a day of labor, to give them energy for the day to come, and to stimulate their minds" (Carlson, 1993, p. 317).

The popular also bespeaks a sense of broad cultural ownership. Pregones member Jorge Merced describes a performance at a high school that began really badly but when the Latino music and poetry started, the whole event turned around (Lopez, 2002). Associate director Alvan Colon Lespier identifies as major influences the Latin American Popular Theatre and New Theatre trends whose origins can be traced to the late twenties when Latin American theatre artists begin experimenting with Stanislavski, Meyerhold, Piscator, and later Brecht (Lespier, personal communication, November, 2003). These sources share popular theatre's emphasis on theatre as a communal event, participating in the celebratory, political, and effective life of the populace: "little or no fourth wall, travel to people rather than expecting them to come to you" (R. Rolon, personal communication, November, 2003). Not infrequently, Pregones' performances are part of larger events like street parties and festivals. On the other hand, the ensemble does not exhibit blind devotion to tradition. Says Rolon, "There are some traditions we don't value. But we rarely take up an issue without going back 100 years. Because we realize it was probably done already" (personal communication, November, 2003). Even when they think they are inventing something, they find a common thread in earlier Latino work. So they have made it a habit to know those sources.

Storytelling

All struggles against oppression in the modern world begin by redefining what had previously been considered private, non-public and non-political issues as matters of public concern, as issues of justice, and sites of power.

—Seyla Benhabib (1992, p. 100)

While productions take a range of aesthetic forms, the most pervasive method of community-based performance building is story gathering. In what follows, I tease out the significance of this approach vis-à-vis "the problem democracy is supposed to solve." The central dynamic characterizing the political use of story is redefining the personal, as Benhabib writes, "as matters of public concern, as issues of justice, as sites of power" (1992, p. 100).

I begin with *common green/common ground (cg2),* a 21-month play building and performance project I initiated about New York City community gardens—their

creation, flourishing, and then struggle to survive. Sabrina Peck, a founding member of Cornerstone Theater, coconceptualized, directed, and choreographed the project with 43 community gardeners and NYU Tisch School of the Arts students. Peggy Pettitt facilitated community storytelling and Michael Keck was musical director. We began *cg2* by holding storycircles with people with community gardening experience. The format was very simple: we'd pose a question like, "What nourishes you most in the garden?" and people would respond with a story, one by one, as everyone else listened. There would be no general conversation until all the people in the circle had had a chance to tell their stories. The play we built together under Peck's direction was largely based on these stories.

Cg2's basis in story created a level playing field apparent to everyone from the first storycircle. People were going to be respected here not for their educational or economic level but for their relationship to gardening:

Rosa: I shared something I knew with the Brooklyn Botanic Garden here—they said it couldn't be done but it can. You take any plant that's dead or you figure can't grow. You take a grain of corn, put a hole in it, and put it in the ground where the ailing plant is planted. When the corn sprouts, the plant catches on and it grows. I have a rose bush that was looking like it was dead. Miss Oliver said to me, "You can't grow that. Leave it be." I put it in the ground with the corn and the other day she said, "Your rose bush look good." (Cohen-Cruz, 2000)

Because stories come out of everyone's experience, not only those designated exceptional, the events they recount feel like actions any of us could emulate. Here's Toby Sanchez:

Our garden started out as a dump just like all the others. There were suitcases in there and you didn't know if there were dead bodies or what. Our neighborhood association was always complaining, oh the lot it's so terrible, it's ruining property values, but

I have to say they mainly whined. So I went downtown and found out that Banco de Ponce owned the land and I wrote them a letter saying, "You're causing slums and blight. Why don't you give the lot to the association and we'll create a garden? I promise we'll take good care of it." Well, they threw that in the waste can. Then I called some friends who told me the correct language to use with banks and the right agencies to send copies to. I wrote the letter again on behalf of our neighborhood association and said, "Federal money has just been used to renovate two buildings next to this lot, and you are creating slums and blight" and I put c.c. to the right agency. That bank manager called up the very next day and said, "I'll do whatever you want." So the association agreed—the bank pays to clean up the lot and put up a fence and the neighbors will garden. (Cohen-Cruz, 2000)

In the same vein, stories promote solidarity. As cultural consultant Caron Atlas avows, "I especially like stories of resistance that help people speak out and feel less isolated."[4]

Story-based theatre is more generally accessible to audiences, too. According to South African theatre critic Zakes Mda,

Why should "art" as in "art theatre" be used to distinguish between theatre that is composed in the codes of national elites, and uses techniques that are appreciated only by them and are beyond the comprehension of the rest of the society, from theatre that has a broad appeal within the society and is rooted in the community? Popularity does not make a work inartistic. It merely means the artist has utilised codes that are shared by the whole of the community. (1993, p. 49)

African American storyteller Lorraine Coleman relies on stories because, "Minority communities only trust what comes from the heart."[4]

Suzanne Lacy is a community-based performance artist who integrated personal story into her work in the early 1970s, largely influenced by feminist consciousness-raising (CR)

groups. The CR group was a grass-roots strategy in the women's movement of that time whereby groups of 6–12 women met in each other's living spaces and told personal stories that bespoke structural inequalities in gender relationships. Lacy had studied with community organizer Saul Alinsky before entering the Feminist Studio Workshop directed by Judy Chicago. In the hands of Lacy and other feminist artists in the 1970s, the processes of CR groups became interviews with women about rape, about aging, about invisibility, that were woven into performance pieces.

Lacy has been equally influenced by aesthetic and conceptual tools she learned from Allan Kaprow, best known for the creation of happenings. She explains: "Although the visual matters, the shape of the concept is more important—emphasizing daily life, everyday actions such as brushing one's teeth as art, and the ideas of contingency, intentionality, and framing" (personal communication, 2003). So it is not surprising that Lacy finds limits to the value of story. In the tradition of the avant-garde, Lacy's interest in contingency shapes her desire for unscripted and unpredictable expressions of personal experience, rather than fixed narrative. While participants of Lacy's projects have extensive conversations among themselves, these conversations, and ultimately performance components, are as likely to be philosophical and idea-driven as they are to be personal and narrative. Lacy distrusts singular narrative, but is drawn toward multiple, simultaneous narratives improvisationally exercised by nontrained actors around a series of predetermined questions. Lacy speculates that part of her aversion to fixed story is that prioritizing individual narrative inevitably distorts the bigger picture:

Everyone operates within a personal narrative history and present that centralizes them within a very vast world. One of the problems with race relations today [Lacy has worked intensively in cross-racial contexts] is how white people centralize the narrative.

Like, "I hurt so much because you are oppressed." (personal communication, 2003)

John O'Neal, cofounder in 1963 of the Free Southern Theater, has also used personal story for political engagement. Rather than tell people what to do, the Free Southern Theater strived to create performances that stimulated postshow discussion, thus serving their goal of supporting the development of southern black communities. The exchange of stories proved to be a better way of having dialogue than argument because, explains O'Neal,

> Adversarial debates reward people who are trained in their techniques. Those tend to be people who have the largest vocabularies and largest egos and most willingness to claim ground and hold it. Which merely affirms the problem you're starting with in the first place. So instead of standing on stage and answering questions, I moved off the stage and sat in the audience and said, "Why don't you tell me a story that the experience of the theatre evoked in you?" (personal communication, 2002)

Story circles frequently lead to other activities; O'Neal, now artistic director of Junebug Productions, is using story in his current project, *The Color Line,* to document civil rights history. He sees this as a step in the rebuilding of a movement for social justice. One artist, one educator, and one activist in each of several towns are bringing their communities' attention to the local legacy of civil rights. The artist is responsible for gathering personal stories on the subject. Stories must be used in some way thereafter, with the help of the educator and the activist.

Storytelling offers what Dudley Cocke calls a "counter-history" to that written by those with the power to articulate official histories (personal communication, June, 2002). Local stories, explains Cocke, often provide a viewpoint that is otherwise suppressed. Cocke and Don Baker's production with Roadside Theater of *Red Fox/Second Hangin'*

(1976/1994) opposed written versions of an Appalachian figure known as "Red Fox" with oral accounts. Officially a villain, Red Fox appears as a hero in local stories. Roadside took the oral stories up a notch by corroborating them with material evidence such as old newspaper articles and court records.

Stories are a valuable tool for building participation because of their contagious nature. Donna Porterfield of Roadside describes a play, *South of the Mountain,* written by company member Ron Short,

> that was his family's personal story, in which real family members were portrayed using their real names. The story, however, was the same story experienced by many in the mountains, so it became archetypal. The play was immensely popular in the mountains, and in working class communities nationally. Audiences always wanted to stay after the show to tell their stories to the actors. (Porterfield, personal communication, June 17, 2003)

Indeed, stories evoke what people know they have in common and affirm the group. In the three plays in John O'Neal's Junebug series, O'Neal portrays a storyteller of that name. SNCC (the Student Nonviolent Coordinating Committee, a civil rights organization) invented Junebug as a "title," i.e., not one character but representative of the wisdom of the common person. The stories themselves came from many African Americans during the civil rights movement. The stories serve multiple community goals, central among them a counter-history from the point of view of those without power who did not get to write the official history. They also celebrate African American wit, language, and spirit.

According to literary theorist Paul Cobley, narrative helps maintain and recall identity; the memories embodied therein have served in the "formation and maintenance of the self-image of a people" (2000, p. 38). This may prove liberating when a group is under pressure to assimilate or simply deserves more respect. Roadside Theater was founded in order to strengthen its Appalachian region. According to Cocke,

> Roadside's home community had no experience creating or attending plays created from its local life. . . . Roadside has had an open field to invent itself, always ready to try something different based on what it originally identified as its core theatrical resources: storytelling, oral history, bluegrass and mountain music, and lively church services. (personal communication, June, 2002)

Narratives representing a people may also prove oppressive, depending on how "we" is defined. Take the case of Swamp Gravy, an annual theatre project conceived in Colquitt, Georgia (pop. 2,000) by a local woman who had met director Richard Owen Gere in a creativity workshop in the north. Wanting to bring a story-based playmaking experience to her small town, she invited Gere to Colquitt. For a half dozen years, in partnership with playwright Jo Carson, Gere made an annual play on local issues with local people. The project was unprecedented in bringing together people from both the black and white communities. But more recently, with a different director and writer, the show became so demanding of people's time that almost only white, more affluent people had time to participate. Consequently, who was represented in the annual, story-based was "Colquitt community" production?

Storytelling as a traditional form of education passes on values, practices, experience, and knowledge that affirm the collective identity of the group. Popular education also affirms collective identity but is based on rethinking received wisdom in a dialectic with lived experience. Brazilian theatre maker Augusto Boal's direct translation of Freire's "pedagogy of the oppressed" into Theatre of the Oppressed (TO) evidences this dynamic. Boal moved from agit-prop, a form of theatre that *tells audiences* what they *should* do, to a story-based approach that engages audiences in discussions about what *they want to* or *could* do. Boal and his middle-class actors from Sao Paolo were performing for peasants in the northeast of Brazil. Holding their prop rifles over their heads, they called for all peasants to mobilize against the landowners and take control of the means of production. The leader of the peasants rushed up to Boal after the show and said, "Yes! You are right! We have a stash of rifles back at our hideout. Let's all go have lunch and then fight the landowners and take the land!" Boal was ashamed. He and his troupes were actors, not fighters. He realized then the fallacy of telling a group of people a solution to a problem that he did not share and whose ramifications he would not experience. This led Boal to the creation of Forum Theatre (2001, pp. 194–195).

In Forum Theatre, several people who share a particular social oppression each tell a story that localizes how that oppression plays out in their lives. The stories all end badly; otherwise, they would not need to find solutions for the problem. Using the stories as building blocks, the group makes a scene in which they all feel represented and perform it for an audience called "spect-actors" who also identify with that problem. Because the one story stands for the many, after performing the scene, the liaison between actors and audience known as "the joker" can discuss the problem with those assembled and ask, "Can anyone imagine something the protagonist might do to ameliorate the situation?" If anyone has an idea—and I've never seen a Forum Theatre where no one did—the scene is replayed, stopping at whatever points spect-actors want to become the protagonist and try it out. Storytelling as critical pedagogy rather than a receptacle of unquestionable knowledge thus provides a way for people who identify with one another to imagine different behavioral choices leading to different outcomes.

As stories are told, paradoxically, they are no longer just one person's tale. That's the basis of storytelling in community-based performance—each person's story is but the raw material from which the performance, which must be meaningful to and representative of the whole group, is created.

Boal, O'Neal, *cg2*, and Lacy all fulfill what Benhabib (1992) calls contextualizing the personal as a "struggle for justice" but they do so in different ways. Boal proposes a structured approach to illuminating the political realities embedded in personal stories. For in Theatre of the Oppressed, the subject of the stories is always oppressions encountered, struggled with, but not overcome. Whether in workshops or Forum performances, spect-actors first warm up so as to be ready to participate. Although the structure of O'Neal's storycircles is looser than that of TO, at their best (from O'Neal's perspective) they are part of a movement for social justice whence their efficacious potential emanates. So did participants in *cg2* see themselves as part of a movement, to save community gardens, and thus the play was experienced at once as an aesthetic and an advocacy experience. And whereas Boal's Forum Theatre begins with people identifying an oppression and then bringing specifics of their lives to illustrate it, Lacy and consciousness-raising groups begin with personal stories to lead to political revelations. For example as long as rape was considered a private matter, it was beyond the ken of political regulation. The very act of speaking about it publicly helped move it into the domain of issues that could be politically regulated.

But neither personal stories manifesting political implications nor any other methodology necessarily leads to justice. Sometimes the heightened political consciousness of the times propels a performance into political efficacy; ACT UP's work in the late 1980s and 1990s is a case in point (see Solomon, 1998). Or a political link is necessary. Boal made such a connection when he became a city councilor of Rio de Janeiro and treated the revelations of Forum Theatre as a dossier pointing the way to

laws that needed to be passed. And indeed, thirteen laws were passed on that basis (see Boal, 1998). Lacy, too, has allied herself with institutions capable of making changes. A decade of work in Oakland, California, was closely coordinated with the police and eventually led to better police training especially in regard to male teens of color, who voiced bitter stories of their treatment at the hands of Oakland's finest. O'Neal originally allied Free Southern Theater with SNCC, and now regularly partners artists with activists and educators. All three of these artists situate story-based performance in relationship to institutions able to lessen the inequities that the stories make public, propelling me to my last point, the overlap of art and other disciplines.

An Expanded Notion of Art

Washington, DC, Yom Kippur, October 2003. I am with choreographer Liz Lerman and some 400 congregants at Temple Micah, dancing our atonement on this, the most solemn day of the Jewish calendar. Ten days ago, on the Jewish New Year, Rabbi Danny Zemel invited worshippers to write down their sins of the past year so they could be used as part of today's danced prayer. Lerman has chosen the following sins that were inscribed most frequently: For the sin I sinned by losing my temper, by being impatient, for my smart mouth, my pride, and for not listening. Five congregants join her on the *bima* (stage) and each reads a sin. Lerman has choreographed a movement for each which she teaches all 400 of us now. The gestures are of the hands, face, arms, and fingers; we can do them standing in place. We all do each gesture as the five congregants each read the corresponding line. Then we join in speaking and embodying all five lines and gestures. Next we do the gestures as we sing a song with different words but the same spirit of praying for forgiveness for our sins. Then instrumental music is added. Each time, the totality of the words and gestures take me to a deeper place. All of me is asking for forgiveness.

Through her work in the Washington Jewish community, Lerman is investigating bringing people of wealth and status into this field. If we really want to hear everyone's story we must include the rich and powerful; they could benefit from this kind of work even as do people on the other end of the economic spectrum. Indeed, all of us need to hear from people in different circumstances than our own. Lerman has taken the opportunity to get people to participate by chance—because her Yom Kippur dance is for the whole congregation and not just a subset interested in creative Jewish experiments, she hopes the power of art to open our hearts and minds will be experienced by the entire congregation. In the same spirit, Lerman worked with both military personnel and those against their use of nuclear weapons in the Portsmouth, New Hampshire, *Shipyard Project,* believing that people of different positions and opinions must be brought to the same table if we all are to move forward together.

Community-based performance is thus inherently educational, teaching participants *how to express themselves and listen to others* in a collective setting. For the main problem with Guinier and Torres' theory of participatory democracy is that most of us lack processes for envisioning our future together. It is idealistic to imagine the political establishment taking art so seriously, yet there is precedent (such as the aforementioned experiments of Augusto Boal as a city councilman).

Moreover, the educational potential of art is impeded by the breach between art makers and thinkers, an area that community-based practitioners must also take up to fulfill art's political promise. Just as the field suffers from lack of recognition of the artistic skills required, so does it undermine itself in not always accepting the other kinds of expertise that a project with multiple goals requires. Though economic constraints pose a challenge, so does habitual

thinking about who is needed to guide a performance project with not only aesthetic goals. As community-based performance fully translates its principles into practice, it will create ever broader participatory spaces for people to imagine their collective future. By providing an accessible process and leadership for thinking our situation through collectively and publicly expressing it, community-based performance could be a viable response to what Guinier and Torres call "the problem democracy is supposed to solve."

NOTES

1. In the newly formed Soviet Union, festivals were a means to educate a large population and forge identification with the new state. Intertwining experimentation, politics, and popular entertainment enabled audiences to grasp ideology by rendering ideas visually and capturing the audience's attention.

2. Cultural democracy has a particular resonance given my focus here on the United States. There are often correlations between cultural and political systems. The Nazi Nuremberg rallies of the 1930s, for example, immortalized in Leni Riefenstahl's film *Triumph of the Will* (1935/ 1993), is a terrifying example of totalitarianism in art reflecting totalitarianism in politics.

3. Liz Lerman's Critical Response Process[SM] and the Critical Response Process[SM] are service marks of the Dance Exchange, Inc. (Liz Lerman Dance Exchange). Use of and reference to Liz Lerman's Critical Response Process[SM] and the Critical Response Process[SM] requires prior permission of the Dance Exchange. For editorial purposes the service mark has been purposely omitted from the text of this publication.

4. From author's notes from Critical Perspectives Writers Gathering held in November 2002 in San Francisco, organized by Animating Democracy Initiative.

REFERENCES

Adams, D., & Goldbard, G. (2001). *Creative community: The art of cultural development.* New York: Rockefeller Foundation.

Bacon, B. S., Yuen, C., & Korza, P. (1999). *Animating democracy: The artistic imagination as a* force in civic dialogue [Electronic version]. Washington, DC: Americans for the Arts.

Baker, D., & Cocke, D. (1994). Red fox, second hangin'. In K. deNobriga & V. Anderson (Eds.), *Alternate ROOTS: Plays from the southern theater* (pp. 57–102). Portsmouth, NH: Heineman. (Work first produced 1976)

Bakhtin, M. (1981). *The dialogic imagination* (C. Emerson & M. Holquist, Trans.). Austin: University of Texas Press.

Benhabib, S. (1992). *Situating the self: Gender, community and post-modernism in contemporary ethics.* New York: Routledge.

Berger, A. A. (1992). *Popular culture genres.* Newbury Park, CA: Sage.

Boal, A. (1998). *Legislative theatre, (A. Jackson, Trans.).* London: Routledge.

Boal, A. (2001). *Hamlet and the baker's son, (A. Jackson & C. Blaker, Trans.).* London: Routledge.

Brady, S. (2000). Welded to the ladle: Non-radicality in community-based theater. *The Drama Review, 44*(3), 51–74.

Broyles-Gonzalez, Y. (1994). *El teatro campesino.* Austin: University of Texas Press.

Carlson, M. (1993). *Theories of the theater.* Ithaca, NY: Cornell University Press.

Cobley, P. (2000). *Narrative.* London: Routledge.

Cohen-Cruz, J. (2000). Transcriptions of story circles for *common green/common ground.* Unpublished.

Fields, M. (2002). *Wild card* [Unpublished dramatic text].

Freire, P. (1987). *Pedagogy of the oppressed* (M. B. Ramos, Trans.). New York: Continuum. (Original work published 1968)

Friedman, D. (1985). Workers theatre of the 1930s. In B. McConachie & D. Friedman (Eds.), *Theatre for working-class audiences: 1830–1980* (pp. 111–120). Westport, CT: Greenwood Press.

Gennep, A. V. (1960). *The rites of passage.* Chicago: University of Chicago Press.

Glassberg, D. (1990). *American historical pageantry.* Chapel Hill: University of North Carolina Press.

Guinier, L. & Torres, G. (2002). *The miner's canary.* Cambridge, MA: Harvard University Press.

Kretzman, J. & McKnight, J. (1993). *Building communities from the inside out.* Chicago: ACTA Publications.

Lewis, F. (2002). Case study: Cornerstone Theater Company. In R. Leonard, A. Kilkelly, L. Burnham, & S. Durland (Eds.), *Performing communities.* http://www.communityarts.net/readingroom/archive/perfcomm/cornerstone/index.php

Lewis, F. (Ed.). (2003). *Cornerstone community collaboration handbook.* Self-published draft.

Lopez, A. (2002). Teatro Pregones. In R. Leonard, A. Kilkelly, L. Burnham, & S. Durland (Eds.), *Performing communities.* www.communityarts.net

Lovelace, A. (2002). Resolving conflict: A poet's residency in Tulsa. www.communityarts.net

McKenna, M. (2002a). Case study: The Dell'Arte Company. In R. Leonard, A. Kilkelly, L. Burnham, & S. Durland (Eds.), *Performing communities.* http://www.communityarts.net/readingroom/archive/perfcomm/dellarte/index.php

McKenna, M. (2002b). Dell'Arte Players: Field Notes. In R. Leonard, A. Kilkelly, L. Burnham, & S. Durland (Eds.), *Performing communities.* http://www.communityarts.net/~commarts/readingroom/archive/perfcomm/dellarte/dellarte-fieldnotes.php

Mda, Z. (1993). *When people play people.* Johannesburg, South Africa: Witwatersrand University Press.

Neal, L. (1968). The black arts movement. *The Drama Review, 12*(4), 29–39.

Nochlin, L. (1985). The Paterson strike pageant of 1913. In B. McConachie & D. Friedman (Eds.), *Theatre for working class audiences in the U.S., 1830–1980* (pp. 87–96). Westport, CT: Greenwood Press.

O'Neal, J. (1968). Motion in the ocean. *The Drama Review, 12*(4), 70–77.

Peeps, C. (2000). Conclusion: Getting in history's way. In M. Cieri & C. Peeps (Eds.), *Activists speak out* (pp. 269–272). New York: Palgrave.

Riefenstahl, L. (1993). *Triumph des willens* [Triumph of the will] [Motion picture]. United States: Connoisseur/Meridian Films. (Work first produced 1935)

Rukeyser, M. (1974). *The life of poetry.* New York: Morrow.

Schechner, R. (1985). *Between theater & anthropology.* Philadelphia: University of Pennsylvania Press.

Solomon, A. (1998). AIDS crusaders ACT UP a storm. In J. Cohen-Cruz (Ed.), *Radical street performance.* New York: Routledge.

Watkins, N. (2002). Carpetbag Theater. In R. Leonard, A. Kilkelly, L. Burnham, & S. Durland (Eds.), *Performing communities.* www.communityarts.net.

Zinn, H. (2003). *A people's history of the United States, 1492–present.* New York: HarperCollins.

25

Black Performance Studies

Genealogies, Politics, Futures

E. PATRICK JOHNSON

Performance maps a space in which to theorize the radicalization of what we might call "black performance studies." Undoubtedly, each of these terms signifies differently and within the specifics of its historicity. Wedded together in dialogic and dialectic tension, however, these terms are at the interstices of black life, politics, and cultural production. "Black" and "performance": These two tropes complement one another in a dialectic that becomes an ontology of racialized cultural production. "Blackness," for instance, is a simulacrum until it is practiced— i.e., performed. The epistemological moment of race manifests itself in and through performance in that performance facilitates self- and cultural reflexivity—a knowing made manifest by a "doing." Far from undergirding an essentialist purview of blackness, performance, as a mode of representation, emphasizes that, "it is only through the way in which we represent and imagine ourselves that we come to know how we are constituted and who we are" (Hall, 1992, p. 30).

Blackness, however, is not only a pawn of and consequence of performance, but it is also an effacement of it. The implication of this construction of blackness in relation to performance is not that performance is, as suggested by its naysayers, "antiintellectual." Rather, it suggests that performance may not fully account for the ontology of race.

Racial performativity informs the process by which we invest bodies with social meaning (Manning, 2001, p. 4). Yet, I must reemphasize that, following Rinaldo Walcott (1997), "to read blackness as merely 'playful' is to fall into a willful denial of what it means to live 'black'" (p. iv). Indeed, blackness offers a way to rethink performance theory by forcing it to ground itself in praxis, especially within the context of a white supremacist, patriarchal, capitalist, homophobic society. While useful in deconstructing essentialist notions of selfhood, performance must also provide a space for meaningful resistance of oppressive systems. Taken together, then, these two terms are both degenerative in that to a degree, they represent a double bluff—their face value always promising more than they can provide. They are also generative forces, pressed into service to create and demarcate cultural meaning. Therefore, black performance has the potential of simultaneously forestalling and enabling social change.

The interanimation of blackness and performance necessitates the codification of this relationship through intellectual inquiry—thus "black performance *studies*." While black performance has been a sustaining and galvanizing force of black culture and a contributor to world culture at large, it has not always been recognized as a site of theorization in the academy. Similarly marginalized as the black bodies with which it is associated, black performance, while always already embedded within institutionally sanctioned and privileged forms of performance, has often been neglected as a intellectual site of inquiry.

Accordingly, this essay seeks to (1) rehearse the history of black performance studies as endemic to the field of interpretation and performance studies; (2) discuss the ways in which blacks have used performance as epistemology and resistance; and (3) engage the various political struggles over what constitutes black performance within black culture by offering examples of the ways in which the signifier *black* within black performance studies has been expanded by the political interventions of black women's and gay and lesbian's artistic work.

THE ERASURE OF
BLACK PERFORMANCE

There has always been a black performative presence within the field of interpretation and performance studies, whether it has been acknowledged as such or not. I am thinking here of Toni Morrison's intervention in the construction of the literary canon. Morrison deploys the term "Africanism" to suggest the process through which black folk are interpellated in the white imaginary and how that interpellation gets represented in literature. "As a trope," Morrison writes,

> little restraint has been attached to its uses. As a disabling virus within literary discourse, Africanism has become, in the Eurocentric tradition that American education favors, both a way of talking about and a way of policing matters of class, sexual license, and repression, formations and exercises of power, and meditations on ethics and accountability.

She continues,

> through the simple expedient of demonizing and reifying the range of color on a palette, American Africanism makes it possible to say and not say, to inscribe and erase, to escape and engage, to act out and act on, to historicize and render timeless. It provides a way of contemplating chaos and civilization, desire and fear, and a mechanism for testing the problems and blessings of freedom. (1992, p. 7)

Morrison's definition and deployment of "Africanism" rings true for the ways in which black performance has remained for years on the periphery of interpretation and now performance studies. That is, although always already a viable contributor to the field, disciplinary practices of exclusion—e.g., the exclusion of black-authored texts in interpretation or the marginalization of black performance scholars in performance studies and the willing omission of the ways that black oratory contributed to the elocutionary moment, an historical epoch many performance scholars locate as the founding moment of the field—have reified the field as a colorless enterprise.

Some might argue that this critique of the field is anachronistic—indeed, that within this historical context, racism was in vogue and should not be read back into the present as exemplary or typical of the field. Touché. But that does not explain the current excision of the role black performance has played in the development of interpretation and black performance in histories being written about the field.[1] Nor does it explain the current miniscule number of black scholars located within interpretation and performance studies programs and departments around the country. Or perhaps it does. The same racist practices of exclusion, omission, or derision in the past only provided a fertile ground for the perpetuation of those same practices today. Despite the lacuna in the recounting of the field's history and the marginalization of black scholarship on performance theory, however, black performance is imbricated in the codified markers of "whiteness."

Dwight Conquergood's essay, "Rethinking Elocution: The Trope of the Talking Book and Other Figures of Speech" (2000), revises this whitened history of the field by demonstrating how racial "others," whose designation as inarticulate and degenerate was reified by the very practice and discourse of elocution, redeployed bourgeois elocutionary practices by performing their own "black counterpublic readings" (p. 333). Similar to Morrison's critique of American literature and criticism, Conquergood's essay argues that while the elocutionary movement highlighted the "performativity of whiteness naturalized," there was another counter performance of race in dialectic tension with this movement that "brings into sharp focus the complex performative cultural politics of this speech tradition" (p. 325): the black oral tradition. Drawing on what A. Hampaté Bâ calls "the great school of life" (p. 168), enslaved and newly emancipated blacks signified on the elocutionary movement by redeploying its tenets toward their own liberation and humanity.

Conquergood's historical intervention notwithstanding, the refusal to acknowledge the coexistence of subaltern voices within the field's history coincides with the disavowal of black literature in interpretation's closely allied field of English. Indeed, performance studies' subjugation of black cultural production reeks of the same arrogant racism in the literary tradition that, according to Morrison,

> holds that traditional, canonical American literature is free of, uniformed, and unshaped by the four-hundred-year-old presence of, first, Africans and then African-Americans in the United States. It assumes that this presence—which shaped the body politic, the Constitution, and the entire history of the culture—has no significant place or consequence in the origin and development of that culture's literature. (1990, p. 5)

And yet, as in the "Africanist" presence in the literary tradition, so too has there been a "black" presence in interpretation and performance studies. Quietly, yet radically transforming departments, black artist-scholars such as Njoki McElroy at Northwestern University and Wallace Ray Peppers at the University of North Carolina at Chapel Hill insisted on foregrounding the literature, folklore, and performance traditions of black writers and scholars by cracking open the white canon that was reified as "Literature" over and above all "others." These black cultural workers not only demanded inclusion, but they also developed courses that were dedicated to the study and analysis of black literature, paving the way for scholars of color who would come after them—myself included. McElroy, Wallace and others were enacting what Conquergood calls an "emancipatory pedagogy and performative cultural politics" (2000, p. 336)—emancipatory in the sense that they no longer felt bound by the strictures of a curriculum that ignored or tokenized the literature, art, music, and artistic expression of their culture; and political in the sense that their intervention occurred during a time when the material consequences of their insubordination could have threatened their employment and even their lives.

Because of the interventions of these foremothers and forefathers, younger black performance scholars continue to press the field and the academy in general to recognize the material, intellectual, and aesthetic matrix that is black performance.[2] But just as they appropriated "performance" in other disciplines, and similar to the ways in which some of those disciplines' current deployment of performance ignores a whole body of work in interpretation and performance studies that preceded its own fetishization and exoticization of performance, interpretation and performance scholars are also guilty of ignoring a whole body of black performance theory that preceded the current proliferation of black performance theory by younger scholars. Nonetheless, at this critical juncture, there is no question that any genealogy of interpretation and performance studies within or outside the National Communication Association must consider the role of black performance and theory in the shaping and codification of interpretation and performance studies as a site of intellectual inquiry.

One might ask how such a rich and vital site of knowledge could have been excluded or gone unnoticed within a field that narrates its own history as one fraught with political debates with the academy about its own status as a legitimate discipline (see Lee, 1999; Thompson, 1983). Institutionalized racism is one culprit, but another one is the inability of academic institutions and individuals to read and value the discreet and nuanced performances and theorizing of African Americans. Outside the purview of what many scholars would hardly recognize as a legitimate object of inquiry, black expressive culture has, until recently, been illegible and unintelligible to the undiscerning eyes and ears, and perhaps minds, of some scholars. The subjugated knowledge embedded within black expressive culture, therefore, is not always ameliorated by those who lack the cultural capital to read it or who are altogether disinterested in these forms. It is the research of the self-reflexive, self-conscious, and humble who may potentially read more than the writing of black people and provide a space, according to D. Soyini Madison, for subjugated knowledge to "enter to articulate—to translate and to unveil—extant philosophical systems to those who (without this knowledge) are unable to find, much less hear them" (1998, p. 321).

Beyond providing an explanation as to why black expressive culture is not always discernible to the researcher, Madison, in her theorization of subjugated knowledge, also implicitly suggests black performance as epistemology. That is, as other scholars have argued about performance in general, black performance provides a space for black culture to reveal itself to itself—to come to *know* itself, in the process of *doing*. Below, I cite a few examples of how black folks use performance as epistemology.

BLACK PERFORMANCE AS EPISTEMOLOGY

Scholars of various African cultures have long since argued the primacy of ritual performance as a site of knowing (Drewal, 1991; Fabian, 1990; Turner, 1969, 1982, 1983, 1986). Consequently, ritual survived as a key component of diasporic black performance and expressive traditions. If, as Victor Turner has argued, cultural performances set in motion "a set of meta-languages whereby a group or community not merely expresses itself, but more actively, tries to understand itself in order to change itself" (1983, p. 383), then, arguably, ritual is the cornerstone of the performative process through which African Americans come to understand, reinforce, and reflexively critique who they are in the world.

One site of such ritual performance is the black church. Indeed, the processual nature of the black church service—the simultaneous improvisational, yet internalized structure— is undergirded by rhythm and repetition, which sustains focus on a renewal of faith and commitment to serving God. From the more formalized roles and procedures of the preacher, choir, ushers, deacons and deaconesses, trustees, minister of music, and "nurses,"[3] to the improvisational call-and-response dynamic and shouts, the central galvanizing force is ritual performance accomplished through repetition and rhythm. As African poet and cultural critic Léopold Senghor argues:

> Rhythm is the architecture of being, the inner dynamic that gives it form, the pure expression of the life force. Rhythm is the vibratory shock, the force which, through our sense, grips us at the root of our being. It is expressed through corporeal and sensual means; through lines, surfaces, colours, and volumes in architecture, sculpture or painting; through accents in poetry and music, through movements in the dance. But, doing this, rhythm turns all these concrete things towards the light of the spirit. In the degree to which rhythm is sensuously embodied, it illuminates the spirit. (quoted in Jahn, 1961, p. 164)

The "vibratory shock" of rhythm and repetition, of which Senghor speaks, appears in the "vamp" or the repetitive chorus of gospel music, which sustains the focus on and generates the spirit. The conjuring of the spirit through the force of rhythm and repetition reinforces the participants' belief that it exists which, in the gestalt of performance, becomes the epistemological moment. The use of repetition to focus attention on a central idea within black American musical traditions encourages emotional engagement on the part of the audience as well as intensifies the emotional engagement of the performer. This active participation occurs through a call-and-response dynamic whereby the rhythm created by the repetitive force effects active participation on the part of the audience and, according to Paul Carter Harrison, "emotionally and cognitively

galvanizes the spirit toward a highly intuitive sense of creation" (1989, p. xxv).

Moreover, the expression of faith in gospel music is animated, culminating in stylized as well as personalized movement of the body. In her autobiography, Mahalia Jackson relives her early exposure to the performative nature of gospel music:

> Those people had no choir and no organ. They used the drum, the cymbal, the tambourine, and the steel triangle. Everybody sang and they clapped and stomped their feet and sang with their whole bodies. They had a beat, a powerful beat, a rhythm we held on to from slavery days, and their music was so strong and expressive it used to bring the tears to my eyes. (1960, p. 72)

The rhythm, beat, and movement of gospel music culminate in joyful expression. Whether it be through a verbalization of "Amen," "Hallelujah," "Thank you Jesus," or "Yes, Lord," or through nonverbals such as waving the hand, stomping the feet, shouting, or crying, gospel faith is always expressed physically through embodied performance.

The same is true in the structure and delivery of the black folk sermon, which also sustains focus on a topic or issue vis-à-vis rhythm and repetition. When describing the effect of the folk preacher's performance style, literary and cultural critic Hortense Spillers notes,

> The thrust of the sermon is passional, repeating essentially the rhythms of plot, complication, climax, resolution. The sermon is an oral poetry—not simply an exegetical, theological presentation, but a complete expression of a gamut of emotions whose central form is the narrative and whose end is cathartic release. In that regard the sermon is an instrument of a collective catharsis, binding once again the isolated members of community. (1974, p. 4)

The notion that the folk sermon is oral poetry, that it evokes catharsis and that it binds members of a community are reflected in the Reverend Jesse Jackson's speech delivered at the 1988 National Democratic Convention. Throughout this speech Jackson draws upon the folk preacher tradition through his use of repetition, rhythm, and metaphor to bring the factions of the Democratic Party together. Transforming his grandmother's quilt into a metaphor for the Democratic Party, Jackson sermonizes,

> Now, Democrats, we must build such a quilt. Farmers, you seek fair prices and you are right, but you cannot stand alone. Your patch is not big enough. Workers, you fight for fair wages. You are right, but your patch labor is not big enough. Women, you seek comparable worth and pay equity. You are right. But your patch is not big enough. Women, mothers, who seek Head Start, and day care and pre-natal care, on the front side of life, rather than jail care and welfare on the back side of life, you're right, but your patch is not big enough. Students, you seek scholarships. You're right, but your patch is not big enough.
> . . . But don't despair; be as wise as my grandmamma. Pull the patches and the pieces together, bound by a common thread. When we form a great quilt of unity, and common ground, we'll have the power to bring health care and housing and jobs and education and hope to our nation. (quoted in Tannen, 1989, pp. 188–189)

The repetition of the phrase "you're right, but your patch is not big enough" and its variation creates a rhythmic force that draws in the listener by creating suspense about who he will refer to next. By including representatives from the Democratic Party's entire constituency, Jackson works toward "binding" those "isolated members of the community." The collective catharsis comes at the end of this excerpt when Jackson summarizes all of the things the different factions cannot achieve alone—health care, housing, jobs, etc.— appealing to their sense of "common ground." Thus rhythm established through repetition in Jackson's speech becomes a generative force,

which heightens emotions and serves as an "opportunity to revitalize a shared cosmogony through social and sacred rituals" (Harrison, 1989, p. xxvi).

Gerald L. Davis also argues that the use of repetition and rhythm in the black folk sermon affects organization and general language use. He writes,

> In sermon performance, the African-American preacher is principally concerned with the organization and the language of his sermon. The notion of meter in the sense of a rhythmic, mnemonic environment for the logical, pragmatic development of ideas, is not subordinate to the language focus. Rather, it is concurrent with it. The generation of structures for language usage and the structuring of rhythmic environments for the preacher's message are complementary, concurrent processes in the performance of African-American sermons. (1985, p. 51)

To support his argument, Davis provides an excerpt from a sermon by Bishop Cleveland entitled, "He Wants Your Life: The Search for the Religion of Christ":

God is studying your tongue

God is studying your aspirations

God ain't studying your manipulations

God ain't studying your demonstrations

God ain't studying your words and your wisdom

God don't want your delay

God wants your life

(Davis, 1985, pp. 51–52)

In this passage from Cleveland's sermon, we immediately recognize a generative formula ("God is studying") and how that formula structures and organizes ideas, and how it serves as a mnemonic device. But we also see that the rhythm and meter is not sacrificed for structure. The two are concurrent.

These examples of black performance suggest that black expressive culture is not merely artifice nor without consideration of aesthetic criteria. Rather, there is an admixture of both as black performative practices, especially those which privilege ritual, sustain the epistemological frame in which black people and culture reflect, reshape, and revitalize.

BLACK PERFORMANCE AS A SITE OF RESISTANCE

In her essay, "Performance Practice As a Site of Opposition," cultural critic and feminist scholar bell hooks suggests that there are two modes of black performance—one ritualistic as a part of culture building and one manipulative out of necessity for survival in a oppressive world (1995, p. 210). Hooks suggests that these two modes are not mutually exclusive but bound together in dialogic tension given the way the skills endemic to black expressive culture are both required and deployed for ritual play and for resistive action. For my purposes here, I focus on the latter to buttress my argument that black performance has always been and will always be a part of any liberationist struggle.

From the minute nonverbal expressions of the slave to the pensive sway of the weary domestic to the collective marches on Washington and throughout the South, black performance has been the galvanizing element of black folks' resistance to oppression. Indeed, in the early years of the antebellum South, black performance was a crucial component of the formation of a black public sphere, which Mark Anthony Neal argues was "invaluable to the transmission of communal values, traditions of resistance, and aesthetic sensibilities" (1999, pp. 1–2). According to bell hooks,

> Performance was important because it created a cultural context where black people could transgress the boundaries of accepted speech, both in relationship to the dominant white culture, and to the decorum of African-American cultural mores. . . .

Performance practice was one of the places where the boundaries created by the emphasis on proving that the black race was not civilized could be disrupted. Radical ideas could be expressed in this arena. Indeed, the roots of black performative arts emerge from an early nineteenth century emphasis on oration and the recitation of poetry. In a number of narratives relating slave experience, African-Americans cite learning to read and recite as crucial to their development of a liberatory consciousness. (1995, p. 212)

Following this logic, we might concede that black performance is at the interstices of black political life and art, providing the lynchpin that sustains and galvanizes arts and acts of resistance.

Hooks offers her own personal narrative about the importance the "live arts" played in her child rearing. Like hooks, I, too, recall how members of my small black community in rural, western North Carolina staged black plays and encouraged us children to memorize and recite the poetry of Paul Lawrence Dunbar, Countee Cullen, and Langston Hughes as a way to instill race pride and to counter the lack of exposure to black writers and artists in the public schools. This grass-roots organizing speaks to the employment of the only available resources to the community—orality. Without the political clout to demand a change in the curriculum, these community leaders drew upon their indigenous expressive forms to transgress the white, bourgeois culturally sanctioned protocols of reading, by making us memorize—and thereby corporeally experience—the literature privileged by black culture.

Some of the best examples of this use of performance are found in the African American oral tradition and literature—tenets of the field of interpretation and performance studies. Within the black oral tradition animal trickster tales in which the weaker animals—rabbit and monkey—outwits the stronger animals—fox and lion—serve as tropes for the master and slave. Given the physical and psychological constraints of slave culture, the slaves' modes of resistance manifested in the form of tales of these anthropomorphic animals whose relationship parallels that of the slave and master. Creating and performing these tales provided temporary psychological relief from slave existence, but some forms of verbal double entendre afforded material results in the way of freedom. The coding of geographic locations such as "heaven," "the river," and "home" in spirituals sung on plantations, for example, served as directions for where to meet to plan a revolt or to escape to the North. This is not to say that slaves only relied on indirect discursive means of resistance. They also employed embodied performances of resistance as well. According to Lawrence Levine,

> The tactics slaves resorted to in order to resist the compulsions of their situation would have been familiar enough to the creatures of their animal tales. The records left by nineteenth-century observers of slavery and by the masters themselves indicate that a significant number of slaves lied, cheated, stole, feigned illness, loafed, pretended to misunderstand the orders they were given, put rocks in the bottom of their cotton baskets in order to meet quota, broke their tools, burned their masters' property, mutilated themselves in order to escape work, took indifferent care of the crops they were cultivating, and mistreated the livestock placed in their care to the extent that masters often felt it necessary to use the less efficient mules rather than horses since the former could better withstand the brutal treatment of the slaves. (1977, p. 122)

These performances of resistance were sometimes met with punishment of the lash, dismemberment, starvation, and even death—many of which are chronicled in animal trickster tales in which Brer Rabbit is caught by Brer Fox, or the monkey in the "Signifying Monkey" tales slips from his tree and is trounced by the lion. Surely, the threat of such retaliation limited the number of such subversive performances, but more times than not, the will to be treated as a human outweighed the potential threat.

After emancipation, these tales evolved into the "John and Old Master" cycle of tales. No longer under the threat of the master's lash, the emancipated black person could speak freely of the cruelty of former slaveholders and took pride in performing tales in which John, the slave, outsmarts his master. Similar to the function of the animal trickster tales, the function of this cycle of tales was both to indict whites for their inhuman treatment of slaves and to demonstrate the slaves' intellectual and physical acumen at resisting such treatment. As Daryl Dance argues, "By belittling and ridiculing whites and by picturing them as foolish victims, Blacks mitigate some of the frustrations of their daily lives and enhance their sense of dignity and pride" (1989, p. 180). Dance's statement suggests that it is not only the content of these tales but also the performance of them by the storyteller that provides a sense of agency to resist struggle. In Hurston's *Mules and Men*, for example, Black Baby, one of the taletellers of Eatonville, Florida, exemplifies both the power of the content of the slave-master folktale and the teller in the following story:

> De first colored man that was ever brought to dis country was named John. He didn't know nothin' mo' than you told him and he never forgot nothin' you told him either. So he was sold to a white man.
> Things he didn't know he would ask about. They went to a house and John never seen a house so he asked what it was. Ole Massa tole him it was his kingdom. So dey goes on into the house and dere was the fireplace. He asked what was that. Ole Massa told him it was flame 'vaperator. The cat was settin' dere. He asked what it was. Ole Massa told him it was his round head.
> So dey went upstairs. When he got on the stair steps he asked what dey was. Ole Massa told him it was his Jacob ladder. So when they got up stairs he had a roller foot bed. John asked what was dat. Ole Massa

told him it was his flowery-bed-of-ease. So dey came down and went out to de lot. He had a barn. John asked what was dat. Ole Massa told him dat was his mound. So he had a Jack in the stable, too. John asked, "What in de world is dat?" Ole Massa said: "Dat's July, the God Damn."

So the next day Ole Massa was up stairs sleep and John was smokin.' It flamed the 'vaperator and de cat was settin' dere it got set afire. The cat goes to de barn where Ole Massa had lots of hay and fodder in de barn. So de cat set it on fire. John watched the Jack kicking up hay and fodder. He would see de hay and fodder go up and come down but he thought de Jack was eating the hay and fodder.

So he goes upstairs and called Ole Massa and told him to get up off'n his flowery-bed-of-ease and come down on his Jacob ladder. He said: "I done flamed the 'vaperator and it caught de round head and set him on fire. He's gone to de mound and set it on fire, and July the God Damn is eatin' up everything he kin git his mouf on."

Massa turned over in de bed and ast, "Whut dat you say, John?"

John tole 'im agin. Massa was still sleepy so he ast John again whut he say. John was gittin' tired so he say, "Aw, you better git out of dat bed and come on down stairs. Ah done set dat ole cat afire and he run out to de barn and set it afire and dat ole Jackass is eatin' up everything he git his mouf on." (Hurston, 1990a, pp. 79–80)

It is clear that the teller of this tale has to demonstrate a level of verbal dexterity to make the punch line effective. Not only must he keep the series of events clear in the mind of the listener, but he must also underscore, undoubtedly through vocal inflection, the irony of the slave's knowledge of standard English. Moreover, the content of the story reveals that the slave discerned all along the master's concealment, or the "appearance that approximates what, ideally, [he wants the slave] to see" (Scott, 1990, p. 50). Thus, the slave sheds his performance of deference and ignorance and provides a glimpse into what James C. Scott (1990) might call his

"hidden transcript" of insubordination and knowledge. This subversive performance is motivated by the slave's frustration with the master in a time of crisis (the cat and barn are on fire); instead of maintaining the ruse of ignorance, he deploys shock to get the master to react.

The slave's use of language here is also an example of "signifying," which refers to the use of indirection to comment negatively on something or someone. In this folktale, the slave's use of "proper" speech after feigning ignorance signifies on the master's own inability to discern that the slave has knowledge of the possessions the master calls by other highfalutin names, and this makes the master look foolish. In *The Signifying Monkey*, Henry Louis Gates, Jr. (1987) argues that the black person's ultimate sign of difference is her "blackness of tongue" (p. 2). While Gates makes this claim to buttress his argument about the signification of black literature on the western literary canon, the same can be argued about signification as a site of resistance within black performance. As in the case of the folktale above, signifying functions as both a source of ritual insult and survivalist strategy or both depending on the context. When deployed in the dozens, a verbal art game of ritual insult, verbal dexterity for "play" may just as easily slip into a critical technology of self-assertion and resistance.

In Zora Neale Hurston's *Their Eyes Were Watching God,* Janie, the protagonist, engages her husband in a dozens contest which results in her enacting her own agency as a woman and as an apt verbal dueler when she exposes her husband's sexual impotence. Trying to put her in her place, Jody, her husband, stands in the middle of their store in front of a crowd of customers and onlookers (dozens contests, to be effective, must always have an audience) and says to Janie, "Whut's de matter wid you, nohow? You ain't no young girl to be gettin' all insulted 'bout yo' looks. You ain't no young courtin' gal. You'se uh old woman, nearly forty." Janie replies,

> Naw, Ah ain't no young gal no mo' but den Ah ain't no old woman neither. Ah reckon Ah looks mah age too. But Ah'm uh woman every inch of me, and Ah know it. Dat's uh whole lot more'n you kin say. You big-bellies round here and put a lot of brag, but 'tain't nothin' to it but yo' big voice. Humph! Talkin' 'bout me lookin' old! When you pull down yo' britches, you look lak de change uh life. (1990b, p. 75)

Drawing on the signifying tradition Janie levels the playing field by countering her husband's ageist and sexist depiction of her as unattractive housewife. Her retort is deft not only because it is delivered with confidence, but also because its content cuts the quick of her husband's manhood, subverting his patriarchal gaze and control over her body.

Black folks employ performative modes of resistance such as signifying beyond interpersonal relationships to transgress institutionalized forms of oppression. This is particularly true for those who do not benefit from "trickle down" economics, urban gentrification, welfare reform, state surveillance, and other regressive policies that maintain the nation-state. A political economy in which governmental taxation laws benefit the top one percent of the population necessitates discreet, but strategic and effective performative modes of resistance or what Scott (1990) refers to as "discourse that takes place 'offstage,' beyond direct observation by powerholders" (p. 4).

I refer again to my own upbringing as an example of a community of black folk who devised all kinds of guileful ruses and hidden scripts because their survival depended on it. Because I was raised in public housing the proximity of our neighbors was such that everyone knew the intricate details of families' personal lives. This situation was inconvenient to the extent that one never felt any semblance of privacy about what would be considered "delicate" family matters. On the other hand, neighbors' knowledge of such intimate details could also work to one's advantage when it came to deploying subversive tactics against "the man." Most of our neighbors as well as my family had parents (usually single mothers) who worked jobs that did not provide health or life insurance. These women were domestics, factory workers, or cooks in low wage earning positions. Therefore, they acquired insurance from insurance salesmen who came door to door selling health and life insurance policies at exorbitant premiums and that actually paid very little if one were to be hospitalized or die. The insurance agents would also go door to door to collect these premiums weekly or monthly. As was to be expected, many families did not have the money to pay these fees yet they were in dire need of insurance in case of emergencies. The performances we devised to avoid payment or distract the salesmen were ingenious. When we children saw them coming, we would run into the house and warn our mothers, who would do one of three things: immediately pull the shades, close the door and pretend not to be home; hide in a closet or bathroom after rehearsing with us the lie to tell the insurance man; or invite the insurance man in and distract him with idle chit chat followed by an invitation to supper (which he sometimes accepted). While these tactics provided only a temporary reprieve from the payment due or overdue, they were performances deployed to stave off institutionalized forms of race and class oppression.

Terry McMillan's elderly black woman narrator in the short story "Ma' Dear," offers another example of subversive performances exemplary of those in which many black working-class and poor people engage to resist devolving further into poverty. Just as my community evaded the calls of insurance salesmen for premium payments, the narrator of McMillan's story pretends that she lives alone and receives no other income beyond her social security payments, which are too low for her to make ends meet. She devises this performance for her social worker, an agent of the state employed to maintain the status quo. The narrator tells the reader:

> That old case worker think she gonna get the truth out of me. She don't scare me. It ain't none of her business that I got money coming in here besides my social security check. How they 'spect a human being to live off $369 a month in this day and age is what I wanna know. Every time I walk out of my front door it cost me at least two dollars. I bet she making thousands and got credit cards galore. Probably got a summer house on the Island and goes to Florida every January. If she found out how much I was getting from my roomers, the government would make me pay back a dollar for every two I made. I best to get my tail on upstairs and clear everything off their bureaus. I can hide all the nurses' stuff in the attic; they won't be back till next month. Juanita been living out of trunks since she got here, so if the woman ask what's in 'em, I'll tell her, old sheets and pillowcases and memories. (McMillan, 1990, p. 465)

This elderly woman's resistance to the state's surveillance succeeds because she alters the visual economy of her home such that "evidence" of upward mobility (i.e., her boarders' things) is hidden in plain sight of the case worker. She also employs the oral tradition as political resistance in her willful commitment to withholding the "truth" about her income. Rather than divulge the truth, she theorizes her situation to her advantage in the way that Zora Neale Hurston describes:

> The white man is always trying to know into somebody's business. All right, I'll set something outside the door of my mind for him to play with and handle. I'll put this play toy in his hand, and he will seize it and go away. Then I'll say my say and sing my song. (1990a, p. 3)

 The "play toy" that McMillan's narrator puts in the case worker's hand is the lie of one

income, single occupancy, and below poverty existence. She astutely discerns that the case worker is an agent of the state and is visiting her home to impose its hegemony while, at the same time, the state buttresses the case worker's middle class lifestyle that affords her "credit cards galore," "summer homes," and trips to Florida in the winter. Attuned to the state's desire to "know her business" as its official hidden transcript, she develops her own "convincing performance," which requires "both the suppression or control of feelings that would spoil the performance and the simulation of emotions that are necessary to the performance" (Scott, 1990, pp. 28–29). In her encounter with the case worker then, the narrator performs deference and ingratiating behavior, disguises evidence of social mobility, thus allowing her to "say [her] say and sing [her] song."

Other subversive performances existed in my community that demonstrated its agency against hegemonic capitalism. There were women who took "orders" for clothing that they would then shoplift from popular department stores. Indeed, their skill at stealing clothes developed into such an art that they became known for their ability to lift clothes from mannequins in store windows. Their craft subsidized the low wages they earned from factory and domestic work and provided access to commodities they would not otherwise be able to afford. The price of the goods stolen was negotiated with buyers on an individual basis, but was usually no more than half of the ticketed price. Many of my siblings' and my Easter suits and Christmas presents were the result of these women's craft, allowing my mother, a single parent, to provide for her family.

When my grandmother worked as a domestic she also employed subversive performances to resist exploitation. Like so many domestics, in the presence of her employer, she adhered to the "public transcript" of subservience and deference by never raising her voice when dissatisfied with her conditions. She contends that if she did not like something, she "nevah did say nothin'," for "saying something" might have cost her her job or caused unnecessary tension in the home. Instead, she was silent. She firmly held her mask in place until she had the opportunity to score a victory—however fleeting. But when asked to participate in one of her white charges' marriage ceremony as "mammy," by sitting next to the biological white mother, she refused by inventing a story about a sick brother whom she had to take care of. This story not only got her out of participating in the wedding, but it also provided her an opportunity to quit her job as she did not return to work for the family (Johnson, 2003, pp. 151–59). As James Scott reminds us: "The hidden transcript is not just behind-the-scenes griping and grumbling; it is enacted in a host of down-to-earth, low profile stratagems designed to minimize appropriation" (1990, p. 188). My grandmother's "stratagem" was her silence, which minimized her appropriation of being put on public display as the domestic mammy and removed her from the oppressive space of her employer.

Black performance as a mode of resistance functions to suture the gap between the oppressor and the oppressed, the vocal and voiceless, the dominator and the dominated—indeed, to make the "bottom rail become the top riser" (Dance, 1978, p. 8). Many of these performances are necessary for survival in a white supremacist patriarchal society, while others are deployed for sheer play. Whatever their motivations, these resistive performances do not evolve in an ahistorical vacuum. They take shape according to the historical and sociopolitical context in which they exist. They are also not deployed unilaterally or toward the same aim as they are bound by geopolitical and social circumstances. Because no performance exists outside the politics of representation, ideology is embedded within them and thus thrusts black performance into

the center of identity politics as performers struggle over the most effective or "proper" performances to deploy against racism. Hooks suggests that

> for performance to continue to be subversive, to engage cultural practice in ways that are disruptive and transformative, African-American artists must claim a space for ongoing critical vigilance, where we can dialogue about the impact of the live act and where performance can be interrogated to see what works as meaningful intervention. (1995, p. 220)

The dialogue that hooks insists must occur often becomes the site where the boundaries of black performance begin to emerge, depending on the political and social climate. Therefore the next section engages the policing of black performance.

THE BOUNDARIES OF BLACK PERFORMANCE

Historically, the boundaries of black performance have been circumscribed by both the art produced by black folks and by the critics of that art. As early as 1926, W. E. B. DuBois, in a speech to the NAACP in Chicago entitled "Criteria of Negro Art," argued that all art is and must be propagandistic. He writes,

> All art is propaganda and ever must be, despite the wailing of the purists. I stand in utter shamelessness and say that whatever art I have for writing has been used always for propaganda for gaining the right of black folk to love and enjoy. I do not care a damn for any art that is not used for propaganda. But I do care when propaganda is confined to one side while the other is stripped and silent. (DuBois, 1926, p. 22)

DuBois is speaking to the rhetoric of performance, the power of performance to persuade, move and cajole an audience to action or to maintain the status quo. In the racial terms of the early twentieth century, this meant the limiting of particular kinds of representations of blackness. DuBois continues,

> It is not the positive propaganda of people who believe white blood divine, infallible and holy to which I object. It is the denial of a similar right of propaganda to those who believe black blood human, lovable and inspired with new ideals for the world." (p. 22)

While arguing for a broader range of black artistic expression, one that would allow for black artists to depict black people as more than the image of themselves lodged in the white imaginary, DuBois' deployment of blackness here still signifies the black, heterosexual male, for black women and especially black homosexual artists were not born with the "veil" or gift of "second sight" of which DuBois writes in his 1903 *Souls of Black Folk*. I am actually not invested, as was DuBois, in an equal right to propagandistic art for black women, lesbians, transgendered individuals, and gays, but rather the expansion of blackness itself such that the artistic and cultural work of these dissident subjectivities might always already be included in what one might call black performance studies.

Zora Neale Hurston was already intervening in DuBois' construction of the criteria for Negro art because of her gender, her art, and her politics. Indeed, Hurston's first play, *Color Struck*, written in the same year as DuBois's address to the NAACP, dislodges essentialist notions of blackness by deconstructing the binaries of middle-class vs. folk, black vs. white, male vs. female, etc., especially through what Sandra Richards calls the "absent potential" of performance. According to Richards (1995), this particular Hurston play, at first glance, falls within the category of the "race" or "propaganda" play which DuBois and others promote. In performance, however, the play moves beyond such limitations because of the contingencies of value placed on the bodies on stage by the viewing audience. Richards

writes: "Given this potential interlock in performance of competing energies, one has a text that again generically rejects the binarism of folk versus propaganda/race play and . . . hints at the possibility of some confounding third category" (1995, p. 79). An enigma herself in the context of the "black nigerati" as she referred to other artists of her era, Zora Neale Hurston the woman and her work defied a parochial view of blackness and black performance. But the material reality of being a black queer rebel in life as in art was such that she and her work would spiral out of existence only to be resurrected during the beginning of what would become a black feminist movement.

Curiously enough, the backdrop for the black feminist intervention in third wave feminist movement would be the Black Arts movement of the 1960s. What a paradox. The poetic and theatrical expressions of Amiri Baraka [LeRoi Jones], Haki Madhubuti [Don L. Lee], Sonia Sanchez, Nikki Giovanni, and others again reflected the imbrication of aesthetics and politics, black performance with black people. These artists and performers saw their art as weapons against oppression as well as the vanguard of black creative expression of that era. Kimberly Benston argues that for these black artists of the '60s "writing, properly reconceived and directed as utterance and as act, was advanced as a signal instrument of cultural liberation" (2000, p. 2). Moreover, he suggests that performance was key to this liberationist struggle:

> For this revolutionary alignment of voice and purpose to be achieved, the 'new breed' . . . of black artists would need to fashion a dynamic new poetics: expression would become preeminently theatrical . . . performance would become transitive and transformative . . . and, finally, the artist would herself become an exemplary performance. (p. 2)

Beyond employing performance as a site of resistance and toward "revolutionary" aims, these artists' work circumscribed black-ness in specific terms that disavowed black women (even black women were guilty of this disavowal), gays, lesbians, and transgendered people, and the black middle class.

In the poem "Black Art," for example, Amiri Baraka/LeRoi Jones says that he desires

Black poems to smear on griddlemamma
 mulatto bitches
whose brains are red jelly stuck
between 'lizabeth taylor's toes. Stinking
Whores! We want poems that kill.
Assassin poems, Poems that shoot
guns. Poems that wrestle cops into alleys
and take their weapons leaving them dead
with tongues pulled out and sent to
 Ireland.

(1971, p. 223)

In this poem, "blackness" is an exemplary simulacrum until activated by the literary per-formance that is the poem or by the various performances of the poem by Baraka and others. Black poetry is action put into motion via performance. Once activated through per-formance, however, "blackness" is defined in relation to what it is not—namely "mulatto bitches," and "whores" as well as other irri-tants outside the purview of Baraka's defini-tion. While the intention in the performance of this poem is to, as Manthia Diawara (1995) suggests, "redefine the tools of Americanness," as well as to install black creative expression with politicized agency against racism, it comes at the expense of the Other within—the sub-jectivity of those who would also like to claim a part of the category "black" that Baraka so strongly advocates and valorizes. I agree with Diawara on the one hand that "a performance must be based on a tradition that the audience can verify, and rate the performer against" (p. 209), but on the other, I have questions about the very tradition in which the perfor-mance is housed. What does it mean, for

example, to perpetuate a tradition that occludes segments of its constituency? What are the ethics of the tradition? Of our criticism? Of our performances?

In his 1968 treatise on the Black Arts Movement, Larry Neal argues that the "Black Arts Movement is an ethical Movement. Ethical, that is, from the viewpoint of the oppressed. And much of the oppression con-fronting the Third World and Black America is directly traceable to the Euro-American cultural sensibility" (1994, p. 186). I would suggest, however, that Neal's definition of ethics is based on the false assumption that the "oppressed" is a static category. Does it include, for instance, the "mulatto bitches" and "whores" of Baraka's poetry? The "fag-gots" in contemporary stand-up routines and theatre productions (what I call "church-on-stage" shows)?[4] Similar to the performances of resistance prior to this period, black arts poetry remained steeped in the quagmire of essential-ized blackness, privileging race as the single most important identity marker. Moreover, these performances moved beyond race privi-leging to actually denigrating members of the black community who were also female, les-bian, gay, transgendered, or middle-class.

Suturing the gap across the river of essen-tialism were the gendered and sexualized "others" of the black community. Namely, black women and black LGBT artists' work expanded and continue to expand the bound-aries of blackness by infusing it with their crit-ical voices. For example, Ntozake Shange's now canonized *For Colored Girls* represented, according to Benston, "a vigorous rethinking of authenticity, authorship, and production that alters the landscape of Black Arts theatri-cal practice" (p. 83). Indeed, Shange's play set the stage ablaze because it pushed not only the form and content of traditional theatre prac-tice, but it also stretched the black body politic by moving from margin to center the voice of the black woman. The impact has been an unprecedented number of riffs and spoofs of Shange's titular performance, all of which, however, have been deployed to continue Shange's radical intervention: Keith Antar Mason's *for colored boys who have considered homicide when the streets were too much* and Marvin K. White's *for colored boyz who have considered the s-curl when the hot comb was too much,* to name two. Shange's work also paved the way for other black artists to challenge and extend the boundaries of black performance to reflect a messier more complex identity marker, namely, the now defunct black gay performance troupe Pomo Afro Homos (Freeman, Branner, and Gupton, 1996) who in *Fierce Love: Stories From Black Gay Life,* handled such topics as homophobia in black communities, internalized homophobia among black gay men, and racism in white gay communities. The actors of Pomo Afro Homo deftly critique heteronormative constructions of blackness such as those that circulate within Black Nationalist discourse by declaring their presence as black men who are constantly under surveillance and threat, but who nonetheless persevere because of the strength garnered from their ancestors. In the opening scene of the play, the actors perform the poem "We Are," which ends with the stanza:

> We are
> an endangered species
> But our stories must be told
> our lives
> forever real
> must be cherished
> and our love
> forever rising
> must be
> has got to be
> no doubt about it
> as strong as our ancestors'
> and twice as fierce.
>
> (1996, p. 259)

This poem frames the performance as it is reprised at the play's end, punctuating the

performers' insistence that they are indeed a part of the black community and that, in some regards, their love of black community is perhaps stronger than that of their heterosexual counterparts—indeed, "twice as fierce."

Pomo Afro Homo, as well as other performance artists and playwrights such as Rhodessa Jones, Shay Youngblood, George C. Wolfe, Suzan Lori Parks, and Craig Hicks, have continued to expand the concept of "black" in black performance studies by bringing to the fore questions of gender and sexuality. In this way, these artists have radicalized the roots of the black performance tradition by deploying a new ethics of the tradition—a critical praxis engaged not in occlusion, exclusion, and delusion, but rather in liberation.

Some might suggest that one way to emerge from this quagmire is to move away from any form of identity politics, for they ultimately lead to what Judith Butler (1990) has referred to as the "embarrassed, etc." (p. 143). Yet, the disavowal of any kind of identity politic in the realm of black performance does not provide for the cultural distinctiveness that this aesthetic produces and contributes to society. It also imbues black cultural production with an unrelenting relativism with which I am uncomfortable—one that black conservative critic of the Harlem Renaissance George Schuyler used to justify the nonexistence of "Negro Art." In 1926 Schuyler wrote, "Negro art 'made in America' is as nonexistent as the widely advertised profundity of Cal Coolidge, the 'seven years of progress' of Mayor Hylan, or the reported sophistication of New Yorkers" (Schuyler, 1926/1994, p. 51). Rather than attend to Schyuler's extreme polemics, I am more apt to believe, as Harry Elam, that while blackness is a fragile fiction, its experiential effects materialize in and through performance. Elam writes,

> From the arrival of the first African slaves on American soil, the discourse on race, the

definitions and meanings of blackness, have been intricately linked to issues of theater and performance. Definitions of race, like the processes of theater, fundamentally depend on the relationship between the unseen and the seen, between the visibly marked and unmarked, between the 'real' and the illusionary. (2001, p. 4)

Other attendant subject positions around which race may pivot, such as gender and sexuality, then, may also come to the fore and be negotiated in relation, rather than subordination, to race in the process of performance. The recognition of this complicated process must not only evolve in the artistic work produced, but in the criticism of this work as well.

We, who currently do black performance studies under the auspices of theatre and performance studies, stand primed to transform the way black performance studies gets theorized. The work of those I have cited as well as that of Bryant K. Alexander, Jennifer Brody, Thomas DeFranz, Joni Jones, Jason King, David Román, José Muñoz, and many others has already begun to intervene and transform the field from within and without. Their work has been a bulwark against the hegemony of a well-meaning yet ill-informed white liberalism or, what Charles Nero (2001) calls "white tribalism," as well as the parochial and conservative discourse of those from within black intellectual circles.

Black performance, like the bodies of those associated with it, has, in the words of the national Negro anthem, "Lift Every Voice And Sing," "come over a way that with tears has been watered." Forever on the periphery of the white bourgeois elite intellectual traditions codified as "the academy," it has, nonetheless, functioned as a specter of "colored contradictions" to the discourse of whiteness—a palimpsestic documentation of an "Africanist" presence. The rhetorical, political, and aesthetic dimensions of black performance served its constituency well as a mode of resistance in those particularly challenging times—and still

do. But as with all representational discourses, black performance is not beyond the reaches of ideology and the power struggles that such battles ensue. We must conceive of black performance as Hortense Spillers suggests conceiving of black community—"as a layering of negotiable differences" (2003, p. 461). Indeed, if this tradition we call black performance studies continues to be generative as opposed to gravitating toward implosion, we must continue to ask, rather then attempt to answer, the question, "What is this "black" in black performance studies? How do we go about creating an ethics of such an endeavor without policing boundaries, silencing opposing or dissenting or dissident voices, while, at the same time, holding true to a politics of social change and transformation that moves us forward in the liberation of black peoples?

NOTES

1. Marvin Carlson's book, Performance: A Critical Introduction (1996), for example, provides scant coverage of the contributions of black performance scholars or black performance in general.

2. Since 1996, there has been an annual meeting of young black performance theory scholars. Since their first meeting at New York University, this group of black performance theorists has met annually to workshop performances, critique each other's written work, and generate new theoretical paradigms. The group has generated one book (see DeFrantz, 2002) and they are at work on another.

3. In many black churches, a group of women who are not medically trained professionals, but who nonetheless attend to parishioners who become filled with the holy spirit and faint, hold the title of nurse and dress in nursing uniforms.

4. These particular shows are also referred to as the "chitlin' circuit." They are usually low budget gospel musicals that travel from city to city. They appeal to mass audiences perhaps because of their formulaic plots, which usually consist of a long-suffering black matriarch who has a wayward child who she prays will "find God" and come home. They also have stereotypical gay

characters, usually hairdressers, who function as comic relief in the play, but who have no real substance. For two different takes on these plays, see Gates (1997) and Burdine (1999).

REFERENCES

Bâ, A. H. (1981). The living tradition. In J. Ki-Zerbo (Ed.), *Methodology and African prehistory* (pp. 166–205). Berkeley: University of California Press.

Baraka, A. (1971). Black art. In D. Randall (Ed.), *The black poets* (pp. 223–224). New York: Random House.

Benston, K. (2000). *Performing blackness: Enactments of African-American modernism.* New York: Routledge.

Burdine, W. B. (1999). The gospel musical and its place in the black American theatre. In A. Bean (Ed.), *A sourcebook of African-American performance: Plays, people, movements* (pp. 190–203). New York: Routledge.

Butler, J. (1990). *Gender trouble: Feminism and the subversion of identity.* New York: Routledge.

Carlson, M. (1996). *Performance: A critical introduction.* New York: Routledge.

Conquergood, D. (2000). Rethinking elocution: The trope of the talking book and other figures of speech. *Text and Performance Quarterly, 20*(4), 325–341.

Dance, D. (1978). *Shuckin' and jivin': Folklore from contemporary black Americans.* Bloomington: Indiana University Press.

Davis, G. L. (1985). *I got the word in me and I can sing it, you know: A study of the performed African-American sermon.* Philadelphia: University of Pennsylvania Press.

DeFrantz, T. F. (Ed.). (2002). *Dancing many drums: Excavations in African American dance.* Madison: University of Wisconsin Press.

Diawara, M. (1995). Cultural studies/Black studies. In M. Henderson (Ed.), *Borders, boundaries, and frames: Cultural criticism and cultural studies* (pp. 202–211). New York: Routledge.

Drewal, M. T. (1991). *Yoruba ritual: Performers, play, agency.* Bloomington: Indiana University Press.

DuBois, W. E. B. (1994). Criteria of Negro art. In A. Mitchell (Ed.), *Within the circle: An anthology of African American literary criticism from the Harlem Renaissance to the present* (pp. 60–69). Durham, NC: Duke University Press.

Elam, H. J. (2001). The device of race: An introduction. In H. J. Elam & D. Krasner (Eds.), *African American performance and theater history: A critical reader* (pp. 3–16). Oxford, England: Oxford University Press.

Fabian, J. (1990). *Power and performance: Ethnographic explorations through proverbial wisdom and theatre in Shaba, Zaire.* Madison: University of Wisconsin Press.

Freeman, B., Branner, D., & Gupton, E. (1996). Fierce love: Stories from black gay life. In H. Elam & R. Alexander (Eds.), *Colored contradictions: An anthology of contemporary African-American plays* (pp. 255–285). New York: Plume.

Gates, H. L. (1987). *The signifying monkey: A theory of Afro-American literary criticism.* Oxford, England: Oxford University Press.

Gates, H. L. (1997, February 3). The chitlin circuit. *New Yorker,* pp. 44–55.

Hall, S. (1992). What is this "black" in black popular culture? In G. Dent (Ed.), *Black popular culture* (pp. 21–33). Seattle: Bay Press.

Harrison, P. C. (1989). Black theatre in the African continuum: Word/song as method. In P. Harrison (Ed.), *Totem voices: Plays from the black world repertory* (pp. xi–lxiii). New York: Grove Press.

hooks, b. (1995). Performance practice as a site of opposition. In C. Ugwu (Ed.), *Let's get it on: The politics of black performance* (pp. 210–221). Seattle: Bay Press.

Hurston, Z. N. (1990a). *Mules and men.* New York: Harper & Row.

Hurston, Z. N. (1990b). *Their eyes were watching god.* New York: Harper & Row.

Jackson, M. (1961). *Moving up.* New York: Hawthorne Books.

Jahn, J. (1961). *Muntu: African culture and the western world.* New York: World Weidenfield.

Johnson, E. P. (2003). *Appropriating blackness: Performance and the politics of authenticity.* Durham, NC: Duke University Press.

Lee, J. (1999). Disciplining theater and drama in the English department: Some reflections on 'performance' and institutional history. *Text and Performance Quarterly, 19*(2), 145–158.

Levine, L. W. (1977). *Black culture and black consciousness: Afro-American folk thought from slavery to freedom.* New York: Oxford University Press.

Madison, D. S. (1998). That was my occupation: Oral narrative, performance, and black feminist thought. In D. Pollock (Ed.), *Exceptional spaces: Essays in performance & history* (pp. 319–342). Chapel Hill: University of North Carolina Press.

Manning, S. (2001). Modern dance, negro dance, and Katherine Dunham. *Textual Practice, 15*(3), 487–506.

McMillan, T. (1990). Ma'dear. In T. McMillan (Ed.), *Breaking ice: An anthology of contemporary African-American fiction* (pp. 457–465). New York: Penguin.

Morrison, T. (1990). *Playing in the dark.* New York: Random House.

Neal, L. (1994). The black arts movement. In A. Mitchell (Ed.), *Within the circle: An anthology of African American literary criticism from the Harlem Renaissance to the present* (pp. 184–193). Durham, NC: Duke University Press.

Neal, M. A. (1999). *What the music said: Black popular music and black popular culture.* New York: Routledge.

Neal, M. A. (2002). *Soul babies.* New York: Routledge.

Nero, C. I. (2001). Black gay men and white gay men: A less than perfect union. In C. L. Dews & C. L. Law (Eds.), *Out in the south* (pp. 115–126). Philadelphia: Temple University Press.

Reed, J. & Wake, C. (Trans. & Eds.). (1976). *Senghor: Prose and poetry.* London: Heinemann.

Richards, S. (1995). Writing the absent potential: Drama, performance, and the canon of African-American. In A. Parker & E. Sedgwick (Eds.), *Performativity and performance* (pp. 64–88). New York: Routledge.

Schuyler, G. S. (1994). The Negro-art hokum. In A. Mitchell (Ed.), *Within the circle: An anthology of African American literary criticism from the Harlem Renaissance to the present* (pp. 51–54). Durham, NC: Duke University Press. (Original work published 1926)

Scott, J. C. (1990). *Domination and the arts of resistance: Hidden transcripts.* New Haven, CT: Yale University Press.

Spillers, H. (1974). *Fabrics of history: Essays on the black sermon.* Unpublished doctoral dissertation, Brandeis University, Waltham, Massachusetts.

Spillers, H. (2003). *Black, white, and in color: Essays on American literature and culture.* Chicago: University of Chicago Press.

Tannen, D. (1989). *Talking voices: Repetition, dialogue, and imagery in conversational discourse.* Cambridge, England: Cambridge University Press.

Thompson, D. (Ed.). (1983). *The performance of literature in historical perspectives.* Lanham, MD: University Press of America.

Turner, V. (1969). *The ritual process: Structure and anti-structure.* Chicago: Aldine.

Turner, V. (1982). *From ritual to theatre: The human seriousness of play.* New York: Performing Arts Journal Publications.

Turner, V. (1983). A review of "ethnopoetics." In J. Rothenberg & D. Rothenberg (Eds.), *Symposium of the whole: A range of discourse toward an ethnopoetics* (pp. 338–342). Berkeley: University of California Press.

Turner, V. (1986). *The anthropology of performance.* New York: Performing Arts Journal Publication.

Walcott, R. (1997). *Black like who?* Toronto, ON: Insomniac.

26

Lethal Theatre

Performance, Punishment, and the Death Penalty

DWIGHT CONQUERGOOD

I'm not going to struggle physically against any restraints. I'm not going to shout,
use profanity or make idle threats. Understand though that I'm not only upset, but
I'm saddened by what is happening here tonight. . . . If someone tried to dispose of
everyone here for participating in this killing, I'd scream a resounding, "No." I'd
tell them to give them all the gift that they would not give me, and that's to give
them all a second chance. . . . There are a lot of men like me on death row—good
men—who fell to the same misguided emotions, but may not have recovered as I
have. Give those men a chance to do what's right. Give them a chance to undo their
wrongs. A lot of them want to fix the mess they started, but don't know how. . . .
No one wins tonight. No one gets closure.

—Napoleon Beazley[1]

There will be no lasting peace either in the heart of individuals or in social customs
until death is outlawed.

—Albert Camus[2]

Conquergood, Dwight. "Lethal Theatre: Performance, Punishment, and the Death Penalty." *Theatre Journal* 54:3 (2002), 339–367. © The Johns Hopkins University Press. Reprinted with permission of The Johns Hopkins University Press.

Like it or not, you are putting on a show.

—John Whitley[3]

Show, spectacle, theatre, these representational media are central to the rituals of state killing.

—Austin Sarat[4]

In 1975 Michel Foucault published *Discipline and Punish: The Birth of the Prison,* a landmark book that opened with two astonishing chapters, "The Body of the Condemned" and "The Spectacle of the Scaffold," harrowing accounts in gruesome detail of the performance of capital punishment in the premodern era.[5] These chapters served as points of departure for charting the historical shift from the dramatic infliction of corporal and capital punishment to modernity's more subtle and insidious infiltrations of power through mechanisms of discipline linked with knowledge. Punishment transformed, Foucault argued, from a theatre of violence and repression to a medical model of rehabilitation metonymically connected to other normalizing mechanisms and internalized techniques of coercion, compliance, and surveillance. According to Foucault, the performance of power in modern society has changed radically from spectacular capital punishments—that point at which the violence of the state is most nakedly displayed—to undercover capillary penetrations, insinuations, secretions, and circulations of power that are difficult to flesh out. He closed the book with the confident claim that "we are now far away from the country of tortures," the spectacle of the scaffold, because contemporary legal punishment "appears to be free of all excess and all violence."[6]

I reread *Discipline and Punish* in the summer of 2001, during the same time that I traveled twice in eight days to Terre Haute, Indiana, to march and stand in vigil outside the prison death chamber to protest the serial executions of Timothy McVeigh and Juan Raul Garza, the first federal prisoners put to death since 1963. I found Foucault's opening chapters on executions more resonant and familiar than later chapters titled "The Gentle Way of Punishment." Emotionally drained from attending the June 11 and June 19 executions, I kept writing "not in June, 2001" in the margins of passages about how modern judicial punishment had advanced well beyond the deployment of raw, physical force. I drew an incredulous exclamation point across from this passage in the conclusion: "There is nothing in it now that recalls the former excess of sovereign power when it revenged its authority" on the body of the condemned.[7]

To be fair, Foucault wrote *Discipline and Punish* in 1975, at a time when the medical model of rehabilitation was in the ascendancy in penological thought and practice. The death penalty was rarely deployed, and France, along with the rest of Europe, was on the verge of abolishing capital punishment for good. Although it is amazing to think of it now, the United States was in step with and even ahead of the international community on the issue of the death penalty. In 1975, there were no executions in the US, not even in Texas. In 1972 the Supreme Court in Furman vs. Georgia had declared capital punishment—"as then practiced," which proved to be a fatal loophole phrase—"cruel and unusual punishment" and therefore unconstitutional. Many assumed that the death penalty had been abolished for good, instead of temporarily suspended. After World War II and the shock of Holocaust atrocities, executions had declined steadily. In 1965, the same year that Britain abolished the death penalty, there were seven executions, compared to the peak decade of the depression-ravaged 1930s when there were 167 executions a year on average. Then in the next year, 1966, there were two, and the following year, 1967, only one. No executions were performed in the five years leading up to the Supreme Court's formal ruling against the death penalty in 1972, and in particular the Federal government had not executed anyone since 1963. From the vantage point of May, 2002 (the time of the final draft of this article), when we have already put 31 people to death in the first five months of this year, it is astounding to think that from 1968 through 1976 there was not a single execution in America.[8]

How have we come so far from the social sensibility that Foucault indexed in *Discipline and Punish?* Since 1975 there has been a major shift of societal attitudes toward punishment. Current support for the death penalty hovers between 70 and 75 percent, having peaked at 80 percent in 1994, the year of the conservative Republican takeover of congress. As of April 1, 2002, there are 3,701 men and women—including 83 juvenile offenders—awaiting execution on Death Row compared to 334 in 1972 when the Supreme Court struck down the death penalty.[9] So deep is the revanchist enthusiasm for spectacles of the scaffold that when Senator Dianne Feinstein, the former mayor of San Francisco, ran for governor of California in 1990 she displayed images of the San Quentin gas chamber in her television campaign commercials. She came from behind to win the Democratic primary by nineteen percent after campaigning on the slogan, "the only Democrat who supports the death penalty."[10] Especially with the resurgent popularity of capital punishment, it is important to remember that the history of the death penalty in the United States has been one of challenge and contention.[11] Almost from the beginning, capital punishment has been a fraught and contested performance practice. The performance genealogy of executions periodically requires fresh blood to keep this macabre tradition alive. Contemporary defenders of capital punishment shore up its shaky premises, not by logic or rational argument, but by invoking scapegoats, poster boys for the death penalty: Timothy McVeigh, John Wayne Gacy, Jeffrey Dahmer, Richard Speck—and now Osama bin Laden and his henchmen. With each exemplary monster executed, capital punishment is legitimated and revitalized. Thus it is no surprise that George W. Bush, who has presided over 156 executions during his relatively short time in public life, issued executive orders very soon after September 11, 2001, to create military tribunals designed to expedite executions with an efficiency and speed that would exceed that of Texas.[12] Theatre and performance studies have an ethical as well as intellectual obligation to examine this resurgent theatre of death that anchors conservative politics in the United States. The very word "execute" means to accomplish, to carry out, and to perform, to do. "Execution" also means "a mode or style of performance."[13] The death penalty cannot be understood simply as a matter of public policy debate or an aspect of criminology, apart from what it is pre-eminently: performance.

PERFORMANCE RITUALS OF STATE KILLING

Executions are awesome rituals of human sacrifice through which the state dramatizes its absolute power and monopoly on violence. We know from the anthropological record that a key to the efficacy of rituals is their capacity to embrace paradox, to gloss contradictions, to mediate profound oppositions, tensions, ambivalences, anxieties. The ritual frame is elastic enough to encompass conflict and chaos, yet sufficiently sturdy to channel volatile forces and disruptive tensions into an aesthetic shape, a repeatable pattern. Rituals draw their drama, dynamism, and intensity from the crises they redress. A host of important anthropologists, notably Victor Turner, Mary Douglas, Clifford Geertz, Roy Rappaport, and others, have noted that ritual performance proliferates along social faultlines, pressure points, cracks in the system, the jagged edge of belief.[14] Rituals carry their weight and earn their cultural keep by restoring, replenishing, repairing, and re-making belief, transforming vague ideas, mixed feelings, and shaky commitments into dramatic clarity and alignment. As embodied performances, rituals incarnate and make visible abstract principles and inchoate concepts—such as "Justice." What is Justice? Justice is an abstraction, a spirit that commands tremendous faith, power, and huge investments both economic and emotional. Like religion and other powerful abstractions, Justice—to paraphrase Victor Turner—lives only in performance, "only in so far as its rituals are 'going concerns'"; Justice can be seen only when it is acted out.[15] All the interlocking rituals of criminal punishment—arrest, detention, interrogation, trial, conviction, incarceration, execution—are performed so that citizens can see "justice done": "All of justice is a stage; it is the appearance—the ritual—that is the meaningful thing."[16]

Moreover, rituals are neither static nor discrete. They draw their meaning, structure, style, and affective resonance from the traditions they reenact. But they never simply repeat a given form, but, like all "restored behavior," they reverberate within the traditions they simultaneously reinvent and re-deploy for historically situated needs and purposes.[17] The ritual replaying of traditional form always plays with, and plays off and against, the performance genealogy that it recites.[18] Rituals of execution in the United States are part of a dynamic performance genealogy that has undergone profound shifts in feeling, form, and dramaturgy. The seismic shift has been from the public, open-air, communal, hortatory rituals of redemption in colonial and revolutionary era America to the privatized, elite, class-stratified rituals of retribution and exclusion that were created in the early nineteenth century to accommodate an emergent middle-class ethos of restraint, propriety, gentility and new standards of bourgeois taste and refinement. Beginning in the 1830s, execution rituals moved from the public square where they drew diverse audiences numbering in the thousands to inside prison walls where, withdrawn from public view, they became private performances for a small, homosocial, invitation-only audience of elites. Historian Louis Masur summarizes the wider social significance of this change in the mise-en-scène of execution rituals:

> The creation of private executions [during the 1830s] . . . was an act charged with multiple meanings: it marked the triumph of a certain code of conduct and set of social attitudes among the middle and upper classes; it symbolized a broader trend toward privatization and class segmentation; it turned the execution of criminals into an elite event centered around class and gender exclusion.[19]

The withdrawal and relocation of executions from the public green to censored enclosures signaled a major shift in structures of feeling about criminals and capital punishment.

To understand better this profoundly meaningful change in dramaturgy, let us examine the execution rituals characteristic of early America. Public hangings in seventeenth- and eighteenth-century New England were mass spectacles that drew the largest audiences ever assembled for any occasion. Especially in Puritan New England, with no maypoles, carnivals, staged theatre, or even Christmas celebrations, a public hanging was an avidly attended "Tragical Spectacle."[20] For the 1686 execution of John Morgan, crowds began gathering in Boston a week before the hanging. According to John Dunston, a book-seller from London visiting Boston at the time, some "have come 50 miles to see it."[21] On the morning of March 11, more than 5,000 people jammed into Boston's Second Old North Church to see the condemned prisoner prominently seated in front of the pulpit to hear Cotton Mather preach his execution ser-mon, a key part of the dramaturgy of hanging day rituals. When the floor and walls of the church gallery began to crack and buckle under the tremendous weight and pressure of the crowd, Mather interrupted his sermon to move the audience to Samuel Willard's Third Old South Church, which had a larger gallery.[22] And the outdoor staging of the gallows accom-modated multitudes who could not squeeze into the church or were inclined to skip the sermon. One scholar estimated that executions in colo-nial New England attracted as many as 12,000 spectators.[23] In terms of sheer audience size, executions were the most popular performance genre in seventeenth- and eighteenth-century America: "Well into the nineteenth century, execution crowds still outnumbered crowds gathered for any other purpose."[24]

Puritan executions were elaborately staged and exquisitely paced ritual dramas seething with suspense, tension, ambivalence, crisis, reversals, revelations, and breath-taking spec-tacle. The hanging day ritual included the pub-lic procession from the jail to the church, where the prisoner was displayed as a "sor-rowful spectacle" and embodied "example," a focal point and prop for the minister's fiery execution sermon.[25] The celebrated ministers appointed to preside at these high profile events rose to their greatest oratorical heights, knowing that they were addressing the largest audiences of their careers, and given the mag-nitude of an execution, the sermons were often published and sold, thus circulating in print to an ever widening audience.[26]

After the sermon, there was the doleful parade to the gallows, which often took one or more hours. The prisoner typically was carried slowly through the crowd elevated on a cart, sometimes with a rope around his or her neck, and with the coffin conspicuously alongside. At the gallows, there were more speeches and audible prayers, and often hymns were sung communally to pitch the emotions of the audi-ence. Then the sheriff read the death warrant aloud. All of the dramaturgy at the foot of the gallows was designed to anticipate, draw out, and heighten the spellbinding moment when the prisoner climbed the ladder and, precari-ously perched, delivered a speech to the rapt audience thronged below. This long-awaited speech from the prisoner—who, more often than not, was a young servant or slave, a per-son of little or no education and low social standing—could eclipse the rhetorical grandeur of the elite, Harvard-trained minister-orators. The "last Dying Words"[27] of the condemned gathered compelling presencing powers pre-cisely because they were uttered from a space of death and disappearance that impressed on the audience the urgency of their vanishing: "I am upon the brink of Eternity."[28] Then the hood was lowered and the noose tightened around the neck. To clinch the climactic force of the condemned's dying speech, the hang-man kicked the ladder out from under the pris-oner's feet, and, as one historian put it, "then came a riot of motion."[29]

The suspense that excited and transfixed execution audiences was not about the tempo-ral plot or unfolding physical action—the hanging day scenario was well known and predictably choreographed. All the suspense hovered over the fate of the prisoner's immor-tal soul. What riveted audience attention was whether or not the condemned had truly repented, and, even if so, would her or his faith hold fast under the tremendous distress and horror of "the present circumstances for Terrification"?[30] Executions, like every other temporal aspect of life in Puritan New England, were inserted within a cosmic spiri-tual drama of sin and salvation. The real suspense was not about anything so mundane as whether the condemned would get a last-minute reprieve, but would the condemned confess convincingly, manifest true repentance, and be able to deliver an affecting dying speech that would serve as warning to sinners and inspiration to the sanctified? If that happened—no easy feat, by any measure—then the worst malefactor could hope for eternal life. Puritan audiences scrutinized the body and speech of the condemned for "Signals of Divine Grace," and when they recognized true penitence then they could interpretively reframe the hideous torture of a hanging into a catalyst for salvation: "This Serves only to draw the Curtain, that thou mayst behold a Tragick Scene, strangely changed into a Theater of Mercy."[31]

To appreciate better the complex theatricality of executions in early America, let us look more closely at one particular case. On July 31, 1701, Esther Rodgers, a twenty-one-year-old indentured servant convicted of infanticide, was hanged outside the town of Ipswich before a crowd estimated between four and five thousand.[32] She had confessed to fornication, "Carnal Pollution with the Negro" with whom she worked in the same household, and to killing the "bastard" newborn "begotten in Whoredom."[33] After arraignment and imprisonment for this heinous crime, she confessed to another, earlier murder: when she was seventeen she had fallen into "that foul Sin of Uncleanness, suffering my self to be defiled by a Negro Lad" and she had killed that mixed-race baby as well. In between the two pregnancies, she had lived in a tavern, "giving my self up to other wicked Company and ways of Evil."[34] A vast multitude of spectators assembled at the gallows, the largest audience "as was scarcely ever heard of or seen upon any occasion in any part of New England."[35] They had come "to behold the Tragical End" of this young but "very great Criminal."[36] In addition to the notoriety and sexual-racial sensationalism of her crimes, part of the draw could have been the

circulating reports of her "marvelous change" from the pastors and pious townspeople who had visited and ministered to her during her eight months in prison awaiting execution.[37] As one of the ministers attested: "a poor Wretch, entering into Prison a Bloody Malefactor, her Conscience laden with Sins of a Scarlet Die . . . she came forth, Sprinkled, Cleansed, Comforted, a Candidate of Heaven."[38]

For all its "antitheatrical prejudice," Puritan life was saturated with a performance consciousness that delighted in transformations, metamorphoses, reversals, astonishing wonders, and the language of theatrical representation: "tragical spectacle," "tragick scene," "tragick end," "theater of mercy."[39] Everyday people and events could become spectacles, displays, signs, examples, monuments. Esther was depicted as "a Pillar of Salt Transformed into a Monument of Free Grace."[40] But Puritan ways of seeing increased the dramatic tension because any "monument of grace" was unstable and fallible, always in danger of falling, of debasing itself, of shape-shifting into "a Monument of shame and Ignominy."[41] The drama of the fall and the relentless conflict with evil suffused the workaday world where everyday action, gesture, and speech suddenly could shimmer with spiritual significance to the discerning eye. The execution sermon provided a figural proscenium arch, the theological frame, through which a Puritan audience viewed a public hanging. Puritan ministers endeavored, at great discursive length, to turn the earthly scene of capital punishment into a stunning morality play, a vivid acting out of the allegory of divine wrath and judgment, and, if the ritual succeeded, "an Instance of Converting Grace and Mercy."[42] They uplifted the physical action of the state "Business of Death" onto a sacred plane of performative metaphors, images, and symbols.[43] Thus when describing the vast multitude of thousands gathered to watch Esther Rodgers hang, one minister commented, "Which could not but put all serious and thoughtful Spirits in mind of the Great and General Assembly that will appear at the Great Day to receive their final Sentence."[44]

Puritan theology underpinned robust "interpretive communities" of active spectators for whom, in a very deep sense, all the world was a stage, a place for seeing.[45] They inculcated "watchfulness"—of themselves and their neighbors—as part of the habitus of daily life.[46] According to their Calvinist outlook, everyone was innately depraved, and conversion, never final, was an arduous and incessant struggle. For several weeks prior to her execution, Esther Rodgers consistently enacted the role of an exemplary sinner, showing all the signs of repentance and conversion. Nonetheless, she emerged from prison on the morning of her execution as a "*Candidate* of Heaven*," her salvation by no means yet assured.[47] She still had to face the greatest and most severe test and trial of her new found faith. The sabbath before her hanging she had dictated a written message to be read aloud in church enlisting the support and prayers of the congregation, "that the Lord would Strengthen and Uphold her, and carry her through that hard and difficult Work when called thereunto, that she may not be dismayed at the Sight and Fear of Death."[48] These same congregants formed part of the vigilant and expectant circle of spectators around the gallows who scrutinized every move she made. Everyone wondered: what was the state of her mind, heart, and soul as she looked death in the face? Had she accomplished the laborious work of conversion sufficiently?

And if these questions were not already in many spectators' minds, they certainly would have been stirred up by the attending clergy who continuously questioned her conversion as they cross-examined her throughout the grim proceedings. Toward the end of this execution morning sermon, the Reverend Rogers challenged her:

But what preparation hast thy Soul made to appear at Gods Tribunal before this Day be ended? . . . Hast thou desired and laboured for Holiness to Sanctify thee, as well as Righteousness to justify thee? What means hast thou used to get thy Soul purged as well as sin pardoned . . . ? Hast thou waited and prayed with David, Psal[m] 51. *Wash me throughly from my sins, purge me with Hyssop* . . . or hast thou thought a few Tears sufficient for this?[49]

And as she walked the long "dolorous way" to the gallows, the accompanying ministers pressed her with frightening questions, "mixing with words of Consolation, something of Terrour":

O Esther, How can your heart abide! Don't you here behold terrible displays of Justice: you are surrounded with Armed men. . . . The terrible place and Engines of Destruction, are but a little before us, where you must in a few Minutes Expire; and there lyes your Coffin that must receive your perishing Body: How can you bear the sight of all these things?[50]

And even after she had climbed the scaffold ladder, and delivered a deeply moving speech to the audience of thousands, and an even more emotionally pitched and passionate prayer, and after the sheriff had tied the blindfold over her face, just moments before he placed the noose over her head, another attending minister, Reverend Wise, stepped forward and took that moment to cross-examine her again: "Now is the great Crisis of Time. Does your Faith hold in God and Christ still? She answers, *God be thanked it does, God be thanked*." Then, with the rope around her neck, and after her final, almost frantic, outcry—"O Lord Jesus, Now Lord Jesus, I am a coming. . . ."—even at that most vulnerable, plaintive moment, as she waited for the drop, "Lifting up her Hands to Heaven," the unflappable Reverend Wise stepped forward again, and extended her only the conditional comfort of the subjunctive mood: "If your Hopes can lay hold upon the irresistible Grace and Mercy of God in Christ, and [if] you can cast your self into His Armes, you are Happy for Ever. And so we must bid you Fare-Well."[51]

The Ipswich pastors seized the occasion of Esther Rodgers's execution to dramatize and drive home the point that conversion was a moment-by-moment contingency: at any instant mortals could be "assaulted with Temptations to Unbelief or Fear."[52] Esther died a saint, but throughout the protracted drama of her execution-*cum*-salvation her state of grace was both affirmed and deferred, contrapuntally played out and kept in agonizing suspense right up until the end. The processual, equivocal, anxious, contested dynamics of conversion heightened the tension and turned a familiar execution scenario into a cliffhanger. The moral drama was heightened and made compelling by this deep interplay between knowing, and not knowing, for sure.

Further, Puritan sermons were filled with warnings against dissemblers, hypocrites, and charlatans who masqueraded piety: "Lyars: Such as are deceitful, and dissembling, who speak otherwise then they think; and do otherwise then they speak; such as accustom themselves to speak falsly" and those are "partial and feigned in their repentance."[53] Esther Rodgers was a person who knew how to keep secrets, how to feign and hide: she had concealed not one, but two pregnancies, carried the babies to term, secretly delivered, and no one knew, not even the fathers. And she had successfully covered up the first murder. At least one supporter felt the need to preempt questions about the sincerity of her jailhouse conversion: "Neither shall any need to question the truth of the repentance of the person Condemned, and after Executed, from the shortness of the time of her Experiences: The Thief that Commenced Converted on the Cross . . . is a proof of the possibility hereof."[54]

The ambivalence of her spiritual condition, the gap between closure and uncertainty that the ministers pried open, also provided a space for multiple ways of seeing and other spectatorial positions unbounded by Puritan orthodoxy. Executions encouraged spectators to gaze intently at the body on display and granted extraordinary ritual license for the condemned, especially if they were women, to make spectacles out of their bodies.[55] Just as the sentence of death had to be "executed on her body," so also the signs of grace had to be manifested bodily.[56] Execution audiences closely monitored the prisoner's gesture, carriage, countenance, demeanor, deportment, vocal intonation, inflection, timber. An "admiring observer" noted Esther's "Composure of spirit, Cheerfulness of Countenance, pleasantness of Speech, and a sort of Complaisantness in Carriage towards the Ministers who were assistant to her."[57] But was there slippage in the frames through which she was viewed? And did even a pious allegorical reading pivot on a doubling of vision, an interplay of perspectives that saw her as both a wanton woman and an aspiring Christian? She had been, until very recently, a harlot. Everyone knew the sexual nature of her crime and her "scarlet" past. She had confessed that she was a creature wholly given over to "lust."[58] Reverend Rogers reminded her, and everyone else, in his morning execution sermon: "Thy ways have been all filthy, thy whole Walk, a walk after the Flesh; thy course a course of filthy Communication and Conversation."[59]

With that phrase still ringing in their ears, how did spectators view her "Walk" to the gallows? Her choice to forego the customary cart and to "walk on foot"?[60] How did they observe the moving body of this young, sexually active woman, surrounded by men, as it paraded by them? Was she a walking palimpsest, the imprint of her harlot past shadowing and alternating with her Christian image? Which image came into sharper and more sustained focus for whom, at what points in the procession? How did bystanders interpret her vivacious physicality, especially the remarkable moment when she responded to a minister's question by "turn[ing] about, and looking him in the face with a very smiling countenance"?[61] What did various spectators make of the moment when she stumbled upon first seeing the gallows, and then, after this "Reluctancy of the Flesh," her recovery when "she lift up her Feet, and Marched on with an Erected, and Radiant Countenance"?[62] How did different audience members construe "the very affecting Gestures" with which she took her leave of the ministers at the foot of the gallows?[63] How did they watch her as she paused, composed herself, "and so without stop or trembling went up the Ladder"? And what went through their minds during the physically delicate moment of "turning herself about" on the narrow ladder so that she could face the crowd? And how did they take in her spectacularly displayed body, especially when she arched it, "being bid [by the sheriff] to lean her Head back upon the Ladder, to receive the Halter"?[64]

We can be sure that profane ways of looking commingled with pious perspectives within this huge gathering. The sheer size of the crowd, numbering in the thousands, must have created a social effervescence. Executions in England during the same time period were rowdy, rambunctious, "carnivalesque" affairs.[65] And the large number of young people in the audience—"great Numbers whereof were expected" and their large presence was "accordingly" noted—must have charged the event with libidinal energy.[66] Puritan sermons reverberated with warnings about "youthful lusts."[67] The massive ideological pressure of the execution sermons attests indirectly to the excitement and desire that the preachers struggled so forcefully to rein in and control. If we read these official documents against the grain of their orthodoxy, we can understand that all the appeals to "serious and

thoughtful spirits" were pulling against other, more unruly and irreverent dispositions.[68] Moreover, sensuality was not banished from Puritan piety. Recent historical research disputes the stereotype of the dour, sexually repressed Puritans and argues that they exuberantly "conjoined earthly and spiritual passion" and that a striking aspect of their religious life was "the eroticisation of the spiritual."[69]

Execution audiences were encouraged to identify deeply with the condemned as fellow sinners. They did not shrink in moral revulsion from even the most despised and heinous criminals. The typical response was "there but for the grace of God, go I." At the 1674 execution of Benjamin Goad for sodomy, Samuel Danforth vehemently denounced his horrid and unnatural "lasciviousness" but then reminded the audience: "there are sins with the Spectators, as well as with the Sufferers. . . . If we ransack our own hearts . . . we shall finde such sins with us. . . . The holiest man hath as vile and filthy a Nature, as the Sodomites. . . ."[70] This way of seeing encouraged a deeply sympathetic, theatrical identification in which the spectators could imaginatively exchange places with the condemned, instead of holding themselves aloof in distanced judgment. The ideal spectator at executions became a deeply engaged, co-performative witness.

The Puritan structure of feeling that embraced wrongdoers as members of the same moral community in need of repentance was superceded in the nineteenth century by a gothic view of criminals as "moral aliens" and "moral monsters."[71] The dramaturgy of executions changed from large-scale public rituals of redemption and reincorporation to exclusive, privatized rituals of retribution and expulsion. This new, bourgeois structure of feeling about criminals is registered powerfully in an 1848 *American Whig Review* article, "On the Use of Chloroform in Hanging."[72] Criminals are now seen as "miserable wretches whom we simply wish to cast contemptuously out of existence."[73] Class lines are now sharply drawn and patrolled by social performances of civility and respectability, all based on bodily deportment: "the rude have one species, the refined another."[74] A "gentlemanly nation" should be "severe towards crime"; therefore the respectable classes "must overcome sympathy"[75] to criminals who are "aliens to the race":

> The reason should condemn them, the fancy recoil from them, and the pride scorn them. All that can spring from the deepest determination to wipe out such stains from humanity, or express the universal strong disgust which they inspire, should be brought to bear against them. Mankind are bound to affect towards them the manners of loathing and horror.[76]

Peck proposed chloroforming prisoners before hanging them, not out of any compassion for the condemned, but because some of the loathsome creatures had the bad manners to struggle and convulse while being executed, "thus tending to disturb the nervous peace, which is the support of refinement." A botched execution was "against good manners, and unbecoming in a civilized Christian people."[77] Coming midway between the 1701 execution of Esther Rodgers and the 2001 executions of Timothy McVeigh and Juan Raul Garza, Peck's pivotal document registers the profound shift in structure of feeling about the death penalty and prefigures the modern interest in new methods and technologies for sanitizing death. Although Peck's idea to anesthetize criminals before executing them was not adopted in his day, it resurfaced in 1977 when Oklahoma invented lethal injection as the preferred mode of capital punishment for the modern age. The lethal injection protocol includes a first dose of sodium pentothal, which puts the prisoner to sleep, followed by a muscle relaxant that paralyzes the lungs, and then potassium chloride that stops the heart.[78]

Putting the prisoner to sleep before killing him or her is more about cosmetics than compassion; it keeps up the appearance of decency, protects the witnesses from messy scenes, and masks the violence of state killing with a humane medical procedure.

THE MAGICAL REALISM OF MODERN CAPITAL PUNISHMENT

The multibillion dollar business of incarceration with its ramified rituals of punishment provides the bodies—and they are disproportionately racialized and working-class bodies—that serve as the concrete referents for society's ideas about "justice," "law and order," and "public safety."[79] Executions anchor belief in the criminal justice system, dramatizing in an especially vivid way that "something is being done," that the system is in control, order has been restored. Foucault argued: "without the right to kill, would the judicial system be anything more than a public utility a bit less efficient than the post office? The right to kill is the last emblem of its supremacy."[80] Never has Foucault's insight been demonstrated more clearly than in the FBI bungling of the McVeigh evidence in the most high-profile capital trial in recent history; the FBI lost 4,400 documents, evidence that should have been turned over to the defense team. This was such a breach of due process that Attorney General John Ashcroft had to issue a one-month stay of execution.[81] If the judicial system can break down and bungle a case of this magnitude, under an international media spotlight, imagine what happens with everyday prosecutions. This crisis of confidence was redressed by speedy review, and within a few weeks the McVeigh execution bandwagon was back on track and a new death warrant signed for June 11. These events dramatically drive home Foucault's larger point that executions justify Justice, that they provide a satisfying sense of closure and cover for a shaky system that pretends to be infallible. Northwestern University's Center for Wrongful Convictions has documented more than one hundred cases of men and women who were sentenced to death and then exonerated. In Illinois, 13 men in recent years have been freed from death row; that is one more than the state has executed since the United States reinstated capital punishment in 1976. One of these released men, Anthony Porter, came within 48 hours of being put to death; he had already ordered his last meal and been measured for his coffin.[82]

Contemporary execution rituals work their magic and derive their efficacy from the effusive power of the effigy. Here I draw together Joseph Roach's performance theory of the effigy in *Cities of the Dead* with Michael Taussig's rereading of the anthropological literature on effigies and magic in *Mimesis and Alterity*.[83] Effigies are crudely fashioned surrogates that bear little resemblance to the person for whom they stand in. They produce magical power from parts, pieces, effluvia, operating on principles of contiguity and synecdoche—the piece, the part that stands for the whole—more than likeness or resemblance. Effigies are rough fabrications made from distorted parts of a person, often excrements such as saliva, blood, hair, fingernail parings, semen, fingerprints, footprints, which are then performatively deployed to put the real person in harm's way. An effigy is the fusion of image and body, symbol and source, the figurative and the physical. Because a jury will never vote to kill a human being, the fundamental task of the prosecutor is to turn the accused into an effigy composed of his or her worst parts and bad deeds. Before they are strip-searched and strapped down to the execution gurney, the condemned must first be stripped of all human complexity and reduced to human waste, the worst of the worst. These waste parts are then crafted onto prefabricated figures: stereotypes of the violent criminal, cold-blooded killer, animal, beast, brute, predator, fiend, monster. Thus a young,

attractive, completely rehabilitated, devoutly spiritual Karla Faye Tucker was transformed into an effigy, a scarecrow, and methodically put to death as "the Pick-Axe Killer." These effigies take on manifest powers and become not just surrogates for the accused, but stand-ins for crime and all anti-social forces of evil that threaten law and order. When the Federal government strapped Juan Garza onto a gurney on June 19, 2001, and stuck a needle into the calf of his right leg, it was not killing a loving father of young children who was much, much more than the single worst thing that he had ever done. They were sticking pins into an effigy: "Drug Kingpin," the headlines blared on execution day. And they did this in the name of Justice and for the sake of Order to ward off omnipresent social dangers and the specter of crime.

Race figures prominently in the construction of these effigies. Glaring racial disparities at every level of the death penalty system are shocking and egregious. Of the 760 people put to death since capital punishment was reinstated in 1977, 44 percent have been minorities, when minorities are only 29 percent of the population. And this disproportion is even more skewed if we focus on blacks: 35 percent of the people executed were black, when blacks are only 12 percent of the population (Table 26.1). And 43 percent of the prisoners currently on death row are black (Table 26.2). The racial profile of people put to death becomes even more stark when we look at juvenile offenders. First, I need to point out that the United States is one of a small number of countries in the world that still has a juvenile death penalty. Not only is the US out of step with other western democracies that long since have stopped putting their citizens to death—abolition of the death penalty is a condition of membership in the European Union—but also only five countries that still retain capital punishment execute minors: Iran, Nigeria, Pakistan, Saudi Arabia, and the United States. And no nation in the world has reported executions of minors since 1997, except the United States: we have executed seven juvenile offenders since 1998, three in 2000, one in May, 2002 (Napoleon Beazley, the young African American man, whose last words I quoted in the epigraph for this essay). Not even China, the world leader in number of executions per year, still executes juvenile offenders. Of the 38 states with death penalty statutes, 23 authorize the execution of children; 18 states allow the execution of children as young as 16 (Table 26.3). Texas has executed 11 of the 19 juvenile offenders

Table 26.1 Race of 760 Defendants Executed, 1977–2002

			(US pop.)
White	430	56%	(71%)
Minority	330	44%	(29%)
Black	265	35%	(12%)
Latino	50	7%	(12%)
Other	15	2%	(5%)

U.S. Census 2000
Execution count up to February 19, 2002

Table 26.2 Race of Death Row Inmates

Minority		54%
Black		43%
Latino		9%
Other		2%
White		46%

January 1, 2002

Table 26.3 Juvenile Death Penalty

23 of the 38 Death Penalty States Permit the Execution of Minors	
Minimum Age	
16	(18 states)
17	(5 states)
18	(15 states)

Table 26.4 19 Juvenile Offenders Executed Since 1985

Texas Executed 11	
7 Minority	64%
6 Black	
1 Latino	
4 White	36%

May, 2002

Table 26.5 83 Juvenile Offenders on Death Row

26 on Texas Death Row	
22 Minority	85%
11 Black	42%
10 Latino	39%
1 Asian	4%
4 White	15%

February, 2002

who have been put to death since 1985, and 64 percent of that group were minorities (Table 26.4). And 26 of the 83 juvenile offenders currently awaiting execution are on Texas' death row: 85 percent of them are minorities (Table 26.5).[84]

Furthermore, if we look at other jurisdictions in addition to the 38 states with death penalty statutes, the racial disparities are even more glaring. The United States military has its own death penalty statute, and 86 percent of the military prisoners on death row are minorities (Table 26.6). This statistic does not augur well for the military tribunals that President Bush has authorized by executive order to adjudicate capital cases in the wake of September 11. The federal government also has its own death penalty statute that authorizes the execution of prisoners in the name of every citizen in the nation. 84 percent of the prisoners on federal death row are minorities (Table 26.7). Because of these statistics, the federal government went to great lengths to

Table 26.6   U.S. Military Death Row

Total 7		
Minority	6	86%
Black	5	71%
Asian	1	14%
White	1	14%

Reinstated in 1984 by executive orders of
Pres. Ronald Reagan

Last military execution in 1963 (hanging)

Table 26.7   Federal Death Row

Total 19		
Minority	16	84%
Black	14	74%
Latino	2	10%
White	3	16%

(Four cases pending: 3 Black, 1 Asian)

January, 2002

assure that McVeigh would precede Mexican-born Garza to the federal death chamber. The federal government had not put anyone to death in thirty-eight years, so whoever inaugurated the newly built state-of-the-art federal execution chamber in Terre Haute, Indiana—strategically chosen as the geographic "crossroads of America"—would attract extraordinary media attention. Garza originally had been scheduled to go to the gurney first, August 5, 2000, but two stays of execution pushed back his date to June 19, 2001, behind Timothy McVeigh who was scheduled for May 16, 2001. The shocking revelation on May 10 that the FBI had failed to turn over 4,400 documents of evidence to the McVeigh defense team, as they were required to do by law, threatened to derail McVeigh's timely execution. However, Attorney General John Ashcroft granted only a one-month reprieve, which kept McVeigh just in front of Garza, absorbing the full media spotlight as the "first" prisoner executed by federal government in 38 years. In this sense, McVeigh's high profile execution was a perverse form of whiteface minstrelsy, a whiteout of the glaring racial inequities in the way capital punishment is meted out in America. Juan Raul Garza, a Mexican American who came to this country as an impoverished migrant laborer, was far more representative of death row inmates than Timothy McVeigh, especially on the federal death row, which is 84 percent minorities. A similar whiteface staging occurred in 1979 when there was much maneuvering around who would be the historic "first" person executed since the Supreme Court reinstated the death penalty with the 1976 Gregg decision. John Spenkelink, a working-class white man, was cast in that leading role. Despite his lawyer's argument that his execution was speeded up for purely political reasons, that as a white man Spenkelink's execution "would inoculate Florida from 150 years of racial discrimination in capital cases," Spenkelink was carried, terrified, to Florida's electric chair on May 25, 1979, to become the first person executed involuntarily since the 1976 restitution of capital punishment."[85]

Race refracts and distorts other parts of the death penalty system as well. 95 percent of all the prosecutors responsible for death penalty cases are white. Because only a tiny fraction of all homicides are prosecuted as capital cases it is very disturbing to see such systemic racial asymmetry with an overwhelmingly white group of people holding the power and responsibility to decide which cases are prosecuted for death and at the other end a staggeringly disproportionate number of people of color sentenced to death (Table 26.8). Race registers its greatest impact when we look at the race of victims in capital cases.[86] Even though only 50 percent of all murder victims are white, 81 percent of murder victims in capital cases are white. And interracial murders compound the effects of race: "African Americans who

Table 26.8   Race of Prosecutors Responsible
for Death Penalty Cases

95% White, 2% Black, 3% Latino			
State	*White*	*Black*	*Latino*
Texas	137	0	11
Virginia	113	8	0
Missouri	115	0	0
Florida	19	1	0
Oklahoma	26	0	0
1998			

murder whites are 19 times as likely to be executed as whites who kill blacks."[87]

And in America, race articulates with class. Middle and upper class people who can afford to hire skilled lawyers do not end up on death row. Mumia Abu-Jamal, currently on Pennsylvania's death row, observed: "Them's that got the capital don't get capital punishment."[88] All of the whites on death row are working class and poor. According to Stephen Bright, a seasoned death penalty lawyer, defendants get the death sentence "not for the worst crime but for the worst lawyer."[89] Even though statistics on the class status of people sentenced to death and executed are not systematically collected or as accessible as those on race and gender, there are other ways of ascertaining class status. Anyone who doubts that people sentenced to death in this country are overwhelmingly impoverished and working class should go to the web site of the Texas Department of Criminal Justice. For some bizarre reason, it posted the last meal requests of all the people it has put to death.[90] Because food preferences are shaped and bounded by class "tastes," it is a very revealing and poignant experience to read through the last meals requested by the Texas condemned.[91]

There is also some evidence of the role that homophobia plays in creating execution effigies. Because of the fluidity of sexualities, as well as the difficulty of collecting data on

sexual orientation—prison is not a safe place to be "out," notwithstanding the non-normative sexual activity that is encouraged by these enforced homosocial environments—it is difficult to know exactly how many queers are on death row. However, one 1992 article in *Advocate* estimated that 40 percent of the women on death row are lesbians.[92]

The death penalty is a potent political symbol, a sign and litmus test for tough-on-crime politicians. The symbolic center of the "war" on crime, it is a gendered symbol, a mantle of "political macho" that female politicians, like Dianne Feinstein and Jeanne Shaheen, the first woman governor of New Hampshire who vetoed the legislation to abolish that state's death penalty, can wear to masculinize themselves in the public sphere. Male Democratic politicians can use their vigorous support of the death penalty to counter charges of "soft" liberalism.[93] Bill Clinton masterminded this New Democrat centrist strategy. He infamously left the presidential campaign trail in 1992 to return to Arkansas to oversee the execution of Rickey Ray Rector, a young African American man so mentally impaired that at his last meal he asked the guards if he could save the piece of pecan pie for later.[94] During the year 2000, when he campaigned for the presidency, George W. Bush presided over 40 Texas executions, which broke the record for the largest number of annual executions ever performed by a state in the history of the nation.

In 1984, Velma Barfield, a North Carolina grandmother, probably became the first woman executed since 1962 because a trial judge set her clemency hearing four days before the general election. Her execution became a political issue because Democratic Governor James Hunt was locked in a tight race for the United States Senate against ultra-conservative Jesse Helms. It has been twenty-two years since a woman had been put to death in this country, and there was strong support and pressure for Governor Hunt to grant clemency to this sweet-natured grandmother who had become a model prisoner. But fearing a political backlash in his closely contested senate race with Helms, Hunt allowed the execution of Barfield to proceed. The prison personnel responsible for killing Barfield, who was affectionately called "Granny," as well as the entire prison staff who had come to know and like her were absolutely devastated by her execution.[95] It took fourteen years before another state had the stomach to execute a woman. In 1998 Karla Faye Tucker became the first woman put to death in Texas since before the Civil War. Her execution, which attracted widespread media coverage, seemed to break the execution chamber glass ceiling for women. In 2001, three women were executed, all in Oklahoma. The last time three women were executed was 1953, when the Federal government electrocuted Ethel Rosenberg in New York, gassed Bonnie Headley in Missouri, and electrocuted Earle Dennison in Alabama. Wanda Jean Allen, one of the three women executed in 2001, became the first black woman put to death in 47 years. The prosecution highlighted her lesbianism in arguing for the death penalty.[96]

Federal Judge Robert Bork provides insight into the expressive and performative politics of the death penalty. In a brief he filed in support of the 1976 Supreme Court decision that reinstated the death penalty—the Gregg Decision—he argued that capital punishment "serves a vital social function as society's expression of moral outrage."[97] This thinking releases capital punishment from accountability as a crime-fighting tool a deterrent, and reframes it as a theatre of retribution and revenge. It becomes a form of "poetic justice," a "revenge tragedy" that operates on the principle of mimetic magic: the belief that only violence can cross out violence. Timothy McVeigh was caught at both ends of this contagious chain of mimetic violence. He bombed the Murrah Federal Building in Oklahoma City to express his moral outrage and mimetically respond to the FBI's botched raid and burning of the Branch Davidian Compound in Waco, Texas. He chose April 19, 1995 as the date for blowing up the federal building because it was the second year anniversary of the Waco conflagration and the 220th anniversary of the Battle of Lexington and Concord.[98] In his warped imagination and twisted aesthetics, the violence he perpetrated in Oklahoma City was the performative reparation for the violence that the federal government wreaked on the Branch Davidian Compound. He, in turn, paid with his life when the federal government responded in kind by killing him. At McVeigh's execution, anti-death penalty activists exposed the circular absurdity of mimetic violence with this question carried on placards and emblazoned on T-Shirts: "Why Do We Kill People, Who Kill People, to Show that Killing People Is Wrong?"

The persistence of the death penalty defies logic and exceeds rational explanation. There are at least four troubling problems with capital punishment. (1) It is not a deterrent to crime. Even conservative criminologists no longer justify it as a deterrent to crime. (2) It is meted out in an inconsistent and capricious way. There are glaring racial and geographical disparities in its application. (3) The system sometimes executes the wrong person: one scholar estimates an error rate of one innocent person out of every seven executed.[99] (4) It is extremely expensive. Each execution (from trial to death chamber) costs on the average 1.5 million dollars, far more expensive than a life sentence.[100] Why then does it persist? When logic cannot uphold it, when it does not work, and then it is not cost-effective? It is adhered to for emotional and expressive purposes that can be exploited for political gain. Like other rituals of sacrifice, executions tap the generative power of violence and harness the volatile energies surrounding death for political purposes. Newt Gingrich once explained that the two cornerstones for building a conservative majority in the United States are (1) tax cuts, and (2) the Death Penalty.[101] A close reading of the dramaturgy of contemporary execution rituals reveals the deep and terribly fraught contradictions, conundra, tensions, and anxieties that are never fully reconciled.

THE DRAMATURGY OF CONTEMPORARY EXECUTIONS

The central performance challenge of execution rituals is to differentiate between judicial killing and murder.[102] This distinction is dramatized through the careful and elaborate staging of props, participants, and players: the entire scenography and choreography of the event signal order, control, propriety, and inevitability. The real violence of state killing is veiled behind protocols of civility and the pretense of courtesy toward the condemned— hence the hollow gestures of permitting the condemned to order his or her last meal and to speak his or her last words. Some guards and wardens even eat with the condemned to give them some company during the ceremony of the last meal. The prison staff show an unusual attentiveness and air of concern for the condemned during the final countdown hours of the death-watch.[103]

But all this consideration is as much about controlling the performance, making sure that it proceeds smoothly without a glitch, as it is about compassion or empathy for the condemned. Inasmuch as possible, spontaneity and improvisation are foreclosed in the execution scenario. Everything is carefully scripted, choreographed, rehearsed, and directed— micro-managed right down to the tiniest of details, nothing left to chance. The condemned must order his or her last meal seven days in advance. Ritual theatre intersects with management science to produce the bizarre contemporary form of modern executions.[104] Much of the debate surrounding the death penalty since the 1890 invention of the

electric chair has focused on the performance technology of executions.

Officials are anxious to control the performance because condemned prisoners, although acutely vulnerable, are not without agency. They can fight back and force the guards to drag them kicking and screaming to their death. In June 2000, Gary Graham, also called Sankofa, refused to cooperate and go quietly to the execution chamber. A helmeted "extraction team" maced and forcibly removed him from his holding cell. Protesting his innocence he resisted every step of the way, and even as the poison was dripping into his veins, he loudly protested, "They're killing me tonight, they're murdering me tonight."[105] On the other hand, prisoners sometimes panic and collapse in terror at the moment of the final walk to their premeditated death. Either response— defiant resistance or terrified hysteria—rips off the mask of civility, the illusion of order, inevitability, procedure, due process, the fiction that what is taking place is "natural," "clean," "solemn," "dignified," and "humane," an acceptable performance of Justice in a modern democracy.[106]

Sometimes executions are botched simply because of the performance anxiety or ineptitude of the executioners. Each one of the methods for putting people to death requires a mastery of technique, and none guarantees a death that is quick, painless, and clean. Hanging involves an intricate calculus between the length of the rope and the weight of the prisoner. If the drop is too short, the neck is not broken, and the condemned kicks and writhes in the agony of slow strangulation. If the drop

Table 26.9 All Nations Have Abolished the Juvenile Death Penalty Except Five

Iran, Pakistan, Nigeria, Saudi Arabia, and the United States

The U.S. has executed seven juvenile offenders since 1998 (three in 2000)

is too long, the head is ripped off. The electric chair requires skillful application of electrodes to the shaved head and leg to ensure a good connection, and the careful measurement of voltage and timing of the jolts. With too powerful a charge, the condemned catches on fire, which happened twice in Florida's electric chair in 1990 and 1997. But even when electrocutions go smoothly they are messy affairs. The eyes bulge, sometimes popping out of their sockets, and the condemned urinate and defecate in the chair. The gas chamber was supposed to be a technological improvement over the rope and the chair, but it proved no more efficient or humane than the other technologies. Prisoners had different reactions to the poison gas. Some convulsed violently, thrashed and foamed at the mouth, and bashed their head against the back metal pole. Even lethal injections, the most antiseptic and clinical of all the modes, are sometimes botched. Sometimes the technicians cannot find a good vein; there are documented cases of them searching and pricking both arms, ankle, and finally going to the neck, taking 45 minutes to insert the needle. Sometimes the needle pops out under the pressure of execution, spewing the toxic drugs and spraying the witnesses. Some prisoners heave and violently choke. Botched executions knock down the ritual frame and expose the gruesome reality of actually putting a human being to death. The illusion of nonviolent decency is torn away. Botched executions also are the stuff of sensational news stories and political embarrassments. Graphic images and grisly reports of botched executions erode the public faith in the "ultimate oxymoron: a humane killing."[107] To prevent embarrassing glitches and disruptions, modern executions have become ever more controlled, engineered, and bureaucratized performances.[108]

The regular rehearsals, precise stage directions, and obsessive planning and detail reveal the fragile and volatile nature of these modern rituals of state killing. *The Execution Protocol*, a 56-page manual issued by the Federal Bureau of Prisons, outlines the procedures (see below).[109] Leaving no detail to the imagination, the last page of the execution manual instructs that the execution chamber should be cleaned by staff "trained in hygiene and infectious disease control."

Section V. "THE FINAL THIRTY MINUTES PRIOR TO THE EXECUTION"

A. Final Sequence of Events: Preparation

1. Bringing the Condemned Individual to the Execution Room: At a time determined by the warden, the condemned individual will be:
   a. removed from the Inmate Holding Cell by the Restraint Team
   b. strip-searched by the Restraint Team and then dressed in khaki pants, shirt, and slip-on shoes
   c. secured with restraints, if deemed appropriate by the Warden;
   d. escorted to the Execution Room by the Restraint Team

2. Restraint Team Procedures

   In the execution room the ambulatory restraints, if any, will be removed, and the condemned individual will be restrained to the Execution Table. . . .

VI: FINAL SEQUENCE OF EVENTS: EXECUTION

A. Staff Witnesses

1. Staff participating in the preparation for the execution will exit the Execution Room but stand by in an adjacent area

2. Staff members remaining to participate in and observe the execution will include the:
   a. Designated United States Marshal
   b. Warden
   c. Executioner
   d. Other staff authorized by the Director of the Bureau of Prisons

B. Countdown

1. Once the condemned individual has been secured to the table, at the direction of the Warden, staff inside the execution room will open the drapes covering the windows of the witness room

2. The Warden will ask the condemned individual if he/she has any last words, or wishes to make a statement. The condemned individual will have been advised in advance by the warden that this statement should be reasonably brief. . . .

3. At the conclusion of the remarks, or when the Warden determines it is time to proceed, the Warden will read documentation deemed necessary to the execution process. The Warden will then advise the Designated United States Marshal that, quote, "We are ready." Close quote. A prearranged signal will then be given by the Designated United States Marshal to the Warden, who will direct the executioner to administer the lethal injection.

4. If the execution is ordered delayed, the Designated United States Marshal will instruct the Executioner to step away from the execution equipment and will notify the condemned individual and all present that the execution has been stayed or delayed. the Warden will direct stand down procedures and return the institution to normal operations after the condemned individual has been returned to appropriate living quarters.

C. Execution

After receiving the signal from the Designated United States Marshal, the Warden will direct the executioner to administer the lethal injection.

And the condemned prisoner is enlisted as a cooperative player within this grisly script. The condemned face a devil's bargain. When all hope for reprieve is gone, the only option left is in common phraseology "getting through this," with as much dignity and as little pain as possible. Perhaps one of the most perverse cruelties is the way the prisoner is coerced into a pact of complicity with his or her executioners. This is perversely apparent with the gas chamber, with the customary final admonition to the condemned as some form of: "Breathe deeply, it'll go easier for you that way." But the life-force is so strong that few comply, and that's why the gas chamber was soon dubbed a chamber of horrors. Norms of masculinity are deployed when wardens exhort prisoners in cliched fashion to "go to your death like a man, take your medicine like a man." My interview with the warden at the Terre Haute Federal Prison revealed a new innovation in the casting of execution scenarios. With federal executions, the administrators now bring in staff from other institutions, just for the executions, As explained by the warden: "It's too traumatic for the local staff who know the prisoner and in some cases have formed a relationship with him or her over the years on death row." And I hasten to add that I interviewed the new warden, David Olson, who is now in charge of the Federal "execution facility," as it is called in the bureaucratic manuals. His immediate predecessor, Harley Lappin, scored high marks for directing the June, 2001 executions of McVeigh and Garza, again the first federal executions since 1963. By the time I was able to return to Terre Haute in September, 2001 to tour the prison and talk with staff, Lappin already had been rewarded with a promotion and transfer. He is now the Director of the Mid-Atlantic Region, with twenty prisons under his supervision.

Even the demonstrators who come to protest the executions are carefully monitored and controlled. No one is permitted onto the prison grounds with his or her own transportation. At both the McVeigh and Garza executions, we had to meet at a designated park, walk down a fenced corridor, and get searched before being permitted to board the Bureau of Prisons busses. We were required to take a "Pledge of Nonviolence," which included: "we will not swear or use insulting language. We will not run in public or otherwise make threatening motions. We will honor the directions of the designated coordinators. In the event of serious disagreement, we will remove ourselves from the Vigil Action." Once on the bus, two guards with rifles accompanied us, one riding up front, the other in the back. Each bus was escorted to the prison by two police cars with flashing lights, one car in front, one in the rear.

"What is at stake," Sarat asks, "when the state imagines itself killing painlessly, humanely?"[110] When it invents new and improved technologies for putting people to death with "decency" and "dignity"? What do the shifting modes and methods of execution say about public standards of taste and thresholds of squeamishness? The quest for quick, efficient, and clean modes of execution that do not disfigure the corpse is for the sake of spectators more than the condemned. When Ronald Reagan was governor of California, he was one of the first government officials to imagine lethal injection. He observed, "as a former rancher and horse raiser, I know what it's like to eliminate an injured horse by shooting him," recommending instead, "a simple shot or tranquilizer."[111] Reagan's point was not to spare the defendant pain, but to shield the executioners—and by extension, civil society—from the horror and anguish of exterminating a human being.

In 1977 Oklahoma reinvented capital punishment for the modern age by developing the new performance technology of "lethal injection." In 1982 in Texas, Charles Brooks became the first prisoner executed by lethal injection. Outside the United States, China first used lethal injection in 1997, which it deemed more scientific than shooting a kneeling prisoner in the back of the head at close range. When lethal injection was first discussed in the Oklahoma legislature, advocates argued the merits of: "No pain,

no spasms, no smells or sounds—just sleep, then death." Governor David Boren pointed out that it provided "a nice clean exit plan."[112] Susan Blaustein, a media witness to a lethal injection in Texas, described the experience in a *Harper's Magazine* article titled, "Witness to Another Execution in Texas: Death Walks an Assembly Line." She wrote: "The lethal injection method has turned dying into a *still life*, thereby enabling the state to kill without anyone involved feeling anything at all. . . . We have perfected the art of institutional killing to the degree that it has deadened our natural, quintessentially human response to death."[113]

Tulsa Republican representative William Wiseman, Jr., was the principal architect of Oklahoma's lethal injection bill. He argued that the needle would "make the death penalty more humane by eliminating the brutality and violence of electrocution"—Oklahoma's then current method for executing criminals. In June 2001, Wiseman published an apologia in the *Christian Century*. He admitted: "The dramatic irony of my action as a legislator is that what purported to be a means of reducing violence became instead a means of increasing it. The moral burden I carry is that, if it were not for my *palatable technique* of death, many who have now been executed would likely have been spared by squeamish juries." He left politics and is now pursuing a Master's of Divinity degree at a theological seminary in Tulsa.[114]

Lethal injection, the favored method of modern capital punishment, borrows props from the medical profession and eerily mimics a therapeutic intervention. Missouri's lethal injection chamber at Potosi Correctional Center is right in the center of the prison hospital ward.[115] One of the uncanny consequences of this slippage between curing and killing is that there is a new emergent justification for executions: executions are justified so that the families of victims can heal and achieve "closure." This is a new development in the history of justifications for capital punishment. We have moved from support of capital punishment as a deterrent, as retribution, and now as an extension and necessary part of the grieving process and form of group therapy. This link between capital punishment and mourning is aligned with the politics of the powerful victims rights movement: "By transforming courts into sites for the rituals of grieving, that movement seeks to make private experiences part of public discourse."[116] Appellate Judge Alex Kosinski says that when he reviews and signs off on executions, he "hear[s] the tortured voices of the victims calling out to [him] . . . for vindication."[117]

The execution of McVeigh demonstrates the political efficacy of mourning. The same group of mourning survivors and family and friends of victims who planned the Oklahoma City National Memorial also campaigned for passage of the 1996 Antiterrorism and Effective Death Penalty Act, legislation that restricts the right of appeal and habeas corpus in order to streamline and speed up the execution process. They also successfully lobbied Attorney General Ashcroft to telecast McVeigh's execution to an invited group of designated mourners in Oklahoma. In an unprecedented move, Attorney General Ashcroft authorized the closed circuit telecast of McVeigh's execution to an arena filled with relatives of victims and survivors of the Murrah building bombing. He infamously said that survivors and families of victims need to be able to see McVeigh executed "to help them meet their need to close this chapter in their lives."[118] Over one thousand people were invited to the live telecast of McVeigh's execution, more than half declined, and on the morning of June 19, 2001, 232 showed up at the telecast site, a federal prison.[119]

Several of the invited people went directly from watching the telecast of McVeigh's execution to the Oklahoma City National Memorial Center, thus collapsing the execution into personal rituals of bereavement.

One of them, Tom Kight, placed the blue federal badge identifying him as "Witness 223" at the execution telecast on the commemorative chair for his stepdaughter killed in the blast.[120] Several newspapers reinforced this conflation of capital punishment with rites of mourning by running full color photographs of the Oklahoma City National Memorial Center underneath banner headlines announcing McVeigh's execution. On June 12, the *New York Times* ran "McVeigh Dies for Oklahoma City Blast" headline above a photograph of family members kneeling and grieving by the chair commemorating their mother at the Oklahoma City National Memorial Center. The caption explained that the family members had just come from watching the execution on closed-circuit TV.[121] The same day the *Chicago Tribune* ran "U.S. Executes Its Worst Terrorist" banner headline above a panoramic photograph of the Oklahoma City National Memorial Center likewise showing grieving family members just arrived from viewing the execution, kneeling at memorial chairs. On an inside page, there was another photograph of a woman holding a radio and listening intently while kneeling in front of one of the memorial chairs. The caption read: "Renee Pendley listens to a radio report on the execution as she kneels near the memorial chair for her friend Teresa Lauderdale."[122]

Two of the relatives of Oklahoma City bombing victims, who won the lottery to witness the McVeigh execution live in Terre Haute, pressed photographs of deceased loved ones against the window as they watched McVeigh die. What does it mean when the rituals of state killing are conflated and enfolded within rituals of mourning and bereavement? In the wake of September 11, 2001, with its massive trauma to the national psyche, we can expect to see the death penalty figure prominently in the politics of grief as executions are argued for and justified as necessary therapies of collective healing and closure.

Author's note: I have delivered earlier versions and different parts of this essay at four conferences where I received helpful and incisive comments, critiques, and suggestions. I thank Jill Dolan and David Román for inviting me first to present this new work as part of the "Fresh Print" series at the ATHE convention in Chicago, August, 2001. I thank Janelle Reinelt for inviting me to present another version at the "Performance, Policy and Culture: *Dead Man Walking* and the Death Penalty in America" conference at University of California, Irvine, March, 2002. I am grateful to Helen Schwartzman, Chair of Northwestern's Anthropology Department, who invited me to present an extended version as the annual Frontier Lecture in Anthropology, March, 2002. I thank Peggy Phelan for inviting me to present and curate a panel on the death penalty at the "Theatres of Life" Performance Studies International conference at New York University, April, 2002. I am especially grateful to my colleagues Micaela di Leonardo and Lisa Merrill for their sustained and generous responses to this work. And I thank Leigh Bienen, Tracy Davis, Harry Haines, E. Patrick Johnson, Dwight McBride, Denise Quirk, Sandra Richards, Mary Strine, Sunwolf, and Mary Weismantel for bracing discussions and sharing resources.

NOTES

1. These are the last words of Napoleon Beazley, a young African American man, who was executed in Huntsville, Texas, May 28, 2002. His last words are posted on the web site of the Texas Department of Criminal Justice.

2. Albert Camus, "Reflections on the Guillotine," *Resistance, Rebellion, and Death* (New York: Vintage, 1995 [1960]), 234.

3. John Whitley, the warden responsible for directing executions at Louisiana's Angola State Prison, quoted in Ivan Solotaroff, *The Last Face You'll Ever See: The Private Life of the American Death Penalty* (New York: HarperCollins, 2001), 34.

4. Austin Sarat, *When the State Kills: Capital Punishment and the American*

Condition (Princeton: Princeton University Press, 2001), 242.

5. Michel Foucault, *Discipline and Punish: The Birth of the Prison*, trans. Alan Sheridan (New York: Vintage, 1979 [1975]).

6. Ibid., 307.

7. Ibid., 302.

8. There are several excellent books that track this history: Stuart Banner, *The Death Penalty: An American History* (Cambridge: Harvard University Press, 2002); Hugo Bedau, ed., *The Death Penalty in America: Current Controversies* (New York: Oxford University Press, 1997); Jesse L. Jackson, Sr., Jesse Jackson, Jr., and Bruce Shapiro, *Legal Lynching: The Death Penalty and America's Future* (New York: New Press, 2001); Robert Jay Lifton and Greg Mitchell, *Who Owns Death?: Capital Punishment, the American Conscience, and the End of Executions* (New York: Morrow, 2000). See also Thomas Laqueur, "Festival of Punishment," *London Review of Books*, 5 October 2000: 17–24; Gary Wills, "The Dramaturgy of Death," *New York Review of Books*, 21 June 2001: 6–10.

9. The most authoritative source for updated data on the death penalty is the Death Penalty Information Center, Washington, D.C. Their excellent web site address is http://www.deathpenalty info.org/.

10. See John D. Bessler, *Death in the Dark: Midnight Executions in America* (Boston: Northeastern University Press, 1997), 146.

11. See especially Banner, *The Death Penalty*.

12. The White House, Office of the Press Secretary, *Military Order: Detention, Treatment, and Trial of Certain Non-Citizens in the War Against Terrorism*, 13 November 2001.

13. *The American Heritage Dictionary of the English Language*, 4th ed. (Boston: Houghton Mifflin, 2000).

14. See Mary Douglas, *Purity and Danger* (London: Routledge & Kegan Paul, 1966); Clifford Geertz, *The Interpretation of Cultures* (New York: Basic, 1973); Victor Turner, *The Ritual Process: Structure and Anti-Structure* (Ithaca: Cornell University Press, 1969) and *From Ritual to Theatre: The Human Seriousness of Play* (New York: Performing Arts Journal Publications, 1982); Roy Rappaport, *Ritual and Religion in the Making of Humanity* (Cambridge: Cambridge University Press, 1999). See also Catherine Bell, *Ritual Theory, Ritual Practice* (New York: Oxford University Press, 1992), and *Ritual: Perspectives and Dimensions* (New York: Oxford University Press, 1997). For important studies of political rituals, see Katherine A. Bowie, *Rituals of*

National Unity: An Anthropology of the State and the Village Scout Movement in Thailand (New York: Columbia University Press, 1997); David I. Kertzer, *Ritual, Politics, and Power* (New Haven: Yale University Press, 1988); Richard J. Evans, *Rituals of Retribution: Capital Punishment in Germany, 1600–1987* (New York: Oxford University Press, 1996). For a historical case study of execution rituals, see Mark Fearnow, "Theatre for an Angry God: Public Burnings and Hangings in Colonial New York, 1741," *Drama Review* 40, T150 (1996): 15–36.

15. Victor Turner, *The Anthropology of Performance* (New York: Performing Arts Journal Publications, 1986), 48.

16. Robert Johnson, *Death Work: A Study of the Modern Execution Process*, 2nd ed. (Belmont: Wadsworth, 1998), 20.

17. Richard Schechner, *Between Theater and Anthropology* (Philadelphia: University of Pennsylvania Press, 1985), 36–37. See also Schechner's *The Future of Ritual: Writings on Culture and Performance* (New York: Routledge, 1993).

18. For pathfinding analyses of the processual and improvisatory dynamics of ritual see Nicholas B. Dirks, "Ritual and Resistance: Subversion as a Social Fact," in *Culture/Power/History: A Reader in Contemporary Social Theory*, ed. Nicholas B. Dirks, Geoff Eley, and Sherry B. Ortner (Princeton: Princeton University Press, 1994), 483–503; Margaret Thompson Drewal, *Yoruba Ritual: Performers, Play, and Agency* (Bloomington: Indiana University Press, 1992).

19. Louis P. Masur, *Rites of Execution: Capital Punishment and the Transformation of American Culture, 1776–1865* (New York: Oxford University Press, 1989), 6. See also Norbert Elias, *The Civilizing Process: The History of Manners*, trans. Edmund Jephcott (New York: Urizen Books, 1978); John R. Kasson, *Rudeness and Civility: Manners in Nineteenth-Century Urban America* (New York: Hill & Wang, 1990); Lawrence W. Levine, *Highbrow/Lowbrow: The Emergence of Cultural Hierarchy in America* (Cambridge: Harvard University Press, 1988).

20. Cotton Mather, *Faithful Warnings to Prevent Fearful Judgments. Uttered in a Brief Discourse, Occasioned, by a Tragical Spectacle, In a Number of Miserables Under a Sentence of Death for Piracy* (Boston: printed and sold by Timothy Green, 1704).

21. John Dunston, quoted in Edwin Powers, *Crime and Punishment in Early Massachusetts, 1620–1692: A Documentary History* (Boston: Beacon, 1966), 295.

22. Ibid., 296.

23. Wayne Minnick, "The New England Execution Sermon, 1639–1800," *Speech Monographs* 35 (1968): 80.

24. Banner, *The Death Penalty*, 25. Theatre historian Peter G. Buckley concurs: "Of all colonial ritual, executions drew the largest crowds." See Peter G. Buckley, "Paratheatricals and Popular Stage Entertainments," in *The Cambridge History of American Theatre* I, ed. Don B. Wilmeth and Christopher Bigsby (Cambridge: Cambridge University Press, 1998), 428.

25. Cotton Mather, *A Sorrowful Spectacle. In Two Sermons, Occasioned by a Just Sentence of Death, on a Miserable Woman, for the Murder of a Spurious Offspring. The One Declaring, The Evil of an Heart Hardened, under and against all Means of Good. The Other Describing, The Fearful Case of Such as in a Suffering Time, and much more such as in a Dying Hour, are found without the Fear of God* (Boston: printed by T. Fleet & T. Crump, 1715).

26. See "Hanging Day" in Banner, *The Death Penalty*, 24–52 and "The Design of Public Executions in the Early American Republic" in Masur, *Rites of Execution*, 25–49. See also Ronald A. Bosco, "Lectures at the Pillory: The Early American Execution Sermon," *American Quarterly* 30 (1978): 156–76; Daniel E. Williams, "'Behold a Tragic Scene Strangely Changed into a Theater of Mercy': The Structure and Significance of Criminal Conversion Narratives in Early New England," *American Quarterly* 38 (1986): 827–47.

27. John Rogers, *Death the Certain Wages of Sin to the Impenitent: Life the Sure Reward of Grace to the Penitent: Together with the only Way for Youth to avoid the former, and attain the latter. Delivered in Three Lecture Sermons; Occasioned by the Imprisonment, condemnation and Execution, of a Young Woman, who was guilty of Murdering her infant begotten in Whoredom* (Boston: Printed by B. Green and T. Allen, 1701), 147.

28. See Peggy Phelan, *Unmarked: The Politics of Performance* (New York: Routledge, 1993).

29. Banner, *The Death Penalty*, 44.

30. Rogers, *Death the Certain*, 144.

31. Ibid., 2, 118. For important historical studies of Puritan culture, see Daniel A. Cohen, *Pillars of Salt, Monuments of Grace: New England Crime Literature and the Origins of American Popular Culture, 1674–1860* (New York: Oxford University Press, 1993); David D. Hall, *Worlds of Wonder, Days of Judgment:*

Popular Religious Belief in Early New England (New York: Knopf, 1989).

32. Ibid., 153.

33. Ibid., 124.

34. Ibid., 123.

35. Ibid., 2.

36. Ibid., 2, 142.

37. Ibid., 3.

38. Ibid., 118.

39. Jonas Barish, *The Antitheatrical Prejudice* (Berkeley: University of California Press, 1981).

40. Rogers, *Death the Certain*, 118.

41. Samuel Danforth, *The Cry of Sodom Enquired Into: Upon Occasion of the Arraignment and Condemnation of Benjamin Goad, For his Prodigious Villany. Together with a Solemn Exhortation to Tremble at Gods Judgements, and to Abandon Youthful Lusts* (Cambridge: printed by Marmaduke Johnson, 1674).

42. Rogers, *Death the Certain*, 3.

43. Ibid., 119. On "performative metaphors," see James Fernandez, *Persuasions and Performances: The Play of Tropes in Culture* (Bloomington: Indiana University Press, 1986).

44. Rogers, *Death the Certain*, 2.

45. On "interpretive communities," see Stanley Fish, *Is There a Text in this Class?: The Authority of Interpretive Communities* (Cambridge: Harvard University Press, 1980).

46. John Williams, *Warnings to the Unclean: In a Discourse from Rev. XXXI. 8. Preacht at Springfield Lecture, August 25th. 1698. At the Execution of Sarah Smith* (Boston: Printed by B. Green and J. Allen, 1699), 7.

47. Rogers, *Death the Certain*, 118, emphasis added.

48. Ibid., 133.

49. Ibid., 115–16.

50. Ibid., 119, 144.

51. Ibid., 152.

52. Ibid., 132.

53. Williams, *Warnings*, 12, 37.

54. Rogers, *Death the Certain*, 3.

55. For important works on spectatorship see Jill Dolan, *The Feminist Spectator as Critic* (Ann Arbor: University of Michigan Press, 1988); Lisa Merrill, *When Romeo Was a Woman: Charlotte Cushman and Her Circle of Female Spectators* (Ann Arbor: University of Michigan Press, 1999).

56. Rogers, *Death the Certain*, 133.

57. Ibid., 153.

58. Ibid., 122.

59. Ibid., 114.

60. Ibid., 143.

61. Ibid., 144.

62. Ibid., 119.

63. Ibid., 146.

64. Ibid., 152.

65. See Thomas W. Laqueur, "Crowds, Carnival, and the State in Early English Executions, 1604–1868," in *The First Modern Society: Essays in English History in Honour of Lawrence Stone*, ed. A. L. Beier, David Cannadine, James M. Rosenheim (Cambridge: Cambridge University Press, 1989), 305–55.

66. Rogers, *Death the Certain*, 113.

67. Danforth, *The Cry of Sodom*, i.

68. Rogers, *Death the Certain*, 2.

69. Richard Godbeer, *Sexual Revolution in Early America* (Baltimore: Johns Hopkins University Press, 2002), 55.

70. Danforth, *The Cry of Sodom*, 10.

71. See Karen Halttunen, *Murder Most Foul: The Killer and the American Gothic Imagination* (Cambridge: Harvard University Press, 1998); Leigh B. Bienen, "A Good Murder," in *The Death Penalty in America*, ed. Hugo Bedau (New York: Oxford University Press, 1997), 319–32.

72. G. W. Peck, "On the Use of Chloroform in Hanging," *American Whig Review* 8 (1848): 283–97. Peck opens with an extended "essay on manners" and does not even mention capital punishment until page 292, ten pages into the essay. Peck is much more interested in the everyday performativity of class—manners, deportment, refinement, cultivation of speech and gesture—than he is in the cultural performance of executions. His essay resonates with other elocutionary texts of the period. For a discussion of the class and racial exclusions upon which the elocutionary movement was based, see my "Rethinking Elocution: The Trope of the Talking Book and Other Figures of Speech," *Text and Performance Quarterly* 20 (2000): 325–41.

73. Ibid., 295.

74. Ibid., 286.

75. Ibid., 291.

76. Ibid., 292.

77. Ibid., 296.

78. See Johnson, *Death Work*.

79. See Michael Taussig, *The Magic of the State* (New York: Routledge, 1997), 187. On the massive incarceration campaign and prison building boom, see Elliott Currie, *Crime and Punishment in America* (New York: Metropolitan

Books, 1998); Joseph T. Hallinan, *Going Up the River: Travels in a Prison Nation* (New York: Random House, 2001); Marc Mauer and The Sentencing Project, *Race to Incarcerate* (New York: Free Press, 1999); Christian Parenti, *Lockdown America: Police and Prisons in the Age of Crisis* (New York: Verso, 1999).

80. Michel Foucault, *Power,* ed. James D. Faubion (New York: New Press, 1994), 435–36.

81. See David Johnston, "Ashcroft Delays Death of McVeigh Over FBI's Lapse," *New York Times,* 12 May 2001, A1.

82. See the Center On Wrongful Convictions web site: http://www.law.northwestern.edu/depts/clinic/wrongful/index.htm.

83. Joseph Roach, *Cities of the Dead: Circum-Atlantic Performance* (New York: Columbia University Press, 1996), 36–41; Michael Taussig, *Mimesis and Alterity: A Particular History of the Senses* (New York: Routledge, 1993).

84. The Death Penalty Information Center is a reliable source for demographic data on the death penalty. See also, Deborah Fins, *Death Row USA,* Quarterly Report, NAACP Legal Defense and Educational Fund, 2002.

85. See William S. McFeely, *Proximity to Death* (New York: Norton, 2000), 69. Gary Gilmore was executed by a firing squad in Utah in 1977, making his the first post-Furman execution. But because he refused all appeals, he was considered a "volunteer."

86. See U.S. General Accounting Office, "Death Penalty Sentencing: Research Indicates Pattern of Racial Disparities," in *The Death Penalty in America,* ed. Hugo Bedau, 268–74. See also Bienen, "A Good Murder," 327.

87. Jackson, Jackson, and Shapiro, *Legal Lynching,* 75.

88. Mumia Abu-Jamal, quoted in ibid., 35. For an astute historical analysis of the codependent connection between capitalism and capital punishment, see Peter Linebaugh, *The London Hanged: Crime and Civil Society in the Eighteenth Century* (Cambridge: Cambridge University Press, 1992).

89. Stephen Bright, "Counsel for the Poor: The Death Sentence Not for the Worst Crime But for the Worst Lawyer," in *The Death Penalty in America,* ed. Hugo Bedau, 275–309.

90. http://www.tdcj.state.tx.us/stat/finalmeal.htm

91. See Mary Douglas, "Food as a System of Communication," in *The Active Voice* (London: Routledge & Kegan Paul, 1982), 82–124; Pierre Bourdieu, *Distinction: A Social Critique of the Judgment of Taste,* trans. Richard Nice (Cambridge: Harvard University Press, 1984).

92. Victoria Brownworth, "Dykes on Death Row," *The Advocate,* June 1992, 62–64. See also Victor Streib, "Death Penalty for Lesbians," *National Journal of Sexual Orientation Law* 1 (1995): 105–26; Richard Goldstein, "Queer on Death Row," *Village Voice,* March 2001.

93. Lifton and Mitchell, *Who Owns Death?,* 135.

94. Ibid., 101.

95. See Bessler, *Death in the Dark,* 142. For studies of the stress and trauma that executions wreak on the prison staff whose job it is to actually carry out this grisly work, see Donald A. Cabana, *Death at Midnight: The Confession of an Executioner* (Boston: Northeastern University Press, 1996); Johnson, *Death Work,* 109–16; Ivan Solotaroff, *The Last Face You'll Ever See: The Private Life of the American Death Penalty* (New York: HarperCollins, 2001).

96. Tonya McClary, "Sexuality and Capital Punishment: The Execution of Wanda Jean Allen," *Outfront: Amnesty International's Program for Lesbian, Gay, Bisexual, and Transgender Human Rights,* Winter, 2002, 1, 4, 6.

97. Robert Bork, quoted in Sarat, *When the State Kills,* 33.

98. Lou Michel and Dan Herbeck, *American Terrorist: Timothy McVeigh and the Oklahoma City Bombing* (New York: HarperCollins, 2001), 226.

99. Sarat, *When the State Kills,* 258.

100. Jackson, Jackson, and Shapiro, *Legal Lynching,* 110.

101. Sarat, *When the State Kills,* 17–18.

102. Timothy McVeigh's death certificate listed the cause of death as "Homicide." See "Coroner Prepares to Sign Death Certificate," *Terre Haute Tribune-Star,* 11 June 2001, A6.

103. See Johnson, *Death Work.*

104. See Jon McKenzie, *Perform Or Else: From Discipline to Performance* (New York: Routledge, 2001).

105. See Frank Bruni and Jim Yardley, "Inmate is Executed in Texas as 11th-Hour Appeals Fail," *New York Times,* 23 June 2000, A18. See also, Amy Dorsett, "Execution Day," *San Antonio Express-News,* 22 June 2000, 1A, 8A.

106. For scathing critiques of the hypocrisy of sanitized lethal injection as a modern and humane method, See Lifton and Mitchell, *Who Owns Death?,* 43–69; Sarat, *When the State Kills,* 60–84.

107. Lifton and Mitchell, *Who Owns Death?*, 44. For examples of botched lethal injections, see ibid., 65–66. Bungled executions are so commonplace that the Death Penalty Information Center documents them under the special topic, "Botched Executions." See http://www.deathpenaltyinfo-.org/botched.html.

108. Modern executions conflate the three performance paradigms that Jon McKenzie identifies as "the efficacy of cultural performance," the efficiency of organizational performance," and "effectiveness of technological performance." See McKenzie, *Perform or Else*, 27–135.

109. A redacted version of the *Execution Protocol* is posted on the internet at http://www.thesmokinggun.com/archive/bopprotoc011.shtml.

110. Sarat, *When the State Kills*, 69.

111. Quoted in Jackson, Jackson, and Shapiro, *Legal Lynching*, 113. In 1984, Reagan issued an executive order that reinstated the Military Death Penalty.

112. William J. Wiseman, Jr., "Inventing Lethal Injection," *Christian Century*, 20 June 2001, 6.

113. Susan Blaustein, "Witness to Another Execution," in *Death Penalty in America*, ed. Hugo Bedau (New York: Oxford University Press, 1997), 387–400.

114. Wiseman, Jr., "Inventing," 6. See also James Walsh, "The Medicine that Kills: Lethal Injection for Execution," *Lancet*, 7 February 1998, 441.

115. See Lifton and Mitchell, *Who Owns Death?*, 97.

116. Sarat, *When the State Kills*, 35. On victims' rights movement, see Wendy Kaminer, *It's All the Rage: Crime and Culture* (New York: Addison-Wesley, 1995); for trenchant critique of the privatization of public discourse, especially the way victims are cast in the role of exemplary citizen, see Lauren Berlant, *The Queen of America Goes to Washington City: Essays on Sex and Citizenship* (Durham: Duke University Press, 1997).

117. Alex Kosinski, quoted in Lifton and Mitchell, *Who Owns Death?*, 162.

118. See Mike Dorning, "Hundreds Will Watch McVeigh Die," *Chicago Tribune*, 13 April 2001, 1, 20.

119. See Rick Bragg, "McVeigh Dies for Oklahoma City Blast," *New York Times*, 12 June 2001, A1, A19; Lisa Anderson, "In Oklahoma City, Some Feel Cheated by 'Easy' Death," *Chicago Tribune*, 12 June 2001, 1, 14.

120. Anderson, "In Oklahoma City, Some Feel Cheated," 14. For an excellent study of the politics of memory and how this played out in the contested process of planning, designing, and building the Oklahoma City National Memorial Center, see Edward T. Linenthal, *The Unfinished Bombing: Oklahoma City in American Memory* (New York: Oxford University Press, 2001).

121. Bragg, "McVeigh Dies," A1.

122. "The McVeigh Execution," *Chicago Tribune*, 12 June 2001, 14.

27

Who Is This Ancestor?

Performing Memory in
Ghana's Slave Castle-Dungeons
(A Multimedia Performance Meditation)

SANDRA L. RICHARDS

I initially wrote this piece in spring, 2003 in order to formally inaugurate my tenure as the Leon Forrest Professor of African American Studies at Northwestern University. Luckily, my endowed chair represented more than a name from a distant past, for the late novelist and department chair had recruited me to Northwestern. Thus, the event occasioned multiple, bittersweet rememberings. I was revisiting the recent loss of a colleague who at times acted like a wonderful mirror that could capture and reflect my potential in ways that I had not suspected. Defying logic as memory often does, I wished that Leon could be present to enjoy how the university was honoring his 24 years of academic service and his stellar contributions to the fields of African-American and American literature. In that he was deeply engaged by performance— the sermonic styles of black preachers; the

elegance of a Mahalia Jackson, Nat King Cole, or Michael Jordan; and interdisciplinary collaborations with sculptor Richard Hunt and composer T. J. Anderson[1]—the occasion also gave me a certain license. I would not have to deliver the usual academic lecture; his creative history authorized me to move back towards my own past as a theatre director and to transform it. After years of watching my faculty colleagues and graduate students in the performance studies department, I could take center stage and attempt to enact my research.

Like many other college-educated African-Americans, I had grown up with poet Countee Cullen's question, "What is Africa to me?" made all the more provocative by intellectual and social structures that posited Africa as lack. Perhaps I had been haunted by its challenge without realizing it, and my subsequent focus first on African-American and later,

489

African theatre had been a way of answering. More recently, I had begun to study African-American tourists to slave sites in the Black Atlantic. In conducting ethnographic research in West Africa, I was keeping journals of my own reactions, but I did not know quite how to incorporate them into academic texts in a way that preserved the emotional integrity of my responses. Further, as I discuss in this text, one particular memory of my trips to Ghana kept recurring: The grave site of eighteenth century Anglican priest Philip Quaque repeatedly came to mind, challenging me to come to terms with his history.

"The real magic happens when the word hits your breath," says Anna Deavere Smith (Roach, 1995, p. 45). In choosing to perform the letters that Quaque wrote to the Society for the Propagation of the Gospel in England from his post at Cape Coast Castle, I had to confront questions like the following: Where does my subject stand in time? How do I understand the historical quality of the emotion that animated Quaque and then translate that intellectual apprehension into my own emotional responses? Why does his biography both repel and attract me? What is my investment in now attempting to inhabit his words?

These are some of the challenges that memory also poses. Thus, in my script readers will encounter memory, not as the recuperation of a fixed past, but rather as a social and moral practice through which individuals labor to constitute the remembered object even as the object determines their experience and sense of identity (Antze & Lambek, 1996, p. xii). As a social practice, memory insists upon a collective identity in which we posit ourselves as descendants in a genealogy to which we may have no actual, blood relationship; we see ourselves as the inheritors of a legacy transmitted by those who preceded us and enact various rituals, like elementary school Thanksgiving Day pageants, in order to deposit into the body and naturalize constructions of collective identity. In addition, as social practice memory

operates "strategically" (Simon, Rosenberg, & Eppert, 2000), for we visitors to heritage sites treat it as a pedagogical exercise that teaches a lost history and orients students towards the present and future. We explain our activities through such truisms as "those who don't know their history are destined to repeat it," or "you can't know where you're going unless you know where you came from." Closely related to this instrumental deployment of memory is the moral demand that we honor the sacrifices of the dead by making our present world better. In the case of black people, whose communities worldwide have historically been under siege, this moral demand is intensified. The suffering of the past is redeemed, so this line of thinking argues, by the quality of the lives we presently lead.

But memory at times defies this neat teleology. Like performance, it can confound time so that past, present, and possible future seemingly become one undifferentiated force field of emotion and identification. For example, African-American travelers to slave dungeons sometimes conflate their persons with enslaved ancestors. Film maker Shirikiana Aina, whose work I excerpt in my performance, speaks of the Cape Coast castle-dungeon from which "*we* were sent away" (*Through the Door of No Return*, 1997). Further, she imagines contemporary Ghanaians as surrogates (Roach, 1996, p. 2) for indigenous populations of some two to three hundred years ago when she wonders whether the people left behind will remember her identity. Not only is memory operating as imagination, but in this instance of collective trauma, it is also functioning as the desire to reverse history. The victims will perform their history differently this time: Enslaved Africans were driven through the castle-dungeon door to be shipped across the Atlantic, and European traders arrogantly proclaimed that exit "the door of no return." Now free Africans, in the surrogates of Aina and other diasporans, have made the trip *back* across the ocean and walked through these same castle doors. As one professor, who undertook a similar journey, triumphantly exclaimed, "Now there *is* a door of return. Their spirits have come back" ("The Great Homecoming," 1998).[2] Not only have the long-lost returned, but as enacted in naming ceremonies staged for diasporans, they have taken their place within the family lineage. Orphaned in the Americas, answering the seductive trope of family used by American and Ghanaian tourism, we journey across the waters hoping to be able to re(?)locate ourselves within the clan, thereby achieving full personhood and freedom.[3]

But our capacity to imagine ourselves as surrogates standing in the place of long-gone ancestors is not without danger. We run the risk of displacing the past entirely, planting ourselves center on the stage of the past rather than seeking to negotiate our relationship to that past. Given the denigration of blackness that connects the transatlantic slave trade to present day aggression on Africa-descended people, very often the gesture of erasure happens quickly and goes unnoticed. Thus, for example, in the video segment included in the performance, the expatriate African-American guide leading visitors on a tour of Ghana's slave dungeons moves effortlessly from recalling the distress of enslaved ancestors to that of black children growing up in America's ghettos. What is unclear is whether, assaulted by the heat, smells, and oppressive history of this slave monument,[4] he and his listeners recognize their location as relational rather than identical. As Deborah Britzman (2000), writing about the trauma of the Jewish holocaust, has observed, "For part of what must be worked through are the projective identifications that impede our capacity to make an ethical relation to the stranger, to encounter vulnerability as a relation" (p. 35). We are challenged to recognize that our pain is twofold, constituted by the contemporary conditions we are undergoing and by "the secondary effects of distress, helplessness, and loss that the [earlier] pain symbolizes" (p. 39).

Because Philip Quaque's history as an Anglican priest, whose religious practice facilitated European penetration of the then-Gold Coast of Ghana, was a memory that I initially did not want to claim, I thought I had been spared the risk of superimposing my narratives onto his. But as I admit in my script, I did want him to speak to my identification with those shipped to the Americas. "I know the memory I want to have," I protested, but he continued to haunt me, refusing my desires yet demanding that I attempt to see him and understand how we are connected. In other words, I was not spared the challenge of determining what would constitute a productive remembering that deployed empathy but recognized difference, disjuncture, and irrecoverable loss as a starting point for reconfiguring the present and imagining another future (Simon et al., 2000). In performing his words and mine, in now writing about the text, I continue to be haunted by Quaque who returns to ask: "For what purposes are you using your research? How does inhabiting my words change how you move through your world?" I suspect that Quaque knows better than I that with each reappearance of memory, his significance and my answers to his questions will be different.

In introducing this script, there is one other observation I wish to make. It relates to what I term "the politics of citation." Readers will see that I refer to the pressures of memory with Yoruba and Ibo terms (*abiku* and *obanje,* respectively) rather than with Freudian terminology. I do not deny that a concept such as "the return of the repressed" is equally appropriate, but I wish to stress that Africa-descended peoples produce(d) knowledge and generate(d) theories of the world that are as viable as those grounded in European history and experience. With the institutionalization of black, ethnic, women's, and performance studies, this emphasis has in one sense become passé, as the academy has moved to recognize the contingent, perspectival quality of truth claims. Yet, too often relevant articulations emanating from the so-called margins are still treated as having no validity for their own cultures as well as for the mainstream; they do not appear in bibliographies or are cited as simply repeating what has already been pronounced in a western metropole. In speaking of abiku and not of Freud or Lacan, I insinuate a reversal in the directional flow of knowledge production.

As scholars, we are challenged to use and develop effective—that is, deeply informed and sufficiently nuanced—analytical tools that describe particular phenomena. As Philip Quaque's biography attests, the globalization that linked Europe, Africa, Asia, and the Americas produced societies that were simultaneously distinct and hybrid. And, as his reappearance asserts, we must enact answers to the challenge: Knowledge and memory for what purposes?

WHO IS THIS ANCESTOR? PERFORMING MEMORY IN GHANA'S SLAVE CASTLE-DUNGEONS

Voices

SLR who at various points is the Scholar, the Tourist and Journal Writer, and the Performer now divulging her subtext. She is dressed not in her usual, western-style clothing but in an African print and style, purchased during a trip to the continent.

Video Travelers

Philip Quaque noted in the script as KWAKU in order to remind SLR of the correct pronunciation.

Mr. Adoy

Setting

An ordinary, campus lecture hall with a proscenium stage. This one has two aisles on the right and left sides, allowing SLR to circle the audience.

I. GREETINGS

(*In the tradition of welcoming and listening to what the a cappella singing group "Sweet Honey in the Rock" terms "the ancestors' breath" [Barnwell, 1993], this event begins and ends with music that the ancestors enjoy.*)

(*Music: "Exu" from* Odum Orim *[Afro-Brazilian music] [Grupo Ofa, 2000])*

SLR the Performer

Having studied Yoruba belief systems in Nigeria, Brazil, and other parts of the Americas, I know that no undertaking is safe from mishap if Esu is not acknowledged at the outset. With this music and movement, I greet the so-called trickster god, the divine messenger who reminds us that each day is unique, presenting the traveler with choices as to how she will craft her life-script. May Esu, ancestors known and unknown who have accompanied me so far, and the spirits of Mahalia Jackson and Leon Forrest who loved her so, be pleased and guide me.

(Music: "Summertime" [Gershwin, Gershwin, and Heyward, 1935], followed by "Motherless Child" from The Best of Mahalia Jackson [1956/1995])

> Summer time and the livin is easy
> Fish are jumpin and the cotton is high
> Oh, your daddy is rich and your ma is good lookin
> so hush little baby, do . . . n't you cry.
> One of these mornings
> you gonna rise up singin
> you gonna heist your wings—ohhh—and take to the sky
> And til that mornin
> nothin will harm you
> with daddy and mammy, they'll be standin by.

(During "Summertime" SLR enters from house right and proceeds counterclockwise through the auditorium, handing out programs and greeting audience members.)

SLR the Performer thinks

The slow, gentle tinkle of a piano and the clear, sweet moanin' of Mahalia Jackson. She uses the "Summertime" melody for both songs. In moving seamlessly from the popular, *Porgy and Bess* folk opera song "Summertime" to the traditional spiritual "Motherless Child," Jackson belies her protests that she sang only religious music. Both feel like a blues of longing for the security that a family presumably provides. Why in the good times of summer, with material plenty, does the baby cry? What danger does the mother anticipate and hope to preempt with the image of the child assuming a bird's form? Will daddy and mammy—in a later verse, Mahalia substitutes "mommy"—indeed protect the child/me from a world of racist violence? As if responding to my question, Mahalia switches and acknowledges her/my sense of latent danger.

(With the beginning of "Motherless Child" SLR picks up her baggage and continues circling the space.)

> Sometime I feel like a motherless chile
> Sometime I feel like a motherless chile
> Sometimes i feeeel like a motherless chile
> just a long way from my home oh lord
> just a long . . . way from home

(Jackson hums and repeats "Summertime.")

SLR the Performer continues (thinking)

The deliberate, bass notes on the piano sound as though someone is moving resolutely through the world. A whole race of motherless people, diaspora people, torn from our places of origin, hated in the world in which we have been forced to make a home. And so, some of us attempt the trek back . . . back to the "green beginning of the world," as playwright Derek Walcott would have one of his characters say (1970, p. 326). The "green beginning" of imagination and desire, come face to face with the realities of contemporary West Africa. Though Mahalia coos, "don't you cry," the juxtaposition of the soaring, crystalline beauty of her voice against the awe-filled history back to the present and future, sketched by that voice, seems to predict that tears will be part of the journey.

(SLR sets props—big Bible and file of Quaque's letters to Society for the Propagation of the Gospel—in Quaque's space, stage left [SL] and then sets down her own props—books, candle—in her space, stage right [SR])

II. THE LECTURE-PERFORMANCE

SLR the Scholar *(Speaking from podium downstage right [DSR])*

Why, you might ask, is someone trained in theatre scholarship and practice researching tourism to slave sites? What intellectual credentials validate her venturing into such an area? Consider some of the parallels between tourism and theatre. Travel mobilizes a variety of calculations concerning the possible roles that both hosts and tourists can adopt: As host, how do I represent/re-present my hometown and identity therein, so that visitors, in search of some emotional experience that they may not be able to define, will discover something sufficiently distinct or different from what they left at home? How must I disguise my required labor and economic interests as open, voluntary hospitality? As tourist, how do I present myself or perform an identity in relation to what I have read about, hope to find, or encounter at my destination? Or think of a heritage site, like the slave-castle dungeons of Ghana, as a large set on which the tourist audience joins a local troupe of host-actors. That is, through its arrangement of artifacts, narration of history, and interactive engagement with visitors, a successful heritage site, much like a play in the theatre, seeks to create an illusion or transform an abstract absence into a palpable presence.

To these issues of identity and difference, role playing, and mediated authenticity, cultural travel to slave sites adds several more: How is a history of pain to be represented so that people will want to visit (and revisit) the site? Whose story is to be narrated? In that enslavement meant being dispossessed of one's body, let alone of material possessions, how is absence to be memorialized?

African-Americans who travel to Ghana's slave castles often explain their motivation in terms of ancestors. They speak of hearing the ancestors' voices urging remembrance of a painful history, demanding descendent recognition of links and obligations to that past.

Video: "Ghana Slave Dungeon Document: St. Paul Trip to Ghana"

(Visuals of well-fed, middle class travelers, dressed in African print, weighted down with photo and video cameras and water bottles, and waiting to begin their tour of the Cape Coast castle. An unseen male voice intones)

This [video] is for my ancestors who are unknown because they were omitted from the history books,

> This is for my ancestors murdered and left to rot in unmarked graves on land and in the sea . . .
>
> This is for my ancestors who worked plantations from sunup to sundown with disgust and mistrust of anyone who tried to justify their enslavement . . .
>
> Time has not let their spirits rest . . .
>
> Join me in paying homage to them whose spirits are still living in the shadows, riding the wind, restless because they will always be unknown.
>
> This tribute is written in anger, in tears.
>
> It is a reminder to those of us who are here today and have no knowledge of yesterday
>
> The spirit of our unknown live in all of us.
>
> You honor them when you take time to acknowledge them.
>
> Join me so that they can be free.

(Brown, 1996)

Video: "Through the Door of No Return"

(Next seen is a match being lit in the darkness. Gradually becoming discernible are water and Cape Coast Castle from the perspective of the Atlantic Ocean. As an unseen boat approaches the castle, a woman's voice confesses:)

My father's voice joined my ancestors' voice to call me back, as they called him . . . "Our arms reach up from the depths of the ocean to guide you. Come back home. Come back home . . . We wait for you, with never-closing eyes, to return home . . ." Millions of hands from billions of bones reach up through the leagues of cold, cold water . . . hands of weavers, hands of carpenters, . . . and painters and children loving to play.

(As the castle comes more clearly into view, the voice says:)

Here it is. Here it is. The point of departure, the door of no return. Here it is. It is from here that we were sent away at night by the water, and it is at night by the water that I return. Do they remember us? Do they remember us? Is our memory buried here? Is our memory buried here? Can I find my father's memory here? my ancestors' memory? my memory? Can I find our memory? Who's here? Who can answer me? Can these walls talk?

(The unseen voice has joined a group of diasporic Africans on a private castle tour and ritual of healing conducted by One Africa founders, IMAKHUS, and Nana Okofu Iture Kwaku I. Now deep underground in the slave dungeons, the voice wonders:)

Is this where my father stood, on the very ground on which my ancestors stood before being shipped out into the horrible time of the Middle Passage? How do we face this history of exile? The legacy of the lash on our backs now imprinted on our souls seems to give us the strength to remember.

(Nana reminds these tourists/pilgrims:)

We are here today to come back forward and to give thanks and praise that the Almighty has spared our life . . . These are the monuments that have been built to corral us, to house us. So we come forward today to say thank you to our ancestors: Help us to go back and pull that youngster or that brother, that sister together and say, "Hang on. Stay strong. You're gonna make it. . . ." *His voice begins to break.* Hallelujah . . . hallelujah, hallelujah . . .

(Then, he instructs the group:)

Blow out the candles. Take a moment. Call out the names of those ancestors who have gone on. Harriet Tubman. Frederick Douglass . . . Rosa Parks . . . the local post-man, Maude Robinson, my son Kelly. Don't be ashamed. Call them out. Let those ancestors know that we're still fighting. Amen.

(Aina, 1997)

(SLR joins the circle of video travelers, picking up her candle, blowing it out when instructed, and repeating names as they do. The video fades to black.)

SLR the Scholar *(moving downstage center [DC]:)*
   The former bondswoman, Sethe in Toni Morrison's (1987) *Beloved,* knows what her traveler descendants will experience when she counsels her daughter:

> If a house burns down, it's gone, but the place—the picture of it—stays, and not just in my rememory, but out there in the world. . . . Someday you be walking down the road and you hear something or see something going on. So clear. And you think it's you thinking it up. A thought picture. But no. It's when you bump into a rememory that belongs to somebody else. . . . The picture is still there and what's more, if you go there—you who never was there—if you go there and stand in the place where it was, it will happen again; it will be there for you, waiting for you . . . nothing ever dies. (p. 36)

But, as Denver soon learns, sometimes even if you never go there, what was there, the past, will come to you, unexpectedly, when your defenses have relaxed, when your rational mind has taken a coffee break. Memory is an abiku, an obanje, an unruly child who torments its parents by being born and dying again and again; it keeps coming back, appearing to accept our inducements to lead a domesticated, ordered life, and then mysteriously disappearing yet again. Memory is an abiku, an obanje demanding that we confront the past (Davies, 1994; Ogunyemi, 1996; Okri, 1992). "To repress memory, 'to keep the past at bay,'" says literary critic Helene Moglen (1997) "is to divert it into the dark silences and crippling diversions of hysteria" (p. 206). On all sides of the Atlantic—in the United States and Canada, in Britain, in Ghana and Senegal—nations of hysterics, exhausted perhaps from doing battle with ghosts, are beginning to look at the past, yet are tempted to transmute it into palatable, comprehensible, theme park narratives that will take away the pain and shame of genocide, slavery, and unjust privilege.

Memory is also like grandmother's crazy quilt, made out of scraps of cloth that lie next to each other in no immediately apparent pattern. Thus, one bit of memory sometimes stimulates another scrap that logically does not belong with the first, and together they engender even more pieces whose coherence may promise an emotional, if not a factual, truth.

So what happens when, warmed by grandmother's crazy quilt, we begin to listen to ancestors? What happens, when the ancestral world complies with the desire of humans to remember but with a perverse logic, sends representatives whose stories we would rather forget? I found out in 1998, after I had returned home from a month-long tour of slave routes in Ghana and Benin, sponsored by Northwestern's Institute for Advanced Study and Research in the African Humanities in collaboration with the African Humanities Institute at the University of Ghana, Legon. Jet-lagged from the transatlantic flight home and stimulated by a performance of Leon Forrest's *Divine Days*, I remember my trip to Cape Coast Castle and then *(look at SLR's chair upstage right—(UR)—look back at audience, and then)* watch myself remembering *(moving into SLR's personal space)*, as I record in my journal: *(SLR reads from the journal.)*

> Temporarily located betwixt Ghana and Illinois time zones, I awaken in the early Chicago hours to read a chapter of Morrison's *Paradise.* I can't go back to sleep and thus decide to meditate. The grave of Philip KWAKU (Quaque) comes clearly into my vision. Why have you come to me, Philip? You who were the first African, Anglican missionary, trained in England and posted to the trading company at Cape Coast?
> At least you help my memory's eye/I to differentiate between Cape Coast

(Slide of Cape Coast Castle appears[5])

> and Elmina,

(Slide of Elmina appears)

> merged into one site of horror, the one castle-dungeon barely distinguishable from the other unless I force myself to linger over the memory and recall carefully. In remembering the site of your grave there at Cape Coast,

(Slide: Philip Quaque's grave)

> there in the blazing sun on the ground floor of the castle, I realize that at Cape Coast, one can at least see the sea, hear its roar from the ground floor.

(Slide: Cape Coast Castle with its cannons facing the sea)

> In contrast, when I picture myself standing at ground level in Elmina castle, all I can see are the various rooms built by the Portuguese and later, by the Dutch.

(Another slide of Elmina: This time of the Portuguese chapel, later converted into a slave market hall.)

> No glimpse of the sea beyond, only the confines that are Elmina. This recall of the sea at Cape Coast gives me a momentary lift: at least present in that place was some sense of nature, of something beyond man's control into which a captive could escape for a

brief comfort. But then later, I realize that my perspective is wrong: I am seeing from the vantage of the sailors and merchants, those free to walk about on the ground floor of the castle. No, I need to readjust my view to where it "belongs"

(Three slides of dungeons)

down below in that dungeon, where there were too many people, too little air, too much stench, too much fear and despair (2 March 1998).

SLR the Scholar *(now rises and moves slightly downstage)*

Years have passed, I have begun to research and write—in academic tones—about the experience of visiting Cape Coast and Elmina castle-dungeons. But like an abiku or obanje, you Philip KWAKU (Quaque) keep returning. Why have you captured my attention, demanding that I learn more about you? Let me then recite the history of this ancestor who has taken a seat at the memorial table.

SLR the Performer *(moving center towards Quaque's space)*

Along with two other boys, you left your Cape Coast home in 1754, at the age of 13, to sail to England and acquire a Western education. In 1766, now as the *Reverend* Philip KWAKU (Quaque), first *African,* Anglican priest, you returned as "Missionary, Catechist, and School Master" to the indigenous people on the Gold Coast" and as "Chaplain" to the English "gentlemen"—as the merchants and officers were called— and to the soldiers at Cape Coast Castle. For the next 50 years, you dutifully wrote letters to your sponsor, the Society for the Propagation of the Gospel in Foreign Parts, even though in all that time, the Society rarely wrote back. *(No longer the composed scholar, SLR quarrels):* Preaching the Christian gospel to *slave* traders, inside and out- side the castle fort! What was this Christian education supposed to do? Render believers more humane in their trade?

The story I want is the one of what happened under the ground, in the dungeons. I pore over your letters, searching for the clear assertion of repulsion or distress at what is transpiring below. I know the memory I want to have, so I continue to read, squinting at your handwriting preserved on microfilm. But along the way, I become seduced by the life your letters reveal. I devour them, read the missionary accounts of your mentor, the Reverend Thomas Thompson, and even turn to *Stories of a Strange Land and Fragments from the Notes of a Traveller,* authored by one Mrs. R. Lee who traveled with her young daughter to the Gold Coast in the mid-1820s. Even though she approaches the castle from the sea, and I have seen it only from land- side, we agree that it is impressive. She writes,

I had ample time to contemplate the lovely appearance this place presents, when viewed from the sea. The castle. . . is a large white stone building. . . . The native houses, interspersed with the more tasteful dwellings of European merchants, lie to the right; and everywhere the hills rise from the water's edge, covered with the richest and most luxuriant forest. (p. 302)

For me, such an incongruous, natural beauty that belies the manmade horrors. Somehow, I would have more easily understood an ugly physical site, but no, Cape

Coast, the even larger castle-dungeon of Elmina, clearly visible in the distance, and the mighty Atlantic ocean with its plumes of water hitting the rocks are beautiful.

(Moves stage left–[SL]–to Quaque's–[Q's] — table)

Did you notice the beauty of the landscape as you returned to the Gold Coast in February 1766 with your English wife, the former Catherine Blunt? *(Now sitting in Q's chair)* Lodged in Cape Coast Castle and beginning his ministry, the Reverend KWAKU (Quaque) wrote to his benefactors *(finding the letter on Q's table)* in September of that year, that given the recent death of the more religiously minded castle governor, he had little hopes for success, because the men are *(searching for the exact wording)* "all Scotch and Irish people, rank Presbyterians" (1766/1972); illiterate, they "defile" themselves by having multiple liaisons with local women. Further, the Caboceer or Fanti chief is ambivalent about Christian conversion and education.

SLR the Scholar *(Shifting in her seat, SLR is the Scholar once again)*
What emerges from these letters is a picture of the precariousness of life on the Gold Coast, given the formidable health challenges that many Europeans fought against—and lost—and given the political instability, violence, and ambition that the slave trade unleashed upon African populations. The terms "whites" and "blacks" are used, indicating that racial significations are operative, yet they are crosscut by more powerful ethnic, religious, and class identities: Thus, the reverend writes of rivalries that fracture the whites into Scotch and "rank Presbyterians" versus English and Anglican, English versus Dutch, officer versus soldier. The "blacks" include Ahantas who possess *(consulting letters again)* a "quiet temper, a ready mind and [are]easy to be governed" (Quaque, 1766/1972, p. 125), versus the Fantis who, though allied to the English, are nonetheless "strangers to civil discipline . . . enemies of public tranquillity" (Quaque, July 30, 1775/1972), and the even more menacing Asantes, who for more than 40 years waged wars against their neighbors in order to build an empire that extended from Kumasi down to the coast, some 140 miles away.

Literally related to both groups, negotiating both worlds are biracials or "mulattoes," as they were termed, who were acquiring the cultural capital to advance in the new world brought about by Portuguese "discovery" in 1471. Also evident is the fact that Philip KWAKU (Quaque) is operating in a world where racism does not yet exist. Europeans seem to treat him as an equal who is tolerated or disliked, because they find his religious commitment to saving *their* souls, irrelevant or annoying. He, in turn, condemns or looks down upon his countrymen—and he does use that term of collective identification—because of their wily refusal to convert to Christianity.

Two topics capture my attention, as I pursue my mission of remembering, namely, KWAKU (Quaque)'s comments about his wives—he married three times—and his relentless proselytizing. Though he never mentions any of his wives by name, it is clear that KWAKU (Quaque) felt closest to the English Catherine Blunt, for she, like him, was schooled in Christian doctrine and behavior. Thus, he writes that some six or seven months after their arrival, she is dying; *(consulting next document)* in March of 1767, he admits a "piercing loss," made even sharper in "these sullen and cruel climates," as he records for the Society's benefit Blunt's last testament of faith. Some two years later, he wrote informing the Society that he had married Blunt's former waiting maid in hopes of silencing those reproaching his widowerhood. By 1772, KWAKU (Quaque) had buried his second wife and married a third "girl" whom he first baptized. He says only, "She is very tractable and seems willing and mindful for the little time she has been with me, which is now two months and better," and in the next sentence states the numbers of people whom he has buried (March 8, 1772/1972).

(SLR the Scholar rises and moves center, hoping that this simple movement captures the attention of those whose interest may be wandering)

But even the brief references to these unnamed African women offer painful, yet telling insights. Painful because seemingly, no one thought these African women—who are my ancestors too—important enough to remember them by name. Telling because of the shift in Fanti life from a clan-focused, collective, or corporate identity to an individual perspective. "Wretchedly reduced" to debilitating illness and concerned about the confusion that rumors of war are engendering, KWAKU (Quaque) also complains in one of his last letters in 1811:

(Returning to Q's table for the relevant document)

> My own family, whom I have brought up . . . are plotting my ruin, particularly by raising up a malicious dispute with Mrs. KWAKU (Quaque) merely through jealousy and hatred and envy, and opposing every measure I take for the future benefit of my wife, as if a man has not power and authority to do and dispose of his own property as he pleaseth, without the controlling or interferring of anyone. (Priestley, 1967, p. 138).

SLR the Scholar *(puts the letter down and continues her lecture.)*

This dispute over inheritance is intimately related to the reverend's larger project of winning converts, for according to Fanti custom, descent and the resources accruing therefrom are traced through the mother. KWAKU (Quaque) was apparently related to Cudjo Caboceer, an important chief and brother to the King Amrah KoFI (Coffi) (Thompson, 1970, p. 34). Cudjo Caboceer served as chief linguist or negotiator between the British and the locals and had selected KWAKU (Quaque) for scholarship abroad. By custom, KWAKU (Quaque) was obligated to Cudjo Caboceer and expected to contribute to the collective wealth of his extended, maternal family. Yet, as his letter suggests, the reverend was planning to defy custom by passing along his inheritance to his wife.

KWAKU (Quaque) never ceased hoping that his "uncle" or head of the family, the Caboceer, would convert to Christianity, for if the chief did, many of the other relatives and townspeople would follow his example. In seeking to enlighten his countrymen, the reverend was engaged in an elaborate dance in which each party in this cultural "contact zone" of shifting and uneven power relations (Pratt, 1992, pp. 6–7) acquiesced, resisted, masked, and tested the resolve of the other. *(Here SLR uses appropriate hand gestures to emphasize her point about the subtle negotiations that occurred. These gestures will change to resemble a waltz in the story that follows.)* Let me illustrate my point with a story about events over a three-week period in August 1767.

SLR the Performer *(taking up a position SL, near Q's pulpit)*

One Sunday morning, Reverend KWAKU (Quaque) prepares for service in the castle *(moves forward SL 2 steps as in an assertion)* but is summarily ordered to remove all the sacred items *(backs up 2 steps)*. Disappointed but not defeated, *(moving forward)* he does so and then goes to town *(forward again)* where he casts his "lot" with "my own countrymen who behaved laudably and very decent, much beyond my expectation: although attended w/ a little inconveniency of noised and clamour." (Quaque, 1767/1972). No longer fluent in Fanti—or in the customary modes of social interaction—KWAKU (Quaque) explains the sacrament of baptism as best he can, promising to send for Mr. Frederick Adoy, who will serve as his translator.

(Mr. Adoy comes through the auditorium and waits DSL of Q's pulpit. SLR is now standing SR of the pulpit.)

SLR the Performer continues:

The next week, Mr. Adoy comes from his village, and together they preach the word of God to some 25 townspeople. On the following day *(SLR moves sideways, SR)* two elders arrive to thank him and to assert that now that he has made them Christians by reading and showing them the word of God or NYANCUMPONG (Yancumpong), he should give them something to drink. *(Two steps back)* KWAKU (Quaque) gives them a flask of liquor, because as he reports to his superiors, he reasoned that through such a device, he will lead them to God. But when next *(moving forward on a diagonal)* he tries to hold service with the townspeople, they respond that they are involved in the critical duties of making sacrifices *(back again 2 steps!)* to restore the health of sick neighbors. The following Sunday, Reverend KWAKU (Quaque), with Mr. Adoy as his translator, begins his service before 20 congregants

(SLR the Performer moves to Q's pulpit, opens the Bible, and assuming Q's role, motions for Mr. Adoy to take his position DSR. But Mr. Adoy remains SL)

Adoy:
Excuse me, sir, but Mr. Adusain says liquor will aid their ability to follow your teachings.

Quaque:
But—Mr. Adoy, please translate *(Q gestures again for him to take up his position. Mr. Adoy complies, moving DSR.)*

Quaque and Adoy:
You know that my predecessor Reverend Thompson always preached that we must take care not to drink immoderately of spiritual liquor. *(Q pauses, waiting for the translation and their response. Sensing their restiveness, he adds)*. I am a "young fellow, unexperienced in Life, *(pause)* surrounded with many difficulties, [and] temptations to encounter in this wicked and degenerate land," (Quaque, 1767/1972). *(Mr. Adoy stops after "temptations." Adoy and Reverend KWAKU (Quaque) exchange glances.)* *(Q repeats his words)* . . . wicked and degenerate land. But, *(pause)* if you will remain silent *(pause, pleading with congregants)* until the service is over, then we can partake, *(pause)*in friendship.

(Still as Quaque, SLR the Performer moves away from the pulpit and sits at Q's table)

SLR the Performer

I admit, most Venerable and Worthy Benefactors, I hoped in this way to win these unthinking people over to our form.

(Switching back into her Scholar mode, SLR rises)

SLR the Scholar

In citing the Reverend Thompson as his authority for initially resisting and then acceding to their expectations, KWAKU (Quaque) was deploying the local custom of demonstrating respect for one's elders. Indeed, the Reverend Thompson, who was the Society's first missionary to the Gold Coast, had written of similar resistance in his *An Account of Two Missionary Voyages* (1937), for not only did the Fanti locals comment upon the immorality of the Christians in their midst (p. 36), but they are also reported as saying in perhaps yet another dance of assertion, masked deference, and reassertion:

> *(Using forward dance step again)* The Christian religion is white man's fashion. White men know best, *(moving back)* but *(moving forward and firmly taking a position)* black man follow black man's fashion. (Thompson, 1937, p. 68)

And so, for the next 49 years, KWAKU (Quaque) and the local people danced in this way, with a small number of "thinking" people converting to Anglicanism. Sometimes as many as seventeen, and sometimes as few as two mulatto boys and girls attended his school, held in his castle rooms.

But, looking at pictures of the castle, replaying the physical landscape in my mind's eye, *(glancing towards Q's space)* I wonder: What did you do when a new convoy of captives, weary from trekking hundreds of miles, were finally brought through the castle gates? From the "gentlemen's" quarters above, did you hear the men led into the underground dungeons? Did you see the shackled women herded across the courtyard to the pens near what would become the gate of no return? Did you reach for your Bible then?

(Addressing her audience directly, SLR the Scholar says)

SLR the Scholar

In the entire fifty years of corresponding with the Society, Philip KWAKU (Quaque) seems to have made only two explicit comments on slavery. In February 1876 he reports first on an uprising that occurred on a Dutch ship about to set sail for the Americas. About 150 captives overpowered the ship's crew, in the captain's absence. KWAKU (Quaque) continues: *(SLR sits at Q's table and reads)*

> But the most dreadful circumstance of all is that after having laid their scheme with subtlety and art, and decoying as many as their countrymen who came far and near to plunder on board and near the ship, and also some white sailors from an English ship in hopes of relieving them, were all indiscriminately blown up to upwards of three or four hundred souls. This revengeful but very rash proceeding we are made to understand to be entirely owing to the Captain's brutish behavior, who did not allow even his own sailors, much more the slaves, a sufficient maintenance to support nature. If this is really the case, can we but help figuring to ourselves the true picture of inhumanity those unhappy creatures suffer in their miserable state of bondage, under the different degrees of austere masters they unfortunately fall in with, in the West Indies? (Priestley, 1967, p. 133)

Interesting, that though KWAKU (Quaque) documents the captives' ingenuity, he attributes the rebellion to the captain's negligent behavior rather than to any basic, human drive for personal autonomy.

Immediately following these sentences, KWAKU (Quaque) mentions a revolt that domestic, castle slaves carried out in November of that same year. Now, *(crossing SR out of Q's space)* I should interject here that in my tours of Cape Coast and Elmina castles, guides say virtually nothing about castle slaves; they tend to deploy a passive voice in which there are victims subjected to unidentified agents. But walking through these large, stone fortifications and catapulting myself back into the past, I can not help but wonder: Who fed, cleaned up, or doctored those captives destined for international markets? How did these people interact with locals, what did they tell locals about events that transpired inside the castle-dungeons? Written histories, such as Lawrence's (1964) *Trade Castles and Forts of West Africa*, provide some of the answers; undoubtedly, proverbs, songs and other documents in indigenous languages provide others. Retaining men, women, and children, all the European trading companies used castle slaves to perform skilled, artisanal, and agricultural tasks, domestic chores such as laundering and cooking, and unskilled labor such as portering. They, like all the inhabitants of the castle or the smaller forts, were compensated for their work in goods that could be bartered in the market; presumably, their "pay" was sufficient only to keep them alive, but through careful husbandry, these slaves might amass a small surplus. They could not be sold into the transatlantic trade, unless they had committed serious crimes (Priestley, 1967, p. 134, footnote 76; Lawrence, 1964, pp. 49–50).

Well, Philip KWAKU (Quaque) writes that on November 14, all these slaves deserted their posts—a sort of *Day of Absence!* Excuse me, but I can't help but think of Douglas Turner Ward's 1960s comedy, in which all the black folks desert a small, Southern town, leaving their white employers to figure out how to empty the trash and to plead for the return of their "nigras" (1966). Except this day lasted a month, and though KWAKU (Quaque) says that no one has yet understood "the real cause of their desertion," he posits—but does not elaborate upon—an analogy between their complaints and the sufferings of the Biblical children of Israel under Egyptian pharaohs.

(SLR the Scholar moves further upstage as though headed for the security of her books)

SLR the Scholar

I attempt an explanation of why the reverend fails to recognize those enslaved beneath his feet as his brothers and sisters in Christ: They weren't, in fact, Christians. Besides, as his counterpart, the former slave and Dutch-educated Reverend Jacobus Capitein had argued, freedom is constituted by spiritual apprehension, not physical status. "Now the Lord is the Spirit, and where the Spirit of the Lord is, there is freedom" (2 Cor 3:17; Capitein, 2001, pp.105–107; Prah, 1989, pp. 59–61). But this line of reasoning feels like sophistry; it does little to assuage KWAKU's (Quaque) periodically demanding, *abiku* resonance in my memory. Sylvia Wynter's (1992) theory of the science of the human, articulated both in dense, analytical terms and in an affective, folk language provides a stronger answer. She argues that our bioculturally programmed, altruism-inducing mechanism enables us to recognize an affinity and obligation not to "human beings" but to a particular mode of the human. Ideologically blind to the partial character of this human whom we think of as universal, we tolerate all kinds of inhumane treatment of those who are defined as outside (Wynter, 1992, pp. 237–250).

> Within the clan, everything.
> Outside the clan, nothing.
> Family have, you have! Outside the family, tough!
> Lineage fight lineage like the Dutch fight the British. The British fight the Prussia.

> (Wynter, 1963/rev.1983 p. 62)

says one of Wynter's dramatic characters in explaining the African origins of the Jonkonnu mask in Jamaica.

But as one descends into the bowels of the earth, into the small pens in which hundreds of captives were housed, this intellectual understanding of how constructions of identity necessitate an excluded other is hard to maintain. My body overrides historical particulars to empathize with the captives. Later in remembering those bodily responses, I am tempted to dismiss Philip's life work, his faith and perseverance in the face of educating so few students and enduring the scorn or indifference of those to whom he was supposed to minister. *(Moving USR to settle in her chair)*

Yet, once you turn down the chatter of daily events and begin to pay real attention to grandmother's crazy quilt, you also discover that the ancestors send a variety of messages in order to disturb your arrogance. First were the newspaper accounts of enslaved boys in the Sudan. Then, Philip KWAKU (Quaque), I suspect, "sent" graduate student Mark West with an even more direct challenge. Mark came with his performance studies piece about more than one million young Indian and Nepalese girls who are presently captives in brothels in South Asia (West, 2003). Even without his use of quotations from Frederick Douglass and Toni Morrison's *Beloved,* the ancestors' message was clear: How does your remembrance of a past catastrophe translate into action against this present disaster? Or, are you/we content to view slavery as a past event which we mourn and about which we can congratulate ourselves for the distance traveled away from that inhumanity?

Perhaps Philip KWAKU (Quaque), you have come to this memorial event to issue a challenge. Perhaps you have come to demand of me and others a "productive remembering" that does not impose our current distress on the historical specificities of the past. A both/and remembering that uses empathy as one avenue to knowledge of and connection to the past and at the same time, acknowledges the differences that will always keep that past beyond our desiring grasp. A difficult, both/and memory of continuity and disruption that in our acts of re-membering *(using a gesture that suggests a putting back together)* challenges us to act differently, to interrogate and reconfigure our present (Simon, 2000, pp. 118–123; Simon, et al., 2000, pp. 4–8).

(SLR the Scholar closes her book and looks SL towards Q's space)
I take one, small step in the direction of your challenge, Philip KWAKU (Quaque).

(SLR picks up the candle, rises and begins to move SL)
Medaase, thank you, my ancestor.

(SLR exits, SL. As she begins to exit:)

III. L'ENVOI (FAREWELL MUSIC FOR THE ANCESTORS)

(Music: "Nature Boy" from Unforgettable *[Nat King Cole, 2000])*

There was a boy, . . .
A little shy and sad of eye
But very wise was he . . .
A magic day he passed my way,
And while we spoke of many things—
This he said to me:
The greatest thing you'll ever learn
Is just to love and be loved in return.

SLR the Performer remembers to herself

This song was one of Leon Forrest's favorites. The orchestral arrangement is lush, yet Nat King Cole's delivery sounds effortless, his message, simple but profound. Like Cole, Leon had a gentle, seemingly unassuming manner in interacting with people. His writing was another matter: voluble, pulsating, attuned to and unflinching in representing the hidden desires, foibles, triumphs, and sometimes sad jokes in people's lives. His was a fierce love affair with life. May I learn from Cole and Forrest to explore the apparent contradiction, to temper my scrutiny with humility, to remain open to magic.

(Music: "So Sa So (Eleggua)" from Orishas *[Afro-Cuban] [Sintesis, 1997])*

SLR the Performer continues

This song comes from Yoruba beliefs as they were adapted to the harsh conditions of slavery in Cuba. Hopefully, Esu has enjoyed our time together and departs happily. Certainly, we will meet again—and again—at the crossroads. Oriented by the memory of what I have learned from these life travels, when I meet you as Esu, Eleggua, or High John the Conqueror, may I respond to your challenges with grace. Ase. Amen.

NOTES

1. See such Forrest (1994) essays as "In the Light of the Likeness—Transformed," "Souls in Motion," "Michael's Mandate," or "A Solo Long-Song: for Lady Day."

2. Ghanaians—or at the least the state—share in this desire to rewrite history. Emancipation Day ceremonies, celebrated on the African continent—in Ghana—for the first time in 1998 included the transportation of the remains of two Africans enslaved in the Americas back through Cape Castle for final interment in Assin Manso.

3. See Aidoo's (1970) play *Anowa* where a lineage-less person is a synonymous term for slave. Frederick Cooper, Thomas C. Holt, Rebecca J. Scott (2000), and Orlando Patterson (1982) have argued that for enslaved Africans, freedom was conceptualized less as the absence of bondage and more as grounding in a familial network.

4. There is an absence of consensus as to whether these structures do indeed memorialize slavery. See Bruner (1996) and Richards (in press).

5. Readers may want to consult the visual archive compiled by Handler and Tuite (n.d.) at http://hitchcock.itc.virginia.edu/Slavery

REFERENCES

Aidoo, A. A. (1970). *Anowa* [Script]. London: Longman Drumbeat.

Aina, S. (1997). *Through the door of no return* [Videotape]. Washington, DC: Mypheduh Films.

Antze, P., & Lambek, M. (Eds.). (1996). *Tense past: Cultural essays in trauma and memory*. New York: Routledge.

Barnwell, Y. (1993). We are. [Recorded by Sweet Honey in the Rock]. On *Sacred ground* [Compact disk]. Redway, CA: Earthbeat! Records. (1995).

Bartels, F. L. (1955). Philip Quaque, 1741–1816. *Transactions of the Gold Coast and Togoland Historical Society, 1*(5), 153–177.

Braun, N. K. Slides of Elmina and Cape Coast Castles.

Britzman, D. P. (2000). If the story cannot end: Deferred action, ambivalence, and difficult knowledge. In R. I. Simon, S. Rosenberg, & C. Eppert (Eds.), *Between hope and despair: Pedagogy and the remembrance of historical trauma* (pp. 27–57). Lanham, MD: Rowman & Littlefield.

Bruner, E. M. (1996).Tourism in Ghana: The representation of slavery and the return of the black diaspora. *American Anthropologist 98*(2), 290–304.

Brown, C. (1996). Ghana slave dungeon document: St. Paul trip to Ghana. [Videotape]. Brooklyn: Trans-Atlantic Productions.

Capitein, J. (2001). *The agony of Asar: A thesis on slavery by the former slave, Jacobus Elisa Johannes Capitein, 1717–1747* (G. Parker, Trans.). Princeton, NJ: Markus Wiener.

Cole, N. K. (2000). Nature boy. On *Unforgettable* [Compact disk]. Los Angeles: Capitol Records.

Cooper, F., Holt, T., & Scott, R. (2000). Beyond slavery: Explorations of race, labor, and citizenship in postemancipation societies. Chapel Hill: University of North Carolina Press.

Davies, C. B. (1994). *Black women, writing and identity: Migrations of the subject*. New York: Routledge.

Forrest, L. (1992). *Divine days*. New York: W.W. Norton & Company.

Forrest, L. (1994). *The furious voice for freedom: Essays on life*. Wakefield, RI: Asphodel Press.

Gershwin, G., Gershwin, I., & Heyward, D. (1935). *Summertime*. Los Angeles: Warner Chappell Music.

The great homecoming [Videotape]. (1998). Accra, Ghana: Visionlink Productions.

Grupo Ofa. (2000). Exu. On *Odum orim, festa da musica* [Compact disk]. Salvador, Brazil: Geleia Geral–Warner Music Brasil.

Handler, J. S., & Tuite, M. L., Jr. (n.d.). *The Atlantic slave trade and slave life in the Americas: A visual record*. Retrieved April 27, 2004, from http://hitchcock.itc.virginia.edu/Slavery

Iabolish (the anti-slavery portal). http://www.iabolish.com

Jackson, M. (1995). Motherless child. On *The best of Mahalia Jackson* [Compact disk]. New York: Sony Music Entertainment.

Lawrence, A. W. (1964). *Trade castles and forts of West Africa*. Palo Alto, CA: Stanford University Press.

Lee, Mrs. R. (former Mrs. Edward T. Bowdich). (n.d.). *Cape Coast Castle; or, the adventures of Sir Thomas Fitzosborne among the people of Fanti*. London: Griffith and Farran.

Lee, Mrs. R. (former Mrs. Edward T. Bowdich). (1835). *Stories of strange lands; and fragments from the notes of a traveler*. London: Edward Moxon.

Moglen, H. (1997). Redeeming history: Toni Morrison's *Beloved*. In E. Abel, B. Christian, & H. Moglen (Eds.), *Female subjects in black and white: Race, psychoanalysis, feminism* (pp. 201–220). Berkeley: University of California Press.

Morrison, T. (1987). *Beloved*. New York: New American Library.

Okri, B. (1992). *The famished road*. New York: Doubleday.

Ogunyemi, C. O. (1996). *African wo/man palava: the Nigerian novel by women*. Chicago: University of Chicago Press.

Patterson, O. (1982). *Slavery and social death: A comparative study*. Cambridge, MA: Harvard University Press.

Pratt, M. L. (1992). *Imperial eyes: Travel writing and transculturation*. New York: Routledge.

Priestley, M. (1967). Philip Quaque. In P. Curtin (Ed.), *Africa remembered: Narratives of West Africans from the era of the slave trade* (pp. 99–139). Madison: University of Wisconsin Press.

Prah, K. K. (1989). *Jacobus Eliza Johannes Capitein, 1717–1747: A critical study of an eighteenth century African*. Braamfontein, South Africa: Skotaville.

Quaque, P. (1972). Letters of Philip Quaque 1766–1811 [Microfilm]. Wakefield: EP Group, Microform Division.

Richards, S. L. (in press). What is to be remembered? Tourism to Ghana's slave castle-dungeons. *Theatre Journal*.

Roach, J. (1995). Culture and performance in the circum-Atlantic world. In A. Parker & E. Kosofsky Sedgwick (Eds.), *Performativity and performance* (pp. 45–63). New York: Routledge.

Roach, J. (1996). *Cities of the dead: Circum-Atlantic performance.* New York: Columbia University Press.

Simon, R. I. (2000). The paradoxical practice of zakhor: Memories of "what has never been my fault or my deed." In R. I. Simon, S. Rosenberg, & C. Eppert (Eds.), *Between hope and despair: Pedagogy and the representation of historical trauma* (pp. 9–25). Lanham, MD: Rowman & Littlefield.

Simon, R. I., Rosenberg, S., & Eppert, C. (2000). Introduction: Between hope and despair: The pedagogical encounter of historical remembrance. "In R. I. Simon, S. Rosenberg, & C. Eppert (Eds.")*, Between hope and despair: Pedagogy and the representation of historical trauma* (pp. 1–8). Lanham, MD: Rowman & Littlefield.

Sintesis. (1997). So sa so (eleggua). On *Orishas* [Compact disk]. Burbank, CA: Milan Music Entertainment.

Thompson, T. (1937). *An account of two missionary voyages.* London: Society for Promoting Christian Knowledge.

Walcott, D. (1970). *Dream on Monkey Mountain and other plays.* New York: Farrar, Straus & Giroux.

Ward, D. T. (1966). *Happy ending and day of absence: Two plays.* New York: Dramatists Play Service.

West, M. (2003, March 15). Go to the deep pine woods: Trafficking, war, and broken-down ethnography in South Asia [Performance]. Mussetter-Struble Theater, Northwestern University, Evanston, Illinois.

Wynter, S. (1992). Rethinking "aesthetics": Notes toward a deciphering practice. In M. Cham (Ed.), *Ex-iles, Essays on Caribbean cinema* (pp. 237–279). Trenton, NJ: Africa World Press.

Wynter, S. (1983, March 6). Maskarade. Revised unpublished manuscript. (Original version written 1963)

28

The Polemics and Potential of Theatre Studies and Performance[1]

JILL DOLAN

This essay offers a brief history of the relationship between theatre studies and performance studies, and describes the trajectory of the theory/practice debate within both fields. My aim is pedagogical, in that I want to help students and practitioners of the field recall its theoretical past, and pragmatic, in that I'm concerned with how we use theatre and performance studies to teach students and ourselves productive ways to be what I like to call "citizen/scholar/artists" (Becker, 2000). Since my commitment is to the politics of performance and its scholarship, I'm most concerned with how we can think about teaching, creating, and theorizing performance as a public intellectual practice with the potential to intervene in restrictive or oppressive representations of human capabilities. In making this argument, I will trace the ways in which identity politics, the first theoretically inflected project to reject the more empiricist bent of the field, began to transform theatre studies from a more conventional academic pursuit to one

with radical possibilities. I'll go on to describe the burgeoning of theatre and performance studies as interdisciplinary gold mines for scholars interested in the workings of culture; launch an argument about "teaching the conflicts" through performance; and then end with an exhortation for theatre and performance scholars and practitioners to return to a capaciously humanist, utopian performative approach to our mutual work.

IDENTITY POLITICS AND ITS INFLUENCE ON THEATRE STUDIES

In the last 20 or so years, the objectivity and empiricism of traditional theatre departments have been challenged mostly on the basis of identity politics, an approach to the social in which categories like gender, race and ethnicity, class, sexuality, and ability offered primary lenses through which to view its workings. Identity politics as methodological tools rooted themselves in the critical and theoretical traditions of feminism, queer studies, critical race studies, and most recently disability studies, all of which prompted ideological adjustments with enormous impact on the field. In particular, feminism's application to theatre has insured that universal "man" can no longer be presumed as the objective or "real" subject of any performance, contemporary or historical. Along with feminism, critical race studies has had perhaps the largest, most visible influence, so that racial and ethnic categories, as well as gender, can no longer be elided responsibly, or located purely in instances of cultural impersonation like minstrelsy and black-face that absented people of color as subjects even while they derided them as objects of an imperialist white gaze. Margaret Wilkerson (1991), in an article that stresses the changing demography of American theatre, reminds theatre scholars that they will have to continue to rethink the Eurocentric history of their theory and practice if theatre programs are to succeed further into the twenty-first century. Wilkerson says, "Theatre provides an opportunity for a community to come together and reflect on itself . . . It is not only the mirror through which a society can reflect upon itself—it also helps to shape the perceptions of that culture through the power of its imaging" (p. 239; see also Elam & Alexander, 2002; Hatch & Hill, 2003; Hatch & Shine, 1996; Uno & Burns, 2002). Wilkerson's aspiration for theatre requires that the discipline, and the scholars who teach it, look elsewhere than the Eurocentric canon for knowledge.

James Hatch (1989) offers a similar reminder of the continuing importance of criticizing racial and cultural exclusions in the contents and methods of theatre studies. Hatch excoriates theatre programs for continuing to overlook African influences in theatre history and African-American work in contemporary theatre. He suggests, "The roots of the problem are woven inextricably into America's social history and perpetuated by graduate programs in theatre departments. This continuing apartheid in an era when our scholars show increasing sophistication in national and multiethnic theatre history is unfair to students—and dishonest" (p. 149). Hatch and Wilkerson propose using knowledge gained from identity politics to infuse theatre studies' practices and methods with difference. Wilkerson says, "We can no longer teach or even study theatre as we have in the past. Those of us in theatre production programs will find ourselves increasingly marginalized or isolated in our institutions if we do not include in very fundamental ways the new population (students of color and others) constituting our student bodies. . . . The path-breaking scholarship in [other] fields is revolutionizing the ways in which we see ourselves and the places where we look for knowledge" (1991, p. 240).

Despite their location in academic institutions that sometimes militate against such thinking, university theatres, for example, could respond to Wilkerson's and Hatch's admonishments by offering a forum for embodying and enacting new communities of performers and spectators and by using their laboratories to enact the possibilities of difference. By doing so, they could become sites for more radical interventionist work. University theatres are spaces that might productively be given over to theories and practices of identity in all its complex intersectional variety, and studies of performance in all its aspects, rather than protected as museums to house imitations of the canonical white masterpieces of dramatic literature. Yet such moves remain surprisingly difficult. Panels at many professional conferences continue to address the unequal or misaligned representations of race and gender in the industry, in the profession, and in theatre departments, and panelists and participants continue to bemoan the lack of opportunities on their campuses for production work that includes attention to minoritarian experience. Even when the curriculum has improved attention to new ways of thinking about social identity in performance—through the addition of courses on women in theatre, gays and lesbians in theatre, people of color in theatre—and to critical approaches to the experience reified in canonical drama, production programs tend to lag far behind. Sometimes, these imbalances stem from the separation between theory and practice in many theatre and performance studies departments; sometimes, the excessively conventional seasons our departments offer come from an unimaginative notion of what audiences want to see and the kinds of theatre they're willing to attend. These shopworn ideas about spectatorship need to be overhauled to reinvigorate how our production seasons speak to our students' needs and those of the communities in which we work.

As Joseph Roach (1992) reiterates, after Raymond Williams, "The convergence of material productions with signifying systems inheres in the fundamental nature of theatrical performance" (p. 11). Because of such a productive convergence, theatrical performance offers a temporary and usefully ephemeral site at which to think through various important questions about the representation not only of individual identities but of social relations within, across and among identity categories, and across communities and cultures. For instance, questions of the signifying body that determine how we read what bodies mean, by considering them as "signs" of meaning, are readily available by looking at actors' gestures and their relationships to each other in the physical space of the stage. Questions of how bodies in space exemplify social relations can be studied in the embodiment of texts as performance, and in a director's choices to position actors around a set or within an empty space. Because performance demonstrates the ways in which any reading is always multiple, and illustrates the undecidability of visual as

well as written meanings, it provides a way of seeing identity as complex, as crossed with difference, and never as the static, innate, unchangeable thing it's described to be in other venues of social life. Performance allows an investigation of the materiality of the corporeal, since the presence of bodies requires direct and present engagement. Such questions can be brought to bear in the temporary communities that theatre-producing and theatre-going construct. Theatre scholars might productively borrow the language of science to explain their goals and methods. As Wilkerson has remarked, research universities understand the workings of "laboratories."[2] Theatre studies might use the analogy, even while it discards its positivist trappings.

PERFORMATIVITY, PERFORMANCE STUDIES, AND THEATRE STUDIES: A PERSONAL GENEALOGY

The importation of identity politics to the academy, and their inflection with postmodern understandings of culture that privilege undecidability rather than truth, gave rise to theories that described identity as malleable and social, superficial and constructed, rather than innate and fixed. Theorists like Judith Butler described identity as performed, which gave rise to new notions of "performativity" as a way to talk about gender and sexuality, especially, as functions of surface rather than depth (Butler, 1990; see also Austin, 1962). The new language of performativity propelled performance to new visibility in academic discourse and participated in the project of unsettling white hegemony in the academy and in theatre studies. But the theorists who used the metaphor of performance to talk about identity itself were mostly interested in the performance of identity constructions in everyday life, rather than in performance *qua* performance. As a result, feminist, queer, and critical race theorists seem to borrow the language of theatre without giving serious consideration to the artifacts that we prize in our study—the richness of performance itself.

The general introduction to Janelle Reinelt and Joseph Roach's edited volume, *Critical Theory and Performance* (1992), is insightful about the peculiar status of theatre studies as a discipline; performance scholarship, the editors note, has always crossed institutional disciplinary lines. Yet theatre scholarship belongs to a particular tradition,[3] one that Reinelt and Roach recall has had a long history of theoretical speculation, now bolstered by the interest in critical theory across the academy. "Ironically," Reinelt and Roach write,

> the history of the discipline of theatre studies is one of fighting for autonomy from English and Speech departments, insisting on a kind of separation from other areas of study. It was necessary, politically necessary, to claim this distinctiveness, even at the expense of becoming somewhat insular and hermetic— a result that unfortunately became true of many departments of theatre. Now, however, it is even more necessary to recognize and insist on the interdependency of a related series of disciplines and also on the role of performance in the production of culture in its widest sense. (Reinelt & Roach, p. 5; see also Bottoms, 2003; Jackson, 2004)

The field of performance studies has come to encompass this broader approach to cultural production.

While theatre studies traces its genealogy through speech departments that once focused on the oral interpretation of literature, as well as English departments that focus on dramatic literature, performance studies has also branched off from several different genres of academic study. One prevalent form of performance studies incurs an equal debt to the transformation of texts from page to stage in speech departments, while another grounds itself in methods and theory borrowed from literary criticism, folklore, social science, and the study of popular culture and performance in

everyday life. The Department of Performance Studies at New York University has perhaps been the primary proponent of this latter, interdisciplinary, social sciences–based branch of the field, and Richard Schechner, an experimental theatre director working actively since the 60s, and a long-standing faculty member in NYU's performance studies department, historically has been one of its preeminent spokespeople. At a conference of the Association for Theatre in Higher Education (ATHE) in the mid-1990s, and in a "Comment" in *The Drama Review* (TDR) he published shortly after, Schechner argued that professional theatre training programs sell "snake oil" to students, and that they should be dismantled so that theatre can return to the humanities (and social sciences) through performance studies, in all its cultural variety (see Schechner, 1992, 1995).[4] Essentially, he was arguing that so-called "professional theatre training programs," or any program that purports to prepare young students for a theatre industry in which they can hardly make a living, is offering a corrupt sense of possibility, and training undergraduates for a future that doesn't exist.

Schechner's comments, and a slowly building consensus among some scholars in the professional organizations that theatre studies could well be amplified by a broader attention to performance, led to various public debates about the relationship between the two fields. That debate saw the establishment of a performance studies focus group in ATHE, which eventually led to the formation of Performance Studies international (PSi) as a freestanding professional organization. In addition, performance studies divisions or subgroups have been established in the National Communications Association and in the American Studies Association, and the field has come to influence more and more the direction of work presented in the relatively august Drama Division of the Modern Languages Association. This infiltration of the professional organizations, which provide important venues for visionary work and its distribution, has had a large impact on the visibility of performance studies in theatre departments around the country, and has changed the status of "drama" as a genre study in English departments.

I was a graduate student at New York University just after it had converted its graduate drama department into the Department of Performance Studies in 1981. I originally returned to grad school because I wanted a supportive intellectual context in which to think about feminist theatre criticism. I had an activist artistic agenda that the feminist political community in which I then lived in Boston wouldn't support, so I decided to see how the academy might facilitate and nourish my thinking. As I learned more about performance studies, it appeared that although I hardly knew what I was getting into, I'd made the right choice. In performance studies, I'd landed in a program that was proud of its resistance to traditional modes of knowledge, and that wanted to give students the tools to produce knowledge differently, through popular culture studies, interculturalism, and folklore. Performance Studies was nonconventional enough to enable feminism to carve out a niche there, which was important to my own nascent interest in feminist criticism and theory.[5] The notion of performance could accommodate the marginalized productions of women's theatre. It offered methods through which to account for women creating texts of their bodies and their lives, whether as mimes in front of Greek theatres, or in upper-middle-class salons. A performance paradigm helped analyze these women's rejection of public architecture, which was in any case out of their reach, to create new meanings in private spaces in which they wielded some power.

As Dwight Conquergood (1991) notes, "Particularly for poor and marginalized people denied access to middle-class 'public' forums, cultural performance becomes the venue for 'public discussion' of vital issues

central to their communities, as well as an arena for gaining visibility and staging their identity" (p. 187). Performance not only broadened what I could study, but it helped me understand how feminism could profit from thinking through performance as an embodied relationship to history and to power. The notion of performance could let me find Dick Hebdige's book *Subculture: The Meanings of Style* (1979), and use it to theorize about lesbian erotics and style as a performance of resistance. I charted my own itinerary through my own desires and, through performance studies, helped establish for myself an embodied relationship to poststructuralist theory, which was just beginning to be applied in feminism.

Through poststructuralism, I escaped from the essentialisms of some forms of feminism that promoted strict and rather conservative understandings of gender, race, and sexuality as innate; I moved outside the hegemony of authorship into an understanding of performance and theatre as "readerly" texts open to multiple interpretations, which I found very helpful politically in making my arguments; and I freed myself from searching for "true" politics to assert against the dominant, hegemonic "truths" from which I thought theatre and performance could dissent. Although I later came to reassert some of the values that poststructuralist criticism and theory taught me to suspect (such as the usefulness of metaphysics and notions of truth), when I first applied poststructuralist ideas to my research on feminist performance, I found that they revolutionized my thinking in performance studies.

When I confronted a class of students as a first-time teacher in the School of Drama at the University of Washington in 1987, I had to explain my training in performance studies, and entice students to go with me as we revised the frame of reference through which to look at theatre. My performance studies education let me persuade them that the plays we read extended well outside the classroom, that they were artifacts of culture (what James Clifford calls "survivals") that needed to be engaged, studied, and contested to figure out what they might tell us about how we live, but more importantly, how we might live (Clifford, 1993, p. 68). I encouraged students to stage cross-gendered versions of scenes from the canon in my play analysis class. We delighted in the fact that gender was a performative practice (although we didn't have that language then) that was part of our performances. Feminism brought me to an embodied approach to learning for which performance offered a strategy. Using performance in the classroom became a different epistemology, a way of knowing not just our selves, but also the world. Performance studies refused to privilege the text, and connected theatre and performance as what Schechner calls "restored behavior" (Schechner, 1985; see also Carlson, 1996; Schechner, 1988). These ideas invigorated my interventions into a more traditional theatre studies curriculum, and the classroom became a new site of my feminist activism around gender and representation.

USING PERFORMANCE STUDIES TO REINVIGORATE THEATRE STUDIES AND PRODUCTION PROGRAMS

I needed a politicized performance paradigm to generate ways of looking at theatre that aren't gilded with the rhetoric of highbrow culture, and with what Lawrence Levine (1998) calls its missionary attitude toward saving or guarding itself against an "uncivilized" public. I wanted to help find rationales for theatre studies and performance in the academy and in culture that aren't about how they rescue people from degeneracy, but that clearly and forcefully articulate tools for cultural intervention, ways of engaging and thinking about social relations as we know them and as they could be. This remains a continuing struggle for several reasons: The

ways in which theatre is viewed in the academy too often restrict it to something precious, or expensive, or irrelevant; the divide between theory and practice in our departments tends to work against a more broad-based commitment to performance as a public cultural practice; and American culture still predominantly views theatre as "entertainment," rather than as an important site of social understanding and political coalition-building.

For example, when I chaired the Department of Theatre and Drama at the University of Wisconsin–Madison in the mid-1990s, bemused administrators tolerated my impassioned explanations of our work in theatre studies, but never appeared to take our department seriously. Our productions seemed pale imitations of work they hoped to see in New York, the real center of what they understood as theatre production.[6] Our scholarship seemed odd in its interdisciplinarity; I recall the Dean of Graduate Studies, as I was trying to impress upon him the connections theatre studies has made with a number of different fields, asking why we needed to work in a theatre department. As Marvin Carlson (1992) has written, we have to be able to "say clearly what distinguishes theatre history from [other histories]," or the "university administrators, legislators, or funding agencies . . . may . . . begin to wonder why our activity cannot be as easily taken care of by one or several of these other disciplines" (p. 92). The very interdisciplinarity that's invigorating the field could endanger it within universities and colleges always looking to streamline their administrative and academic structures.

At the City University of New York Graduate Center, where I chaired the PhD program in the late 1990s, I was impressed that, this being New York, people presumed they knew what it was we did in the Theatre Program. They still couldn't quite grasp that ours was a solely academic study of theatre, and turned to us occasionally for cheap entertainments. One year Carlson, my colleague at

CUNY, was irate during the student demon-strations against the budget cuts when he was asked if the Program could put together some sketches, or something dramatic that might be effective on the streets. I had mixed responses to this request. On the one hand, I agreed with Carlson that we have to educate our institu-tional colleagues against the notion that our labor is simply available to throw together skits. On the other hand, following more of a perfor-mance studies itinerary through this anecdote, I do think it would have been interesting to encourage our students and faculty to work with the protesters to integrate performance into their activist strategies. For the Theatre Program to be perceived in this new way would require a different kind of institutional educat-ing.[7] How can we offer what we know to student demonstrators and striking workers, to people without large public forums to share what they know, through performance? How can we offer performance as a tool that can be embraced and harnessed toward exactly that kind of public educational process, a process of difficult social change? Implicit here is a ratio-nale for theatre and performance that extends well beyond the academy.

Theatre studies is in a unique position to experiment with the construction of knowledge and new ways of learning, precisely because many of its departments include production components that can embody the questions of content, context, theory, and history raised by its scholars. Through a performance studies model, we can think of performance as research, as part and parcel of the ideas we have to offer to the store of knowledge. Yet there remains something fundamentally divi-sive in how theatre departments are structured, carefully mixing and matching and sometimes blending practice and intellectual work rather than premising both on the other. The conven-tions of theatre training too often jealously guard the theory/practice split that hobbles our field. Caught up in still romantic notions of artistry as unthought, as unmediated by choice

and work and modes of production, academic theatre practice often aspires to imitate "real theatre" that happens elsewhere and strives to replicate the high-art, elite centers of produc-tion that progressive cultural critics, often in their own departments, are simultaneously challenging. Preprofessional BFA and MFA programs often virulently insist on unexamined discourses of high-art elitism, as they prepare students to enter what is described monolithi-cally as "the profession." And as Roach (1999) has suggested, even the architecture of theatre buildings tends to separate our departments from the rest of the campus, removing theatre to sometimes isolated locations with ample parking and room to build shops, fly lofts, and large auditoriums (pp. 3–10).

Some departments, working through the challenges of identity politics, have built cur-riculum and created production projects to challenge traditional understandings of theatre as an art, and have immersed their students in performance as an art practice with multiple articulations in the sociopolitical world.[8] But the theory/practice split that rends the field has allowed many production programs to con-tinue to describe the actor, especially, as out-side of history, as objective, empirical, inspired not by context but by genius and canonical knowledge. As a result, these departments are often considered naive or irrelevant to the larger intellectual project of the university or college. Theatre departments generally haven't done very well at teaching new models for how to be artists.[9]

Theatre scholar Sandra Richards (1995) says that "given the evanescence of theatre, and its insistence upon subjectivity as part of its methodological approach, academics from other disciplines all too often view the schol-arly validity of drama departments with vary-ing degrees of skepticism; that ambiguity," she goes on, "reproduces itself within departments as a contentious divide between practitioners and scholars, such that each group jostles to privilege its mode of activity, and the insights of one often do not inform those of the other" (p. 67). To counter this unproductive standoff, Richards considers herself as a "critic working in theatre . . . whose directing constitutes a critical praxis addressed to a non-professional audience, and whose subsequent writing to an academic audience is partially shaped by those experiences" (p. 69). Such a dialectical movement keeps Richards from foundering in an unproductive debate.

Production could come to mean something much more vital in theatre departments and the communities in which they're located. Rather than succumb to the marketplace pressures of theatre, film, and television for which they're grooming some students, university theatres could take more risks, producing texts that might share with the academic and public communities something new about theatre, and about people's contemporary situation in culture. Too often, university theatres fail to use their resources to introduce their faculty and students and others to a new writer, a new performance style, a new issue or identity in the space of their stages. Rather than employing a pedagogical model of theatre production and practice, they adopt the market strategies of the industry they seek to emulate. The Broadway productions they replicate are more and more driven by market research, by audience surveys that determine the structure, shape, and narratives of mainstream product (Kakutani, 1998, p. 26). The cultural capital of seeing a Broadway show and reproducing it in a university theatre builds intellectual capital in theatre departments. But shouldn't university theatres reach higher than that, and try to create performances that reach deeper, intellectually, artistically, and even spiritually?

Theatre departments, of course, are hardly free from the market pressures that influence their students. The circulation of academic, cultural, and financial capital drives their teaching and their research and the productions they select for their seasons in one way or another (Bourdieu, 1984). Departments need majors to

survive in academic institutions that are now economically motivated, and they must be responsible for training their students toward some sort of financially viable future. But how can faculty more responsibly train theatre majors to think of their skills as critical tools, rather than encouraging their students' fantasies about their future stardom, inspired by an excessive American culture of celebrity? How can faculty persuade students that theatre degrees might make them employable later, or that a thoughtful use of their degrees can mean more, personally and politically, especially when they're young, than secure employment prospects? It sounds excessively privileged to suggest that an arts education is more important than a livelihood. But faculty committed to the arts know that they can offer important ways of structuring identity, of seeing the world critically, of thinking about and experimenting with social relations and their potential. Such critical and social thinking should be a vital part of any student's education.

STAGING THE ARGUMENTS IN THEATRE STUDIES

In addition to focusing the ways we teach theory and practice on their potential use in a wider social world, theatre and performance studies are ideal places to engage public debate through the methods of performance. Theatre studies might use performance and the built environment in which our departments are housed to engage students with the larger world, encouraging them to be not only scholar/artists but *citizen*/scholar/artists, not to participate in unselfreflexive nationalism but to use art and research, aesthetics and intellect to participate in a civic conversation about what "America" is and what it does. Such a vision of the university, in which various constituencies might cooperate to find a common social voice or political vision, has long made conservatives fearful, perhaps partly because such an activist intellectual environment would clearly contribute to shaping public life. Carol Stabile (1995), in fact, argues that the "culture wars" and the debates about political correctness that have long divided college campuses were engineered by the first Bush administration during the Gulf War as a way to contain campus protests against this conflict and to manufacture consent (pp. 108–125).[10] Whether or not one agrees with Stabile, the culture wars have succeeded, to a certain extent, in isolating progressive academics by making them appear doctrinaire and ridiculous (Gitlin, 1995; see also Rorty, 1998). Conservative rhetoric about political correctness has made progressives seem against a democratic notion of human community and for the "special interests" that have been disparaged in public culture in recent legislative initiatives against gays and lesbians, against affirmative action, and against welfare. The very identity politics that have opened up our field remain threatening to a government that retains a vested interest in supporting a powerful, "unmarked" elite (Phelan, 1993).

The terms of scholars' work need to change to connect more directly to a diverse public. Henry Giroux, for example, argues that literacy has to be reconceptualized as a critical cultural practice in which students become agents of their own lives by learning to understand the representational practices through which they're often excluded. "This is not merely about who speaks and under what conditions," he writes. "It is about seeing the university as an important site of struggle over regimes of representation and over ownership of the very conditions of knowledge production" (Giroux, 1995, p. 249). Gregory Jay and Gerald Graff (1995) suggest that rather than trying to resolve them, we should "teach the conflicts. . . . The 'politicized' university . . . would look to turn the campus into . . . a community where empowered citizens argue together about the future of their society, and in so doing help students become active

participants in that argument rather than passive spectators" (pp. 210, 212).

Actually staging arguments in theatre studies would make faculty and students more self-conscious of the public, progressive possibilities of theatre and performance. A good example of such a staging occurred in fall 1996, when white, Harvard/American Repertory Theatre–based *New Republic* critic Robert Brustein and the noted, often-produced African-American playwright August Wilson waged their own battle over universal versus particular knowledge, identity politics, and ways that theatre might engage with deeply contentious cultural issues. In the pages of the trade magazine *American Theatre*, Wilson argued that African-American plays should not be produced by white theatres, and spoke against color-blind and cross-race casting. Wilson's argument, though persuasive in some respects, was an essentialist and modernist vision of identity politics. But Brustein's universalist, blindly humanist response suggested that art conquers difference, which makes attention to the specifics of identity irrelevant. In a later issue of *American Theatre*, Patti Hartigan, a cultural reporter from Boston, suggested that Brustein and Wilson should give their debate over to African-American performer/playwright Anna Deavere Smith to stage as a polemical performance in the style of her *On the Road* pieces. Smith, Hartigan suggested, could perform it for Brustein and Wilson and the theatre community, investigating its ideologies and its implications much as she did for Crown Heights and East LA. (Smith, 1994; see also Smith, 1997; Smith, 2004). Through performance, this debate about the meaning of theatre, and how it structures representations of our culture, might enter the lives and imaginations of a much larger community. Theatre people, Hartigan implied, should assume responsibility as public intellectuals and make our work accessible and relevant to a broad public audience.

In fact, in January 1997, Smith moderated a public debate between Brustein and Wilson at Town Hall in New York City. Sponsored and organized by Theatre Communications Group, the sold-out event was one of the high points of the season, attracting a more ethnically and generationally diverse audience than typically appears for theatre productions in midtown Manhattan (Grimes, 1997, p. C9). The theatre buzzed with interest and excitement; people felt each other's presence as a necessary anchor. The liveness of the moment, and the investment in a very material commitment to a theatre community our presence represented, buoyed the spirits of the people in the large, cold hall. The evening was contentious and the power dynamics disconcerting, as Brustein and Wilson refused to cede ground to each other's arguments. Despite Smith's mediating presence, the debate framed poles of power in contemporary theatre, and still managed to leave out a wide spectrum of work and invested viewpoints. Many of the people attending were theatre-makers in their own right, who were discouraged from speaking publicly into the forum, making the evening two separate monologues instead of a true public forum about race and theatre in America. Smith read questions solicited from the audience in the second half of the evening, but Brustein and Wilson's responses only demonstrated the multiple layers of issues involved, rather than profitably untangling them to clarify, and the audience often groaned in frustration when either of the two men would drastically miss the point. And although the evening focused on race, both men displayed blind spots when confronted with gender or sexuality issues. Still, the event was invigorating and moving, a heartening demonstration of how much people care about theatre. Why don't theatre departments and performance studies departments open their theatres to just this sort of debate, about racial issues, gender issues, sexuality issues, about affirmative action, gay/lesbian civil rights, immigration and welfare, or even about the ways in which academic courses and productions create knowledge in theatre and performance studies?

Another productive example of such public debate was staged at the ATHE conference in 1998, when the organization's Advocacy Committee programmed a plenary session on arts funding called "Showdown on the Arts in San Antonio." The debate was prompted by the city council's decision to cut the local arts budget by 15 percent, and to deny funding completely to the Esperanza Peace and Justice Center, one of the city's most progressive producing organizations for the Latino and gay and lesbian communities. The city's defunding of Esperanza was widely seen as political—in fact, one of the city council members, who attended the ATHE panel, stood up in the audience to identify himself and to wave a flyer for Esperanza's gay and lesbian film festival as "evidence" of the organization's depravity. Although he was in the minority in the mostly liberal crowd, the panel framed various sides in the contentious local struggle and extended the questions raised into the national arena. The panelists disagreed vocally, and the audience lined up at microphones in the house to participate in the debate. The event proved one of the most stimulating hours at the conference and inspired much heated discussion that continued through the meetings. The plenary was an example of a more effective town hall meeting than the one that was actually held at Town Hall between Brustein and Wilson in New York. That is, the ATHE event allowed everyone who came to line up at the microphones strategically placed in the house so that they, too, could have a turn to speak into the public forum. The variety of comments, and the vehemence and urgency with which they were delivered, were themselves highly performative; the whole event was a wonderful example of performance in the public sphere.[11] Why shouldn't theatre faculty teach these and other conflicts, so that faculty and students can assume the moral accountability that publicly engaging difficult debate requires? Wouldn't it be exciting, relevant, and educationally stimulating to regularly program town hall meetings in our departments for our students and for our community? Shouldn't there be contentious talkbacks after every performance that raise important issues about the production and how it relates to our lives? For example, theatre faculty might make their decisions about season selection open to faculty, students, and a wide public, who would discuss the kinds of plays that might be produced and why, taking into consideration the new knowledge and aesthetic values they might share and with whom. They might sponsor debates about curriculum with students, faculty, and staff from theatre and other departments, which could address how to balance new knowledge with canonical knowledge. They might explain the decisions they make as teachers and administrators about why they teach what and how they do, so that their choices are historicized and contextual.

In a graduate seminar I teach at the University of Texas at Austin, under the auspices of the MA/PhD program's emphasis in performance as public practice, we investigate what it means to be a public intellectual in the arts, trying to find ways to make our intellectual and artistic practices relevant to a wider public constituency that might follow or extend the town hall format. Students in this seminar have practiced these skills by producing speculative dramaturgical and critical and creative work that allows them to practice methods for centering performance in public debate and discourse. One student, for example, wrote an article for the UT student newspaper that contextualized an upcoming production of Wendy Kesselman's play *My Sister in This House* in the complex history of the real events on which it's based, arguing that the UT Department of Theatre and Dance productions could be made more vital for the wider UT student population. Another pair of students offered ways to situate the very complicated politics of Rebecca Gilman's play, *Boy Gets Girl*, thinking of a university theatre department as the site of its production and anticipating that its very complicated sexual politics would need some interrogation to escape the incipient sexism of the piece.

Another student staged a reading of a cut from Naomi Wallace's play *In the Heart of America* for the occasion of a conference on human rights at the UT law school, and another described a performance of *A Song of Greenwood*, which premiered in 1998 and was remounted in 2001 in honor of the anniversary of the Tulsa race riots in Oklahoma, describing, in the process, the movement of history across these two public events. Another student wrote to Austin's local weekly newspaper, suggesting a new mode of arts reviewing in which "critic colleagues" would engage each other's work without the presumption of objectivity that too often limits the local dialogue about what the arts are and how they function in our community. Another student practiced for her colleagues portions of a site-specific, traveling performance that eventually took us all out into the streets of a local Austin neighborhood where we watched, as spectators moving and moved, an elegiac public performance that referred to losses we all incurred on 9/11. All of these projects and more exemplified the possibility for widening the public discussion of local arts practices, and for embedding those practices in larger discussions about pressing social issues.[12]

RADICAL HUMANISM AND SITUATED UTOPIA AS THE POTENTIAL OF PERFORMANCE

After nearly twenty years of progressive scholars using identity politics to open up the sphere of discovery in the field, at the beginning of the twenty-first century, we seem poised to reembrace a more radical humanism, one infused with the lessons about difference so useful to questioning the historically white, male canon. That is, the way we are subjects, or people in the world, is more complex now than ever. Our identities are less coherent; we see ourselves not just through one identity category (immigrant, African-American, lesbian, Jew), but through several simultaneously. As a result, how we identify within communities is also more and more complex. Theatre producing organizations often try to appeal through identity categories to spectators who are actually linked by geography or by desires that transcend the specifics of identity—they might live near the theatre, or they might share a common desire to attend the theatre, to see how it might speak to them, inspire them, and teach them something about their lives. Who they *are* can't be captured in simple categories, and what they *do* with performance—how they engage it and use it in their lives—is much more complex (Wolf, 1998, pp. 7–23). As a result, the idea of doing an "African-American play," or an "Asian-American play," simply to appeal to those presumptively clear identities, even in a theatre with a mixed-race population, is rather ludicrous, as the category is much too simplistic and too narrowly identity-based to be meaningful. Likewise, it's become more and more difficult to teach courses about only one area of identity, like "gender" or "race," and much more important to find ways to teach all the vectors of identity as mutually influencing our theatre and performance practice and reception. I find that when I combine all the terms of identity into a course syllabus, other themes sometimes become more pressing and apparent. Considerations of race, gender, sexuality, class, ability, and the other categories of identity are urgent in the work my students and I study, but often, our materials are organized around issues like contemporary production practice more generally, or around a question like what it means to be a public intellectual in the arts. More and more, I'm interested in pedagogy

that looks at performance as a public practice, and concentrates on what it can *do* in the larger world.

As I've demonstrated throughout this essay, one of my primary goals is to train my students to use performance as a tool for making the world better, to use performance to incite people to profound responses that shake their consciousness of themselves in the world. Perhaps this is a utopian belief, the idea that theatre can do any of those things. Yet that's the depth of reaction for which I long when I go to the theatre—I don't think we should expect anything less. Theatre remains, for me, a space of desire, of longing, of loss, in which I'm moved by a gesture, a word, a glance, in which I'm startled by a confrontation with mortality (my own and others'). I go to theatre and performance to hear stories that order, for a moment, my incoherent longings, that engage the complexity of personal and cultural relationships, and that critique the assumptions of a social system I find sorely lacking. I want a lot from theatre and performance.

I've argued here for the ways in which theatre studies in the academy might be engaged as a site of progressive social and cultural practice. I urge students to be advocates for the arts, to be theatre-makers committed to creating performances of insight and compassion, and to become spectators who go to see performance because they want to learn something about their culture that extends beyond themselves and the present circumstances of our common humanity (Dolan, 2001a). I've argued that theatre and performance create citizens and engage democracy as a participatory forum in which ideas and possibilities for social equity and justice are shared, and I've suggested how we might reimagine theatre studies programs to meet these goals. The final thought of this essay takes the same beliefs, the same faith in theatre's transformative impact on how we imagine ourselves in culture, and applies it more closely to performance itself. While I'm still addressing the ways in which theatre and performance studies promote citizenship and subjectivity, I'd like to end by imagining how a commitment to theatre and performance as transformational cultural practices might offer us, in fact, glimpses of utopia.

As theatre and performance scholars and practitioners, we might revel in what Peggy Phelan (1993) calls the nonreproductive capacity of performance, while arguing that its ephemerality is partly what helps it build community. And as performance scholar Diana Taylor (2003) argues, despite its ephemerality, performance also offers an archive of human experience, and a repertoire of cultural practices on which we can rely to ground our histories and build our futures. How can performance, in itself, be a utopian gesture? Why do people come together to watch other people labor on stage, when contemporary culture solicits their attention with myriad other forms of representation and opportunities for social gathering? Why do people continue to seek the liveness, the present-tenseness that performance and theatre offer? Is the desire to be there, in the moment, an expression of a utopian impulse? I believe that people are often drawn to attend live theatre and performance for emotional, spiritual, or communitarian reasons. Desire, perhaps, compels us there, whether to the stark, ascetic "spaces" that house performance art, or to the aging opulence of Broadway houses, or to the serviceable aesthetics of regional theatres.[13] Audiences are compelled to gather with others, to see people perform live, hoping, perhaps, for moments of transformation that might let them reconsider and change the world outside the theatre, from its macro to its micro arrangements. Perhaps part of the desire to attend theatre and performance is to reach for something better, for new ideas about how to be and how to be with each other. I believe that theatre and performance can articulate a common future, one that's more just and equitable, one in which we can all participate more equally, with more chances to live fully and

contribute to the making of culture. Such desire to be part of the intense present of performance offers us if not expressly political, then usefully emotional, expressions of what utopia might feel like.

Seen through the lens of performance, the possibility for utopia doesn't only happen when the lights go down and the "play" begins. I've argued in this essay for the importance of considering production, and the "backstage" work of performance, as equally important sites of inquiry into how identities are constructed, rewarded, made visible, and understood. Extending this investigation into the possibility for utopia, for instance, might let us see rehearsals as a place to practice not only the performance at hand. Director Anne Bogart, in fact, says, "I often see my rehearsal situation as utopian. Rehearsal is a possibility for the values I believe in, the politics I believe in, to exist in a set universe which is within the room" (Bogart, 1995, p. 182). She suggests that rehearsals are the moment of utopian expression in theatre, when a group of people repeat and revise incremental moments, trying to get them right, to get them to "work." Anyone who considers herself a theatre person knows when something "works"—it's when the magic of theatre appears, when the pace, the expression, the gesture, the emotion, the light, the sound, the relationship between actor and actor, and actors and spectators, all meld into something alchemical, something nearly perfect in how it communicates in that instance. We all rehearse for the moments that work, and critics look out for them, when they're still idealistic enough to believe in them. Through an itinerary of performance, we can enlarge the potential territory in which something might "work" to the social frame of performance and look more widely for a glimpse of utopia (see Schechner, 1988).

I've been moved by the palpable energy that performances that "work" generate; I've felt the magic of theatre; and I've witnessed the potential of the temporary communities formed when groups of people gather to see other people labor in present, continuous time, time in which something can always go wrong.[14] Surely any gathering can promote community. But Herb Blau (1982) once said that watching live performance is watching the actor dying onstage; I think sharing that liveness promotes a necessary and moving confrontation with mortality.[15] The actor's willing vulnerability perhaps enables our own and prompts us toward compassion and greater understanding. Such sentiments can spur emotion, and being moved emotionally is a necessary precursor to political movement (see Cohen, 1991, pp. 84–85). Anna Deavere Smith (1995) says, "The utopian theatre would long for flesh, blood, and breathing. It would be hopelessly old-fashioned in a technical world, hopelessly interested in presence, hopelessly interested in modes of communication requiring human beings to be in the same room at the same time" (pp. 50–51). By clinging to the fleshy seductions of old-fashioned primal emotion and presence, Smith's work spurs political action by reminding us, perhaps, that however differently we live, our common, flesh-full cause is that in performance, we're dying together.

Theatre can move us toward understanding the possibility of something better, can train our imaginations, inspire our dreams, and fuel our desires in ways that might lead to incremental cultural change.[16] My concern here is not with the content of performance—not necessarily with plots or narratives that *address* utopia, but with how utopia can be imagined or experienced affectively, through feelings, in small, incremental moments that performance can provide. As Richard Dyer (1992) says, "Entertainment does not . . . present models of utopian worlds. . . . Rather the utopianism is contained in the feelings it embodies. It presents . . . what utopia would feel like rather than how it would be organized. It thus works at the level of sensibility, by which I mean an affective code that is characteristic of, and

largely specific to, a given mode of cultural production" (p. 18).[17] These feelings and sensibilities, in performance, give rise to what I'm calling the "utopian performative." In many ways, utopian performatives gesture toward my own desire to knit together performativity and performance, bringing real performance to the site of so much invigorating theoretical discourse. Borrowing from J. L. Austin (1962), utopian performatives describe moments which, through their *doing*, allow audiences to experience, for a moment, a sense of what utopia would feel like were the claims of social justice movements realized.

A utopian performative is like a Brechtian *gestus*; it represents, in a crystalline moment of performance, an understanding of social relationships full of potential, full of warmth, desire, caring, and love. Utopian performatives sometimes derive from a kind of performed romanticism found, for example, in solo performances by Peggy Shaw or Deb Margolin (see Dolan, 2001b, 2003). Romanticism is an affective address that, like love, has been perhaps banished too long from our discussions of performance or research (see Domínguez, 2000).[18] Dyer notes, "Romanticism is a particularly paradoxical quality of art to come to terms with. Its passion and intensity embody or create an experience that negates the dreariness of the mundane and everyday. It gives us a glimpse of what it means to live at the height of our emotional and our experiential capacities—not dragged down by the banality of organized routine life" (Dyer, 1995, p. 413). This intense, utopian romanticism is what creates those moments of magic and communion in performance that I'm calling utopian performatives; they lift us from our more prosaic lives, into an almost exalted sense of what life *could* be like, if we lived the "what if" instead of the "as is."[19]

Anthropologist Victor Turner's (1982) notion of "communitas" in social drama very much describes what I'm calling utopian performativity in performance. He says,

"Spontaneous communitas is 'a direct, immediate and total confrontation of human identities,' a deep rather than intense style of personal interaction. 'It has something "magical" about it. Subjectively there is in it a feeling of endless power.'" Turner asks, "Is there any of us who has not known this moment when compatible people—friends, congeners—obtain a flash of lucid mutual understanding on the existential level, when they feel that all problems, not just their problems, could be resolved, whether emotional or cognitive, if only the group which is felt (in the first person) as 'essentially us' could sustain its intersubjective illumination?" (Turner, 1982, pp. 47–48). These moments of communitas offer springboards to utopia.

I've also argued, earlier in this essay, the importance of teaching students to be critical, engaged citizen/scholar/artists, people who can bring their passion to spectatorship just as easily as they can to their artistry. I was struck recently, teaching a class of graduating senior theatre majors, how rarely some of them even go to see theatre or performance, and realized how important it was for me, as one of their last instructors, to instill a sense of commitment to our mutual artistic pursuits. As performance scholars and students, one of our primary goals should be creating a new generation of passionate spectators, who'll become the new arts advocates and intellectuals, as well as the artists. The passion of the audience explains why live performance continues; the desire to see it, to participate in its world-makings persists. People in my generation must instill such desire in people in the next. I want to perpetuate experiences of utopia in the flesh of performance that might performatively hint at how a different world could feel.

I know that at the end of a more sober essay about the possibilities for institutional change around the production of theatre and performance knowledge, I'm suddenly risking sentiment; I know that community and theatre, like utopia, can be coercive, that nothing is outside of ideology, and that nothing is ever, truly, perfect. But I believe in the politically progressive possibilities of romanticism in performance, what Dyer (1992) calls "the intensity of fleeting emotional contacts . . . and the exquisite pain of [their] passing" (p. 413). I believe that in performance, we can achieve moments of spontaneous communitas, which Turner (1982) says "is sometimes a matter of 'grace'" (p. 58). "Communitas," he says, "tends to be inclusive—some might call it generous" (p. 51). This, for me, is the beginning (and perhaps the substance) of the utopian performative: in the performer's grace, in the audience's generosity, in the lucid power of intersubjective understanding, however fleeting. These are the moments when we can believe in utopia. These are the moments theatre and performance make possible.[20]

NOTES

1. This essay was adapted and rewritten from the author's book *Geographies of Learning* (2001a) and her article in *Theatre Journal* (2001b).

2. She made this remark as an audience member at an ATHE conference panel in 1998 on emerging scholarship and institutional issues in the field. This panel took place on 14 August 1998. Panelists included Shannon Jackson, Jay Plum, and Stacy Wolf, and I moderated.

3. See some of the essays in Postlewait and McConachie, particularly Vince, for narratives of theatre scholarship's "tradition."

4. Schechner (1992) is quoted as saying, "Get out of the phony training business and into the culture business." A performance studies focus group is now well established in ATHE, and has been instrumental in the formation of a new association called Performance Studies international. PSi intends to remake the practices of professional associations, attempting to resist the typically conservative impulses of institutionalization while it charts new territory in this still growing field.

5. Bottoms (2003) raises important questions about what he sees as the implicit homophobia of performance studies as Schechner espoused it early in its development. Although a certain amount of misogyny was also present in the NYU training in the early 1980s, the department as a whole

still provided a context in which nascent radical critiques could flourish.

6. For further explanation of the centrality of New York as the scale by which all theatre is measured, university and otherwise, see Wolf, 1994 and 1998.

7. These misreadings of our program as only about entertainment or theatre practice persisted. In preparation for the opening of the Graduate Center's new building at Thirty-fourth Street and Fifth Avenue in fall 2000, I was asked to serve on the "Arc of Celebration" committee. People couldn't fathom why I wasn't interested in encouraging students to do some performances to honor this event. My explanation that our program is strictly academic, rather than one in which students act and direct, was completely opaque to my colleagues on the committee. This seems to me a misunderstanding of the intellectual, as well as the practical, value of theatre studies. And while, had students been interested in performing for the event, that would have been just fine, the administrators' presumption was about "entertainment," not about performance as research or social intervention.

8. For instance, the undergraduate program in theatre at San Francisco State University has a curriculum that encourages the theory and practice of performance to be applied to activism. And the Performance as Public Practice emphasis in the MA/PhD Program at the University of Texas at Austin, which I head, is committed to investigating through scholarship and performance research the ways in which people engage performance as a social act with larger political and cultural ramifications. These two examples offer just a glimpse of the kind of more culturally inflected curricula now beginning to appear in theatre and performance studies departments in the United States.

9. See Becker, 1996b, for a creative, politicized, and pragmatic approach to training artists in a postmodern era. See also Becker, 1996a, and Becker, 1994.

10. The "culture wars" generally refer to a public discourse of the late 1980s through the 1990s in the United States in which conservative commentators accused leftist academics of dogmatism and "political correctness," which they defined as a doctrinaire attitude towards social identity (see Gitlin, 1995, for example, and Dolan 2001a, for a counterargument). The culture wars also tend to refer to the public funding debates of this era, in which, for instance, artists Andres Serrano and Robert Mapplethorpe, and queer performance artists Holly Hughes, Tim Miller, John Fleck, and Karen Finley were denied funding

by the National Endowment for the Arts for reasons that were egregiously political. For a discussion of and bibliography on this aspect of the culture wars, see Dolan 2001a.

11. Jaclyn Pryor has kindly pointed out that Esperanza has regular events called *platicas*, which are similar to town hall meetings in that they allow Esperanza to practice civic engagements in large public forums. I'd like to thank her for this insight.

12. These presentations/performances were by Abigail Self, Elia Nichols and Kim Dilts, Shannon Baley, Kevin Hodges, Paul Bonin-Rodriguez, and Jaclyn Pryor. Baley and Hodges went on to create Living Newspaper performances based on international workers' rights for the "Working Borders" Human Rights Conference at the University of Texas at Austin in February 2005. Bonin-Rodriguez, Jaclyn Pryor, and I are now collaborating on a project of revisionary writing about performance that we call, inspired by Bonin-Rodriguez, "colleague criticism." And Pryor's piece became *floodlines* [sic], her MA thesis at the University of Texas, which was performed in April 2004 and remounted in April 2005 as part of the Refraction Arts Fusebox Festival in Austin.

13. As Holly Hughes says ironically, "Theater tends to happen in theaters, whereas performance art tends to happen in spaces. A theater will be defined . . . as somewhere with a stage, some lights, a box office, a dressing room, head shots, and people who know how to run these things. A theater is a place that has been designed for theater, whereas a space has been designed for some other purpose: it's a gas station, an art gallery, somebody's living room, a church basement, and it's always better suited for pancake suppers and giving oil changes than for performing" (Hughes 1996, p. 15).

14. Playwright Sarah Schulman quotes performance artist Jeff Weiss, who said to her in reference to the AIDS crisis, "We have a moral and ethical obligation to persist in the living of real (as opposed to 'reel') time. That is the power of theater. We're all in this together, at the *same* time. We're totally engaged in being human together, sharing the identical instants as our time advances, parallel, in unison" (Schulman, 1998, p. 61).

15. Blau's comment is actually, "When we speak of what Stanislavski called Presence in acting, we must also speak of its Absence, the dimensionality of time through the actor, the fact that he who is performing can die there in front of your eyes; is in fact doing so. Of all the performing arts, the theater stinks most of mortality" (Blau, 1982,

p. 83). I'd like to thank Amy Steiger, who reminded me of the exact quotation by citing it in her MA thesis in the Department of Theatre and Dance at the University of Texas at Austin, spring 2001.

16. These ideas, of course, resonate with the important work of Brazilian radical theatre theorist and practitioner Augusto Boal, who sees theatre as a "rehearsal for revolution" (Boal 1979).

17. See also Jameson, in which he suggests, "The hypothesis is that the works of mass culture cannot be ideological without at one and the same time being implicitly or explicitly Utopian as well: they cannot manipulate unless they offer some genuine shred of content as a fantasy bribe to the public about to be so manipulated" (1979, p. 146).

18. Domínguez argues that love and affection have a place in cultural (even in scholarly) discourse. Domínguez is writing specifically to scholars in anthropology, but her comments on the necessity for love and affection in our discourse resonate usefully here. See also Sandoval (2000). See also Dolan (2005) for a discussion of German philosopher Ernst Bloch, whose theories of utopia were quite influenced by romanticism. Bloch's philosophies undergird my ideas here.

19. For a useful discussion of the utopian implications of exploring the "what if" instead of the "as is," see Wickstrom and the other essays in the special issue of *Modern Drama* devoted to utopian performatives (Dolan, 2004).

20. I'd like to thank my research assistant Jaclyn Pryor for her perceptive editorial advice and her patience with the mechanics of citation in preparing this essay for publication.

REFERENCES

American Studies Association. http://www.george town.edu/crossroads/asainfo.html

Association for Theatre in Higher Education. http://www.athe.org

Austin, J. L. (1962). *How to do things with words.* Oxford, England: Clarendon Press.

Becker, C. A. (1994). *The subversive imagination: Artists, society, and social responsibility.* New York: Routledge.

Becker, C. A. (Ed.). (1996a). *Zones of contention: Essays on art, institutions, gender, and anxiety.* Albany: SUNY Press.

Becker, C. A. (1996b, November 8). A new generation of artists and art schools. *Chronicle of Higher Education,* B8–9.

Becker, C. A. (2000). The artist as public intellectual. In G. Bradford, M. Gary, & G. Wallace (Eds.), *The politics of culture: Policy perspectives for individuals, institutions and communities* (pp. 236–246). Washington DC: New Press.

Blau, H. (1982). *Take up the bodies: Theater at the vanishing point.* Champaign-Urbana: University of Illinois Press.

Boal, A. (1979). *Theatre of the oppressed.* New York: Urizen Books.

Bogart, A. (1995). Utopia forum. *Theater, 26*(1/2), 182.

Bottoms, S. (2003). The efficacy/effeminacy braid: Unpacking the performance studies/theatre studies dichotomy. *Theatre Topics, 13*(2), 173–187.

Bourdieu, P. (1984). *Distinction: A social critique of the judgment of taste* (R. Nice, Trans.). Cambridge, MA: Harvard University Press. (Original work published 1979)

Brustein, R. (1996). Subsidized separatism. *American Theatre, 13*(8), 26–27, 100–107.

Butler, J. (1990). *Gender trouble: Feminism and the subversion of identity.* New York: Routledge.

Carlson, M. (1992). Theatre history, methodology, and distinctive features. *Theatre Research International, 20*(2), 90–96.

Carlson, M. (1996). *Performance: A critical introduction.* New York: Routledge.

Clifford, J. (1993). On collecting art and culture. In S. During (Ed.), *The cultural studies reader* (pp. 49–73). New York: Routledge.

Cohen, E. (1991). Who are "we"? Gay "identity" as political (e)motion (a theoretical rumination). In D. Fuss (Ed.), *Inside/out: Lesbian theories, gay theories* (pp. 71–92). New York: Routledge.

Conquergood, D. (1991). Rethinking ethnography: Towards a critical cultural politics. *Communication Monographs 58,* 179–194.

Department of Theatre and Dance. University of Texas at Austin. Performance as Public Practice MA/PhD Program. www.utexas.edu/cofa/the atre/grad.html

Dolan, J. (2001a). *Geographies of learning: Theory and practice, activism and performance.* Middletown, CT: Wesleyan University Press.

Dolan, J. (2001b). Performance, utopia, and the "utopian performative." *Theatre Journal 53,* 455–479.

Dolan, J. (2003). Finding our feet in the shoes of one (an)other: Multiple character solo performers and utopian performatives. *Modern Drama, 45*(4), 495–518.

Dolan, J. (Ed.). (2004). Utopian performatives [Special issue]. *Modern Drama, 47*(2), 165–332.

Dolan, J. (2005). *Utopia in performance: Finding hope at the theatre*. Ann Arbor: University of Michigan Press.

Domínguez, V. R. (2000). For a politics of love and rescue. *Cultural Anthropology, 15*(3), 361–393.

Dyer, R. (1992). *Only entertainment*. New York: Routledge.

Dyer, R. (1995). In defense of disco. In C. K. Creekmur & A. Doty (Eds.), *Out in culture: Gay, lesbian, and queer essays on popular culture* (pp. 407–415). Durham, NC: Duke University Press.

Elam, H., & Alexander, R. (Eds.). (2002). *The fire this time: African-American plays for the 21st century*. New York: Theatre Communications Group.

Giroux, H. (1995). Beyond the ivory tower: Public intellectuals and the crisis of higher education. In M. Bérubé & C. Nelson (Eds.), *Higher education under fire: Politics, economics, and the crisis of the humanities* (pp. 238–258). New York: Routledge.

Gitlin, T. (1995). *Twilight of common dreams: Why America is wracked by the culture wars*. New York: Metropolitan Books.

Grimes, W. (1997, January 29). Face-to-face encounter on race in the theatre. *New York Times,* C9.

Hatch, J. V. (1989). Here comes everybody: Scholarship and black theatre history. In T. Postlewait & B. McConachie (Eds.), *Interpreting the theatrical past* (pp. 148–165). Iowa City: University of Iowa Press.

Hatch, J. V., & Hill, E. G. (2003). *A history of African American theatre*. Cambridge, England: Cambridge University Press.

Hatch, J. V., & Shine, T. (Eds.). (1996). *Black theatre USA: Plays by African Americans*. New York: Free Press.

Hebdige, D. (1979). *Subculture: The meaning of style*. London: Methuen.

Hughes, H. (1996). *Clit notes: A sapphic sampler*. New York: Grove Press.

Jackson, S. (2004). *Professing performance: Theatre in the academy from philology to performativity*. Cambridge, England: Cambridge University Press.

Jameson, F. (1979). Reification and utopia in mass culture. *Social Text, 1,* 130–148.

Jay, G., & Graff, G. (1995). A critique of critical pedagogy. In M. Bérubé & C. Nelson (Eds.), *Higher education under fire: Politics, economics, and the crisis of the humanities* (pp. 201–213). New York: Routledge.

Kakutani, M. (1998, March 1). Portrait of the artist as a focus group. *New York Times Sunday Magazine, 26.*

Levine, L. W. (1988). *Highbrow/lowbrow: The emergence of cultural hierarchy in America*. Cambridge, MA: Harvard University Press.

Modern Languages Association. http://www.mla.org

National Communication Association. http://www.natcom.org

Performance Studies international. http://www.psi-web.org

Phelan, P. (1993). *Unmarked: The politics of performance*. New York: Routledge.

Postlewait, T., & McConachie, B. (Eds.). (1989). *Interpreting the theatrical past*. Iowa City: University of Iowa Press.

Reinelt, J., & Roach, J. (Eds.). (1992). *Critical theory and performance*. Ann Arbor: University of Michigan Press.

Richards, S. (1995). Writing the absent potential: Drama, performance, and the canon of African-American literature. In A. Parker & E. K. Sedgwick (Eds.), *Performance and performativity* (pp. 64–88). New York: Routledge.

Roach, J. (1992). Introduction. In J. Reinelt & J. Roach (Eds.), *Critical theory and performance* (pp. 1–6). Ann Arbor: University of Michigan Press.

Roach, J. (1999). Reconstructing theatre/history. *Theatre Topics, 9*(1), 3–10.

Rorty, R. (1998). *Achieving our country: Leftist thought in twentieth-century America*. Cambridge, MA: Harvard University Press.

Sandoval, C. (2000). *Methodology of the oppressed*. Minneapolis: University of Minnesota Press.

Schechner, R. (1985). *Between theatre and anthropology*. Philadelphia: University of Pennsylvania Press.

Schechner, R. (1988). *Performance theory* (Rev. ed.). New York: Routledge.

Schechner, R. (1992, September). Schechner advocates radical rethinking. *ATHENEWS, 6*(4), 1.

Schechner, R. (1995). Transforming theatre departments. *The Drama Review, 39*(2), 8.

Schulman, S. (1998). *Stagestruck: Theater, AIDS, and the marketing of gay America*. Durham, NC: Duke University Press.

Smith, A. D. (1994). *Twilight, Los Angeles, 1992; on the road: A search for American character*. New York: Anchor Books.

Smith, A. D. (1995). Systems of light. *Theater, 26*(1/2), 50–51.

Smith, A. D. (1997). *Fires in the mirror: Crown Heights, Brooklyn, and other identities*. New York: Dramatists Play Service.

Smith, A. D. (2004). *House arrest: A search for American character in and around the White House, past and present; and Piano: Two plays*. New York: Anchor Books.

Stabile, C. A. (1995). Another brick wall: (Re)contextualizing the crisis. In M. Bérubé & C. Nelson (Eds.), *Higher education under fire: Politics, economics, and the crisis of the humanities* (pp. 108–125). New York: Routledge.

Taylor, D. (2003). *The archive and the repertoire*. Durham, NC: Duke University Press.

Theatre Arts Department. San Francisco State University. www.sfsu.edu/~tha/academics.html

Turner, V. (1982). *From ritual to theatre: The human seriousness of play*. New York: PAJ Publications.

Uno, R., & Burns, L. M. S. P. (Eds.). (2002). *The color of theatre: Race, culture, and contemporary performance*. New York: Continuum.

Vince, R. W. (1989). Theatre history as an academic discipline. In T. Postlewait & B. McConachie (Eds.). *Interpreting the theatrical past* (pp. 1–18). Iowa City: University of Iowa Press.

Wickstrom, M. (2004). Wonder in the heart of empire: Deborah Warner's Medea and the Angel Project. *Modern Drama, 47*(2), 177–199.

Wilkerson, M. (1991). Demographics and the academy. In S. Case & J. Reinelt (Eds.), *The performance of power: Theatrical discourse and politics* (pp. 238–241). Iowa City: University of Iowa Press.

Wilson, A. (1996). The ground on which I stand. *American Theatre, 13*(7), 14–16, 71–74.

Wolf, S. (1994). *Theatre as social practice: Local ethnographies of audience reception*. Unpublished doctoral dissertation: University of Wisconsin, Madison.

Wolf, S. (1998). Civilizing and selling spectators: Audiences at the Madison Civic Center. *Theatre Survey, 39*(2), 7–23.

Index

About the Editors

D. Soyini Madison is Associate Professor in the Department of Communication Studies in the area of Performance Studies at the University of North Carolina at Chapel Hill. She received her PhD from Northwestern University in 1989 under the direction of Dwight Conquergood. She is author of *Critical Ethnography: Methods, Ethics, and Performance (2005)* and editor of *The Woman That I am: The Literature and Culture of Contemporary Women of Color* (1994). Madison's several publications in journals and edited volumes focus on black diaspora performances and the intersections between the global political economy and human rights. She is recipient of several university teaching awards including the Tanner Award for "outstanding and inspirational" teaching.

Madison lived in Ghana, West Africa as a Senior Fulbright Scholar conducting field research on women's human rights, traditional religion, and globality from 1998 to 2001. She received a Rockefeller Foundation fellowship in Belagio, Italy in 2004 for her current book project, *"The White Girl Upstairs": Ethnography, Performance, and Human Rights*, based on her field research in Ghana. Madison has also adapted and directed ethnographic and oral historical materials for *I Have My Story to Tell*, a performance reflecting the labor struggles of UNC service workers, and for *Mandela, the Land, and the People*. She is currently working on an ethnographic performance entitled *Water Rites* based on local human rights activism in the global South and the struggle against the privatization of waters.

Judith Hamera received her BA (1980) in Mass Communication from Wayne State University and her MA (1982) and PhD (1987) in Interpretation and Performance Studies respectively from Northwestern University. She is currently Professor and Head of the Department of Performance Studies at Texas A&M University. She has served as editor of *Text and Performance Quarterly*, the journal of the National Communication Association Division of Performance Studies. She is the author of *Dancing Communities: Performance, Culture, and Community in a Global City* (forthcoming) and editor of *Opening Acts: Performance in/as Communication and Cultural Studies* (2005). Her essays have appeared in *Cultural Studies*, *TDR: The Drama Review*, *Modern Drama*, *Text and Performance Quarterly*, *Theatre Topics*, and *Women and Language*. She is the recipient of the National Communication Association's Lilla Heston Award for Outstanding Scholarship in Interpretation and Performance Studies, and was named President's Distinguished Professor at California State University, Los Angeles, in 2004.

About the Contributors

Bryant Keith Alexander is Professor of Communication Studies and is currently the acting chair of the Department of Liberal Studies at California State University, Los Angeles. His research in performance, cultural, and pedagogical studies appears in a wide variety of journals and books. He is a contributing author to the *Handbook of Qualitative Research* (3rd ed.), and is the coeditor of *Performance Theories in Education: Power, Pedagogy, and the Politics of Identity*. He is currently finalizing a book-length project entitled *Contesting Performances: Ethnographic Explorations of Culture, Subjectivity, and Social Relations*.

Michael S. Bowman teaches performance studies at Louisiana State University, where he is Associate Professor and Director of Graduate Studies in the Department of Communication Studies. He serves as the current editor of *Text and Performance Quarterly*, the National Communication Association journal of performance studies.

Ruth Laurion Bowman is an Associate Professor of Communication Studies at Louisiana State University, where she teaches courses in performance studies and is the producing director of the HopKins Black Box, an experimental lab theatre. Her essays have appeared in *Text and Performance Quarterly*, *Theatre Topics*, and various collections.

Barbara Browning is the author of *Samba: Resistance in Motion* (1995), which received the De la Torre Bueno Prize for the best book on dance in that year, and *Infectious Rhythm: Metaphors of Contagion and the Spread of African Culture* (1998). Her research concerns African diasporic expressive culture, and the conjunction of medical anthropology and performance analysis. From 2001 to 2005 she served as the Chair of the Department of Performance Studies at NYU. Browning is a member of the governing boards of the Society of Dance History Scholars and the Congress on Research in Dance. She is also a member of the editorial collective of the journal *Women & Performance*.

Gay Gibson Cima is Professor of English and Director of the Humanities Initiative at Georgetown University. Her book manuscript, *Early American Women Critics: Performance, Politics, Religion, Race,* is under contract with Cambridge University Press. She has published widely on feminist performance history, dramaturgy, and criticism in a number of critical anthologies and journals. Her book *Performing Women: Female Characters, Male Playwrights, and the Modern Stage* was published in 1993. She is Secretary of the American Society for Theatre Research and a member of the American Council of Learned Societies Conference of Administrative Officers.

Jan Cohen-Cruz is a scholar/practitioner of activist and community-based performance. An Associate Professor in the NYU Tisch School of the Arts Drama Department, she coordinates a minor in applied theatre, guiding young artists who facilitate cultural projects in city neighborhoods. She coedited *Playing Boal: Theatre, Therapy, Activism* and edited *Radical Street Performance: An International Anthology.* Her book on community-based performance in the United States, *Local Acts,* was published in March, 2005. Another edited text with Mady Schutzman, *A Boal Companion,* should be available in late 2005.

Dwight Conquergood was former chair of the Department of Performance Studies at Northwestern University where he served as Director of Graduate Studies and Interim Director of the Center for Interdisciplinary Research in the Arts. He was also a member of the Research Faculty for the Center for Urban Affairs and Policy Research. He served as site consultant for the International Rescue Committee and other human rights organizations. Professor Conquergood conducted several workshops for public defenders and consulted pro bono on capital cases involving indigent, minority, and immigrant defendants. He taught at the Bryan R. Shechmeister Death Penalty College, School of Law, Santa Clara University. His research interests were in cultural studies and performance ethnography. He conducted ethnographic fieldwork in refugee camps in Thailand, the Gaza Strip, and with street gangs in Chicago. In addition to numerous publications in journals and edited volumes, he coproduced two award-winning documentaries based on his ethnographic fieldwork: *Between Two Worlds: The Hmong Shaman in America* (1985), and *The Heart Broken in Half* (1990). Before his death in November 2004, he was completing a book on performance ethnography grounded in his long-term transnational field research with refugees and new immigrants in Chicago.

Tracy C. Davis is Barber Professor of the Performing Arts at Northwestern University. She is general editor of the Cambridge University Press series *Theatre and Performance*

Theory and recently joined *TDR* as a consulting editor. A book on nuclear civil defense practices in Canada, Britain, and the United States. is in process. This study explores the staging of preparations for catastrophe by various populations within governmental, scientific, engineering, and social communities as they coordinate civil defense exercises affecting neighborhoods, cities, and nations on local and international scales.

Norman K. Denzin is Distinguished Professor of Communications, College of Communications Scholar, and Research Professor of Communications, Sociology, and Humanities at the University of Illinois, Urbana-Champaign. He is the author, editor, or coeditor of numerous books including *Performance Ethnography: Critical Pedagogy and the Politics of Culture, Screening Race: Hollywood and a Cinema of Racial Violence; Performing Ethnography;* and *9/11 in American Culture.* He is past editor of *The Sociological Quarterly,* coeditor of *The Handbook of Qualitative Research* (2nd ed.), coeditor of *Qualitative Inquiry,* editor of *Cultural Studies Critical Methodologies,* and series editor of Studies in Symbolic Interaction.

Greg Dimitriadis is Associate Professor in the Graduate School of Education and Adjunct Professor of American Studies at the University at Buffalo, SUNY. He is author, coauthor, or coeditor of nine books, including *Performing Identity/Performing Culture: Hip Hop as Text, Pedagogy, and Lived Practice.*

Jill Dolan holds the Zachary T. Scott Chair in Drama in the Department of Theatre and Dance at the University of Texas at Austin. She is the author the *The Feminist Spectator as Critic* (1989), *Presence and Desire: Essays on Gender, Sexuality, Performance* (1993), *Geographies of Learning: Theory and Practice, Activism and Performance* (2001), and *Utopia in Performance: Finding Hope at* *the Theatre* (2005). Her research projects include a critical memoir on lesbian feminism in the United States and a critical history of queer theatre since the 1960s. She coedits, with David Roman, the Triangulations: Lesbian/Gay/QueerDrama/Theatre/Performance series at the University of Michigan Press. She is the past president of the Women and Theatre Program of the Association for Theatre in Higher Education (ATHE), and a past president of ATHE itself. She is former Executive Director of the Center for Lesbian and Gay Studies at the Graduate Center of the City University of New York. Her articles have been published in *Theatre Journal, The Drama Review, Modern Drama,* and *Theatre Topics,* among other publications. She heads the Performance as Public Practice MA/PhD Program at UT-Austin.

Paul Edwards is Director of Undergraduate Studies in the Department of Performance Studies at Northwestern University and the recipient of the 2002 NU Alumni Excellence in Teaching Award. He has directed more than 40 original stage adaptations of fiction for campus and professional settings. His adaptation of John Barth's *The End of the Road* received a 1993 Joseph Jefferson Citation (for non-Equity production); his adaptation of Geoff Ryman's *Was* received a Joseph Jefferson Award (for Equity production) and an After Dark Award. From the National Communication Association he has received two awards: the Leslie Irene Coger Award, honoring lifetime achievement in performance, and the Lilla A. Heston Award for outstanding scholarship in performance studies. His essays and monographs have appeared in such publications as *Shakespeare Quarterly, Text and Performance Quarterly,* and *Theatre Annual.*

Derek Goldman is an Assistant Professor of Theatre and Performance Studies at Georgetown University and is Founding Artistic Director of the StreetSigns Center for

Literature and Performance, an award-winning professional theatre company that has produced over 50 productions in 13 years. He has also directed Off-Broadway and at numerous other venues including the Steppenwolf Theatre in Chicago, and he has had more than a dozen of his own plays and adaptations produced professionally. Current projects include his adaptation of Studs Terkel's *Will the Circle Be Unbroken: Death, Rebirth, and Hunger for a Faith* (Steppenwolf); his jazz musical *My Swan: the Passions of F. Scott Fitzgerald* (New York), and *Hymn to Elsewhere,* an original piece inspired by the life and work of Salman Rushdie and the iconography of *The Wizard of Oz.*

Bruce Henderson is Professor of Speech Communication at Ithaca College, where he also served as department chair for five years and is currently coordinator of Health Communication. He is co-author with Carol Simpson Stern of *Performance: Texts and Contexts* and also serves as an Associate Editor of *Text and Performance Quarterly.* He has written about modern poetry, children's literature, queer theory, and disability studies.

Shannon Jackson is Professor of Rhetoric and of Theater, Dance, and Performance Studies at the University of California, Berkeley. She is head graduate advisor of the doctoral program in Performance Studies, core faculty of the Art Research Center, and affiliated faculty in the Department of Women's and Gender Studies. She has published *Lines of Activity: Performance, Historiography, Hull-House Domesticity* (2000), *Professing Performance: Theatre in the Academy from Philology to Performativity* (2004), and dozens of articles in edited collections and journals of theatre, performance, and cultural studies. Jackson has received publication awards from the American Studies Association, the American Society for Theatre Research, and the Association for Theatre in Higher Education, and fellowships from the Radcliffe Institute for Advanced Study, the Townsend Center for the Humanities, and the Spencer Foundation.

E. Patrick Johnson is Associate Professor and Director of Graduate Studies in the Departments of Performance Studies and African American Studies at Northwestern University. He is author of *Appropriating Blackness: Performance and the Politics of Authenticity* and coeditor (with Mae G. Henderson) of *Black Queer Studies: A Critical Anthology*. He is currently working on a book manuscript entitled, *Sweet Tea: An Oral History of Black Gay Men of the South*.

Joni L. Jones/Olorisa Omi Osun Olomo is an Associate Professor of Performance Studies in the Department of Theatre and Dance, and Associate Director of the Center for African and African-American Studies at the University of Texas at Austin. She is an artist/scholar who is currently engaged in performance ethnography around the Yoruba deity Osun, and is writing a collaborative ethnography on the use of a jazz aesthetic in theatre. While on a Fulbright Fellowship in Nigeria (1997–98), Dr. Jones taught at Obafemi Awolowo University and contributed theatre for social change workshops to the Forum on Governance and Democracy in Ile-Ife. Her articles on performance and identity have appeared in *Text and Performance Quarterly*, *The Drama Review*, *Theatre Topics, and Black Theatre News*. Her performance ethnography includes *Searching for Osun*, *sista docta*, and *Broken Circles: A Journey Through Africa and the Self*.

Kristin M. Langellier is Mark and Marcia Bailey Professor at the University of Maine where she teaches communication, performance studies, and women's studies. Her research interests are narrative performance, family storytelling, and Franco American cultural identity. Her numerous publications include *Storytelling in Daily Life: Performing Narrative* (2004), coauthored with Eric E.

Peterson. She is a former editor of *Text and Performance Quarterly*.

Jon McKenzie is Assistant Professor of English at the University of Wisconsin–Milwaukee, where he teaches courses in performance studies and civil disobedience. His works include *Perform or Else: From Discipline to Performance* (2001), the essays "Democracy's Performance," "Laurie Anderson for Dummies," and "Towards a Sociopoetics of Interface Design: etoy, etoys, and TOYWAR," and a 1996 broadcast commemoration of the 1986 shuttle disaster titled "CINC: A Challenger Radio Drama." Jon's texts have been translated into Croatian, French, German, Japanese, Polish, and Portuguese. He has also worked in the new media industry as a writer and information architect.

Lisa Merrill is Professor in the Department of Speech Communication, Rhetoric, and Performance Studies at Hofstra University. Merrill is a gender and performance historian and specialist in American studies. Her research focuses on nineteenth century theatrical and everyday performances of nationality, race, gender, and sexuality and their reception. Merrill is a recipient of a National Endowment for the Humanities senior scholar award, the Lilla Heston Prize for Outstanding Scholarship in Interpretation and Performance Studies, and visiting fellowships and professorships at Cambridge University, England; La Trobe University, Melbourne, Australia; and Northwestern University, United States. Her most recent book, *When Romeo Was a Woman: Charlotte Cushman and Her Circle of Female Spectators* was awarded the Joe A. Callaway Prize for Best Book in Theatre or Drama by an American author.

Lynn C. Miller is Professor of Theatre and Dance in the Performance as Public Practice program at the University of Texas at Austin. Miller is the coeditor of *Voices Made Flesh: Performing Women's Autobiography* (2003) and author of the novels *The Fool's Journey*

(2002) and *Death of a Department Chair* (in press, 2006). Miller has adapted the works of many contemporary writers for the stage and has toured performances of Edith Wharton, Gertrude Stein, and Katherine Anne Porter. Miller teaches courses in adaptation of literature for stage and screen, performing autobiography, performance art, and performance and culture. Currently, she's writing a libretto for her play (coauthored with Laura Furman), *Passenger on the Ship of Fools*, which has been performed in Saratoga Springs and at Louisiana State University.

José Esteban Muñoz is Chair of the Department of Performance Studies, Tisch School of the Arts, New York University. He is author of *Disidentifications: Queers of Color and the Performance of Politics* (1999) and the coeditor of several volumes including *Pop-Out: Queer Warhol* and *Everynight Life: Music and Dance in Latin/o America*. He is completing two manuscripts, *Feeling Brown: Ethnicity, Affect and Performance* and *Cruising Utopia*.

Eric E. Peterson is Professor at the University of Maine where he teaches in the Department of Communication and Journalism. His research and teaching interests are in narrative performance, media consumption, nonverbal communication, and communication diversity and identity. He is coauthor with Kristin M. Langellier of *Storytelling in Daily Life: Performing Narrative* (2004) and coeditor of *Public Broadcasting and the Public Interest* (2003).

Della Pollock is Professor of Communication Studies in the areas of performance and cultural studies at the University of North Carolina at Chapel Hill. She is the author of *Telling Bodies Performing Birth* (1999) and editor of *Exceptional Spaces: Essays in Performance and History* (1998) and *Remembering: Oral History Performance* (2005). She coedits the journal *Cultural Studies* with Lawrence Grossberg.

Sandra L. Richards's teaching interests center on American drama, African-American and African theatres, and black feminist theories. She has taught dramatic literature and directed African-American, Caribbean, and African plays at Stanford University, San Francisco State University, Northwestern University, and the University of Benin (Nigeria), where she was a Fulbright lecturer from 1983 to 1985. She has published articles on such African-American playwrights as Amiri Baraka, Ntozake Shange, August Wilson, and on Nigerian dramatists Wole Soyinka, Bode Sowande, and Zulu Sofola in *Theatre Journal, New Theatre Quarterly*, and in the collections *Critical Theory and Performance* and *Performance and Performativity*. Her full-length study, *Ancient Songs Set Ablaze: The Theatre of Femi Osofisan*, was selected by *Choice* as one of the outstanding academic publications of 1997. Other collections in which her work has appeared include *Horror and Human Tragedy Revisted, African Drama and Performance*, and *The African Diaspora: African Origins and New World Self-Fashioning*. From 1998 to 2001, Richards served as the Chair of the African American Studies Department, and from 2001 to 2004, she held the Leon Forrest Professorship of African American Studies, both at Northwestern University. Currently, she is researching issues of cultural tourism to slave sites throughout the Black Atlantic.

Rebecca Schneider is Associate Professor and Head of the MA and PhD programs in Theatre and Performance Studies at Brown University. She is the author of *The Explicit Body in Performance* as well as numerous essays, most recently "Solo Solo Solo" in *After Criticism: New Responses to Art and Performance*. She is a contributing editor to TDR and coeditor, with Gabrielle Cody, of *Re:Direction: A Theoretical and Practical Guide* on twentieth century directing theory and practice.

Mady Schutzman is a writer, scholar, and theatre artist. She is author of *The Real Thing:*

Performance, Hysteria, and Advertising and coeditor with Jan Cohen-Cruz of two anthologies on the work of Augusto Boal. Her performative essays have been published in journals ranging from *The Drama Review* to *The Journal of Medical Humanities*. Schutzman's current research focuses on humor as resistance and divinatory practices. She teaches and serves as Assistant Dean of the School of Critical Studies at California Institute of the Arts.

Nathan Stucky is the Chair of the Department of Speech Communication at Southern Illinois University at Carbondale where he writes and directs performances and teaches courses in performance studies. He is coeditor of *Teaching Performance Studies*, and he formerly edited *Theatre Annual: A Journal of Performance Studies*. His essays have appeared in *Cultural Studies ↔ Critical Methodologies*, *Text and Performance Quarterly*, *Communication Education*, *Journal of Pragmatics*, and *The Journal of Language and Social Psychology*.

Jacqueline Taylor is the Director of the DePaul Humanities Center and teaches performance studies, women's studies, and gender and communication at DePaul University. She is the author of *Grace Paley: Illuminating the Dark Lives*, and of chapters in *Queer Words, Queer Images* and *Readings in Cultural Contexts*. Her essays have been published in *Text and Performance Quarterly*, *Southern Speech Communication Journal*, and *Women's Studies in Communication*. Her coedited volume (with Lynn C. Miller and M. Heather Carver), *Voices Made Flesh: Staging Women's Autobiography* contains fourteen scripts and essays on women's autobiographical performance.

Kristin Bervig Valentine is Professor Emeritus of Communication and Women's Studies at Arizona State University. Her research within communication is focused on performance studies and ethnography. For more than 30 years she has been a volunteer teacher for incarcerated women and continues to work for alternatives to prisons. Valentine has published earlier information about her work with incarcerated women in *Women's Studies in Communication*, 21 (1998) and will contribute to a white paper on incarcerated persons to be published by NCA in 2006.